Environmental Impacts of Ecotourism

Edited by

Ralf Buckley

*Director, International Centre for Ecotourism Research,
Griffith University, Queensland, Australia*

CABI Publishing

CABI is a trading name of CAB International

CABI Head Office
Nosworthy Way
Wallingford
Oxfordshire OX10 8DE
UK

CABI North American Office
875 Massachusetts Avenue
7th Floor
Cambridge, MA 02139
USA

Tel: +44 (0)1491 832111
Fax: +44 (0)1491 833508
Email: cabi@cabi.org
Web site: www.cabi.org

Tel: +1 617 395 4056
Fax: +1 617 354 6875
Email: cabi-nao@cabi.org

A catalogue record for this book is available from the British Library, London, UK

The Library of Congress has cataloged the hardcover edition as follows:
Environmental impacts of ecotourism / edited by Ralf Buckley.
     p.   cm.—(Ecotourism book series)
Includes bibliographical references and index.
  ISBN 085199-810-0 (alk.paper)
  1. Ecotourism—Environmental aspects. 2. Ecotourism. I. Buckley,
Ralf. II. Title. III. Series.
G156.5.E26E58 2004
577.27 – dc22

                                     2003023660

ISBN-13: 978-0-85199-810-7 (hardback edition)
ISBN-13: 978-1-84593-456-9 (paperback edition)

First published 2004
Paperback edition 2008

Printed and bound in the UK by Biddles Ltd, King's Lynn.

Contents

_____

Contributors

Lilian Alessa, *Department of Biological Sciences, University of Alaska Anchorage, 3211 Providence Drive, Anchorage, Alaska 99508, USA. E-mail: afla@uaa.alaska.edu*

Angela H. Arthington, *Centre for Riverine Landscapes, Griffith University, Nathan, Queensland 4111, Australia. E-mail: a.arthington@griffith.edu.au*

James Bacon, *Park Studies Laboratory, School of Natural Resources, University of Vermont, Burlington, Vermont 05405, USA.*

Suzanne Becken, *Environment, Society and Design Division, Lincoln University, New Zealand. E-mail: beckens@lincoln.ac.nz*

Ralf Buckley, *International Centre for Ecotourism Research, Griffith University, Parklands Drive, Gold Coast, Queensland 9726, Australia. E-mail: r.buckley@griffith.edu.au*

Megha Budruk, *Park Studies Laboratory, School of Natural Resources, University of Vermont, Burlington, Vermont 05405, USA.*

Troy Byrnes, *International Centre for Ecotourism Research, Griffith University, Parklands Drive, Gold Coast, Queensland 9726, Australia*

Vera P. Chizhova, *Faculty of Geography, Moscow State University, Moscow, Russia. E-mail: chizhova@ru.ru*

David N. Cole, *Aldo Leopold Wilderness Research Institute, Forest Service, PO Box 8089, Missoula, Montana 59807, USA. E-mail: dcole@fs.fed.us*

Maria Isabel Amando de Barros, *Outward Bound Brasil, Rua Suíça, 415, 01449-030 São Paulo-SP, Brazil. E-mail: isabelbarros@obb.org.br*

Bruce Forbes, *Arctic Center, University of Lapland, Box 122, FIN-96101, Rovaniemi, Finland. E-mail: bforbes@urova.fi*

James Higham, *Department of Tourism, University of Otago, Dunedin, New Zealand. E-mail: jhigham@business.otago.ac.nz*

Jerry Johnson, *Department of Political Science, Montana State University, Bozeman, Montana 59717, USA. E-mail: jdj@montana.edu*

Narelle King, *International Centre for Ecotourism Research, Griffith University, Parklands Drive, Gold Coast, Queensland 9726, Australia.*

Andrew Kliskey, *Department of Biological Sciences, University of Alaska Anchorage, 3211 Providence Drive, Anchorage, Alaska 99508, USA. E-mail: afadk@uaa.alaska.edu*

Daniel Laven, *Park Studies Laboratory, School of Natural Resources, University of Vermont, Burlington, Vermont 05405, USA.*

Steven Lawson, *Park Studies Laboratory, School of Natural Resources, University of Vermont, Burlington, Vermont 05405, USA.*

Yu-Fai Leung, *Parks, Recreation and Tourism Management, North Carolina State University, 4012F Biltmore Hall, Raleigh, North Carolina 27695-8004, USA. E-mail: leung@ncsu.edu*

Carolyn J. Littlefair, *International Centre for Ecotourism Research, Griffith University, Parklands Drive, Gold Coast, Queensland 9726, Australia. E-mail: carolyn.littlefair.reps@aph.gov.au*

David Lusseau, *Department of Zoology, University of Otago, Dunedin, New Zealand. E-mail: lusda563@student.otago.ac.nz*

Teresa Cristina Magro, *Departamento de Ciências Florestais, ESALQ/USP, Av. Pádua Dias, 11, 13418.900 Piracicaba-SP, Brazil. E-mail: tecmagro@esalq.usp.br*

Robert E. Manning, *Park Studies Laboratory, School of Natural Resources, University of Vermont, Burlington, Vermont 05405, USA. E-mail: robert.manning@arm.edu*

Jeffrey L. Marion, *Patuxent Wildlife Research Center, US Geological Survey, Virginia Tech/Forestry (0324), Blacksburg, Virginia 24061, USA. E-mail: jmarion@vt.edu*

Christopher A. Monz, *Assistant Professor of Environmental Studies Program, St Lawrence University, Canton, New York 03617, USA. E-mail: cmonz@stlawu.edu*

Thorsten D. Mosisch, *Moreton Bay Waterways and Catchments Partnership, GPO Box 1434, Brisbane, Queensland 4001, Australia.*

Peter Newman, *Park Studies Laboratory, School of Natural Resources, University of Vermont, Burlington, Vermont 05405, USA.*

David Newsome, *School of Environmental Science, Murdoch University, Perth WA 6150, Western Australia. E-mail: dnewsome@essun1.murdoch.edu.au*

Julianna Priskin, *School of Earth and Geographical Sciences, The University of Western Australia, 35 Stirling Highway, Crawley, WA 6009, Australia.*

Martin Robards, *Department of Biological Sciences, University of Alaska Anchorage, 3211 Providence Drive, Anchorage, Alaska 99508, USA.*

David G. Simmons, *Environment, Society and Design Division, Lincoln University, New Zealand. E-mail: dsimmons@lincoln.ac.nz*

Anne Tolvanen, *Department of Biology, University of Oulu, Box 3000, FIN-90014, Oulu, Finland.*

Paul Twardock, *Assistant Professor of Outdoor Studies, Alaska Pacific University, Anchorage, Alaska 99508, USA.*

William Valliere, *Park Studies Laboratory, School of Natural Resources, University of Vermont, Burlington, Vermont 05405, USA.*

Jan Warnken, *International Centre for Ecotourism Research, Griffith University, Parklands Drive, Gold Coast, Queensland 9726, Australia. E-mail: j.warnken@griffith.edu.au*

Wiebke Warnken, *International Centre for Ecotourism Research, Griffith University, Parklands Drive, Gold Coast, Queensland 9726, Australia.*

Tatia Zubrinich, *International Centre for Ecotourism Research, Griffith University, Parklands Drive, Gold Coast, Queensland 9726, Australia.*

Foreword

_____

In 1991, I sat at a large wooden table in Arlie House, an historic country inn outside of Washington, DC. It was a beautiful spring day, and around the table with me sat a group of conservationists, tour operators, NGO representatives and donor agency officials. We had come to Arlie House from Africa, Asia and the Americas on the occasion of the first board meeting of a new organization called The Ecotourism Society. One of our most important tasks was to succinctly define the word, 'ecotourism'. After lengthy discussion, the group reached consensus on a brief but fundamental definition for this newly emerging idea: 'Ecotourism is responsible travel to natural areas that conserves the environment and improves the welfare of local people'.

Since that day, much has changed. But the basic tenets of ecotourism – conserving nature and benefiting local communities – have remained the same. During the 1990s, tourism exploded across the world stage. According to the World Travel and Tourism Council, tourism generates nearly 11% of global gross domestic product (GDP), employs some 200 million people and transports nearly 700 million international travellers per year – a figure expected to double by 2020. The World Tourism Organization reports that tourism is one of the top five exports for 83% of countries and the main source of foreign currency for at least 38% of countries. Even if we account for any possible statistical errors, the bottom line fact is indisputable – tourism is growing, and growing fast in many places.

At the top of that growth curve is nature and adventure travel, which has emerged as a leading tourism sector. Whether it is cruise ships plying the remote waters of Glacier Bay in Alaska, hikers flocking to the lush rainforests of northern Australia, or city dwellers heading to luxury safari lodges in Africa, more and more tourists are seeking out nature and the beauty of wild places.

Just as tourism has grown and changed, ecotourism also has gone through a kind of metamorphosis. In its early days, ecotourism was seen more as a type of travel and a specific market niche. Today, it is increasingly viewed as a travel concept or philosophy, based upon a set of principles that can, and should, be applied across the widest possible spectrum of the global tourism industry in an effort to make tourism truly sustainable and a positive benefit to the natural and cultural heritage of our planet. In that sense, ecotourism and nature travel should not be viewed as the same thing. A river-rafting trip through the jungle may be fun, may be interesting and may provide a great family vacation. But only if that trip directly promotes the protection of nature and tangibly contributes to the well-being of local people does it become ecotourism.

At this time in our history, we find ourselves at a crossroads where the Earth's last wild areas, the make-or-break world of economic survival for millions of people and the ever-expanding world of tourism meet. We know what ecotourism should be and, in a number of positive examples from around the world, we know what ecotourism can be – a catalyst for protecting nature and supporting cultural heritage. But for ecotourism to achieve its true potential, we must fully understand its impacts – both at the site-specific level and on a global scale. We need to know where it works and why, and we need to learn from its mistakes and understand its limitations. *Ecological Impacts of Ecotourism* helps us to do that, by collecting together a variety of research efforts that attempt to both define and then evaluate different kinds of environmental impacts, both positive and negative, that ecotourism may be having. It is an important step forward providing much-needed research on the ecological footprint of ecotourism.

Costas Christ
Senior Director, Ecotourism, Conservation International,
Washington, DC, USA

Preface

Ecotourism is widely recognized as the most rapidly growing sector within the global tourism industry. By definition, ecotourism is travel to minimally impacted natural areas and associated cultural locales. Ecotourists enjoy nature, and cultures that coexist harmoniously with the natural environment; they are conscious of minimizing their impacts on nature and local cultures and aim to improve socio-economics of local populations. Given this relatively noble profile, compared to other tourist types, can the ecotourist actually have adverse ecological impacts on places and peoples visited, the land, water and air traversed, and the animals and plants viewed?

The papers compiled in this volume attempt to answer questions of ecological impacts of ecotourism. They derive from case studies in countries such as Australia, Brazil, Canada, New Zealand, Russia and the USA. Some chapters, e.g. Impacts of Ecotourism on Terrestrial Wildlife by Ralf Buckley, also provide a broad overview of literature on the subject. Despite insufficient data and country- or site-specificity of analyses presented, the evidence is sufficient to caution ecotourists and their promoters against complacency with regard to the adverse impacts of ecotourism on natural areas. The volume raises important questions and issues that must be addressed if ecotourism, as a nature- and culture-friendly industry, is to benefit socio-economics of peoples and regions in less developed parts of the world.

At the Fifth World Parks Congress, convened in Durban, South Africa, from 8 to 17 September 2003, the global community celebrated the fact that about 12% of the world is under some form of legal protection for nature and associated cultural features. At that congress, tourism, particularly ecotourism, was frequently hailed as the most promising industrial partner for nature conservation and protected area management. Yet, the number of protected areas among more than 44,000 now recognized worldwide in which we have been able to clearly demonstrate benefits for both nature conservation and local economies are few. This paucity of success stories applies even for the sub-set of protected areas designated as World Heritage by UNESCO.

Of the 754 sites that are recognized as World Heritage, 582 are cultural. Many of them are monuments, e.g. the Taj Mahal of India. The remaining 172 sites contain natural (149) and mixed, natural/cultural (23) sites, respectively. The 172 sites comprise more than 500 protected areas. The Great Barrier Reef of Australia and the Serengeti of Tanzania are amongst the well-known World Natural Heritage sites; mixed sites include Machu Picchu of Peru, Tikal National Park in the Mayan Region of Guatemala and Australia's Uluru Kata-Tjuta National Park.

Despite the 'iconic' status of the 172 natural and mixed sites among the world's protected areas, tourism's performance in those sites is rather mixed. In Queensland, Australia, a thriving ecotourism enterprise, centred on the Wet Tropics World Heritage area, has almost fully replaced timber-extraction as a basis for the regional economy within a decade. Jiuzhaigou and Huanglong World Heritage areas in Sichuan, China have fostered multi-million dollar tourism enterprises, corrected unsustainable visitor management practices and transfer millions of dollars for the benefit of local peoples, including some Tibetan communities. In the past, however, China, fast becoming the world's most important importer and exporter of tourists, had to resort to drastic measures in the Mount Huangshan World Heritage area, to curtail and reverse impacts of unsustainable tourism practices.

Assumptions of our ability to convert mass tourism to ecotourism rely on changes we anticipate and influence in society as a whole. Continuous growth of a literate and educated public, interested to know more about nature, biodiversity, wildlife and local cultures are a necessary condition for an ecotourism economy. Without the growth of that part of the mobile public that is curious about natural and cultural histories of places and people, and are eager to see and learn about them in modest comfort, travel and tourism will merely result in crowded cities and beaches. Conservationists and the industry need to invest more time, effort and resources into educational schemes to ensure that markets for ecotourism will grow continuously.

Education that can sustain the creation and growth for a market for ecotourism cannot solely be dependent on opportunities for viewing large charismatic species in land and water, in selected parts of the world. It must re-create an interest and curiosity about nature, wildlife and cultures through different approaches and techniques in outdoor education that can continue to expand the repertoire of natural and cultural heritage that can fascinate and inspire the visitor. Research on nature and culture, including how we impact those natural and cultural treasures that we seek out to view, study and learn about, is a necessary condition to building a knowledge base critical to the success of the ecotourism enterprise.

Natarajan Ishwaran PhD Chief,
Natural Heritage Section
UNESCO World Heritage Centre
Paris, France

Introduction

Ralf Buckley
International Centre for Ecotourism Research, Griffith University, Gold Coast, Queensland, Australia

Ecotourism has been espoused widely as a tool for commercial profit, community development and environmental conservation (UNEP/WTO, 2002). It can indeed achieve all these on occasion (Buckley, 2003). In the process, however, it does produce impacts on the natural environment. In particular, many ecotourism products rely on protected areas, where environmental impacts are of particular concern. As pressure on conservation areas from ecotourism and recreation continues to rise, an understanding of impacts and ways to manage them becomes increasingly important for land managers and tour operators alike (Eagles and McCool, 2002; Buckley, 2003; Buckley and King, 2003).

There is now a substantial literature on ecotourism as a component of the tourism industry (Fennell, 1999; Weaver, 2001a,b; Newsome *et al.*, 2002). This literature does consider environmental impacts, but rather briefly (Buckley, 2001; Newsome *et al.*, 2003, pp. 79–145). There is also a substantial literature on outdoor recreation and recreation ecology (Hammitt and Cole, 1987; Liddle, 1997; Manning, 1999); and since much of ecotourism is commercialized outdoor recreation, this literature is highly relevant to the impacts of ecotourism. In addition, there is a longstanding body of research and practice on the management of protected areas and wilderness (e.g. Eagles and McCool, 2002; Hendee and Dawson, 2002), some of which refers to visitor impacts.

This volume aims to review and synthesize available information worldwide on the environmental impacts of ecotourism. From a management perspective, we need to know the impacts of different numbers of people with different skills and backgrounds, in groups of various sizes, undertaking a range of different activities in various different ecosystems at different times of year under different management regimes, on a variety of specific environmental parameters of ecological concern. However, research data are available only for a rather limited set of activities, ecosystems, environmental parameters and management regimes. Some of the impacts of some activities in some countries have been studied in detail; others much less so or not at all. Both the choice and content of the following chapters necessarily reflects the availability of relevant research data.

As there are many factors that influence the environmental impacts of ecotourism, there are correspondingly many criteria on which to classify those impacts. For example, impacts may be classified by ecosystem, by activity, by impact mechanism or by the ecosystem component affected.

Different formats are useful to address different management issues. In considering whether and where to allow high-impact uses such as helicopters, off-road vehicles or horses, for example, land managers need to know all the various impacts that such uses are likely to create. In considering how best to protect endangered wildlife, or how to manage wildlife watching so as to provide tourism opportunities without threatening wildlife populations, it is more useful to consider all the impacts that a range of different activities might have on the species concerned. Different chapters in this volume use different classification criteria, reflecting the structure of available research information.

The overall chapter structure follows a pragmatic approach, with reviews of more heavily studied topics, and case studies of impacts which are significant but as yet little analysed. In practice, there are few topics where a realistic choice is needed between classification by ecotourist activity, by impact mechanism or by ecosystem component. As one example, the impacts of off-highway vehicles (OHVs) on wildlife are equally relevant to management of OHVs, and to conservation of endangered or otherwise significant fauna. In this particular instance, we chose the activity classification, on the grounds that impacts of wildlife are a major cause for concern in management of OHVs, whereas OHVs are only one of many ecotourism activities with ecological impacts on animal species.

The focus of this book is the on-site environmental impacts of ecotourism: the recreation ecologists' contribution to the ecotourism literature. However, those on-site impacts do not occur in isolation, and the book's first three chapters aim to provide a context. The ecotourism sector benefits greatly from conservation of the natural environment and can also make positive contributions on occasion. The first chapter summarizes some of the mechanisms and the overall balance between positive and negative impacts. A detailed quantitative assessment is beyond the scope of this volume and would need another book.

Ecotourists often travel considerable distances to reach preferred destinations, and this long-distance travel also has significant environmental impacts, summarized by Simmons and Becken in Chapter 2. Notably, whereas ecotour operators and land management agencies have a range of tools to reduce environmental impacts on site, during long-distance

travel most ecotourists produce precisely the same *per capita* impacts as any other tourist. Finally, whereas most ecotourists visit briefly and head home, other visitors to the world's scenic places move there permanently. In some regions this so-called amenity migration completely eclipses both tourism and primary industries in its social, economic and environmental consequences. Perhaps the best-known examples are in the mountain states of the western USA: the Sierra Nevada of California; the Rocky Mountains of Colorado and Arizona; and the Greater Yellowstone Region (GYE) in Idaho, Montana and Wyoming. Migration to the GYE and adjacent areas of south-western Canada is particularly dynamic at present, and the issues involved are examined by Johnson in Chapter 3.

In the second section of the volume, the impacts of four common ecotourism activities are reviewed in turn. The effects of trampling by hikers are perhaps the most heavily studied of all recreational impacts, particularly in the montane ecosystems of North America, and one of the first where anyone attempted a quantitative synthesis of the research literature. That approach was taken by Cole in the mid-1980s, and in Chapter 4 he updates his previous reviews to the current state of the art. Similar, but more intense, impacts on soil and vegetation are produced by horse-riding and off-road vehicles, and these are reviewed in the two subsequent chapters. Impacts of recreational boating, the marine equivalent of off-road vehicles, are also reviewed in this section.

A corresponding review for freshwater locations, by Mosisch and Arthington, emphasizes the ecosystem more than the activity, and is placed accordingly in the book's third section. It is followed by a review of tourism impacts in polar ecosystems, compiled by the transatlantic team of Forbes, Monz and Tolvanen. This section also includes reviews of ecotourism impacts on the more heavily studied groups of animal species – whales and their relatives, birds and terrestrial wildlife.

The fourth section examines impacts specifically from a management perspective. Marion and Leung discuss how best to manage the hiking and camping impacts reviewed in earlier chapters; and Manning and his colleagues address how impacts are perceived by ecotourists themselves, rather than by managers or scientists; and how they may be managed through various rationing and allocation tools.

In the first four sections of this volume, the authors set out specifically to review established fields of research, synthesizing the global scientific literature on the better-studied environmental impacts of ecotourism. The fifth, and final, section presents case studies from recent research, little-studied impacts and continents where English is not the primary language.

Education and interpretation is a commonly used approach in reducing impacts, but its effectiveness has very rarely been tested in any rigorous way. A recently completed 3-year study in a World Heritage rainforest in subtropical Australia is presented here by Littlefair. Protocols for rapid assessment of impacts at seakayak campsites have been developed by Monz on behalf of the US National Outdoor Leadership School, and an Alaskan case study is presented by Monz and Twardock.

Introduction and dispersal of plant and animal pathogens, initially invisible, may ultimately produce far more severe ecological consequences than more readily apparent impacts. Two examples from Australia are presented: a review of impacts caused by the jarrah dieback fungus, and a detailed experimental study of recreational swimming impacts on waterborne bacteria. Both of these are of particular significance for management. For the dieback fungus, only complete quarantining of entire water catchments from any human access seems to be effective in preventing the spread of the disease, which causes major ecological change in a wide range of Australian plant communities. For recreational swimming, the use of a carefully designed monitoring approach can identify impacts below the threshold of human health concern, as an early warning indicator for management action.

A somewhat different management approach is taken by Priskin in her study of off-road vehicles on a section of coastline in Western Australia. In this case the localized impact is easily identifiable: complete removal of vegetation. From a management perspective the critical issues are the aggregate broad-scale loss of plant cover, flow-on effects on dune stability and management tools to curtail continued proliferation of new tracks.

Finally, much of the internationally accessible research literature derives from the North American continent and is written in the English language. However, similar ecotourism activities, impacts and management issues occur equally in other continents and are described in other languages. We are fortunate to include case studies from Brazil and Russia, contributed by Magro and De Barros, and Chizhova, respectively. We trust there will be many more such studies in future.

Acknowledgements

This volume forms part of the Ecotourism Series published by CAB International. My thanks to Series Editor David Weaver and CAB International Commissioning Editor Rebecca Stubbs. Thanks also to all the chapter authors, in particular for their willingness to divide up topics by consensus. Thanks in particular to our contributors from Brazil and Russia for writing in English. All the chapters have been double-blind peer refereed, and I am greatly obliged to the referees for their time and expertise. Thanks also to Karen Sullivan, Administrator for ICER, for managing the refereeing and revision process, following up citations and other information deficiencies, and assisting throughout the editorial process.

References

Buckley, R.C. (2003) Ecological indicators of tourist impacts in parks. *Journal of Ecotourism* 2, 54–66.

Buckley, R.C. and King, N. (2003) Visitor impact data in a management context. In: Buckley, R.C., Pickering, C.M. and Weaver, D. (eds) *Nature-based Tourism, Environment and Land Management.* CAB International, Wallingford, UK, pp. 89–101.

Eagles, P.F.J. and McCool, S.F. (2002) *Tourism in National Parks and Protected Areas: Planning and Management.* CAB International, Wallingford, UK.

Fennell, D.A. (1999) *Ecotourism: an Introduction.* Routledge, New York.

Hammitt, W.E. and Cole, D. (1987) *Wildlife Recreation: Ecology and Management.* John Wiley & Sons, New York.

Hendee, J.C. and Dawson, C.P. (ed.) (2002)

Wilderness Management, 3rd edn, Fulcrum, Golden, Colorado.

Liddle, M.J. (1997) *Recreation Ecology*. Chapman & Hall, London, UK.

Manning, R.E. (1999) *Studies in Outdoor Recreation*, 2nd edn. Oregon State University Press, Corvallis.

Newsome, D., Moore, S. and Dowling, R. (2002) *Natural Areas Tourism: Ecology, Impacts and Management*. Channel View, Clevedon UK.

UNEP and WTO (2002) *Quebec Declaration on Ecotourism*. Available at website http://www.uneptie.org/pc/tourism/documents/ecotourism/WESoutcomes/Quebec-Declar-eng.pdf (verified 20 September 2002).

Weaver, D. (2001a) *Ecotourism*. John Wiley & Sons, Brisbane.

Weaver, D. (2001b) *Encyclopedia of Ecotourism*. CAB International, Wallingford, UK.

1

Impacts Positive and Negative: Links Between Ecotourism and Environment

Ralf Buckley

International Centre for Ecotourism Research, Griffith University, Gold Coast, Queensland, Australia

Introduction

Ecotourism is widely touted for its positive impacts, actual or potential, for communities and conservation as well as for companies and consumers. In arguing for access to protected areas, for example, tourism lobbyists and ecotourism operators commonly argue not only that they will take steps to minimize their environmental impacts, but that ecotourism also generates benefits. However, protected areas also provide very significant benefits for the tourism industry. This chapter therefore summarizes these costs and benefits as a context for the detailed reviews and case studies of specific impacts in the rest of the book.

Every year more of the planet's natural resources are consumed or contaminated by its human population. Human survival needs drinkable water, breathable air and usable biological diversity. Natural ecosystems are the world's primary reservoirs for each of these. Ecosystems worldwide have been modified by human activities to various degrees. Areas of near-pristine wilderness and other little-modified environments are continually reduced. Areas of nearly completely modified environments, such as city centres, garbage dumps, mines and monocultures, continue to expand. The much larger areas with significant but not total modification, such as rural residential, broadacre pastoral and logged native forests

are also continuing to expand, and to encroach on the least-modified areas. To arrest and reverse these trends will only be possible with large-scale and far-reaching changes in human social structures and human behaviour. However, without such changes in the short term, far larger disruptions will be forced upon us.

The single most critical component of any long-term strategy for sustainability, and indeed human survival, is hence to maintain representative areas of the world's various ecosystems in a reasonably intact and functional state. This, of course, is the principal aim of the global system of protected areas, including World Heritage Areas, Biosphere Reserves, national parks and other conservation areas. However, on their own, parks are not enough to prevent continued loss of biological diversity: first, because they are too small and not fully representative; and, secondly, because they are not fully protected. Currently, there are other areas of public and private lands outside the protected area system, which contribute significantly to conservation of biodiversity and air and water quality. These include: polar, high montane, desert and marine ecosystems where there are few people; forests, woodlands and rangelands which are used for timber and livestock production but which none the less retain much of their original character function and biological diversity; and tribal and community lands where human lifestyles do not involve intensive modification to the natural environment.

As human population and resource consumption continue to grow, however, all these unprotected areas are subject to increasing exploitation and modification, as logging, agricultural clearance and similar impacts accelerate. In particular, some of these areas are contiguous with conservation reserves, and increasing population pressures are leading to land clearance and settlement right up to reserve boundaries, and sometimes encroachment within reserves themselves. In areas where protected area boundaries are not well defined or patrolled on the ground, such encroachment may commonly include poaching, illegal harvesting, small-scale settlement and sometimes military manoeuvres. However, even in areas where national park boundaries are well established and enforced, encroachments can still occur. In some cases, relevant legislation may allow certain classes of development inside protected areas. Also, development outside park boundaries can increase the pressure of weeds, pathogens, feral animals, water pollution and fire sources around the perimeter of the protected area, and these can then spread inside the protected area without further human intervention.

Conservation of representative ecosystems can therefore be improved either by adding to the protected area estate, by improving the effectiveness of protection in existing reserves, or by reducing modification to land outside reserves so as to improve its conservation value.

In purely financial terms, it would be within the scope of the world economy for richer governments and corporations simply to buy all the remaining areas of high conservation value worldwide at current market prices, and declare them as protected areas (Pimm, 2002). However, for many political reasons, this is very unlikely to happen. Many protected area management agencies don't have enough money to manage their existing estate, let alone add to it. The total area of national parks and similar reserves worldwide has continued to grow slowly (Eagles, 2002; Eagles and McCool, 2002; Eagles et al., 2002), and funding for some protected area management agencies has increased significantly over recent years. However, on a global scale, public protected areas are increasingly short of funds. At the same time, they are subject to increasing human pressures, both from around outside their borders, and from increasing visitor numbers and expectations. As a result, only the largest and most remote protected areas can simply be set aside to survive on their own. Most require continued management action to control ongoing conservation threats; and these management actions require operational funding.

Note that whereas a significant component of this funding is required for managing visitors, most parks agencies cannot solve funding shortfalls simply by closing their gates and keeping visitors out, for several reasons. Funds are still needed for basic conservation management, including control of fire, feral animals and weeds. Most parks don't have gates: and if there are no rangers to stop them, people will continue to enter and exploit protected areas, legally or not.

In addition, few parks agencies have a legal mandate to close parks to the public completely, except in very unusual circumstances; though they generally do have the power to impose a wide variety of specific restrictions. Even where the legal mandate exists, e.g. to limit numbers or ban particular historical uses, such as horse-riding or snowmobiles, it can be difficult for parks agencies to impose such restrictions in practice, unless they first muster strong political support from groups who favour conservation and low-impact recreation only. In addition, although the legal and financial systems that support parks and their management agencies can survive short-term political opposition, laws and budgets are themselves human social constructs and need continued political support to survive in the longer term. Parks agencies therefore need to maintain political constituencies who will support their continued existence; and the greater the external pressures they face, the more such support is needed.

Such political support may derive from four major groups, namely those who support protected areas for: existence values, conservation and global ecosystem services; local ecosystem services such as drinking water supplies; individual recreational opportunities; and commercial opportunities, such as tourism.

The first two of these groups have little or no negative impact on specific protected areas. However, the former provide rather diffuse and generalized support, rarely linked to marginal electorates or practical powerbrokers. The second is relevant only for a limited number of protected areas, such as those associated with municipal water catchments.

The recreational group is quite large, but does create on-site impacts, and will generally only maintain its support as long as recreational opportunities are still available. Indeed, if these opportunities are withdrawn, support may change to antagonism. For protected area management agencies, this group presents several management dilemmas. More outdoor recreation means more political support, but restricting numbers or activities to control impacts causes political contention. Different activities cause widely different *per capita* impacts, but higher-impact activities, which use expensive equipment, are likely to have greater funds for political lobbying. Demographics and interests change, and people of different ages, origins and, indeed, ethnic backgrounds may often want to use parks for different activities; but it can be difficult for parks agencies to provide a correspondingly changing spectrum of opportunities (Haas, 2002). And, finally, conflicts can be commonplace between different recreational groups, and between private recreational visitors and commercial tourism operations.

Until recently, commercial tour operators were not a significant stakeholder in protected area management, and in most of the world this is still the case. However, in some countries and areas, large-scale tourism operations, industry associations and government tourism portfolios have recognized the economic significance of protected areas for commercial tourism operations, and are exerting strong pressure for increased access and opportunities, and in some cases for a say in management. The rhetoric for such involvement is couched in terms such as partnership (Buckley, 2002a; DeLacy et al., 2002; Charters, 2002; IUCN, 2002); but the reality seems to be about the tourism industry wanting rights of access to national parks to run commercial ventures, with little mention of what the parks agencies and the public might receive in return. The

degree and direction of political debate on this topic differs considerably between nations.

In this volatile political landscape, and particularly in the context of political negotiations over so-called partnerships, it is timely to consider the current balance sheet between tourism and conservation. What are the benefits and costs of conservation to tourism, and what are the benefits and costs of tourism to conservation?

Trying to use any commercial industry, including tourism, as a conservation tool is perhaps grasping at straws. Human impacts on the planet continue to grow apace, however, and there seem to be remarkably few practical conservation tools which are both rapid and effective. Stringent laws and strong enforcement are most effective, but they are slow to establish and improve, not least because of international trade law. Markets can move quickly, but they are unprincipled and unpredictable. Tourism can muster considerable economic power, but tourism developers and entrepreneurs are in business for private profit, not public good. It is commonly in their commercial interests to gain access to natural tourist attractions as cheaply as possible, and it is not in their commercial interests to protect the natural environment, except as required to maintain their income. Here, therefore, I examine the principal mechanisms by which tourism may have either positive or negative impacts on the natural environment, and some of the political factors that affect the balance.

Benefits of Protected Areas for Ecotourism

Seas and scenery, wildlife and waterfalls, forests and mountains are major tourist attractions worldwide, and many of them owe their attractiveness, and indeed their continuing existence, to conservation reserves. People visit parks in ever-increasing numbers, and World Heritage Areas, national parks and similar reserves are major destinations for domestic and international tourists alike.

Although plants, animals, water and scenery occur in other public and private lands as well as parks, parks provide a number of additional advantages for commercial tour operations. Many national parks, and World Heritage Areas in particular, incorporate icon attractions which are well-known or, indeed, internationally famous, and which are effectively advertised through information materials produced for the general public by a protected area management agency. They have publicly funded access and publicly funded visitor infrastructure, including carparks, toilets, tracks and trails, lookouts, visitor centres and interpretive materials.

The economic scale and significance of conservation benefits to tourism are not well quantified, but they are very large. A number of estimates internationally indicate that at least half of the world's tourism and travel is so-called geotourism (Stueve et al., 2002), i.e. travel to specific geographic attractions, and much of this is to natural attractions, many of them within protected areas. Since the global tourism and travel industry is currently worth around US$500 billion per annum (p.a.) (WTO, 2002), this would suggest that conservation is worth around at least US$250 billion p.a. to tourism. Indeed, in North America alone it has been calculated that national parks contribute around US$250 billion p.a. to the tourism economy, including private recreation and other factors as well as commercial tourism (Eagles, 2002). In Australia, at least one-quarter to one-third of the tourism industry is in the so-called nature, eco- and adventure tourism (NEAT) sector (Buckley, 2000); i.e. around US$10 billion p.a. In many African and Latin American nations, almost the entire tourism industry is based on conservation reserves. In the Yukon area in northern Canada, every Can$1.00 invested by Parks Canada yields an increase of Can$3.50 in tourism revenues (Thompson and Peepre, 2002).

At its most basic, commercial opportunities exist wherever people visit parks and businesses can sell them tourist services. Such opportunities increase in value if they are restricted, so that one or more companies have a monopoly or oligopoly on providing such services. Values increase further where access is restricted and retail demand exceeds supply, so that businesses can charge an increasing premium over the costs of the service provided. And most valuable of all are opportunities to provide a tourism service where supply is restricted, demand is high and growing, and in addition, the right to provide the service is tradeable.

Thus, for example, a licence to run commercial tours in a national park provides a commercial opportunity even where licences are issued to all applicants, free of charge. For rafting trips on the Colorado Grand Canyon, however, the total number of people on the river is restricted by regulatory quotas which are effectively set by the physical availability of campsites, and there is a 17-year waiting list to run private trips. Only a small number of tour operators have permits to run rafting tours, with quota grandfathered from pre-permit times. Since quotas are expressed as person-launch-days and expire unless used, tour operators can simply increase prices until demand drops to match their quota, and increase profits accordingly. These permits are correspondingly valuable.

Costs of Protected Areas for Ecotourism

Costs of conservation for tourism fall into two main categories. First, designation as a protected area restricts activities by private property developers. However, since it also provides the attraction that interests the developers in the first place, the opportunity outweighs the restrictions. Secondly, many protected areas charge fees for commercial tour operations as well as for individual visitors. These fees are a cost to ecotourism businesses (Watson and Herath, 1999; Buckley et al., 2001; Lindberg and Halpenny, 2001; Haas, 2002). Commonly, however, these fees are very small, far below the value of the assets and services provided, and a very small component of total costs for the tour operator. They are also levied equally on all operators for the areas concerned, and in most cases also on independent visitors, so they do not generate any competitive differentials between operators or any disincentive to use commercial tour services. Conceivably they could differentiate between destinations, where some fees are higher than others, but currently they are too small to have a significant effect, relative to travel and tour costs overall.

Benefits of Ecotourism for Protected Areas

There are many potential mechanisms by which ecotourism could contribute to conservation (Buckley, 1998, 2000). Potentially the most significant contribution would occur if large-scale tourism businesses, tourism industry associations and government tourism portfolios were to lobby governments to reallocate public land from higher-impact primary industries to tourism and conservation. For various political reasons this rarely happens in practice, even in areas where tourism is many times more profitable than logging or similar activities. Except in the USA (USFS, 2002), public forestry agencies have been very slow to recognize the economic potential of tourism, although this is now changing slowly. Their political links are with the timber industry, including multi-national logging corporations and equipment manufacturers. Timber towns are slow to switch to tourism, because of internal social barriers (Forbes, 1998), and the tourism industry lobbies for access to national parks rather than public forests or rangelands, because parks are better known and already have publicly funded visitor infrastructure (Buckley, 2000). Tourism is indeed replacing primary industries in many areas, but mainly through grassroots initiatives by landowners and management agencies, not government tourism policies.

Rather than lobbying government for political action, a smaller-scale but much more reliable way for tour operators to increase the area of protected plant and animal habitat is to buy or lease the land themselves, and establish private reserves funded from tourism revenues. Perhaps the classic examples of this are the private game reserves of sub-Saharan Africa (Buckley, 2003; Carlisle, 2003).

Tourism companies can also contribute in cash or in kind to conservation organizations or conservation agencies. Some businesses specialize in running tours for not-for-profit organizations, where the tour price includes a contribution to the organization; and some of these organizations are conservation non-governmental organizations (NGOs). In some countries, there are individual tour operators that pay salaries for park rangers or have pro-

vided their field vehicles or communication systems (Buckley, 2003). However, such contributions seem to be relatively rare.

Other potential mechanisms by which tourism can contribute to conservation remain much less tangible. It is possible, but unproven, that clients of commercial ecotours may subsequently become political advocates for conservation, or may change their own lifestyles to reduce their own personal ecological footprints. It has also been suggested that ecolodges may be able to test low-impact technologies to the point where they are commercially viable for the retail residential market (Buckley, 1998). Again, this does not yet seem to have been demonstrated in practice.

Although there are a small number of private companies that do indeed make a significant contribution to conservation, these are currently the exceptions rather than the rule. Most of the companies that do make contributions are very small, and the few larger companies that follow suit generally make very small proportional contributions, e.g. a few tenths of 1% of total revenue. By far the majority of tourism companies operating in conservation areas make no corporate contribution at all to conservation management. Tour operators pay mandatory licence fees, but often these do not cover even the costs of running the parks permits system. They pay mandatory *per capita* entrance and camping fees, but these are typically the same as for individual visitors, and in some areas are even discounted to lower rates for commercial tour clients (Buckley *et al.*, 2001).

None of the above is surprising. Tourism is an industry, and most tourism operations are private ventures established to turn a profit, not NGOs with the public interest at heart. In addition, it is relatively rare for a single company to control all phases of a tourism development. Rather, various different corporations or individuals are involved at different stages. Some make a profit from land speculation and rezoning, some from construction, some from operating a going concern, and some from manufacturing and selling recreational equipment. None of these has any particular interest in conserving the natural environment, as long as there is more land to buy and sell, more buildings to construct, more hotels to run, and continuing sales of recreational equipment and clothing.

Similarly, most tourists are not environmental advocates: they are on holiday. Learning a little about the environment may be an interesting add-on, but it is not likely to change their life.

Also, since tourism is a business, tourism ventures are subject to the same risks as any other commercial enterprise. There are indeed examples where dedicated individuals or community groups have established successful tourism businesses that do contribute to conservation. Often, however, these businesses may then be undercut by copycat competitors, bought out by larger concerns or conglomerates, swamped by other industry sectors which destroy their primary attraction, or bankrupted by fluctuations in travel patterns, currency exchange rates or share prices.

One of the principal conclusions from a recent global audit of over 170 ecotourism enterprises (Buckley, 2003) was that ecotourism only contributes to conservation if a strong conservation framework is in place first, including both a legal mandate and management resources. Within such a framework, ecotourism can generate considerable revenue, sufficient to contribute to conservation of natural resources as well as paying dividends to shareholders. However, with rather few exceptions, the tourism industry tends to be reluctant to make such contributions, for the obvious reason that these payments reduce profits and dividends.

A distinction may perhaps be drawn between operators that have a primary long-term interest in a particular piece of land, with tourism as one way to generate a living from it; and those with primary interests in a tourism business, where access to land is simply one of the supplies to produce a marketable retail product. Communities, private reserves, protected area management agencies and, indeed, farmers and forestry agencies are more likely to have a long-term interest in a particular area of land, and are therefore more likely to reinvest tourism profits into conservation. However, for most of the tourism industry, the primary interest is simply in commercial tourism opportunities, and cheap or free access to land simply provides a commercial opportunity.

Costs of Ecotourism for Protected Areas

On the red side of the ledger, there is no doubt that tourism, even ecotourism, produces a wide range of negative impacts on the natural environment. A large part of the tourism industry is simply an incremental addition to urban accommodation and infrastructure, and existing transport networks. In addition, the production of goods and services for tourism involves most other sectors of the human economy, with consequential increases in consumption of energy, water and other resources, and production and disposal of wastes. Tourism developers and operators of all kinds, urban as well as nature-based, may adopt environmental technologies and management which reduce impacts to some extent. However, relatively few adopt measures beyond those required by development approval, pollution control and similar legislation, except for resource and energy conservation measures, where the principal consideration is reducing financial costs rather than environmental impacts.

As in any other industry sector, there is considerable variation between enterprises in the efficiency of energy and resource consumption, and in measures taken to minimize wastes. It is these 'brown' aspects of environmental management which are the principal targets of mainstream tourism ecocertification programmes such as Green Globe 21 (2002). If such programmes do in fact yield significant improvements in environmental management performance by large-scale public and private enterprises, this will indeed represent a contribution to the sustainability of the tourism industry (Honey, 2002). However, this is by no means certain (Font and Buckley, 2001). Whether intentionally or inadvertently, any form of industry self-regulation, such as ecocertification, may delay the establishment of more effective environmental management measures, such as new legislation or regulations. This happened, for example, with the so-called Responsible Care initiative in the chemical industry (Gunningham and Grabowsky, 1998).

Industry ecocertification schemes such as Green Globe 21 are themselves private enterprises which must maintain profits to survive. They are hence under strong commercial pressure to increase their membership base and to cut costs. They offer certification to operators that already have high environmental performance, e.g. those certified under other schemes. They may adopt multiple levels of certification, not necessarily distinguishable by the retail public, so as to lower entry-level standards and expand membership. And they may devote more of their budget to marketing than to audit. This contrasts with the introduction of new environmental legislation and regulations, which has little effect on industry leaders but which forces laggards to improve environmental management practices to a new baseline level. This is critical, since any attempt to reduce the aggregate environmental impacts of an entire industry sector depends far more on raising performance of laggards rather than leaders.

Although tourism and travel may make up around 10% of the global economy, it is not clear what proportion it contributes to global environmental impacts. On one hand, the economic scale of tourism is measured at a retail level, exaggerating its size relative to primary industries, which are quantified at a commodities level. On the other hand, tourism uses products from all other industry sectors, and hence contributes *pro rata* to their environmental impacts. Either way, tourism is certainly a large enough sector that it is worthwhile trying to reduce its contributions to air and water pollution and to resource consumption.

More critically, however, as noted earlier, the tourism industry can have direct and differential impacts in areas particularly significant for conservation of biological diversity; and these 'green' aspects of environmental management, largely ignored by ecocertification schemes, are at least as important as the 'brown' aspects. In established protected areas, ecotourism itself may well be the principal source of impacts, if management agencies have sufficient resources to prevent damage to biodiversity from weeds and pests, livestock encroachment or mining, and illegal activities such as fish and wildlife poaching and plant and timber harvesting.

Tourism can produce negative impacts on the natural environment through a wide variety of mechanisms at a wide variety of scales (Liddle, 1997; Manning, 1999; Buckley, 2001; Newsome, *et al.*, 2001; Eagles and McCool,

2002). These range from a single minimal-impact backcountry hiker, to large-scale infra-structure within protected areas, and intensive tourist accommodation and residential development immediately around its borders. The growth of adventure tourism and associated activities, including multi-sport races and similar competitive events, is significant, since for commercial adventure clients and competitors, the activity is more important than the environment, and minimal-impact practices are commonly ignored. Adventure tour operators and multi-sport event organizers do have an interest in minimizing impacts, so as to use the same site repeatedly, in the same way as local residents and outdoor recreation clubs. Whereas residents and club members continue to frequent the same area, commercial clients and event competitors generally do not.

Amenity migration is significant because it increases infrastructure, subdivision and residential development on the immediate borders of protected areas. This does not necessarily lead to complete vegetation clearance, as commonly happens for agricultural land uses, but it does commonly increase: the number of fences, which act as a barrier to wildlife movements; the number of dogs and cats, which prey on native birds and wildlife and may escape into protected areas and establish feral populations; cars and noise, which kill and disturb native birds and animals; and the introduction of garden plants and weeds, which may also disperse into protected areas. Many of the world's worst weeds were first introduced as garden plants, and many of the world's worst animal pests were first introduced as household pets.

In wilderness areas and other relatively pristine protected ecosystems, any human use produces some impacts, even if the greatest skills and care are used to minimize them. The impacts and management of outdoor recreation, small-scale commercial nature tourism, and public visitor infrastructure in national parks and similar areas have been reviewed on a number of occasions under the rubric of recreation ecology (Liddle, 1997; Manning, 1999; Buckley, 2001; Newsome *et al.*, 2001). The type and degree of impacts depend on a range of factors, including: number of people, group size, activity, equipment, minimal-impact skills and practices, ecosystems, season and management regime. For the same activity and equipment, minimal-impact practices, and management regime, more people means more impact. However, any of these factors can change per capita impacts by orders of magnitude, and can therefore outweigh the effects of numbers alone.

The ecological significance of different impacts differs considerably between different ecosystems. Impacts that are localized, obvious and easy to measure have been studied in much more detail than those that are diffuse, hidden and hard to measure. For most types of impacts, research data are very sparse. Even for the most heavily studied types of impacts, such as trampling of vegetation by hikers, there is nowhere near enough information to construct general predictive models that apply across a broad range of ecosystems (Buckley, 2001). There seems to be very little appreciation within the tourism industry, or even within protected area management agencies, of the complexity of ecological impacts, or the time and resources required to carry out scientifically valid ecological research (Buckley, 2002b).

To summarize all the different impacts of tourism on the natural environment is beyond the scope of this chapter, but a few general patterns are worth noting. Different activities cause widely different impacts. Impacts can include noise, air pollution, water pollution, groundwater depletion, modification to surface water flows, soil erosion or compaction, changed fire regimes, damage and disturbance to plants and vegetation, death and disruption of animal species and communities, introduction and dispersal of weeds and pests, introduction of plant and animal diseases and pathogens, disruption of plant and animal reproduction, interference with interspecies interactions, and a wide range of more subtle and complex higher-order effects.

Individual *per capita* impacts can vary by several orders of magnitude, depending on activities and equipment, place and timing, and minimal-impact skills and practices. The ecological significance of different types of impact, and hence of the activities that cause them and the minimal-impact practices and management regimes which may reduce them, differ greatly from one ecosystem to another. The most heavily studied impacts tend to be those that are obvious, localized and easy to measure. Many impacts of this type are also self-limiting, in the sense that they do not spread beyond the initial impact site unless the human disturbance continues. Some are also reversible, by appropriate management actions. In consequence, they are typically less significant for ecological integrity than impacts that are hidden and diffuse, hard to measure and manage, irreversible, and self-propagating, in the sense that once initiated, the impact continues to spread or intensify even if the original disturbance ceases. However, these distinctions are not always straightforward, since: (i) some impacts may be self-limiting in one ecosystem but self-propagating in another; (ii) some impacts may be self-limiting at low intensity, but become self-propagating if the initial impact exceeds a particular threshold of disturbance; and (iii) impacts which are minor and self-limiting in themselves may produce far-reaching secondary effects in some circumstances.

As an example, trampling of soils and vegetation by hikers can quickly cause quite significant damage to arctic–alpine ecosystems, whereas in the dense understorey of a tropical or subtropical rainforest, stinging plants and hooked vines may do more damage to the hiker than vice versa. However, even a barely detectable backcountry trail in dense forest may have secondary impacts if it is used by native or feral predators to hunt smaller native wildlife. Depending on the vegetation type, low-intensity trampling may do no lasting damage, since the vegetation can recover once the impact is removed. Beyond a certain threshold, which varies with the plant species concerned, however, trampling causes the plants to die, though often not immediately, and this may then lead to soil erosion, even if there was none initially. This may occur on steep hill slopes with friable soils, for example, or in permafrost areas which melt out and subside where insulating vegetation has been destroyed.

Conclusions

Comparing these various credits and debits, it is clear that conservation interests, agencies and land tenures make a very large net positive contribution to the tourism industry, by providing tourist attractions, protecting them from deterioration, and subsidizing access and facilities. This applies in developed and developing countries alike, although facilities may be fewer in the latter.

The net positive or negative contribution of tourism to conservation is less straightforward. Mainstream transport, accommodation and urban attractions have a range of negative impacts with no immediate positive offset. For the nature tourism subsector specifically, there are many mechanisms for potential positive contributions to conservation, either by lobbying for new national parks, setting up private reserves, helping to protect existing parks or changing land use in public land outside parks. However, to date, the practical quantitative contribution has been small (Buckley, 2003). There are many ways in which tourism has detracted from conservation by producing environmental impacts within public protected areas, and by building, contributing to or lobbying for large-scale infrastructure and/or residential development in and around protected areas. To date the monitoring and management of these has been limited. Additionally, most nature tourism products also rely on urban accommodation and transport internationally and in gateway towns.

Overall, in developing countries where conservation frameworks are often less effective, the net effect of tourism on conservation is probably positive: not because tourism itself is necessarily lower-impact, but because impacts from other sectors pose a greater risk. In developed nations with more effective protected area systems and management agencies, the net effect of tourism on conservation is probably negative, particularly if amenity migration is included.

As human populations and land-use pressures continue to grow worldwide, protected area management agencies face growing political challenges in maintaining public support for protected areas, so as to get the financial resources and public cooperation necessary for visitor and conservation management. In addition to traditional tasks such as controlling weeds, fires and feral animals, therefore, they now need to build and maintain political constituencies which will either lobby for public funding, or support the imposition of user charges, or both.

While some people appreciate the significance of protected areas for global sustainability and are glad to lend support for this reason alone, others are more likely to provide such support if they can make some immediate personal use of the areas concerned. And whereas minimal-impact backcountry bushwalking or birdwatching are preferred activities for more traditional users of the protected area estate, there are also social groups who want to use national parks simply for an out-of-town picnic, or for adventure activities such as rock climbing, mountain biking or whitewater kayaking.

In addition, some parks and other public lands have a history of use for horse-riding or motorized activities such as snowmobiling. Such uses can cause major environmental impacts, such as trampling by horses' hooves, introduction of pathogens in horse manure, and noise and air pollution from snowmobiles. They may also generate strong conflicts with other park users. However, despite these factors, there are strong political lobbies which make it difficult for protected area management agencies to control such uses. In some cases at least, it appears that such lobby groups are so-called 'astroturf', i.e. political lobby organizations that masquerade as grassroots groups, but are, in fact, established and funded by large-scale commercial interests, such as equipment manufacturers. Large-scale global trends, such as the increasing commercialization of the adventure recreation sector, therefore, and its increasing links with the clothing and entertainment industries, affect protected areas through political constituencies as well as on-ground impacts.

In both developed and developing nations, therefore, the overall balance of credits and debits between tourism and conservation is increasingly dependent on politics on local, national and international scales.

It was not coincidental, therefore, that tourism and conservation interests worldwide intensified their political efforts during the International Year of Ecotourism. Global social and environmental megatrends take time to turn around, whereas in politics it is said that 'a day is a long time'. However, short-term political manoeuvring, often in secret, affects the long-term future credits and debits between tourism and conservation.

References

Buckley, R.C. (1998) Can ecotourism yield net global environmental benefits? *National Ecotourism Conference 98*. Ecotourism Association of Australia, Margaret River, Australia.

Buckley, R.C. (2000) NEAT trends: current issues in nature, eco and adventure tourism. *International Journal of Tourism Research* 2, 437–444.

Buckley, R.C. (2001) Environmental impacts. In: Weaver, D. (ed.) *Encyclopaedia of Ecotourism*. CAB International, Wallingford, UK, pp. 189–212.

Buckley, R.C. (2002a) Public and private partnerships between tourism and protected areas. *Journal of Tourism Studies* 13, 26–38.

Buckley, R.C. (2002b) Ecological indicators of tourist impacts in parks. *Journal of Ecotourism* 2, 54–66.

Buckley, R.C. (2003) *Case Studies in Ecotourism*. CAB International, Wallingford, UK.

Buckley, R.C., Witting, N. and Guest, M. (2001) *Managing People in Australian Parks. 2. Commercial Operations Management*. CRC Tourism, Gold Coast, Australia.

Carlisle, L. (2003) Nature tourism and the environment: the Conservation Corporation Africa model. In: Buckley, R.C., Pickering, C.M. and Weaver, D. (eds) *Nature-based Tourism, Environment and Land Management*. CAB International, Wallingford, UK, pp. 17–24.

Charters, T. (Chair) (2002) *Draft Cairns Charter on Partnerships for Ecotourism*. Available at website www.ecotourism.org.au/charter.cfm (verified 26 November 2002).

DeLacy, T., Battig, M., Moore, S. and Noakes, S. (2002) *Public/Private Partnerships for Sustainable Tourism*. CRC Tourism, Gold Coast, Australia.

Eagles, P.F.J. (2002) Trends in park tourism: economics, finance and management. *Journal of Sustainable Tourism* 10, 132–153.

Eagles, P.F.J. and McCool, S.F. (2002) *Tourism in National Parks and Protected Areas: Planning and Management*. CAB International, Wallingford, UK.

Eagles, P.F.J., McCool, S.F. and Haynes, C.D. (2002) *Sustainable Tourism in Protected Areas: Guidelines for Planning and Management*. IUCN, Gland, Switzerland.

Font, X. and Buckley, R.C. (eds) (2001) *Tourism Ecolabelling*. CAB International, Wallingford, UK.

Forbes, W. (1998) Curry County sustainable nature-based tourism project. In: Hall, C.M. and Law, A.A. (eds) *Sustainable Tourism. A Geographical Perspective*. Longman, Harlow, UK, pp. 119–131.

Green Globe 21 (2002) *Sustainable 21st Century Tourism*. Available at website www.greenglobe21.com (verified 9 October 2002).

Gunningham, N. and Grabowsky, P. (1998.) *Smart Regulation*. Clarendon, Oxford, UK.

Haas G. (2002) *Visitor Capacity on Public Lands and Waters: Making Better Decisions*. National Recreation and Park Associates, Ashburn, Virginia.

Honey, M. (ed.) (2002) *Ecotourism and Certification: Setting Standards in Practice*. Island Press, Washington, DC.

IUCN (2002) *Vth World Parks Congress Provisional Programme*. Available at website http://iucn.org/themes/wcpa/wpc/programme/programme.html (verified 27 November 2002).

Liddle, M. (1997) *Recreation Ecology*. Chapman & Hall, London, UK.

Lindberg, K. and Halpenny, E. (2001) *Protected Area Visitor Fees*. Available at website www.ecotourism.org/protareavisgfees_summary.pdf (verified 3 December 2002).

Manning, R.E. (1999) *Studies in Outdoor Recreation*, 2nd edn. Oregon State University Press, Corvallis, Oregan.

Newsome, D., Moore, S.A. and Dowling, R.K. (2001) *Natural Area Tourism: Ecology Impacts and Management*. Channel View, Clevedon, UK.

Pimm, S.L. (2002) *The World According to Pimm: a Scientist Audits the Earth*. McGraw-Hill, New York.

Stueve, A.M., Cock, S.D. and Drew, D. (2002) *The Geotourism Study: Phase I Executive Summary*. Available at website www.tia.org/pubs/geotourismphasefinal.pdf (verified 12 June 2002).

Thompson, J. and Peepre, J. (2002) *Economic Benefits of Protected Areas*. Canadian Parks and Wilderness Society, Whitehorse. Available at website www.cpaswyukon.org/07-A Different Way of Business/ecben (verified 12 December 2002).

US Department of Agriculture, Forest Service (USFS) (2002) America's Wildland Playground. Available at website www.fs.fed.us/news/agenda/wildland_playground (verified 22 November 2002).

Watson, A.E. and Herath, G. (1999) Societal response to recreation fees on public lands. *Journal of Leisure Studies* 31, 325–334.

World Tourism Organisation (2002) Latest data. Available at website www.world-tourism.org/market_research/facts&figures/latest_data (verified 26 November 2002).

2

The Cost of Getting There: Impacts of Travel to Ecotourism Destinations

David G. Simmons and Suzanne Becken

Environment, Society and Design Division, Lincoln University, New Zealand

Introduction

This chapter discusses energy use and carbon dioxide emissions associated with ecotourism. To date most research has focused on the visible and direct effects of ecotourism activities; however, the analysis presented here suggests that far greater attention needs to be paid to the invisible effects, especially those arising from the travel inputs throughout the 'ecotourism system'. Data presented are drawn from recent research in New Zealand which, while not assembled for this specific analysis, have been extended to discuss ecotourism in New Zealand.

Much of this volume focuses on defining and measuring the outcomes from ecotourism at the site level. Increasingly ecotourism has been described to represent, or at least encourage, sustainable forms of tourism in natural areas. *Sustainable tourism* is focused on 'using resources sustainably' and 'reducing overconsumption and waste' (Tourism Concern, 1991). Accordingly, ecotourism has also been defined as

> . . . environmentally responsible travel and
> visitation to relatively undisturbed natural
> areas, in order to enjoy and appreciate nature
> (and any accompanying cultural features –
> both past and present) that promotes
> conservation, has low visitor impact, and
> provides for beneficially active socio-
> economic involvement of local populations
> (Ceballos-Lascurain, 1996, p. 20).

However, travel or mobility are mostly associated with considerable resource use in the form of fossil fuels, and it therefore directly challenges the principles set out above for sustainable tourism.

For ecotourism, a travel component can occur at three distinct scales: first, transport directly associated with the ecotourism experience, for example a boat trip around an ecotourism site; secondly, travel between various ecotourism sites or operations; and thirdly, transport from the home location to the destination, where the ecotourism experiences take place. Ecotourism often occurs in remote areas (Boyd and Butler, 1996) and in developing countries or island states (Gössling, 1999), which means that this third travel component often requires international long-distance air travel. It is argued in this chapter that at each of these travel components ecotourism is associated with substantial energy use and greenhouse gas emissions, and that future concepts and developments need to take into consideration measures to mitigate these effects. We argue that ecotourism will fail to be on the 'deep green' or sustainable side of the nature tourism spectrum, if these criteria of environmental sustainability are not met in the future.

Interestingly, most ecotourism research and product development focuses on local, on-site environmental impacts resulting from ecotourism activities (Cole, 1995; Buckley, 2000a, 2001), with the wider global consequences rarely being analysed. Transport, as a main contributing factor to resource use associated with ecotourism activities, has, at most, been dealt with as a source of local air pollution, congestion or habitat destruction for infrastructure construction. Research on environmental impacts mostly deals with the broader concepts of nature tourism or sustainable tourism, rather than with the very specific niche product of ecotourism, which has been difficult to distinguish sufficiently from these other forms of tourism (Buckley, 2000b).

In the same way as there is disagreement as to what exactly ecotourism comprises, it is problematic to identify and capture 'ecotourists', and to separate them from other visitors to natural areas. Following criteria for ecotourists in Kenya by Ballantine and Eagles (1994), for example, the large majority of holiday visitors to a 'green' destination such as New Zealand would qualify as ecotourists. Taking the stricter definition of Butler (1992) (given in Higham and Lück, 2002), however, only few tourists would meet the criteria. While most tourists to New Zealand consider 'learning about nature' and visiting natural areas as important (criteria from Ballantine and Eagles), they probably rarely 'benefit the natural resource', and the experience is mostly not 'intrinsic', 'biocentric' and not 'thrill-seeking' (selected criteria from Butler). For this reason, we would define tourists to New Zealand more broadly as nature tourists and do not specify to what degree they would qualify as ecotourists in the purist sense. This reflects the perspective that during their visit most tourists engage in some sort of 'ecotourist' activity (for example visiting a National Park), or by undertaking a tour that possibly could qualify as an 'ecotour' (for example wildlife scenic boat cruises or cultural performances).

This chapter discusses energy use and carbon dioxide emissions associated with ecotourism in New Zealand, and is structured according to the three dimensions of travel identified above. The local level (on-site activity) is considered first, and is followed by a discussion of national travel patterns (between-site travel, or itineraries), and international travel by tourists. Throughout, New Zealand is used as a case study, as our analysis has been able to draw on unique datasets and recently completed analyses.

On-site Travel

Clearly, ecotourism forms an important part of the tourism industry in New Zealand, building on a long tradition of tourism in natural areas (Dowling, 2001). To the present, there are no ecotourism accreditation programmes in New Zealand, although following the International Year of Ecotourism in 2002 the Nature and Ecotourism Accreditation Programme (NEAP-GG21) is being introduced in New Zealand. In an effort to develop a national database of ecotourism operators in New Zealand, Higham *et al.* (2001) identified 400 businesses that offer some sort of nature-based tourism product. Of these operators, 247 (62%) promoted themselves as ecotourism providers. The differentiation between ecotourism and nature or adventure tourism seems to be experience-based rather than impact-based, which means that more emphasis is put on the educational part of the product than on its environmental outcomes. One key issue in this context is on-site transport, which is often a fundamental component of most nature tourism operations.

Previous research on the New Zealand tourist attraction and activity sector (Becken and Simmons, 2002) revealed that many tourist activities require some form of motorized transport. As part of a broader study on energy use in tourism, data were collected on energy use from a cross-section of activity providers ($N=107$) broken down by different energy sources; for example, diesel for transport and electricity for building functions. It became evident that nature-based 'tourist activities' are considerably more energy intensive on a per visitor basis than the more urban-based 'tourist attractions' (for example, visiting museums or botanical gardens). 'Ecotours', in particular, were found to be built around taking visitors to natural assets by various types of motorized vehicles; for example, four-wheel drive vehicles or boats. In fact, the further activities explore remote areas, the larger the energy use due to the increasing transport requirements (Table 2.1). The highest per capita energy use is associated with scenic flights (344 MJ) and jet-boat excursions (200 MJ). Our data also indicate that combination activities such as watching wildlife (400 MJ) are very energy intensive, because in New Zealand most wildlife operations focus on marine mam-

Table 2.1. Energy use per visitor for different tourist activities (source: Becken and Simmons, 2002).

Activity	N	Mean energy use per visitor (MJ)	Standard deviation
Walking	4	3.2	3.2
Shopping	3	3.4	2.5
National Park visitor centre	11	3.5	4.4
Historic site	5	4.0	1.8
Botanical garden	3	6.2	1.3
Farm show	3	6.9	3.2
Museum and art gallery	9	9.7	11.4
Golf	3	12.0	9.7
Theatre or concert	3	21.5	15.5
Experience centre	6	29.2	14.4
Rafting	4	36.4	17.0
Adventure	4	56.9	46.7
Horse-riding	4	117.9	127.0
Scenic boat cruise	5	164.7	110.4
Wildlife in natural setting	3	234.3	164.8
Jet-boating	4	255.3	147.4
Scenic flight	3	344.4	91.7

mals that are viewed from a boat. In contrast, more general tourist activities, such as playing golf (12 MJ) or visiting a visitor centre (3.5 MJ), are low-energy tourist activities.

Between-site Travel

Most tourists to New Zealand are likely to have some interest in nature, and, in fact, it proves difficult to select a sample of 'ecotourists' out of the existing database on international tourists (annual International Visitor Survey). For example, 25% of all international tourists visit geo-thermal areas, 17% undertake a boat cruise and 12% engage in trekking (Tourism New Zealand, 2002). Moreover, New Zealand is generally characterized as a touring destina-tion, with attractions being widely dispersed, which induces multi-destination itineraries (Oppermann, 1994; Becken *et al.*, 2003).

For this reason it is difficult to compare holiday itineraries of 'ecotourists' with 'non-ecotourists'. For the purposes of this analysis, it was therefore decided to discuss transport energy use associated with a hypothetical self-drive itinerary that is promoted on the web-site homepage of Tourism New Zealand, the national marketing agency. These general self-drive itineraries are tailored for different lengths

of stay, and also include reference to a variety of local tourist attractions and activities en route, among them numerous ecotourism attractions. The analysis brings with it the assumption that a potential nature tourist (as are most tourists to New Zealand) searching the Internet selects one of the suggested multi-day itineraries, or builds a similar one based on their specific interests, from one of the many other promotional sources that support Tourism New Zealand's marketing efforts. Based on an average length of stay of 20 days (Statistics New Zealand, 2000), the 22-day itinerary (being the nearest surrogate) was chosen (Table 2.2). This suggested route combines the North Island with the South Island through a flight from Auckland to Christchurch. Energy use is calcu-lated assuming the use of a rental car (average occupancy 2.5 passengers; Becken, 2002a), which has an energy intensity of 0.94 MJ per passenger-kilometre (62.7 g CO_2 per passenger-kilometre). The energy intensity of domestic air travel is 2.75 MJ per passenger-kilometre (EECA, 1999), resulting in CO_2 emissions of 188.9 g per passenger-kilometre.

The suggested itinerary covers 3773 km and results in a total transport energy use of 6388 MJ and concomitant release of 430 kg of CO_2. The inland flight alone makes up one-third of this energy use. This compares with an

Table 2.2. Tourism New Zealand's suggested self-drive itinerary (TNZ, 2003) and associated energy use and carbon dioxide emissions.

Day	From – to	Eco-activity	Distance (km)	Transport mode	Energy use (MJ)	CO$_2$ (kg)
1	Auckland – Whitianga	Karaka bird hide	214	Rental car	201	13
2	Whitianga – Tauranga	Boat cruise, kayak trips, fishing	167	Rental car	157	10
3	Tauranga – Rotorua	Dolphin encounters, geothermal attractions	86	Rental car	81	5
4	Rotorua – Gisborne	Horse trekking	286	Rental car	269	18
5	Gisborne – Napier	Wine and food trails	216	Rental car	203	14
6	Napier, day trip to Taupo	Cape Kidnapper gannet colony	286	Rental car	269	18
7	Napier – Wellington	Kapiti Island	335	Rental car	315	21
8	Wellington	Guided walking tours		Rental car	0	0
9	Wellington – New Plymouth	Whanganui National Park	355	Rental car	334	22
10	New Plymouth – Waitomo	Mt Taranaki	173	Rental car	163	11
11	Waitomo – Auckland	Glow worm caves	200	Rental car	188	13
12	Auckland – Christchurch		744	Domestic air	2046	141
13	Christchurch – Dunedin	Royal Albatross Colony, Penguin Place	362	Rental car	340	23
14	Dunedin – Te Anau	Trout fishing, caves	290	Rental car	273	18
15	Day trip to Milford or Doubtful Sound	Boat cruise, ecology tours	121	Rental car	114	8
16	Te Anau – Queenstown	Maori culture	170	Rental car	160	11
17	Queenstown – Wanaka	Flightseeing	117	Rental car	110	7
18	Wanaka – Franz Joseph	Haast information centre	287	Rental car	270	18
19	Franz Joseph – Greymouth	Okarito Lagoon, white heron colony	177	Rental car	166	11
20	Greymouth – Nelson	Pancake rocks	327	Rental car	307	21
21	Nelson – Blenheim	Sea kayaking	138	Rental car	130	9
22	Blenheim – Christchurch	Kaikoura whale watching	312	Rental car	293	20

average transport energy use of 2830 MJ across all international tourists in New Zealand in 2000 (Becken, 2002b). Calculated on a daily basis, the suggested tour consumes 290 MJ/day for transport alone. In addition, a tourist would require energy for accommodation, which in New Zealand ranges between 25 MJ per night on a campground to 155 MJ for an average night in a hotel (Becken *et al.*, 2001). (For New Zealand's international tourism, transport within the destination has been estimated to consume 69% of all energy deployed across the sector; Becken, 2002b.) The participation in eco-activities requires additional energy input, as indicated in Table 2.1.

As mentioned previously, it is very difficult to draw a line between ecotourists, nature tourists and other tourists to New Zealand. However, it becomes clear that visiting ecotour-

ism sites and operations in New Zealand is most likely associated with a multi-destination or touring holiday. This style of travel induces considerable energy use, in which energy deployed for transport dominates other energy required for accommodation and recreational activities.

It is also instructive to make comparisons among different travel styles. At the other end of the spectrum from an ecotourism holiday in New Zealand (as described above) would be an all-inclusive holiday in a resort, such as those found in tropical destinations such as the Caribbean. This type of mass-tourism has often been stigmatized by being potentially environmentally harmful (due to high levels of energy use to meet guests' expectations of 'luxury'), socially incompatible and culturally dangerous. On the basis of energy use, however, it appears that tourists who stay comparatively immobile in one single resort consume less energy compared with so-called ecotourists. The UK Centre for Economic and Environmental Development (UK CEED, 1998) analysed the impacts of all-inclusive resorts in Santa Lucia, and found that one guest-night is equivalent to about 109 MJ (own calculations derived from figures provided by UK CEED). In addition to this base energy consumption, tourists are picked up from the airport and undertake occasional excursions. However, most activities are on-site and therefore do not require transportation. Notwithstanding the climatic differences, the hypothetical ecotourism holiday in New Zealand discussed above is therefore about three times as energy intensive on a per-day basis as the Santa Lucia example. Within New Zealand a separate analysis of international tourism has indicated that energy intensities vary considerably across six identified tourist types: coach (536 MJ/day), soft comfort (431 MJ/day), auto (321 MJ/day), camper (310 MJ/day), backpacker (250 MJ/day), tramper (hiker) (212 MJ/day), and visiting friends and relatives (205 MJ/day) (Becken *et al.*, 2003).

It appears therefore that curbing energy use associated with ecotourism holidays fundamentally requires reducing travel distances. Hence, a more regional approach, where tourists stay longer in one region, needs to be considered. Tourism New Zealand has reported a trend that 'fewer tourists want to race along the traditional "golden route". The new rule in travel is to "go slow and savour" – meaning visitors want to do fewer regions, but in greater depth' (Anon., 2002). In the promotion of regional travel lies a great challenge for regional and national marketing agencies, but also a great potential to achieve synergetic effects of reducing transport energy use and supporting regional development. Such measures will not be easy policy options, however, as much ecotourism development is promoted under the aegis of regional economic development, and in so doing differing regions are set to compete against each other.

Travel to the Destination

Ecotourism destinations and sites are often located in developing countries, while ecotourists tend to originate from Western countries, typically Europe or North America (Gössling, 2000). For this reason air travel is the most common transport mode used for ecotourism holidays. Aviation has been identified as an important contributor to climate change, with passenger air travel comprising about 3.5% of worldwide greenhouse gas emissions (IPCC, 1999). In spite of external 'shocks', such as the sudden acute respiratory syndrome (SARS) outbreak, and increasing terrorist activity, The World Tourism Organization continues to predict an increasing long-term trend of long-distance travel to exotic destinations combined with an increasing interest in nature activities. Nature tourists often originate from the wealthy countries in Europe, North America and Oceania and travel to destinations such as South America, Asia and Africa. As a result of this geographical distribution, considerable migrations are involved to transport nature tourists to their destination. This global situation is particularly evident in the case of New Zealand, an isolated destination in the South Pacific where the average one-way flying distance of international visitors was found to be 12,000 km (Becken, 2002c). Clearly, from a global perspective the enormous energy consumption associated with this travel makes any energy reduction achievements at the destination look minor. The emission of 430 kg of CO_2 for the self-drive itinerary presented above is about the same as the one-way flight for Australian visitors to New Zealand. Visitors from Britain emit about six times the emissions of their destination-based travel on their one-way flight to New Zealand (Table 2.3).

When looking at the importance of different nationalities at representative ecotourism operations in New Zealand (Higham *et al.*, 2001), it is evident that most 'ecotourists' travel a long way to New Zealand, mostly from Europe. This fact alone may lead to the conclusion that tourism in natural areas in New Zealand can be classified at most as nature tourism, but not ecotourism, unless measures are taken to mitigate the impact of the long-distance flight.

Discussion

A generally accepted model of resource use would suggest that one either reduces inputs at

Table 2.3. Nationalities of visitors to New Zealand ecotourism operations alongside calculated carbon dioxide emissions from their international travel to New Zealand (one-way flight).

Nationality	Per cent[a]	CO_2 emissions (tonnes)[b]
New Zealander	28.3	NA
British	26.1	2.4
American	15.1	1.4
German	5.0	2.5
Australian	4.7	0.4
Canadian	4.0	1.8
Dutch	2.8	2.3
Swiss	1.9	2.3
Danish	1.3	2.5[c]
Belgian	1.0	2.3[c]

NA, not applicable.
[a] Source: Higham *et al*. (2001).
[b] Source: Becken (2002c).
[c] Danish equated with German and Belgian with Dutch.

source, reviews and changes technologies (resource transformation systems) or, failing that, mitigates the outcomes, for example through carbon offsetting schemes. Each of these has application to the ecotourism system and resource use we have described above.

In the first instance, ecotourism has been promoted as an environmentally positive form of tourism – indeed many contemporary definitions list a 'positive contribution to nature' as one, if not the, core requirement. To the present, local and directly visible effects have been treated with much greater interest and attention in the ecotourism literature. However, as our above data demonstrate, it may be that ecotourism's more insidious effects lie in those that remain invisible. Increasing evidence of the invisible effects of ecotourism activities may lead those who call themselves ecotourists to consider changing their behaviour. Modifications to tourist behaviour could include both less frequent and less extensive (between and within destinations) travel. Increased length of stay either regionally, or at key sites, is certainly another possibility that could reduce travel costs. The fact that in this year (2003) the World Tourism Organization is hosting a conference on tourism and global climate change suggests that greater attention is being focused on the energy costs of tourism

overall. Among all forms of tourism, it might be reasonable to assume that ecotourists might be the most susceptible to change messages.

An increasing number of initiatives seek to encourage better practice through providing general tips on how to reduce energy use and emissions, and through describing case studies of good practice (Commonwealth Department of Tourism, 1995; Green Globe Asia Pacific, 2000). Key options include: (i) reducing the need to travel, for example by linking several single trips to one multipurpose trip (trip-chaining); (ii) increasing transport efficiency, for example through occupancy levels, fuel efficiency, cleaner fuels, driving behaviour, and vehicle size; and (iii) offsetting carbon dioxide emissions by investing into renewable energies or tree-planting schemes (carbon sinks). Table 2.4 provides a list of suggestions to reduce tourist transportation.

In terms of technology, considerable progress has been made in air technology in the past two decades (IPCC, 1999), but these gains appear to have been overrun by the pervasive growth of tourism demand. None the less, options do exist for ongoing marginal gains and more fuel-efficient engines (for both air and land applications) and in traffic management. Notwithstanding these gains, the sheer distances covered by air transport and the overwhelming contribution of origin-destination or intra-destination linkages makes air transport the single significant driver of tourism energy emissions.

To embrace fully the concept of ecotourism as sustainable tourism, a tourist can choose between a number of operators at, and between, destinations, including those who market themselves as ecotourism businesses. For major airlines, however, there are none operating as ecotourism businesses *per se* although there is an emerging trend for some to benchmark their environmental performance, with views to increasing resource efficiency and possible carbon sequestration.

Carbon sequestration is a medium-term process whereby carbon dioxide emissions from the combustion of hydrocarbon fuels is (re)-bound into carbon storage, via the growth of plant materials, most often in the form of mature forest systems. Carbon sequestration offers some promise, but only for those destinations that can

Table 2.4. On the way to better practice (after Commonwealth Department of Tourism, 1995).

Action	How
Encourage longer stays in one area	Through attractive packages (discounts), attraction chaining
Encourage tourists to use energy-efficient transport modes	Public transport (provide timetables), collective transport (e.g. shuttle bus), attractive tour packages with interpretation, meals enroute and stops at interesting places, promote fuel-efficient cars, diesel cars
Transport behaviour by staff members	Carpooling of staff, minibuses, encourage public transport or cycling, combine guest transport and delivery of supplies, use telecommunication
Reduce vehicle use	Encourage walking and biking, plan trips to reduce travel distance
Driving behaviour and vehicle performance	Tyre pressure, regular service and tuning, speed of 90 km/h instead 110, driver training courses, switch off idling engines, use air-conditioning wisely

offer real opportunities due to their geographical possibilities. In New Zealand, carbon sequestration from tourism (among other sectors) can address general biodiversity goals as previously modified landscapes are re-established in native flora. Kaikoura, a Green Globe 21 benchmarked community, which is often seen as an ecotourism destination because of its focus on marine mammal watching, has calculated the need to plant 2 million trees to sequester the carbon from its tourism sector (McNicol *et al.*, 2002). To some, at least, this represents the opportunity for new tourist experiences as they 'bury' their carbon and receive appropriate recognition [e.g. a global positioning system (GPS) reference, and/or a digital image] for their action. Preliminary estimates for New Zealand as a whole also indicate that all carbon from internal travel could be sequestered. In a bold move, the New Zealand Tourism Strategy Group (2001) has signalled an intention for the sector to be 'carbon neutral' by the implementation date (2010). Elsewhere there are already a number of initiatives at the level of the individual firm, including the Green Globe 21 programme, which has energy management as the first of its ten criteria towards sustainable tourism businesses.

Thus, in the realm of energy and emissions management, ecotourism may again become a lead segment for more sustainable tourism practices. Within the above discussion of a tourism 'production function' for ecotourism, it remains yet to be seen what role, if any, will be played by various government interventions – be they incentives or regulations. Shadow pricing of external costs, via carbon taxes, are a possible mechanism under the Kyoto Protocol, coming into force in New Zealand in 2007. If at a later stage international travel was to be included in the Kyoto Protocol, this could have significant effects on the long-haul ecotourism market, as could refocusing market efforts as governments are challenged to meet their Kyoto obligations. One implication of the above that has yet to be exposed to international debate is the potential consequence of reduced travel to the Third World. Earlier in this discussion we had indicated that, on a global scale, many destinations offering ecotourism opportunities are to be found in Third World destinations. Modifications to the demand for long-haul travel may arise from a number of means, including price, as well as moral or ethical pressures. If this were to happen, then this could set in train a wider set of problems, as many Third World destination areas have a much higher dependency on (eco)tourism as an earner of foreign exchange than most, if not all, of their major source markets.

The data and analyses reported here represent a preliminary analysis of ecotourism viewed through the lens of energy use and emissions. Much of these data were assembled for other broader analyses, and the itinerary analysis, while being based on publicly available recommendations, remains hypothetical.

Notwithstanding these caveats, the early indications are that ecotourism in its present configuration (certainly in New Zealand at least) is a highly energy-dependent form of travel.

Aside from re-examining the data and analyses presented here, the immediate implication is for ecotourism operators' associations and national policy makers to examine the wider tourism systems in which they operate. Without such considerations, ecotourism may merely present a scattering of relatively well-managed sites within an expansive and expensive tourism system that leads both tourism and development away from their overarching goals of sustainability.

References

Anon. (2002) Research shows visitors want to savour. *Inside Tourism* 425, 7.

Ballantine, J.L. and Eagles, P.F.J. (1994) Defining Canadian ecotourists. *Journal of Sustainable Tourism* 2(4), 210–214.

Becken, S. (2002a) *Tourism and Transport in New Zealand – Implications for Energy Use.* Report No. 54, July. TRREC, Lincoln University.

Becken, S. (2002b) Energy use in the New Zealand Tourism Sector. PhD thesis. Environment, Society and Design Division, Lincoln University.

Becken, S. (2002c) Analysing international tourist flows to estimate energy use associated with air travel. *Journal of Sustainable Tourism* 10(2), 114–132.

Becken, S. and Simmons, D. (2002) Understanding energy consumption patterns of tourist attractions and activities in New Zealand. *Tourism Management* 23(4), 343–354.

Becken, S., Frampton, C. and Simmons, D. (2001) Energy consumption patterns in the accommodation sector – the New Zealand Case. *Ecological Economics* 39(3), 371–386.

Becken, S., Simmons, D. and Frampton, C. (2003) Energy use associated with different travel choices. *Tourism Management* 24(3), 267–278.

Boyd, S. and Butler, R. (1996) Managing ecotourism: an opportunity spectrum approach. *Tourism Management* 17(8), 557–566.

Buckley, R. (2000a) Tourism in the most fragile environments. *Tourism and Recreation Research* 25, 31–40.

Buckley, R. (2000b) Neat trends: current issues in nature, eco- and adventure tourism. *International Journal of Tourism Research* 2, 437–444.

Buckley, R. (2001) Environmental impacts. In: Weaver, D.B. (ed.) *The Encyclopaedia of Ecotourism.* CAB International, Wallingford, UK, pp. 379–394.

Ceballos-Lascurain, H. (1996) *Tourism, Ecotourism and Protected Areas: the State of Nature-based Tourism Around the World and Guidelines for its Development.* IUCN, Gland, Switzerland.

Cole, D.N. (1995) Experimental trampling of vegetation. Relationship between trampling intensity and vegetation response. *Journal of Applied Ecology* 32, 203–214.

Commonwealth Department of Tourism (1995) *Best Practice Ecotourism. A Guide to Energy and Waste Minimisation.* Commonwealth Department of Tourism, Canberra, Australia.

Dowling, R.K. (2001) Oceania (Australia, New Zealand and South Pacific). In: Weaver, D.B. (ed.) *The Encyclopedia of Ecotourism.* CAB International, Wallingford, UK, pp. 379–394.

Energy Efficiency Conservation Authority (EECA) (1999) *Energy-wise Monitoring Quarterly. New Zealand's Transport Sector Energy Use: Highlights.* Issue 14, December. EECA, Wellington, New Zealand.

Gössling, S. (1999) Ecotourism: a means to safeguard biodiversity and ecosystem functions? *Ecological Economics* 29, 303–320.

Gössling, S. (2000) Sustainable tourism development in developing countries: some aspects of energy use. *Journal of Sustainable Tourism* 8(5), 410–425.

Green Globe Asia Pacific (2000) *A Research Report on Exemplary Environmental Practice in Key Tourism Sectors.* Green Globe Asia Pacific, Canberra, Australia.

Higham, J. and Lück, M. (2002) Urban ecotourism: a contradiction in terms? *Journal of Ecotourism* 1(1), 36–50.

Higham, J., Carr, A. and Gale, S. (2001) *Ecotourism in New Zealand: Profiling Visitors to New Zealand Ecotourism Operations.* Research Paper Number Ten. Department of Tourism, School of Business, Dunedin, New Zealand.

Intergovernmental Panel on Climate Change (IPCC) (1999) *Aviation and the Global Atmosphere.* Available at website http://www.grida.no/climate/ipcc/aviation (verified 2 December 2001).

McNicol, J., Shone, M. and Horn, C. (2002) *Green Globe 21 Kaikoura Community Benchmarking Pilot Study.* Report No. 53. Tourism Research and Education Centre (TREC), Lincoln University.

Oppermann, M. (1994) Comparative analysis of escorted tour packages in New Zealand and North America. In: Ryan, C. (ed.) *Tourism Down-Under: a Tourism Research Conference.* Massey University, Palmerston North.

Statistics New Zealand (2000) *International Visitor Arrivals to New Zealand.* Available at website http://www.stats.govt.nz (verified 1 February 2001).

Tourism Concern (1991) *Beyond the Green Horizon.* Tourism Concern and World Wildlife Fund, Roehampton Institute, London, UK.

Tourism New Zealand (TNZ) (2002) International Visitors' Surveys. Available at website http://www.trcnz.govt.nz/Surveys/International + Visitor + Survey/ (verified 15 March 2003).

Tourism New Zealand (TNZ) (2003) Suggested drive itineraries. Retrieved from website http://www.purenz.com/index.cfm/purenz_page/01D07FC2-C58B-4AED-A653-0DD8FCCCAC16.html (verified 15 March 2003).

Tourism Strategy Group (TSG) (2001) *New Zealand Tourism Strategy 2010.* TSG, Wellington, New Zealand.

UK CEED (1998) *An Assessment of the Environmental Impacts of Tourism in St Lucia.* Report 5/98. British Airways and British Airways Holidays, Cambridge, UK.

3

Impacts of Tourism-related In-migration: the Greater Yellowstone Region

Jerry Johnson

Department of Political Science, Montana State University, Montana, USA

Introduction

Tourism and recreation, like most entertainment businesses, are dependent on an ever-expanding market for an ever-changing product that appears novel and exciting. In the face of a flat, and even declining, ski industry since the mid-1980s, the successful Rocky Mountain resort (e.g. Vail, Colorado; Sun Valley, Idaho; Jackson, Wyoming) is, in large part, subsidized by a thriving market for second homes and recreational ranch properties. The buyers are an increasingly affluent, ageing population. In the many tourism towns that dot the West, construction and home sales are two of the most vigorous business activities in local economies.

While tourists and their related activities may bring negative impacts to a community or region (Rotham, 1998) the consequences may well be short term or manageable by governments or markets. For example, minimizing the degradation of environmental resources as a result of too much visitation can be mitigated by temporary closures, a permit system that limits visitation, alternative means of experiencing the attraction, or discriminatory pricing.

The same may not be true for real estate development and the infrastructure that comes with tourism-stimulated migration (Clifford, 2002). This chapter provides a discussion of two categories of impacts resulting from rural residential development in resort towns and tourist destinations in the Greater Yellowstone Region (USA). The first category includes those that affect the physical, administrative and public service infrastructure. The second includes those that accrue to the social, economic and quality of life elements of a community. Both categories bring with them positive and negative attributes of change. On one hand, rural residential development pressure may present challenges to local jurisdictions in terms of public service provision. On the other hand, development may enhance the local economy or quality of life in small towns that are partially or wholly dependent on tourism activity.

Background: the Greater Yellowstone Region and Tourism

The lands that comprise the Greater Yellowstone Region (Fig. 3.1) are home to key predator species (grizzly bear and grey wolf), prey species (elk, deer, moose), and a host of birds and smaller mammals (Hansen *et al.*, 2002). Several species in the region are listed under the Endangered Species Act or are 'species of special concern'. The landscape is a mosaic of wild and domestic vegetation, including coniferous forests, arid shrub and grasslands, cultivated crops that include wheat, maize, potatoes, lucerne and hay, as well as domestic

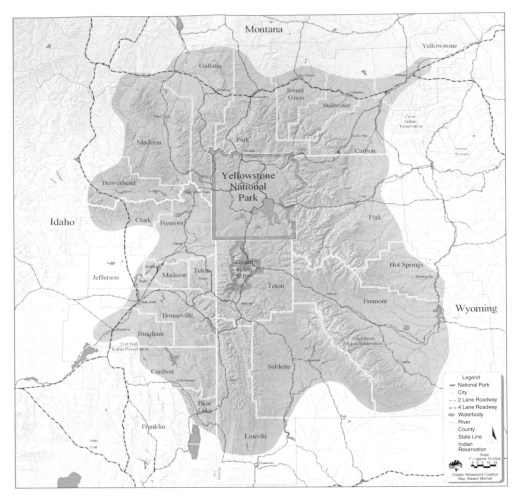

Fig. 3.1. Greater Yellowstone Region, USA.

animal production. Several major river systems originate in the region; many are highly developed for agriculture and the private lowland river valleys (<1800 m above sea level) are much sought-after rural homesites. The scenery can be spectacular. Several major mountain ranges in the area exceed 3000 m above sea level. Most of these spectacular vistas are found on public land (80% of the land base) and the remaining 20% of the land is privately owned. Public land managers are increasingly consumed with the tradeoff between commodity production (minerals, timber, grazing and recreation) and its impacts (i.e. off-road vehicles, snowmobiles, wilderness boundary enforcement). Long-time private landowners are chal-

lenged by rapidly escalating land prices and the difficulty of continuing to make a living from the land.

The region is home to over 370,000 residents, many recently arrived in the past decade. Several counties are among the fastest growing in the nation. During the past decade the growth rate was nearly 19%, compared to 13% nationally (US Bureau of the Census, 2000). In the region there are a few micropolitan centres (Vias *et al.*, 2002) where most residents live and work, and many others live in neighbouring small towns or in the rural countryside.

Slightly over 3.5 million tourists visit Yellowstone National Park each year. The regional tourism industry is comprised of an assortment of activities, ranging from high-value alpine skiing, snowmobiling, big-game hunting, and fly-fishing to lower-value activities such as bike-touring, hiking and river-running. The tourism industry thrives in a full spectrum of public and private settings. The majority of recreation takes place on public land comprised of the two national parks and the seven national forests in the region. Private lands development include the Yellowstone Club – an exclusive resort home development and ski area – and many luxurious fishing lodges on large ranch properties; many of these lodges enjoy exclusive access to 'spring creeks' located on ranch property. The single feature that ties all tourist activity in the Greater Yellowstone together is that it takes place primarily in a sparsely populated rural setting; this differentiates it from some other tourist destinations in America, located in an urban setting (e.g. Disneyland, Niagara Falls, Las Vegas).

Tourism as an Attractant for New Residents

From the mid-1980s through the 1990s non-metro population growth in the western states outpaced any other region in the USA (Cromartie and Wardwell, 1999). Researchers speak of a 'rural renaissance' as increasing numbers of people fled the urban centres and sought out high-amenity rural settings in which to live (Beyers and Nelson, 2000). Part of the quality of life these urban refugees were looking for was outdoor recreation (Johnson and Rasker 1995; Power, 1996).

Tourism- and recreation-related activity is a magnet for the recently arrived, but the in-migration of residents to resort towns and 'touristic' destinations is not new. In the Greater Yellowstone Region the land that is now Yellowstone National Park had been a popular tourist destination prior to when the Park was established in 1872. Indeed, during the last great Indian war of 1877, when Colonel Nelson Miles' army pursued Chief Joseph across much of Montana, tourists were taken hostage within the Park boundaries (they were later released unharmed). At the turn of the century wealthy English gentry maintained an exclusive fox-hunting preserve in Gallatin County, Montana.

As early as the 1930s avid skiers and Hollywood stars alike were attracted to deliberate resorts such as Sun Valley, Idaho and Aspen, Colorado. One effective method of promoting the emergent ski industry and resorts was to lure the rich and famous to the million dollar lodges and to encourage them to own property in the area. By the 1950s Sun Valley and Aspen, in particular, became known as playgrounds for the social and economic élite. Others soon followed.

Throughout the 1960s and into the 1970s 'ski bums' vigorously pursued a lifestyle based on achieving maximum ski days with minimum work. The original resorts matured into functional communities. Many of the original lifestyle migrants remained to become local business owners, real estate developers, and holders of public office. They contributed a sense of permanence and history to the communities that transient visitors could not. In the Greater Yellowstone, Jackson Hole Ski and Summer Resort, Wyoming and Big Sky Resort, Montana began operations during this period.

More recently, Johnson and Beale (2002) found that rural counties with large concentrations of recreational activity have had population growth rates over 5% greater than that of the US overall since 1990, and five times the rate of other non-recreation non-metropolitan counties. Most of the growth they document has come from in-migration rather than natural increase.

The reasons for the high growth vary, but a map of recreation counties shows clearly that in the western US many recreation counties are in close proximity to mountains, the deserts of the south-west and the Pacific Northwest (Fig. 3.2). Almost no recreation counties are located in the eastern parts of the Rocky Mountain States, eastern Oregon or Washington or in southern California. Many recreation counties in the West are adjacent to national parks and most are in close proximity to national forests.

Johnson and Beale (2002) find that while most recent research on rural population growth suggests that high-amenity areas attract significant numbers of older migrants, they found that recreational counties attract migrants at every age above 30. What this means is that the contemporary recreation in-migrant is no longer only a young 'footloose'

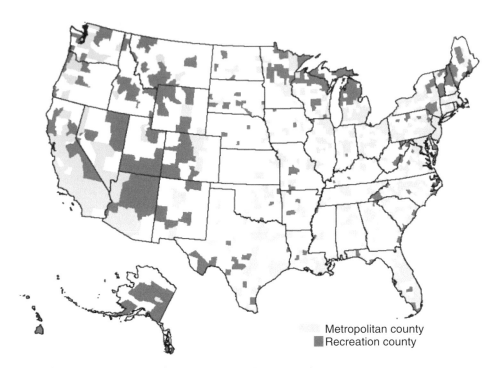

Fig. 3.2. US recreational counties (from Johnson and Beale, 2002).

individual; rather, many are later in their life cycle and perhaps bring more skills and desire for community identity and permanence.

For the young, tourism employment is still primarily in the lower-paid service sector – maids, taxi drivers, ski-lift attendants or in retail outlets. Such employment tends to be short term and with little commitment to the employer or community. Their commitment is to recreation and they move to locations that can provide high-quality skiing, fishing, kayaking, backcountry travel, etc. A second, somewhat older group may tend towards more permanence in the community. These tourism entrepreneurs are outfitters, restaurant and hotel operators, B&B owners, tour bus operators and travel consultants, all of whom can find meaningful and lucrative work in a local tourism economy. They own property and locate to recreation areas for reasons of both quality of life and employment. The third group of residents is the retired or semi-retired. This group is looking for similar recreation outlets as the two previous groups, but also demand quality health care, personal safety, a good transpor-

tation infrastructure and a vast array of personal services (Beyers and Lindahl, 1996). Taken together, these three groups comprise a dynamic and exciting demographic of lifestyle migrants to rural communities that can offer recreation and quality of life in a attractive geographical setting.

The Greater Yellowstone Region was, and still is, one of the primary destinations for the new lifestyle migrant, and tourism seems to play a significant role in introducing would-be residents to the region. Snepenger *et al.* (1995), for example, found that 4 out of 10 business owners surveyed in 1995 reported that they had first experienced the Greater Yellowstone Region as a tourist. These 'travel-stimulated entrepreneurs' either moved or started a business in the region subsequent to their tourist experience.

Another indicator of the region as a tourist destination that attracts new residents is the number of second or vacation homes. According to the latest census, approximately 13% of the total housing stock in the region is classified as either a second or a vacation home (US Bureau of the Census, 2000). Some will even-

Table 3.1. Second homes in the Greater Yellowstone ecosystem (source US Census Bureau, 2000).

	Percentage of housing stock
Montana	
Carbon	18.5
Gallatin	5.9
Madison	24.5
Park	9.6
Stillwater	12.0
Sweet Grass	10.9
Idaho	
Bear Lake	22.3
Bonneville	1.2
Caribou	8.1
Clark	24.0
Franklin	4.3
Fremont	33.9
Madison	0.9
Teton	12.5
Wyoming	
Fremont	4.2
Hot Springs	5.4
Lincoln	13.4
Park	6.8
Sublette	26.2
Teton	20.7

tually be the permanent residence as the owners age and retire. Table 3.1 indicates the relative percentages by county.

What makes the contemporary in-migration to recreation counties remarkable is the extent of the migration and the impact on communities and land stewardship. The scale of the migration is as large as any migration experienced in US history. Between the 1990 and 2000 census the American West grew by over 10 million people, and 67% of rural counties grew at rates faster than the national average (Beyers and Nelson, 2000; US Bureau of the Census, 2000). In terms of the affected communities, the number of new residents, homes and businesses has led to significant benefits as well as certain detrimental effects. Land use has also shifted in ways that could not have been foreseen at the beginning of the growth period, as the demand for recreation ranches, for example, has continued to increase and production patterns shift towards conservation of natural amenities and away from commodity and agricultural production.

Impacts of Tourism-related In-migration

Tourism activity in general is known to bring with it a variety of direct positive and negative economic, social and environmental impacts to host resident communities, and they are well documented in the professional literature (Allen *et al.*, 1988; Var and Kim, 1989; Long *et al.*, 1990; Allen *et al.*, 1993; Andereck and Vogt, 2000). The economic impacts, and concomitant multiplier effect, are the object of a great deal of research (Stynes and Propst, 1992; Teisl and Reiling, 1992); however, other indirect impacts as a result of tourism-related in-migration have received less attention. Two clusters of impacts are identified in Table 3.2.

Public service/administration impacts

The first cluster of growth impacts are those that accrue to the community as a functional service and administrative unit (Teisl and Reiling, 1992). These include: increased construction of primary and recreation homes, increases to local economic activity and resultant tax revenue, diversification of the tax revenue income stream, changes in local property values, increased maintenance of public buildings and infrastructure and issues of public safety.

In some cases there are obvious benefits from these changes. For example, in the Greater Yellowstone Region, construction is a dynamic component of the regional economy as the demand for primary and second homes continues. The construction trade, in turn, supports the building materials industry. These jobs employ local labour and are typically locally owned small businesses. The home construction industry also supports a considerable ancillary business component in architectural services, interior decorating, landscaping and home furnishings. Many of the jobs in those sectors are high value and offer quality employment opportunities. Figure 3.3 depicts the changes to regional employment patterns for the past three decades.

The flow of general tax revenue from tourism is difficult to track and controversial. In most communities, enhancement and diversification of tax revenues would be a positive

Table 3.2. Public administration and qualitative infrastructure impacts from tourism-stimulated in-migration.

Public service/administration impacts	Qualitative impacts
Construction of seasonal and recreation homes	Diversified employment opportunity
Increase in local/state sales tax	Enhanced entertainment and shopping
Diversification of tax revenues	Environmental degradation/improvements
Cost of public service provision – sewer, water, schools, etc.	Enhanced social capital
	Upward pressure on housing prices
Enhanced property values	Downward pressure on wages
Healthy seasonal and recreation home market	Traffic congestion

change. However, in rapidly growing recreation communities the costs of hosting tourists can, in some cases, exceed the revenues they generate. In one of a handful of studies, Teisl and Reiling (1992) attempted to determine the costs incurred by towns in Maine to provide public services to tourists. They found that while some costs, such as police, sanitation and administration, were associated with higher levels of tourism, others costs did not increase (i.e. fire protection). They do point out that the relatively large number of seasonal homes in some Maine communities did increase police expenditures because of the need for additional labour costs during the peak season of use.

In those areas with significant amounts of tourism-related in-migration the tax impacts are negative. Even as local economic development due to construction enhances property values and results in higher tax revenues, the unanticipated tax burden due to the increased cost of public service provision to rural house sites can outweigh those revenues. Of the six Rocky Mountain communities that have been studied in the past decade by the American Farmland Trust (1998), on average, residential development cost county government US$1.22 in public service expenditures for every dollar of tax revenue. A statewide study in Wyoming found that rural residential development cost US$2.01 in public expenditure for every dollar in tax revenue, and similar results were reported for a regional study (Coupal *et al.*, 2000). These findings strongly suggest that the newcomer's home in the rural countryside is subsidized by other taxpayers, even as that home may erode the viewshed for others in the region.

Tax revenue in those counties where

the tourist sector is targeted directly can be a positive impact. One case study – West Yellowstone, Montana – illustrates the magnitude of tourist spending in a small gateway community. Roughly 1 million visitors enter the Park's west entrance each year through the small town of population 1200. Montana has no statewide sales tax, but does allow for a local option sales tax (4%) in communities where tourism is demonstrated to be the major component of the local economy. The tax was implemented in West Yellowstone in 1985 and has generated considerable revenues. This source of revenue, derived largely from tourist expenditures, has funded infrastructure improvements to local water, roads and public safety, and recreational trails, while some is spent on tourism promotion. The diversification of public funds has helped transform West Yellowstone into a community with better pubic services, an improved physical appearance and allows the community to offset some of the negative impacts of large numbers of visitors to the community.

Like many aspects of tourism or other forms of economic development, the impacts that accrue to a specific jurisdiction or region are mixed. However, the evidence seems to indicate that, for the public sector, tourism, and especially tourism-induced in-migration, results in a net loss to the economic balance sheets of local governments – due in large part to the cost of public service provision. On the other hand, for those private recipients of tourist spending, and for those who supply the construction and personal services to tourism-induced in-migrants, the rewards can be significant, and they pay taxes and add to the overall regional economy. Clearly, further research is

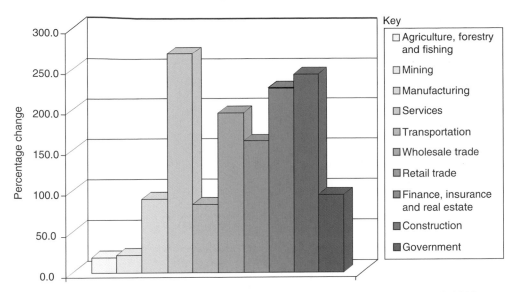

Fig. 3.3. Percentage change in Greater Yellowstone Regional employment by industry, 1970–2000 (source: US Bureau of the Census, 2000).

needed to fully understand the indirect costs and benefits of tourism-related in-migration on public revenues and costs and the relative equity of distribution of cost and benefits.

In communities experiencing a high demand for property a common impact is the upward pressure on housing costs – sometimes so high that locals who work in the mainstream economy can no longer afford a home in the community in which they live. The result is long commutes from the 'downstream' communities. This downward economic spiral (Hartman, 2002) of ever-increasing costs of living has reached absurd proportions in the Roaring Fork Valley of Colorado, where tourist service workers drive 2 h each way to work in Aspen – a county where the median home price is US$2.4 million and there is a 2- to 4-year waiting list for apartments. A report on Pitkin County's housing estimated that for every new 6000-square-foot home, two domestic workers are brought into the work force. But, in Aspen's current housing shortage, job creation produces a need for affordable housing, which does not exist.

Housing shortages, like those found in Colorado, are not yet widespread in the Greater Yellowstone. However, long commutes to work in the tourism service sector are increasingly

common. Based on census data, Fig. 3.4 shows the over 2000% increase in the number of workers who live in Teton County, Idaho (Driggs, Victor) but commute over a major mountain pass in excess of 1 h to Teton County, Wyoming (Jackson). The costs of the commute are easily explained by the disparity in the median cost of housing: in Teton County, Wyoming this is US$365,400 as compared to the median cost in Teton County, Idaho of US$133,000 in 1999.

Finally, the seasonal home market is often discussed in the literature as a detriment to the natural and social community (Gartner, 1987). In the Greater Yellowstone Region the typical second home is in an existing recreation/tourism community (i.e. Jackson, Red Lodge, Big Sky) or a recreational ranch property. Second home development may occur disproportionately in environmentally sensitive areas adjacent to bodies of water or the forest edge – both areas of prime wildlife habitat – and some ecological impacts of building the home are realized even if the home is not inhabited (Gartner, 1987). Second homes may have less impact than other forms of rural residential development. First, because they are part-time residences there are fewer public service demands placed on local governments. Part-time residents do not place

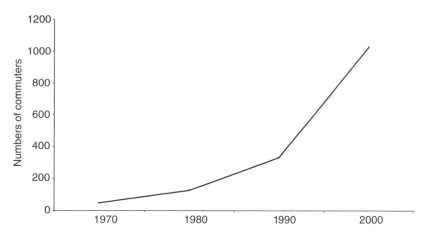

Fig. 3.4. Numbers of commuters living in Teton County, Idaho and working in Teton County, Wyoming, 1970–2000 (source: US Bureau of the Census, 2000).

their children in local schools, use the health-care system less, and place less demand on public infrastructure in general. Additionally, they may exert less impact on the environment because they use less in terms of natural resources (i.e. power and water). At the same time, they pay property and sales taxes to local jurisdictions.

Qualitative impacts

Tourism is an activity that affects many 'non-participants' of the industry, who are affected directly and/or indirectly by the process of hosting tourists and, specifically, through tourism-related in-migration and resultant population growth. The presence of large numbers of second homes and the attendant amenity-based location phenomenon is often stated as if the impacts are inevitably negative: the source of erosion of community and quality of life, the impacts on the ecological setting. Hansen *et al.* (2002) and Johnson (2003, p.14) and others (Gersh, 1995; Knight *et al.*, 2000; Hansen and Rotella, 2002) document some of the negative ecological impacts of rural residential development. However, the focus of this examination is on social and economic considerations.

First, and most obviously, as tourism diversifies the historical economic base of a region, population growth follows, and the diversifica-tion of employment opportunities will predict-ably expand. Timber harvest, mining and agri-cultural production are still much in evidence in the Greater Yellowstone Region, but at much reduced levels. Today, service-related employ-ment, non-labour income, small business start-ups, light manufacturing, retail, and construction jobs dominate much of rural employment and job opportunity in urban, as well as rural, centres (Beyers and Nelson, 2000). Important components of the business mix are services that cater to the second home buyer, recent arrivals and tourists. These include personal services, such as guides and outfitters, decorating consultants and invest-ment advisers; high-value producer services, such as architects, building engineers and art-ists; and curio shops, restaurants and photo processing outlets. In many cases, personal and producer services can be some of the better-quality jobs in the newly diversified economy (Beyers and Nelson, 2000), and these jobs may be accessible to those in small rural commu-nities who may not have enjoyed the same edu-cational benefits as those educated in wealthier urban centres.

For those not involved in the tourist indus-try, the expanded range of goods and services provide for more consumer choice at two levels. First, many retail outlets that serve the 'new economy' are small, locally owned busi-nesses. When residents shop in these stores the local economy can realize a higher multiplier

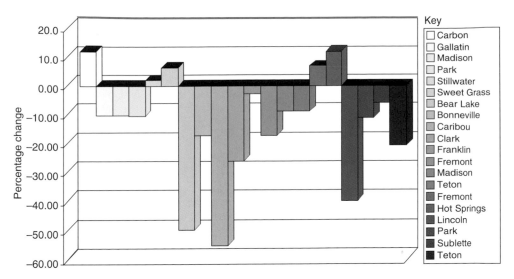

Fig. 3.5. Percentage change in the amount of land in agriculture in the Greater Yellowstone, 1974–1997 (source: US Census of Agriculture, 1997).

effect for local purchases than is possible with large national retail outlets or via mail order. Secondly, for those towns that attract the large retail outlets, the expansion of consumer choice may still benefit locals. In Jackson, Wyoming, for example, before the opening of a large grocery chain, it was cost effective to drive to Idaho Falls, Idaho – over 2h away – to 'stock up' on bulk food purchases. Now, prices and selection are competitive in Jackson, and residents can shop nearby, thereby saving time and supporting 'community' business.

Similar benefits accrue to residents for entertainment of all forms. Tourist towns typically provide 'summer stock' theatre, entertaining tours, or summer music and arts festivals. For residents, a more important form of local enjoyment may be 'window shopping' at tourist-oriented boutiques, art galleries and gift shops. These activities are free and can be augmented with a visit to the upscale coffee shops and eateries ubiquitous on 'Main Street' in every tourist town in the West. Surveys conducted in Bozeman, Montana in 1995, and since replicated in several other Greater Yellowstone locations, found that locals actively utilize the so-called 'tourist-oriented' segments of downtown at a high rate and, further, over a third were very positive about the touristic nature of downtown 'Main Street'. It serves as inexpensive

entertainment and met most of their shopping needs. For 16% of the community, the touristic nature of downtown was a negative attribute of their community experience (Snepenger *et al.*, 1998).

The environmental impacts of in-migration have received a great deal of attention from researchers and public interest groups alike. Regional environmental interest groups rightly point to locations of high population growth as having detrimental effects. In the Greater Yellowstone, analysis of the US Census of Agriculture data suggests that widespread loss of farmland to rural residential development is probably not as widespread as anecdotal or modelling data might suggest.

Most observers would agree there are clearly 'hotspots' of growth and landscape change throughout the ecosystem, as evidenced by the high rates of growth in most of the counties and the decline of farmland (Fig. 3.5). The issue is the scale at which these changes are occurring and the impact on natural resources and local quality of life. And while rural residential development attracts a great deal of attention in the ecological and social science literature as well as the popular press, the reality of most settlement patterns is that they are in relatively close proximity to existing micropolitan centres (i.e. Bozeman and Red

Table 3.3. Social and ecological impacts of rural land-use change (from: Johnson *et al.*, 2003).

Social and community effects of rural land-use change
    Changes in landowner structure (Turner *et al.*, 1996)
    Changes to community history and culture (Jobes, 1988; Williams and Jobes, 1990; Beggs *et al.*, 1996; Rudzitis *et al.*, 1996)
    Impact on agricultural land (Heimlich and Vesterby, 1992; Greene and Harlin, 1995)
    Impact on open space/view (Gersh, 1998; Johnson and Maxwell, 2001)
    Uneven cost of residential service (American Farmland Trust 1998; Haggerty, 1996; Kelsey, 1996)
    Changing political/economic structure (Beyers and Lindahl, 1996; Alm and Witt, 1997)
    Quality of life effects (Decker and Crompton, 1993; Johnson and Rasker, 1995; Jobes, 2000)
Ecological effects of rural land-use change
    Water pollution and sewage (LaGro, 1998; Gersh, 1998)
    Fragmented habitat (Theobald, 1998)
    Threats to biodiversity (Pimental *et al.*, 1992; Farrier, 1995; Forester and Machlis, 1996; White *et al.*, 1997)
    Land-use conversion (Riebsame *et al.*, 1996; Bean and Wilcove, 1997; Johnson and Maxwell, 2001)
    Source/sink effects (Hansen and Rotella, 2002; Hansen *et al.*, 2002)

Lodge, Montana; Jackson and Cody, Wyoming; Idaho Falls and Rexburg, Idaho). Of course, the demand expressed for high-quality outdoor recreation and natural resource quality is highest near these population areas, so the policy issues are pressing.

    The negative impacts of uncontrolled rural residential development are well documented and have been discussed in depth by Riebsame *et al.* (1996), Hansen *et al.* (2002) and Johnson *et al.* (2003). The social, economic and ecological impacts are summarized in Table 3.3.

    That these changes are taking place in the Greater Yellowstone Region and other western locations is not at issue. Almost anyone who has lived in the region for any length of time can point to a favourite piece of land that was once a working agricultural operation but is now roaded and crowded with homes. Others

tell of ranches where they once hunted but where, now, access is leased to an outfitter that caters to wealthy out-of-state hunters. But, while the negative impacts of such change receive the bulk of attention from activist groups, researchers and others, there is evidence that some positive effects may result.

    No data, as such, exist for the amount of reclaimed streams, wetlands game fish habitat and grazing land contracted by the many buyers of recreational properties in the Greater Yellowstone Region. However, the growth of stream habitat firms and private fisheries/wetlands consultants provides a good indicator of the interest recreational property owners have in clean and healthy natural resources. One example is the Baker Springs residential development in Gallatin County, Montana. The developers restored and enhanced a neglected spring creek back to maximize all the fisheries resources on the property and create new ones for the property owners. The development plan increases fishing opportunities throughout the property, restoring the small spring creeks that flow into Baker Creek and the West Gallatin River. These restored steams will provide additional spawning habitat and fishing opportunities for the public, and expand the creek's spawning habitat and holding waters. They have also re-engineered formerly grazed land into a limited number of homesites with conservation setbacks. Another example is the Flying D Ranch in Montana where significant private investments have resulted in enhanced, albeit private, habitat for big game (elk, bison) and fish – including the rare westslope cuthroat trout, upland birds and waterfowl.

    Another positive secondary effect of land-ownership change is the growth of conservation easements across the state. A conservation easement is a legal contract between a land trust, a governmental entity or other qualified organization, and a willing landowner. In exchange for a tax deductible contribution for the value of the protected land, the easement permanently limits uses of the land in order to protect its conservation values. The restrictions run permanently with the land. A conservation easement protects the land from unlimited subdivision and development, while also protecting the rights of private ownership. Examples of uses generally permitted by a conservation easement include:

continued agricultural use, sale or gift of the property or selective timber harvest. Examples of uses generally restricted by a conservation easement are: subdivision for residential development, surface mining or the elimination of wildlife or fisheries habitat protected by the easement. The landowner continues to own and pay taxes (at a reduced rate) on the land.

In the Greater Yellowstone Region several entities can negotiate conservation easements, including various agencies within the three states and many local regional and national land trusts. However, the reality of conservation easement is that it is a tool aimed primarily at the new wealthy landowners – they possess the income and gross tax liability that will result in significant tax savings.

Large ranches purchased for recreation property are less likely to be overgrazed or managed in such a way as to be detrimental to native species (Knight, 2002). The result to the public is that the large tracts of land protected and managed as 'habitat friendly' produce scenic open space and act as population sources for native species – many of whom migrate to nearby public lands.

Communities experiencing an increased in-migrant population find themselves faced with a myriad of both problems and opportunities. The incoming population may bring a newly skilled workforce to a community, who will compete with the existing, possibly economically downtrodden, population for jobs. In economically stricken areas, this competition could create a great deal of tension among neighbours.

Generally, areas experiencing increased population due to immigration are those prospering economically. In contrast, areas experiencing out-migration are usually areas experiencing economic decline. Traditionally, individuals migrate in order to secure employment or advance their personal opportunities. However, as discussed above, migration can also be attributed to non-economic factors such as quality of life, preference for rural areas and availability of eco-amenities in a given area. Regions such as the Greater Yellowstone seem to experiencing three categories of immigrants: return migrants, retirement migrants and new migrants.

Return migrants are those individuals who initially left the region but subsequently come back to where they were raised. Reasons for returning include: the improvement of economic conditions in a given area, desire to be near family and friends, or the ability to apply newly acquired skills to the work force in the place of origin. Data for the State of Montana indicate that as many as two-thirds of those immigrating to Montana from outside its borders are return migrants. In other words, of the approximately 48,000 person gain in the past decade, almost 32,000 are individuals who previously lived in Montana (Sylvester and Polzin, 1995). Depending on the length and/or success of the return migrant's time outside of the home state, they may return with new political ideology, economic theories and financial resources. These fundamental changes in ideology and social status may also greatly affect the social cohesion of a community; but they may also create an atmosphere that allows for new political ideas and thought.

Migrants categorized as 'retirement migrants' come to an area to live after a career spent elsewhere. These migrants may not necessarily be return migrants, but some overlap does exist. Retirees make migration decisions based on nearness to family, climate, cost of living and recreation opportunities. Finally, 'new migrants' are those individuals migrating to an area for the first time, usually citing economic advantages and personal opportunity as reasons for relocating.

While the majority of immigrants are those returning 'home', the others are largely from urban settings in Washington, California or Minnesota, and are white, middle-class, well educated and wealthier than locals. Research by Johnson and Shell-Beckert (2004) indicates that, as a group, in-migrants influence their new communities by bringing neoconservative political values with them. A 'curious mixture of Old-West gun culture and high-tech individualism'; the new west conservative is one that holds a quasi-religious belief in private property rights but also values highly the conservation efforts of government and public-interest groups that maintain the attributes that make the Greater Yellowstone Region a clean and beautiful place to live.

Many of the new residents bring with them ideas and experiences, and are a valuable

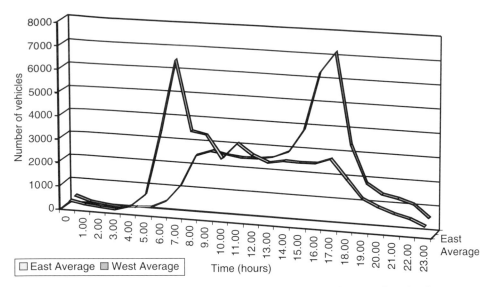

Fig. 3.6. Average east- and west-bound traffic over Teton Pass in 2002 (source: Wyoming Department of Transport, personal communication 2002).

source of social capital to rural communities. Social capital is the concept of the stock of active connections among people: the trust, mutual understanding, shared values and behaviours that bind the members of human networks and communities, and make cooperative action possible. Manifestations of social capital are high levels of civic engagement in community organizations. In a recent study of social capital conducted in 2001, almost no volunteers for civic and social organizations were native to the community (Velasquez, 2001).

Several socio-economic costs are typically cited in the current literature with respect to the impacts of growth on the costs of housing and wages in tourism and resort communities. A major economic effect of rapid land-use conversion is the inflationary pressure on homes and cost of living for locals. Communities that provide high-quality recreation, and are good places to live, work and raise a family are increasingly unaffordable for many would-be residents working local blue-collar jobs. In many communities in the Rocky Mountain region the cost of a home is well over the national average (Doyle, 2002). The high cost of housing is disturbing, given that some of the Rocky Mountain States rank among the highest in the nation for populations that work multiple

jobs, and whose pay is among the lowest in the nation (US Bureau of the Census, 2000).

Adjacent to the highest priced communities are service communities requiring long commutes for little pay and high housing costs. Across the West, most measures of economic well-being are on the decline, as fewer workers are able to save for a home or more people qualify for welfare payments (Montana State University Local Government Center, 2003). For many tourism and resort towns there is tremendous pressure to provide larger roadways to facilitate the commuter traffic and thereby unintentionally encourage sprawl even further away from the economic centre (Hartman, 2002).

Longer commutes to work also result in increased traffic congestion. Figure 3.6 depicts the commuter traffic pattern over a 24-h day on Teton Pass, Wyoming, as Teton County, Idaho residents travel to and from work.

The connection between tourism-related in-migration and transportation is increasingly understood to be autocatalytic in nature. Very simply, as quality roads help push development beyond the urban fringe, businesses and homes follow, thereby spreading consumer travel patterns over a larger geographic area. This can lead to malls and shopping centres locating new operations away from the historic downtown business district and, in the process, the social function of downtown erodes as a functional centre for the community (Snepenger *et al.*, 1998). The community loses its sense of place and solidarity (Huang and Stewart, 1996), and this may help contribute to the high turnover of new residents, as documented by Jobes (2000).

Conversely, increased mobility through automobile usage and the infrastructure that facilitates it is clearly a contributing factor to the 'livability' of rural settings (Dunn, 1998) and the economic vitality many of them currently enjoy. Roads and highways can make rural living possible by shortening travel time to work, thereby enabling more people to live in the small towns that typically surround larger micropolitan centres. Likewise, small towns themselves become desirable destinations for those who can make a living in a rural setting. Airports, another form of transportation infrastructure investment, may be key location factors for many growing rural communities (Rasker and Hansen, 2000).

Further Research

There is no question that tourism is a powerful stimulus for some visitors to relocate their primary residence or to purchase a second home in the tourism destination area. It is also abundantly clear that there is a paucity of research aimed at understanding the complexity of the tourism-stimulated in-migration system. The political agendas of many public-interest groups, local government jurisdictions and public lands agencies, at both ends of the pro/anti-development spectrum, do not lend themselves to objective research to assess the effects of growth and change in tourism and resort communities.

Some areas of study are well developed, and models exist that can be applied directly to further study. The cost of services methodology developed by American Farmland Trust and others (Coupal *et al.*, 2000) is already in use in many high-growth settings, and has been adapted to large- and small-scale development (Mitchell, 2000). Additionally, the role that recreation and other quality of life factors play in rural development is also well understood.

Johnson and Rasker (1995), Beyers and Nelson (2000), Rasker and Hansen (2000), Power and Barrett (2001) and others have demonstrated unequivocally the importance of non-economic amenities in helping to explain rural growth patterns. Integral to their argument is the tourism and recreation experience as an attractant for rural communities.

Two impact themes deserve the attention of researchers. First, based on the recognition that land use not only influences transportation outcomes, but that transportation investments also influence land-use decisions, there is a growing interest in integrating transportation and land-use planning in rural communities (Humstone, 2002; Waddell, 2002; Johnson, 2003). The majority of these studies focus on urban centres, with their networks of public transportation, arterial highways and movement of large volumes of traffic. Rural locations have diseconomies of scale for public transport, and large-scale highway construction projects are not politically efficient in sparsely populated rural areas. Small-scale redesign of the rural transportation network has been shown to impart large-scale land-use effects (Johnson *et al.*, 2002). These connections are poorly modelled, but emerging computer simulations can enhance the capacity of local jurisdictions to influence rural growth patterns through management of transportation infrastructure (Johnson, 2003).

The second area, the role of private conservation efforts and how they might influence public resources, is a potentially rich area of study. Expanded economic well-being has stimulated the demand for high-quality, private ecological surroundings. These emergent values can be found in the personalized ecotourism market, private recreational preserves, and on the recreational ranchlands across the Rocky Mountain West. High-value private hunting and fishing, skiing, wildlife viewing, and personalized sightseeing tours all show steadily increasing demand, and the resources needed to provide high-quality tourism services reside on large tracts of private lands. To what degree do qualities such as clean, free-flowing streams, large herds of migrating ungulates and healthy predator populations, undeveloped open spaces and private wilderness provide ecological improvement to public lands for enjoyment by the public? Ecosystem services accounting for private lands may prove to have large benefits for recreation on public lands.

Conclusion

Adding to the political and scientific complexity of rural residential development is the uncertainty of the global tourism industry. The September 11 terrorist attack altered the travel habits of many Americans, and domestic tourism excursions to national parks and historic places continue to increase. These family-oriented experiences will expose urbanites to the beauty and relative safety of rural America, and some will choose to relocate there. Some will build second homes and eventually retire to communities that offer recreation, an interesting cultural heritage and small-town values.

Planning and policy adapting to continued rural population growth and resultant sprawl has reached a high level of national attention in the USA and other developed countries. Local politicians, environmentalists, and public lands managers in the Greater Yellowstone Region are increasingly concerned with the myriad of ecological, social and economic impacts of unrestrained growth in the rural countryside. Many jurisdictions have adopted anti-sprawl local government ballot initiatives and some support the concept of 'smart growth' to help local governments manage the effects of sprawl. National environmental groups (i.e. the Sierra Club) have made sprawl a major focus of their political activity. Others, such as the American Farmland Trust, cooperate with the agricultural community to safeguard farmland from development. Largely missing from the policy debate is the countervailing view of tourism-stimulated growth as a positive trend for rural communities.

While population growth in the Greater Yellowstone Region and other amenity-rich areas will most likely continue at least into the next decade, local government officials and residents will begin to assimilate both the positive and negative long-term impacts of tourism-stimulated in-migration. With better understanding of growth impacts, continued education by tourism planners and community leaders, and a continued informed dialogue, political conflict

over 'old-timers' and 'newcomers' or 'us' and 'them' may eventually give way to recognition of community solidarity. If and when that happens, local jurisdictions can concentrate on the preservation of scenic vistas and the regional quality of life that attracts visitors and permanent residents to the Greater Yellowstone Region and other special places in rural America.

References

Allen, L., Long, P.T., Perdue, R.R. and Kieselbach, S. (1988) The impact of tourism development on residents perceptions of community life. *Journal of Travel Research* Summer 16–21.
Allen, L.R., Hafer, H.R., Long, P.T. and Perdue, R.R. (1993) Rural residents' attitudes toward recreation and tourism development. *Journal of Travel Research* Spring 27–33.
Alm, L.R. and Witt, S.L. (1997) The rural–urban linkage to environmental policy making in the American West: a Focus on Idaho. *Social Science Journal* 34, 271–284.
American Farmland Trust (1998) Living on the Edge: the Costs and Risks of Scatter Development. Available at website http://farm.fic.niu.edu/cae/scatter/e-loe.htm (verified 18 June 2003).
Andereck, C.A. and Vogt, A. (2000) The relationship between residents' attitudes toward tourism and tourism development options. *Journal of Travel Research* 39, 27–37.
Bean, M.J. and Wilcove, D.S. (1997) The private-land problem. *Conservation Biology* 11, 1–2.
Beggs, J.J., Haines, V.A. and Hurlbert, J.S. (1996) Revisiting the rural–urban contrast: personal networks in nonmetropolitan settings. *Rural Sociology* 61, 306–325.
Beyers, W.B. and Lindahl, D.P. (1996) Lone eagles and high fliers in rural producers services. *Rural Development Perspectives* 11, 2–10.
Beyers, W.B. and Nelson, P.B. (2000) Contemporary development forces in the nonmetropolitan west: new insights from rapidly growing communities. *Journal of Rural Studies* 16, 459–474.
Clifford, H. (2002) *Downhill Slide: Why the Corporate Ski Industry is Bad for Skiing, Ski Towns, and the Environment.* Sierra Club Books, San Francisco, California.
Coupal, R., Taylor, D.T. and McLeod, D.M. (2000) Available at website http://agecon.uwyo.edu/EconDev/pubs.htm (verified 18 June 2003).
Decker, J.M. and Crompton, J.L. (1993) Attracting footloose companies: an investigation of the business location process. *Journal of Professional Services Marketing* 9, 69–94.

Doyle, R. (2002) Affording a Home. *Scientific American* September, 32.

Dunn, J.A. (1998) *Driving Forces: the Automobile, its Enemies and the Politics of Mobility.* The Brookings Institution, Washington, DC.

Farrier, D. (1995) Conserving biodiversity on private land. *Harvard Environmental Law Review* 19, 304–305.

Forester, D.J. and Machlis, G.E. (1996) Modeling human factors that affect the loss of biodiversity *Conservation Biology* 10, 1253–1263.

Gartner, W.C. (1987) Environmental impacts of recreational home developments. *Annals of Tourism Research* 14, 38–57.

Gersh, J. (1995) The Rocky Mountain West at risk. *Urban Land* 54, 32–35.

Gersh, J. (1998) Subdivide and conquer. *Amicus Journal* 18, 14–23.

Greene, R.P. and Harlin, J.M. (1995) Threat to high market value agricultural lands from urban encroachment: a national and regional perspective. *The Social Science Journal* 32, 137–155.

Haggerty, M. (1996) Costs of county and education services in Gallatin County, Montana. *Montana Policy Review* 6(1), 13–21.

Hansen, A.J. and Rotella, J.J. (2002) Regional source–sink dynamics and the vulnerability of species to extinction in nature reserves. *Conservation Biology* 16, 1112–1122.

Hansen, A.J., Rasker, R., Maxwell, B.M., Rotella, J.J., Johnson, J.D., Wright-Parmenter, A., Langner, U., Cohen, W.B., Lawrence, R.L. and Kraska, M. (2002) Ecological causes and consequences of demographic change in the New West. *BioScience* 52, 151–162.

Hartman, R. (2002) Downstream and down valley: essential components and directions of growth and change in the sprawling resort landscapes of the Rocky Mountain West. In: Clark, T. (ed.) *Mountain Resort Development in an Era of Globalization Conference, Steamboat Springs, Colorado, September.* University of Colorado, Denver, p. 27

Heimlich, R. and Vesterby, M. (1992) Farmland loss to urban encroachment no threat to U.S. agriculture. *Rural Development Perspectives* 8, 2–7.

Huang, Y. and Stewart, W.P. (1996) Rural tourism development: shifting basis of community solidarity. *Journal of Travel Research* 34, 26–31.

Humstone, E. (2002) Improving environmental policy through land use planning and providing assistance to communities to aid in the redevelopment of brownfield sites. Testimony to: Senate Committee on Environment and Public Works. Available at website http://www.vtsprawl.org/Initiatives/research/HPW_testimony.htm (verified 18 June 2003).

Jobes, P.C. (1988) Nominalism, realism and planning in a changing community. *International Journal of Environmental Studies* 31, 279–290.

Jobes, P. (2000) *Moving Nearer to Heaven: the Illusions and Disillusions of Migrants to Scenic Rural Places.* Praeger, Westport, Connecticut.

Johnson, J.D. (2003) *Land Use and Transportation Infrastructure Models for Application in Rural Settings.* Western Transportation Institute, Montana State University.

Johnson, J.D. and Maxwell, B.M. (2001) The role of the conservation reserve program in controlling rural residential development. *Journal of Rural Studies* 17, 323–332.

Johnson, J.D. and Rasker, R. (1995) The role of economic and quality of life values in rural business location. *Journal of Rural Studies* 11, 405–416.

Johnson, J.D. and Shell-Beckert, L. (2004) Reshaping of the political environment in Montana: implications for Montana fish, wildlife and parks. In: Miller, S. (ed.) *Changing Times, Changing Values* (in press).

Johnson, J.D., Maxwell, B.M., Brelsford, M. and Dougher, F. (2002) Transportation infrastructure and rural residential development. In: Clark, T. (ed.) *A Tourism Region. Mountain Resort Planning and Development in an Era of Globalization, Steamboat Springs, Colorado, September.* University of Colorado, Denver, pp. 25–28.

Johnson, J.D., Maxwell, B.M. and Aspinall, R. (2003) Moving nearer to heaven: growth and change in the Greater Yellowstone region. In: Buckley, R.C., Pickering, C.M. and Weaver, D. (eds) *Nature-based Tourism, Environment and Land Management.* CAB International, Wallingford, UK.

Johnson, K.M. and Beale, C.L. (2002) Recreational counties in nonmetropolitan America. Available at website http://www.luc.edu/depts/sociology/johnson/p99webr.html (verified 18 June 2003).

Kelsey, T.W. (1996) The fiscal impacts of alternative land uses: what do costs of community service studies really tell us? *Journal of Community Development and Sociology* 27, 78–89.

Knight, R.L. (2002) The ecology of ranching. Available at website http://www.colostate.edu/Depts/forages/PDF/LTB_02-1/Chap.%2001%20-%20Knight,%20R.L.PDF (verified 18 June 2003).

Knight, R.L., Smith, F.W., Buskirk, S.W., Romme, W.H. and Baker, W.L. (eds) (2000) *Forest Fragmentation in the Southern Rocky Mountains.* University Press of Colorado, Boulder.

LaGro, J.A. Jr (1998) Landscape context of rural development in Southeastern Wisconsin *Landscape Ecology* 13, 65–77.

Long, P.T., Perdue, R.R. and Allen, L. (1990) Rural resident tourism perceptions and attitudes by community level of tourism. *Journal of Travel Research* 31, 27–33.

Mitchell, S. (2000) Cited in: Bozeman, M.T. (ed.) Cost of services study. Unpublished Masters thesis, Department of Earth Sciences, Montana State University.

Montana State University Local Government Center (2003) Montana County indicators of family well-being. Available at website http:// www.montana.edu/wwwlgc/comap1.htm (verified 18 June 2003).

Pimental, D., Takacs, D.A., Brubaker, H.W., Dumas, A.R., Meaney, J.J., O'Neill, J.A.S., Onsi, D.E. and Corzilius, D.B. (1992) Conserving biological diversity in agricultural/forestry systems *BioScience* 42, 354–362.

Power, T.M. (1996) *Lost Landscapes and Failed Economies: the Search for a Value of Place.* Island Press, Washington, DC, USA.

Power, T.M. and Barrett, R.N. (2001) *Post Cowboy Economics: Pay and Prosperity in the New American West.* Island Press, Washington, DC.

Rasker, R. and Hansen, A. (2000) Natural amenities and population growth in the greater Yellowstone Region. *Research in Human Ecology* 7, 30–40.

Riebsame, W.E., Gosnell, W. and Theobald, D.M. (1996) Land use and landscape change in the Colorado Mountains I: theory, scale and pattern. *Mountain Research and Development* 16, 395–405.

Rotham, H. (1998) *Devil's Bargain: Tourism in the Twentieth Century American West.* University of Las Vegas Press, Las Vegas, Nevada.

Rudzitis, G., Hintz, J. and Watrous, C. (1996) Snapshots of a changing Northwest. University of Idaho Department of Geography: Working Paper From The Migration, Regional Development and Changing American West Project.

Snepenger, D.J., Johnson, J.D. and Rasker, R. (1995) Travel stimulated entrepreneurial migration. *Journal of Travel Research* 34, 40–44.

Snepenger, D.J., Reiman, S., Johnson, J.D. and Snepenger, M. (1998) Is downtown mainly for tourists? *Journal of Travel Research* 36, 5–12.

Stynes, D.J. and Propst, D.B. (1992) A system for estimating local economic impacts of recreation and tourism. In: Reiling, S. (ed.) *Measuring Tourism Impacts at the Community Level.* Maine Agricultural Experiment Station. Available at website http://www.nsue.msu.edu/msue/imp/modtd/33519758.html (verified 18 June 2003).

Sylvester, J.T. and Polzin, P.E. (1995) Montana or bust: Montana migration patterns. *Montana Business Quarterly* Autumn, pp. 5–8.

Teisl, M.F. and Reiling, D.D. (1992) The impact of tourism on local government public service expenditures. In: Reiling, S. (ed.) *Measuring Tourism Impacts at the Community Level.* Maine Agricultural Experiment Station, pp. 61–91. Available at website http://www.msue. msu.edu/ msue/imp/modtd/33519758.html (verified 7 August 2003).

Theobald, D.M. (1998) Fragmentation by inholdings and exurban development. In: Knight, R.L., Smith, F.W., Buskirk, S.W., Romme, W.H. and Baker, W.L. (eds) *Forest Fragmentation in the Central Rocky Mountains.* University Press of Colorado, Boulder, Colorado, pp. 155–174.

Turner, M.G., Wear, D.N. and Flamm, R.O. (1996) Land ownership and land-cover change in the Southern Appalachian Highlands and the Olympic Peninsula. *Ecological Applications* 6, 1150–1172.

US Bureau of the Census (2000) Census Bureau Reports. Available at website http://www. census.gov (verified 18 June 2003).

US Census of Agriculture (1997)

Vias, A.C., Mulliagan, G.F. and Molin, A. (2002) Economic structure and socioeconomic change in America's Micropolitan Areas, 1970–1997. *The Social Science Journal* 39, 399–417.

Var, T. and Kim, Y. (1989) Measurement and findings on the tourism impact. Unpublished paper, Department of Recreation, Park and Tourism Sciences, Texas A&M University, College Station.

Velasquez, T. (2001) Utilizing social capital in a Western Boomtown: The 2001 Campaign for the Bozeman Public Library Bond. Unpublished Masters Thesis, Montana State University Department of Political Science, Bozeman, Montana.

Waddell, P. (2002) UrbanSim: modeling urban development for land use, transportation and environmental planning. *Journal of the American Planning Association* 68, 297–315.

White, D.W., Minotti, P.G., Barczak, M.J., Sifneos, J.C., Freemark, K.E., Santelmann, M.V., Steinitz, C.F., Kiester, A.R. and Preston, E.M. (1997) Assessing risks to biodiversity from future landscape change *Conservation Biology* 11, 349–360.

Williams, A.S. and Jobes, P.C. (1990) Economic and quality of life considerations in urban–rural migration. *Journal of Rural Studies* 6(2), 187–194.

4

Impacts of Hiking and Camping on Soils and Vegetation: a Review

David N. Cole

Aldo Leopold Wilderness Research Institute, Forest Service, Missoula, Montana USA

Introduction

Ecotourism affects local environments in many ways. Although some of the most dramatic environmental changes result from development of the infrastructure to support tourism, more widespread impacts result from the recreational activities that tourists engage in. For ecotourists engaged in adventurous pursuits, hiking and camping are perhaps the most common activities that can have profound ecological impacts. This is particularly true in more remote places, protected as parks or wilderness.

Of the many environmental effects of hiking and camping, impacts on soil and vegetation have been most thoroughly explored. Consequently, the literature on this subject is voluminous and is a challenge to review thoroughly. The strategy of this chapter is to provide an historical context for the development of this literature, discuss the types of studies that have been employed (each with inherent strengths and weaknesses) and briefly assess the geographical distribution of research. Emphasis is placed on development of generalities from the literature and identification of critical knowledge gaps, rather than a comprehensive review of many site- and context-specific descriptive studies. I try to identify the early papers that provided the genesis of ideas and concepts, as well as recent papers that extend earlier work conceptually and geographically. Inevitably I have drawn more examples from my own work than might be representative because I am most familiar with their details. Additional sources can be found in several textbooks (Liddle, 1997; Hammitt and Cole, 1998; Newsome *et al.*, 2002) and reviews of the literature (Cole, 1987, 2002; Leung and Marion, 2000).

In this chapter, I do not distinguish between recreation and tourism. From the point of view of impacts to soils and vegetation, differences between the two seem negligible. Ecotourism suggests environments characterized by near-natural conditions, low levels of development and crowding. Fortuitously, most of the literature on recreation impacts has been conducted in such environments, making application to ecotourism straightforward.

Hiking and Camping as Activities

Humans have walked and camped for as long as they have existed. Only in recent centuries, particularly in developed countries, has there been little need for large portions of the population to walk from place to place. In the past half century, this trend has reversed. As the proportion of people with substantial leisure time has increased, people are turning to hiking and camping as recreational activities (Fig. 4.1). In the USA, for example, two-thirds of the population engages in walking for pleasure and

Fig. 4.1. Recreational hiking and backpacking have increased dramatically in the past few decades.

about one-quarter hikes and camps (Cordell and Super, 2000). Increased interest in ecotourism reflects this trend and its dissemination around the globe.

Hiking has always been more ubiquitous than camping, particularly in more developed and less remote places. In road-accessible places, with well-developed infrastructure, most hiking may occur on highly engineered trails designed to absorb the impacts of hiking and to confine those impacts to the designed trail system and nodes of activity (e.g. viewpoints, picnic sites, etc.). Most hiking is of short duration, less than 1 day and often for just an hour or two, with tourists staying the night in some sort of lodging. In addition to staying in overnight lodging, many people camp in road-accessible developed campgrounds, which ideally are designed to confine traffic to surfaces that are hardened to absorb use. In these situations, impacts to soils and vegetation can be limited despite very high visitation levels. Where people venture off the trail system, however, impacts can be pronounced.

Less-developed and more remote areas are used in more variable ways. Day hiking on engineered trails still occurs, but overnight hiking on less-developed trails and even off-trail travel also occurs. In certain parts of the world (e.g. much of Europe, Nepal and New Zealand), long-distance trekkers usually overnight in lodges or shelters, but, in many places, the tradition involves overnight camping. Camping may occur on designated campsites; informal, long-established sites; and even on places that have never been camped on before.

The value of research on recreation impacts to soils and vegetation seems generally greater in less-developed and more remote lands. This has nothing to do with the relative amount or importance of recreation in these places. In less-developed and more remote places, management is more complex, and the knowledge required to manage effectively is greater. Management relies less on engineering and on separating the natural environment from recreational use. Therefore, it is more critical to understand the inherent durability of the natural environment, and how much of what types of use the environment can support. The standards for acceptable levels of impact are also likely to be more stringent, and concern about the obtrusiveness of management is likely to be greater. This management complexity, I think, explains the fact that although most visitation occurs on more developed lands, most research has been conducted in less-developed parks and wilderness areas.

Historical Context of Research

Research on the ecological impacts of recreation has a short history. Although there were a few isolated early studies of the ecological impacts of tourists (Meinecke, 1928) and of vegetation subjected to trampling (Bates, 1935), the 1960s was the decade when interest in recreation impacts first developed widely. Not coincidentally, it was the 1960s when the demand for outdoor recreation first exploded in much of the developed world. This earliest work was descriptive, highly site-specific, seldom published, and largely confined to the USA and western Europe. Few researchers ever conducted more than one study.

By the early 1970s, interest had grown enough for collaborative and cumulative research to be supported. The term 'recreation ecology', the most common descriptor of research on the environmental effects of recreation, was probably coined about this time. By 1973, in Great Britain, the Recreation Ecology Research Group was convening regularly to share information. The first pioneers in recreation ecology also began work in the early 1970s. Neil Bayfield (1971, 1973, 1979) developed the first sustained programme of recreation ecology research, a 20-year programme of government-funded work on trampling and footpath impacts in the mountains of Scotland and England. He was among the first to propose methods for monitoring trail impacts and to investigate means of restoring damaged recreation sites. Michael Liddle began a lifetime of work in academia on recreation impacts, first in Great Britain (Liddle and Greig-Smith, 1975) and later in Australia (Liddle and Kay, 1987). Notably, Liddle (1975a,b) was among the first to search for generalities about recreation impacts and his career culminated in a comprehensive textbook on recreation ecology (Liddle, 1997).

The earliest students of recreation ecology in the USA did not pursue careers in the field. Nevertheless, their contributions were vital. Al Wagar conducted the first simulated trampling experiments, and provided initial conceptual development of the carrying capacity concept (Wagar, 1964). Sid Frissell conducted the first study of campsites that received differing levels of use (Frissell and Duncan, 1965). This research showed that impact occurs wherever use occurs, leading Frissell to suggest that the decision facing recreation managers is how much impact is acceptable – not whether or not to allow impact. This observation provided the conceptual foundation for planning processes such as the Limits of Acceptable Change (Stankey *et al.*, 1985). Frissell's data also illustrated the curvilinear nature of the relationship between amount of use and amount of impact, although it was another 15 years before the generality of this finding and its significance to recreation management was articulated (Cole, 1981a). Frissell (1978) was also among the first to publish suggested methods for monitoring wilderness campsites.

Efforts to develop generalities and the management implications of recreation ecology were substantially increased when governmental research institutions hired recreation ecologists. Since the late 1970s (Cole, 1978), my position with the US Forest Service has allowed me to focus my professional work on recreation ecology. Jeff Marion has held a similar position with the National Park Service (now the US Geological Survey) since the mid-1980s. This has provided the opportunity for more rigorous study of recreation ecology. It has been possible to use multiple methodologies to examine impacts (Marion and Cole, 1996), to develop models of factors that influence impacts (Cole, 1987, 1992), to search for generality across different environments (Cole, 1995a), to study trends over time (Cole, 1993) and to work at multiple spatial scales (Cole, 1996). It has also provided more opportunity to apply research results to the development of management strategies (Cole, 1987, 2002; Hammitt and Cole, 1998; Leung and Marion, 2000) and monitoring techniques (Cole, 1989a; Marion and Leung, 2001).

The geographic distribution of recreation ecology research has also expanded. Prior to the 1980s, recreation ecology research was largely confined to North America and Europe. Research continues to be conducted throughout Europe, but nowhere is recreation ecology an established discipline. Occasional studies have been conducted in Japan since at least the late 1960s (Tachibana, 1969) and that traditional continues today (Yoda and Watanabe, 2000) – there and in Hong Kong (Jim, 1987;

Fig. 4.2. Much of the research in recreation ecology has been conducted in mountainous environments.

Leung and Neller, 1995). In the 1980s, research expanded in developed countries around the world, most notably in South Africa (Garland, 1987) and Australia. Notable in Australia is the work of Liddle and his students (Liddle and Thyer, 1986; Sun and Liddle, 1993a,b) and research related to management of World Heritage Areas in Tasmania (Whinam *et al.*, 1994; Whinam and Chilcott, 1999) and the Great Barrier Reef (Liddle and Kay, 1987).

In the 1990s, perhaps in response to increased ecotourism and recognition of its potential environmental consequences, recreation ecology research has expanded into developing countries and ecotourism destinations around the globe. Recent studies have been conducted in the Middle East – in Israel (Kutiel and Zhevelev, 2001) and Egypt (Hawkins and Roberts, 1993) – as well as in the tropics – in Central and South America (Boucher *et al.*, 1991; Farrell and Marion, 2001a), Africa (Obua and Harding, 1997) and South-East Asia (Jusoff, 1989). It has expanded throughout the temperate lands of the southern hemisphere – in New Zealand (Stewart and Cameron, 1992) and in Chile (Farrell and Marion, 2001b) – and even the sub-Antarctic (Scott and Kirkpatrick, 1994). Much of this generation of research has drawn directly from the research techniques and protocols developed by the original generation of recreation ecologists. Buckley and Pannell

(1990) applied the findings of recreation ecology to ecotourism and Tracy Farrell applied Jeff Marion's impact monitoring procedures in Central and South America (Farrell and Marion, 2001a,b).

The ecosystems in which recreation ecology research has been conducted has expanded along with the geographical distribution of studies. The earliest work occurred in mountainous and coastal environments, due to the attraction of tourists to these locations (Fig. 4.2). To this day, the preponderance of work is still conducted in the mountains and, to a lesser degree, along coasts. Although the earliest work in the mountains was typically in the alpine and subalpine zones, recently more research has been conducted at lower elevations (e.g. Hall and Kuss, 1989; Leung and Marion, 1999a). Much of the recent coastal work has shifted to recreational impacts on reefs and intertidal areas (Liddle and Kay, 1987; Hawkins and Roberts, 1993; Rouphael and Inglis, 2002). Other environments recently studied include riparian (Marion and Cole, 1996) and desert environments (Cole, 1986).

Research Designs

Four different research designs have been employed as a means of studying recreational impacts (Cole, 1987). Each of these designs has strengths and weaknesses. The valuable perspective of each design is reflected in the fact that each was used in early recreation ecology research and each continues to be used today. The most common design, particularly in highly applied research, designed to assess impacts to an entire park, campground or trail system, is the descriptive field survey. Vegetation and soil parameters on recreation sites are measured for the purpose of assessing current conditions. Environmental and use characteristics are often simultaneously assessed and then correlated with variation in impacts to soil and vegetation. Examples of this approach include Bayfield's (1973) work on Scottish trails, as well as the work of Marion and his students on trails and campsites in the eastern USA and in Central and South America (Leung and Marion, 1999a,b; Farrell and Marion, 2001a,b). The value of this approach is that impact conditions can be surveyed over large areas rapidly and with minimal training. Surveys provide a snapshot of conditions at a point in time and, when repeated, can be used to assess trends over time. Consequently, such studies can provide much of the foundational information needed to guide day-to-day management. However, if one's goal is to understand cause-and-effect, this is the least useful of the research designs. One can speculate about cause and effect from correlational analyses, but apparent relationships can be spurious and true relationships can be missed due to the confounding of intervening variables.

A common variant of the descriptive survey is the addition of measures taken on undisturbed control sites that, when compared with recreation sites, provide an estimate of change resulting from recreation use. This amounts to using spatial differences (used versus unused) to infer temporal change (pre- versus post-use). In such studies, it is common to compare impacts on categories of sites that vary either in use or environmental characteristics. An early example is Frissell and Duncan's (1965) study of variation in impact, related to amount of use, on canoe campsites. This approach, though more time-consuming than the simple descriptive survey, has the advantage of providing an estimate of the extent to which conditions reflect recreational use.

However, control sites are never perfect replicates of pre-existing conditions and, in some situations, the difficulty of finding good controls makes it impossible to use this approach.

A further variant of the descriptive field survey is the before-and-after natural experiment. This design involves assessing conditions before and after recreational use occurs, or before and after a change in management regime. Ideally, identical measures are taken on control sites that are not subjected to use or a change in management. In this case, change resulting from management is measured directly. An early example of this approach is Merriam and Smith's (1974) study of impacts resulting from initial use of newly opened campsites. Spildie *et al.* (2000) used this design to assess the effectiveness of a management programme designed to confine and reduce campsite impacts associated with packstock. Typically, such studies are conducted in one place at one point in time. Consequently, it can be difficult to assess the general applicability of results.

The three variants of the descriptive field survey have the advantage of realism and providing highly relevant site-specific information, but they all suffer, to varying degrees, in their ability to identify cause-and-effect and to contribute to general knowledge. The alternative is the simulated experimental approach. With this approach, researchers carefully control use and environmental factors in a replicated design that maximizes insights into cause and effect. Bayfield (1971) was perhaps the first to employ experimental trampling by humans, although Wagar (1961) trampled vegetation using an artificial 'tamp'. More recently, Cole and Bayfield (1993) developed a standard protocol for conducting trampling experiments. This protocol has been applied in many different vegetation types, from mountainous areas of the USA (Cole, 1995a) to such places as Arctic tundra (Monz, 2002), sand dunes in France (Lemauviel and Rozé, 2003) and forested communities in Uganda (Pratt, 1997). Widespread application of similar field techniques increases the ability to develop broad generalizations and to understand the causes of variability.

Each of these research designs has inherent strengths and weaknesses. The most appropriate approach to take will depend on the goals of the study. Maximum insight can be gained by utilizing several approaches simultaneously. For example, Marion and Cole (1996) combined: (i) descriptive field surveys of campsites, stratified according to amount of use and vegetation type, along with measures taken on adjacent controls; (ii) natural experiments on previously undisturbed sites, before and after being opened for camping; (iii) natural experiments on established campsites, before and after being closed to use, as well as before and after management actions designed to reduce campsite size; and (iv) trampling experiments.

Progress in recreation ecology is hampered by minimal attention given to conceptual and theoretical development. Early exceptions include Liddle's (1975a,b) conceptual model of trampling processes and his hypothesis that trampling tolerance is related to primary productivity. Cole's (1992) simplified model of campsites represents one of the few attempts to use analytical models to build foundational concepts regarding how various factors operate in determining impact magnitude. Rigorous analyses of the efficiency of impact assessments are also lacking, although Leung and Marion (1999c) is a notable exception.

Research Results

Descriptive information about recreational impacts can be divided into information about the nature and magnitude of impacts caused by different recreational activities, spatial aspects of impacts, and temporal patterns of impact. There is also an extensive body of information about use and environmental characteristics that influence the nature and magnitude of impacts. This knowledge provides the basis for insight into management actions that might effectively control impacts. Finally, a substantial amount of work has developed regarding the effectiveness of impact management techniques, as well as efficient ways to monitor impacts.

The nature and magnitude of impacts

Much of the research into hiking and camping impacts on soil and vegetation is focused on either linear travel routes, usually trails, or nodes of concentrated use, usually campsites but also picnic sites and viewpoints. The other tradition has been to study the effects of trampling, which occurs on trails and campsites but also away from these places of concentrated use.

Trampling has at least three effects: abrasion of vegetation, abrasion of organic soil horizons and compaction of soil (Fig. 4.3). Plants can be bruised, crushed, sheered off and even uprooted by trampling. Trampling effects include reductions in plant height, stem length and leaf area, as well as in the number of plants that flower, the number of flower heads per plant and seed production (Liddle, 1997). Reduced height and leaf area decrease the photosynthetic area of plants, resulting in depleted carbohydrate reserves (Hartley, 1999). These changes typically result in reductions in plant vigour and reproduction. Many plants are killed by trampling. At moderate levels of trampling, however, some species increase in abundance, often as a result of decreased competition or a change in microhabitat. Generally, where trampling is intense, plant cover and biomass are low, most plants are short, species richness is reduced and species composition has shifted.

Trampling compacts soils, reducing porosity, particularly the volume of macropores (Monti and Mackintosh, 1979). This reduces the water-holding capacity of soil, except in some coarse-textured soils. Compaction reduces water infiltration rates, leading to increased runoff and erosion potential. These physical soil changes alter soil chemistry and biota, although such changes are poorly understood. Compacted soils can also inhibit seed germination and plant growth. Alessa and Earnhart (2000) have shown that plants in compacted soils may be less able to utilize available nutrients because they grow fewer lateral roots and root hairs and because cytoplasmic streaming within root hairs is reduced. Soil compaction effects are exacerbated by abrasion and loss of organic soil horizons, which shield underlying mineral soil horizons from excessive compaction and erosion.

Loss of organic litter directly affects plant and animal populations, both above and below the ground. Since certain plant species germinate most frequently on organic soil surfaces,

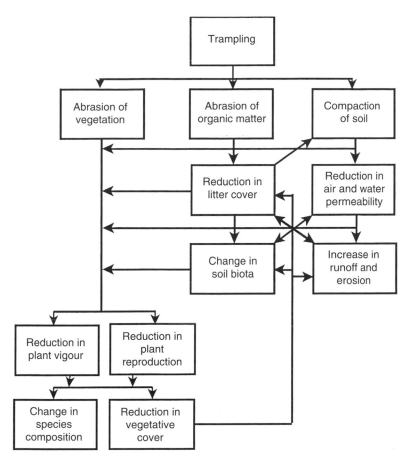

Fig. 4.3. A conceptual model of trampling impacts. Note the numerous reciprocal and cyclic relationships.

loss of litter can cause species composition to shift towards species that germinate most frequently on mineral soil. Loss of organic matter from the soil typically reduces the water-holding capacity of the soil and has an adverse effect on soil microbial populations, which depend on soil organic matter and root exudates from above-ground plants for their energy. Zabinski and Gannon (1997) report substantial reductions in the functional diversity of microbial populations on a backcountry campsite. Microbial populations contribute to ecosystem functioning by metabolizing nutrients, transforming soil organic matter, producing phytohormones and contributing to soil food webs.

The impacts of camping include all the effects of trampling, as well as some unique impacts. Numerous studies have quantified the magnitude of soil and vegetation impact on campsites. The data in Table 4.1 are typical. They describe vegetation and soil conditions on 29 paired canoe-accessible campsites and undisturbed control sites in low-elevation riparian forests in the eastern USA (Marion and Cole, 1996). On most campsites, most of the vegetation has been eliminated and the vegetation that remains consists primarily of graminoids. Forbs dominate undisturbed control sites. Organic horizons on campsites are only about one-third as thick as on controls; mineral soil is exposed over most of the campsite. These mineral soils are compacted – exhibiting increased bulk density and penetration resistance. Substantial numbers of trees have been damaged (cut branches or scarred trunks) or

Table 4.1. Vegetation and soil conditions on 29 campsites and undisturbed control sites at Delaware Water Gap National Recreation Area, 1986 (from Marion and Cole, 1996).

	Campsite		Control		
Impact parameter	Mean	Range	Mean	Range	P
Ground vegetation cover (%)	15	0–63	72	1–95	0.001
Floristic dissimilarity (%)	75	23–100		Not applicable	
Graminoid cover (%)	58	0–100	26	0–92	0.023
Forb cover (%)	23	0–78	59	5–100	0.001
Mineral soil cover (%)	61	21–94	1	0–15	0.001
Organic horizon thickness (cm)	0.5	0–1.4	1.5	0.2–3.1	0.002
Soil bulk density (g/cm^3)	1.26	1.0–1.4	1.06	0.7–1.4	0.001
Soil penetration resistance (kPa)[a]	275	137–382	49	0–226	0.001
Soil moisture (g/cm^3)	18	8–32	17	8–31	0.710
Felled trees (%)	19	0–53		Not applicable	
Damaged trees (%)	77	25–100		Not applicable	
Tree reproduction (stems/ha)	936	0–6275	10,090	0–56,400	0.001
Non-vegetated area (m^2)	181	0–696	0	0–15	0.001
Campsite area (m^2)	269	51–731		Not applicable	
Shoreline disturbance (m)	9	0–20		Not applicable	

[a] 1 kPa = the pressure corresponding to 1.01971×10^{-2} kg/cm^2

felled, and tree reproduction has been dramatically reduced. Along with the felling of tree saplings, lack of tree reproduction suggests that overstorey trees will not be replaced on campsites when they eventually die.

Camping also can cause off-site impacts. The most common off-site impacts are informal trailing (between the campsite and water sources, other campsites or the main trail) and impacts caused by the collection of wood to be burned in campfires. Hall and Farrell (2001) documented 25–63% reductions (depending on size class) in abundance of woody material on and around campsites. Taylor (1997) found that the density of saplings around campsites was reduced within an area that extended 45 m on average from the centre of the campsite. The most pronounced off-site impacts are often those associated with the confinement of horses and other pack animals used to transport people and gear (see Newsome *et al.*, Chapter 5, this volume).

Impacts on trails have also been studied. However, it is difficult to separate the impacts of hiking on trails from the impacts associated with trail construction and maintenance, and the impacts that would occur on trails in the absence of hiking (e.g. erosion by rainwater channelled down a trail tread). Major impacts

of trail construction and maintenance include opening up tree and shrub canopies, the building of a barren, compacted trail tread that may alter drainage patterns, and the creation of a variety of new habitats, including cut slopes above the trail and fill below (Cole, 1981b). Except where hiking use is extremely high, it is probably rare for the impacts of hiking on trails to exceed the impacts caused by trail construction. However, these rare cases of profound hiking impact can be highly problematic. For example, the deep, peaty soil of tracks in much of the Tasmanian Wilderness World Heritage Area can be churned into deep quagmires by a small number of hikers (Calais and Kirkpatrick, 1986; Whinam and Chilcott, 1999).

Impacts adjacent to trails are similar to those caused by trampling. Although trampling adjacent to trails can reduce vegetation cover (Cole, 1978; Boucher *et al.*, 1991), it is common for vegetation cover to be greater adjacent to trails than on undisturbed sites (Hall and Kuss, 1989), presumably due to increased light, water and nutrients there. Organic matter can decrease and soil compaction increase (Adkison and Jackson, 1996). Vegetation composition adjacent to trails is usually very different from undisturbed site controls. It can be less diverse (Boucher *et al.*, 1991), but often is more diverse (Hall and Kuss, 1989), partially due to the invasion of exotic species that use trails as conduits for movement (Benninger-Truax *et al.*, 1992).

Of more practical significance and concern is the impact of hiking on the constructed and maintained trail surface. Constructed trails are barren and compacted by design. So, the interest here is not impacts on native soil and vegetation but impacts on the trail itself. This is a concern because hikers can increase soil erosion from trails, either by detaching or transporting soil particles. Two recent experimental studies provide insight into the process by which this occurs. They show that sediment yield and trail erosion is detachment-limited rather than transport-limited (Wilson and Seney, 1994; DeLuca *et al.*, 1998). Trail use loosens soil particles, making them easier to detach and, therefore, available to be transported by such erosive agents as running water.

Most trail-impact studies document trail characteristics, such as width and depth, without regard for the complex factors (of use, environment and management) that combine to influence these characteristics. Bayfield and Lloyd (1973) developed survey techniques for periodically assessing trail width and depth, as well as censusing the presence or absence of 'detracting' features, such as rutting and bad drainage. Coleman (1977) developed a technique for measuring trail cross-sectional area. More recent assessments of trail conditions, in such places as Guadalupe Mountains National Park (Fish *et al.*, 1981), the Selway-Bitterroot Wilderness, (Cole, 1983) and Great Smoky Mountains National Park (Leung and Marion, 1999b), are largely extensions of this early work. These studies provide descriptive statistics (means and ranges) for such metrics as trail width and depth, as well as frequency and extent of trail problems (Bayfield's 'detracting' features). For example, mean trail width and depth were 115 cm and 10 cm, respectively, on trails in the Selway-Bitterroot Wilderness (Cole, 1991). On trails in Great Smoky Mountains National Park (Leung and Marion, 1999b) there were 470 occurrences of multiple tread. A total of 10.3 km of trail (1.8% of the trail system) had multiple treads. These studies typically search for correlations between trail conditions and characteristics of use, environment and man-

agement. For example, in Great Britain, Bayfield (1973) found that trail width was positively correlated with soil wetness, roughness and steepness, and Coleman (1981) found that trail width was positively related to recreation use.

The most significant impacts of hiking on native soils and vegetation are probably those associated with proliferation of user-created trails along hiking routes where a trail tread is never constructed. Lance *et al.* (1989), describe this process in Scotland, noting that trail development usually starts with formation of a single track. As this path widens and erodes, secondary paths are created. These widen and merge with other paths, ultimately creating a braided, eroding web (Fig. 4.4). On the tallest peaks in Colorado, user-created trails to the summits have eroded so severely that they are now being replaced by constructed trails. Restoration of abandoned sections of user-created trail, which are often steep and eroding, is difficult (Ebersole *et al.*, 2002).

Spatial patterns of impact

Most studies of impact report the intensity of particular types of impact – the amount of impact per unit area (e.g. the campsite lost 50% of its vegetation cover). Assessments of magnitude of impact must also consider the area over which this impact occurs. The magnitude of a 50% cover loss on a $1000 \, m^2$ campsite is twice that of a 50% cover loss on a $500 \, m^2$ campsite – although the intensity of impact is the same. Magnitude of impact (sometimes referred to as aggregate impact) is minimized when both the area of impact and the intensity of impact per unit area are minimized (Cole, 1981a). Certain impact parameters only describe impact intensity (e.g. vegetation cover loss), while others only describe area of impact (e.g. campsite area). A few parameters describe both. For example, the area of vegetation loss on a campsite (Cole, 1989b) expresses vegetation loss, in m^2, as the product of campsite area and the difference between vegetation cover on the campsite and an adjacent control site. This metric makes it possible to compare the magnitude of vegetation impact on sites that vary greatly in size (e.g. Marion and Farrell, 2002).

Spatial aspects of impact have received

Fig. 4.4. Trail braiding is a common type of trail impact in certain environments.

little attention, beyond recognition that assessments of the magnitude of impact must consider the area that has been impacted, as well as the intensity of impact. In addition to the intensity and aggregate area (magnitude) of impact, other potentially important descriptors of impact include the size of impacts and the spatial distribution (pattern) of impacts. Given a constant aggregate area of impact, there may be many small impacts or a few large impacts. Theoretically, these impacts can be distributed in a pattern that is either more clumped (aggregated or underdispersed) or more regular (overdispersed) than a random pattern. In reality, spatial impact patterns are almost always more clumped than random. Campsites are clustered in campgrounds or around lakes and in places accessed by trails. Hiking impacts are concentrated along trail corridors, with little impact off trail.

Quantitative descriptions of impact vary with the spatial scale of analysis that is selected. For example, vegetation loss may be 100% at the centre of a campsite but only 50% when the entire campsite is surveyed. At the scale of a lake basin, vegetation loss associated with camping might amount to only 1 or 2% and, at the scale of the park or wilderness, less than 1% of the vegetation is likely to be lost (Cole, 1981b). Impacts might be considered few and large at a 10ha scale but many and

small at the scale of 10,000 ha. They may be regularly distributed at a 10ha scale but clumped at the scale of 10,000 ha. What this suggests is that any quantification of impacts is only valid at the chosen scale of analysis.

Although generally ignored, spatial descriptors of impact and scaling issues are important considerations, particularly in assessing how much of a problem impacts are, and in devising strategies for managing them. Cole (1981b) noted that hiking and camping impacts on soil and vegetation, while severe when measured at small scales, are minimal at large spatial scales. This suggests that while recreation impacts can be serious for individual plants and animals, and perhaps localized rare populations, they are generally of little significance to landscape integrity or regional biotic diversity. Moreover, unless much of a population is impacted by a single impacted site, the intensity, size and distribution of impacts are not relevant to the significance of impacts assessed at large spatial scales. If animal populations are considered, however, spatial patterns in which impacts are clustered, leaving large expanses undisturbed, might be the ideal.

Recreation impacts on soil and vegetation are highly significant at the scale of human perception – the scale humans can readily observe. Studies of wilderness campers show that most campers view small areas of impact as 'posi-

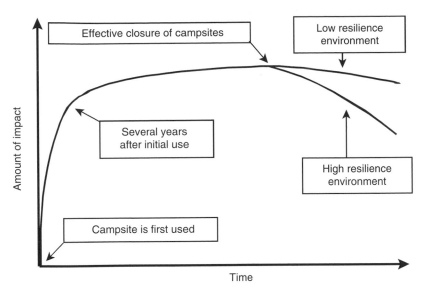

Fig. 4.5. The typical life history of a campsite, from initial use through a period of closure and recovery.

tive', 'pretty natural, healthy' (Farrell *et al.,* 2001), because they make the site function well as a temporary dwelling for humans. Perhaps from the human perspective, many small impacts are preferable to a few large impacts, because small impacts are perceived as 'healthy' dwelling sites, while large impacted areas (several hectares or more) suggest abuse, damage and unhealthy conditions. Moreover, dispersal of impacts at this scale provides more solitude and privacy for tourists. This line of thinking leads to the conclusion that, when impacts on soils, vegetation, animals and humans are all considered, they are least problematic when: (i) aggregate impact (intensity in combination with area) is minimized; and (ii) impacts are concentrated at the site scale, dispersed at intermediate scales (within a destination area such as a lake basin) and clustered at larger scales (within a park or wilderness) (Hammitt and Cole, 1998). Although little attention has been devoted to these spatial issues, Leung and Marion (1999d) suggest some spatial strategies for managing impacts.

Temporal patterns of impact

The tendency to study impacts at one point in time has contributed to a lack of data on tempo-ral patterns of impact, much as the tendency to conduct studies at just one spatial scale leaves us with little insight into spatial patterns. Available studies suggest that individual campsites have a typical 'life history', moving successively through stages of development, dynamic equilibrium and recovery (Fig. 4.5). Impact occurs rapidly during the development phase, shortly after a campsite is first used. For example, on newly established canoe campsites, most of the impact that occurred over the 6 years following creation of the campsite occurred during the first year of use (Marion and Cole, 1996). Impact did increase over the first 3 years, but at a decelerating rate. This phase is followed by a more stable phase in which impacts change little unless there are dramatic changes in amount of use. For example, on long-established campsites in the Eagle Cap Wilderness, mean vegetation cover was 15% in 1979, 12% in 1984 and 19% in 1990 (Cole and Hall, 1992). Vegetation cover on these campsites might be expected to fluctuate between about 10% and 20%, as long as use characteristics are relatively stable. These patterns are relatively consistent across diverse ecosystem types and types of recreation, although impacts occur more rapidly (the development phase is shorter) as amount of use increases and site durability decreases. Moreover, aberrant behaviour

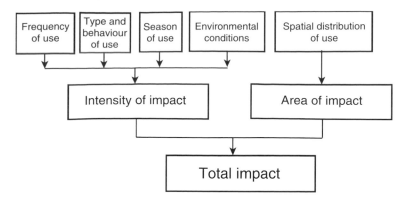

Fig. 4.6. Factors that influence the intensity and area of impact and, therefore, the total amount of impact.

(e.g. someone cutting down a tree) can cause dramatic spikes in impact at any time.

The recovery phase is almost invariably longer than the development phase, because deterioration occurs more rapidly than recovery. Recovery rates also vary greatly with kinds of impact, magnitude of impact and environment. Variation in the resilience of different ecosystem types is pronounced. Hartley (1999) reports residual effects of trampling after 30 years, in alpine meadows in Glacier National Park, while most evidence of camping on closed riparian campsites disappeared within 6 years (Marion and Cole, 1996). Cole and Monz (2002) report that an alpine grassland trampled 1000 times recovered more rapidly than a neighbouring forest, with an understorey of low shrubs, that was trampled just 75 times. Given the same environmental setting, sites that receive more use and that are more heavily impacted will take longer to recover.

Temporal patterns at larger spatial scales have generally been ignored. They are particularly important, however, because impacts tend to proliferate and spread across the landscape where use distribution is not tightly controlled. For example, in two drainages in the Eagle Cap Wilderness, the number of campsites increased from 336 in 1975 to 748 in 1990 (Cole, 1993), even though the condition of most of the sites that existed in 1975 changed little between 1975 and 1990. Site proliferation occurs because, as use shifts across the landscape, new campsites appear more rapidly than old campsites disappear.

Temporal patterns on trails and hiking routes are likely to be similar, though they have seldom been studied. Trail impacts occur rapidly; most segments on established trail systems are generally stable (Fish *et al.*, 1981; Cole, 1991); and recovery of closed trails is typically slow, except where it is assisted (Eagen *et al.*, 2000). However, trail segments that are poorly located or inadequately designed and maintained may deteriorate substantially. At large spatial scales, impacts have increased over time due to: (i) lack of recovery on re-routed trail segments; and (ii) the pioneering of routes into trailless places. This latter trend can be particularly problematic because development of a trail makes access easier, which can lead to a cycle of ever-increasing use and impact.

Factors that influence magnitude of impact

The types of research that have probably been most useful to management are studies of the factors that influence the magnitude of impacts – why impacts are minor in some situations and severe in others. The principal factors that influence intensity of impact (Fig. 4.6) are: (i) frequency of use; (ii) type and behaviour of use; (iii) season of use; and (iv) environmental conditions, while area of impact is primarily a result of the spatial distribution of recreation use (Cole, 1981a, 1987). An understanding of each of these influential variables suggests strategies for managing the impacts of hiking

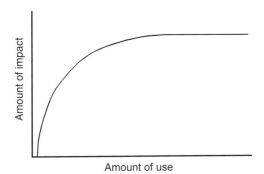

Fig. 4.7. The relationship between amount of use and amount of impact is curvilinear (asymptotic).

and camping on soils and vegetation (Cole *et al.*, 1987; Marion and Leung, Chapter 13, this volume).

The relationship between frequency of use and intensity of impact is generally asymptotic (Fig. 4.7). At first, small increases in use frequency cause pronounced increases in impact; however, the rate of increase in impact decreases as use intensity increases. Where use is light, sites that receive even small differences in amount of impact can have very different impact levels. However, where use is heavy, sites that receive substantially different amounts of use may have similar impact levels. Frissell and Duncan (1965), the first researchers to document this relationship in a field situation, concluded that 'if any use is to be allowed in the wilderness areas, some immediate loss of the natural vegetation will have to be tolerated' (p. 258). Similar results have been found in numerous field surveys of recreation sites and in experimental studies. The further implication of this relationship is that the magnitude of impacts can usually be minimized by encouraging the repetitive use of as small a number of sites as possible (i.e. concentrating use) (Cole, 1981a). This strategy involves accepting a slight increase in the intensity of impact to realize the benefits of a large decrease in the area of impact.

The type and behaviour of use can also have a profound effect on both the type and magnitude of impact. For example, campers who build fires cause both more and different types of impact than campers who do not build fires. Several studies have compared the im-

pacts of hikers with those of groups who use horses or llamas for transport. Generally, these studies have found that horses cause more impact than hikers or llamas, which cause equivalent levels of impact (Cole and Spildie, 1998; DeLuca *et al.*, 1998). Recreation ecology research has provided the scientific foundation for minimum-impact educational programmes (Cole, 1989c). These programmes teach techniques of trip planning, route selection, hiking behaviour, campsite selection and camping behaviour that minimize the *per capita* impacts of use.

Season of use is a less critical factor for hikers than it is for horses and heavy pack animals that can cause severe damage to trails and meadows when soils are water-saturated and plants are growing rapidly. During seasons when snow banks are melting, hikers also need to avoid walking off trail and on water-saturated soils.

A substantial body of research has developed regarding characteristics that make different environments more or less durable as campsites or as trail locations. Experimental applications of both trampling (e.g. Bayfield, 1979; Cole, 1995b) and camping (Cole, 1995c) have been particularly insightful in building this knowledge. Field surveys of trails and campsites that develop correlations between impact parameters and environmental variables have also been helpful (e.g. Leung and Marion, 1999a,b). Experimental studies show that some vegetation types can tolerate more than 30 times as much use as others, with no more damage (Cole, 1995a).

Experimental studies suggest that there is an important difference between a site's resistance (its ability to tolerate use without being damaged) and its resilience (its ability to recover from damage). Cole (1995b) has shown, for groundcover plants, that resistance decreases with erectness and that broadleaved herbs are typically less resistant than grass-like plants and shrubs. Herbs growing in shade are particularly intolerant of trampling because adaptations to shading – possession of large, thin leaves and tall stems – make these plants vulnerable when trampled. This explains the common finding that trampling of forested sites generally results in more rapid loss of vegetation than trampling of open woodlands or

Fig. 4.8. The area of vegetation loss on this campsite is small, due to the durability of the graminoid vegetation cover.

meadows. Low shrubs, such as heather, are relatively resistant to trampling stress, but their resilience is low. Once damaged, they recover slowly. Grass-like plants are most tolerant of trampling.

At the risk of overgeneralizing about a very complex subject (refer to reviews in Cole, 1987; Liddle, 1997; Hammitt and Cole, 1998; and Leung and Marion, 2000, for further details), a few conclusions about site durability seem warranted. Characteristics of durable campsites and other nodes of concentrated use include: (i) either lack of groundcover vegetation or presence of resistant vegetation (Fig. 4.8); (ii) an open, rather than closed, tree canopy; (iii) thick organic soil horizons; or (iv) a relatively flat but well-drained site. Marion and Farrell (2002) also note the importance of designing campsites to confine impacts to a small area, in the absence of natural features such as rocky terrain that serve this purpose.

Leung and Marion (1996) provide a useful overview of knowledge regarding how environmental characteristics influence trail condition. Terrain and topography have a major influence on trail conditions. Steep trail slopes, steep side slopes and trail alignments in which the trail directly ascends slopes all tend to be more degraded, usually because more water is chan-

nelled, with more force, down the trail tread. Trail problems are also common where soils are fine-textured, stone-free and homogeneous, or highly organic and where soils are poorly drained or have high water tables. Trails also tend to widen where the ground surface is wet or rough (Bayfield, 1973).

Management and monitoring

Management and monitoring of trails and campsites are covered in detail in Leung and Marion (Chapter 14 this volume). The scientific foundation for knowledge about effective management strategies was derived from hundreds of studies of the nature and magnitude of impacts, and how they are influenced by characteristics of use and the environment. Along with the experiential knowledge developed from decades of implementing recreation management programmes, a wide array of effective management strategies has evolved (Hammitt and Cole, 1998). Similarly, decades of recreation ecology research, developing methods of measuring impact, have contributed to the campsite and trail monitoring methods employed today (Cole, 1983, 1989a; Marion, 1991; Leung and Marion, 1999b).

Conclusions and Future Directions

Although the field of recreation ecology is only about 30 years old, somewhere around 1000 studies have been conducted. A majority of these have focused on the impacts of hiking and camping on recreation and soils. Specific details about the nature, magnitude and spatial aspects of impact vary with the context of every situation (with amount and type of use, environment, management, etc.). In addition, the management objectives of every park, wilderness or other tourist destination also vary. Therefore, in every place where recreation impacts are a concern, it is worthwhile to have recreation ecology studies conducted in that area, so results can be interpreted in reference to the specific context and management objectives of the area. However, in the absence of site-specific studies and information, much insight can be gleaned from generalizations suggested by the recreation ecology literature.

Since the late 1970s, there have been several attempts to synthesize the recreation ecology literature. Each attempt, including this one, is somewhat unique but there is substantial consensus as well. The following five generalizations are among the most important and generally agreed upon.

1. Impact is inevitable with repetitive use. Numerous studies have shown that even very low levels of repetitive use cause impact. Therefore, avoiding impact is not an option unless all recreation use is curtailed. Managers must decide on acceptable levels of impact and then implement actions capable of keeping use to these levels.

2. Impact occurs rapidly, while recovery occurs more slowly. This underscores the importance of proactive management, since it is much easier to avoid impact than to restore impacted sites. It also suggests that relatively pristine places should receive substantial management attention, in contrast to the common situation of focusing most resources in heavily used and impacted places. Finally, it indicates that rest-rotation of sites (periodically closing damaged sites, to allow recovery, before re-opening them to use) is likely to be ineffective.

3. In many situations, impact increases more as a result of new places being disturbed than from the deterioration of places that have been disturbed for a long time. This also emphasizes the need to be attentive to relatively pristine places and to focus attention on the spatial distribution of use. It suggests that periodic inventories of all impacted sites is often more important than monitoring change on a sample of established sites.

4. Magnitude of impact is a function of frequency of use, the type and behaviour of use, season of use, environmental conditions, and the spatial distribution of use. Therefore, the primary management tools involve manipulation of these factors.

5. The relationship between amount of use and amount of impact is usually curvilinear (asymptotic). This has numerous management implications and is also fundamental to many minimum impact educational messages. It suggests that it is best to concentrate use and impact in popular places and to disperse use and impact in relatively pristine places.

New insights into recreation ecology have been generated as researchers have adopted multiple methodologies and expanded both the temporal and spatial scales of analyses. However, further progress is hampered by a lack of theory and conceptual thinking. Now that the field is 30 years old, the time seems ripe for conceptual and theoretical work that can build a framework for organizing the knowledge gained from the multitude of idiosyncratic field studies that have been conducted.

Two critical gaps in knowledge also limit maturation of the field. First, research needs to move beyond the easily observable and measurable effects of recreation. In particular, we need to better understand relationships between the physical, chemical and biological effects of recreation on soil, and how these soil impacts affect, and are affected by, plants. In the absence of such knowledge, attempts to restore damaged sites often fail. Plants are placed in soil that has not held plants for a half-century and the plants die (Moritsch and Muir, 1993). Soil amendments are needed before plants can survive (Cole and Spildie, 2000; Zabinski *et al.*, 2002). Restoration has been called the acid test of our ecological knowledge (Jordan *et al.*, 1987) because our ability to restore ecosystems will be dependent on the depth of our under-standing and insight into how ecosystems work. By this definition, our understanding of recrea-tion ecology is still wanting.

The lack of attention that recreation ecolo-gists have given to the spatial aspects of recre-ation impacts is also problematic. Impacts have almost always been evaluated at the meso- or site-scale. Populations and communities of plants and soil pedons have been the primary unit of analysis. We have generally done a good job of describing impacts that occur at the human scale. As mentioned above, lack of research at smaller scales hampers our ability to restore damaged sites. Lack of research at larger spatial scales – regarding how landscapes and regions are impacted by recreation – limits our insight into the significance of recreation impacts. How do we answer the 'so what' ques-tions? Hiking and camping impacts on soil and vegetation are generally severe but localized disturbances. Evaluations of these impacts at larger spatial scales would result in wiser judgements about how much of a problem these impacts are, and the most appropriate balance between impacts and access for recre-ation and tourism.

References

Adkison, G.P. and Jackson, M.T. (1996) Changes in ground-layer vegetation cover near trails in Midwestern U.S. forests. *Natural Areas Journal* 16, 14–23.

Alessa, L. and Earnhart, C.G. (2000) Effects of soil compaction on root and root hair morphology: implications for campsite rehabilitation. In: Cole, D.N., McCool, S.F., Borrie, W.T. and O'Loughlin, J. (comps) *Wilderness Science in a Time of Change Conference*. Vol. 5. *Wilderness Ecosystems, Threats and Management*. Proceedings RMRS-P-15-VOL-5. U.S. Department of Agriculture, Forest Service, Rocky Mountain Research Station, Ogden, Utah, pp. 99–104.

Bates, G.H. (1935) Vegetation of footpaths, side-walks, cart-tracks, and gateways. *Journal of Ecology* 23, 470–487.

Bayfield, N.G. (1971) Some effects of walking and skiing on vegetation at Cairngorm. In: Duffey, E. and Watt, A.S. (eds) *The Scientific Management of Plant and Animal Communities for Conserva-tion*. Blackwell, Oxford, UK, pp. 469–485.

Bayfield, N.G. (1973) Use and deterioration of some Scottish hill paths. *Journal of Applied Ecology* 10, 639–648.

Bayfield, N.G. (1979) Recovery of four montane heath communities on Cairngorm, Scotland, from disturbance by trampling. *Biological Conservation* 15, 165–179.

Bayfield, N.G. and Lloyd, R.J. (1973) An approach to assessing the impact of use on a long distance footpath – the Pennine Way. *Recreation News Supplement* 1973, 11–17.

Benninger-Truax, M., Vankat, J.L. and Shaefer, R.L. (1992) Trail corridors as habitat and conduits for movement of plant species in Rocky Mountain National Park, Colorado. *Landscape Ecology* 6, 269–278.

Boucher, D.H., Aviles, J., Chepote, R., Dominguez-Gil, O.E. and Vilchez, B. (1991) Recovery of trailside vegetation from trampling in a tropical rain forest. *Environmental Management* 15, 257–262.

Buckley, R.C. and Pannell, J. (1990) Environmental impacts of tourism and recreation in national parks and conservation reserves. *Journal of Tourism Studies* 1, 24–32.

Calais, S.S. and Kirkpatrick, J.B. (1986) Impact of trampling on natural ecosystems in the Cradle Mountain-Lake St Clair National Park. *Australian Geographer* 17, 6–15.

Cole, D.N. (1978) Estimating the susceptibility of wildland vegetation to trailside alteration. *Journal of Applied Ecology* 15, 281–286.

Cole, D.N. (1981a) Managing ecological impacts at wilderness campsites: an evaluation of tech-niques. *Journal of Forestry* 79, 86–89.

Cole, D.N. (1981b) Vegetational changes associated with recreational use and fire suppression in the Eagle Cap Wilderness, Oregon: some manage-ment implications. *Biological Conservation* 20, 247–270.

Cole, D.N. (1983) *Assessing and Monitoring Back-country Trail Conditions*. Research Paper INT-303. US Department of Agriculture, Forest Service, Intermountain Research Station, Ogden, Utah.

Cole, D.N. (1986) Recreational impacts on back-country campsites in Grand Canyon National Park, Arizona, USA. *Environmental Manage-ment* 10, 651–659.

Cole, D.N. (1987) Research on soil and vegetation in wilderness: a state-of-knowledge review. In: Lucas, R.C. (comp.) *Proceedings – National Wilderness Research Conference: Issues, State-of-knowledge, Future Directions*. General Tech-nical Report INT-220. US Department of Agriculture, Forest Service, Intermountain Research Station, Ogden, Utah, pp. 135–177.

Cole, D.N. (1989a) *Wilderness Campsite Monitoring Methods: a Sourcebook*. General Technical

Report INT-259. US Department of Agriculture, Forest Service, Intermountain Research Station, Ogden, Utah.

Cole, D.N. (1989b) *Area of Vegetation Loss: a New Index of Campsite Impact.* Research Note INT-389. US Department of Agriculture, Forest Service, Intermountain Research Station, Ogden, Utah.

Cole, D.N. (1989c) *Low-impact Recreational Practices for Wilderness and Backcountry.* General Technical Report INT-265. US Department of Agriculture, Forest Service, Intermountain Research Station, Ogden, Utah.

Cole, D.N. (1991) *Changes on Trails in the Selway-Bitterroot Wilderness, Montana, 1978–89.* Research Paper INT-450. US Department of Agriculture, Forest Service, Intermountain Research Station, Ogden, Utah.

Cole, D.N. (1992) Modeling wilderness campsites: factors that influence amount of impact. *Environmental Management* 16, 255–264.

Cole, D.N. (1993) *Campsites in Three Western Wildernesses: Proliferation and Changes in Condition over 12 to 16 years.* Research Paper INT-463. US Department of Agriculture, Forest Service, Intermountain Research Station, Ogden, Utah, USA.

Cole, D.N. (1995a) Experimental trampling of vegetation. I. Relationship between trampling intensity and vegetation response. *Journal of Applied Ecology* 32, 203–214.

Cole, D.N. (1995b) Experimental trampling of vegetation. II. Predictors of resistance and resilience. *Journal of Applied Ecology* 32, 215–224.

Cole, D.N. (1995c) Disturbance of natural vegetation by camping; experimental applications of low level stress. *Environmental Management* 19, 405–416.

Cole, D.N. (1996) Wilderness recreation in the United States – trends in use, users, and impacts. *International Journal of Wilderness* 2, 14–18.

Cole, D.N. (2002) Ecological impacts of wilderness recreation and their management. In: Hendee, J.P. and Dawson, C.P. (eds) *Wilderness Management: Stewardship and Protection of Resources and Values.* Fulcrum Publishing, Golden, Colorado, USA, pp. 413–459.

Cole, D.N. and Bayfield, N.G. (1993) Recreational trampling of vegetation: standard experimental procedures. *Biological Conservation* 63, 209–215.

Cole, D.N. and Hall, T.E. (1992) *Trends in Campsite Condition: Eagle Cap Wilderness, Bob Marshall Wilderness and Grand Canyon National Park.* Research Paper INT-453. US Department of Agriculture, Forest Service, Intermountain Research Station, Ogden, Utah.

Cole, D.N. and Monz, C.A. (2002) Trampling disturbance of high-elevation vegetation, Wind River Mountains, Wyoming, U.S.A. *Arctic, Antarctic, and Alpine Research* 34, 365–376.

Cole, D.N., Petersen, M.E. and Lucas, R.C. (1987) *Managing Wilderness Recreation Use: Common Problems and Potential Solutions.* General Technical Report INT-259. US Department of Agriculture, Forest Service, Intermountain Research Station, Ogden, Utah.

Cole, D.N. and Spildie, D.R. (1998) Hiker, horse, and llama trampling effects on native vegetation in Montana, USA. *Journal of Environmental Management* 53, 61–71.

Cole, D.N. and Spildie, D.R. (2000) Soil amendments and planting techniques: campsite restoration in the Eagle Cap Wilderness, Oregon. In: Cole, D.N., McCool, S.F., Borrie, W.T. and O'Loughlin, J. (comps) *Wilderness Science in a Time of Change Conference.* Vol. 5. *Wilderness Ecosystems, Threats and Management.* Proceedings RMRS-P-15-VOL-5. US Department of Agriculture, Forest Service, Rocky Mountain Research Station, Ogden, Utah, pp. 181–187.

Coleman, R.A. (1977) Simple techniques for monitoring footpath erosion in mountain areas of northwest England. *Environmental Conservation* 4, 145–148.

Coleman, R. (1981) Footpath erosion in the English Lakes District. *Applied Geography* 1, 121–131.

Cordell, H.K. and Super, G.R. (2000) Trends in American's outdoor recreation. In: Gartner, W.C. and Lime, D.W. (eds) *Trends in Outdoor Recreation, Leisure and Tourism.* CAB International, Wallingford, UK, pp. 133–144.

DeLuca, T.H., Patterson, W.A., Freimund, W.A. and Cole, D.N. (1998) Influence of llamas, horses, and hikers on soil erosion from established recreation trails in western Montana, USA. *Environmental Management* 22, 255–262.

Eagen, S., Newman, P., Fritzke, S. and Johnson, L. (2000) Restoration of multiple-rut trails in Tuolumne Meadows of Yosemite National Park. In: Cole, D.N., McCool, S.F., Borrie, W.T. and O'Loughlin, J. (comps) *Wilderness Science in a Time of Change Conference.* Vol. 5. *Wilderness Ecosystems, Threats and Management.* Proceedings RMRS-P-15-VOL-5. US Department of Agriculture, Forest Service, Rocky Mountain Research Station, Ogden, Utah, pp. 188–192.

Ebersole, J.J., Bay, R.F. and Conlin, D. (2002) Restoring high-alpine social trails on the Colorado Fourteeners. In: Perrow, M.R. and Davy, A.J. (eds) *Handbook of Ecological Restoration.* Vol. 2, *Restoration in Practice.* Cambridge University Press, Cambridge, UK, pp. 389–391.

Farrell, T.A. and Marion, J.L. (2001a) Identifying and assessing ecotourism visitor impacts at eight protected areas in Costa Rica and Belize. *Environmental Conservation* 28, 215–225.

Farrell, T.A. and Marion, J.L. (2001b) Trail impacts and trail impact management related to visitation at Torres del Paine National Park, Chile. *Leisure* 26, 31–59.

Farrell, T., Hall, T.E. and White, D.D. (2001) Wilderness campers' perception and evaluation of campsite impacts. *Journal of Leisure Research* 33, 229–250.

Fish, E.B., Brothers, G.L. and Lewis, R.B. (1981) Erosional impacts of trails in Guadalupe Mountains National Park. *Landscape Planning* 8, 387–398.

Frissell, S.S. (1978) Judging recreational impacts on wilderness campsites. *Journal of Forestry* 76, 481–483.

Frissell, S.S. and Duncan, D.P. (1965) Campsite preference and deterioration in the Quetico-Superior canoe country. *Journal of Forestry* 65, 256–260.

Garland, G.G. (1987) Rates of soil loss from mountain footpaths: an experimental study in the Drakensberg Mountains, South Africa. *Applied Geography* 7, 41–54.

Hall, C.N. and Kuss, F.R. (1989) Vegetation alteration along trails in Shenandoah National Park, Virginia. *Biological Conservation* 48, 211–227.

Hall, T.E. and Farrell, T.A. (2001) Fuelwood depletion at wilderness campsites: extent and potential ecological significance. *Environmental Conservation* 28, 241–247.

Hammitt, W.E. and Cole, D.H. (1998) *Wildland Recreation: Ecology and Management*, 2nd edn. John Wiley & Sons, New York.

Hartley, E.A. (1999) Visitor impact at Logan Pass, Glacier National Park: a thirty-year vegetation study. In: Harmon, D. (ed.) *On the Frontiers of Conservation*. George Wright Society, Hancock, Michigan, pp. 297–305.

Hawkins, J.P. and Roberts, C.M. (1993) Effects of recreational scuba diving on coral reefs: trampling on reef-flat communities. *Journal of Applied Ecology* 30, 25–30.

Jim, C.Y. (1987) Trampling impacts of recreationists on picnic sites in a Hong Kong country park. *Environmental Conservation* 14, 117–127.

Jordan, W.R., Gilpin, M.E. and Aber, J.D. (eds) (1987) *Restoration Ecology*. Cambridge University Press, Cambridge, UK.

Jusoff, K. (1989) Physical soil-properties associated with recreational use of a forested reserve area in Malaysia. *Environmental Conservation* 16, 339–342.

Kutiel, P. and Zhevelev, Y. (2001) Recreational use impact on soil and vegetation at picnic sites in Aleppo pine forests on Mount Carmel, Israel. *Israel Journal of Plant Sciences* 49, 49–56.

Lance, A.N., Baugh, I.D. and Love, J.A. (1989) Continued footpath widening in the Cairngorm Mountains, Scotland. *Biological Conservation* 49, 201–214.

Lemauviel, S. and Rozé, F. (2003) Response of three plant communities to trampling in a sand dune system in Brittany (France). *Environmental Management* 31, 227–235.

Leung, Y. and Marion, J.L. (1996) Trail degradation as influenced by environmental factors: a state-of-knowledge review. *Journal of Soil and Water Conservation* 51, 130–136.

Leung, Y. and Marion, J.L. (1999a) Characterizing backcountry camping impacts in Great Smoky Mountains National Park, USA. *Journal of Environmental Management* 57, 193–203.

Leung, Y. and Marion, J.L. (1999b) Assessing trail conditions in protected areas: application of a problem assessment method in Great Smoky Mountains National Park, USA. *Environmental Conservation* 26, 270–279.

Leung, Y. and Marion, J.L. (1999c) The influence of sampling interval on the accuracy of trail impact assessment. *Landscape and Urban Planning* 43, 167–179.

Leung, Y. and Marion, J.L. (1999d) Spatial strategies for managing visitor impacts in national parks. *Journal of Park and Recreation Administration* 17, 20–38.

Leung, Y. and Marion, J.L. (2000) Recreation impact and management in wilderness: a state-of-knowledge review. In: Cole, D.N., McCool, S.F., Borrie, W.T. and O'Loughlin, J. (comps) *Wilderness Science in a Time of Change Conference*. Vol. 5. *Wilderness Ecosystems, Threats and Management*. Proceedings RMRS-P-15-VOL-5. US Department of Agriculture, Forest Service, Rocky Mountain Research Station, Ogden, Utah, pp. 23–48.

Leung, Y. and Neller, R.J. (1995) Trail degradation along the Pat Sin Range: an example of environmental geomorphology. *Hong Kong Geologist* 1, 79–87.

Liddle, M.J. (1975a) A selective review of the ecological effects of human trampling on natural ecosystems. *Biological Conservation* 7, 17–36.

Liddle, M.J. (1975b) A theoretical relationship between the primary productivity of vegetation and its ability to tolerate trampling. *Biological Conservation* 8, 251–255.

Liddle, M.J. (1997) *Recreation Ecology*. Chapman & Hall, London, UK.

Liddle, M.J. and Greig-Smith, P.J. (1975) A survey of tracks and paths in a sand dune ecosystem. *Journal of Applied Ecology* 12, 893–930.

Liddle, M.J. and Kay, A.M. (1987) Resistance, survival and recovery of trampled corals on the Great Barrier Reef. *Biological Conservation* 42, 1–18.

Liddle, M.J. and Thyer, N. (1986) Trampling and fire in a subtropical dry sclerophyll forest. *Environmental Conservation* 13, 33–39.

Marion, J.L. (1991) *Developing a Natural Resource Inventory and Monitoring Program for Visitor Impacts on Recreation Sites: a Procedural Manual.* Natural Resources Report NPS/NRVT/NRR-91/06. US Department of Interior, National Park Service, Denver, Colorado.

Marion, J.L. and Cole, D.N. (1996) Spatial and temporal variation in soil and vegetation impacts on campsites. *Ecological Applications* 6, 520–530.

Marion, J.L. and Farrell, T.A. (2002) Management practices that concentrate visitor activities: camping impact management at Isle Royale National Park, USA. *Journal of Environmental Management* 66, 201–212.

Marion, J.L. and Leung, Y. (2001) Trail resource impacts and an examination of alternative assessment techniques. *Journal of Park and Recreation Administration* 19, 17–37.

Meinecke, E.P. (1928) *The Effect of Excessive Tourist Travel on the California Redwood Parks.* California Department of Natural Resources, Division of Parks, Sacramento, California.

Merriam, L.C. and Smith, C.K. (1974) Visitor impact on newly developed campsites in the Boundary Waters Canoe Area. *Journal of Forestry* 72, 627–630.

Monti, P. and Mackintosh, E.E. (1979) Effect of camping on surface soil properties in the boreal forest region of northwestern Ontario, Canada. *Soil Science Society of America Journal* 43, 1024–1029.

Monz, C.A. (2002) The response of two arctic tundra plant communities to human trampling disturbance. *Journal of Environmental Management* 64, 207–217.

Moritsch, B.J. and Muir, P.S. (1993) Subalpine revegetation in Yosemite National Park, California: changes in vegetation after three years. *Natural Areas Journal* 13, 155–163.

Newsome, D., Moore, S.A. and Dowling, R.K. (2002) *Natural Area Tourism: Ecology, Impacts and Management.* Channel View Publications, Clevedon, UK.

Obua, J. and Harding, D.M. (1997) Environmental impact of ecotourism in Kibale National Park, Uganda. *Journal of Sustainable Tourism* 5, 213–223.

Pratt, J. (1997) The effect of human trampling on three vegetation communities in Mount Elgon National Park. Available at website http://

www.env.leeds.ac.uk/elgon/trampling.html (verified 30 January 2003).

Rouphael, A.B. and Inglis, G.J. (2002) Increased spatial and temporal variability in coral damage caused by recreational scuba diving. *Ecological Applications* 12, 427–440.

Scott, J.J. and Kirkpatrick, J.B. (1994) Effects of human trampling on the sub-Antarctic vegetation of Macquarie Island. *Polar Record* 30, 207–220.

Spildie, D.R., Cole, D.N. and Walker, S.C. (2000) Effectiveness of a confinement strategy in reducing pack stock impacts at campsites in the Selway-Bitterroot Wilderness, Idaho. In: Cole, D.N., McCool, S.F., Borrie, W.T. and O'Loughlin, J. (comps) *Wilderness Science in a Time of Change Conference.* Vol. 5. *Wilderness Ecosystems, Threats and Management.* Proceedings RMRS-P-15-VOL-5. US Department of Agriculture, Forest Service, Rocky Mountain Research Station, Ogden, Utah, pp. 199–208.

Stankey, G.H., Cole, D.N., Lucas, R.C., Petersen, M.E. and Frissell, S.S. (1985) *The Limits of Acceptable Change (LAC) System for Wilderness Planning.* Research Paper INT-176. US Department of Agriculture, Forest Service, Ogden, Utah.

Stewart, D.P.C. and Cameron, K.C. (1992) Effect of trampling on the soils of the St. James Walkway, New Zealand. *Soil Use and Management* 8, 30–36.

Sun, D. and Liddle, M.J. (1993a) A survey of trampling effects on vegetation and soil in eight tropical and subtropical sites. *Environmental Management* 17, 497–510.

Sun, D. and Liddle, M.J. (1993b) Plant morphological characteristics and resistance to simulated trampling. *Environmental Management* 17, 511–521.

Tachibana, H. (1969) Vegetation changes of a moor in Mt. Hakkoda caused by human treading. *Ecological Review* 17, 177–188.

Taylor, J.Y. (1997) Leave only footprints? How backcountry campsite use affects forest structure. *Yellowstone Science* 5, 14–17.

Wagar, J.A. (1961) How to predict which vegetated areas will stand up best under 'active' recreation. *American Recreation Journal* 1, 20–21.

Wagar, J.A. (1964) The carrying capacity of wild lands for recreation. Forest Science Monograph 7. Society of American Foresters, Washington, DC.

Whinam, J. and Chilcott, N. (1999) Impacts of trampling on alpine environments in central Tasmania. *Journal of Environmental Management* 57, 205–220.

Whinam, J., Cannell, E.J., Kirkpatrick, J.B. and Comfort, M. (1994) Studies on the potential impact of recreational horseriding on some alpine environments of the Central Plateau, Tasmania. *Journal of Environmental Management* 40, 103–117.

Wilson, J.P. and Seney, J.P. (1994) Erosional impact of hikers, horses, motorcycles, and off-road bicycles on mountain trails in Montana. *Mountain Research and Development* 14, 77–88.

Yoda, A. and Watanabe, T. (2000) Erosion of mountain hiking trail over a seven-year period in Daisetsuzan National Park, central Hokkaido, Japan. In: Cole, D.N., McCool, S.F., Borrie, W.T. and O'Loughlin, J. (comps) *Wilderness Science in a Time of Change Conference*. Vol. 5.

Wilderness Ecosystems, Threats and Management. Proceedings RMRS-P-15-VOL-5. US Department of Agriculture, Forest Service, Rocky Mountain Research Station, Ogden, Utah, pp. 172–178.

Zabinski, C.A. and Gannon, J.E. (1997) Effects of recreational impacts on soil microbial communities. *Environmental Management* 21, 233–238.

Zabinski, C.A., DeLuca, T.H., Cole, D.N. and Moynahan, O.S. (2002) Restoration of highly impacted campsites in the Eagle Cap Wilderness, Oregon. *Restoration Ecology* 10, 275–281.

5

Environmental Impacts Associated with Recreational Horse-riding

David Newsome,[1] David N. Cole[2] and Jeffrey L. Marion[3]

[1]School of Environmental Science, Murdoch University, Perth, Western Australia; [2]Aldo Leopold Wilderness Research Institute, Forest Service, Missoula, Montana, USA; [3]Patuxent Wildlife Research Center, US Geological Survey, Virginia Tech/ Forestry (0324), Blacksburg, Virginia, USA

Introduction

This chapter provides a state of knowledge review of some of the most recent research concerned with the environmental impacts of horse-riding. Our perspective is derived from studies carried out in the USA and Australia, but the results and conclusions derived from this work are applicable in the global situation. The focus is largely on trail examples from the USA but also considers the case of free range riding in Australia. We provide the context of horse-riding as a recreational activity and summarize the spectrum of impacts brought about by recreational horse-riding. This is followed by three case studies concerned with the assessment and measurement of impacts in important conservation areas. The case study from Yosemite National Park in the USA considers the associated impact of grazing effects, while the Big South Fork study, also from the USA, highlights impacts on trail networks. The final case study explores the quantifiable damage to soils and vegetation when horse-riding occurs in a random dispersed fashion off-trail networks. The final section of this chapter provides insight into three different management situations. The first relates to reducing impacts at campsites used by horse-riders in the USA, the second management perspective, also from the USA, explores the management of horse-riding in a multiple-use recreation area. The third manage-

ment scenario examines the management of horse-riding in Australian protected areas.

Horse-riding as a Recreational Activity

Horses originally evolved to live in open environments in North America. Today wild equids can be found living on the grasslands and plains of Mongolia (Przewalski's horse), the Russian steppe (tarpan), and in the grasslands of Africa (zebra). The domestic horse (*Equus caballus caballus*) has been associated with humans for about 4000 years. Initially utilized for meat and their milk, domestication of horses also meant they could be used as draft animals. Once horses could be tamed and trained for riding, they became inextricably linked with humans and were used to carry people in armed conflict and as a means of travel to new lands. Recreational pursuits in the form of horse racing are recorded from the time of the ancient Greeks. Today horses are still used for a variety of purposes, but globally their role as a recreational animal is highly significant as indicated by the science, health aspects, business and retailing, printed matter, clubs and societies devoted to horses and associated activities. Furthermore, horses have also been introduced into a range of environments (e.g. forests) that are quite different from those in which they originally evolved (grasslands and open areas). These aspects raise three important points in relation to the recreation ecology of horse riding. First, horse-riding will continue to be a significant recreational activity in an increasingly crowded world with diminishing and increasingly impacted natural ecosystems. Secondly, horse-riding is seen by many as a legitimate activity in natural areas that are already under pressure from a variety of recreational interests that may be competing for the same space. Thirdly, protected areas are often poorly funded and frequently lacking in adequate management. This presents natural area managers with the difficult task of achieving conservation objectives in an atmosphere of increasing recreational pressures.

Horse-riding today is a major tourist/ recreational activity and takes place in a wide spectrum of environmental situations and countries. Horse-riding tours and treks, for example, are widely marketed and available in Australia, New Zealand, Scotland, Spain, USA, Canada, Thailand and South Africa. Such tours are often combined with other activities such as camping and fishing. In addition to this, particularly in the USA, Europe and Australia, there are a large number of private individuals and horse-riding clubs (e.g. 1.3 million people engage in horse-riding activities each year in the UK), who seek to ride in natural areas such as local open spaces, nature reserves and national parks. In these areas horse-riders can utilize multipurpose trails, specifically designated horse trails that non-horse-riders may or may not use, and engage in cross-country riding where there is no designated pathway. Even though, in many cases, access is approved and available to horse-riders, conflicts continue to arise in two situations. The first concerns conflicts where other users, such as hikers and mountain-bike riders, object to impacts such as horse faeces on the track, the increased incidence of flies that are attracted to dung, and the sheer presence of large domestic animals in conservation reserves. Secondly, non-horse-riders also state that the erosion caused by horse-riding far exceeds any that is caused by other users, such as cyclists or hikers. Moreover, these assertions are supported by research (for example, see Dale and Weaver, 1974; Wilson and Seney, 1994; Deluca et al.,

1998). The fact that horse-riders (lobby groups and commercial operators) argue they also have the right to use reserved areas brings them into potential conflict with natural area resource managers over issues of restricted access to reserved areas, perceived environmental impacts and the fact that managers have to respond to complaints from non-horse-users.

Newsome et al. (2002) considered the experience horse-riders sought or operators marketed in the context of Australian national parks. The experience is advertised by many commercial horse-riding operations as an 'ecotourism experience'. Horse-riders wish to experience natural environments and enjoy working with the animals as they move through the landscape, but Newsome et al. (2002) questioned whether this really reflected ecotourism, where minimal impact is the key feature in entering and utilizing natural areas. In contrast to a dominantly environmentally sensitive approach, the image portrayed in many horse-riding operations is more of a historical pioneering concept. There is now irrefutable evidence that horse-riding is an environmentally damaging activity (e.g. Widner and Marion, 1993; Phillips and Newsome, 2002). It also appears that in many cases horse-riders are indifferent to or unaware of their effects on the environment (UK CEED, 2000; D. Newsome, personal observation).

In the USA, horse-riding has been an important recreational activity for more than a century. At one time, packstock (primarily horses and mules) were the primary mode of transportation in large wild lands (e.g. wilderness areas and the backcountry of national parks). Packstock were such a traditional part of wilderness recreation that Leopold (1921) defined wilderness as lands large enough to absorb a 2-week packstock trip. Similarly, when Sumner (1942) first introduced the carrying capacity concept (referred to as the recreation saturation point) he was commenting on concerns about excessive packstock use in California's Sierra Nevada. Packstock use of wilderness lands probably exceeded backpacker use until sometime in the 1960s (McClaran and Cole, 1993). However, the proportionate increase in backpacker use results more from increased backpacking than from decreased use of packstock. McClaran and

Cole (1993) estimated that about 11% of wilderness use in the USA, in 1990, was by people with packstock.

In wildlands of the USA, some horse-riding involves people riding horses for the day. This use causes impacts to the trails and to any places where people stop and tie up their horses. Much more problematic, however, are the impacts that occur when riders take overnight trips. On such trips, riders bring along pack animals, to carry their gear, as well as the animals they ride on. In the past, some groups rode through the wilderness with more than 100 animals, and outfitters would sometimes leave their horses and mules in the backcountry for the entire summer. Today, most wilderness areas place limits on the maximum number of animals in one group. However, the most common limit, 25 animals (Cole, 2002), is suggestive of the magnitude of impact that a single group can still cause.

In addition to damage to trails, overnight stock use damages campsites and grazing areas (Cole, 1983). Horses are usually allowed to graze freely and they need to be confined for long periods. While grazing, they defoliate plants, urinate and defecate, and trample soils (McClaran and Cole, 1993). The soils of meadows, where forage is abundant, are frequently moist, making them particularly prone to trampling impact. They are often tied to trees, which results in loss of soil and damage to tree roots. Sometimes, they are tethered to a stake in the ground. Unless they are moved frequently, this can also be highly damaging. Less destructive – but still problematic – confinement techniques include tying stock to a rope tied between trees (a high line) and confining stock inside an electric fence.

Overview of Environmental Impacts

Horses have the potential to cause considerable damage to soils and vegetation (Table 5.1). While many of these impacts can also be caused by hikers, impacts caused by horses generally occur to a greater degree. Horse-riding impacts are quantitatively greater than those caused by walkers (e.g. see Liddle, 1997). There is also a qualitative difference, in the sense that certain types of impacts, such as grazing and confinement, are unique to horse-riding.

Of all the impacts that have been identified, the most common and widely recognized is the ground-level damage caused by horses' hooves. The main problem is the large force applied to the ground because the horse's weight is transferred to ground level on four relatively sharp points – the hooves. As the horse and rider move along a trail or across vegetation there is much potential for the activity to damage vegetation and soils, particularly in fragile plant communities.

Direct impacts on horse trails include damage to stable soil systems, in the form of displaced sediments and surficial soils. Horses' hooves dig into the surface, pushing particles across the surface. This is often associated with some form of compaction in clay soils, but predominantly manifests as displacement in sandy, weakly cohesive soils. As Wilson and Seney (1994) noted, a critical issue in bringing about erosion is the detachment of soil particles that can then be readily transported by water, especially on steep slopes. Figure 5.1 illustrates the way surficial soil is damaged by horses' hooves. The hoof incision has destabilized the surface, displacing soil to one end and forming a depression at the other. The displaced soil can be mobilized more easily because any organic layers are disrupted and/or surface crusts are broken, allowing rain-drop splash dispersion of soil particles to be more effective. Soil structure is also broken down, especially at the embedded end of the hoof print (Fig. 5.1). In fine-grained and organic soils, such depressions can fill with water and can become quagmires with frequent horse use. On sloping ground and in wet climates the displaced soil is readily mobilized and can be transported downhill. Such processes can lead to deepening of trails and trail proliferation as users seek to avoid wet and/or deeply incised segments of trail.

Such trail degradation also constitutes a social and potential ecological impact. Other users find degraded trails unsightly and not in keeping with the overall concept of natural area integrity. Other users of such degraded trails may exacerbate the situation by developing parallel informal trails in order to avoid unsafe, deeply incised or boggy segments. Widespread erosion problems may undermine the soil-rooting zone

Table 5.1. Environmental impact of horse-riding in natural areas.

Activity	User conflict	Damage to soils and trail incision	Trail deepening	Erosion	Degradation of existing trail network	Development of multiple informal trail networks	Loss of vegetation height and cover	Browsing of shrubs and grazing	Seed dispersal of introduced species	Transport of fungal pathogens	Change in plant species composition	Nutrient enrichment from faeces and urine scalds	Fouling of water holes	Collapse of wildlife burrows	Disturbance to wildlife
											Recognized impacts				
Multiple-use trails	✓	✓	✓	✓	✓**	✓	✓**	✓	✓	✓	✓□	✓			✓
Designated horse-riding trails		✓	✓	✓	✓**	✓	✓**	✓	✓	✓	✓□	✓			✓
Cross-country riding (no designated pathway)	✓	✓	✓	✓			✓	✓	✓	✓	✓	✓	✓	✓	✓
Horse party camping and tethering sites	✓*			✓			✓	✓	✓		□		✓	✓	✓

* If also used by other recreationists; ** if horses stray off trails; □ weed communities often well established.

of nearby vegetation, causing localized loss of individual plants and an extension of the erosion problem, as the protective function of plant cover continues to be lost. The extent to which all of this occurs is somewhat dependent on the intensity and frequency of use, although even low levels of usage can cause significant damage (Phillips and Newsome, 2002). Clearly, if large numbers of horse-riders utilize a wide area there is a greater degree of biophysical impact and area at risk of being impacted. However, the level of damage is also dependent on the nature of soils, slope, climate, relative sensitivity of the vegetation and the effectiveness of any management that may be in place. Horse-riding that takes place on erodible soils in steeply sloping terrain in the absence of management constitutes a major impact risk.

Ecosystem-level impacts can especially occur when there is widespread damage to vegetation as a result of trampling or the accidental spread of introduced organisms. Plant damage should not be a feature on designated trail systems except where trail proliferation has occurred in response to trail degradation, or where horses are allowed to stray off the trail. Loss of vegetation height and cover readily occurs where horse-riding occurs off designated pathways (Weaver and Dale, 1978; Cole and Spildie, 1998; Newsome *et al.*, 2002). Vegetation is particularly at risk where upright and shrub forms readily snap in response to trampling. This, in combination with slow-growing species/plant communities that are adapted to coping with natural limiting factors such as aridity, low temperatures and nutrient poverty, means that the vegetation is likely to have a long recovery time and may even continue to die after the initial impact has occurred (Whinam and Comfort, 1996; Whinam and Chilcott, 1999; Newsome *et al.*, 2002; Phillips and Newsome, 2002).

Local-scale impacts can evolve into larger scale impacts as a result of widespread erosion,

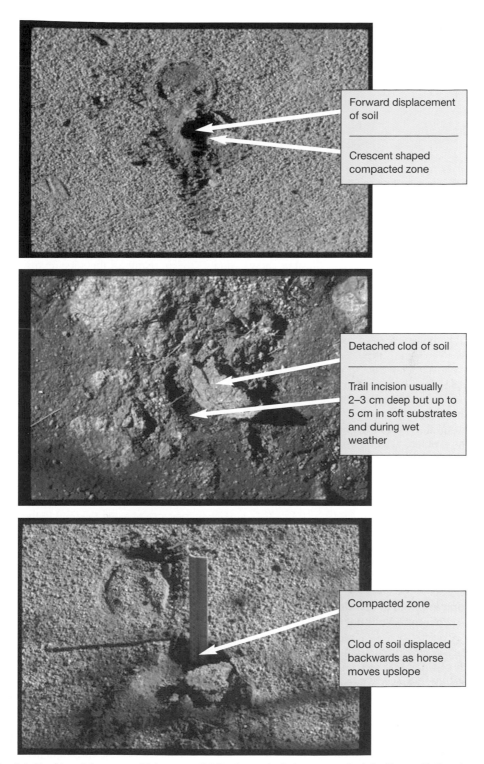

Fig. 5.1. Hoof imprints on a multiple-use trail following a single horse pass in John Forrest National Park, Western Australia.

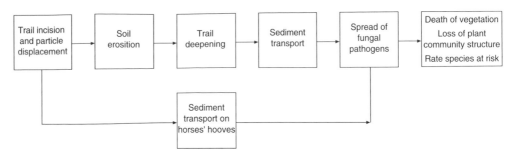

Fig. 5.2. Direct, indirect and potential extended biophysical impacts of horse-riding in Australian ecosystems.

weed invasion and the introduction of fungal pathogens. For example, Fig. 5.2 illustrates how pathogenic organisms may be translocated from an infected area to what was a disease-free area. This is a pertinent issue in Western Australia, where the accidental transport of fungal pathogens poses a serious risk to biodiversity (Newsome, 2003). Because horses disturb soil, particles can be readily transferred from place to place on their hooves. The presence of horses in conservation areas that are at risk because of existing infection by exotic organisms thus poses a major risk of exacerbating the problem and/or spreading the problem from one site to another. Soil erosion on horse trails can therefore bring about wider and extended impacts if soil is moved from one site to another.

Assessing and Measuring the Environmental Impacts of Horse-riding

Grazing impacts to subalpine meadows in Yosemite National Park, USA

The lack of empirical information regarding the effects of grazing by recreational packstock on remote meadows in wilderness and national parks was the motivation for a study of grazing impacts in Yosemite National Park (Cole *et al.*, 2004). Three different meadow types were studied: (i) a high elevation (3100 m), xeric shorthair sedge (*Carex filifolia*) meadow; (ii) a somewhat mesic shorthair reedgrass (*Calamagrostis breweri*) meadow (2600 m); and (iii) a more mesic

tufted hairgrass (*Deschampsia cespitosa*) meadow (2285 m). None of the specific meadows that were studied had been grazed in the past century.

In each of the three meadows, horses and mules were allowed to graze at specified intensities each year for four successive years. The intention was to have four replicate blocks of four grazing intensities (0, 25, 50 and 75% forage removal) in each meadow. This was accomplished by tethering animals to a stake, using a 4-m-long rope, for as long as was required to remove the target level of forage. This produced ~50 m^2 grazing plots, which were monitored before and after grazing for each of the 4 years of grazing, as well as 1 year after the final grazing treatment (Fig. 5.3).

As described in Moore *et al.* (2000), grazing at these intensities caused substantial changes in meadow conditions. In all three meadows, meadow productivity (vegetation biomass 1 year after grazing) was reduced significantly after the second season of grazing. Other changes apparent in all meadows after two seasons were increases in basal cover of bare soil and changes in species composition. Basal vegetation cover declined in one meadow, but not the others.

The most consistent and predictable impact of grazing was the reduction in meadow productivity. In the shorthair sedge meadow, for example, our data fit the regression equation $Y = 16 + 0.0075X + 0.02X^2$, where X is the percentage of biomass removed by grazing and Y is the percentage decline in productivity ($r^2 = 0.68$). Based on this type of data, managers can establish grazing intensities that are likely to

Fig. 5.3. Researchers taking field measurements on grazed plots in the shorthair reedgrass meadow, Tuolumne Meadows, Yosemite National Park, USA.

avoid unacceptable impacts on meadow productivity. In the three meadows we studied, if a limit of 10% decline in productivity is established, maximum permissible levels of forage removal range from 17% in the tufted hairgrass meadow to 36% in the shorthair sedge meadow. A common rule of thumb for grassland vegetation is to leave 50% of the biomass at the end of the grazing season. Our data suggest that this level of defoliation would result in a loss of productivity on the order of 25–30% in these meadow types.

Much less consistent and predictable were changes in species composition. Although differences in species composition between grazed plots and control plots increased with each successive season of grazing, ordinations suggest that the magnitude of shift in composition due to grazing was minor. Using canonical correspondence analysis, plots and species were ordinated such that the first axis of the ordination was constrained to reflect grazing intensity (percentage utilization). Eigenvalues for the first axis indicate that, after 4 years of grazing, grazing intensity explains only 6–10% of the variation in species composition between plots. Eigenvalues for the second axis, not constrained to reflect grazing intensity, are three to five times as great. The ordination of

plots and species (Fig. 5.4) shows little variation between plots, no consistent distinction between control plots and plots grazed at different intensities, and little influence of grazing intensity on composition.

In detrended correspondence analysis, axes are not directly constrained to reflect grazing intensity. We did multiple regression analyses using first- and second-axis detrended correspondence analysis (DCA) scores as the dependent variable and percentage utilization, seasons grazed and dummy variables for replicate blocks as independent variables. In all meadows, the influence of grazing intensity was minimal, with replicate block usually being the primary influence on species composition. Plot ordinations typically showed plots clustered by replicate block rather than treatment. Together, these analyses suggest that species compositional changes due to grazing, although measurable, were less substantial than compositional differences between replicate blocks that existed prior to grazing.

Given that species compositional change was small in magnitude, it is not surprising that effects of grazing on species diversity measures (species richness, Shannon's evenness and Shannon's diversity) were generally small and inconsistent. In all three meadows, variation

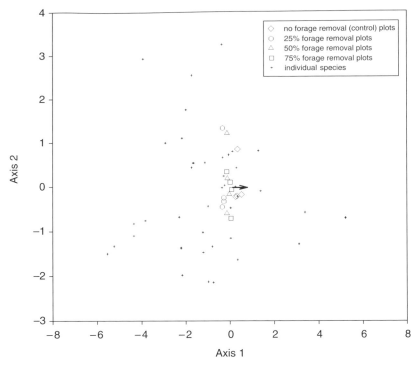

Fig. 5.4. Ordination of plots and species, using canonical correspondence analysis, after 4 years of grazing. The degree to which plots cluster in locations divergent from other treatments, and the length of the arrow (located at the centre of the ordination) along Axis 1 are indicative of the influence of grazing intensity on species composition. (After Cole *et al.*, 2004.)

between years in mean number of vascular plant species per 1.25 m² sample was virtually identical on grazed and control plots. Grazing reduced the relative cover of graminoids in all three meadows, but differences were statistically significant only in the shorthair reedgrass meadow. No other growth forms differed significantly between grazed and ungrazed plots.

This case study illustrates the difficulties of conducting research on the impacts of grazing. Environmental heterogeneity, variation in the behaviour of grazing animals, the lag time between cause and effect and the need to assess long-term effects, all conspire to reduce the precision of attempts to estimate the likely effects of specific levels of grazing. Nevertheless, this research clearly shows that even modest levels of grazing can cause substantial impacts to meadows intended for preservation. Moreover, these data provide a first approximation of the likely effects of specific grazing

intensities. It also suggests that monitoring of productivity (biomass) may be more effective than monitoring species composition.

Assessing and monitoring the impacts of horse use in a multiple-use recreation area: Big South Fork, USA

The Big South Fork National River and Recreation Area is a US National Park Service unit encompassing 50,588 ha in northern Tennessee and southern Kentucky. The area consists of upland plateaux separated by cliff lines from deeply cut river and stream drainages. Big South Fork (BSF) receives nearly 900,000 visitors annually, with trail-related activities accounting for a large portion of total use. The area has 365 km of trails and primitive roads that have become popular among horseback riders, although off-road/all-terrain vehicle (ORV/ATV) use and hiking are also common recreational activities. Preparation of a road and trail management plan prompted research to develop and apply trail impact assessment and monitoring methods, which are considered here.

Many of Big South Fork's trails are multiple use, including many that receive heavy horse traffic and/or motorized uses. Resource impacts associated with these activities are substantial on some trails, few of which have received adequate management work, due to limited agency budgets and staffing. Trail system impacts are further aggravated by: (i) highly erodible soils and steep terrain; (ii) improper construction and maintenance; (iii) inappropriate stream crossings; (iv) high use by horseback riders and motorized vehicles; and (v) improper location (e.g. steep grades or floodplain settings). Lack of information regarding horse-trail use and impact, and the identification and management of sustainable horse trails, prompted managers to issue a moratorium on new horse-trail construction. This research sought to provide essential information for planning and management decision-making purposes by: (i) identifying and characterizing current resource impacts through development of trail-monitoring procedures; (ii) collecting baseline data from a random sample of Big South Fork trails; and (iii) conducting relational analyses to evaluate the role and influence of causal and non-causal factors to inform the selection of effective management interventions.

The park's Geographic Information System included a database for roads and trails. Improved roads and graded gravel roads were removed from the sample population, along with some gravelled 4-wheel drive roads not considered part of the recreational trail system. Longer trails were subdivided into 9.5 km segments to avoid undersampling. This process yielded a sample population of 365 km and 182 segments, from which a statistical randomizing procedure was used to select a 34% sample. This large sample (48 trail segments, 124 km) was necessary to ensure adequate representation of diverse use-related, environmental and managerial factors, and adequate documentation of baseline conditions for comparison with future monitoring. A knowledgeable park man-

ager assigned percentage use estimates for each use type (horse, ATV and hiking) to each surveyed segment; segments with 75% or more use from a single-use type were categorized as representative of that type of use for analyses (including 91 km of trails).

Elements of two trail survey methodologies were integrated in developing monitoring procedures for the BSF. A point measurement method with a systematic sampling scheme at 152 m intervals, following a randomized start, was the primary method (Leung and Marion, 1999b; Marion and Leung, 2001). At each sample point, a transect was established perpendicular to the trail tread, with endpoints defined by visually pronounced changes in non-woody vegetation height (trampled versus untrampled), cover, composition, or, when vegetation cover is minimal or absent, by disturbance to organic litter. Representative photo sets were used to promote consistent judgement. The objective was to select boundaries that contain the majority (>95%) of traffic. Temporary stakes were placed at these boundaries and the distance between was measured as tread width. Maximum depth from a taut string, tied to the base of these stakes, to the trail surface was measured as maximum incision, an indicator of soil erosion (Farrell and Marion, 2002). Tread composition characteristics (e.g. vegetation cover, organic litter, soil, mud, rock) were defined to be mutually exclusive and assessed as a percentage of tread width.

A problem assessment method was integrated into the monitoring procedures to provide census information on specific trail-impact problems, including excessive erosion and muddiness (Leung and Marion, 1999c). Excessive erosion was defined as sections of tread (>3 m long) with tread incision exceeding 13 cm. Excessive muddiness was defined as sections of tread (>3 m long) with seasonal or permanently wet, muddy soils that show imbedded foot- or hoof prints (>1.3 cm deep). This approach provides data on the frequency, lineal extent of occurrence, and location of specific pre-defined problems, facilitating management efforts to rectify such impacts. A trail-measuring wheel was pushed along each trail to measure distance to each sampling point and beginning/ending distances of each trail problem.

Table 5.2. Big South Fork trail condition assessment data from the point sampling method.

Indicator	N	Mean	F	P
			ANOVA statistic	
Tread width (cm)			273.2	0.000
Horse	276	208 (a)[1]		
Hiker	300	82 (b)		
ATV	29	238 (c)		
Max. incision (cm)			49.7	0.000
Horse	276	7.7 (a)		
Hiker	300	2.3 (b)		
ATV	29	9.7 (a)		
Muddiness (%)			15.6	0.000
Horse	276	9.3 (ac)		
Hiker	300	0.0 (b)		
ATV	29	2.6 (c)		

ATV, all-terrain vehicle.
[1] Means with the same letters are not statistically different; Duncan's test (*P*<0.05).

Table 5.3. Big South Fork trail condition assessment data from the problem assessment method.

Indicator	Occurrences (No.)	(No./km)	Lineal distance (m)	(%)	(m/km)
Soil erosion					
Horse	232	4.8	3302	7	69
ATV	30	6.8	1039	24	236
Hiker	53	1.4	565	1	15
Muddiness					
Horse	203	4.2	3762	8	79
ATV	29	6.6	345	11	78
Hiker	15	0.4	234	1	6

ATV, all-terrain vehicle.

Representative monitoring data are presented in Tables 5.2 and 5.3 and Fig. 5.5, to illustrate the types of trail condition data yielded by the two survey methods. The point sampling method provides the most efficient, accurate and precise measures for monitoring trail characteristics that are continuous (e.g. tread width, incision and composition) (Marion and Leung, 2001). For example, Table 5.2 compares tread width, incision and muddiness measures taken at sampling points for horse, hiking and ATV trails. Horse trails were significantly wider (2.5×) and deeper (3.3×) than hiking trails, although ATV trails were in the poorest condition (Table 5.2). Muddiness was not a problem on hiking trails but, on average, 9.3% of horse-trail treads were muddy. An examination of tread compositions for the different trail use types (Fig. 5.5) reveals other substantial differences. Organic litter comprised an average of 61% of tread surfaces for hiking trails, reduced to 32% on ATV and 25% on horse trails. Gravel, applied on high-use horse trails to enhance their resistance, comprised 19% of horse trail tread substrates. Interestingly, hiking and horse trails had 5% vegetation cover but ATV trails had more than four times as much (Fig. 5.5). Field staff attributed this to the growth of vegetation between

wheel ruts and to vegetative recovery occurring between the autumn, when most of the hunting-related ATV use occurs, and early summer, when fieldwork was conducted. These data may also be used for comparing conditions among different trails, or for the same trail or group of trails over time.

A problem assessment method is a preferred method for characterizing uncommon characteristics (e.g. muddiness) and for documenting the frequency, lineal extent and location of specific trail-impact problems (Marion and Leung, 2001). Horse trails were intermediate in the number of occurrences of soil erosion (4.8/km) and lineal distance (69 m/km) but had the greatest lineal extent (3302 m), due to the larger sample size of horse trails (47.9 km) (Table 5.3). ATV trails were the most severely eroded, however, with 23 m/km of soil erosion exceeding 13 cm, 24% of their length. Similarly, horse trails were intermediate in the number of occurrences of excessive muddiness (4.2 per km) and lineal distance (79 m/km), though similar to that of ATV trails (78 m/km) (Table 5.3). Muddiness affected only 1% of hiker trails but was more prevalent on horse trails (8%) and ATV trails (11%). These results are similar to those found in other studies (see Table 5.1 and Fig. 5.1), which have concluded that horse impacts to trails are similar to, but more pronounced than, hiking impacts (Nagy and Scotter, 1974; Weaver and Dale, 1978; Cole, 2002; Newsome *et al.*, 2002).

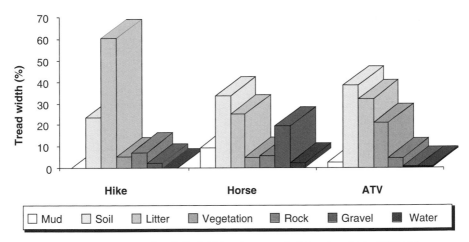

Fig. 5.5. Tread composition for Big South Fork hiking, horse and all-terrain vehicle (ATV) trials.

Quantifying horse-riding damage to soils and vegetation: D'Entrecasteaux National Park, Western Australia

D'Entrecasteaux National Park is situated on the southern coastline of south-west Western Australia. Soil-vegetation systems comprise various age fixed dune communities that contain a mosaic of vegetation types, ranging from heath and low sedgelands to woodlands and forests. At present, casual public horse-riding is prohibited in the park, but commercial horse-riding tours are allowed, according to a permit system that allows for riding on 'off-road' vehicle and designated bridle trails. In addition to this, free-range or off-track riding is allowed in designated areas where low, open vegetation occurs. Until recently there were no data on the nature and degree of damage to soils and vegetation as a result of horse-riding in the park or anywhere else in Western Australia. Experiments carried out by Phillips (2000) and Phillips and Newsome (2002) quantified horse-riding damage on transects under controlled conditions, and provided an important reference point from which to assess the nature of horse-riding impacts where horses ride in un-tracked areas.

The assessed parameters were soil microtopography, penetrometry, species composition and extent of bare ground, vegetation cover and height of vegetation. Changes to all parameters occurred after only very low levels of horse trampling.

Figure 5.6 shows a typical cross-sectional profile of changes in soil surface condition following various intensities of horse trampling. In the most impacted central portion of the trample line, microtopography has decreased by 17.9 mm between 0 and 300 horse passes (Fig. 5.7). These changes demonstrate the capacity for soil disturbance. The same transect line also showed a decrease in soil penetration resistance from baseline condition, reflecting a dominance of soil loosening and particle detachment (Fig. 5.8). However, in most cases horse trampling, will result in soil displacement in association with some degree of soil compaction (see Fig. 5.1). This combined feature of horse damage to soils is evident in the data set provided by Phillips and Newsome (2002), where transect line DE1 shows a decrease in soil penetration resistance, contrasting with transect line DE3, which shows a progressive increase in soil compaction with increasing intensities of horse passes.

The changes in soil surface condition mentioned before are also reflected in a progressive increase in bare ground. Data collected from transect line DE2 show a baseline condition of 5.4% bare ground, increasing to 8.9% following 20 horse passes. This value increased to 25.6% after 300 passes. Changes in the relative frequency of various plant species are also evident, with the low-growing (<60 cm) shrub *Loxocarya cinerea* decreasing from 65.9% to 56.7%, and *Pimelea rosea* decreasing from

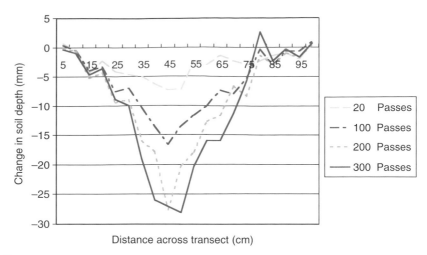

Fig. 5.6. The change in soil depth from the baseline microtopography across 5–100 cm of the cross-sectional profile of the treatment transects, after various intensities of horse trampling. Transect DE2, D'Entrecasteaux National Park, Western Australia. (From Phillips, 2000.)

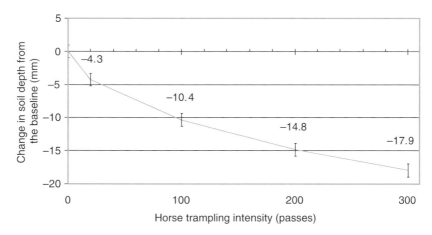

Fig. 5.7. The change in the soil depth from the baseline microtopography averaged across the central 30–75 cm of the cross-sectional profile of the treatment transects, after various intensities of horse trampling. Transect DE2, D'Entrecasteaux National Park, Western Australia. (From Phillips, 2000.)

17.8% to 9%, following 300 horse passes (Fig. 5.9). The data clearly demonstrate the potential for change in species composition.

Figure 5.10 shows the corresponding loss in overlapping vegetation cover on transect DE2. Cover declined from 122% to 112% following 20 horse passes and was reduced to 56% following 300 passes (Fig. 5.11). Structural changes to vegetation are depicted in Fig. 5.12. The largest decrease in vegetation height, along the most impacted central portion of the

trample line, occurred between 0 and 100 horse passes (Fig. 5.13). In comparing these data it is noteworthy that a tenfold increase in horse use decreased cover by about 50%, whereas a fivefold increase reduced vegetation height by about 50% (Figs 5.11 and 5.13), demonstrating that structure is rapidly altered and is a sensitive indicator of horse-riding damage to vegetation (Fig. 5.14).

The changes and damage to soils and vegetation described here are especially important

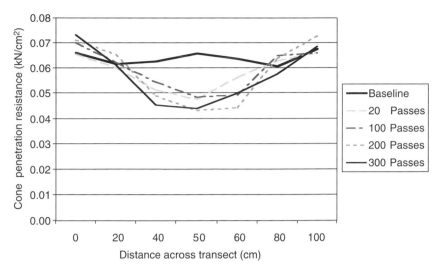

Fig. 5.8. Cone penetration resistance at a soil depth of 5 cm, measured across 5–100 cm of the cross-sectional profile of the treatment transects, after various intensities of horse trampling. Transect DE2, D'Entrecasteaux National Park, Western Australia. (From Phillips, 2000.)

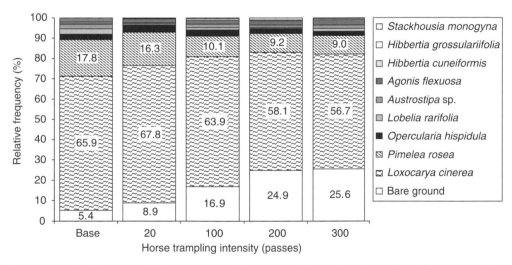

Fig. 5.9. Relative frequency of plant species and bare ground after various intensities of horse trampling. Transect DE2, D'Entrecasteaux National Park, Western Australia. (From Phillips, 2000.)

in sensitive environments that exhibit slow recovery rates and low resilience, as in the case of arctic–alpine areas, many arid environments and in the nutrient-poor ecosystems of much of Australia. Moreover, soil movement both on and off designated tracks is a critical issue in those ecosystems that are vulnerable to plant disease and important as biodiversity hotspots, as in the case of Western Australia.

Managing the Environmental Impacts of Horse-riding in Natural Areas

North American perspectives 1: the case of a confinement strategy for reducing impacts at campsites

Cole (2002) provides an overview of the five primary strategies available for managing

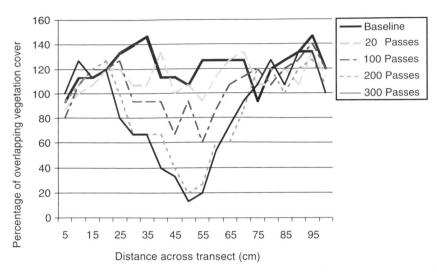

Fig. 5.10. Percentage of overlapping vegetation cover across 5–100 cm of the cross-sectional profile of the treatment transects, after various intensities of horse trampling. Transect DE2, D'Entrecasteaux National Park, Western Australia. (From Phillips, 2000.)

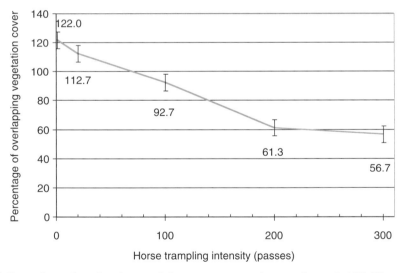

Fig. 5.11. Percentage of overlapping vegetation cover averaged across the central 30–75 cm of the cross-sectional profile of the treatment transects, after various intensities of horse trampling. Transect DE2, D'Entrecasteaux National Park, Western Australia. (From Phillips, 2000.)

packstock impacts in wilderness areas and national parks in North America. Amount of use can be reduced, for example by prohibiting stock use or by closing overgrazed meadows. Behaviour can be changed, either through restrictions or low-impact education. Critical behaviours include group size, stock-confinement techniques, carrying feed, and steps to insure against the introduction of exotic species. The timing of use can be managed. It is often critical for horses to stay off trails and out of meadows shortly after snowmelt, when soils are water-saturated. Trail impacts, particularly, can be mitigated by hardening trails, such as

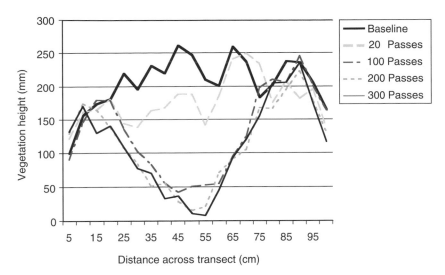

Fig. 5.12. Vegetation height across 5–100 cm of the cross-sectional profile of the treatment transects, after various intensities of horse trampling. Transect DE2, D'Entrecasteaux National Park, Western Australia. (From Phillips, 2000.)

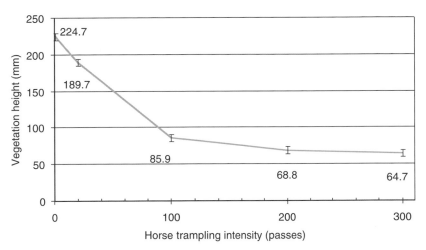

Fig. 5.13. Vegetation height averaged across the central 30–75 cm of the cross-sectional profile of the treatment transects, after various intensities of horse trampling. Transect DE2, D'Entrecasteaux National Park, Western Australia. (From Phillips, 2000.)

reinforcing the trail with log cribbing. Finally, impacts can be confined by only allowing stock use on certain trails and in certain locations.

Management generally involves balancing demand for access with the desire to avoid impairment of the natural environment sought out by ecotourists. Particularly where tourist activities have a high potential to cause impact, as is the case with horse-riding, confinement of activities is a highly effective way to minimize impacts without curtailing use. This management strategy has also been referred to as use concentration and use containment (Cole, 1981; Leung and Marion, 1999a; Marion and Farrell, 2002). A good example of the efficacy of this strategy is provided in the following case study of Seven Lakes basin in the Selway-Bitterroot Wilderness, USA, a destination area

Fig. 5.14. Experimental transect (DE1) in D'Entrecasteaux National Park, Western Australia, showing damage to vegetation following 200 horse passes. (From Phillips, 2000.)

nate most of the stock-holding areas and reduce the number of intensively impacted campsites, while leaving at least one campsite open for stock use at each of the major lakes.

These objectives were to be met by implementing the following management actions: (i) the designation of three day-use stock containment areas and six overnight stock containment areas, where stock were to be tethered between designated trees with a high line, rope or electric corral; (ii) the prohibition of stock containment on other campsites or other parts of designated campsites; and (iii) the prohibition of all camping on four campsites. Tying stock directly to trees or in places where tree roots can be damaged was prohibited. Stock numbers were limited to a maximum of ten animals per group. Regulations on where to camp and contain stock were communicated to the public on a brochure, signs on bulletin boards at the trailhead and at the entry point to the lake basin on all trails, in local newspapers and by frequent visits of wilderness rangers to the area. Compliance was enforced through special orders and heavy ranger presence.

Some trails in the basin were reconstructed; about 1 km of trail was re-routed, and another 1 km of trail was closed and rehabilitated. Two bridges were built. Forty-seven former stock-holding areas were closed to stock containment. These areas were generally adjacent to clumps of trees with roots and mineral soil exposed by decades of tying horses to trees. These 47 areas were on 12 campsites that were closed to stock use, six campsites that remained open to stock use and one former campsite where day-use containment only of stock was allowed. Designated high-line trees were signed at each of the six open stock campsites with a designated stock-holding area and the three day-use stock-holding areas. These campsites, where stock use was still allowed, were signed, as were four campsites that were closed to all use. Most closed areas were intensively restored. Seeds were collected, and about 2000 seedlings of three species were propagated in nurseries and packed up to the basin. Soils were scarified, organic matter was added to soils, and large rocks were used as 'icebergs' (placed to protrude from the ground, making the site undesirable for camping). Stumps were flush-cut and tree wells were filled with soil.

in which there were excessive numbers of campsites, many of which were severely degraded by stock use (horses and mules). More detail on this case example can be found in Spildie *et al.* (2000).

The Seven Lakes basin (an area of about 500 ha) contains 11 lakes and is located at an elevation of 1860–2000 m. It can be accessed within 1 day but requires a climb of about 1000 m in the last 10 km of the 19 km trail. Use levels in the basin are moderate. Records show that there are virtually never more than four other groups in the basin at one time. Monitoring showed that previous recreation use, particularly by groups with packstock, had left 26 substantially impacted campsites in the area. Associated with these campsites were 47 distinct stock-holding areas that had been damaged by tying horses and mules to trees, often overnight. Management objectives were to reduce campsite density by about 50%, elimi-

Pitch and charcoal were applied to trees to minimize evidence of tree scarring. Propagated seedlings, locally collected seed and local transplants were used to revegetate areas. Finally, some areas were covered with a mulching material. Campsite impact conditions were monitored over the period.

This work was largely accomplished, over a 5-year period, by two people who shared one seasonal wilderness ranger position. They were assisted by volunteer crews who provided a total of almost 4000 person hours of volunteer labour over the 5 years.

In its first 5 years, the Seven Lakes basin restoration programme was highly successful in reducing impacts associated with camping. Campsite densities decreased slightly. The magnitude of impact decreased on virtually all campsites and decreased greatly on many sites. In just 5 years, the total area of disturbance in the Seven Lakes basin decreased by 37%, from 3518 m² to 2205 m². Total bare area (places devoid of vegetation) decreased by 43%, from 1222 m² to 699 m². Disturbed area and bare area declined by at least 10% on 16 of the 26 campsites. Tree scarring declined, although primarily from masking scars with pitch and charcoal. Vegetation cover has increased and mineral soil exposure has decreased. Only root exposure has worsened. Moreover, if the management programme is continued, the greatest positive changes are still to come. Disturbed area and bare area are likely to decline in a few decades to just 36% and 24%, respectively, of what they were in 1993.

Most of these positive changes came from confining where camping could occur, particularly by groups with packstock. Improving conditions on former stock-holding areas have more than compensated for the increased impact on newly designated stock-holding areas. The closure of some campsites to all use and efforts to reduce the size of open campsites, through both closure and restoration of portions of large sites, have also been highly effective. Reductions in maximum group size have undoubtedly contributed to success. For these benefits to continue or increase in the future, the programmes need to remain in effect.

These management actions clearly reduce the original freedom that horse-riders had to go and to camp wherever they wanted. However, since there are no limits on amount of use, no lakes where camping is not allowed, and no groups excluded from visiting the basin, experiential costs seem minor. Fiscal costs of this programme are another matter. The 5-year costs exceeded US$135,000, although the Forest Service was able to reduce out-of-pocket costs by more than 50% by using volunteer groups extensively.

In conclusion, the Seven Lakes basin management programme illustrates that the confinement strategy can be highly effective, particularly with types of use that have high impact potential, such as stock groups. It also illustrates the need to prevent problems in the first place, rather than attempt to correct them after they have already occurred, particularly with the types of use that can cause substantial disturbance. It is important to anticipate where impact is likely to occur and to take effective, preventive actions, even if they need to be restrictive. Finally, in addition to being costly, restoring recreation impact will be a slow and never-ending process. At Seven Lakes, the management programme can now shift into a maintenance mode. However, in the maintenance mode, restrictions must be kept in force, and frequent ranger presence is still needed to obtain reasonable compliance. Given the minimal budgets for on-the-ground management, even the maintenance mode will stretch available resources.

North American perspectives 2: the horse-trail management experience at Big South Fork

The trail assessment and approaches to monitoring discussed earlier set the scene for the following comments relating to issues surrounding horse-trail management at Big South Fork. Historically, the application of gravel to replace or cap wet or eroding tread soils has been the primary management response at Big South Fork. Initial work along riparian trails that had become muddy quagmires employed full-size bulldozers and dump trucks to replace wet soils with up to 30 cm of gravel (up to 3 cm in diameter). Horseback riders complained about the use of these 'road-construction' techniques, particularly the excessive trail width and clearing of vegetation. The use of gravel also drew complaints, though after several years the gravel packed down and became less conspicuous and artificial in appearance. Vegetation growth has narrowed the treads, which have remained in excellent condition despite heavy horse traffic. Seasonal mowing, vegetation trimming and occasional grading are the only maintenance actions required on gravelled horse trails in flatter terrain.

The park maintenance division recently purchased narrower-gauge equipment for trail construction and maintenance work. Current horse-trail standards for high-use trails call for hard surfaced (gravel) treads 1.8–2.4 m wide, with water-bars constructed of a soil and gravel mixture. Vegetation clearing is 4.5 m wide by 3 m high. Standards for intermediate-use trails call for application of gravel only as needed for muddy or eroding sections. Tread width is 1.8–2.4 m wide, with earth water-bars and vegetation clearing as above.

The application of gravel on trails in sloping terrain has been less successful. Horses' hooves and water runoff during heavy rainstorms move gravel downslope, particularly on grades exceeding 8%. Efforts to apply larger gravel (4–7 cm) capped with finer gravel (up to 3 cm) have met with limited success. Horses' hooves and water move the finer material downslope, exposing the larger gravel. The size and angular edges of the large gravel are uncomfortable to horses. Grading work to move gravel back upslope or to reshape treads also mixed the gravels, bringing some of the larger material to the surface. Furthermore, the use of heavy equipment for such grading restricts the type of tread drainage features to tread outsloping, drainage dips and grade dips (reversed grades). Frequent grading has been required to maintain proper outsloping and drainage dips. Shorter sections of horse trails that descend steeply through gaps in the cliff line have required wooden structures filled with rock and gravel. These locations are often difficult to access and require shifting the gravel from large trucks, to smaller trucks, to motorized tracked wheelbarrows.

The numerous stream crossings throughout Big South Fork have been a particular management challenge. Wooden bridges have been constructed for stream crossings on the heaviest-use horse trails. Trail erosion into streams is a substantial and continuing problem within the park, which has inadequate funding to bridge every stream crossing. Most horse-trail bridges have planking along the edges to contain a bed of soil that covers the bridge deck. This is done to allow use by horses that shy away from travel across wood planking. Unfortunately water often drains to the bridges, contributing to tread muddiness and overflowing directly into streams during storms (Fig. 5.15).

In preparing the Road and Trail Management Plan, park staff have been re-evaluating all park roads and trails for their suitability to sustain horse use. Careful attention to the relative resource resistance of alternative routes, including trail grade, alignments and substrates, will avoid the inclusion of trails that would require substantial reconstruction or ongoing maintenance. Management emphasis will continue to rely primarily on tread-hardening techniques. Experimentation with geotextiles is just beginning, and managers expect their use will resolve problems in some of the worst locations, while reducing the need for large amounts of gravel in less accessible settings.

An Australian perspective

Landsberg *et al.* (2001) provide a useful overview of the issues surrounding the management of horse-riding in Australia. They note that where horses are allowed to stray off trails, or where horse-riding takes place on poorly maintained or constructed trails, or in steep and/or waterlogging prone environments, a high impact potential exists. The first part of any management system should therefore consider the risk potential for horse-riding damage. Conservation reserves and highly valued natural areas with at-risk environmental characteristics, such as steep slopes, high soil erosivity, poorly drained areas and those infected with readily transportable fungal pathogens, should not be available for horse-riding activities. In some areas, however, where horse-riding is already established because of tradition or precedent, prohibiting horse-riding may be dif-

Fig. 5.15. Muddiness on a Big South Fork horse-trail bridge.

ficult to achieve. In relation to this, Landsberg *et al.* (2001) also raise the issue of equity in providing outdoor recreational opportunities. Indeed, it is worth noting that hiking and mountain-biking also pose a risk of environmental damage in susceptible environments, and raise the question that if horse-riding is prohibited, why not also prohibit other recreational activities. Restricting horse-riding, however, can be justified on the basis that the activity causes the greatest amount of impact.

Landsberg *et al.* (2001) have developed ten principles (Table 5.4) to guide the management of public horse-riding in a peri-urban nature reserve in eastern Australia. These principles provide a useful basis from which to develop management strategies elsewhere in Australia.

Newsome *et al.* (2002) explored various options for managing horse-riding in more remote locations, such as D'Entrecasteaux National Park in Western Australia. One important issue to arise from their work was the assertion that if a management strategy was in place, management capacity was often insufficient to police, enforce and monitor the situation. Moreover, interpretive material, public seminars, education and voluntary codes of conduct are ostensibly a good idea, but it only takes a small percentage of users to ignore them and significant impacts can occur.

Newsome *et al.* (2002) explored three management options in relation to the situation in D'Entrecasteaux National Park in Western Australia. Prohibiting use, although the most effective in eliminating impacts, was seen to be problematic, because national park policy provides for a spectrum of recreational opportunities and raised questions of equity and honouring traditional usage of the area. Despite this, Newsome *et al.* (2002) assert that national parks should not be opened up to any new horse-riding operations. They also viewed unrestricted open access in conservation reserves as unacceptable, due to the dispersed and possibly cumulative nature of impacts, especially where plant disease is present in vulnerable plant communities.

One of the most effective means of managing horse-riding in conservation areas would be to prohibit random, unsupervised public access and authorize access via licensed tour operators. Licensing and the allocation of permits provides incentives for the operator to reduce impacts, via controlling the numbers of users, adhering to guidelines and keeping horses to designated bridle trails. This, in conjunction with applying the principles developed by Landsberg *et al.* (2001), provides for a management framework in which horse-riding can occur alongside other recreational activities in conserved environments (Table 5.4).

Table 5.4. Principles to guide management of public horse-riding in a peri-urban nature reserve in Australia (according to Landsberg et al., 2001).

1. Provide for recreational horse-riding only
2. No dogs allowed
3. Confine horse-riding to specific trails
4. Locate trails near perimeter of reserves and/or in modified zones
5. Construct and maintain trails to a standard (drained and hardened/stable surface of suitable width)
6. Exclude horse-riding from ecologically sensitive areas
7. Rationalize existing trail networks where horse-riding is currently allowed with a view to closing trails and developing alternative routes and/or construct trails to acceptable standard
8. Develop a code of conduct that fosters rider compliance to management system in place
9. Develop monitoring systems to measure rider compliance and impacts of horse-riding
10. Modify management programme if unacceptable impacts are detected

Conclusion

Recreational horse riding is a legitimate and important recreational activity. However, it is well established that the activity carries a high impact potential. The nature, extent and degree of impact are related to the intensity of usage. High-use situations, as in some parts of the USA, can result in high levels of campsite and trail degradation. Furthermore, differing environmental resilience may dictate that some parts of the world are more susceptible to ecological degradation that others. This is certainly the case where horse-riding occurs in fragile Australian ecosystems. In response to the need to predict and manage impacts, many recreation ecologists and natural resource managers are developing methods for assessing and monitoring horse-riding damage and activities. However, there is still scope for the development of a database on the relative sensitivity of different environments around the world to horse-riding damage.

Given the plethora of environmental impacts associated with horse-riding, natural-area managers need to assess existing activities and operations, and balance the activity with other recreational uses and wider conservation objectives. Because of the high impact potential, it needs to be emphasized to horse-riders that, for continued access, management is critical. Only with 'best practice' management should horse-riding be allowed in national parks and similar areas. With sustained horse traffic, management may have to include some or all aspects of the following: trail location and design; trail construction (drainage and erosion control); trail hardening, such as the use of gravel, geotextiles or geoblock; trail maintenance; visitor regulation (confinement, amount of use, timing of use); education (user behaviour, codes of conduct); policing and enforcement.

Both land managers and users must take this need seriously. In addition, a universally valid model for natural area planning, such as the Limits of Acceptable Change Planning Framework, needs to be applied in multi-use recreation areas, to help determine what sorts of impacts are acceptable and to guide monitoring of change and application of management actions. Horse-riding is likely to be deemed inappropriate where unacceptable impacts are occurring and where trails and sites need rehabilitation. Where significant conservation and biodiversity values are threatened, it might be necessary to prohibit horse-riding entirely.

Acknowledgements

We thank Nate Olive and Sarah Janes for their dedicated field survey work at Big South Fork National River, and for their perseverance despite mud, ticks and poorly signed trails. We would also like to acknowledge the contributions that Nick Phillips and Rodney Annear made with field work in D'Entrecasteaux National Park. Thanks also go to John Gillard and to all staff members of the Pemberton District Office of the Western Australian Department of Conservation and Land Management. We also thank A. Rossow for cartographic work. Special thanks go to Kevin Henderson and Joe Melville for supplying accommodation and the use of horses.

References

Cole, D.N. (1981) Managing ecological impacts at wilderness campsites: an evaluation of techniques. *Journal of Forestry* 79, 86–89.

Cole, D.N. (1983) *Campsite Conditions in the Bob Marshall Wilderness, Montana*. Research Paper INT-312. US Department of Agriculture, Intermountain Research Station, Ogden, Utah.

Cole, D.N. (2002) Ecological impacts of wilderness recreation and their management. In: Hendee, J.C. and Dawson, C.P. (eds) *Wilderness Management: Stewardship and Protection of Resources and Values*, 3rd edn. Fulcrum Publishing, Golden, Colorado, pp. 413–460.

Cole, D.N. and Spildie, D.R. (1998) Hiker, horse and llama trampling effects on native vegetation in Montana, USA. *Environmental Management* 53, 61–71.

Cole, D.N., van Wagtendonk, J., McClaran, M., Moore, P. and McDougald, N. (2004) Response of mountain meadows to grazing by recreational pack stock. *Journal of Range Management* (in press).

Dale, D. and Weaver, T. (1974) Trampling effects on vegetation of the trail corridors of north Rocky Mountain Forest. *Journal of Applied Ecology* 11, 767–772.

Deluca, T.M., Patterson, W.A., Freimund, W.A. and Cole, D.N. (1998) Influences of llamas, horses and hikers on soil erosion from established recreation trails in Western Montana, USA. *Environmental Management* 22(2), 255–262.

Farrell, T.A. and Marion, J.L. (2002) Trail impacts and trail impact management related to ecotourism visitation at Torres del Paine National Park, Chile. Leisure/Loisir: *Journal of the Canadian Association for Leisure Studies* 26(1/2), 31–59.

Landsberg, J., Logan, B. and Shorthouse, D. (2001) Horse riding in urban conservation areas: reviewing scientific evidence to guide management. *Ecological Management and Restoration* 2, 36–46.

Leopold, A. (1921) The wilderness and its place in recreational policy. *Journal of Forestry* 19, 718–721.

Leung, Y.-F. and Marion, J.L. (1999a) Spatial strategies for managing visitor impacts in national parks. *Journal of Park and Recreation Administration* 17, 20–38.

Leung, Y.-F. and Marion, J.L. (1999b) The influence of sampling interval on the accuracy of trail impact assessment. *Landscape and Urban Planning* 43(4), 167–179.

Leung, Y.-F. and Marion, J.L. (1999c) Assessing trail conditions in protected areas: Application of a problem assessment method in Great Smoky

Mountains National Park, U.S.A. *Environmental Conservation* 26(4), 270–279.

Liddle, M. (1997) *Recreation Ecology: the Ecological Impact of Outdoor Recreation and Ecotourism*. Chapman & Hall, London, UK.

Marion, J.L. and Farrell, T.A. (2002) Management practices that concentrate visitor activities: camping impact management at Isle Royale National Park, USA. *Journal of Environmental Management* 66, 201–212.

Marion, J.L. and Leung, Y.-F. (2001) Trail resource impacts and an examination of alternative assessment techniques. *Journal of Park and Recreation Administration* 19(1), 17–37.

McClaran, M.P. and Cole, D.N. (1993) *Packstock in Wilderness: Use, Impacts, Monitoring, and Management*. General Technical Report INT-301. US Department of Agriculture, Intermountain Research Station, Ogden, Utah.

Moore, P.E., Cole, D.N., van Wagtendonk, J.W., McClaran, M.P. and McDougald, N. (2000) Meadow response to pack stock grazing in the Yosemite Wilderness: integrating research and management. In: Cole, D.N., McCool, S.F., Borrie, W.T. and O'Loughlin, J. (eds) *Wilderness Science in a Time of Change*. Vol. 5: *Wilderness Ecosystems, Threats, and Management*. Proceedings RMRS-P-15-Vol-5. USDA Forest Service, Rocky Mountain Research Station, Ogden, Utah, pp. 199–208.

Nagy, J.A. and Scotter, G.W. (1974) *A Qualitative Assessment of the Effects of Human and Horse Trampling on Natural Areas, Waterton Lakes National Park*. Canadian Wildlife Service, Edmonton, Alberta, Canada.

Newsome, D. (2003) The role of an accidentally introduced fungus in degrading the health of the Stirling Range National Park ecosystem in South Western Australia: status and prognosis. In: Rapport, D.J., Lasley, W.L., Rolston, D.E., Nielsen, N.O., Qualset, C.O. and Damania, A.B. (eds). *Managing for Healthy Ecosystems*. Lewis Publishers, Boca Raton, Florida.

Newsome, D., Phillips, N., Milewskii, A. and Annear, R. (2002) Effects of horse riding on national parks and other natural ecosystems in Australia: implications for management. *Journal of Ecotourism* 1(1), 52–74.

Phillips, N. (2000) A field experiment to quantify the environmental impacts of horse riding in D'Entrecasteaux National Park, Western Australia. Unpublished Honours thesis, School of Environmental Science, Murdoch University, Perth, Western Australia.

Phillips, N. and Newsome, D. (2002) Understanding the impacts of recreation in Australian protected areas: quantifying damage caused by horse riding in D'Entrecasteaux National Park, Western Australia. *Pacific Conservation Biology* 7, 256–273.

Spildie, D.R., Cole, D.N. and Walker, S.C. (2000) Effectiveness of a confinement strategy in reducing pack stock impacts at campsites in the Selway-Bitterroot Wilderness, Idaho. In: *Wilderness Science in a Time of Change.* Vol. 5. *Wilderness Ecosystems, Threats, and Management* Proceedings RMRS-P-15-Vol-5. USDA Forest Service, Rocky Mountain Research Station, Ogden, Utah, pp. 199–208.

Sumner, E.L. (1942) The biology of wilderness protection. *Sierra Club Bulletin* 27(4), 14–22.

UK CEED (2000) *A Review of the Effects of Recreational Interactions within UK European Marine Sites.* UK Marine SACs Project. Countryside Council for Wales, Cambridge, UK.

Weaver, T. and Dale, D. (1978) Trampling effects of hikers, motorcycles and horses in meadows and forests. *Journal of Applied Ecology* 15, 451–457.

Whinam, J. and Chilcott, N. (1999) Impacts of trampling on alpine environments in central Tasmania. *Journal of Environmental Management* 57, 205–220.

Whinam, J. and Comfort, M. (1996) The impact of commercial horse riding on sub-alpine environments at Cradle Mountain, Tasmania, Australia. *Journal of Environmental Management* 47, 61–70.

Widner, C. and Marion, J. (1993) *Horse Impacts: Research Findings and their Implications.* Master Network, a publication of the National Outdoor Leadership School, Lander, Wyoming, Part 1 – 1993, No. 5, pp. 5–14; Part 2 – 1994, No. 6, p. 56.

Wilson, J.P. and Seney, J.P. (1994) Erosional impacts of hikers, horses, motorcycles and off-road bicycles on mountain trails in Montana. *Mountain Research and Development* 14, 77–88.

6

Environmental Impacts of Motorized Off-highway Vehicles

Ralf Buckley

International Centre for Ecotourism Research, Griffith University, Gold Coast, Queensland, Australia

Introduction

Motorized transport is a component of many tourism products, including tours that are advertised as ecotours, and tours that operate in protected areas. Four-wheel-drive (4WD) and other off-highway vehicles (OHVs) many be used in ecotours for a number of reasons:

- to transport inexperienced clients safely amidst potentially dangerous wildlife, e.g. in African game safaris;
- to transport and control clients amongst wildlife more easily disturbed by pedestrians than by vehicles;
- to transport equipment for non-motorized activities, e.g. whitewater rafts, sea kayaks, mountain bikes;
- to transport camping equipment and food for tour clients travelling by non-motorized means;
- as the primary means of travel in terrain types where travel on foot is too slow or arduous for the distances involved; e.g. level arid landscapes with little surface water.

Realistically, therefore, the impacts of ecotourism include the impacts of OHVs, but only where OHVs are legally permitted, where they are needed as part of an ecotour product, and where they are driven with due regard to mini-mize environmental impacts. There are also many recreational users of OHVs, both private and commercial, who drive them with no concern for environmental impacts and in places of high conservation value. Such use is clearly not ecotourism.

This review therefore considers the impacts on the natural environment of commonly used OHVs including 4WD vehicles, smaller all-terrain vehicles (ATVs), larger tundra buggies, trailbikes and snowmobiles. Note that the terms OHV and ORV (off-road vehicle) are sometimes used interchangeably, but strictly speaking the former term includes vehicles used on dirt roads and tracks which are recognized routes but not legal highways. This review does not, except incidentally, refer to tracked, military, construction or large-scale industrial vehicles. Nor does it cover non-motorized transport such as mountain bikes, riding animals or packstock. It does not focus on tours or recreational groups which set out deliberately to use OHVs in an environmentally damaging manner, such as enduro racing or competitive mudbogging, though it does mention the types of ecological damage that can result from such use. It does not consider social impacts such as conflicts with non-motorized users (McCool, 1981; Wilkinson, 1999), though from a land management perspective these may be as important as environmental impacts. In addition, any impact on soil or vegetation which is recorded for hiking boots (Cole, Chapter 4, this volume) can generally also be produced by vehicle tyres.

Types, intensity and ecological significance of impacts differ considerably between ecosystems (Liddle, 1997; Yorks et al., 1997; Buckley, 2001a, 2003; Newsome et al., 2002). Impacts also depend considerably on driving practices. Most off-highway travel by motorized ecotours is on established dirt roads and tracks in parks, forests and farms, with relatively little being completely off-track. For example, safari vehicles in the private game reserves of Africa commonly stay on tracks except where icon species such as lion, leopard or rhino are sighted, and off-track travel is needed for a closer approach. The environmental impacts of motorized ecotours hence include those of track formation and traffic, as well as those of off-track use. There is quite an extensive literature on the impacts of roads on wildlife, especially through noise disturbance and barrier effects, which is also relevant to 4WD tracks. Likewise, there is an extensive literature on the impacts of logging roads on soil erosion and stream sedimentation, some of which is relevant to other recreational 4WD tracks.

The ecological impacts of vehicles driving off-road have been recognized for over 70 years. Meinecke (1928) recorded damage to the roots of redwood trees by vehicles driving over them, and recommended that vehicles be kept away. More detailed study commenced in the late 1950s and the 1960s (Green and Knight, 1959; Westhoff, 1967). During the 1970s and 1980s there was more intensive research on OHV impacts in particular ecosystems, and a number of reviews and bibliographies (e.g. California Parks and Recreation, 1975; Webb and Wilshire, 1983; Albrecht and Knopf, 1985; Leatherman and Steiner, 1987). The majority of this research was in North American ecosystems, with a focus on sandy coasts and the arid south-west. Concern over the impacts of snowmobiles and other over-snow vehicles (OSVs) prompted research, especially in northern USA (Bloomfield, 1969; Lazan, 1969; Bissill, 1970; Dorrance et al., 1975; Bury, 1978; Richens and Lavigne, 1978; McCool, 1978, 1981; Eckstein et al., 1979); and, more recently, concern over the impacts of swamp buggies and other ATVs has prompted

research in south-eastern USA (Duevers, 2002). There have been recent reviews by Liddle (1997) and James (2000, pp. 18–28).

Environmental impacts of OHVs have been studied much more intensively in some areas and environments than others. Examples include:

- the arid landscapes of south-western USA (Vollmer et al., 1976; Eckert et al., 1979; Foreman, 1979; Iverson et al., 1981; Kay et al., 1981; Webb, 1982, 1983; Hinkley et al., 1983; Lathrop, 1983; Webb and Wilshire, 1983; Belnap, 1995; Brainard, 1998; Lovich and Bainbridge, 1999; Kutiel et al., 2000; Milchunas et al., 2000);
- coastal beaches, especially in north-eastern USA (Steiner and Leatherman, 1981; Wolcott and Wolcott, 1984; Anders and Leatherman, 1987; Mackay, 1997) but also in Australia (Priskin, Chapter 22, this volume);
- coastal dunes in various parts of the USA (Brodhead and Godfrey, 1977; Wilshire et al., 1978; Hosier and Eaton, 1980; Godfrey et al., 1980; Godfrey and Godfrey, 1981; Luckenbach and Bury, 1983) and also in southern and south-western Australia (Gilbertson, 1983; Priskin, 2003) and Israel (Kutiel et al., 2000);
- arctic tundra (Bellamy et al., 1971; Rickard and Slaughter, 1973; Rickard and Brown 1974; Slaughter et al., 1990; Forbes, 1992) and cool temperate bogs and moors (Bayfield, 1986; Ross, 1992);
- grasslands in east Africa (Onyeanusi, 1986) and north-western Australia (Hercock, 1998, 1999);
- subtropical south-eastern USA (Duevers, 2002).

There are thus a number of major ecosystems worldwide where OHVs are used extensively in tourism and recreation, but where their impacts remain largely unstudied. Examples include:

- grasslands of south-eastern South America;
- savanna grasslands of sub-Saharan Africa and northern Australia;
- eucalyptus woodlands of south-western and south-eastern Australia;

- mixed conifer woodlands of south-western Canada and north-western USA;
- rainforests of south-eastern Asia, north-eastern Australia, central West Africa and Central America.

Even in those areas and ecosystems which have been studied most intensively, quantitative knowledge of impacts remains scanty. As with many impacts from tourism and recreation, the more obvious direct impacts are identified but rarely quantified, and the less obvious indirect impacts may remain unknown (Buckley, 2001a, 2003).

The ecological impacts of OHVs may be considered from various perspectives:

- type of ecosystem, e.g. coastal, arid, montane, arctic;
- ecosystem component affected, e.g. air, water, soil, plants, animals;
- type of OHV, e.g. 4WD, buggy, ATV, snowmobile;
- type of activity or tour, e.g. wildlife safari, adventure activity;
- impact mechanism, e.g. tyres, noise, exhaust, indirect.

Impact mechanisms include, for example:

- the physical action of tyres on soils, vegetation and fauna;
- secondary physical effects, such as increased slopewash and stream sedimentation;
- collisions, especially with animals;
- air pollution from exhaust;
- water pollution from fuel spills, oil, etc.;
- noise and associated effects on wildlife;
- transport of progagules, notably weed seeds and pathogens;
- impacts of tracks, e.g. on waterflow and animal movements;
- impacts of humans travelling in OHVs to areas they would not otherwise visit: e.g., increased fires, litter, hunting, etc.

Soils

The action of vehicle tyres on soil has been analysed extensively (Freitag, 1971; Liddle, 1997).

Impacts depend on topography and slope, soil type and moisture content, how the vehicle is driven, and on the vehicle's weight and number of passes.

Pressures applied to the soil surface by 4WD vehicles and trailbikes travelling at constant speed on level ground range from 1000 to 2300 gm/cm^2, about 5–15 times the pressure applied by a hiking boot (e.g. Eckert *et al.*, 1979; Slaughter *et al.*, 1990; Liddle, 1997). Pressures may be up to ten times greater when OHVs are braking, accelerating or skidding (Liddle, 1997). The immediate effects are to break up soil crusts, erode or displace upper soil layers to form tracks or wheel ruts, and compress and compact deeper soil layers (Wilshire and Nakata, 1976; Liddle, 1997). Damage to soil crusts, and to surface lags of pebbles or shells, has been described in a range of environments (Davidson and Fox, 1974; Godfrey *et al.*, 1980; Hosier and Eaton, 1980; Adams *et al.*, 1982; Brown and Schoknecht, 2001). In tundra areas, ruts form by a different mechanism, as the removal of insulating vegetation leads to melting of the permafrost, to 150 cm depth or more (Rickard and Slaughter, 1973; Rickard and Brown, 1974; Walker and Walker, 1991). Recovery of the soil surface from the passage of a single OHV may take only days or hours on active sand dunes, but has been estimated at up to 680 years or more for crusted desert soils (Liddle, 1997; Brainard, 1998).

The relation between the number of passes, weight of vehicle, and degree of erosion and compaction seems to differ considerably between soil types. Broadly, erosion effects seem to be more marked for a small number of passes, and compaction effects for a large number of repeated passes, on the same track.

Erosive effects by OHVs include wind and water erosion of disturbed soil, and mechanical displacement by vehicle tyres. Wind erosion (Brodhead and Godfrey, 1977; Godfrey and Godfrey, 1981; Wilshire, 1989; Stebbins, 1990) can also disperse pesticides in agricultural soils (Leys *et al.*, 1998) or asbestos from mineral soils (Popendorf and Wenk, 1983). Mechanical displacement of soil has been recorded on a variety of soil types (Anders and Leatherman, 1987), with erosion rates recorded at 150,000 cm^3/m^2/year after 100 4WD passes on a coastal dune (Godfrey, 1975), and 250,000 cm³/m²/ year on an arid sand dune (Eckert et al., 1979). Erosion rates in Alaska were recorded at 450,000 cm³/m²/year by Rickard and Slaughter (1973), but not only by mechanical displacement. Erosion is commonly greater on steep slopes, wet areas, and fine-grained soils (Bellamy et al., 1971; Anders and Leatherman, 1987; Wilson and Seney, 1994). Trailbikes climbing steep slopes produced 15 times as much erosion as hikers (Weaver and Dale, 1978).

The effects of OHV tyres can increase surface runoff and slopewash, promote waterborne debris flows, and, in some cases, lead to burial of plants (Webb et al., 1978; Eckert et al., 1979; Iverson et al., 1981; Gilbertson, 1983; Nakata, 1983; Webb, 1983; Lovich and Bainbridge, 1999). Eckert et al. (1979), for example, found that 50 passes by a trailbike doubled slopewash, and 20 passes by a truck increased it five times. Off-road tracks and forest roads can lead to water erosion further upslope than in undisturbed areas (Montgomery, 1994). Forested areas traversed by logging tracks, often used by recreational OHVs, suffer significantly more erosion than untracked areas (Swanson and Dyrness, 1975; Rice and Lewis, 1991; Grayson et al., 1993; Forman et al., 1997; Forman and Mellinger, 1998; Forman and Alexander, 1998, p. 223). Forested areas with a high density of tracks are more prone to flooding (Forman and Alexander, 1998 p. 218). Sediment from slopewash degrades forest streams, in North America (Bilby et al., 1989) and Australia (Brown, 1994).

Compaction effects include increased bulk density and penetration resistance, and decreased porosity, infiltrability and hydraulic conductivity (Liddle, 1997). Loamy sands and coarse gravels are particularly susceptible to compaction, and wet soils commonly more susceptible than dry (Webb, 1983). In lightly affected areas, compaction effects seem to be roughly proportional to the total applied weight, i.e. load times number of passes. In more heavily impacted areas, at least for certain soil types such as dune sands, compaction impacts seem to stabilize beyond a threshold number of passes. For trailbikes in desert soils, the first few passes yielded greatest impacts on bulk density, and the rate of change decreased with additional passes (Webb, 1982). In this instance, even a single pass produced a significant reduction in the number of larger soil pores in the top 30 cm. After 200 passes, all pore sizes were reduced, and compaction effects occurred to 60 cm depth. In coastal sand dunes, Liddle and Greig-Smith (1975) found greatest compaction at 15 cm depth. For up to 256 passes of a 4WD vehicle within 3 days, the bulk density of this soil increased proportionally with the number of passes, and the logarithm of penetrability decreased proportionately.

Infiltration rates are also reduced by OHVs and, indeed, even by hikers (e.g. Brown et al., 1977; Eckert et al., 1979; Liddle, 1997, Buckley, 2001a). In some soils, compaction reduced infiltration rates by 97%. Less commonly studied impacts on soil include increased temperature on dune sands bared of vegetation (Liddle and Moore, 1974); and a reduction in fertility, particularly nitrogen (Duggeli, 1937; Whisler et al., 1965; Belnap, 1995; Liddle, 1997).

OHVs, and other forms of trampling, have been shown to reduce a wide range of soil infauna (Bellamy et al., 1971; Brown et al., 1977) including springtails (Little, 1974; Yur'eva et al., 1976), mites (Chappell et al., 1971), cranefly larvae (Newton and Pugh-Thomas, 1979), woodlice and spiders in surface litter (Ingelog et al., 1977), and earthworms (Cluzeau et al., 1992). Different species are affected differently, and larger individuals of the same species may survive better, perhaps by using deeper soil layers (Ingelog et al., 1977; Bayfield, 1979; Piearce, 1984).

Vegetation

OHVs affect vegetation by: crushing and bruising individual plants; modifying soil properties; introducing weed seeds and plant pathogens; increasing ignition sources for wildfires; and producing air pollution from engine exhausts (Duevers, 2002). Direct impacts of tyres have been studied most intensively, with a strong focus on particular ecosystems. These include:

• coastal sand dunes in east-coast USA, South Africa, Israel and elsewhere (Godfrey, 1975; Blom, 1976; Brodhead and Godfrey, 1977; Godfrey *et al.*, 1978, 1980; Hosier and Eaton 1980; Godfrey and Godfrey 1981; Gilbertson, 1983; Luckenbach and Bury, 1983; van der Merwe, 1988; Rickard *et al.*, 1994; Kutiel *et al.*, 2000; Brown and McLachlan, 2002);

• arid and semi-arid landscapes, largely in the south-western USA but also in the Middle East (Davidson and Fox, 1974; Vollmer *et al.*, 1976; Webb and Wilshire, 1980, 1983; Lathrop, 1983; Webb *et al.*, 1983; Milchunas *et al.*, 2000; Brown and Schokrecht, 2001);

• tundra (Rickard and Slaughter, 1973; Greller *et al.*, 1974; Rickard and Brown, 1974; Slaughter *et al.*, 1990; Walker and Walker, 1991; Forbes, 1992); bogs (Ross, 1992); fens (Barry and Schlinger, 1978) and montane landscapes (Wilson and Seney, 1994).

Forest and woodland vegetation has received much less attention (Brown *et al.*, 1977; Ingelog *et al.*, 1977; Weaver and Dale, 1978); and grasslands even less (Onyeanusi, 1986; Hercock, 1998, 1999).

The number of OHV passes that causes a 50% reduction in plant cover differs by a factor of over 100 times between different ecosystems (Liddle, 1973, 1997; Kendal, 1982). OHVs cause 5–30 times as much damage to vegetation as hikers (Cole, 1993, 1995a,b). Different vegetation types differ greatly in susceptibility to the impacts of OHV tyres (Wright 1989; Liddle, 1997; Yorks *et al.*, 1997; Milchunas *et al.*, 2000). In general, grasses and graminoids are both most resistant and most resilient to OHV impacts, with other plant growth forms differing in relative resistance and resilience (Yorks *et al.*, 1997). In many vegetation types, relatively few passes by OHVs can cause major reductions in plant cover and density. In a marsh area, for example, 40 crossings reduced plant cover to zero (Ross, 1992). However, on temperate coastal dunes in Massachusetts, USA, 12% of plant biomass remained after 675 OHV crossings (Godfrey, 1975). OHVs cause more damage to vegetation on slopes and turns than on straight, level ground, and skilled drivers can reduce impacts relative to unskilled ones (Rickard and Brown, 1974; Weaver and

Dale, 1978; Godfrey *et al.*, 1980; Onyeanusi, 1986; Woodward, 1995; Buckley, 2001b).

There are positive feedbacks between OHV damage to soil and vegetation. Loss of plant cover increases soil erosion, nutrient loss and sometimes soil surface temperature, and all these factors contribute further to vegetation loss.

Plants can suffer physiological damage from OHVs even if not broken or killed (Hylgaard and Liddle, 1984), which can lead to leaf abscission and reduced growth rates (Liddle, 1997). Plant species assemblages along OHV tracks are often modified relative to untracked vegetation, through a variety of mechanisms. These include: changes to soil properties; differential damage to some species relative to others; trapping windblown seeds in tyre ruts (Brown and Schoknecht, 2001); and the introduction of seeds in mud on tyres and vehicle bodies.

OHVs spread weeds by carrying seeds in radiator grilles and in mud, soil and sludges on tyres and underbodies (Wace, 1977; Marion *et al.*, 1986). Smaller seeds are carried differentially. During the wet season in Nigeria, Clifford (1959) recorded an average of 100 seeds/kg of dry mud on cars, and this increased to 180 seeds/kg during the dry season. Schmidt (1989) germinated 124 plant species from seeds carried on a single vehicle in Göttingen. In Kakadu National Park, Australia, Lonsdale and Lane (1994) found 1505 individual seeds in 84 different plant species on 384 parked cars, but 80% of these were seeds from only seven species. In Colorado, USA, weeds are more abundant in areas used heavily by OHVs (Milchunas *et al.*, 2000); and in the coastal dunes of southern Australia, Gilbertson (1983) found that once established, weed species are more resistant than natives to further OHV damage.

In some areas, OHVs are also a major dispersal mechanism for plant pathogens. A particularly well-known example is provided by the cinnamon fungus *Phytophthora cinnamomi*, the causal agent of jarrah dieback disease in plant communities throughout southern Australia (Marks and Smith, 1991; Newell and Wilson, 1993; Gillen and Napier, 1994; Barker and Wardlaw, 1995; Hill *et al.*, 1995; Shearer and Dillon, 1996; Buckley *et al.*, Chapter 20, this volume).

Animals

Impacts by OHVs have been recorded for a wide variety of vertebrates and invertebrates, including endangered species. Impact mechanisms include:

- crushing animals, nests and burrows under tyres;
- collisions and roadkill;
- physiological damage from noise;
- disturbance through noise, vibration and visual impact, leading to displacement, habitat loss, increased energy consumption, and increased predation, especially on juveniles;
- barriers to movement from wheel ruts, tracks and dirt roads;
- indirect impacts of increased human access, including feral animals, hunting and fires.

The precise mechanisms are not always known. There are many cases where significant decreases in populations of particular animal species have been recorded in areas used by OHVs, relative to control areas without OHVs, but without further experimental evidence. Densities of species such as bears, wolves, elk, deer and lizards decrease in areas with more tracks, OHVs or snowmobiles, in various parts of the world (Dorrance et al., 1975; Vollmer et al., 1976; Elgmork, 1978; Rost and Bailey, 1979; Lyon, 1983; Paquet and Callaghan, 1996). Wolves and cougar are displaced entirely from areas with road densities >0.6 km km^{-2} (van Dyke et al., 1986; Mech, 1989; Forman and Alexander, 1998, p. 123). In some cases the mechanism can be inferred, e.g. for marmots on Vancouver Island (Dearden and Hall, 1983); or newts, frogs and tadpoles in Florida (Duevers, 2002).

Significant impacts by OHVs on beaches have been recorded for a variety of birds, turtles, crabs, clams, beetles, isopods and other species. Eggs and chicks of shore-nesting birds, and nests and hatchlings of marine turtles, are crushed by OHV tyres, and predation increases sharply when brooding adults are driven from nests, even briefly. Feeding by adult birds is also interrupted by OHV disturbance. This is of particular concern in highly seasonal climates and

for birds resting during migration. Interestingly, Watson et al. (1996) found that OHV drivers on South African beaches did not notice shorebirds even when there were several species in close range.

Shorebirds affected by OHVs include a variety of terns, oystercatchers, plovers and dotterel, some of them endangered (Lord et al., 1977; Godfrey and Godfrey, 1981; Pfister et al., 1992; Melvin et al., 1994; Palacios and Mellink, 1996; Watson et al., 1996). OHVs are the greatest threat to least terns in the Gulf of California, for example (Palacios and Mellink, 1996). OHVs are also a major threat for the endangered little tern on the beaches of central eastern Australia (NSW National Parks and Wildlife Service, personal communications, 2001, 2002). Significant OHV impacts have also been recorded for turtles on beaches in Israel (Kuller, 1999). Ghost crabs, Ocypode spp., seem to be particularly susceptible to OHV impact, since they dig shallow burrows in the upper sections of sandy beaches. In Maryland USA, OHVs reduced population of O. quadrata by 97% (Steiner and Leatherman, 1981); and in nearby Virginia, 100 passes by an OHV reduced ghost crab populations by 98% (Wolcott and Wolcott, 1984). In south-western Australia, ghost crab populations are 90% less on urban beaches than in rural areas (Barros, 2001), even though more food is available in urban areas.

Significant OHV damage has been recorded for a range of sandy-beach infauna, including: softshell clams in the USA (Godfrey et al., 1978); wedge clams, Donax harleyanus, in Uruguay (Defeo and de Alava, 1995); sand dollars, Echinodiscus spp., in New Zealand (Brown and McLachlan, 2002); and isopods Tylos spp. in South Africa (van der Merwe, 1988; van der Merwe and van der Merwe, 1991; Brown, 2000). The proportion of isopods killed or injured increases directly with the number of OHV passes ($P < 0.008$), and OHVs are a major factor in the decline of isopod populations.

In other environments, OHVs have significant impacts on desert tortoise (Bury and Marlow, 1973); sand scarab beetles (Luckenback and Bury, 1983); tiger beetles (Mackay, 1997); and a variety of litter-inhabiting invertebrates (Duffey, 1975). Similar impacts occur from snowmobiles and other over-snow vehicles (OSVs). For example, OSVs crush the undersnow burrows of the northern bog lemming in eastern Washington (Leys and Burke, 1973). By compacting overlying snow, OSVs also reduce insulation for overwintering burrows of various species (Schmid, 1970).

OHVs kill a variety of animals by direct collision, the off-highway equivalent of roadkill. Most of the information available on vehicle collisions with large mammals is from on-road traffic, but much of this is also relevant to logging roads, dirt tracks and other OHV routes. Roadkill is by no means insignificant as a source of wildlife mortality (Hodson, 1962, 1966; Oetting and Cassell, 1971; Bennett, 1991; Ellenberg *et al.*, 1991; Harris and Scheck, 1991; Forman and Alexander, 1998). Over 1 million vertebrates are killed on roads each day in the USA, for example (Forman and Alexander, 1998, p. 213). Roads have been described as ecological traps which consistently kill wildlife attempting to cross.

Up to 1991, for example, the annual roadkill of the Florida panther, *Felis concolor coryi*, was equal to 10% of the total population (Evink *et al.*, 1996). Annual roadkill of key deer, *Odocoileus virginianus clavium*, in Florida is even higher, 16% of the total population (Forman and Alexander, 1998, p. 213). Large and medium-sized mammals seem to be most susceptible on narrower roads; birds and small mammals on wider roads; reptiles on narrow roads with low traffic, such as OHV tracks; and frogs and other amphibians, not surprisingly, on roads and tracks near ponds (Hodson, 1962, 1966; Oxley *et al.*, 1974; Dodd *et al.*, 1989; Langton, 1989; de Maynardier and Hunter, 1995; Ashley and Robinson, 1996; Romin and Bissonette, 1996; Vos, 1997; Forman and Alexander, 1998). Roadkills encourage 'traplining' by predators (Bennett, 1988, 1991; Ellenberg *et al.*, 1991; Forman, 1995), which can lead to further mortality.

Nocturnal and crepuscular species, and diurnal species occasionally active at night, seem to be particularly vulnerable. Highest roadkill of grey kangaroos in Victoria, Australia, for example, occurred during full moon when these kangaroos are particularly active (Coulson, 1982). Interestingly, warning signs for motorists did not reduce kangaroo roadkill

(Coulson, 1982). Correspondingly, in the northern hemisphere, Pojar *et al.* (1975) found that even illuminated and animated warning signs did not reduce roadkill of deer: drivers only slowed down when they saw dead deer carcasses on the roadside.

In addition to direct roadkill, road noise and associated disturbance commonly leads larger mammals to move away from roads. Mountain goats, for example, are visibly disturbed by the noise of an OHV over 1 km away (Singer, 1978). Reindeer and mule deer are highly disturbed by the sounds of snowmobiles, even half a kilometre or more away (Calef, 1976; Freddy *et al.*, 1986; Tyler, 1991). This is perhaps unsurprising, since snowmobilers have often been observed harassing a variety of deer, including both white-tailed and mule deer (Eckert *et al.*, 1979; Freddy *et al.*, 1986). Lieb and Mossman (1974) reported that deer disturbed by OHVs on a beach attempted to swim and were consequently drowned. Occupants of OHVs and OSVs have been recorded shooting deliberately at a variety of birds, including eagles, osprey and even jays (Duevers, 2002). Of course, such behaviour is far from ecotourism. In any area where animals can expect to be chased or shot at, however, the sound of any OHV will trigger physiological and behavioural disturbance. This also applies to areas where licensed hunters operate legally. In Canada, for example, McLellan (1989) and McLellan and Shackleton (1989) reported that a high proportion of grizzly bears shot by licensed hunters are shot from roads. Besides hunters, OHVs may bring dogs, which disturb mammals and birds more than humans alone (MacArthur *et al.*, 1982; Liddle, 1997; Buckley, 2001a; Deuvers, 2002).

Songbirds of various species are easily disturbed by vehicle noise. Particularly sensitive species, such as cuckoo, avoid areas with vehicle noise >35 dB, and typical avoidance thresholds are 42 dB for songbirds in woodland areas, and 48 dB in grasslands (Reijnen *et al.*, 1995, 1996). Even these higher thresholds, incidentally, are equivalent to the sound level in a library reading room (Forman and Alexander, 1998). Birds driven away from areas used by vehicles may be forced into territories occupied by competing individuals, or into less favourable areas for nesting (Yalden and Yalden, 1990;

Buckley, 2001a). ORV noise can also lead to hearing loss in ground-dwelling vertebrates (Brattstrom and Bondello, 1983).

OHV wheel ruts, tracks and roads can act as significant barriers to movement of some animal species. 4WD wheel ruts and lights block and disorientate turtle hatchlings on beaches, for example, leading to exhaustion, predation and increased mortality (Hosier et al., 1981; Witherington, 1997). Tracks in forests act as barriers to small mammals (Burnett, 1992; Goosem, 1997, 2000). Tracks can also block movement by amphibians and invertebrates (Forman and Alexander, 1998). It appears that although wider roads, not surprisingly, are more serious barriers than narrower ones, the actual road surface is unimportant: dirt tracks used by OHVs form just as severe a barrier as a bitumen road of equivalent width (Oxley et al., 1974; Mader, 1984; Fahrig et al., 1995; Forman, 1995; Forman and Alexander, 1998).

Snowmobiles, in particular, can have a severe adverse effect on air quality (Wilkinson, 1995; Wade, 2000). A single snowmobile may emit as much nitrous oxide and hydrocarbons as 1700 cars (Wilkinson, 1995). In Yellowstone National Park USA, for example, snowmobile exhaust fumes are sufficiently concentrated and continuous in some areas that rangers on duty suffer respiratory poisoning symptoms, such as headaches and nausea (Wilkinson, 1995; Wade, 2000).

Conclusions

OHVs are a common component of a wide variety of ecotourism operations, and their environmental impacts cannot be ignored. These impacts, can, however, be reduced considerably through careful driving and access restrictions. A number of organizations have compiled minimal-impact guidelines for OHVs. The most detailed appears to be that of Buckley (2001b), which incorporates 33 individual items on preparation, 55 on driving techniques and 24 on OHV camping. Broadly, these cover items such as: choice of tyres; avoiding marshes, muddy trails, steep dunes and back beaches; crossing dunes and creeks at established ramps and fords; and driving to minimize wheel ruts, noise and wildlife disturbance.

Even if all these precautions are taken, OHVs still cause impacts. Land managers, especially of protected areas, or other sites of high conservation value, may therefore need to impose restrictions on OHV use, backed up with monitoring, enforcement and penalties where appropriate. Common management approaches include:

- restricting OHV use to a small number of heavily used, well-maintained tracks;
- clearly signposting off-track areas as closed for conservation;
- encouraging OHV operators to improve driving skills;
- only allowing OHVs on wide, sandy beaches and only at low tide during the day;
- keeping ORV tracks narrow (Burnett, 1992);
- maintaining a closed canopy above tracks in wooded areas (Turton and Goosem, 2001);
- conducting education campaigns to make ORV operators aware of wildlife (Watson et al., 1996).

There are enormous differences in impacts between different OHV users. Driven carefully at the right speed, with the right tyres, in the right places, by a well-informed user, a 4WD vehicle is a perfectly reasonable and legitimate way to enjoy many landscapes. Driven carelessly, or with deliberate impacts, in fragile areas, by an ignorant or heedless user, OHVs can rapidly cause major and ecologically significant damage to soils, plants and animals.

Acknowledgements

The database of literature on which this review is based has been constructed since 1991 by staff of the International Centre for Ecotourism Research at Griffith University (www.gu.edu.au/centre/icer/staff). It is currently maintained by Karen Sullivan, who also kindly checked references and citations. Coverage, opinions, errors and omissions in this chapter remain my own responsibility.

References

Adams, J.A., Endo, A.S., Stolzy, L.H., Rowlands, P.G. and Johnson, H.B. (1982) Controlled experiments on soil compaction produced by off-road vehicles in the Mojave Desert, California. *Journal of Applied Ecology* 19, 167–175.

Albrecht, J. and Knopf, T.B. (1985) *Off-Road Vehicles – Environmental Impact – Management Response: a Bibliography.* Publication 35-1985. Agricultural Experiment Station, University of Minnesota, St Paul, Minnesota.

Anders, F.J. and Leatherman, S.P. (1987) Disturbance of beach sediment by off-road vehicles. *Environmental Geology and Water Sciences* 93, 183–189.

Ashley, E.P. and Robinson, J.T. (1996) Road mortality of amphibians, reptiles and other wildlife on the Long Point causeway, Lake Erie, Ontario. *Canadian Field Naturalist* 110, 403–412.

Barker, P.C.J. and Wardlaw, T.J. (1995) Susceptibility of selected Tasmanian rare plants to *Phytophthora cinnamomi. Australian Journal of Botany* 43, 379–386.

Barros, F. (2001) Ghost crabs as a tool for rapid assessment of human impacts on exposed sandy beaches. *Biological Conservation* 97, 339–404.

Barry, W.J. and Schlinger, E.I. (1978) Inglenook Fen: a study and plan, Sacramento, California. In: Webb, R.H. and Wilshire, H.G. (eds) *U.S. Geological Survey Open File Report.* Californian Department of Parks and Recreation, Sacramento, California.

Bayfield, N.G. (1979) Some effects of trampling on *Molophilus ater* (Meigen) (Diptera: Tipulidae). *Biological Conservation* 14, 219–232.

Bayfield, N.G. (1986) *Penetration of the Cairngorm Mountains, Scotland, by Vehicle Tracks and Footpaths: Impacts and Recovery.* General Technical Report INT 212, USDA Forestry Service Intermountain Research Station, Fort Collins, Colorado, pp. 121–128.

Bellamy, D., Radforth, J. and Radforth, N.W. (1971) Terrain, traffic and tundra. *Nature* 231, 429–432.

Belnap, J. (1995) Surface disturbances: their role in accelerating desertification. *Environmental Monitoring and Assessment* 37, 39–57.

Bennett, A.F. (1988) Roadside vegetation a habitat for mammals at Naringal, southwestern Victoria. *Victorian Naturalist* 105, 105–113.

Bennett, A.F. (1991) Roads and roadsides and wildlife conservation: a review. In: Saunders, D.A. and Hobbs, R.J. (eds) *Nature Conservation: the Role of Corridors.* Surrey Beatty and Sons, Chipping Norton, NSW, Australia, pp. 99–117.

Bilby, R.E., Sullivan, K. and Duncan, S.H. (1989) The generation and fate of road-surface sediment in forested watersheds in southwestern Washington. *Forest Science* 35, 453–468.

Bissill, L.P. (1970) The social and political impact of snowmobiles. *Proceedings of the 3rd International Snowmobile Congress Portland, Maine,* pp. 58–62.

Blom, C.W.P.M. (1976) Effects of trampling and soil compaction on the occurrence of some *Plantago* species in coastal sand dunes. *Œcologia Plantarum* 11, 225–241.

Bloomfield, H.V. (1969) Snowmobiles – boon or bane? *American Forestry* 75, 4–5, 48 and 50–51.

Brainard, J. (1998) Patton tank marks suggest long recovery. *Science News* 154, 87.

Brattstrom, B.H. and Bondello, M.C. (1983) Effects of off-road vehicle noise on desert vertebrates. In: Webb, R.H. and Wilshire, H.G. (eds) *Environmental Effects of Off-road Vehicles: Impact and Management in Arid Regions.* Springer Verlag, New York, pp. 167–206.

Brodhead, J.M. and Godfrey, P.J. (1977) Off road vehicle impact in Cape Cod National Seashore: disruption and recovery of dune vegetation. *International Journal of Biometeorology* 21, 299–306.

Brown, A.C. (2000) Is the sandy-beach isopod *Tylos granulatus* an endangered species? *South African Journal of Science* 96, 474.

Brown, A.C. and McLachlan, A. (2002) Sandy shore ecosystems and the threats facing them: some predictions for the year 2025. *Environmental Conservation* 29, 62–77.

Brown, G. and Schoknecht, N. (2001) Off-road vehicles and vegetation patterning in a degraded desert ecosystem in Kuwait. *Journal of Arid Environments* 49, 413–427.

Brown, J.M. Jr, Kalisz, S.P. and Wright, W.R. (1977) Effects of recreational use on forested sites. *Environmental Geology* 1, 425–431.

Brown, K.J. (1994) River-bed sedimentation caused by off-road vehicles at river fords in the Victorian Highlands, Australia. *Water Resources Bulletin* 30, 239–250.

Buckley, R.C. (2001a) *Environmental impacts.* In Weaver, D. (ed.) *Encyclopaedia of Ecotourism.* CAB International, Wallingford, UK, pp. 374–394.

Buckley, R.C. (2001b) *Green Guide for 4WD Tours.* CRC for Sustainable Tourism, Gold Coast, Australia.

Buckley, R.C. (2003) Ecological indicators of tourist impacts in parks. *Journal of Ecotourism* 2, 54–66.

Burnett, S.E. (1992) Effects of a rainforest road on movements of small mammals: mechanisms and implications. *Wildlife Research* 19, 95–104.

Bury, R.L. (1978) Impacts of snowmobiles on wildlife. *Transactions of North American Wildlife and Natural Resources Conference* 43, 149–156.

Bury, R.B. and Marlow, R.W. (1973) The desert tortoise: will it survive? *Environmental Journal* June, 9–12.

Calef, G.W. (1976) Numbers beyond counting, miles beyond measure. *Audubon* 78, 42–61.

California Department of Parks and Recreation (1975) *The off-road vehicle: a study report*, pp. 103 (cited in Albrecht, J. and Knopp, T.B. 1985).

Chappell, H.G., Ainsworth, J.F., Cameron, R.A.D. and Redfern, M. (1971) The effect of trampling on a chalk grassland ecosystem. *Journal of Applied Ecology* 8, 869–882.

Clifford, H.T. (1959) Seed dispersal by motor vehicles. *Journal of Ecology* 47, 311–315.

Cluzeau, D., Binet, F. and Vertes, F. (1992) Effects of intensive cattle trampling on soil–plant–earthworm systems in two grassland types. *Soil Biology and Biochemistry* 24, 1661–1665.

Cole, D.N. (1993) *Trampling Effects on Mountain Vegetation in Washington, Colorado, New Hampshire and North Carolina.* Research paper 1NT-464, US Department of Agriculture, Forest Services, Intermountain Research Station, Ogden, Utah.

Cole, D.N. (1995a) Experimental trampling of vegetation. I. Relationship between trampling intensity and vegetation response. *Journal of Applied Ecology* 32, 203–214.

Cole, D.N. (1995b) Experimental trampling of vegetation. II. Predictors of resistance and resilience. *Journal of Applied Ecology* 32, 215–224.

Coulson, G.M. (1982) Road-kills of macropods on a section of highway in Central Victoria. *Australian Wildlife Research* 9, 21–26.

Davidson, E. and Fox, M. (1974) Effects of off-road motorcycle activity on Mojave Desert vegetation and soil. *Madrono* 22, 381–412.

Deardon, P. and Hall, C. (1983) Non-consumptive recreation pressures and the case of the Vancouver Island marmot (*Marmota vancouverensis*). *Environmental Conservation* 10, 63–66.

Defeo, O. and De Alava, A. (1995) Effects of human activities on long-term trends in sandy beach populations: the wedge clam *Donax hanleyanus* in Uruguay. *Marine Ecology Progress Series* 123, 73–82.

de Maynadier, P.G. and Hunter, M.L. Jr (1995) The relationship between forest management and amphibian ecology: a review of the North American literature. *Environmental Review* 3, 230–261.

Dodd, C.J. Jr, Enge, K.M. and Stuart, J.N. (1989)

Reptiles on highways in North–Central Alabama, USA. *Journal of Herpetology* 23, 197–200.

Dorrance, M.J., Savage, P.J. and Huff, D.E. (1975) Effects of snowmobiles on white-tailed deer. *Journal of Wildlife Management* 39, 563–569.

Duevers, L. (2002) *Out of Control: the Impacts of Off-Road Vehicles and Roads on Wildlife and Habitat in Florida's National Forests.* Defenders of Wildlife, Washington, DC, 120 pp. Available on website www.defenders.org/habitat/florvs (verified 11 September 2002).

Duffey, E. (1975) The effects of human trampling on the fauna of grassland litter. *Biological Conservation* 7, 255–274.

Duggeli, J. (1937) Wie wirkt das oftere Betreten des Walbodens auf einzelene physikalische und biologishe Eigenschaften. *Schweizerische Zeitschrift fur Furstwesen* 88, 151–165.

Eckert, R.E. Jr, Wood, M.K., Blackburn, W.H. and Petersen, F.F. (1979) Impacts of off-road vehicles on infiltration and sediment production of two desert soils. *Journal of Range Management* 32, 394–397.

Eckstein, R.G., O'Brien, T.F., Rongstad, O.J. and Bollinger, J.G. (1979) Snowmobile effects on movements of white-tailed deer: a case study. *Environmental Conservation* 6, 45–51.

Elgmork, K. (1987) The cryptic brown bear populations of Norway. *Proceedings of the International Conference on Bear Research Management* 7, pp. 13–16.

Ellenberg, H., Muller, K. and Stottele, T. (1991) Strassen-okologie. In: *Okologie und Strasse, Broschurenreihe der Deutschen Strassenlings.* Broschuerenreihe des Deitschen Strassenverbandes, Bonn, Germany.

Evink, G.L., Garret, P., Zeigler, D. and Berry, J. (eds) (1996) *Trends in Addressing Transportation Related Wildlife Mortality.* Report No. FL-ER-58-96. Florida Department of Transportation, Tallahassee, Florida.

Fahrig, L., Pedlar, J.H., Pope, S.E., Taylor, P.D. and Wegner, J.F. (1995) Effect of road traffic on amphibian density. *Biological Conservation* 73, 177–182.

Forbes, B.C. (1992) Tundra disturbance studies, I: long-term effects of vehicles on species richness and biomass. *Environmental Conservation* 19, 48–58.

Foreman, D. (1979) ORVs threaten a wild canyon. *The Wilderness Society* 43, 14–18.

Forman, R.T.T. (1995) *Land Mosaics: the Ecology of Landscapes and Regions.* Cambridge University Press, Cambridge, UK.

Forman, R.T.T. and Alexander, L.E. (1998) Roads and their major ecological effects. *Annual Review of Ecology and Systematics* 29, 207–231.

Forman, R.T.T. and Mellinger, D.A. (1998) Road networks and forest spatial patterns in ecological models of diverse logging regimes. In: Saunders, D.A., Craig, N.M. and Norton, C. (eds) *Nature Conservation in Production Environments: Managing the Matrix.* Surrey Beatty, Chipping Norton, NSW, Australia.

Forman, R.T.T., Friedman, D.S., Fitzhenry, D., Martin, J.D., Chen, A.S. and Alexander, L.E. (1997) Ecological effects of roads: toward three summary indices and an overview for North America. In: Canters, K. (ed.) *Habitat Fragmentation and Infrastructure.* Ministry of Transport Public Works and Water Management, Delft, The Netherlands, pp. 40–54.

Freddy, D.J., Bronaugh, W.M. and Fowler, M.C. (1986) Responses of mule deer to disturbance by persons afoot and snowmobiles. *Wildlife Society Bulletin* 14, 63–68.

Freitag, D.R. (1971) Methods of measuring soil compaction. In: Barnes, K.K. *et al.* (eds) *Compaction in Agricultural Soils.* American Society of Agricultural Engineers, Michigan, pp. 45–103.

Gilbertson, D. (1983) The impacts of off-road vehicles in the Coorong Dune and Lake Complex of South Australia. In: Webb, R.H. and Wilshire, H.G. (eds) *Environmental Effects of Off-road Vehicles: Impact and Management in Arid Regions.* Springer Verlag, New York, pp. 355–374.

Gillen, K. and Napier, A. (1994) Management of access. *Journal of the Royal Society of Western Australia* 77, 163–168.

Godfrey, P.J. (1975) *The Ecological Effects of Off-road Vehicles in Cape Cod National Seashore, Massachusetts (Phase II).* Report No. 18, University of Massachusetts–National Park Service Cooperative Research Unit. University of Massachusetts, Amherst, Massachusetts.

Godfrey, P.J. and Godfrey, M.M. (1981) Ecological effects of off-road vehicles on Cape Cod. *Oceanus* 23, 56–67.

Godfrey, P.J., Leatherman, S.P. and Buckley, P.A. (1978) Impact of off-road vehicles on coastal ecosystems. *Proceedings of a Symposium on Coastal Zones,* pp. 581–600.

Godfrey, P.J., Leatherman, S.P. and Buckley, P.A. (1980) ORVs and barrier beach degradation. *Parks* 5, 5–11.

Goosem, M.W. (1997) Internal fragmentation: the effects of roads, highways and powerline clearings on movements and mortality of rainforest vertebrates. In: Laurance, W.F. and Bierregaard, R.O. (eds) *Tropical Forest Remnants: Ecology, Management and Conservation of Fragmented Communities.* University of Chicago Press, Chicago, pp. 241–255.

Goosem, M. (2000) Effects of tropical rainforest roads on small mammals: edge changes in community composition. *Wildlife Research* 27, 151–163.

Grayson, R.B., Haydon, S.R., Jayasuriya, M.D.A. and Enlayson, B.C. (1993) Water quality in mountain ash forests – separating the impacts of roads from those of logging operations. *Journal of Hydrology* 150, 459–480.

Green, J.E. and Knight, S.J. (1959) *Preliminary Study of Stresses Under Off-road Vehicles.* Misc. Paper No. 4-362, US Army Corps of Engineers Waterways Experimental Station, Vicksburg, Mississippi.

Greller, A.M., Goldstein, M. and Marcus, L. (1974) Snowmobile impact on three alpine tundra plant communities. *Environmental Conservation* 1, 101–110.

Harris, L.D. and Scheck, J. (1991) From implications to applications: the dispersal corridor principle applied to the conservation of biological diversity. In: Saunders, D.A. and Hobbs, R.J. (eds) *Nature Conservation: the Role of Corridors.* Surrey Beatty and Sons, Chipping Norton, NSW, Australia, pp. 189–200.

Hercock, M. (1998) The challenges posed by four-wheel drive tourists to sustainable tourism in tropical Western Australia. *Australian Parks and Leisure,* September, 15–19.

Hercock, M. (1999) The impacts of recreation and tourism in the remote North Kimberly region of Western Australia. *The Environmentalist* 19, 259–275.

Hill, T.C., Tippett, J.T. and Shearer, B.L. (1995) Evaluation of three treatments for eradication of *Phytophthora cinnamomi* from deep, leached sands in southwest Australia. *Plant Disease* 79, 122–127.

Hinkley, B.S., Iverson, R.M. and Hallett, B. (1983) Accelerated water erosion in ORV-use areas. In: Webb, R.M. and Wilshire, H.G. (eds) *Environmental Effects of Off-road Vehicles.* Springer-Verlag, New York, pp. 81–96.

Hodson, N.L. (1962) Some notes on the causes of bird road casualties. *Bird Study* 9, 168–173.

Hodson, N.L. (1966) A survey of road mortality in mammals (and including data for the grass snake and common frog). *Journal of Zoology London* 148, 576–579.

Hosier, P.E. and Eaton, T.E. (1980) The impact of vehicles on dune and grassland vegetation on a south-eastern North Carolina barrier beach. *Journal of Applied Ecology* 17, 173–182.

Hosier, P.E., Kockhar, M. and Thayer, V. (1981) Off-road vehicle and pedestrian effects on the sea approach of hatchling Loggerhead Turtles. *Environmental Conservation* 8, 158–161.

Hylgaard, T. and Liddle, M.J. (1984) The effect of

human trampling on a sand dune ecosystem dominated by *Empetrum nigrum*. *Journal of Applied Ecology* 18, 559–569.

Ingelog, T., Olsson, M.T. and Bodvarsson, J. (1977) *Effects of Long-term Trampling and Vehicle Driving on Soil, Vegetation and Certain Soil Animals of an Old Scots Pine Stand*. Research Note 27, Royal College of Forestry, Uppsala.

Iverson, R.M., Hinckley, B.S., Webb, R.M. and Hallet, B. (1981) Physical effects of vehicular disturbances on arid landscapes. *Science* 212, 915–917.

James, R.J. (2000) From beaches to beach environments: linking the ecology, human use and management of beaches in Australia. *Ocean and Coastal Management* 43, 495–514.

Kay, J., Bacon, S.K., Bond, V.E., Braun, B.A., Collinson, J.W., Gooding, J.E., Langford, K.S., Meehan, C.S., Murphy, R.G., Petrusky, J.R., Poor, O.H., Sampson, C.E., Warfel, W.R. and Warnek, R.E. (1981) Evaluating environmental impacts of off-road vehicles. *Journal of Geography* 80, 10–18.

Kendal, P.C. McM. (1982) The effect of season and/or duration of trampling on vegetation in an open forest of South East Queensland. Master of Science Thesis, Griffith University, Brisbane.

Kuller, Z. (1999) Current status and conservation of marine turtles on the Mediterranean coast of Israel. *Marine Turtle Newsletter* 86, 3–5.

Kuss, F.R. and Morgan, J.M. (1986) A first alternative for estimating the physical carrying capacities of natural areas for recreation. *Environmental Management* 10, 225–262.

Kutiel, P., Eden, E. and Zhevelev, Y. (2000) Effect of experimental trampling and off-road motorcycle traffic on soil and vegetation of stabilized coastal dunes, Israel. *Environmental Conservation* 27, 14–23.

Langton, T.E.S. (ed.) (1989) Amphibians and roads. *Proceedings of the Toad Tunnel Conference, Rotenburg, Germany*. ACO Polymer Products, Shefford, UK.

Lathrop, E.A. (1983) The effect of vehicle use on desert vegetation. In: Webb, R.H. and Wilshire, H.G. (eds) *Environmental Effects of Off-road Vehicles: Impact and Management in Arid Regions*. Springer Verlag, New York, pp. 153–166.

Layser, E.F. and Burke, T.E. (1973) Northern bog lemming and its unique habitat in north eastern Washington. *Murrelet* 54, 7–8.

Lazan, G. (1969) The thrill killer. *American Forestry* 75, 6–7.

Leatherman, S. and Steiner, A. (1987). *An Annotated Bibliography of the Effects of Off-road Vehicle and Pedestrian Traffic on Coastal Ecosystems*. Vance Bibliographies, Illinois, USA.

Leys, J.F., Larney, F.J., Müller, J.F., Raupach, M.R., McTainsh, G.H. and Lynch, A.W. (1998) Anthropogenic dust and endosulfan emissions on a cotton farm in northern New South Wales, Australia. *Science of the Total Environment* 220, 55–70.

Liddle, M.J. (1973) The effects of trampling and vehicles on natural vegetation. PhD Dissertation, University College of North Wales, Bangor, UK, p. 211.

Liddle, M. (1997) *Recreation Ecology*. Chapman & Hall, London, UK.

Liddle, M.J. and Greig-Smith, P. (1975) A survey of tracks in a sand dune ecosystem. I. Soils. *Journal of Applied Ecology* 12, 893–908.

Liddle, M.J. and Moore, K.G. (1974) The microclimate of sand dune tracks: the relative contribution of vegetation removal and soil compression. *Journal of Applied Ecology* 11, 1057–1068.

Lieb, T.W. and Mossman, A.S. (1974) Elk drowning. *Pacific Northwest Bird and Mammal Society* 55, 39–40.

Little, A.D. (1974) *Betridings-experimenten in een Duinvallei: Effecten op Mesofauna en Vegetatie, Series B: Biologische Aspecten* No. 5. Vrij Universiteit, Amsterdam.

Lonsdale, W.M. and Lane, A.M. (1994) Vehicles as vectors of weed seeds in Kakadu National Park in plant invasions. *Kowari* 2, 167–169.

Lord, A., Waas, J.R. and Innes, J. (1997) Effects of human activity on the behaviour of northern New Zealand Dotterel *Charadrius obscurus aquilonius* chicks. *Biological Conservation* 82, 15–20.

Lovich, J.E. and Bainbridge, D. (1999) Anthropogenic degradation of the Southern California desert ecosystem and prospects for natural recovery and restoration. *Environmental Management* 24, 309–326.

Luckenbach, R.A. and Bury, R.B. (1983) Effects of off-road vehicles on the biota of the Algodones Dunes, Imperial County, California. *Journal of Applied Ecology* 20, 265–286.

Lyon, L.J. (1983) Road density models describing habitat effectiveness for elk. *Journal of Forestry* 81, 592–595.

MacArthur, R.A., Geist, V. and Johnston, R.H. (1982) Cardiac and behavioural responses of mountain sheep to human disturbance. *Journal of Wildlife Management* 46, 351–358.

Mackay, K. (1997) Beetle mania. *National Parks* 41, 40.

Mader, H.J. (1984) Animal habitat isolation by roads and agricultural fields. *Biological Conservation* 29, 81–96.

Marion, J.L., Cole, D.N. and Bratton, S.P. (1986) *Exotic Vegetation in Wilderness Areas*. General Technical Report INT-212, US Forestry Services

Intermountain Research Station, Ogden, Utah, pp. 114–120.

Marks, G.C. and Smith, I.W. (1991) The cinnamon fungus in Victorian forests: history, distribution, management and control. *Lands and Forests Bulletin* 31, 33.

McCool, S.R. (1978) Snowmobiles, animals and man: interactions and management issues. *Transactions of North American Wildlife and Natural Resources Conference* 43, 140–148.

McCool, S.F. (1981) Off-road vehicles in National Park areas: some information needs. *Leisure Sciences* 4, 343–354.

McLellan, B.N. (1989) Dynamics of a grizzly bear population during a period of industrial resource extraction. II Mortality rates and causes of death. *Canadian Journal of Zoology* 67, 1861–1864.

McLellan, B.N. and Shackleton, D.M. (1989) Immediate reactions of grizzly bears to human activities. *Wildlife Society Bulletin* 17, 269–274.

Mech, L.D. (1989) Wolf population survival in an area of high road density. *American Midland Naturalist* 121, 387–389.

Meinecke, P. (1928) *The Effect of Excessive Tourist Travel on the California Redwood Parks.* California Department of Nature and Resources, Division of Parks, Sacramento, California.

Melvin, S.M., Hecht, A. and Griffin, C.R. (1994) Piping plover mortalities caused by off-road vehicles on Atlantic coast beaches. *Wildlife Society Bulletin* 22, 409–414.

Milchunas, D.G., Schulz, K.A. and Shaw, R.B. (2000) Plant community structure in relation to long-term disturbance by mechanized military maneuvers in a semiarid region. *Environmental Management* 25, 525–539.

Montgomery, D. (1994) Road surface drainage, channel initiation, and slope instability. *Water Resources Research* 30, 192–193.

Nakata, J.K. (1983) Off-road vehicle destabilization of hill slopes: the major contributing factor of destructive debris flows in Ogden, Utah. In: Webb, R.H. and Wilshire, H.G. (eds) *Environmental Effects of Off-Road Vehicles: Impacts and Management in Arid Regions.* Springer, New York.

Newell, G. and Wilson, B.A. (1993) The relationship between cinnamon fungus (*Phytophthora cinnamomi*) and the abundance of *Antechinus stuartii* (Dasyuridae: Marsupialia) in the Brisbane Ranges, Victoria. *Wildlife Research* 20, 251–259.

Newsome, D., Moore, S. and Dowling, R. (2002) *Natural Areas Tourism: Ecology, Impacts and Management.* Channel View, Clevedon, UK.

Newton, J. and Pugh-Thomas, M. (1979) The effects of trampling on the soil Acari and Collembola of a heathland. *International Journal of Environmental Studies* 13, 219–223.

Oetting, R.B. and Cassel, J.F. (1971) Waterfowl nesting on interstate highway right-of-way in North Dakota. *Journal of Wildlife Management* 35, 774–781.

Onyeanusi, A.E. (1986) Measurements of impact of tourist off-road driving on grasslands in Masai Mara National Reserve, Kenya: a simulation approach. *Environmental Conservation* 13, 325–329.

Oxley, D.J., Fenton, M.B. and Carmody, G.R. (1974) The effects of roads on populations of small mammals. *Journal of Applied Ecology* 11, 51–59.

Palacios, E. and Mellink, E. (1996) Status of the Least Tern in the Gulf of California. *Journal of Field Ornithology* 67, 48–58.

Paquet, P.C. and Callaghan, C. (1996) Effects of linear developments on winter movements of grey wolves in the Bow River Valley of Banff National Park, Alberta. In: Evink, G.L., Garret, P., Zeigler, D. and Berry, J. (eds) *Trends in Addressing Transportation Related Wildlife Mortality.* Report No. FL-ER-58-96, Florida Department of Transportation, Tallahassee, Florida, pp. 51–73.

Pfister, C., Harrington, B.A. and Lavine, M. (1992) The impact of human disturbance on shorebirds at a migration staging area. *Biological Conservation* 60, 115–126.

Piearce, T.G. (1984) Earthworm populations in soils disturbed by trampling. *Biological Conservation* 29, 241–252.

Pojar, T.M., Prosence, R.A., Reed, D.F. and Woodard, T.N. (1975) Effectiveness of a lighted, animated deer crossing sign. *Journal of Wildlife Management* 39, 87–91.

Popendorf, W. and Wenk, H. (1983) Chrysotile asbestos in a vehicular recreation area: a case study. In: Webb, R.H. and Wilshire, H.G. (eds) *Environmental Effects of Off-road Vehicles: Impacts and Management in Arid Regions.* Springer-Verlag, New York, pp. 375–396.

Priskin, J. (2003) Physical impacts of four-wheel drive related tourism and recreation in a semi-arid, natural coastal environment. *Ocean and Coastal Management* 46, 127–155.

Reijnen, R., Foppen, R., Ter Braak, D. and Thissen, J. (1995) The effects of car traffic on breeding bird populations in woodland. III. Reduction of density in relation to the proximity of main roads. *Journal of Applied Ecology* 32, 187–202.

Reijnen, R., Foppen, R. and Meeuwsen, H. (1996) The effects of traffic on the density of breeding birds in Dutch agricultural grasslands. *Biological Conservation* 75, 255–260.

Rice, R.M. and Lewis, J. (1991) Estimating erosion risks associated with logging and forest roads in northwestern California. *Water Resources Bulletin* 27, 809–818.

Richens, V.B. and Lavigne, G.R. (1978) Response of white-tailed deer to snowmobiles and snowmobile trails in Maine. *Canadian Field Naturalist* 94, 131–138.

Rickard, C.A., McLachlan, A. and Kerley, G.I. (1994) The effects of vehicular and pedestrian traffic on dune vegetation in South Africa. *Ocean and Coastal Management* 23, 225–247.

Rickard, W.E. and Brown, J. (1974) Effects of vehicles on Arctic tundra. *Environmental Conservation* 1, 5562.

Rickard, W.E. and Slaughter, C.W. (1973) Thaw and erosion on vehicular trails in permafrost landscapes. *Journal of Soil and Water Conservation* 28, 263–266.

Romin, L.A. and Bissonette, J.A. (1996) Temporal and spatial distribution of highway mortality of mule deer on newly constructed roads at Lordanelle Reservoir, Utah. *Great Basin Naturalist* 56, 1–11.

Ross, J.B. (1992) Impacts of all-terrain vehicles on bogs of the Cape Breton Highlands, Nova Scotia, Canada. In: Willison, J.H.M., Bondrup-Nielson, S., Drysdale, C., Herman, C.T.B., Munro, N.W.P. and Pollock, T.L. (eds) *Science and Management of Protected Areas*. Elsevier, New York, pp. 533–534.

Rost, G.R. and Bailey, J.A. (1979) Distribution of mule deer and elk in relation to roads. *Journal of Wildlife Management* 60, 363–368.

Schmid, W.D. (1970) Modification of the subnivean microclimate by snowmobiles. In: Haugen, A.O. (ed.) *Proceedings, Symposium on Snow and Ice in Relation to Wildlife*. Iowa Cooperative Wildlife Research Unit, Iowa State University, pp. 251–257.

Schmidt, W. (1989) Plant dispersal by motor cars. *Vegetatio* 80, 147–152.

Shearer, B.L. and Dillon, M. (1996) Impact and disease centre characteristics of *Phytophthora cinnamomi* infestations of *Banksia* woodlands on the Swan Coastal Plain, Western Australia. *Australian Journal of Botany* 44, 79–90.

Singer, F.J. (1978) Behaviour of mountain goats in relation to US Highway 2, Glacier National Park, Montana. *Journal of Wildlife Management* 42, 591–597.

Slaughter, C.W., Racine, C.H., Walker, D.A., Johnson, L.A. and Abele, G. (1990) Use of off-road vehicles and mitigation of effects in Alaska permafrost environments: a review. *Environmental Management* 14, 63–72.

Stebbins, R.C. (1990) A desert at the crossroads.

California Academy of Sciences, Pacific Discovery. 32, 3–16.

Steiner, A.J. and Leatherman, S.P. (1981) Recreational impacts on the distribution of ghost crabs *Ocypode quadrata* Fab. *Biological Conservation* 20, 111–122.

Swanson, F.J. and Dyrness, C.T. (1975) Impact of clear-cutting and road construction on soil erosion by landslides in the western Cascade Range, Oregon. *Geology* 3, 393–396.

Turton, S.M. and Goosem, M.W. (2001) Environmental impacts of linear infrastructure and service corridors in the Wet Tropics of Queensland World Heritage Area. In: Buckley, R.C. (ed.) *Abstracts, Fenner Conference 2001, Nature Tourism and the Environment*. Canberra, Australia.

Tyler, N.J.C. (1991) Short-term behavioural responses of Svalbard reindeer *Rangifer tarandus platyrhynchus* to direct provocation by snowmobiles. *Biological Conservation* 56, 179–194.

Van der Merwe, D. (1988) *The Effects of Off-road Vehicles (ORV's) on Coastal Ecosystems – a Review*. Institute for Coastal Research, University of Port Elizabeth, Port Elizabeth, South Africa.

Van der Merwe, D. and Van der Merwe, D. (1991) Effects of off-road vehicles on the macrofauna of a sandy beach. *South African Journal of Science* 87, 210–213.

van Dyke, F.B., Brocke, R.H., Shaw, H.G., Ackerman, B.B., Hemker, T.P. and Lindzey, F.G. (1986) Reactions of mountain lions to logging and human activity. *Journal of Wildlife Management* 50, 95–102.

Vollmer, A.T., Maza, B.G., Medica, P.A., Turner, F.B. and Bamberg, S.A. (1976) The impact of off-road vehicles on a desert ecosystem. *Environmental Management* 1, 115–129.

Vos, C.C. (1997) Effects of road density: a case study of the moor frog. In: Canters, K. (ed.) *Habitat Fragmentation and Infrastructure*. Ministry of Transport Public Works and Water Management, Delft, The Netherlands, pp. 93–97.

Wace, N. (1977) Assessment of dispersal of plant species – the car-borne flora in Canberra. *Proceedings of the Ecological Society of Australia* 10, 167–186.

Wade, K. (2000) *Record of Decision: Winter Use Plans for the Yellowstone and Grand Teton National Parks and John D. Rockefeller Jr. Memorial Parkway*. US Department of the Interior National Parks Service Intermountain Region, Ogden, Utah, USA.

Walker, D.A. and Walker, M.D. (1991) History and pattern of disturbance in Alaskan Arctic terrestrial ecosystems: a hierarchical approach to analysing landscape change. *Journal of Applied Ecology* 28, 244–276.

Watson, J.J., Kerley, G.I.H. and McLachlan, A. (1996) Human activity and potential impacts on dune breeding birds in the Alexandria Coastal Dunefield. *Landscape and Urban Planning* 34, 315–322.

Weaver, T. and Dale, D. (1978) Trampling effects of hikers, motorcycles and horses in meadows and forests. *Journal of Applied Ecology* 15, 451–457.

Webb, R.H. (1982) Off-road motorcycle effects on a desert soil. *Environmental Conservation* 9, 197–208.

Webb, R.H. (1983) Compaction of desert soils by off-road vehicles. In: Webb, R.H. and Wilshire, H.G. (eds) *Environmental Effects of Off-road Vehicles: Impact and Management in Arid Regions*. Springer, New York, pp. 51–80.

Webb, R.H. and Wilshire, H.G. (1980) Recovery of soils and vegetation in a Mojave Desert ghost town, Nevada, USA. *Journal of Arid Environments* 3, 291–303.

Webb, R.H. and Wilshire, H.G. (1983) *Environmental Effects of Off-road Vehicles*. Springer, New York.

Webb, R.H., Ragland, H.C., Godwin, W.H. and Jenkins, D. (1978) Environmental effects of soil property changes with off-road vehicle use. *Environmental Management* 2, 219–233.

Webb, R.H., Wilshire, H.G. and Henry, M.A. (1983) Natural recovery of soils and vegetation following human disturbance. In: Webb, R.H. and Wilshire, H.G. (eds) *Environmental Effects of Off-road Vehicles: Impact and Management in Arid Regions*. Springer, New York, pp. 279–302.

Westhoff, V. (1967) The ecological impact of pedestrian, equestrian, and vehicular traffic on vegetation. *IUCN Naturalist* 10, 218–223.

Whisler, F.D., Engle, C.F. and Baughman, N.M. (1965) *The Effects of Soil Compaction on Nitrogen Transformations in the Soil*. Agricultural Experimental Bulletin No. 516T, West Virginia State University, West Virginia.

Wilkinson, T. (1995) Snowed under. *National Parks* 69, 32–36.

Wilkinson, T. (1999) Bear necessities. *Audubon* 101, 54–61.

Wilshire, H.G. (1989) *Human Causes of Wind Erosion in California's Desert*. The Desert Protective Council Inc., Palm Springs, California.

Wilshire, H.R. and Nakata, J.K. (1976) Off-road vehicle effects on California's Mojave Desert. *California Geology* 29, 123–132.

Wilshire, H.G., Nakata, J.K., Shipley, S. and Prestegaard, K. (1978) Vehicle impacts on natural terrain at seven sites in the San Francisco Bay area. *Environmental Geology* 2, 295–319.

Wilson, J.P. and Seney, J.P. (1994) Erosional impact of hikers, horses, motorcycles, and off-road bicycles on mountain trails in Montana. *Mountain Research and Development* 14, 77–88.

Witherington, B.E. (1997) The problem of photopollution for sea turtles and other nocturnal animals. In: Clemmons, J.R. and Buchholz, R. (eds) *Behavioural Approaches to Conservation in the Wild*. Cambridge University Press, Cambridge, UK, pp. 303–325.

Wolcott, T.G. and Wolcott, D.L. (1984) Impact of off-road vehicles on macroinvertebrates of a mid-Atlantic beach. *Biological Conservation* 29, 217–240.

Woodward, B. (1995) Drive to get bush bashers back on track. *GEO Australasia* 17, 24–36.

Wright, S. (1989) A review of the impacts of recreation on vegetation. In: *Proceedings of the Leisure Studies Association Annual Conference*, 24–26 April 1987, Bournemouth, UK, pp. 86–101.

Yalden, P.E. and Yalden, D.W. (1990) Recreational disturbance of breeding golden plovers *Pluvialis apricarius*. *Biological Conservation* 51, 243–262.

Yorks, T.P., West, N.E., Mueller, R.J. and Warren, S.D. (1997) Toleration of traffic by vegetation: life form conclusions and summary extracts for a comprehensive data base. *Environmental Management* 21, 121–131.

Yur'eva, N.D., Matyeva, V.G. and Trapido, I.L. (1976) Influence of recreation on soil invertebrate groups in birch woods round Moscow. *Lesovedenie* 2, 27–34.

7

Impacts of Tourboats in Marine Environments

Jan Warnken and Troy Byrnes

International Centre for Ecotourism Research, Griffith University, Queensland, Australia

Introduction

Travellers and tourists have always been attracted to seaside destinations, and their numbers have grown, and continue to grow, since the onset of mass tourism in the early 1900s. Most seaside visitors generally only wish to explore the foreshore area and its beaches; however, a considerable number of visitors still like to expand their activity spectrum by including one or several boat trips in their travel itinerary. In Australia alone, the tour boat industry generated 400,000 trips worth Aus$850 million (based on a survey of 150 operators from seven major destinations, and a conservative estimate of 1500 operators Australia-wide) (Byrnes, unpublished data 2002). Accordingly, marine boat tours represent a prominent sector within the tourism industry, not only in Australia, but probably also in other countries around the world known for their seaside resorts, dive spots, fishing grounds or sailing areas.

The main product of this sector is, in most cases, heavily dependent on the quality of its non-transferable assets, i.e. near-shore coastal waters and their biota. The majority of marine tour operators rely on one or more launching points close to their resident destination, and one or more natural attractions that are: (i) located within a day's travel distance; and (ii) usually limited in extent (e.g. coral reefs) or limited in yield (e.g. fishing grounds). Under such

scenarios, a small number of trips per year would, in the vast majority of cases, cause little threat to the integrity of these natural assets. In practice, however, economic factors require operators, particularly those running a large vessel, to offer as many trips as possible: depending on demand and weather conditions, up to several trips per day for 7 days per week. The resulting number of frequent visits to sites limited in extent and/or yield may eventually put parts or sections of near-shore ecosystems or species under such stress that their ecological status deteriorates to an extent where recovery during off-peak seasons is no longer possible. Ultimately, this would result not only in loss of an area of (usually rare) habitat or a rare species, it would also result in the loss of the primary attraction that generated the demand for the tourboat business in the first place.

Furthermore, most tourboat operators offer activities, sites and/or vessels similar to those enjoyed by recreational users, i.e. boat owners who have no commercial interests in their operations. This triple overlap often makes it impossible to separate impacts of tourist vessels from those of recreational vessels. Accordingly, this review tries to: (i) characterize tourboat operators and their impacts based on technical knowledge and information collected from interviews with Australian operators in seven geographical regions; and (ii) summarize cases published in the peer-reviewed scientific literature that describe impacts of any vessel, or vessels, similar to those used by tourist operators.

Scope

This chapter considers the most common vessels operated by, or for, tourists in near-shore coastal waters, i.e. medium to small boats ranging from sea kayaks to >300 passenger high-speed catamarans. At one extreme of the spectrum, surfboards, windsurfers and kite surfers are excluded because they resemble sporting equipment rather than vessels. At the other extreme, ferries and ocean liners are excluded because their impacts are considered to be similar to those of large commercial vessels (except for solid wastes and sewage), they often operate in international waters, are part of the major international shipping fleet and are therefore regulated by the International Maritime Organization (IMO) under MARPOL 73/78 and other treaties. Vessels used for ferry services as part of a regional public transport network were also excluded from this review, even though many of these vessels are also popular with tourists (e.g. Sydney Harbour ferries, New York City ferries, Hong Kong ferries).

From a more practical point of view, this chapters focuses only on impacts that are directly associated with operating vessels, and not on impacts that can originate from tourist activities *per se*, e.g. snorkelling and diving (fin damage to corals) or fishing (depletion of stocks). Alleviating such impacts is considered the primary responsibility of the owner of the tourism business rather than the master or owner of a vessel used for such tourism operations.

Types of Tourist Vessels

The majority of tourism vessels reviewed in this chapter are used for short trips or day trips to one or more locations/areas that are visited regularly, i.e. up to a maximum of 7 days per week several times/day (weather permitting) during peak season. Only houseboats and bareboat charter vessels are used for periods of up to 1 or 2 weeks (Table 7.1). Typically, many operators establish their business using a single port or

marina or a few launching ramps/beaches close to a well-known coastal destination. Others, particularly those who own or operate large vessels, can diversify their activities by providing services for the fishing industry or moving to another location. Overall, however, their activities can be characterized as summarized in Table 7.1 and detailed below.

Kayaks (mostly specialized sea kayaks) are only suitable for travel in sheltered coastal waters, unless they are taken for extreme tours. Such tours are less common, due to a very limited number of qualified customers and high insurance premiums. Under normal circumstances, kayaks, hired for group tours or individual trips, can be transported by car (on roof racks or a small trailer) and launched from any sheltered beach or ramp. These vessels have no onboard facilities and rely mostly on paddles for propulsion (small sails can be used though). Accordingly, tourists have to be reasonably fit and dedicated to a 'nature-based' experience. As a result, the use of these vessels is not widespread.

Sailing catamarans and dinghies are popular resort vessels with no onboard facilities and are offered for beach hire on an hourly or half-daily basis. The use of these vessels is limited to calm conditions and, usually, a narrowly defined near-shore area. This is to avoid excessive wear and tear on equipment and to prevent lesser-experienced clients from being blown offshore in adverse wind conditions. If not in use, most vessels are kept up on the beach and out of the water.

Personal water crafts (PWCs), also widely known as 'jet skis', have become an increasingly popular recreational vessel over the past decade. Their powerful two-stroke engines can push these vessels along at high speeds and, therefore, users are required to wear protective equipment such as a life vest and, in some countries, a helmet. PWCs are hired on an hourly or half-daily basis mostly for use in a narrowly defined area, or for guided group tours. Apart from small storage compartments, these vessels provide no onboard facilities and, therefore, most trips are taken to enjoy the ride rather than to use the vessel for another activity (e.g. fishing or diving). Most PWCs can be transported on a trailer pulled by an ordinary family car and are mostly refuelled and maintained at

Table 7.1. Basic operational characteristics of common types/classes of tourism vessels in Australia.

Type of vessel	Principal method of propulsion	Passengers/ operators per vessel	Types of trip	Type of operation
Kayak, canoe, sea kayak	Paddle	1–2	Half-day, full-day paddle tours in groups or in single	Self-skippered, mostly inshore or protected open waters
Small sailing catamaran or dinghy	Sail	1–2	1 hour to half-day sailing trips	Self-skippered, inshore, protected waters, usually confined to small area
Personal water craft (PWC)	Two-stroke engine, jet	1–2	1 hour to half-day sightseeing and trips and speed runs, some guided tours	Self-skippered or skippered, usually confined to small area
Outboard tinny and half-cabin cruiser	Two-stroke and four-stroke outboard engine	1–4	Half-day to full-day fishing or sightseeing trips	Self-skippered, inshore, protected waters
Semi-rigid inflatable (SRI)	Two-stroke and four-stroke outboard engine	8–12 (15)	Half-day to full-day dive tours, some megafauna watching	Skippered, mostly near-shore in protected open waters
Sailing yacht (bare-boat charters)	Sail, inboard diesel engine, some outboards	2–6 (8)	Full day to >1 week, sailing trips	Self-skippered or skippered, protected open waters
Speedboat	Two-stroke outboard engine, inboard diesel or four-stroke	2–8 (10)	1 or 2 hours to half-day parasailing trips or speed runs	Skippered, inshore, occasionally open protected waters
Houseboat	Two-stroke outboard engine, inboard diesel	4–10 (12)	Usually >1 day to 1 week	Self-skippered, protected waters
Flybridge fishing cruiser	Inboard diesel	6–10 (12)	Half-day to full-day fishing trips (occasionally overnight, e.g. for game fishing)	Skippered, no restrictions
Ex-commercial fishing vessel, purpose-built dive boat, etc.	Inboard diesel	8–15 (20)	Half-day to full-day (some 2–4 days) fishing or whale watching (whale shark swimming) tours	Skippered, no restrictions
Catamaran registered for around 300 to 400 passengers, incl. high-speed (wave-piercing) vessels	Inboard diesel, jet propelled	50–400	Half-day to full-day pleasure or party cruises, dive and whale-watching tours	Skippered, no restrictions

Note: numbers in parentheses represent maximum values.

petrol stations and workshops located through-out urban built-up areas.

Fishing boats (typically tinnies or half-cabin cruisers with small outboard engines), represent the vast majority of small vessels in most coastal areas with some sheltered waterways. In windy conditions, they are uncomfortable to ride, and they provide only very limited onboard facilities. The stereotypical type of use for this vessel is a fishing trip when either two or more friends, or a small family, hires such a vessel for half a day or a day of exploring unknown fishing grounds while on holidays. Operators can pull smaller vessels in this category (tinnies) up on a beach and out of the water when not in use, whereas the larger half-cabin cruisers are usually kept on a swing mooring somewhere near the operator's rental office. Until the turn of this century, most of the small fishing vessels in this class used fuel-inefficient two-stroke outboard engines for a better power to weight ratio and reliability under saltwater stress. Modern four-stroke designs have overcome most of these problems, and regulating authorities in many parts of the world (notably the USA) are increasingly banning the use of two-stroke outboard engines on confined water bodies.

Semi-rigid inflatables (SRIs) are very popular with dive operators. If well-maintained and operated by a skilled master, these vessels are almost unsinkable. SRIs with two outboard engines (mostly two-strokes) are reliable enough to take dive tourists out to a sheltered location, even if they have to pass through conditions that would be off limits for most other small tour-boats. Apart from tank racks, these vessels provide no other onboard facilities and are primarily used for short trips to a near-shore dive site, where they are anchored or tied to a fixed swing mooring. Upon return, SRIs can be pulled on to a trailer and cleaned and serviced near the operator's dive shop.

Speedboats are best characterized by their powerful inboard or outboard engines in relation to a comparatively small hull and low weight. These vessels are used by many operators for water skiing, parasailing and general speedboat thrill tours. High-speed runs on water are usually uncomfortable and also use large amounts of fuel. Therefore, speedboat trips are mostly short: passengers are either transported back to land via smaller vessels

(parasailing) or boats simply return to their base after half an hour or 1 hour, to pick up new passengers. Accordingly, onboard facilities are not required. However, speedboats have one major advantage: if used regularly, they don't require antifouling, even if moored in a wet berth. The forces created by a hull being pushed over, and slammed on to, the water's surface are enough to clean the hull of most thin-layered biofilms.

Sailing yachts, including catamarans and motor yachts of about 30 ft (9.1 m) and more in length overall (LOA), are the preferred vessels for bareboat charters in near-shore open waters. Vessels in this category allow parties of 2–8, or even 12, people to hire a yacht for several days of exploring coastal islands or estuaries within about a radius of 20–40 nautical miles from the operator's base, i.e. the average distance of a 1- or 2-day sailing trip during daylight hours. For safety, licensing and insurance reasons, vessels are usually set up to limit speeds to less than 10 knots. Onboard facilities, such as galleys with stoves and sinks, refrigerators, showers, toilets and bed spaces, are the norm for any competitive bareboat vessel. The majority of customers hire vessels for more than 1 day. Accordingly, onboard facilities are used many times during an average trip. Most use is likely to occur in protected anchorages: customers take out a bareboat for a holiday trip where comfort is paramount and, therefore, prefer areas where many such anchor sites are available in a 10–20 nautical mile sailing distance, i.e. for lunch breaks and overnight stays. Famous examples of bareboat areas are found amongst the Caribbean Islands, in the Mediterranean Sea along the former Yugoslavian coast, Turkey, and Greece, and around Australia's Whitsunday Islands. All vessels in this category are too large and heavy to be pulled out of the water if not in use: they all require antifouling and sacrificial anodes to protect propeller shafts, rudders, steel keels, etc. when moored in a wet berth.

Fly-bridge cruisers are the preferred vessel for off-shore fishing tour operators, including game fishing expeditions targeting tuna, mackerel, blue marlin and other sailfish species. The main advantages of these vessels is their speed, the extra space and height of their fly-bridge and the open space around the stern. By steering the vessel from the fly bridge, operators can provide additional space for their customers in the main cabin while gaining a good view to spot fish activity (e.g. predator species feeding on schools of bait fish). The vessel's speed can be used to check a large area, or number of distant spots, to increase the customers' chances of catching a fish on a single trip, even if the numbers of target species of legal size are low. Most vessels have onboard facilities such as galleys, toilets and bed spaces. When at a destination, vessels are often left to drift rather than kept at anchor: the vessel has to be ready in case someone on board catches a large fish that starts to fight. To prevent the line from snapping, the vessel has to be moved towards the fish until it has tired and can be lifted on board. Unless hired for large game fishing expeditions, most operators offer half-day, day or night trips.

Ex-commercial fishing vessels, such as line fishing working boats or decommissioned trawlers, or even purpose-built tourist vessels, are often multipurpose vessels for large parties (up to 20 or more). They can be used for diving or fishing trips, sight seeing, whale and whale shark tours, or even surfing tours. During the off-season, these vessels are either moved to another destination, or they are used again as commercial fishing vessels (provided their owners or operators maintain their appropriate licences). Their overall design prohibits planing, which usually limits their top speed to around 20 knots. Onboard facilities are similar to those of fly-bridge cruisers, but usually not very luxurious. Whether operators on these vessels drop anchor during a trip depends on the area visited and the trip's purpose. Furthermore, large vessels in this category could still be using tributyltin (TBT)-based paints for antifouling, depending on local regulations and their enforcement.

Multilevel, large catamarans, with a capacity for 300 or more passengers, have become an increasingly popular vessel for mass tourism operations. A number of these vessels operate in the Great Barrier Reef Marine Park to carry tourists to snorkelling and coral-viewing sites, others are used for sight-seeing or party tours, and even whale-watching trips. Some are modified to improve certain aspects of their performance (e.g. wave-piercing hull designs for high-speed travel in open waters). In general, their double hull design provides for a lot of usable space and good fuel economy, even at higher speed.

Onboard facilities include several toilets, one or even several food outlets or restaurants, and seating, entertainment and party facilities. The overall investment in such a vessel and its crew forces operators to run tours every day, unless weather or technical issues prevent this. Similar to line fishing working boats or trawlers, large tourist catamarans may be antifouled with TBT-based paints, again depending on local regulations (see below for more discussion). Where vessels have to anchor at their trip's destination, operators in Australia are, more often than not, required to install fixed swing moorings.

Risks of Causing Impacts

Numerous studies have investigated the effects that could originate from operating a recreational boat and, similarly, a tourism vessel (for summaries see Chmura and Ross, 1978; Liddle and Scorgie, 1980; Arthington and Mosisch, 1998). Many studies were conducted for lakes and reservoirs or river systems, but, in principle, most of their results are applicable to the marine environment. In theory, vessels can cause impacts to components of the natural and human environment in a number of ways, including:

1. Emitting or releasing polluting substances: heavy metals [mainly copper (Cu) and zinc (Zn)], organometal compounds (e.g. TBT) and booster algicides (e.g. Irgarol 1051) from either antifouling paints or sacrificial anodes; oil and fuel from small engine leaks and spills during refills; CO_2, NO_x and other unburned fuel residues from combustion engines (Jüttner *et al.*, 1995a,b; Tjärnlund *et al.*, 1995).
2. Causing direct physical damage through propeller cuts; dislocation of bottom substrates, corals, etc. by pulling up anchors and accidental groundings; re-suspension of sediments from scouring of anchor chains and propeller or vessel wash; and destruction of shore banks from vessel wash.
3. Disturbance of natural behavioural patterns of sensitive species, thereby causing additional strain on energy budgets when triggering flight responses and increased alertness.
4. Visual interference by placing man-made high-tech items into otherwise little-developed natural scenery.

5. Emission of extensive noise, mostly from inboard or outboard engines.

From an operator's or boat user's point of view, a trip on a tourist vessel can be broken up into three sections, each with its own types and risks of causing an impact:

1. Mooring at, and launching from or near, the operator's base.
2. Travel to and from destination.
3. Staying at destination.

Other impacts can evolve from maintenance work and emergency situations. However, these are not part of routine operations and not considered further here.

The magnitude of impacts associated with a particular category of tourism vessel (see Table 7.1) depends on the number of incidents and the concentration of pollutants emitted per area or volume of water, the resilience and health of the ecosystem or the flushing rate of the water body affected, and, in the case of pollutants, the concentration of neutralizing agents (e.g. particulate organic matter) present (see Equations 7.1 and 7.2). In the marine environment, all these parameters change with time, notably through monthly variations in tidal prisms, wind conditions and general seasonal changes (e.g. wet versus dry season). In other terms, long-term effects depend on the time during which disturbances or pollution events occur and the recovery period between two consecutive events.

$$
\begin{aligned}
&\text{Magnitude of impact}_{\text{(disturbances)}} = \\
&F(\text{incidents, 1/area, 1/resilience} \\
&\text{(or health) of ecosystem (or species)} \\
&\text{affected, } t)
\end{aligned}
\qquad 7.1
$$

$$
\begin{aligned}
&\text{Magnitude of impact}_{\text{(pollutants)}} = \\
&F([\text{pollutant emitted}], 1/\text{volume,} \\
&1/\text{flushing rate, 1/[neutralizing} \\
&\text{agents], } t)
\end{aligned}
\qquad 7.2
$$

In order to characterize the types and impacts of tourboat operations in Australia, a database of operators was compiled from listings in phone books, the Australian Charter Guide and the Tour Finder website of the Department of Conservation and Land Man-

agement (CALM). Entries from this database were summarized based on postcodes, and subsequently displayed on a geographic information system (GIS) map identifying tourism hotspots for different geographical regions (T. Byrnes, PhD thesis, Griffith University, Australia). Boat operators were then surveyed in seven major nodes: Melbourne, Sydney, Gold Coast/Moreton Bay, Whitsundays, Cairns, Broome and Exmouth. Seven hundred and fifty operators were selected randomly from the database and either interviewed directly or asked by postal survey to reply to a questionnaire almost identical to that used during interviews. Furthermore, *in situ* environmental performance audits were conducted for another 40 operators. Information obtained from 50 interviews, 100 questionnaires and 40 audits collected over a 3-year period at seven different geographical regions around Australia's 35,000 km coastline (including remote, subtropical dive and whale-shark-viewing destinations and a major urban centre in a temperate climate), was used, together with the relationships shown in Equations 7.1 and 7.2, to develop impact risk assessment tables for each of the three major sections of boat trips in marine coastal areas (for Tables 7.2–7.4 see Appendix). The data collected from tourboat operators included information about the size and type of their vessels and engines, on board facilities and waste management, fouling and corrosion management, the number of trips and number of persons on board for different times of the year, their primary activity and the overall size of their business. This quantitative information was condensed to develop categories for impact frequencies and extent as shown in Tables 7.2–7.4.

Potential impacts associated with vessels using mooring or launching sites

Without any environmental control and management measures, impacts from pollution, visual interference and noise are likely to be highest at or near purpose-built mooring (e.g. marinas) and launching (e.g. boat ramps) sites. In these areas, boat density is highest, spatial extent limited, and depth shallow, and all activities happen close to the water/land boundary, which often provides a variety of sensitive habitats. Almost all vessels, from yachts to large catamarans, have to be moored in a wet berth and are therefore antifouled and fitted with sacrificial anodes (Table 7.2). As a result, their submersed structures release copper (Cu) at a rate of $3.8\,\mu g/cm^2/day$ to $65\,\mu g/cm^2/day$ (Valkirs *et al.*, 2003), algicides such as Irgarol 1051, and zinc (Zn). Depending on the flushing rate of the marina or boat harbour, the concentration of these substances could build up to levels that could eventually cause acute or chronic toxic effects to sensitive species. Furthermore, mooring and launching sites are selected or built to provide shelter against wind and wave action and currents. During periods of low boating activity, such calm waters allow fine particles, together with other substances adhering to them, to precipitate and, hence, act as a sink for such materials. Accordingly, heavy metals washed off trailers, or Cu and Zn released from antifouling paints and sacrificial anodes, can accumulate in sediments, which, in turn, can be released through resuspension from propeller wash to add to already elevated levels of pollutants. As mentioned previously, these types of impacts are typical examples of situations where it is impossible to distinguish between impacts from tourism vessels and those from recreational vessels.

The use of detergents for cleaning the galley, toilets and other onboard facilities, etc. when preparing a vessel for its next customer(s) cannot be avoided by any tourism operator who provides vessels with such facilities (Table 7.2). Whether these wastes are then released into marina waters depends on the existence and, ultimately, use of holding tanks and on-shore pump-out facilities. Although regulatory authorities in many parts of the world try to increase construction and use of these facilities, only very few (almost none) were easily available to, and therefore used by, tourism operators in Australia up until the beginning of 2002 (T. Byrnes, personal observation 1999–2002).

Smaller incidents of pollution can occur where vessels are refuelled (tanks spill over, or inadequate equipment is used, e.g. not using funnels when refilling from spare tanks that cannot be hooked up to fuel lines) or where minor repair works are conducted. Mooring and launching sites are the most likely areas

that could be subject to such activities (Table 7.2) because they provide refuelling berths, or access to spare parts and mechanical tools that are kept in cars or available at a boat chandlery. The number of such incidents is likely to be correlated to the skills and experience of the boat or fuel berth operator, and the management requirements of the mooring area. The overall amounts of fuel released during each incident are probably small (unless vessel operators act recklessly): operators would be overseeing refuelling and small repair works and, in case of minor accidents, they would intervene. Similar impacts from bilge pump-outs should be rare because such activities are prohibited in most mooring sites, unless a vessel takes in water as a result of an emergency situation.

Solid wastes, such as empty food and beverage containers and other packaging materials, accumulate during most boat trips and need to be discarded when returning to the vessel's mooring or launching site. The exceptions are trips on smaller craft lasting only a couple of hours, e.g. a sail on a small sailing catamaran or dinghy or a PWC. In most cases, operators take all wastes that haven't been lost during the trip off board and discard them in rubbish bins or containers commonly provided at mooring and boat launching sites. One notable exemption is a group of canoes and sea kayaks: these vessels can be launched from any beach that provides car access. Such beach areas may not necessarily have rubbish collection facilities that can cope with a large group of such vessels returning from a longer trip (see Table 7.2).

Disturbance of species is considered rare in mooring or boat-launching places, because most of the more vulnerable species would have either become locally extinct or moved on and left these places, leaving only species that are more adapted to human activities.

Perhaps the largest impacts on the human resident population, and often most controversial ones when it comes to proposals for new boat facilities, are visual impacts and noise. Tall above-deck structures such as masts, antennae, fishing equipment, etc. can be seen from many viewpoints along a coastline, and create a stark contrast against its natural coastal settings. Equally, or even more, annoying for people that are not enthusiastic about boats, is the clatter and noise from loose running gear and the howling noise created by strong winds passing masts, stays, fishing rods, etc. During busy holiday periods and weekends, noise from starting and warming-up engines or, even worse, from flushing out cooling water from outboard engines, adds to the overall noise spectrum. The overall magnitude of such impacts is usually a result of the combined effects from commercial (including tourism) and recreational vessels.

Potential impacts associated with vessels in transit

For many marine tours, the actual time that a vessel is in transit, i.e. moving in open or sheltered waters, constitutes the main reason for undertaking such a tour (e.g. sea kayaking, jet skiing, sailing, etc.). For all other types of tours, time in transit is essential to get to or from a destination, either a fishing spot, specific megafauna or a dive location. Accordingly, all vessels, unless under sail or being paddled, will burn fossil fuels to produce greenhouse gases such as CO_2 and NO_x. Because these gases readily disperse within the atmosphere and are unlikely to cause local effects, they add to global warming in general and are not discussed any further. Other pollutants such as Cu, Zn, algicides and toilet wastes (nutrients and pathogens) are rapidly diluted in the large volumes of water that are used by a vessel when travelling from point A to point B, and are therefore very hard to detect.

More problematic are unburnt fuel residues from two-stroke engines. These are emitted in large quantities (Jüttner et al., 1995a) and their volatile organic compounds (VOC) are highly toxic to marine organisms (Jüttner et al., 1995b; Tjärnlund et al., 1995). As a result, some countries [e.g. the USA (EPA, 1996)] started to introduce emission guidelines for new two-stroke engines, or banned these altogether from many inland water bodies. Marine tourist operators in Australia are still left with the choice to use either two- or four-stroke outboard engines. Many prefer modern direct-injected two-stroke engines for their more favourable power to weight ratio and easier maintenance. However, some have developed a liking for the greater reliability of four-stroke designs. Until late 2001, most PWCs were equipped with two-stroke engines, but enforcement of full compli-

ance with US regulations since 2001 (EPA, 1996) has encouraged manufacturers to now offer a wide range of PWCs with four-stroke engines. However, it remains unclear to what extent these trends have penetrated the current fleet of tourism vessels. The frequency of unburnt fuel release has therefore been ranked as 'always' and 'considerable' in Table 7.3.

Another aspect of pollution is associated with the release of bilge water or water from other compartments that can receive oil, fuel and other pollutants from small engine leaks, small cracks in fuel lines, etc. Most tourism vessels of the size of a 8–10 m sailing yacht or longer have bilge pumps that will be activated shortly after the vessel has left its mooring (or in some cases launching) area. In most cases, operators should want to repair engine leaks immediately, otherwise their clients could lose confidence in the vessel they hired, or that they are being taken for a trip on. As engine oil can cover large areas of a water surface, bilge pump-outs after even small leaks were considered 'minor' rather than 'negligible' (Table 7.3).

Probably the biggest issues in the long term could evolve from disturbance of native fauna, loss of habitat from shore-bank erosion through boat wakes, and accidental loss of solid wastes. In our current world economic system, recreational and tourist activities will increase, and with this, boating activities. Unless vessel speeds are widely restricted and enforced, injuries to marine wildlife as a result of boat strikes and propeller cuts will increase, and more and more shorebirds will be repelled, either through disturbances or direct loss (erosion) from habitats that are adjacent to popular boating areas. Tourism operators may make a significant contribution because of their frequent use of near-shore waterways. However, there is currently little or no quantitative information about these effects in relation to boat use intensities (e.g. trips or boats per area), and, therefore, the extent of such disturbances was classified as 'unknown' (Table 7.3). An increasing number of boat trips would also lead to an increase in chances of losing any inadequately stowed items such as food, hats, towels or packaging wastes. Again, the overall rates at which such items are lost or, even worse, negligently discarded in open waters, are largely unknown. For Table 7.3, it was assumed that most operators are aware of this problem and try to minimize the occurrence of such acts, or that the type of operation would only include so few possibilities for such loss of wastes, that these were not considered (e.g. PWCs).

Noise emitted from combustion engines on vessels in transit is one of the biggest issues that directly affects humans, i.e. mostly residents living at or near coastal waterways and other recreational users of shoreline environments. Apart from sea kayaks and small sailing vessels, all other vessels (even yachts) have to use engines and therefore emit noise (Table 7.3). In some areas, the noise from recreational vessels has become such an issue that relevant authorities banned certain vessels from some parts of their waterways. Tourist operators that predominantly operate in off-shore open waters would only add to this issue when leaving from, and returning to, their mooring sites. Others, such as operators who hire out PWCs or other small engine-driven craft or speedboats, are more likely to use near-shore sheltered waters and could become a target for complaints by residents.

Potential impacts associated with vessels at their destinations in open waters

Many marine boat trips are primarily taken to use a vessel to: (i) get to a destination; and (ii) use this vessel as a base for exploring or enjoying the surrounding marine environment, e.g. scenery, corals or coastal/marine wildlife. Other trips are taken mainly for enjoying the ride, i.e. using the vessel in transit. These are mostly PWCs and small sailing vessels and, consequently, are not considered in Table 7.4.

The majority of vessels that have reached their destination will use anchors or, if available, a fixed-swing mooring. This usually happens in calm waters, which, in turn, provides the best opportunities for passengers and crew to use onboard facilities. This includes marine toilets, food preparation facilities, showers, or whatever else is provided on board. Accordingly, this generates a mostly liquid waste stream that is released directly into the marine environment, unless the vessel is equipped with holding tanks and/or treatment facilities. Most vessels built after the year 2000 would

have such holding tanks, as required by relevant marine pollution legislation in Australia [e.g. the Transport Operations (Marine Pollution) Act 1995 Qld] or overseas. However, many tourism operators in Australia use older vessels, which are difficult to refit with holding tanks. The only places in Australia where sewage discharge limitations were strictly enforced were, until the end of 2002, the waterways around Sydney and sites under a commercial (tourism) permit in the Great Barrier Reef Marine Park (see comments, Table 7.4).

The other major impacts from vessels at their destination in open waters are associated with anchors and anchor chains. Unless vessels anchor in a spot where wind and currents are virtually non-existent, they swing around, thereby dragging their chain, and sometimes even their anchor, over the area's bottom substrate. As a result, bottom sediments are resuspended, which can lead to an increase in turbidity and additional sediment deposits on sensitive species, e.g. corals and seagrasses. Ongoing exposure to such minor, but constant, additional stress can lead to deficiencies in energy budgets and, ultimately, to changes in sessile bottom substrate communities. Inexperienced skippers also drop anchor in spots that are particularly sensitive to physical damage and destroy large sections of their communities, e.g. coral reefs. Some operators recognized these problems and, often in collaboration with relevant management authorities, installed fixed-swing moorings near sites that were frequently visited, most notably popular dive and snorkel sites. Some of the larger dive and snorkel tour operators in the Great Barrier Reef have been allowed or required to install such fixed moorings or floating pontoons at sites that are visited regularly.

Another serious threat to sessile marine organisms at destinations frequently used by tourism vessels are vessel groundings, particularly in areas used by bareboat and houseboat charters. In Australia, most bareboats can be hired without a recreational boating licence, and many first-time customers have little or no local knowledge. Accordingly, they often miscalculate tidal variations and anchor at depths that leave them stranded at low tide. In tropical waters, they are also more prone to hitting coral outcrops (e.g. bommies) that could rise suddenly, even out of waters of 10m depth at low tide. Little is known about the frequency of such events, but based on observations of houseboats and bareboats in the southern Moreton Bay and Whitsunday regions over 10 years (Warnken, personal observation 1993–2003), groundings could not be considered 'uncommon' in Table 7.4.

Another potential for conflict between different users of an anchorage is the noise from parties, loud radios and people shouting and jumping overboard. While the impact of such noise is likely to be minor on native fauna, visitors who wish to enjoy the serenity of an isolated anchor site could perceive such noises as a major nuisance (Table 7.4).

Actual Impacts of Recreational and Tourism Vessels

Pollution from antifouling paints

The concept of small to medium-sized recreational vessels having the potential to cause severe environmental impacts was first demonstrated towards the end of the 1970s, when oyster production in Arcachon Bay, France nearly collapsed because of elevated concentrations of tributyltin (TBT) in its water column and sediments (Alzieu et al., 1981–1982; Alzieu, 2000). The major reason for this drastic effect was the extreme toxicity of TBT, e.g. an LC_{50} of several 100 ng/l (lugworms), growth reduction of oyster spats at less than 10 ng/l and imposex in marine gastropods at levels of less than 1 ng/l (for a review, see Maguire, 1987; Becker and Bringezu, 1992; Cardwell et al., 1999; Alzieu, 2000). Secondly, the environmental half-life of TBT in water and sediments ranges from several hours to almost a year, depending on the type of environment and the mode of degradation (Maguire, 1987; Kawai et al., 1998). Thirdly, the bay of Arcachon hosted about 7800 pleasure craft with only limited exchange rates through a narrow channel to the Atlantic Ocean (Alzieu, 2000). Although Arcachon might have been an extreme example, similar discoveries were soon made in Great Britain (Waldock et al., 1987) and, subsequently, in many other parts of the world. As a result, the use of TBT-based antifouling paints on vessels >25 m length overall (LOA) was banned in most developed nations (e.g.

France, UK, USA, Australia) between 1982 and 1990. Since the mid-1980s a wealth of data has been collected, mapping the distribution of TBT in freshwater and marine water, sediments and practically any biota living in these environments. Even a few years after the ban of TBT on vessels <25 m, many studies found high levels of TBT in sediments and waters of marinas (often highest), boat harbours and commercial ports (Dowson et al., 1993; Fent and Hunn, 1995; Ko et al., 1995; Kubilay et al., 1996; Cardwell et al., 1999). Using imposex in female marine gastropods (e.g. dogwhelks Nucella lapillus, periwinkle Littorina littorea) as probably the most sensitive biological indicator of elevated TBT levels, indicated that, for many areas, TBT levels decreased after the ban (Evans et al., 1996; Smith, 1996; Gibson and Wilson, 2003); however, background concentrations generally remained elevated (e.g. Huet et al., 1996; Harding et al., 1999; Evans and Nicholson, 2000; Axiak et al., 2003). As a result, the International Maritime Organization (IMO) has agreed to implement regulations that should phase out the use of TBT antifouling paints for all vessels, including all tourboats, by 2008 (IMO, 2001).

Cuprous oxide, the other principal component of antifouling paints, has received less attention, mainly because of (i) higher concentrations required to result in toxic effects (e.g. Ahsanulla and Williams, 1991; Claisse and Alzieu, 1993) and (ii) a much greater potential to bind tightly to organic matter (Hall and Anderson, 1999; Voulvoulis et al., 1999). Nevertheless, elevated levels of Cu^{2+} were commonly, but not always, found in sediments and waters of marinas (Turner et al., 1997; Foerster et al., 1999; An and Kampbell, 2003) and even in those used by tourist vessels in Australia (e.g. Cairns and the Airlie Beach; Haynes and Loong, 2002). Recent investigations into in situ Cu release rates from antifouling paints suggest that small to medium-sized vessels moored for some time emit Cu^{2+} in the order of 8.2 μg/cm²/day (Valkirs et al., 2003), and not as high as 18–22 μg/cm²/day as reported previously (Thomas et al., 1999). So far, there is only limited evidence about Cu accumulation in anchorages or waterways due to boating activities (Preda and Cox, 2002).

Irgarol 1051 is an algicide now commonly

used as a substitute for TBT in antifouling paints. It has toxicity values of 136 ng/l (Hall *et al.*, 1999), and has been found at concentrations of up to 1693 ng/l in marine waters (Readman *et al.*, 1993), but usually between 14 and 1571 ng/l in Europe (Hall *et al.*, 1999) and between 12 and 144 ng/l in Japan (Okamura *et al.*, 2003). No Irgarol 1051 was detected in waters of 73 Canadian marinas (Liu *et al.*, 1999). Levels in British estuaries were similar to those in marinas, and highest at the beginning and the end of the boating season. This was considered to be the result of high initial release rates from freshly antifouled hulls in spring and, subsequently, the result of cleaning activities when boats are pulled out of the water in the autumn (Bowman *et al.*, 2003). Overall, Irgarol concentrations outside marinas seemed to be generally below levels of 'no observed effect concentration' (NOEC).

Non-antifouling pollution

Similar to antifouling paints, the need for engines to propel vessels through the water introduces another set of potentially harmful pollutants that can escape into the marine environment as a direct result of operating a vessel. Almost all of the engine-associated pollutants (fuels, lubricating oils, grease, unburnt fuel residues) are chemically similar, if not identical, to those known for land-based combustion engines. Accordingly, it is often difficult to discriminate between vessel-derived inputs and land-based inputs into coastal environments. Several studies, however, have identified the type and amount of fuel residues or additives (e.g. methyl *tert*-butyl ether, MTBE) released when operating two-stroke outboard engines (Jackivjz and Kuzminski, 1973; Gabele and Pyle, 2000) and their toxicological effects on fish (e.g. Tjärnlund *et al.*, 1995) and distribution in the water column (e.g. Mastran *et al.*, 1994; Reuter *et al.*, 1998; Zuccarello *et al.*, 2003). As a response to this, and also amendments to the Clean Air Act in the USA in the early 1990s, engine manufacturers developed improved engines with better fuel-economics and reduced emissions with regard to both unburnt residues as well as greenhouse gas outputs.

The consequences of accidental fuel spills during refuelling events are similar to those widely described for tanker accidents, but at a scale several orders of magnitude smaller. Nevertheless, elevated concentrations of aliphatic and aromatic fuel compounds have been reported for sediments near a powerboat mooring site in sheltered open waters, i.e. Green Island, Australia (Smith *et al.*, 1987). This suggests that sometimes even frequent but small accidents of small to medium-sized vessels, including tourist vessels, can be the principal source of such pollutants.

Zinc emissions from sacrificial anodes can be substantial; however, zinc levels have to be quite high to cause an effect on marine biota. Accordingly, elevated concentrations in the water and sediment have been found for two marinas in the UK (Bird *et al.*, 1996), but were reported as lower than the local Environmental Quality Standard of 40 µg/l. Further studies need to be undertaken to confirm these results for other parts of the world.

One of the most concerning types of pollution from small boats is, in the eyes of the public, the release of untreated or only partly treated sewage, particularly at sites shared by both boats and other recreationists. So far, strong evidence demonstrating a link between boating activities and faecal pollution has so far been rare in the scientific literature. Most attention has been paid to marinas or boat harbours providing permanent moorings and associated facilities, and most of the data collected is only available from commissioned reports or conference proceedings (e.g. Sawyer and Goulding, 1990; Gaines and Solow, 1990; Fisher *et al.*, 1987 – all cited in OWOW 1993; references in Milliken and Lee, 1990, p. 11; Augier *et al.*, 1984, 1985 – quoted in Guillon-Cottard *et al.*, 1998). One study in the Rhode river estuary, Maryland, USA, over one single weekend, demonstrated a link between boat numbers and faecal coliform counts in shallow waters of a narrow estuary (Faust, 1982). A more recent study in France indicated that boating activities could have an effect on faecal coliforms and faecal streptococci in *Mytilus galloprovincialis* mussels (Guillon-Cottard *et al.*, 1998).

Most of these studies used faecal or total coliforms as indicators for sewage pollution. Total coliform counts include many different non-faecal psychotrophic species (Gauthier *et al.*, 1991). Thermotolerant or faecal coliforms

(FCFs) can be isolated from the effluent of industrial paper mills and textile factories (Mates and Schaffer, 1988), and many marinas or anchorage sites are located in estuaries that receive waters which have passed urban and/or industrial discharge points (stormwater drains, licensed discharge pipes). *Escherichia coli* is thought to be a better, though not perfect, indicator of faecal contamination of water, because it is considered to be exclusively of faecal origin (Dufour and Cabelli, 1981; APHA, 1998). Indeed, more recent studies in freshwater systems indicate that even elevated *E. coli* concentrations result from sediment resuspension rather than sewage input (An *et al.*, 2002). Certainly, more research is needed in this area to improve our knowledge about the circumstances under which sewage from small to medium-sized vessels becomes a real threat to natural ecosystems and human health.

Physical damage

One of the greatest concerns about recreational, fishing and tourist vessels was the use of anchors, and accidental groundings, when moored at a destination away from their usual port or mooring area. A lot of anecdotal evidence has long been reported, with surveys of coral reefs from, for example, Florida (Davies, 1977), the Galapagos Islands (Glynn, 1994), the Philippines (McManus *et al.*, 1997), Sri Lanka (Rajasuriya *et al.*, 1998), Zanzibar (Johnstone *et al.*, 1998) and Egypt (Jameson *et al.*, 1999). Similarly, though in somewhat more detail, damage has been reported for seagrass beds in Australia (Walker *et al.*, 1989; Hastings *et al.*, 1995), the Mediterranean Sea (Francour *et al.*, 1999) and in Florida (Zieman, 1976; Dawes *et al.*, 1997). Furthermore, erosion from propeller and vessel wash has been demonstrated, assessed or reviewed for many rivers, freshwater reservoirs or estuarine systems (Moss, 1977; Liddle and Scorgie, 1980; Smart *et al.*, 1985; Nanson *et al.*, 1994; Schoellhammer, 1996; Doyle, 2001). Again, the magnitude of impacts were dependent on the type of vessel, its frequency of use, the type of sediment, coral or seagrass bed affected and, most importantly, the water depth in which the vessel was operated.

Disturbance to fauna

Many of the early research projects focused on waterfowl using inland reservoirs, lakes and river systems (e.g. Batten, 1977; Liddle and Scorgie, 1980; Tuite *et al.*, 1984), but later expanded to cover almost any type of water body and many different bird species (e.g. Mikola *et al.*, 1994; Perry and Deller, 1996; Steidi and Anthony, 1996; Galicia and Baldassarre, 1997; Mori *et al.*, 2001; Ronconi and St. Clair, 2002). It would be far beyond the scope of this chapter to review every single aspect of these disturbances, but many studies concluded that increased flushing responses (in frequency and duration) resulting from boating activities can lead to lower breeding success and, therefore, long-term ecological consequences. More drastic disturbances were reported first for Florida's manatees or sea cows (*Trichenus manatus latirostris*) (see discussion in Marmontel *et al.*, 1997; Langtimm *et al.*, 1998) and later other large marine mammals (e.g. Wells and Scott, 1997; Visser, 1999): individuals of these species were observed with deep propeller scars or found dead, presumably killed as a result of a boat collision (mostly manatees).

More recently, the rapidly increasing number of whale-watching tours have attracted the attention of a number of researchers. An earlier review suggested that response thresholds for a variable or increasing sound, e.g. an approaching boat, are low compared to steady or pulsed sounds such as drilling or seismic noises (Richardson and Würsig, 1997). Further studies confirmed that most whales or dolphins change their behaviour in response to boat noise or appearance (Janik, 1996; Bejder *et al.*, 1999; Nowacek *et al.*, 2001; Van Parijs and Corkeron, 2001), but noise levels don't seem to be capable of causing hearing damage (Au and Green, 2000). Results from these studies also indicated a potential for habituation to the sound and appearance of tourboats; however, this seemed to be dependent not only on the species but also on experiences of individuals or a group of individuals. Indeed, other studies suggested that, where they can avoid boat encounters, some large cetaceans prefer this type of response over habituation (Duffus, 1996).

Visual interference and noise

Many people love boats in which to go fishing, sailing, sight seeing or diving. Possibly an even larger number of people do not share this enthusiasm and regard boats as a nuisance. There is little evidence in the scientific literature to demonstrate such a reaction; however, it often emerges with submissions to environmental impact statements (EISs) for marinas or boat-mooring sites. Classic examples are the many proposals for such structures in and around Sydney and Melbourne. Many projects were considered visually obtrusive and not approved, or downscaled in a substantial manner (Warnken, unpublished data 1996). Noise, particularly that of two-stroke engines from PWCs, has been used by many local resident groups to lobby for a ban of small recreational craft on waterways in urban or rural areas. Some evidence from Alaska and New Zealand suggests that these aspects of boat operations could, in fact, be of relevance to tour operators: opinions of visitors to the Glacier Bay National Park shifted from 'neutral' or 'pleasant' to 'unpleasant' and 'very unpleasant' with increasing hypothetical numbers of cruise ships, tourboats, pleasure craft or aircraft (Manning *et al.*, 1996), and hikers on tracks adjacent to New Zealand's Dart River saw noise as a primary annoying feature of jet-boat activity on the river (Graham, 1999).

Conclusions

This review of the current scientific literature on boat impacts reveals only few studies that directly addressed specific aspects of marine tourboat operations. However, in summary, it is safe to conclude that wherever boats or vessels accumulate in one area, or use a particular area frequently, there is a high probability that such use will cause a detectable change in one or several of the parameters discussed above. Such changes may not necessarily lead to irreversible impacts, e.g. concentration of pollutants over and above guideline values for environmental standards. Where impacts do occur, it is often difficult to separate pollution or disturbances from small to medium-sized boats from those of large commercial vessels,

let alone impacts from tourboats against those from recreational vessels. Notable exceptions from this rule are, of course, impacts associated primarily with tourism, e.g. impacts on large marine vertebrates as a result of wildlife-watching tours.

Many national and international regulatory authorities have recognized these potentials for impacts and enacted or amended regulations that address these problems at a broad scale, e.g. a total ban on TBT-based antifouling paints (IMO, 2001), more stringent exhaust emission standards for two-stroke outboard engines (EPA, 1996), or general requirements for installation of holding tanks (Transport Operations (Marine Pollution) Act 1995 Qld). Even for whale-watching tours, many nations have enacted regulations that define how and to what distance whales can be approached by tourboats. Furthermore, many nature conservation agencies have started to collaborate with operators to organize permanent swing moorings for sensitive anchor sites (e.g. installation of moorings for bareboats by the Great Barrier Reef Marine Park Authority (GBRMPA) and Queensland Parks and Wildlife Services (QPWS) around the Whitsundays Islands, Australia). All in all, most unsustainable impacts on the marine environment can be avoided where tourboat operators: (i) maintain an open mind about their activities and acknowledge their potential for causing impacts; (ii) continue to educate themselves about, and implement, new regulations and technologies; and (iii) collaborate with relevant authorities and other members of the boating community. In the end, it is in the interest of all local users, i.e. fishermen, recreationists and tour operators, to protect their often-limited section of marine environment and, ultimately, their livelihoods.

References

Ahsanulla, M. and Williams, A.R. (1991) Sublethal effects and bioaccumulation of cadmium, chromium, copper and zink in the marine amphipod *Allorchestes compressa*. *Marine Biology* 108, 59–65.

Alzieu, C.L. (2000) Environmental impact of TBT: the French experience. *Science of the Total Environment* 258, 99–102.

Alzieu, C.L., Héral, M., Thibaud, Y., Dardignac, M.J. and Feuillet, M. (1981–1982) Influence des

peintures antisalissures à base d'organostan-
niques sur la calcification de la coquille de
l'huître *Crassostrea gigas*. *Révue des Travaux de
l'Institut des Pêches Maritimes* 45, 101–116.

An, Y.-J. and Kampbell, D.H. (2003) Total, dissolved,
and bioavailable metals at Lake Texoma marinas. *Environmental Pollution* 122, 253–259.

An, Y.-J., Kampbell, D.H. and Breidenbach, P.G.
(2002) *Escherichia coli* and total coliforms in
water and sediments at lake marinas. *Environmental Pollution* 120, 771–778.

APHA (American Public Health Association) (1998)
*Standard Methods for the Examination of Water
and Wastewater*, 20th edn. American Public
Health Association, Washington, DC.

Arthington, A.H. and Mosisch, T. (1998) The impacts
of power boating and water skiing on lakes and
reservoirs. *Lakes and Reservoirs: Research and
Management* 3, 1–17.

Au, W.W. and Green, M. (2000) Acoustic interaction
of humpback whales and whale-watching boats.
Marine Environmental Research 49, 469–481.

Augier, H., Aubert, J. and Guillemeau, C. (1984)
Première contribution a l'étude de la pollution
bactérienne dans les ziones de grande fréquenta-
tion balnéaire estivales des îles d'Hyères. *Science
Report Port-Cros National Park* 10, 27–35.

Augier, H., Aubert, J., Mathonet, S. and Guillemeau,
C. (1985) Estimation de la contamination bacté-
rienne et fongique de la plage du Sud (Parc
National de Port-Cros, Méditerranée, France).
Science Report Port-Cros National Park 11,
41–50.

Axiak, V., Micallef, D., Muscat, J., Vella, A. and
Mintoff, B. (2003) Imposex as a biomonitoring
tool for marine pollution by tributyltin: some
further observations. *Environment International*
28, 743–749.

Batten, L.A. (1977) Sailing on reservoirs and its effect
on water birds. *Biological Conservation* 18,
110–116.

Becker, E.C. and Bringezu, S. (1992) Belastung von
Binnengewässern durch biozide Organozinver-
bindungen – Immissionen, Wirkungen, Quali-
tätsziele, Anwendungsverbote. *Zeitschrift für
Wasser- und Abwasserforschung* 25, 40–46.

Bejder, L., Dawson, S.M. and Harraway, J.A. (1999)
Responses by Hector's dolphins to boats and
swimmers in Porpoise Bay, New Zealand.
Marine Mammal Science 15, 738–750.

Bird, P., Comber, S.D.W., Gardner, M.J. and
Ravenscroft, J.E. (1996) Zinc inputs to coastal
waters from sacrificial anodes. *Science of the
Total Environment* 181, 257–264.

Bowman, J.C., Readman, J.W. and Zhou, J.L. (2003)
Seasonal variability in the concentrations of
Irgarol 1051 in Brighton Marina, UK: including
the impact of dredging. *Marine Pollution
Bulletin* 46, 444–451.

Cardwell, R.D., Brancato, M.S., Toll, J., DeForest, D.
and Tear, L. (1999) Aquatic ecological risks
posed by tributyltin in United States surface
waters: pre-1989 to 1996 Data. *Environmental
Toxicology and Chemistry* 18, 567–577.

Chmura, G.L. and Ross, N.W. (1978) *The Environmental Impacts of Marinas and their Boats: a
Literature Review with Management Considerations*. Marine Advisory Service. University of
Rhode Island, Narragansett, Rhode Island.

Claisse, D. and Alzieu, C. (1993) Copper contamination as a result of antifouling paint regulations?
Marine Pollution Bulletin 26, 395–397.

Davies, G.E. (1977) Anchor damage to a coral reef on
the coast of Florida. *Biological Conservation* 11,
29–34.

Dawes, C.J., Andorfer, J., Rose, C., Uranowski, C. and
Ehringer, N. (1997) Regrowth of the seagrass
Thalassia testudinum into propeller scars.
Aquatic Botany 59, 139–155.

Dowson, P.H., Bubb, J.M. and Lester, J.N. (1993)
Temporal distribution of organotins in the
aquatic environment: five years after the 1987
UK retail ban on TBT based antifouling paints.
Marine Pollution Bulletin 26, 487–494.

Doyle, R.D. (2001) Effect of waves on the early
growth of *Vallisneria americana*. *Freshwater
Biology* 46, 389–397.

Duffus, D.A. (1996) The recreational use of grey
whales in southern Clayoquot Sound, Canada.
Applied Geography 16, 179–190.

Dufour, A. and Cabelli, V. (1981) Membrane filter
method for enumeration of *Escherischia coli*.
Applied and Environmental Microbiology 64,
3079–3083.

EPA (1996) Air pollution control; final rule for new
gasoline spark-ignition marine engines; exemp-
tions for new nonroad compression-ignition
engines at or above 37 kilowatts and new nonroad spark-ignition engines at or below 19 kilowatts. *Federal Register* 61(194), 52087–52169.

Evans, S.M. and Nicholson, G.J. (2000) The use of
imposex to assess tributyltin contamination in
coastal waters and open seas. *Science of the
Total Environment* 258, 73–80.

Evans, S.M., Evans, P.M. and Leksono, T. (1996)
Widespread recovery of dogwhelks, nucella
lapillus (L.), from tributyltin contamination in
the North Sea and Clyde Sea. *Marine Pollution
Bulletin* 32, 263–269.

Faust, M.A. (1982) Contribution of pleasure boats to
faecal bacteria concentrations in the Rhode
River Estuary, Maryland, U.S.A. *Science of the
Total Environment* 25, 255–262.

Fent, K. and Hunn, J. (1995) Organotins in freshwater

harbors and rivers: temporal distribution, annual trends and fate. *Environmental Toxicology and Chemistry* 14, 1123–1132.

Fisher, J.S., Perdue, R.R., Overton, M.F., Sobsey, M.D. and Sill, B.L. (1987) *Comparison of Water Quality at Two Recreational Marinas During a Peak-use Period*. University of North Carolina Sea Grant College Program, Raleigh, North Carolina.

Foerster, J.W., Lamontagne, R.A., Ewing, J.K. and Ervin, A.M. (1999) Copper circulation in two tidally influenced marinas studied with the use of a nafion polymer probe. *Field Analytical Chemistry and Technology* 3, 3–18.

Francour, P., Ganteaume, A. and Poulain, M. (1999) Effects of boat anchoring in *Poseidonia oceania* seagrass beds in the Port-Cros National Park (north-western Mediterranean Sea). *Aquatic Conservation: Marine and Freshwater Ecosystems* 9, 391–400.

Gabele, P.A. and Pyle, S.M. (2000) Emissions from two outboard engines operating on reformulated gasoline containing MTBE. *Environmental Science and Technology* 34, 368–372.

Gaines, A.G. and Solow, A.R. (1990) *The Distribution of Fecal Coliform Bacteria in Surface Waters of Edgartown Harbour Complex and Management Implications*. Woods Hole Oceanographic Institute, Woods Hole, Massachusetts.

Galicia, E. and Baldassarre, G.A. (1997) Effects of motorized tourboats on the behavior of non-breeding American Flamingos in Yucatan, Mexico. *Conservation Biology* 11, 1159–1165.

Gauthier, M., Torregossa, V., Babelona, M., Cornax, R. and Borrego, J. (1991) An intercallibration study of the use of 4-methylumbelliferyl-b-D-Glucuronidase for the specific enumeration of *Escherischia coli* in seawater and marine sediments. *Systematic and Applied Microbiology* 14, 183–189.

Gibson, C.P. and Wilson, S.P. (2003) Imposex still evident in eastern Australia 10 years after tributyltin restrictions. *Marine Environmental Research* 55, 101–112.

Glynn, P.W. (1994) State of coral reefs in the Galapagos Islands: natural vs anthropogenic impacts. *Marine Pollution Bulletin* 29, 131–140.

Graham, O.J. (1999) Measuring the effects of commercial jet boats on the Dart River on the experiences of recreationists in natural settings. *Noise Control Engineering* 47, 104–106.

Guillon-Cottard, I., Augier, H., Console, J.J. and Esmieu, O. (1998) Study of microbiological pollution of a pleasure boat harbour using mussels as bioindicators. *Marine Environmental Research* 45(3), 239–247.

Hall, L. and Anderson, R. (1999) A deterministic eco-

logical risk assessment for copper in European saltwater environments. *Marine Pollution Bulletin* 26, 365–373.

Hall, L.W., Giddings, J.M., Solomon, K.R. and Balcomb, R. (1999) An ecological risk assessment for the use of Irgarol 1051 as an algaecide for antifouling paints. *Critical Review in Toxicology* 29, 367–437.

Harding, M.J.C., Davies, I.M., Bailey, S.K. and Roger, G.K. (1999) Survey of imposex in dogwhelks (*Nucella lapillus*) from North Sea Coasts. *Applied Organometallic Chemistry* 13, 521–538.

Hastings, K., Hesp, P. and Kendrick, G.A. (1995) Seagrass loss associated with boat moorings at Rottnest Island, Western Australia. *Ocean and Coastal Management* 26, 225–246.

Haynes, D. and Loong, D. (2002) Antifoulant (butyltin and copper) concentrations in sediments from the Great Barrier Reef World Heritage Area, Australia. *Environmental Pollution* 120, 391–396.

Huet, M., Paulet, Y.M. and Glémarec, M. (1996) Tributyltin (TBT) pollution in the coastal waters of West Brittany as indicated by imposex in *Nucella lapillus*. *Marine Environmental Research* 41, 157–167.

IMO (International Maritime Organization) (2001) *International Conference on the Control of Harmful Anti-Fouling Systems on Ships, Adoption of the Final Act of the Conference and Any Instruments, Recommendations and Resolutions Resulting Form the Work of the Conference October 18, 2001*. IMO Headquarters, London, UK.

Jackivjz, T.P. and Kuzminski, L.N. (1973) A review of outboard motor effect on the aquatic envirnment. *Journal of the Water Pollution Control Federation* 45, 1759–1770.

Jameson, S.C., Ammar, M.S.A., Saadalla, E., Mostafa, H.M. and Riegl, B. (1999) A coral damage index and its application to diving sites in the Egyptian Red Sea. *Coral Reefs* 18, 333–339.

Janik, V.M. (1996) Changes in surfacing patterns on bottlenose dolphins in response to boat traffic. *Marine Mammal Science* 12, 597–602.

Johnstone, R.W., Muhando, C.A. and Francis, J. (1998) The status of the coral reefs of Zanzibar: one example of a regional predicament. *Ambio* 27, 700–707.

Jüttner, F., Backhaus, D., Matthias, U., Essers, U., Greiner, R. and Mahr, B. (1995a) Emissions of two- and four-stroke outboard engines – I. Quantification of gases and VOC. *Water Research* 29, 1976–1982.

Jüttner, F., Backhaus, D., Matthias, U., Essers, U., Greiner, R. and Mahr, B. (1995b) Emissions of two- and four-stroke outboard engines – II. Impact on water quality. *Water Research* 29, 1983–1987.

Kawai, S., Kurokawa, Y., Harinao, H. and Fukushima, M. (1998) Degradation of tributyltin by a bacterial strain isolated from polluted river water. *Environmental Pollution* 102, 259–263.

Ko, M.M., Bradley, G.C., Neller, A.H. and Broom, M.J. (1995) Tributyltin contamination of marine sediments of Hong Kong. *Marine Pollution Bulletin* 31, 249–253.

Kubilay, N., Yemenicioglu, S.T. and Salihoglu, I. (1996) The distribution of Organotin Compounds in the North-Eastern Mediterranean. *Marine Pollution Bulletin* 32, 238–240.

Langtimm, C.A., O'Shea, T.J., Pradel, R. and Beck, C.A. (1998) Estimates of annual survival probabilities for adult Florida manatees (*Trichechus manatus latirostris*). *Ecology* 79, 981–997.

Liddle, M.J. and Scorgie, H.R.A. (1980) The effects of recreation on freshwater plants and animals: a review. *Biological Conservation* 17, 183–206.

Liu, D., Pacepacivius, G.J., Maguire, R.J., Lau, Y.L., Okamura, H. and Aoyama, I. (1999) Survey for the occurrence of the new antifouling compound Irgarol 1051 in the aquatic environment. *Water Research* 33, 2833–2843.

Maguire, R.J. (1987) Environmental aspects of tributyltin. *Applied Organometallic Chemistry* 1, 475–498.

Manning, R., Johnson, D. and Vande Kamp, M. (1996) Norm congruence among tour boat passengers to Glacier Bay National Park. *Leisure Science* 18, 125–141.

Marmontel, M., Humphrey, S.R. and O'Shea, T.J. (1997) Population viability analysis of the Florida Manatee (*Trichechus manatus latirostris*), 1976–1991. *Conservation Biology* 11, 467–481.

Mastran, T.A., Dietrich, A.M., Gallagher, D.L. and Grizzard, T.J. (1994) Distribution of polyaromatic hydrocarbons in the water column and sediments of a drinking water reservoir with respect to boating activity. *Water Research* 28, 2353–2366.

Mates, A. and Schaffer, M. (1988) Quantitative determination of *Escherichia coli* from faecal coliforms in seawater. *Microbios* 53, 161–165.

McManus, J.W., Reyes, R.B. and Nanola, C.L. (1997) Effects of some destructive fishing methods on coral cover and potential rates of recovery. *Environmental Management* 21, 69–78.

Mikola, J., Miettinen, M., Lehikoinen, E. and Lehtila, K. (1994) The effects of disturbance caused by boating on survival and behaviour of velvet scoter *Melanitta fusca* ducklings. *Biological Conservation* 67, 119–124.

Milliken, A.S. and Lee, V. (1990) *Pollution Impacts from Recreational Boating: a Bibliography and Summary Review.* Rhode Island Sea Grant Publications. University of Rhode Island Bay Campus, Narrangansset, Rhode Island.

Mori, Y., Sodhi, N.S., Kawanishi, S. and Yamagishi, S. (2001) The effect of human disturbance and flock composition on the flight distances of waterfowl species. *Journal of Ethology* 19, 115–119.

Moss, B. (1977) Conservation problems in the Norfolk Broads and rivers of East Anglia, England – phytoplankton, boats and the causes of turbidity. *Biological Conservation* 12, 95–114.

Nanson, G.C., v. Krusenstierna, A., Bryant, E.A. and Renilson, M.R. (1994) Experimental measurements of river-bank erosion caused by boat-generated waves on the Gordon River, Tasmania. *Regulated Rivers: Research and Management* 9, 1–14.

Nowacek, S.M., Wells, R.S. and Solow, A.R. (2001) Short-term effects of boat traffic on bottlenose dolphins, *Tursiops truncatus*, in Sarasota Bay, Florida. *Marine Mammal Science* 17, 673–688.

Okamura, H., Aoyama, I., Ono, Y. and Nishida, T. (2003) Antifouling herbicides in the coastal waters of western Japan. *Marine Pollution Bulletin* 47, 59–67.

OWOW (Office of Wetlands, Oceans and Watersheds) (1993) *Guidance Specifying Management Measures for Sources of Nonpoint Pollution in Coastal Waters*, EPA-840-B-93-001c, Chapter 5. Environmental Protection Authority, Washington, DC, USA.

Perry, M.C. and Deller, A.S. (1996) Review of factors affecting the distribution and abundance of waterfowl in shallow-water habitats of Chesapeake Bay. *Estuaries* 19, 272–278.

Preda, M. and Cox, M.E. (2002) Trace metal occurrence and distribution in sediments and mangroves, Pumicestone region, southeast Queensland, Australia. *Environment International* 28, 433–449.

Rajasuriya, A., Öhmann, M.C. and Svensson, S. (1998) Coral and rock reef habitats in Southern Sri Lanka: patterns in the distribution of coral communities. *Ambio* 27, 723–728.

Readman, J.W., Kwong, L.L.W., Grondin, J., Bartocci, J., Villeneuve, J.P. and Mee, L.D. (1993) Coastal water contamination for a triazine herbicide used in antifouling paints. *Environmental Science and Technology* 27, 1940–1942.

Reuter, J.E., Allen, B.C., Richards, R.C., Pankow, J.F., Goldman, C.R., Scholl, R.L. and Seyfried, J.S. (1998) Concentrations, sources, and fate of the gasoline Oxygenate Metyl *tert*-Butyl Ether

(MTBE) in a multiple-use lake. *Environmental Science and Technology* 32, 3666–3672.

Richardson, W.J. and Würsig, B. (1997) Influences of man-made noise and other human actions on cetacean behaviour. *Marine and Freshwater Behaviour and Physiology* 29, 183–209.

Ronconi, R.A. and St. Clair, C.C. (2002) Management options to reduce boat disturbance on foraging guillemots (*Cepphus grylle*) in the Bay of Fundy. *Biological Conservation* 108, 265–271.

Sawyer, C.M. and Goulding, A.F. (1990) *Marina Pollution Abatement*. International Marina Institute, Wickford, Rhode Island.

Schoellhammer, D.H. (1996) Anthropogenic sediment resuspension mechanisms in a shallow microtidal estuary. *Estuarine, Coastal and Shelf Science* 43, 533–548.

Smart, M.M., Rada, R.G., Nielsen, D.N. and Claflin, T.O. (1985) The effect of commercial and recreational traffic on the resuspension of sediment in navigation pool 9 of the upper Mississippi River. *Hydrobiologia* 126, 263–274.

Smith, J.D., Bagg, J. and Sin, Y.O. (1987) Aromatic hydrocarbons in seawater, sediment and clams from Green Island, Great Barrier Reef, Australia. *Australian Journal of Marine and Freshwater Research* 38, 501–510.

Smith, P.J. (1996) Selective decline in imposex levels in the dogwhelk *Lepsiella scobina* following a ban on the use of TBT antifoulants in New Zealand. *Marine Pollution Bulletin* 32, 362–365.

Steidi, R.J. and Anthony, R.G. (1996) Responses of Bald Eagles to human activity during the summer in interior Alaska. *Ecological Applications* 6, 482–491.

Thomas, K., Raymond, K., Chadwick, J. and Waldock, M. (1999) The effects of short-term changes in environmental parameters on the release of biocides from anti-fouling coatings: cuprous oxide and tributyltin. *Applied Organometallic Chemistry* 13, 453–461.

Tjärnlund, U., Ericson, G., Lindesjöö, E., Petterson, I. and Balk, L. (1995) Investigation of the biological effects of 2-cycle outboard engines' exhaust on fish. *Marine Environmental Research* 39, 313–316.

Tuite, C.H., Hanson, P.R. and Owen, M. (1984) Some ecological factors affecting winter waterfowl distribution on inland waters in England and Wales, and the influence of waterbased recreation. *Journal of Applied Ecology* 21, 41–62.

Turner, S.J., Thrush, S.F., Cummings, V.J., Hewitt, J.E., Wilkinson, M.R., Williamson, R.B. and Lee, D.J. (1997) Changes in epifaunal assemblages in response to marina operations and boating activities. *Marine Environmental Research* 43, 181–199.

Valkirs, A.O., Seligman, P.F., Haslbeck, E. and Caso, J.S. (2003) Measurement of copper release rates from antifouling paint under laboratory and in situ conditions: implications for loading estimation to marine water bodies. *Marine Pollution Bulletin* 46, 763–779.

Van Parijs, S. and Corkeron, P.J. (2001) Boat traffic affects the acoustic behaviour of Pacific humpback dolphins, *Sousa chinensis*. *Journal of the Marine Biological Association of the United Kingdom* 81, 533–538.

Visser, I.N. (1999) Propeller scars on and known home range of two orca (*Orcinus orca*) in New Zealand waters. *New Zealand Journal of Marine and Freshwater Research* 33, 635–642.

Voulvoulis, N., Scrimsha, D.M. and Lester, J.N. (1999) Alternative antifouling biocides. *Applied Organometallic Chemistry* 13, 135–143.

Waldock, M.J., Thain, J.E. and Waite, M.E. (1987) The distribution and potential toxic effects of TBT in UK estuaries during 1986. *Applied Organometallic Chemistry* 1, 287–301.

Walker, D.J., Lukateelich, R.J., Bastyan, G. and McComb, A.J. (1989) Effect of boat moorings on seagrass beds near Perth, Western Australia. *Aquatic Botany* 36, 69–77.

Wells, R.S. and Scott, M.D. (1997) Seasonal incidence of boat strikes on bottlenose dolphins near Sarasota, Florida. *Marine Mammal Science* 13, 475–480.

Zieman, J.C. (1976) The ecological effects of physical damage from motor boats on turtle grass beds in southern Florida. *Aquatic Botany* 2, 127–139.

Zuccarello, J.L., Ganske, J.A. and Green, D.A. (2003) Determination of MTBE in a recreational harbor using solid-phase microextraction. *Chemosphere* 51, 805–810.

Table 7.2. Impacts or disturbances of tourist vessels during mooring/launching.

Vessel type	Pollutants	Freq	Ext	Physical damage	Freq	Ext	Disturbance to fauna	Freq	Ext	Visual interference	Freq	Ext	Emission of noise	Freq	Ext	Comment
Kayak, canoe, sea kayak	Release of urine and faeces (rare on short day trips); disposal of accumulated solid wastes after trip	○ / →	σ / σ	Damage to sediments during launching	→	●	Sensitive species – if vessel is launched close to animal	–	●	Vessels beached on shore, accumulation of trailers unlikely (either transported on car or >1 vessel per trailer)	–	σ	Un-obstrusive, some noise from stowing paddles and gear	–	●	Impacts generally low: vessels usually launched from protected beach, no engine, no antifouling, food and solid wastes common
Small sailing catamaran or dinghy	Unlikely (vessel only used for short trips with little or no food supplies, etc.)	–	●	As for kayaks	○	●	As for kayaks, though less likely (vessels rarely operated in areas occupied by sensitive species)	–	σ	Vessels kept on designated shore area above high-water mark	→	σ	When beached, clatter from sails, running gear	←	σ	Hire vessels usually launched from small designated areas, impacts generally small and localized (no engines, no antifouling, no storage)
Personal water craft (PWC)	Fuel (spillage) during refills; heavy metals from trailers and sacrificial anodes (engine)	○ / ■	σ / σ	Resuspension of sediments in shallow areas	←	?	Most species – mostly through appearance and noise when leaving launch area	?	?	During popular boating times (i.e. sunny weekends), accumulation of empty trailers and beached vessels	←	π	Extensive noise from starting and repairing engines	←	π	Jet-propelled small vessels with powerful engines, launched from boat ramps and often beached to exchange passengers or rest
Outboard tinnie and half cabin outboard cruiser	Fuel spillage similar to PWC; heavy metals similar to PWC; release of CU and booster herbicides from antifouling paints (hire vessels)	← / ■ / →	σ / σ / σ	Similar to PWC	←	σ	Similar to PWC	?	?	Similar to PWC	←	σ	Extensive noise from running outboard engines when flushing out cooling water	←	π	Very common type of vessel in coastal areas, cabin cruiser hire vessels often moored in wet berths

Vessel					
Semi-rigid inflatable (SRI)	← σ Fuel spillage similar to PWC; ■ σ heavy metals similar to PWC	→ σ Similar to PWC	? Similar to PWC	→ σ Similar to PWCs	→ π Vessels used by dive tour operators (limited numbers), most vessels kept on trailers
Speedboat	→ σ (If kept in wet berth) Zn, Cu and booster herbicides similar to sailing yacht; → σ fuel spills during refills; → σ release of oil, grease and fuel residues when draining the bilge after trip	→ π If moored in a wet berth, similar to sailing yacht; otherwise similar to PWC	? If moored in a wet berth, unlikely to encounter sensitive species; otherwise similar to PWC	→ σ Similar to outboard tinnies if kept on a trailer	→ ☾ Fast moving vessels with powerful engines, not as common as outboard tinnies and sailing yachts (expensive to run)
Sailing yacht (incl. racing yachts and historical sailing vessels)	■ σ Continuous release of Cu and booster herbicides from antifouling paints, Zn from sacrificial anodes; ← σ release of detergents and wastes from preparing vessels for next customer; ○ σ diesel fuel spills during refills; ○ σ release from oil, grease and fuel residues during bilge pump-outs	■ σ Sediment resuspension, grounding	– Where moored in a wet berth, unlikely to encounter sensitive species	← π Clatter from running gear, noise from wind howling past mast stays	← ● Masts being visible from many view points along a shore; ← π Slow-moving vessels with small engines, keel (fin or full) deeper than propeller (little chance for sediment re-suspension), apart from small trailer sailers – vessels moored in wet berths
Houseboat	■ σ Zn, Cu and booster herbicides similar to sailing yacht; ← σ detergents and wastes similar to sailing yacht; → σ fuel spills during refills; → σ release of oil, grease and fuel residues during engine well pump-outs	← σ Sediment resuspension similar to PWC or outboard tinnie	– Similar to sailing yacht	○ π Similar to outboard tinnies and half-cabin outboard cruisers	← ● Houseboats have high and square-looking above-deck structures; where vessels are moored in large numbers, they resemble a small floating village; ← π Usually moored in areas designated for a houseboat fleet (often shallow depths)

Continued

Table 7.2. *Continued*

Vessel type	Pollutants	Freq	Ext	Physical damage	Freq	Ext	Disturbance to fauna	Freq	Ext	Visual interference	Freq	Ext	Emission of noise	Freq	Ext	Comment
Fly-bridge fishing cruiser	Zn, Cu and booster herbicides similar to sailing yacht; detergents and wastes similar to sailing yacht; diesel fuel spills during refills; release of oil, grease and fuel residues during bilge pump-outs	■ ↑ ○ ○	σ σ σ σ	Due to powerful engines, greater potential for sediment resuspension	→	π	Similar to sailing yacht	–	π	Fly-bridge and fishing gear being visible from many viewpoints along a shore	○	†	Noise from wind howling past fishing rods, etc.; noise from engine exhausts	→	π	Fast-moving vessel with powerful engines, common in many marinas and often used for offshore or near-shore fishing tours – vessels can accumulate in marinas near popular fishing spots
Ex-commercial fishing vessel	Zn, Cu and booster herbicides similar to sailing yacht; detergents and wastes similar to sailing yacht; diesel fuel spills during refills; release of oil, grease and fuel residues during bilge pump-outs	■ ↑ → →	π σ σ π	Similar to fly-bridge cruiser	↓	π	Similar to sailing yacht	–	π	Similar to fly-bridge cruiser, but usually only a few vessels per launching area	○	†	Similar to fly-bridge cruisers	↑	π	Vessels usually occupy large designated berths (often with small visitor terminal); because of their potential to serve a large number of customers, vessels unlikely to accumulate in a single marina or boat harbour
Catamaran registered for around 300 to 400 passengers	Zn, Cu and booster herbicides similar to sailing yacht; detergents and wastes similar to sailing yacht; diesel fuel spills during refills; release of oil, grease and fuel residues during bilge pump-outs	■ ↑ → →	◐ π π π	Sediment resuspension widespread during mooring manoeuvres	■	◐	Similar to sailing yacht	↑	◐	Large above-deck structures several storeys high and clearly visible from shoreline, but usually only 1 or 2 vessels per visitor terminal	–	†	Noise from engine exhausts (powerful diesel engines)	→	◐	Vessels moored in designated wet berths close to cruise terminals, vessels operated daily except for times of bad weather; because of their capacity to carry up to 300 passengers, a few (1–3) vessels can serve the demand in one destination

Freq = Frequency of effect [based on technical and practical (operational) knowledge from Australian boat tour operators]: unknown, ?; highly unlikely, ?; unlikely, –; uncommon, ↓; common, ○; widespread, π; always, ■.

Ext = Extent of effect [based on technical and practical (operational) knowledge from Australian boat tour operators]: unknown, ?; negligible, ?; minor, †; considerable, σ; widespread, π; ◐.

Cu, copper; Zn, zinc.

Table 7.3. Impacts or disturbances of tourist vessels in transit to destination(s).

Vessel type	Pollutants	Physical damage	Disturbance to fauna	Visual interference	Emission of noise	Comment
Kayak, canoe, sea kayak	Release of urine (rare on short day trips); Loss of solid wastes	None	Sensitive species – if vessel is manoeuvred too close to animal	Little or none (very low hull, hard to see from a distance)	Unobtrusive, some noise from paddles bumping against hull	Impacts generally very low: only accidents (loss of waste, grounding) could lead to very minor impacts
Small sailing catamaran or dinghy	Release of urine	Grounding (vessels often used in shallow areas)	As for kayaks	Vessels can accumulate during peak holidays paired with fine weather	Little or none (no engine)	Impacts generally low, accumulation of vessels (with mostly colourful sails) can be perceived as 'disturbing'
Personal water craft (PWC)	Unburnt fuel residues from two-stroke engines*; Zn from sacrificial anodes (engine)	Resuspension of sediments; boat wakes	Most species – mostly through appearance and noise	During popular boating times (i.e. sunny weekends), accumulation of vessels	Extensive noise from revving high-power engines	Jet-propelled small vessels with powerful engines, launched from boat ramps and often beached to exchange passengers or rest
Outboard tinnie and half-cabin outboard cruiser	Unburnt fuel residues*; release of urine; Zn from sacrificial anodes (engine); loss of solid wastes; release of Cu and booster herbicides from antifouling paints (hire vessels)	Resuspension of sediments; boat wakes; groundings (when trying to manoeuvre to fishing spots, etc. in shallow areas)	Similar to PWC; vessel strikes and propeller cuts from direct hits	Similar to PWC	Noise from running outboard engines	Very common type of vessel in sheltered coastal areas and therefore likely to accumulate in large numbers along popular transit routes (major waterways)
Semi-rigid inflatable (SRI)	Unburnt fuel residues*; Zn from sacrificial anodes (engine); loss of solid wastes	Resuspension of sediments; boat wakes	Similar to PWC	Types of vessel uncommon (only used by a few operators)	Similar to PWCs	Vessels mostly used by dive tour operators for short trip to dive site or as service vessels for bareboat operators, etc.

Continued

Table 7.3. *Continued*

Vessel type	Pollutants	Freq	Ext	Physical damage	Freq	Ext	Disturbance to fauna	Freq	Ext	Visual interference	Freq	Ext	Emission of noise	Freq	Ext	Comment
Speedboat	Unburnt fuel residues; Zn from sacrificial anodes (engine); loss of solid wastes	■ ■ ○	π ↑ ?	Resuspension of sediments; boat wakes	→ →	σ ↑	Similar to PWC; vessel strikes and propeller cuts	? ?	? ☾	High speeds and considerable propeller wash, parachutes from parasailing vessels	↑	π	Noise from running powerful engines	■	☾	Fast-moving vessels used for short trips
Sailing yacht (incl. racing yachts and historical sailing vessels)	Continuous release of Cu and booster herbicides from antifouling paints, Zn from sacrificial anodes; release of detergents and wastes (incl. toilet wastes); release of oil, grease and fuel residues during bilge pump-outs	■ ○ ↑	σ ↑ σ	Sediment resuspension; boat wakes; grounding	– ↑ ↑	↑ σ σ	Sensitive species (most yachts move too slow to trigger panic-like escape reactions)	–	?	Sails visible from many view points along a shore, white sails often perceived as 'positive' effect (sailing nostalgia)	↑	π	Some noise from exhaust when running under engine	↑	↑	Slow-moving vessels with small engines, keel (fin or full) deeper than propeller (little chance for sediment resuspension), apart from small trailer sailers – vessels moored in wet berths
Houseboat	Zn, Cu and booster herbicides similar to sailing yacht; detergents and wastes similar to sailing yacht; release of oil, grease and fuel residues during engine well pump-outs	■ ○ ↑	σ σ σ	Sediment resuspension similar to PWC or outboard tinnie	↑	π	Similar to sailing yacht	–	π	Houseboats are more considered as residential units (not boats) and therefore often perceived as 'out-of-place'	○	?	Similar to outboard tinnies and half-cabin outboard cruisers	○	π	Slow-moving vessel often powered by two outboard engines linked to inboard fuel tanks, shallow draught and small wakes
Fly-bridge fishing cruiser	Zn, Cu and booster herbicides similar to sailing yacht; detergents and wastes similar to sailing yacht; release of oil, grease and fuel residues during bilge pump-outs	■ ↑ ↑	σ σ σ	Sediment resuspension; boat wakes (shore bank erosion)	→ ↑	σ ☾ ?	Most species – mostly through appearance and noise; hull strikes, propeller cuts from direct hits	↑	σ ☾	Fly-bridge and fishing gear being visible from many viewpoints along a shore	↑	π	Noise from exhaust	■	π	Fast-moving vessel with powerful engines, common in many marinas and often used for offshore or near-shore fishing tours – vessels can accumulate in marinas near popular fishing spots

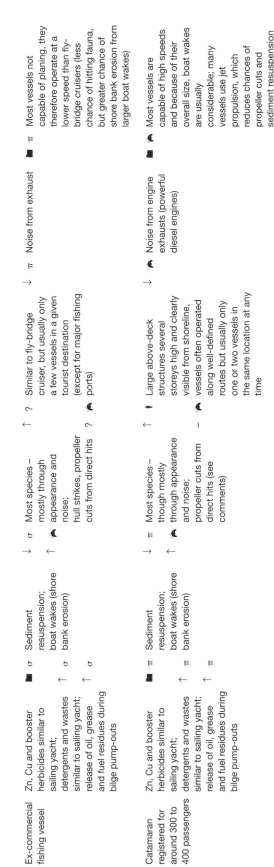

Vessel	Chemical inputs	Freq/Ext	Physical disturbance	Freq/Ext	Fauna	Freq/Ext	Visibility/distribution	Freq/Ext	Noise	Freq/Ext	Comments	Freq/Ext
Ex-commercial fishing vessel	Zn, Cu and booster herbicides similar to sailing yacht; detergents and wastes similar to sailing yacht; release of oil, grease and fuel residues during bilge pump-outs	■ σ; ↑ σ; ↑ σ	Sediment resuspension; boat wakes (shore bank erosion)	↑ σ	Most species – mostly through appearance and noise; hull strikes, propeller cuts from direct hits	↑ ?; 🌙 ?	Similar to fly-bridge cruiser, but usually only a few vessels in a given tourist destination (except for major fishing ports)	↓ ?	Noise from exhaust	→ π	Most vessels not capable of planing, they therefore operate at a lower speed than fly-bridge cruisers (less chance of hitting fauna, but greater chance of shore bank erosion from larger boat wakes)	■ π
Catamaran registered for around 300 to 400 passengers	Zn, Cu and booster herbicides similar to sailing yacht; detergents and wastes similar to sailing yacht; release of oil, grease and fuel residues during bilge pump-outs	■ π; ↑ π; ↑ π	Sediment resuspension; boat wakes (shore bank erosion)	■ π	Most species – though mostly through appearance and noise; propeller cuts from direct hits (see comments)	→ π; 🌙 ↑	Large above-deck structures several storeys high and clearly visible from shoreline, vessels often operated along well-defined routes but usually only one or two vessels in the same location at any time	↑ –; 🌙 –	Noise from engine exhausts (powerful diesel engines)	↓ 🌙	Most vessels are capable of high speeds and because of their overall size, boat wakes are usually considerable; many vessels use jet propulsion, which reduces chances of propeller cuts and sediment resuspension	■ 🌙

Freq = Frequency of effect [based on technical and practical (operational) knowledge from Australian boat tour operators]: unknown, ?; highly unlikely, ≃; unlikely, ↓; uncommon, ○; common, ↑; always, ■.

Ext = Extent of effect [based on technical and practical (operational) knowledge from Australian boat tour operators]: unknown, ?; negligible, ♩; minor, σ; considerable, π; widespread, 🌙.

Cu, copper; Zn, zinc.

* emissions of unburnt fuel residues are likely to be reduced for modern, direct-injection two-stroke engines, and practically no issue for four-stroke outboard engines (uncommon though for PWCs).

Table 7.4. Impacts or disturbances of tourist vessels at destination in open or sheltered waters.

Vessel type	Pollutants	Freq	Ext	Physical damage	Freq	Ext	Disturbance to fauna	Freq	Ext	Visual interference	Freq	Ext	Emission of noise	Freq	Ext	Comment
Kayak, canoe, sea kayak	Release of urine (rare on short day trips)	–	◆	None	–	◆	Sensitive species when taken by surprise	–	◆	Little or none (very low hull, hard to see from a distance)	–	◆	None	–	–	Impacts generally very low: vessels are moved slowly or left to drift
Outboard tinnie and half-cabin outboard cruiser	Release of toilet wastes, burley, fishing gear; release of Cu and booster herbicides from antifouling paints (hire vessels)	← →	σ σ	Resuspension of sediments or damage to coral from anchor and chain	←	σ	Sensitive species when restarting the engine	←	π	Vessels accumulate at popular fishing spots (larger half-cabin cruisers share the same anchor sites with sailing yachts)	←	?	If not used for fishing, noise from people shouting and jumping overboard, etc.	σ	σ	At destination, vessels commonly used for recreational line fishing
Semi-rigid inflatable (SRI)	Loss of dive gear, towels, etc.	→	?	Similar to outboard tinnie	→	?	Similar to outboard tinnie	←	π	Vessels can accumulate at popular dive spots	←	π	Clanking of dive gear against scuba tanks	→	◆	Some dive operators have detailed local knowledge that help to minimize impacts
Sailing yacht (incl. racing yachts and historical sailing vessels)	Continuous release of Cu and booster herbicides from antifouling paints, Zn from sacrificial anodes; release of detergents and wastes (incl. toilet wastes); release of oil, grease and fuel residues during bilge pump-outs	■ ← ○	σ π σ	Similar to outboard tinnie; grounding when miscalculating tides (in shallow areas)	←	σ π	Similar to outboard tinnie	←	π	Vessels can accumulate at popular anchor sites (see also fly-bridge cruiser)	←	π	Parties, radios, people jumping overboard, etc.	←	◆	Vessels are anchored during most trips (if only for a lunch break)
Houseboat	Zn, Cu and booster herbicides similar to sailing yacht; detergents and wastes similar to sailing yacht; release of oil, grease and fuel residues during engine well pump-outs	■ ← ○	σ π σ	Similar to sailing yacht	■	σ	Similar to sailing yacht	←	π	Houseboats can accumulate at popular anchor sites during holidays	○	π	Similar to sailing yacht	←	◆	Because most vessels are so slow, they are anchored for practically every trip and often in shallow areas which can result in frequent groundings

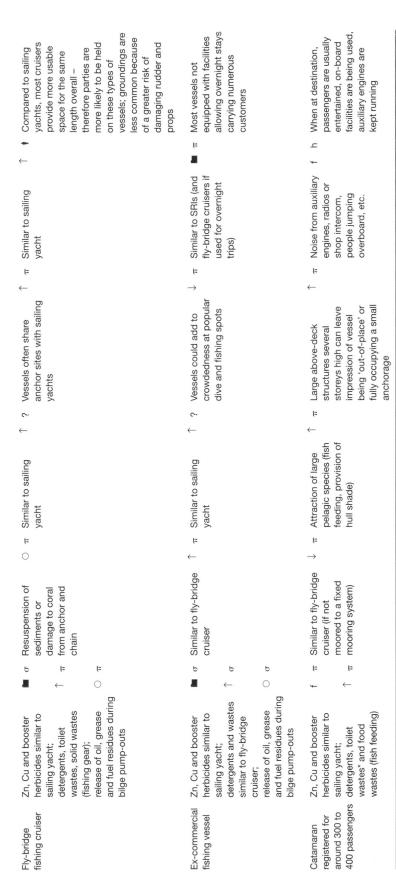

Vessel type						
Fly-bridge fishing cruiser	Zn, Cu and booster herbicides similar to sailing yacht; detergents, toilet wastes, solid wastes (fishing gear); release of oil, grease and fuel residues during bilge pump-outs ■ σ ↑ π ○ π	Resuspension of sediments or damage to coral from anchor and chain ○ π	Similar to sailing yacht ↑ ?	Vessels often share anchor sites with sailing yachts ↑ π	Similar to sailing yacht ↑ ?	Compared to sailing yachts, most cruisers provide more usable space for the same length overall – therefore parties are more likely to be held on these types of vessels; groundings are less common because of a greater risk of damaging rudder and props ↑ ▮
Ex-commercial fishing vessel	Zn, Cu and booster herbicides similar to sailing yacht; detergents and wastes similar to fly-bridge cruiser; release of oil, grease and fuel residues during bilge pump-outs ■ σ ↑ σ ○ σ	Similar to fly-bridge cruiser ↑ π	Similar to sailing yacht ↑ π	Vessels could add to crowdedness at popular dive and fishing spots ↑ ?	Similar to SRIs (and fly-bridge cruisers if used for overnight trips) ↓ π	Most vessels not equipped with facilities allowing overnight stays carrying numerous customers ■ π
Catamaran registered for around 300 to 400 passengers	Zn, Cu and booster herbicides similar to sailing yacht; detergents, toilet wastes* and food wastes (fish feeding) f π ↑ π	Similar to fly-bridge cruiser (if not moored to a fixed mooring system) f π	Attraction of large pelagic species (fish feeding, provision of hull shade) ↓ π	Large above-deck structures several storeys high can leave impression of vessel being 'out-of-place' or fully occupying a small anchorage ↑ π	Noise from auxiliary engines, radios or shop intercom, people jumping overboard, etc. ↑ π	When at destination, passengers are usually entertained, on-board facilities are being used, auxiliary engines are kept running f h

* In certain areas (e.g. the Great Barrier Reef Marine Park) large tourist vessels are required to use holding tanks at anchor sites which can only be discharged at a certain speed and distance from a sensitive area.

Freq = Frequency of effect [based on technical and practical (operational) knowledge from Australian boat tour operators]: unknown, ?; highly unlikely, –; unlikely, ↓; uncommon, ○; common, ↑; always, ■.

Ext = Extent of effect [based on technical and practical (operational) knowledge from Australian boat tour operators]: unknown, ?; negligible, ▮; minor, ▮; considerable, σ; widespread, π.

Cu, copper; Zn, zinc.

8

Impacts of Recreational Power-boating on Freshwater Ecosystems

Thorsten D. Mosisch[1] and Angela H. Arthington[2]

[1]Moreton Bay Waterways and Catchments Partnership, Brisbane, Queensland, Australia; [2]Centre for Riverine Landscapes, Griffith University, Nathan, Queensland, Australia

Introduction

'Water-based recreation forms a major value of water resources to the community . . .' (Office of the Commissioner for the Environment, Victoria, 1988). 'The trail bike, the power boat and the snowmobile are seen as symbolic of a society that arrogantly exploits and consumes resources' (Pigram, 1983). With an increase in leisure time available to the majority of the working population over the years, the opportunities to pursue outdoor recreational activities have risen. In particular, more active, water-based sports, including activities such as water-skiing and power-boating, appear to be high on the list of desirable outdoor leisure pursuits and have grown rapidly in popularity (Jaakson, 1970; Tanner, 1973; Craig, 1977; McCall and McCall, 1977; Pigram, 1983). Power-boating, in particular, has increased quite significantly since the 1960s (Horsfall et al., 1988; Hodges, 1991); this includes both boating *per se* and boating for the purpose of towing water-skiers. In Australia, Mercer (1977) reported that power-boating and water-skiing are increasing at a rate of 20–24% per year, while Prosser (1985) commented on the fast increase in the number of people taking part in water-based recreational activities.

Advances in materials technology (e.g. high-strength plastics) have made water-skiing and boating equipment more affordable, with the result that high-speed, water-based recreation activities have become more popular and readily accessible to a wider section of the community (McCall and McCall, 1977). For example, this is reflected in the fact that the annual growth rate for boat sales in Canada alone is 3% (Jaakson, 1993). During a 1992/93 survey of sporting activities in Australia, responses indicated that 12% of the population participate in water-skiing, with the majority being in the 16–29-year age group (Brian Sweeney and Associates, 1993). Be it due to ease of accessibility, the smoothness of the water, or perceived safety reasons, a large and steadily increasing percentage of recreational boating takes place on inland water bodies (Adams, 1993), and there appears to be an increasing demand by the public for the development of more reservoirs, lakes and streams for recreational activities (Department of Community Services and Health, 1990). Burton (1989) noted that, in south-eastern Australia in particular, water-based recreational activities, including water-skiing, take place mainly in and on these bodies of water. Many tourist centres adjacent to water resources (e.g. major rivers and lakes) now offer commercial water-ski, jet-ski and 'parasailing' experiences, all involving the operation of high-powered water craft. In recent years, problems with jet skis in particular have become increasingly common, as they are easily transported and can be launched virtually anywhere (cf. Ward and Andrews, 1993).

Past research into the effects of power-boating has produced some conflicting results (Australian Water Resources Council, 1984); however, most studies have come to the conclusion that power-boating and water-skiing can create a number of problems for aquatic environments and their surrounding riparian and terrestrial systems; in particular, impacts in lakes and water-storage reservoirs. Pigram (1983) noted that in situations where specialized recreational equipment (e.g. power-boats, trailbikes) is used, their operation will add to the degradation of a recreational site and also affect its chances of recovery.

Jaakson (1970) raised several questions regarding water-based recreation activities on lakes, including whether the flora, fauna and water quality of lakes subjected to high recreational usage are adversely affected, and whether lakes actually have an identifiable capacity limit for carrying this type of recreation. The recreational carrying capacity of a lake can be estimated by taking into account the three main groups of water-based recreational activities (after Jaakson, 1970):

1.   On-water activities (activities taking place on the water surface, e.g. power-boating, jet-skiing, water-skiing).
2.   Contact activities (activities where the body is in contact with the water, e.g. swimming, diving).
3.   Littoral activities (activities taking place on land surrounding the lake and within sight of the water, e.g. picnicking, sightseeing, hiking).

In discussing these recreational categories, Jaakson (1970) stated that while contact and littoral activities are relatively leisurely in nature, on-water activities utilize boats, and are thus associated with noise, speed and pollution through exhaust, fuel and oil discharges, necessitating rigid controls. Water-skiing (and power-boating on its own) does also have an impact on, and may conflict with, many other aquatic and land-based recreational activities (Feilman Planning Consultants, 1987). Power-boat-

based recreational activities can diminish the 'enjoyment quality' of shore-based activities, in particular through noise pollution (cf. Jaakson, 1970: conflict between on-water and contact/littoral activities). Pigram (1983) stated that power-boating and water-skiing are the two water-based activities that are most likely to provoke opposition from people participating in other, more sedate, recreational activities. This is certainly the case at Brown Lake, the subject of our case study, described below. Both Jaakson (1988) and Murphy *et al.* (1995) noted that the impact of a boat on the environment can be related directly to its speed, with disturbance escalating with increasing boat speed. Thus, by their very nature, power-boating and water-skiing are both high-impact recreational activities and have not only the potential for environmental damage, but also to exclude, restrict or endanger other leisure activities taking place in and on a water body (McCall and McCall, 1977; Bate, 1985; Garmann and Geering, 1985a; Edmonds *et al.*, 1987); for example, through noise pollution, exhaust fumes, dangers to other users (especially swimmers) and interfering with recreational fishing.

Three major annotated bibliographies covering the effects of recreational boating on inland water bodies have been published in the past: Pearce and Eaton (1983) covered some 418 research works on this topic, York (1994) produced a bibliography including 111 papers, while Marston and Yapp (1992) have compiled an annotated bibliography on the quality of recreational waters in alpine areas (118 references). Water-skiing effects on their own have been examined less frequently and have mainly been dealt with under the topic of power-boating. Some of the specific effects of power-boating on the ecology of inland water bodies have been addressed in a number of studies (e.g. Liddle and Scorgie, 1980; Horsfall *et al.*, 1988; Adams, 1993; Murphy *et al.*, 1995; Warrington, 1999). However, there are no recent reviews dealing exclusively with the major effects of power-boating and water-skiing on lakes, water-storage reservoirs and rivers.

The aim of this chapter is to provide a concise overall review of the main findings of studies undertaken in the past on the subject of

Table 8.1. Average capacity standards for boating and related activities (adapted from Baud-Bovy and Lawson, 1977; applicable to lakes with a surface area of up to 50 ha).

Activity	Area per boat (m²)	No. of boats per ha	Capacity (Number of users per ha of water)	
			Max. instantaneous capacity	Max. daily capacity
Fishing	2,500–5,000	2	2–4	5–8
Small boats[a]	1,800–5,000	2–6	4–12	10–30
Sailing boats	5,000–10,000	1–2	3–6	10–15
Power-boats	15,000–30,000	0.3–0.6	1–2	5–10
Water-skiing	20,000–40,000	0.25–0.5	0.7–1.5	5–15

[a] 'Small boats' refers to low-powered motor boats, rowing boats, etc.

motorized recreational boating on inland waters and their effects on aquatic ecosystems. The review has been structured around three main types of impact:

- physical impacts;
- chemical impacts;
- ecological impacts.

Each of these impact groups is further subdivided into relevant categories, where the impacts are discussed in detail, including a case study of the impacts, primarily chemical, of power-boating and water-skiing on an Australian freshwater lake.

Impacts of Power-boating and Water-skiing

Bate (1985) stated that both power-boating and water-skiing are sources of disturbance on water bodies, while Pressey and Harris (1988) noted that, in New South Wales, power-boat usage on wetlands can cause substantial environmental damage. Jaakson (1988) considered water-skiers to be 'high-impacting boats', with the boat and the water-skier as a combined unit taking up large areas of water. Tables 8.1 and 8.2 summarize the space requirements for some popular water-based recreational activities. As can be seen from the data presented, power-boating and water-skiing activities are the most space-demanding activities, with their inherent nature of operation allowing only a small number of users to participate in these activities at any one time.

Table 8.2. Recommended density limits for boating (adapted from Council on Environmental Quality, 1975).

Boat type	Max. number of boats per acre of reservoir water
High speed (unrestricted engine size)	0.33
Low speed (10 hp)	1
Non-motorized	2
Fishing	1
Sail	1

Physical Impacts

Wave action

Possibly the most obvious power-boat-related impacts on a body of water are waves and wash. Wave action resulting from recreational power-boating can best be classified as a form of mechanical disturbance, causing far-reaching problems due to damage of banks, in particular by erosion. Kuss *et al.* (1990) reported that the operation of power-boats causes more damage to shorelines by way of erosion than other types of boating (e.g. sailing, rowing). A number of studies have reported on these erosional effects (e.g. Tanner, 1973; Moss, 1977; Liddle and Scorgie, 1980; Fallen, 1985; Garrad and Hey, 1988; Pressey and Harris, 1988; Ward and Andrews, 1993; Liddle, 1997) and the physical damage to both emergent and floating water plants due to power-boating activity (e.g. Cragg *et al.*, 1980; Vermaat and de Bruyne, 1993;

Murphy *et al.*, 1995). In a report on the inland waters of Victoria (Office of the Commissioner for the Environment, Victoria, 1988), erosion was listed as an identified impact due to power-boating. Both Liddle and Scorgie (1980) and Murphy *et al.* (1995) noted that the mechanisms of boat-generated waves can severely erode the roots of plants growing on the bank. Murphy *et al.* (1995) detailed how aquatic plants are damaged through the 'uprooting, drag and tearing' actions of these waves. In their study of the distribution of water plants in a river, Vermaat and de Bruyne (1993) went so far as to consider boat-generated waves as one of the main factors determining the distribution of aquatic plants. Boats do not even have to be operational in order to cause erosion, since the process of launching a boat (especially from a badly constructed launching site) can potentially cause localized erosion (cf. Finlayson *et al.*, 1988).

It is a well-known fact that the action of waves is complex (Jaakson, 1988) and depends on a number of variables, including the size, shape and speed of the boat (Liddle and Scorgie, 1980; Jaakson, 1988; Murphy *et al.*, 1995). The Tasmanian National Parks and Wildlife Service has undertaken a series of speed trials on the Gordon River to determine the relationship between boat speed, wave height and bank erosion (Cook, 1985). Some of the results obtained are reproduced in Table 8.3, where it is shown that a lowering in boat speed and engine speed (r.p.m.) resulted in reduced wave heights, indicating that limiting the speeds of boats would slow down riverbank erosional processes (Cook, 1985; also Garrad and Hey, 1988).

Garrad and Hey (1988) detailed the sequence of boat-generated wave action on river banks and how this affects bank stability: as a vessel passes a given point, there is a rise in the water level at the bank, followed by a sudden drop and finally a series of smaller waves. They also noted that the incidence of boat-induced waves at the shoreline (and thus the risk of erosion) can be reduced by a lowering of boat speed or by increasing the distance between boats and the bank. The erosional actions of power-boat-generated wash and waves are also dependent on the type and consistency of the soil on the bank (Garrad and Hey, 1988). Furthermore, Garrad and Hey

Table 8.3. Results of boat speed/wave height trials performed by the Tasmanian NPWS (adapted from Cook, 1985).

Run No.	Vessel	R.P.M.	Speed	Wave height
1	A	800	20 km/h, 10 knots	>20 cm
2	A	900	22 km/h, 11.8 knots	>30 cm
1	B	900	17 km/h, 8.3 knots	>15 cm
2	B	1000	19 km/h, 9 knots	>20 cm

(1988) stated that the stabilizing nature provided by the root depth and density of any vegetation on the shoreline will contribute to erosional resistance, with plants such as reeds able to act as 'wave-breaks' and reduce the force of incoming waves. It follows from the above that the destruction of any such vegetation, due to, for example, boat launching or mooring, will increase the risks of serious bank erosion where power-boating activities take place. Furthermore, power boat-created waves and wash may also destroy bird nests floating on the water, as reported by Reichholf (1976) and Batten (1977).

However, when reviewing the literature, there appear to be a number of conflicting reports as to the effects of power-boat-induced erosion. Hodges (1991) examined two cases (on rivers) where it was claimed that increased power-boating and water-skiing activity caused serious bank erosion. He reported that, after investigations by the relevant departments, in both cases it was concluded that power-boating only caused negligible, if any, bank erosion. In these two cases, erosion in reaches where power-boating took place stayed at approximately the same level as in areas where there was no boating activity. In the Victorian Department of Conservation and Environment (1991) findings on the effects of water-skiing on a stretch of the Loddon River, it was indicated that 'the relative contribution of water skiing is small in comparison with other forces of erosion . . .', and that there were other areas of the river which showed more signs of erosion than at the site where water-skiing took place.

Another point noted in the paper by Hodges (1991) was that power-boats, due to their design, create very few waves once at operating speed, for example when towing a water-skier. Significantly, it is when this type of boat is turning (e.g. on smaller water bodies or when negotiating slalom courses), that the waves created could present considerable erosion problems, in particular where there is no riparian vegetation. Hodges (1991) concluded that power-boating does not necessarily cause any erosion problems if 'reasonable precautions are taken'. Williamson *et al.* (1989), who investigated impacts of water-skiing on an irrigation water-supply dam, noted that the operation (including launching procedures) of power boats can cause erosion of the shoreline. However, in this case, it was also found that no obvious shore damage resulted from water-skiing activity alone. Bate (1985) noted that while power-boating has the potential to accelerate bank erosion through wave action, negligible effects are likely to be caused on industrial or irrigation water-supply storages. Importantly, Garrad and Hey (1988) noted that in the case of the Broadland waterways (England), which they described as 'low-energy environments', stream-bank erosion directly attributable to boating activity was severe, with channel width increases of up to 1.8 m/year. As a solution to this problem, Garrad and Hey (1988) recommended a reduction in boat speed.

Turbidity

Due to the mechanical action of boat propellers, turbulence is created in the water in an area immediately surrounding an outboard motor propeller, leading to the resuspension of bed sediments, especially in shallow waters, which can then reduce the productivity of a water body (Kirk, 1985). On lakes and smaller rivers, the operation of recreational vessels is most likely the major source of mechanical disturbance of the bed sediments. Moss (1977) investigated the causes of turbidity in the Norfolk Broads wetlands and concluded that turbidity in the water was caused, amongst other things, by the mechanical disturbance (i.e. propeller action) of sediments by recreational boats.

Smart *et al.* (1985) demonstrated that almost every recreational vessel has the capacity to resuspend sediments. While high-speed power-boating and water-skiing activities, in particular, result in increased turbulence and thus turbidity of the water (cf. Longworth and McKenzie, 1986), the severity of this turbulence is, amongst other factors, determined by the design of the boat and the maximum output of the motor (Liddle and Scorgie, 1980).

Turbidity due to power-boat operation is the result of the disturbance of bottom sediments of a lake or river. Outward and downward forces created by the passage of power boats resuspend nutrient- and mineral-containing bed sediments and erode the shoreline (Fallen, 1985). It has been shown that power-boat activity on a body of water can cause the resuspension of sediments and associated turbidity due to the turbulence created by the propeller (e.g. Pressey and Harris, 1988), and, in the case of water storages, may lead to 'premature siltation' (Fallen, 1985). In particular, shallow areas are affected by the stirring actions of boat propellers (Kuss *et al.*, 1990). The magnitude of sediment resuspension will depend on the origin and composition of the sediment itself, for example its clay content (Liddle and Scorgie, 1980; Smart *et al.*, 1985). Clay suspensoids can stay in the water column for days and up to weeks (Kirk, 1985).

However, it appears that, overall, power boating may increase turbidity in a water body for only a relatively short period, as observed by Williamson *et al.* (1989), who stated that while the operation of power boats does result in increased turbidity (in particular in areas close to the banks where erosion occurs; cf. Moss, 1977), it seemed to be only a temporary effect. This was also observed by Horsfall *et al.* (1988), who researched the impacts of recreational power boating on lakes and noted that power-boat-generated turbulence resulted only in a temporary increase in turbidity. Hilton and Phillips (1982) examined the effects of motorized recreational boating on turbidity in a shallow English river. They noted that turbidity due to resuspended bed sediments can affect the growth of submerged macrophytes, and that boats were responsible for most of the turbidity present in the water. However, turbidity levels returned to normal approximately 5.5 hours after boating activities had stopped. One point that has to be considered in this respect is that, in the case of rivers, resuspended sediments would be carried downstream continuously with the flow, and thus turbidity would be expected to clear faster than in lakes. Moss (1977) stated that suspended sediments would sink back to the bottom quite rapidly, unless the water is continuously reagitated by further boating activity. However, Hilton and Phillips (1982) found it unlikely that background turbidity would build up throughout the length of a complete boating season, and Moss (1977) reported that sediments stirred up by outboard motors did not appear to contribute greatly to the sustained turbidity of water in the Norfolk Broads wetlands. In another study by Jackivicz and Kuzminski (1973a), the turbidity of a shallow pond where outboard motors were operated was compared with the turbidity of a control pond. Results indicated that turbidity was not measurably elevated by outboard motor turbulence in the pond where these were operated, even when outboards were running for prolonged periods. However, they stated that turbidity might, in fact, increase in lakes where clay bed sediments prevail.

While there is extensive evidence that the operation of power boats is responsible for the disturbance of sediments and resultant increases in turbidity (Cragg et al., 1980; Garman and Geering, 1985a; Smart et al., 1985; Garrad and Hey, 1988; Williamson et al., 1989), and that a reduction in the operation of boats can improve water quality by controlling turbidity (Garrad and Hey, 1988), there have been inconclusive reports as to the actual impacts of boat-generated turbidity on the lake or stream biota. Increased turbidity affects submerged aquatic plants by inhibiting the penetration of solar radiation by way of scattering and absorbing solar photons and thus changing the primary productivity of a body of water (Kirk, 1985). Murphy and Eaton (1983) found that increases in recreational boat traffic in canals led to a gradual reduction in light available for photosynthesis by submerged macrophytes. Cragg et al. (1980) linked the reduction in the number of submerged macrophytes in a Welsh lake to an increase in turbidity as a result of recreational boating (i.e. again the effect of reduced light penetration), while Murphy et al.

(1995) concluded that the significance of the shading effects of sediment particles settling on the leaves of submerged plants is uncertain.

Boat-generated turbidity of the water may have an adverse effect on the growth of submerged macrophytes (cf. Cragg et al., 1980; Hilton and Phillips, 1982; Murphy et al., 1995); however, it appears that, in the past, few studies have addressed potential problems created by this on freshwater fish and aquatic invertebrates. Thus, any possible effects of turbidity on these would have to be based on studies examining turbidity generated by processes other than boating (Murphy et al., 1995). One effect of fine suspensoids in water on invertebrates was discussed by Liddle (1997), who noted that the gills of aquatic insects, such as stoneflies and mayflies, may become obstructed by an accumulation of silt. The gills of fish may also be affected by boat-induced suspended sediments (cf. Murphy et al., 1995). Murphy et al. (1995) further stated that an increase in turbidity can impair the success of visual feeding by water birds and also reduce their food resources (e.g. a reduction in the number of invertebrates and plants).

Not only does the stirring-up of bed sediments by power boats reduce the amount of light reaching submerged aquatic plants, but nutrient enrichment of the water may also occur, and in some cases, pollutants contained in the resuspended sediment could be mixed into the water (cf. Liddle and Scorgie, 1980; Kuss et al., 1990; Munawar et al., 1991). Phosphorus (phosphate) is usually the element limiting plant growth in freshwater habitats and is generally bound within the sediments (e.g. Hammitt and Cole, 1998). Phosphorus and other nutrients are released from the sediments by the actions of many water-based activities (e.g. boating and swimming; Hammitt and Cole, 1998). This has also been reported by Longworth and McKenzie (1986), who stated that the disturbance of sediments due to power-boating may lead to increased nutrient levels in the water. This nutrient availability may then lead to an increase in the growth of phytoplankton and other aquatic plants. For example, Fallen (1985), while reporting on the effects of water-skiing on a reservoir, noted that nutrients released from resuspended sediments were causing algal blooms. Yousef et al. (1980)

examined the sediment layers of shallow lakes. They stated that disturbance of sediments could have a number of effects on the phosphorus concentrations present therein. They found that, in shallow lakes, changes in the phosphorus content of the sediments were related to changes in turbidity as a result of power-boat operation, with an increase in turbidity and phosphorus concentration in the water following mixing by power boats. However, while looking at a deeper lake with a sandy-bed sediment, Yousef *et al.* (1980) noted that the evidence concerning the relationship between phosphorus and power-boat activity proved less conclusive. While studying the effects of suspensoids in the Upper Great Lakes Connecting Channels, Munawar *et al.* (1991) observed that primary production of phytoplankton was both enhanced and inhibited by the presence of suspended sediments as a result of boating and shipping activity, depending on the type of plankton and whether or not the sediments contained pollutants.

Direct boat contact

Garman and Geering (1985a) stated that power boats have a great impact on the aquatic biota by disturbing benthic organisms and emergent vegetation situated along the shoreline (cf. also Jahrsdoerfer and Leslie (1988): 'boat contact causes damage to riparian vegetation'). In shallow waters, the actions of outboard motor propellers can cause damage to benthic plants (Jaakson, 1979). Physical damage of the aquatic flora and fauna by the direct action of boat movement and boat propellers has been reported in several papers. Tanner (1973), Liddle and Scorgie (1980) and Jahrsdoerfer and Leslie (1988) reported on the cutting action of outboard propellers and how this can leave aquatic macrophytes, especially mat-forming species, severely damaged. Murphy and Eaton (1983) suggested that while the actions of physical damage by direct boat contact with aquatic plants may play the most important controlling role at times of low boat traffic, boat-induced turbidity may play a more important controlling role at high boat densities. Murphy and Eaton (1983) observed differences in the emergent macrophytes present in canals and linked these

to recreational boating densities: areas of highest boating activity frequently featured no emergent plants, while in areas of low boating activity, an extensive macrophyte cover prevailed. They stated that floating-leaved macrophytes are very susceptible to damage by outboard propellers (by cutting, breakage and uprooting), and are thus at a competitive disadvantage. Furthermore, Murphy and Eaton (1983) concluded that this may actually encourage growth of submerged plants, since a reduction of floating-leaved plants will allow more sunlight to penetrate to deeper waters. Cragg *et al.* (1980) also observed that emergent vegetation zones were damaged by recreational boating activities, while Pressey and Harris (1988) noted that the vegetation of wetlands used for boating can be damaged through abrasion (cf. also Murphy and Eaton, 1983). Even activities such as the deliberate clearing of riparian vegetation to provide boat-launching access can create problems; for example, increased bank erosion (Liddle, 1997) especially through repeated boat launching and retrieval actions. Any submerged vegetation at these locations would be adversely affected by these activities.

While Murphy *et al.* (1995) considered injuries to fish due to physical contact with boats to be a relatively rare occurrence, there have been reports of fish receiving wounds by colliding with power boats (e.g. Rosen and Hales, 1980). Rosen and Hales (1980) discussed the effects of power-boating on paddlefish (*Polyodon spathula*) in the Missouri River. They found that 36% of the fish sampled were scarred and 10% had severed rostrums due to collisions with power boats.

Noise and visual disturbance

Amongst other impacts, noise is one of the major factors that makes power boats the dominant recreational impact on the water body where they are operating (Garman and Geering, 1985a). From past studies it appears that waterbirds are much affected by boat motor noise. The unpredictable movements, speed and noise connected with power-boating and water-skiing can cause serious disturbance of waterbirds (Speight, 1973; Tanner, 1973). Marchant and Hyde (1980) and Adams *et al.*

Table 8.4. Breeding densities (pairs/10 km channel) of three widespread species of English waterbirds in canals of varying intensities of boat use (adapted from Murphy et al., 1995).

Species	Disused canal	Used canal
Little grebe (Tachybaptus ruficollis)	5.1	0.2
Coot (Fulica atra)	4.7	2.5
Moorhen (Gallinula chloropus)	37.8	22.5

Table 8.5. Estimates of boating and outboard motor usage (adapted from Jackivicz and Kuzminski, 1973b).

	Year	
Item	1968	1970
Persons participating in recreational boating	42.2×10^6	44.1×10^6
Outboard motors in use	7.0×10^6	7.2×10^6
Fuel consumed (litres)	3.8×10^9	4.0×10^9

(1992) found that birds were disturbed by recreational boat operation. Boat operation can subject birds to psychological stress and affect their breeding (Murphy et al., 1995; Table 8.4). Boyle and Samson (1985) noted that, as a response to power-boating activity, waterfowl exhibited changes in behaviour and moved to areas that are less disturbed. Similar effects were observed by Ward and Andrews (1993): they stated that power boats (usually used for towing water-skiers) were a major agent of disturbance for water birds, and that they quickly evacuated an area subjected to boating and skiing activity. They also noted the displacement of birds due to jet-ski activities. Havera et al. (1992) discovered that up to 78.5% of all disturbances of waterbirds were directly attributable to the operation of boats; however, the effects appear to be only short-lived, since birds take refuge in surrounding vegetation during the disturbance event (Horsfall et al., 1988). Prolonged periods of water-skiing (e.g. during the holiday seasons) may have particularly severe effects if carried out on permanent lakes used as refuges by waterbirds (Lane and McComb, 1988). Often, it is not only the noise emanating from outboard motors, but a combination of sound and sight which may disturb birds (cf. Batten, 1977), reacting at a greater distance to fast-moving power boats than rowing boats or sail boats (Ward and Andrews, 1993).

Noise originating from the operation of powerboats can greatly interfere with other recreational pursuits, such as bushwalking and relaxing in the natural environment (Jaakson, 1970; Garman and Geering, 1985a). A handbook prepared by the Council on Environmental Quality (1975) states that 'the semi-wilderness

quality of reservoirs makes them particularly suited for quiet, solitary enjoyment, and large motorboats have ample opportunities elsewhere. Motor recreation imposes a burden on those who object to it'. This statement would apply to most natural lakes situated in a relatively undisturbed environment sought out as a place for peaceful relaxation.

Chemical Impacts

Fuel, oil and chemical pollution

Amongst the identified impacts on the aquatic environment by the operation of power boats are water pollution due to fuel and oil spills, and motor exhaust fumes (Office of the Commissioner for the Environment, Victoria, 1988; Adams et al., 1992; Adams, 1993). Outboard motor impacts on water bodies are due, to a large extent, to the relatively inefficient mode of operation of two-stroke engines, resulting in fuel spillage and the formation of polycyclic aromatic hydrocarbons (PAHs) (Mastran et al., 1994). Approximately 3.8 billion litres of fuel per year are used by outboard motors; of this, 380–600 million litres are discharged into the water (e.g. Jackivicz and Kuzminski, 1973b; Table 8.5). There will always be a risk of spillage during refuelling procedures or boat breakdowns, for example due to ruptured or dislodged fuel lines or leaking fuel tanks. Longworth and McKenzie (1986) highlighted the introduction of residual hydrocarbons from fuels into the water as potential impacts of power-boating and water-skiing activities. The possible contamination of water by hydrocarbons as a result of the operation of

Table 8.6. Average data on water chemistry in three control and in three motor-use ponds (reproduced from Jackivicz and Kuzminski, 1973a).

Pond	pH	Phenolphthalein alkalinity (p.p.m.)	Total (methyl orange) alkalinity (p.p.m.)	Dissolved oxygen (cc/l)
Control	7.3	14.33	129	5.17
Motor use	7.4	16.00	120	5.27

power boats was also noted in guidelines for the recreational use of water storages and catchments proposed by the Australian Department of Resources and Energy (1987). Murphy *et al.* (1995) stated that 'powered boating causes direct chemical changes to water quality by adding fuel combustion products . . .' and went on to highlight problems for the aquatic environment due to fuel leakage and outboard motor emissions (i.e. hydrocarbons and exhaust gases). Fallen (1985), while discussing the effects of water-skiing on a shallow water storage reservoir, observed significant impacts on the water quality following the onset of water-skiing activities. Kuss *et al.* (1990) noted that fuel and oil pollutants, as a direct result of boat operation, include short- and long-chained hydrocarbons, tetraethyl lead, ethylene dibromide, ethylene dichloride, zinc, sulphur and phosphorus, while exhaust pollutants include carbon, nitrogen oxide, sulphur oxide, hydrocarbons, particulate lead products and a number of oxidation products. Burton (1975) stated that, apart from unburnt fuel, pollutants that can be detected in waters used by outboard-motor-driven boats include phenols, lead and non-volatile and volatile oils. Apart from being present in the water column, oil and lead pollutants can also accumulate in sediments, where they can remain in a toxic form for a long period of time (Kuss *et al.*, 1990). However, Jackivicz and Kuzminski (1973a) noted that the pH, hardness, alkalinity and dissolved oxygen content of the water in ponds were not affected by the operation of outboard motors (Table 8.6).

When operating on water-supply reservoirs, power boats and their motor emissions may also affect the quality of drinking water (Fallen, 1985). Longworth and McKenzie (1986) noted that recreational power-boating may reduce the quality of water by contamination with hydrocarbons from motor fuel and

exhaust components, of which the polycyclic aromatic hydrocarbons (PAHs) may be carcinogenic (Mastran *et al.*, 1994). In their study investigating the presence of PAHs, Mastran *et al.* (1994) found highest levels during times of high boating activity and lowest levels during times of low boating activity, and concluded that boating was 'at least one of the sources of PAH to the water'. Polycyclic aromatic hydrocarbons can accumulate in both the water column and sediments (cf. Neff, 1979; Mastran *et al.*, 1994). The sediment acts as a sink for PAHs, so these compounds can accumulate over time, and the sediments may still provide a source for PAHs even when inputs of these compounds have ceased (cf. Wells and Adams 1991; Mosisch and Arthington, 2001). Further details of the sources and types of PAHs occurring in lakes and other water bodies, and their potential impacts on aquatic biota, are discussed below in our case study of an Australian lake used for power-boating and water-skiing.

In experimental studies, motorboat fuels and emissions have been found to be toxic to fish and invertebrates (e.g. Tarkpea and Svanberg, 1982; cf. Murphy *et al.*, 1995). Surber (1971) examined bluegill sunfish from a lake used for water-skiing, a pond subjected to the operation of outboard motors, and a control pond not subjected to motor usage. Results of this study indicated significant tainting of fish in both ponds subjected to outboard-motor usage, in conjunction with significant increases in threshold odour, hydrocarbons and chlorine demand. Jackivicz and Kuzminski (1973a) concluded that outboard motor emissions can have adverse effects on fish, but that further research is necessary in order to obtain conclusive evidence.

Muratori (1968) stated that in the USA, approximately 90% of power boats employ outboard motors, and that 98% of these operate on the two-stroke engine principle. The very design of the two-stroke motor appears to present a greater number of environmental problems than conventional four-stroke engines (Liddle and Scorgie, 1980). Two-stroke engines require a mixture of petrol and lubricating oil (to protect moving parts within the motor) (Jackivicz and Kuzminski, 1973b; Mele, 1993), thus introducing a wider range of potentially toxic substances than the standard fuel used by four-stroke engines. Kuss *et al.* (1990) reported that water bodies used for motorized recreational purposes are subjected to a high input of polluting agents emitted via engine crank-case drainage points. Unburnt oil and fuel from the crank case is emitted into the water via a drainage point to prevent what is known as 'hydraulic lock', and fuel is also lost by passing over the cylinder and through the engine during operation (Stewart and Howard, 1968; Jackivicz and Kuzminski, 1973a,b). However, two-stroke outboards of newer design recycle much of the crank-case emissions, thus reducing compounds emitted into the water, but still permit unburnt fuel and oil to pass through the engine (Jackivicz and Kuzminski, 1973b). Mele (1993) noted that while part of the lubricating oil is burnt during the combustion process, unburnt oil is expelled into the environment through the exhaust. Bate (1985) also considered pollution by unburnt hydrocarbons to be a problem. On average, two-stroke outboard motors emit between 10 and 20% of the fuel/oil mixture into the water as part of normal operations, and this can be as much as 40% (Muratori, 1968), with all exhaust gases and any unburnt compounds being expelled under water near the propeller to aid in mixing and dispersal of emitted compounds in the water (cf. Muratori, 1968). Mele (1993) provided the following data obtained from a technical paper by the Mercury Marine and Outboard Marine Corporations (USA) on the fuel and oil released from outboard motors: 1529 g of unburnt hydrocarbons are released from a 70 hp outboard motor per hour, which represents 8.3% of the total fuel input (these, in his opinion, being very conservative figures). Mele (1993) further cited figures obtained from the US Environmental Protection Agency (EPA) Certification Division, which showed that 25% of the fuel mixture is being passed through two-stroke outboard motors and into the environment. According to the EPA data, outboard motors discharge 798 kg (1760 lb) of hydrocar-

bons for every 3785 litres (1000 gallons) of fuel they consume (Mele, 1993).

It has been documented that, in particular, the lubricating oils used in two-stroke outboard motors aggregate in the water column and produce visible slicks on the surface (cf. Jackivicz and Kuzminski, 1973a). It has also been demonstrated that engines that are not properly tuned, and those that are run on an incorrect fuel/oil mixture, emit more unburnt fuel and other substances into the water than engines that are tuned properly (Jackivicz and Kuzminski, 1973b). Oil films greater than 0.0001 cm in thickness may lead to a temporary depletion in the oxygen content of the underlying layer of water, and this can affect the reproduction of diatoms (Stewart and Howard, 1968). On the same topic, Wall and Wright (1977) stated that the oxidation of 1.0 g of oil in a lake, originating from the operation of power boats, uses up 3.3 g of oxygen, and that a depletion of oxygen in the upper centimetres of water decreases the production rates of phytoplankton.

Hammitt and Cole (1998) stated that the deposition of a film of unburnt oil on aquatic organisms is the 'primary ecological effect' of the operation of outboard motors. Deleterious effects of these oil depositions on aquatic plants (including unicellular plankton and algae) include interference with respiration and the inhibition of algal growth, ultimately affecting the food chains of fish and other aquatic organisms (Hammitt and Cole, 1998).

There is evidence that recreational powerboat activities can increase the concentration of heavy metals, in particular lead, in water bodies, and introduce other toxic compounds. Jackivicz and Kuzminski (1973b) identified problems with phenols and other organic compounds, while Byrd and Perona (1980) stated that boating is a possible source of lead. King and Mace (1974) noted higher phosphate levels in water around campsites on a lake. They attributed this to the use of detergents and outboard motor fuel in that area (motor-boat oil is a source of phosphate; Hammitt and Cole, 1998).

It has been documented that the lead added to petrol as an anti-knocking agent can accumulate in aquatic systems. Horsfall *et al.* (1988) noted that lead concentrations were highest in a lake that was used for recreational power boating, and accumulated in the lake sediments (cf. also Wall and Wright, 1977). Horsfall *et al.* (1988) were able to calculate from the lead concentrations present that approximately 200 litres of petrol were introduced into the lake due to power-boating, but no obvious effects of this on the phytoplankton of the lake were noted. The presence of lead in a freshwater lake was also investigated by Byrd and Perona (1980), with results indicating that power-boating activities had a minimal effect on lead levels in the main part of the lake. However, boating activity resulted in high lead concentrations in water surrounding the lake's boat launching facility, which Byrd and Perona (1980) attributed to poor water mixing and the possibility of fuel spills.

It appears that no recent studies have re-addressed the problems associated with the use of outboard-motor fuels. In particular, it can only be assumed that with the advent of lead-free fuel, the addition of this element to waters used for the purpose of power-boating has decreased (cf. Murphy *et al.*, 1995). However, there are probably still any number of older-style motors in use today which require fuel containing lead (even though lead levels have been reduced in modern leaded fuel).

Antifouling paints

The hulls of ships and boats are regularly (up to once a year) painted with antifouling paints to prevent attachment of a variety of organisms that increase drag, and thus fuel consumption of the engine (Simmonds, 1986). While copper-based paints were used in the past, organic compounds such as tributyltin (TBT) have been employed as antifouling agents in more recent years (Simmonds, 1986). These have been proven to be highly toxic, even in minute amounts, and to accumulate in organisms, often producing mutagenic effects (cf. Simmonds, 1986; Murphy *et al.*, 1995). Even though mostly applied to ships and boats using marine waters, it is very likely that toxins found in antifouling paints can also be introduced into wetlands and lakes, since many boat owners, especially those who own power boats, use their vessels in both marine and freshwater environments. However, it appears that, at least in some countries, the use of TBT paints is now restricted to vessels over 25 m (Murphy *et al.*, 1995), essentially ruling out their use for power boats. Paints containing copper compounds (copper oxide) are still by far the most widely used antifouling treatments (Simmonds, 1986). To some organisms, copper oxide is only one-tenth as poisonous as TBT, and there have been reports of some organisms having become tolerant to this type of antifouling paint (cf. Simmonds, 1986).

Ecological Impacts

Dispersal of aquatic plants

One frequently overlooked problem with the operation of boats is the dispersal of aquatic plants from one body of water to another. Garman and Geering (1985a,b) raised the question of whether boats could introduce exotic plants and organisms into recreational waters. It has been documented by several authors that reproductive structures and other vegetative fragments can be spread by boating activities (Liddle and Scorgie, 1980). Finlayson *et al.* (1988) also commented that the distribution of weeds and plant seeds by boats and vehicles is a problem that may be difficult to control. Longworth and McKenzie (1986) noted that recreational activities may adversely affect the quality of water by introducing organisms such as exotic flora and fauna into reservoirs. A major study of the dispersal of aquatic macrophytes has been undertaken by Johnstone *et al.* (1985), who examined 107 lakes used for recreational purposes in New Zealand. They found that the distribution of five aquatic weed species (*Ceratophyllum demersum, Egeria densa, Elodea canadensis, Hydrilla verticillata* and *Lagarosiphon major*) was related directly to boating activities: 5.4% of boats being launched in the lakes were found to have viable plant fragments entangled in propellers and other attachments, with 27% of plants originating from previous boating trips to another lake. Significantly, the lakes not used for power-boating or fishing contained none of the five weed species examined in this study (Table 8.7). In contrast to Finlayson *et al.* (1988), Johnstone *et al.* (1985) further noted that the accidental transport of weeds by recreational

Table 8.7. The relationship between the presence of any of the five weed species and human activity in 88 New Zealand North Island lakes that possess a macrophyte flora and could support weed growth (adapted from Johnstone *et al.*, 1985).

Human activity	Weed presence (number of lakes)		
	Present	Absent	Total
No boating, no fishing	0	27	27
No boating, fishing	1	2	3
Boating, no fishing	10	1	11
Boating, fishing	39	8	47
Total	50	38	88

boats could be controlled relatively easily (e.g. by clearing boat-launching areas of weeds). Regular monitoring of the aquatic and littoral vegetation of lakes used for power-boating

would also be easy and potentially very effective, since early detection and eradication of exotic species is a cornerstone of management strategies to combat invasive species (Arthington and Mitchell, 1986; Williamson and Fitter, 1996; Leung *et al.*, 2002).

Other effects on aquatic flora and fauna

Figures 8.1 and 8.2 provide a general overview of how water-based recreational activities impact on aquatic plants and animals, respectively (adapted from Liddle and Scorgie, 1980). While most of the more commonly encountered effects of power boats and water-skiing on the aquatic flora and fauna have been discussed in earlier sections, there are published reports detailing the effects of some more specific situations. For example, the retreat of wild rice from a previously wide distribution in

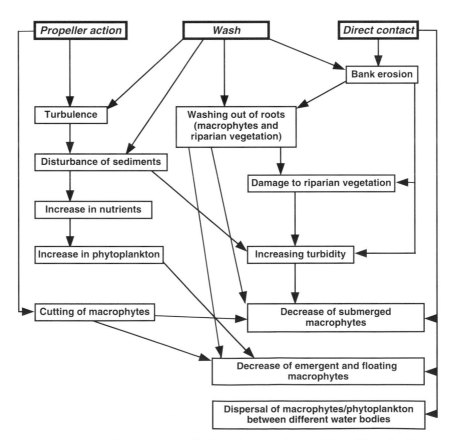

Fig. 8.1. Impacts of power-boating on aquatic plants (adapted from Liddle and Scorgie, 1980).

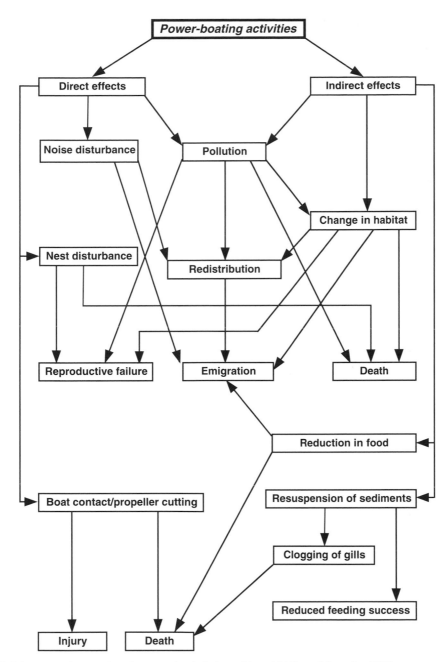

Fig. 8.2. Impacts of power-boating on animals (adapted from Liddle and Scorgie, 1980).

some lakes in Ontario, Canada, to only a few areas inaccessible to powerboats, is a graphic example of how power-boating can seriously affect aquatic biota (Jaakson, 1979). Murphy *et al.* (1995) reported on studies where it was found that silt deposition as a result of power-boat operation can have deleterious effects on invertebrates and fish, including clogging of respiratory structures, reduced feeding rates, increased invertebrate drift, disrupting court-ship displays and spawning behaviour, and reduced hatching rates of fish.

Table 8.8. Maximum overall percentage fatalities of eggs of quinnat salmon, *Oncorhynchus tshawytscha* (Walbaum), subjected to pressure gradients induced in their redds by passages of jet boats in shallow water (reproduced from Sutherland and Ogle, 1975).

Water depth (mm)	150	300	450
Boat speed (m/s)	8.9	5.6	4.0
Fatality (%)	37	39	24

Jet boats, which operate by pumping water through an intake opening and expelling it as a jet at the rear (cf. Sutherland and Ogle, 1975), lack the stirring and damaging effects of propellers and thus are likely to stir up fewer bed sediments. Damaging effects in this boat design appear to be the result of pressure gradients created as the boat passes a set point (Sutherland and Ogle, 1975). Due to their very shallow draught, they can access shoals where fish may have spawned. Sutherland and Ogle (1975) noted that pressure fluctuations created by passing jet boats can kill significant numbers of salmon eggs (Table 8.8).

The ability of fish to cope with disturbance as a result of power-boat operation appears to vary according to species. Jackivicz and Kuzminski (1973a) found that sunfish and bass were able to locate their nests under conditions of normal power-boat operation, while nest-guarding males of bluegill, pumpkinseed and largemouth bass were found to leave their nests when disturbed by power boats. Similar results were obtained by Mueller (1980), who investigated the effects of boating activity upon nest guarding by the longear sunfish (*Lepomis megalotus*) and found that defensive behaviour was altered by boating activities in the nest vicinity, with boat speed and passing distance from the nest being the important factors: slow-moving boats caused the guarding males to abandon the nest more often than fast-moving boats (Table 8.9).

Jackivicz and Kuzminski (1973a) concluded that turbulence from outboard-motor propeller action did not have any major effects directly on fish but that it did reduce the number of bottom-dwelling invertebrates; however, they noted that individuals may just have been moved about by the turbulence created by the propellers.

The Occurrence of Polycyclic Aromatic Hydrocarbons in a Lake Used for Recreational Power Boating: a Case Study

Background and aims

The subject of this case study is Brown Lake, also known as Lake Boumiera by local aboriginal groups. It is situated on North Stradbroke Island, a sand island 27,520 ha in size, located approximately 38 km to the east of the City of Brisbane, Queensland, Australia. Brown Lake is the most accessible lake on the island, attracting visitors from the mainland as well as the island community. In four seasonal surveys of visitor numbers and their recreational preferences, each conducted over 2 days of either a weekend or a school holiday period (June 1996 to March 1997), 2384 individuals and 509 vehicles were counted at Brown Lake, with 78% of visitors citing swimming as their reason for coming to this lake. Brown Lake has been used for power-boating and water-skiing since the early 1960s, and for jet-skiing since 1983, with the intensity of use increasing over time. A total of 60 power boats and jet skis was recorded on Brown Lake during the 1996/97 visitor surveys, and it was not uncommon to find up to 14 power boats and jet skis using the lake simultaneously (Mosisch and Arthington, 2001). Boat engine sizes ranged from 25 cc to 5000 cc in capacity, while jet-ski engine sizes ranged from 500 cc to 1100 cc. The majority of boats and jet skis operated on Brown Lake were run on unleaded two-stroke petrol.

Since the start of power-boating on Brown Lake, sites along its shoreline where boats are launched have become increasingly degraded, especially by the removal/destruction of both littoral and riparian vegetation, resulting in open, destabilized stretches of sand along the shore (Fig. 8.3). Apart from these highly visible physical impacts of powered recreational activities on the littoral and riparian zone, anecdotal evidence of the chemical impacts of boating activities was provided by numerous visitors to the lake. This evidence included reports of boats and jet skis being refuelled from fuel canisters while in the lake, and 'fuel slicks' on the surface of the lake at times of power-boat operations. Written comments received on visitor survey forms indicated that more than 50% of respondents were

Table 8.9. Displacement of guarding longear sunfish males from their nests in relation to propulsion and speed of passing boats (reproduced from Mueller, 1980).

Boat propulsion	Boat speed	Number of boat passes by nest[a]	% of passes causing fish to leave nest
Paddled	1 m/s	43	71%
Motored	1 m/s	20	40%
Motored	>5 m/s	31	3%

[a] At a distance of 0–4.5 m from nests.

Fig. 8.3. Water-skiing on Brown Lake (top) and degraded shoreline at the northern end of the lake due to launching of boats using four-wheel drive vehicles (bottom).

in favour of either complete banning or severely restricting power-boat and jet-ski operations on Brown Lake. Comments included statements such as: 'Prevent the use of power (fuel driven) boats/skis', 'Would like to see powered boating, jet-skiing and four-wheel driving banned from lakes and surrounding areas', 'No powered boats should be permitted', 'Please no power boats'. The major reasons for wishing to limit power-boating were that boats and jet skis are noisy, dangerous and cause water pollution.

Although the physical impacts of power-boat activities around Brown Lake were significant, as discussed above, the particular aims of our study were to: (i) determine the presence of any residues of pollutants arising from motorized recreational activities; (ii) to identify and quantify PAH compounds that may have accumulated in the water and/or sediments of Brown Lake as a result of the operation of powered recreational water craft; and (iii) to evaluate the risk of toxic effects on the aquatic biota, and ecosystem consequences. The study was commissioned by the Local Government (Redland Shire Council) as part of its responsibilities for management of North Stradbroke Island's natural and human resources.

Study area and methods

Both Brown Lake (27°29'30"S, 153°25'45"E; area, 45.7 ha) and a reference lake (Swallow Lagoon, 27°30'00"S, 153°27'15"E; area, 1.5 ha) are naturally acidic, oligotrophic perched lakes situated in dune depressions amidst stabilized high sand dunes, with their aquifers separated from and at a higher altitude than the main water table of the sand mass (cf. Laycock, 1977). Due to their proximity, Brown Lake and Swallow Lagoon are subjected to similar influences of terrain and atmosphere, and feature a very similar littoral and surrounding terrestrial vegetation (cf. Clifford and Specht, 1979). As a result, the two lakes are exposed to comparable inputs of dissolved and particulate organic matter and nutrients from these sources, contributing to their chemically similar water quality. The shoreline and littoral zone of both lakes is composed of siliceous sand, amalgamating with mud in the deeper parts. The bottom layer of these lakes consists of a distinct layer of black

anoxic, compressed organic matter (cf. Bensink and Burton, 1975). This, together with high levels of dissolved organic matter, including tannin from decaying leaves, stains the water in both lakes a distinctive dark brown colour and contributes to its low pH. As a result of this, the aquatic fauna and flora of both Brown Lake and Swallow Lagoon are unusually depauperate; for example, the lakes support no fish, and the aquatic flora is relatively unproductive (cf. Bensink and Burton, 1975). However, the lake supports several rare invertebrate species found only in dune lakes of south-east Queensland (Arthington and Watson, 1982) and Brown Lake has been placed on the Register of the National Estate because of its unusual mode of origin, and its physical, chemical and biological characteristics.

The input of water into perched dune lakes is primarily dependent on rainfall, water runoff from surrounding land, and seepage of rainwater through the sand dunes. Consequently, water levels in the lakes can fluctuate considerably (cf. Laycock, 1975; Lee-Manwar et al., 1980). Brown Lake is also supplied with water from a stream-fed swamp at its southern end. Water loss occurs mainly through seepage through the organic sediment layer and evaporation, as there are no surface stream outflows from these lakes (cf. Laycock, 1977; Lee-Manwar et al., 1980). As a result, any material entering the lakes (e.g. nutrients, pollutants) will tend to accumulate in the sediments and/or the water column and can remain there for long periods of time (Longmore, 1986).

Sites for monitoring water and sediment quality were established on the basis of preliminary visits to both lakes, and data on visitation and usage patterns obtained from visitor surveys. Three sites of high recreational usage, plus two within-lake reference sites, were identified at Brown Lake and used as stations for the collection of replicate water, sand and organic layer samples for three water and sediment quality surveys (Fig. 8.4). Two sites were established for monitoring at Swallow Lagoon, the reference lake (Fig. 8.5). Visitor numbers to this lake are relatively low, and while there were no distinct cleared areas or 'bases' for recreational activities, the southern end of Swallow Lagoon is, on occasion, used for swimming and picnics.

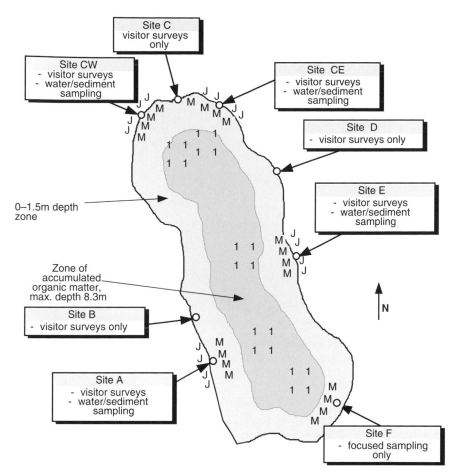

Fig. 8.4. Locations at Brown Lake used for visitor surveys and water/sediment sampling (not to scale). M, Water samples; J, sand samples; I, organic bottom-layer samples.

An extensive testing programme of lake water, sediments and organic bottom layers was devised to determine the presence of any residues of pollutants due to motorized recreational activities. The suite of compounds selected for surveying was based on an extensive review of studies dealing with the effects of motorized recreational activities on lakes and rivers (Mosisch and Arthington, 1998). These compounds included:

- polycyclic aromatic hydrocarbons, short- and long-chained hydrocarbons (e.g. Longworth and McKenzie, 1986; Kuss *et al.*, 1990; Mastran *et al.*, 1994);
- trace metals (e.g. Byrd and Perona, 1980; Kuss *et al.*, 1990);

- phenolic compounds, non-volatile and volatile oils, and other organic compounds (e.g. Jackivicz and Kuzminski, 1973a,b; Burton, 1975);
- total and soluble (dissolved) nutrients (N and P) (e.g. King and Mace, 1974; Longworth and McKenzie, 1986; Hammitt and Cole, 1998);
- tributyltin (e.g. Simmonds, 1986; Murphy *et al.*, 1995).

Water quality of the lakes

Basic water-quality characteristics (e.g. conductivity, pH, major ions, tannins) of Brown Lake and Swallow Lagoon, the reference lake, were

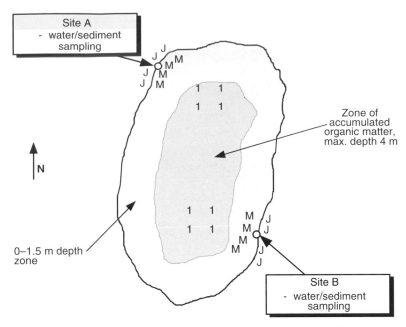

Fig. 8.5. Locations at Swallow Lagoon used for water and sediment sampling (not to scale). M, Water samples; J, sand samples; I, organic bottom-layer samples.

similar and generally within the range for comparable acidic dune lakes located in the southeast Queensland region (Bensink and Burton, 1975; Arthington *et al.*, 1986), giving no indication of any deterioration of water quality in Brown Lake attributable to human usage. Trace metal scans of both water and sediment samples produced results comparable to other similar dune lakes (Arthington *et al.*, 1986). None of these values exceeded the Australian Water Quality Guidelines for Fresh and Marine Waters (ANZECC, 1992), the proposed ANZECC sediment quality guidelines or the draft interim Canadian freshwater sediment quality guidelines (Environment Canada, 1995). Furthermore, there was no evidence of gasoline lead accumulated in the organic sediments of Brown Lake (Mosisch and Arthington, 2001).

Polycyclic aromatic hydrocarbons (PAHs)

No PAH compounds were detected in any of the water samples collected in either lake (Mosisch and Arthington, 2001). If PAHs are detected in water, this usually points to an event of recent or acute pollution, since these compounds have a short residence time in the water column (Mastran *et al.*, 1994). In the case of Brown Lake, power-boating had probably not yet reached the stage where PAHs can be detected in the water column, even when samples were collected at launching and refuelling stations. However, during the five surveys, ten PAH compounds (including heavy molecular weight PAHs, which frequently occur as by-products of the combustion process) were detected in samples taken from the organic bottom layer of Brown Lake (Table 8.10). These compounds were: anthracene, benzo(a)-anthracene, benzo(a)pyrene, benzo(b + k)fluoranthene, benzo(g,h,i)perylene, chrysene, fluoranthene, naphthalene, phenanthrene and pyrene (Mosisch and Arthington, 2001). The most commonly encountered PAHs were benzo(a)pyrene (in 46% of all samples), fluoranthene (in 53% of all samples) and pyrene (in 44% of all samples); these three compounds were detected in the sediments of all five Brown Lake sites. No PAH compounds were detected in any of the samples from the reference lake, Swallow Lagoon.

Table 8.10. Mean PAH values detected in Brown Lake organic sediments during the three basic (*) and two focused (#) sampling trips (all values in µg/kg dry wt ± SE). Total number of positive values recorded during each trip is shown in parentheses.

PAH compound	Trip No. 1 * January 1997	Trip No. 2 * March/April 1997	Trip No. 3 * July 1997	Trip No. 4 # February 1998	Trip No. 5 # September 1998
Anthracene	–	93.33±35.0 (3)	–	27.25±2.49 (4)	–
Benzo(a)anthracene	–	–	42.6 (1)	58.0±37.0 (2)	–
Benzo(a)pyrene	–	314.0±105.0 (2)	245.0±74.5 (3)	130.92±19.19 (26)	394.0±52.34 (28)
Benzo(b+k)fluoranthene	–	–	–	99.0±4.0 (2)	–
Benzo(g,h,i)perylene	–	–	–	–	50.0 (1)
Chrysene	–	–	43.2 (1)	58.0±37.0 (2)	50.0 (1)
Fluoranthene	531.0±234.65 (3)	58.6±10.51 (5)	56.4±7.22 (10)	67.82±20.89 (28)	165.09±24.58 (22)
Napthalene	–	–	17.45±9.75 (2)	–	–
Phenanthrene	–	61.75±9.7 (4)	–	42.0 (1)	–
Pyrene	57.0 (1)	57.0 (1)	40.87±7.46 (11)	48.42±14.13 (26)	111.76±17.61 (17)

Table 8.11. Low and high PAH threshold values in sediments as stated in guidelines proposed by ANZECC (2000) and Environment Canada (1995). The position of Brown Lake PAH values in relation to the sediment guidelines is indicated by arrows (all values in µg/kg dry wt).

PAH compound	ANZECC (2000) guidelines		Draft Environment Canada (1995) guidelines	
	Low	High	Low	High
Anthracene	↑ 85	↓ 1100	n/a	
Benzo(a)anthracene	↓ 261	↓ 1600	↑ 32	↓ 385
Benzo(a)pyrene	↑ 430	↓ 1600	↑ 32	↑ 782
Benzo(b + k)fluoranthene	n/a		n/a	
Benzo(g,h,i)perylene	n/a		n/a	
Chrysene	↓ 384	↓ 2800	↑ 57	↓ 862
Fluoranthene	↑ 600	↓ 5100	↑ 111	↓ 2355
Naphthalene	↓ 160	↓ 2100	n/a	
Phenanthrene	↓ 240	↓ 1500	↑ 42	↓ 515
Pyrene	↓ 665	↓ 2600	↑ 53	↓ 875

↑ At least one sediment sample exceeded the relevant guideline value.
↓ Results of all sediment samples were below the relevant guideline value normalized to 1% organic carbon.
n/a, not available.

The position of PAH concentrations from Brown Lake sediments in relation to published guideline values is shown in Table 8.11. Results falling below the lower guideline values indicate that there is a high probability of no toxic effects on the sediment-dwelling and benthic biota. Results exceeding the higher guideline values indicate that there is a high probability of pronounced effects on sediment-dwelling and benthic organisms. However, some organisms may already be adversely affected when values are within the defined 'low/high' range (cf. ANZECC, 2000).

Levels of PAH contaminants in Brown Lake sediments were generally low; for example, none of the PAH concentrations recorded in Brown Lake sediments exceeded the upper ANZECC (2000) sediment quality guidelines (Table 8.11). However, three PAH compounds exceeded the lower ANZECC guideline values: anthracene (higher in 1.5% of all samples), benzo(a)pyrene (higher in 11% of all samples), and fluoranthene (higher in 0.8% of all samples). Three values for benzo(a)pyrene (830 µg/kg, 955 µg/kg, 1070 µg/kg; 2.3% of all samples) exceeded the upper threshold recommended in the draft interim Canadian freshwater sediment quality guidelines (782 µg/kg; Environment Canada, 1995) (Table 8.11). The following PAH compounds exceeded the respective lower draft interim Canadian sediment quality guidelines, but were still below the upper recommended values (Table 8.11): benzo(a)anthracene (higher in two samples), benzo(a)pyrene (higher in 51 samples; 40% of all samples), chrysene (higher in one sample; 0.8% of all samples), fluoranthene (higher in 19 samples; 15% of all samples), phenanthrene (higher in five samples; 4% of all samples), and pyrene (higher in 26 samples; 20% of all samples).

Discussion

In Brown Lake, sediment monitoring was more useful than water column monitoring in detecting chemical impacts due to motorized recreational activities. PAH compounds introduced into the water column of Brown Lake were likely to be quickly bound to suspended organic and inorganic particulate matter and then deposited into the bottom sediments (cf. Neff, 1979), i.e. the rate of deposition into the sediments is faster than the rate of introduction and resuspension into the water column. It is very likely that the PAHs recorded have accumulated over periods of time, probably since motorized recreational activities started in the lake in the 1960s. As sediments act as sinks of PAHs, these compounds become accumulated in them, and they are still a source for PAHs even when inputs of the compounds have ceased (cf. Wells and Adams, 1991).

Naturally derived (petrogenic) PAH assemblages are characterized by more lower-membered ring structures and a higher number of low molecular weight PAHs, such as naphthalene, acenaphthene and fluorene (Prahl *et al.*, 1984; Mastran *et al.*, 1994). On the other hand, combustion-derived (pyrolytic) PAH assemblages (those that are the product of a combustion process) contain more higher-membered ring structures and a higher number of high molecular weight PAHs, including phenanthrene, fluoranthene, pyrene, benzo(a)pyrene, chrysene, benzofluoranthene and benzo(a-anthracene (Prahl *et al.*, 1984; Mastran *et al.*, 1994). It is well documented that the high molecular weight PAHs, phenanthrene, pyrene and fluoranthene, are reliable indicators ('fingerprints') of a high-temperature combustion PAH source (Prahl *et al.*, 1984; Helfrich and Armstrong, 1986; Mastran *et al.*, 1994). Prahl *et al.* (1984) stated that phenanthrene is commonly contained within mixtures of PAHs from both combustion and unburned fossil fuel sources. This PAH was present at all Brown Lake sites except one, remote from boating activities. Importantly, benzo(a)pyrene, benzo(a)anthracene, chrysene and other PAHs have been classified as probable human carcinogens (Prahl *et al.*, 1984; Mastran *et al.*, 1994; Harvey, 1997).

Mastran *et al.* (1994) reported that only a few PAHs (fluoranthene, phenanthrene and pyrene) were commonly encountered throughout the sediments of the reservoir they studied. This was also the case in the present study, with only three PAHs (benzo(a)pyrene, fluoranthene, pyrene) detected at all sites. As mentioned above, this combination of PAHs is indicative of fossil fuel combustion. These three compounds were also the most commonly encountered in the present study. While Mastran *et al.* (1994) found benzo(a)pyrene, a high molecular weight PAH, in 50% of their study sites, few low weight PAHs were detected. A similar result was observed in the present study: the only low molecular weight PAH compound detected in Brown Lake was found in two sediment samples collected from one site; other low molecular weight PAHs were absent or below the detection limit, further indicating that combustion

Table 8.12. Concentration of benzo(a)pyrene accumulated in the sediments of some lakes and reservoirs (adapted from Neff, 1979), and the levels recorded in Brown Lake.

Lake	Benzo(a)pyrene (μg/kg dry wt)	Country
Plöner See	260–1610	Germany
Lake Constance	443	Germany
Rublevskoye Reservoir	44	Russia
Khiminskoe Reservoir	390–500	Russia
Brown Lake	17–1070	Australia

products were the most likely source of the PAHs present in the lake sediments.

Despite the absence of any major roads and other sources of PAH-carrying runoff, the values recorded in Brown Lake for benzo(a)-pyrene generally fall within the range of values for this PAH compound reported from two lakes located in relatively heavily populated areas in Germany, and are, on average, higher than those recorded in two reservoirs in Russia (Table 8.12). Moreover, benzo(a)pyrene was one of the most frequently encountered and one of the most widespread PAHs in Brown Lake sediments. These results indicate that over the years of power-boat operation on Brown Lake (*c.* 1960–1999), substantial PAH inputs into the sediments have occurred as a result of these recreational activities.

The highest value of fluoranthene detected in this survey (995.0 μg/kg) approached the lower range of this compound recorded by Mastran *et al.* (1994). Yet, unlike Brown Lake, the reservoir surveyed by Mastran *et al.* (1994) is located in a highly urbanized area, featuring three boating marinas, and thus, presumably, subjected to considerably higher power-boat usage than Brown Lake. This indicates that the high values for this compound in Brown Lake are more than likely the result of high power-boat numbers in combination with a relatively small lake volume and the many years of exposure to contamination.

The presence of PAHs in the sediments did not appear to be confined to boat-launching sites. This was evidenced by the presence of the three most common compounds (benzo(a)-pyrene, fluoranthene, pyrene) at all survey sites,

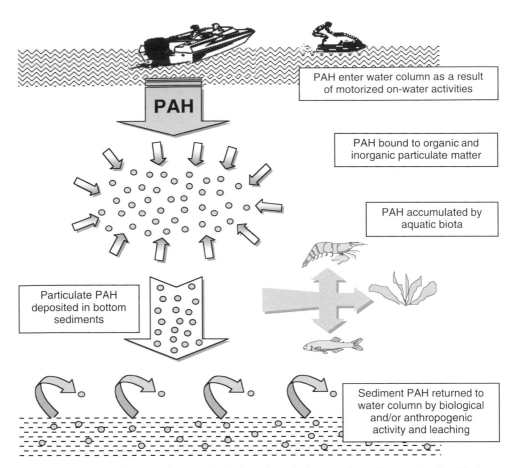

PAH enter water column as a result of motorized on-water activities

PAH bound to organic and inorganic particulate matter

PAH accumulated by aquatic biota

Particulate PAH deposited in bottom sediments

Sediment PAH returned to water column by biological and/or anthropogenic activity and leaching

Fig. 8.6. The pathway of polycyclic aromatic hydrocarbons in the aquatic environment: a simplified conceptual model.

including a site far removed from any boat-launching activities. This suggests that once introduced into the water column, PAHs are mixed throughout Brown Lake before being deposited into the sediments, or that sediments are being resuspended (cf. Mastran *et al.*, 1994). Also, the relatively compact size of Brown Lake, and the fact that power boats and jet skis use most of its length and width, would contribute to easy dispersal and mixing of PAHs.

The high sediment concentrations of the three most prevalent PAHs in Brown Lake (benzo(a)pyrene, fluoranthene, pyrene) indicate that this lake is impacted to a relatively high degree by power-boating activities. Although the biological accumulation of these compounds has not been measured during this

study, this process could be significant, with the uptake of PAHs reported in plankton, vascular aquatic plants, molluscs and fish (e.g. Neff, 1979; Harvey, 1997). A wide range of microscopic and macroscopic animals and plants live in and on the bottom sediments of water bodies, and many of these organisms ingest organic material from these sediments (Neff, 1979). Bioavailability of sediment-bound PAH compounds is an important factor, since this process provides access of PAHs into the aquatic food chain, posing a hazard to many organisms along the way (Neff, 1979). We present a conceptual model of the pathway of PAHs in the aquatic environment in Fig. 8.6.

Brown Lake does not support any fish and mollusc species, but has a varied crustacean and insect fauna in littoral and benthic zones. These invertebrates, closely associated with the sediments, would be exposed to sediment-bound PAHs. The ubiquity and high concentrations of several PAHs can be expected to present a significant risk to these organisms. Of particular concern in Brown Lake are certain rare insect species restricted to oligotrophic lakes in the Queensland sand-dune series (see Bensink and Burton, 1975, Arthington and Watson, 1982; Arthington *et al.*, 1986). Brown Lake is the type locality of one of these rare species, the odonate *Orthetrum boumiera* (Watson and Arthington, 1978).

As a consequence of this investigation of impacts on the lake, and other studies, the use of powered recreational craft has recently been banned on Brown Lake. However, the persistence of PAHs after inputs have ceased (Wells and Adams, 1991), particularly in anoxic sediments (Neff, 1979; Mastran *et al.*, 1994), means that the invertebrates associated with the sediments of this perched dune lake may be exposed to significant concentrations of PAHs for some time to come. Future monitoring of sediment PAH levels in Brown Lake, and bioassay studies, have been recommended to determine the long-term effects of power-boating activities on the lake ecosystem.

Summary and Conclusions

Summaries of the main physical, chemical and biological impacts on aquatic systems by power-boating and water-skiing, as well as the impacts of boat-launching activities, are presented in Figs 8.7, 8.8, 8.9 and 8.10, respectively. Jaakson (1970) stated that 'excessive boating and littoral activity often results, and, in a large way, may contribute to the deterioration of a lake as an attractive recreation area'. Garman and Geering (1985a) and Edmonds *et al.* (1987) noted that power-boating and water-skiing not only had an impact on the aquatic environment itself, but also on the land bordering a water body. An increase in the number of boats operating on a lake might not only put increased pressure on the lake biota but also on the surrounding areas. Not only do the effects of power-boating have to be considered, but also effects on, and possible damage to, the sur-

rounding environment by increases in associated land-based recreational activities and traffic (e.g. four-wheel driving). For example, an increase in the number of visitations (e.g. as a lake becomes a more popular water-skiing venue) will bring with it increases in the number of cars, the amount of rubbish left behind and trampling (and thus destabilization) of the banks (Liddle and Scorgie, 1980). Thus, an area surrounding a site where water-skiing is carried out requires a sufficient infrastructure to support an increase in visitor numbers (e.g. car-parking facilities, picnic areas, constructed paths) and to meet the demands of these visitors (cf. Garman and Geering, 1985a). Garman and Geering (1985a) stated that participants in power-boating and water-skiing activities 'are the least tolerant of management strategies designed to move uses away from sensitive foreshore areas' and that they 'contribute largely to excessive pressures on these areas'. A continuous increase in power-boating and water-skiing on waters where these practices have been carried out in the past will compound possible impacts. Some of the specific requirements for power-boating include good vehicular access to allow boat trailers to be brought in, suitable launching sites (banks with little slope), and a water body free from obstructions (Feilman Planning Consultants, 1987). In addition to this, a dense riparian vegetation is favoured by water-skiers, since this helps in reducing strong winds (Feilman Planning Consultants, 1987).

As recreational boating on inland waters continues to grow, it has become apparent that a sound management strategy is a necessity for the majority of the high-usage waters, in order to avoid a deterioration in both their environmental and recreational qualities (cf. Adams *et al.*, 1992). This need has also been expressed in a report by the Department of Community Services and Health (1990), where it was stated that 'in the absence of proper planning and control, the pressure associated with heavy recreational use can itself rapidly reduce the value of a body of water as a public amenity'. To monitor possible impacts, a baseline study of the aquatic environment concerned would have to be carried out prior to the start of any power-boating or water-skiing activity (cf. Hodges, 1991), or, where this is not possible, an aquatic habitat

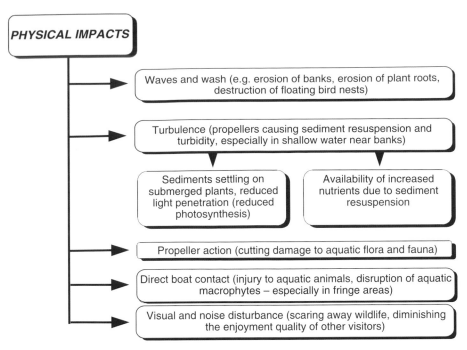

Fig. 8.7. Summary of the main physical impacts on aquatic systems of power-boating and water-skiing activities.

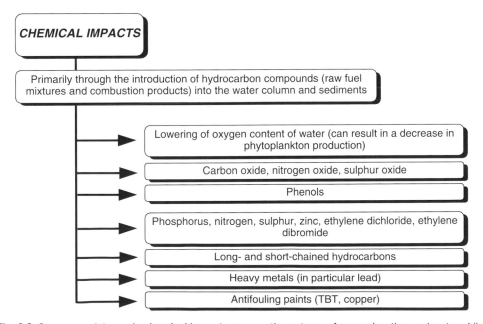

Fig. 8.8. Summary of the main chemical impacts on aquatic systems of power-boating and water-skiing activities. TBT, tributyltin.

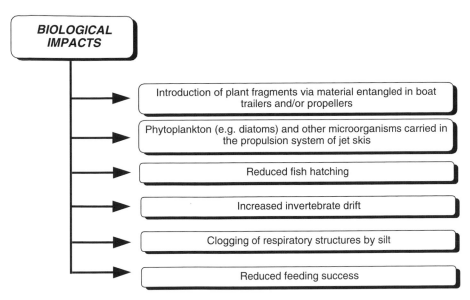

Fig. 8.9. Summary of the main biological impacts on aquatic systems of power-boating and water-skiing activities.

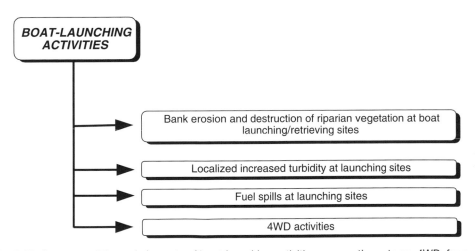

Fig. 8.10. Summary of the main impacts of boat-launching activities on aquatic systems. 4WD, four-wheel drive.

similar to the one used for recreational purposes should be used for comparative studies.

As has been seen from this review, water-based recreational activities such as water-skiing and power-boating can have far-reaching impacts on freshwater ecosystems, many of which are easily recognizable (for example erosional effects, increases in turbidity, noise).

However, not all of the boating-induced impacts are highly visible and may only have an effect after a longer period of motorboat activity (for example, PAHs accumulating in the water column and sediments, resuspended sediments clogging the gills of aquatic insects).

It has become clear that in order to reduce the impact of power-boat operation on water bodies, regulatory measures have to be implemented, either restricting or even totally prohibiting boat usage. Chenoweth (1984) recommended that as one of the specific site requirements, a lake should be greater than 10 ha in size to accommodate power boats, and greater than 50 ha in size in order to safely accommodate water-skiers, stating that each boat takes up 5 ha of space. Jaakson (1979) suggested that on lakes smaller than 50 acres (20.23 ha) water surface, strong consideration should be given to a total ban of all power boats. A lake could easily become congested as a result of uncontrolled power boating, posing a danger to swimmers and other activities, and ultimately resulting in the lake losing its appeal to visitors (Jaakson, 1970). The operation of high-powered motor boats (especially in conjunction with water-skiing) on reservoirs (or lakes) requires patrols to provide a safe environment for activities such as swimming, with the establishment of boat exclusion zones highly recommended to separate swimmers from power boats (Council on Environmental Quality, 1975). In the case where separation between swimmers and powerboats proves to be unsuccessful or impossible, a system where power boating is allowed only on certain days could be implemented (Council on Environmental Quality, 1975). Lane and McComb (1988) reported that on permanent lakes of the Swan Coastal Plain in Western Australia, recreational activities such as swimming and power boating are now prohibited to protect the environment from disturbance, in particular for the benefit of waterbirds.

Power-boating is not permitted on many newly constructed water storages, for example, power-boating and water-skiing have never been allowed on Wivenhoe Dam, south-east Queensland (even though these activities are permitted on the older, nearby Somerset Dam). Recreational activities on the lake are controlled by management policies which stipulate that activities are prohibited where they cause or are likely to cause water pollution, cause or are likely to cause natural resource deterioration, endanger other users of the lake, create an unacceptable nuisance, or involve unacceptable risks to participants (Queensland Premier's Department, 1985). Boats propelled by an electric motor are permitted on the lake.

Jaakson (1979) stated that any attempt to properly manage recreation areas must incorporate measures whereby competition and conflict can be minimized. While the demand for water-based recreation resources is increasing rapidly in most Western countries, attempts to satisfy participants in the conflicting activities (e.g. water-skiers and swimmers) have rarely been successful (cf. Jaakson, 1979).

Authors of the majority of papers and reports consulted during the preparation of this review came to the conclusion that power-boating and water-skiing produce adverse effects on the aquatic environment. However, a small number concluded that 'reasonable levels of use on lakes of reasonable size will produce no adverse consequence' (Australian Water Resources Council, 1984; cf. also Hodges, 1991; Victorian Department of Conservation and Environment, 1991).

While many impacts from power boats and water-skiing on lakes and rivers have been identified and documented, it has become apparent from this review that ecological implications have, in the past, been underestimated. Warrington (1999) commented that 'studies carried out to measure the effects of outboard exhaust on bulk water quality, and on the organisms that live in the water, have not been well designed to answer crucial biological questions and the results are tentative at best'. We concur, and conclude that both the direct and indirect effects of power-boat usage on lake, wetland (including riparian) and river biota warrant further investigation, some critical issues being the impacts of boating on waterbirds and their riparian and wetland habitats, the effects of settled sediments on aquatic flora and fauna, and, in particular, the effects of fuel and combustion products on aquatic biota, including food-chain accumulation processes and ecosystem consequences.

Acknowledgements

This review chapter and the case study are based on two papers published previously by the journal *Lakes and Reservoirs: Research and Management*. We sincerely thank Jenny Dunhill, Blackwell Publishing Ltd. Oxford, for permission to reproduce the contents of these papers in the present form. The Blackwell journal articles we have used are: Mosisch, T.D. and Arthington, A.H. (1998) The impacts of power boating and water skiing on lakes and reservoirs. *Lakes and Reservoirs: Research and Management* 3, 1–17; and Mosisch, T.D. and Arthington, A.H. (2001) Polycyclic aromatic hydrocarbon residues in the sediments of a dune lake as a result of power boating. *Lakes and Reservoirs: Research and Management* 6, 21–32.

The authors thank Professor J. Pigram of the Centre for Water Policy Research, University of New England, Armidale, Australia, for providing access to a number of references. Much of this work was funded by the Redland Shire Council, Queensland, Australia, and supported by the Centre for Catchment and In-Stream Research, Faculty of Environmental Sciences, Griffith University, and the Co-operative Research Centre for Sustainable Tourism.

References

Adams, C. (1993) Environmentally sensitive predictors of boat traffic loading on inland waterways. *Leisure Studies* 12, 71–79.

Adams, C.E., Tippett, R., Nunn, S. and Archibald, G. (1992) The utilization of a large inland waterway (Loch Lomond, Scotland) by recreational craft. *Royal Scottish Geographical Society* 108, 113–118.

ANZECC (1992) *Australian Water Quality Guidelines for Fresh and Marine Waters.* Australian and New Zealand Environment and Conservation Council, Canberra, Australia.

ANZECC (2000) *Australian and New Zealand Guidelines for Fresh and Marine Waters.* Vol. 1. Australian and New Zealand Environment and Conservation Council, Canberra, Australia.

Arthington, A.H. and Mitchell, D.S. (1986) Aquatic invading species. In: Grooves, R.H. and Burdon, J.J. (eds) *Ecology of Biological Invasions.* Australian Academy of Science, Canberra, Australia, pp. 34–53.

Arthington, A.H. and Watson, J.A.L. (1982) Dragonflies (Odonata) of coastal sand-dune fresh waters of south-eastern Queensland and north-eastern New South Wales. *Australian Journal of Marine and Freshwater Research* 33, 77–88.

Arthington, A.H., Burton, H.B., Williams, R.W. and Outridge, P.M. (1986) Ecology of humic and non-humic dune lakes, Fraser Island, with emphasis on the effects of sand infilling in Lake

Wabby. *Australian Journal of Marine and Freshwater Research* 37, 743–764.

Australian Water Resources Council (1984) *Recreational Use of Urban Water Storages and Catchments.* Australian Government Publishing Service, Canberra, Australia.

Bate, J. (1985) Planning and management procedures of the Water Resources Commission of New South Wales. In: *Proceedings of the Workshop on the Recreational Use of Urban Water Storages and their Environs.* Australian Government Printing Service, Canberra, Australia.

Batten, L.A. (1977) Sailing on reservoirs and its effects on water birds. *Biological Conservation* 11, 49–58.

Baud-Bovy, M. and Lawson, F. (1977) *Tourism and Recreation Development.* Architectural Press Ltd, London, UK.

Bensink, A.H.A. and Burton, H. (1975) North Stradbroke Island – a place for freshwater invertebrates. *Proceedings of the Royal Society of Queensland* 86, 29–45.

Boyle, S.A. and Samson, F.B. (1985) Effects of non-consumptive recreation on wildlife: a review. *Wildlife Society Bulletin* 13, 110–116.

Brian Sweeney & Associates (1993) *Australians and Sport.* Brian Sweeney & Associates, South Melbourne, Australia.

Burton, J.R. (1975) *The Recreational Use of Malpas Reservoir.* Report to the Armidale City Council. University of New England, Armidale.

Burton, J.R. (1989) Instream water management: recreational, cultural and scientific aspects. In: Teoh, C.H. (ed.) *Proceedings of the Specialist Workshop on Instream Needs and Water Uses.* Australian Government Publishing Service, Canberra, Australia, pp. 7/1–7/8.

Byrd, J.E. and Perona, M.J. (1980) The temporal variations of lead concentration in a freshwater lake. *Water, Air and Soil Pollution* 13, 207–220.

Chenoweth, A.R.F. (1984) Recreational resources of North Stradbroke Island. In: Coleman, R.J., Covacevich, J. and Davie, P. (eds) *Focus on Stradbroke.* Boolarong Publications, Brisbane, Australia, pp. 371–384.

Clifford, H.T. and Specht, R.L. (1979) *The Vegetation of North Stradbroke Island.* University of Queensland Press, Brisbane, Australia.

Cook, C. (1985) Tourist boats erode banks of the Gordon River. *Australian Ranger Bulletin* 3, 26–27.

Council on Environmental Quality (1975) *Recreation on Water Supply Reservoirs – a Handbook for Increased Use.* US Government Printing Office, Washington, DC.

Cragg, B.A., Fry, J.C., Bacchus, Z. and Thurley, S.S. (1980) The aquatic vegetation of Llangorse Lake, Wales. *Aquatic Botany* 8, 187–196.

Craig, W.S. (1977) Reducing impacts from river rec- reation users. In: *Symposium on River Recrea- tion Management and Research (Proceedings)*. University of Minnesota, Minneapolis.

Department of Community Services and Health (1990) *Australian Guidelines for Recreational Use of Water*. Australian Government Publish- ing Service, Canberra, Australia.

Department of Resources and Energy (1987) *Desirable Guidelines for the Recreational Use of Urban Water Storages and their Catchments*. Australian Government Publishing Service, Canberra, Australia.

Edmonds, H., Whitford, I. and Ford, H. (1987) *A Method for Assessing the Recreational Inland Water Bodies in Victoria*. Environmental Report No. 29. Graduate School of Environmental Science, Monash University, Melbourne, Australia.

Environment Canada (1995) *Interim Sediment Quality Guidelines*. Ecosystem Conservation Directorate Report. CCME Task Group on Water Quality Guidelines, Ottowa, Canada.

Fallen, W. (1985) Effects of power boating upon a water storage. In: *Report on the 11th Seminar for Swimming Pool, Water Supply and Sewerage System Operators*. Department of Local Government, Brisbane, Australia, pp. 1–4.

Feilman Planning Consultants (1987) *Recreational Opportunities of Rivers and Wetlands in the Perth to Bunbury Region*. Vol. 1, Main Report. Western Australian Water Resources Council, Perth, Australia.

Finlayson, C.M., Bailey, B.J., Freeland, W.J. and Fleming, M.R. (1988) Wetlands of the Northern Territory. In: McComb, A.J. and Lake P.S. (eds) *The Conservation of Australian Wetlands*. Surrey Beatty & Sons, Sydney, Australia, pp. 103–126.

Garman, D.E.J. and Geering, D. (1985a) Recreational use of urban water storages and their environs: environmental issues – 1. An analysis. *Australian Parks Recreation* 21, 17–20.

Garman, D.E.J. and Geering, D. (1985b) Recreational use of urban storages and their environs: environ- mental issues. In: *Proceedings of the Workshop on the Recreational Use of Urban Water Storages and their Environs*. Australian Government Printing Service, Canberra, Australia.

Garrad, P.N. and Hey, R.D. (1988) The effect of boat traffic on river regime. In: White, W.R. (ed.) *International Conference on River Regime*. Wiley & Sons, Chichester, UK, pp. 395–409.

Hammitt, W.E. and Cole, D.N. (1998) *Wildland Recreation*, 2nd edn. John Wiley & Sons, New York.

Harvey, R.G. (1997) *Polycyclic Aromatic Hydro- carbons*. Wiley-VCH, New York.

Havera, S.P., Boens, L.R., Georgi, M.M. and Shealy, R.T. (1992) Human disturbance of waterfowl on Keokuk Pool, Mississippi River. *Wildlife Society Bulletin* 20, 290–298.

Helfrich, J. and Armstrong, D.E. (1986) Polycyclic aromatic hydrocarbons in sediments of the southern basin of Lake Michigan. *Journal of Great Lakes Research* 12, 192–199.

Hilton, J. and Phillips, G.L. (1982) The effect of boat activity on turbidity in a shallow broadland river. *Journal of Applied Ecology* 19, 143–150.

Hodges, R. (1991) Riparian damage from boating. *Australian Planner* 29, 101–106.

Horsfall, L., Jelinek, A. and Timms, B. (1988) The influ- ence of recreation, mainly power boating, on the ecology of the Thirlmere Lakes, N.S.W., Australia. *Internationale Vereinigung für Theoretische und Angewandte Limnologie: Verhandlungen* 23, 580–587.

Jaakson, R. (1970) Planning for the capacity of lakes to accommodate water-oriented recreation. *Plan Canada* 10, 29–40.

Jaakson, R. (1979) Shoreline recreation planning: a systems view. In: Wall, G. (ed.) *Recreational Land Use in Southern Ontario*. University of Waterloo, Waterloo, Ontario, Canada, pp. 303–320.

Jaakson, R. (1988) River recreation boating impacts. *Journal of Waterways Port, Coastal and Ocean Engineering* 114, 363–367.

Jaakson, R. (1993) Regulation of recreational boating. *Canadian Water Research Journal* 18, 189–197.

Jackivicz, T.P. Jr and Kuzminski, L.N. (1973a) The effects of the interaction of outboard motors with the aquatic environment – a review. *Environmental Research* 6, 436–454.

Jackivicz, T.P. Jr and Kuzminski, L.N. (1973b) A review of outboard motor effects on the aquatic environment. *Journal of Water Pollution Control Federation* 45, 1759–1770.

Jahrsdoerfer, S.E. and Leslie, D.M. Jr (1988) *Tamaulipan Brushland of the Lower Rio Grande Valley of South Texas: Description, Human Impacts, and Management Options*. Biological Report 88 (36), US Fish and Wildlife Service, Washington, DC.

Johnstone, I.M., Coffey, B.T. and Howard-Williams, C. (1985) The role of recreational boat traffic in interlake dispersal of macrophytes: a New Zealand case study. *Journal of Environmental Management* 20, 263–279.

King, J.G. and Mace, A.C. Jr (1974) Effects of recrea- tion on water quality. *Journal of Water Pollution Control Federation* 46, 2453–2459.

Kirk, J.T.O. (1985) Effects of suspensoids (turbidity) on penetration of solar radiation in aquatic ecosys- tems. *Hydrobiologia* 125, 195–208.

Kuss, F., Graefe, A. and Vaske, J. (1990) *Visitor Impact Management*. Vol. I. National Parks and Conservation Association, Washington, DC.

Lane, J.A.K. and McComb, A.J. (1988) Western Australian wetlands. In: McComb, A.J. and Lake, P.S. (eds) *The Conservation of Australian Wetlands*. Surrey Beatty & Sons, Sydney, Australia, pp. 127–146.

Laycock, J.W. (1975) Hydrogeology of North Stradbroke Island. *Proceedings of the Royal Society of Queensland* 86, 15–19.

Laycock, J.W. (1977) North Stradbroke Island. In: Orme, G.R. and Day, R.W. (eds) *Handbook of Recent Geological Studies of Moreton Bay, Brisbane River and North Stradbroke Island*. Australasian Sedimentologists Group. Department of Geology, University of Queensland, St Lucia, Australia, pp. 52–58.

Lee-Manwar, G., Arthington, A.H. and Timms, B.V. (1980) Comparative studies of Brown Lake, Tortoise Lagoon and Blue Lake, North Stradbroke Island, Queensland. I. Morphometry and origin of the lakes. *Proceedings of the Royal Society of Queensland* 91, 53–60.

Leung, B., Lodge, D.M., Finnoff, D., Shogren, J.F., Lewis, M.A. and Lamberti, G.A. (2002) An ounce of prevention or a pound of cure: bioeconomic risk analysis of invasive species. *Proceedings of the Royal Society of London (Series B -Biological Sciences)* 269, 2407–2412.

Liddle, M. (1997) *Recreation Ecology – the Ecological Impact of Outdoor Recreation and Ecotourism*. Chapman & Hall, London, UK.

Liddle, M.J. and Scorgie, H.R.A. (1980) The effects of recreation on freshwater plants and animals: a review. *Biological Conservation* 17, 183–206.

Longmore, M.E. (1986) Modern and ancient sediments – database for management of ecosystems and their catchments. In: De Dekker, P. and Williams, W.D. (eds) *Limnology in Australia*. CSIRO Melbourne, Dr W. Junk, Dordrecht, The Netherlands, pp. 509–522.

Longworth and McKenzie Pty Ltd (1986) *Survey of Existing and Potential Recreation uses of the Water Board's Catchments and Storages*. Metropolitan Water, Sewerage and Drainage Board, Sydney, Australia.

Marchant, J.H. and Hyde, P.A. (1980) Aspects of the distribution of riparian birds on the waterways in Britain and Ireland. *Bird Study* 27, 183–202.

Marston, F.M. and Yapp, G. (1992) *A Selected Annotated Bibliography of Recreational Water Quality in Alpine Areas*. CSIRO Division of Water Resources, Canberra, Australia.

Mastran, T.A., Dietrich, A.M., Gallagher, D.L. and Grizzard, T.J. (1994) Distribution of polyaromatic hydrocarbons in the water column and sediments of a drinking water reservoir with respect to boating activity. *Water Research,* 28, 2353–2366.

McCall, J.R. and McCall, V.N. (1977) *Outdoor Recreation – Forest, Park and Wilderness*. Bruce, Beverly Hills, California.

Mele, A. (1993) *Polluting for Pleasure*. W.W. Norton & Co, New York.

Mercer, D. (1977) *Leisure and Recreation in Australia*. Sorrett Publishing, Malvern, Australia.

Mosisch, T.D. and Arthington, A.H. (1998) The impacts of power boating and water skiing on lakes and reservoirs. *Lakes and Reservoirs: Research and Management* 3, 1–17.

Mosisch, T.D. and Arthington, A.H. (2001) Polycyclic aromatic hydrocarbon residues in the sediments of a dune lake as a result of power boating. *Lakes and Reservoirs: Research and Management* 6, 21–32.

Moss, B. (1977) Conservation problems in the Norfolk Broads and rivers of East Anglia, England – phytoplankton, boats and the causes of turbidity. *Biological Conservation* 12, 95–114.

Mueller, G. (1980) Effects of recreational river traffic on nest defense by longear sunfish. *Transactions of the American Fisheries Society* 109, 248–251.

Munawar, M., Norwood, W.P. and McCarthy, L.H. (1991) A method for evaluating the impact of navigationally induced suspended sediments from the Upper Great Lakes Connecting Channels on the primary productivity. *Hydrobiologia* 219, 325–332.

Muratori, A. (1968) How outboards contribute to water pollution. *The Conservationist* 22, 6–8.

Murphy, K.J. and Eaton, J.W. (1983) Effects of pleasure-boat traffic on macrophyte growth in canals. *Journal of Applied Ecology* 20, 713–729.

Murphy, K., Willby, N.J. and Eaton, J.W. (1995) Ecological impacts and management of boat traffic on navigable inland waterways. In: Harper, D.M. and Ferguson, A.J.D. (eds) *The Ecological Basis for River Management*. John Wiley & Sons, Chichester, UK, pp. 427–442.

Neff, J.M. (1979) *Polycyclic Aromatic Hydrocarbons in the Aquatic Environment: Sources, Fates and Biological Effects*. Applied Science Publishers, London, UK.

Office of the Commissioner for the Environment (1988) *Victoria's Inland Waters*. Government of Victoria, Melbourne, Australia.

Pearce, H.G. and Eaton, J.W. (1983) Effects of recreational boating on freshwater ecosystems – an annotated bibliography. In: *Waterway Ecology and the Design of Recreational Craft*. Inland

Waterways Amenity Advisory Council, London, UK, pp. 13–68.

Pigram, J. (1983) *Outdoor Recreation and Resource Management.* Croom Helm Ltd, Beckenham, UK.

Prahl, G.F., Crecellus, E. and Carpenter, R. (1984) Polycyclic aromatic hydrocarbons in Washington coastal sediments: an evaluation of atmospheric and riverine routes of introduction. *Environmental Science Technology* 18, 687–693.

Pressey, R.L. and Harris, J.H. (1988) Wetlands of New South Wales. In: McComb, A.J. and Lake, P.S. (eds) *The Conservation of Australian Wetlands.* Surrey Beatty & Sons, Sydney, Australia, pp. 35–57.

Prosser, G. (1985) Planning for recreation needs: the case of urban water storages. *Australian Parks Recreation* 21, 4–9.

Queensland Premier's Department (1985) *The Recreation Plan for Lake Wivenhoe and Environs.* The Co-ordinator-General, Queensland Premier's Department, Brisbane, Australia.

Reichholf, J. (1976) The influence of recreation activities on waterfowl. In: Smart, M. (ed.) *Proceedings of the International Conference on Conservation of Wetlands and Waterfowl.* International Waterfowl Research Bureau, Slimbridge, UK, pp. 364–369.

Rosen, R.A. and Hales, D.C. (1980) Occurrence of scarred paddlefish in the Missouri River, South Dakota – Nebraska. *The Progressive Fish-Culturist* 42, 82–85.

Simmonds, M. (1986) The case against Tributyltin. *Oryx* 20, 217–220.

Smart, M.M., Rada, R.G., Nielsen, D.N. and Claflin, T.O. (1985) The effect of commercial and recreational traffic on the resuspension of sediment in Navigation Pool 9 of the Upper Mississippi River. *Hydrobiologia* 126, 263–274.

Speight, M.C.D. (1973) *Outdoor Recreation and its Ecological Effects: a Bibliography and Review.* Discussion Papers in Conservation, 4. University College, London, UK.

Stewart, R. and Howard, H.H. (1968) Water pollution by outboard motors. *The Conservationist* 22, 6–8.

Surber, E.W. (1971) The effect of outboard motor exhaust wastes on fish and their environment. *Journal of Washington Academy of Science* 61, 120–123.

Sutherland, A.J. and Ogle, D.G. (1975) Effect of jet boats on salmon eggs. *New Zealand Journal of Marine and Freshwater Research* 9, 273–282.

Tanner, M.F. (1973) *Water Resources and Recreation.* Report No. 3, Sports Council, London, UK.

Tarkpea, M. and Svanberg, O. (1982) The acute toxicity of motor fuels to brackish water organisms. *Marine Pollution Bulletin* 13, 125–127.

Vermaat, J.E. and De Bruyne, R.J. (1993) Factors limiting the distribution of submerged waterplants in the lowland River Vecht (The Netherlands). *Freshwater Biology* 30, 147–157.

Victorian Department of Conservation and Environment (1991) *Findings of the Investigation into the Use and Management of the Bridgewater Public Park Reserve.* Victorian Department of Conservation and Environment, Melbourne, Australia.

Wall, G. and Wright, C. (1977) *The Environmental Impact of Outdoor Recreation.* Department of Geography Publication Series, 11. University of Waterloo, Waterloo, Ontario, Canada.

Ward, D. and Andrews, J. (1993) Waterfowl and recreational disturbance on inland waters. *British Wildlife* 4, 62–68.

Warrington, P. (1999) Impacts of outboard motors on the aquatic environment. *North American Lake Management Society.* Available at website www.nalms.org/bclss/impactsoutboard.htm (verified 16 June 2003).

Watson, J.A.L. and Arthington, A.H. (1978) A new species of Orthetrum Newman from dune lakes in eastern Australia (Odonata: Libellulidae). *Journal of Australian Entomological Society* 17, 151–157.

Wells, M.J.M. and Adams, V.D. (1991) Determination of anthropogenic organic compounds associated with fixed or suspended solids/sediments: an overview. In: Baker, R.A. (ed.) *Organic Substances and Sediments in Water.* Vol. 2. *Processes and Analytical.* Lewis Publishers, Chelsea, UK, pp. 409–479.

Williamson, J., Kite, J., Henderson, P. and Bowman Bishaw and Associates (1989) *Waroona Reservoir and Catchment Area Management Plan 1990–2000.* Department of Conservation and Land Management/Water Authority of Western Australia, Perth, Australia.

Williamson, M.H. and Fitter, A. (1996) The characters of successful invaders. *Biological Conservation* 78, 163–170.

York, D. (1994) *Recreational-boating Disturbances of Natural Communities and Wildlife: an Annotated Bibliography.* National Biological Survey, Biological Report 22, US Department of the Interior, Washington, DC.

Yousef, Y.A., McLellon, W.M. and Zebuth, H.H. (1980) Changes in phosphorus concentrations due to mixing by motorboats in shallow lakes. *Water Research* 14, 841–852.

9

Ecological Impacts of Tourism in Terrestrial Polar Ecosystems

Bruce C. Forbes,[1] Christopher A. Monz[2] and Anne Tolvanen[3]
[1]Arctic Centre, University of Lapland, Rovaniemi, Finland; [2]Environmental Studies Program, St Lawrence University, Canton, New York, USA; [3]Department of Biology, University of Oulu, Oulu, Finland

Introduction

Travel to the world's polar regions has been of great interest to 'outsiders' since at least the time of Capt. James Cook. He surveyed extensively around Antarctica and the Arctic for the Royal British Navy on his second and third circumglobal navigations between 1772 and 1779. Early as he was, Cook was firmly within the third wave of European visitors, the second wave having consisted of the key 16th and 17th century expeditions of Ferdinand Magellan (1519–1522), Martin Frobisher (1576–1578), John Davis (1585–1588), Willem Barents (1596), Henrik Hudson (1607–1610), and William Baffin and Robert Bylot (1615–1616). The first wave comprised the Norse, who settled Iceland, southern Greenland and (briefly!) northernmost Newfoundland and explored the coasts of Baffin Island and Labrador. The reports of abundant marine mammals and fish by the second and third waves of explorers set off successive movements to commercially exploit first the Barents Sea, the waters of the Canadian eastern Arctic and, later, the Bering and Beaufort Seas. They sought oil, baleen, ivory and food, not to mention adventure. As a result, by the early 1500s Basques had established fishing and whaling settlements in southern Labrador and by 1614 some 25 ships were whaling in the vicinity of several stations and settlements on Svalbard (Armstrong *et al.*, 1978; Sugden, 1982).

Many of these ventures actually harboured political (nationalist) and scientific, in addition to commercial, intent. The difficult journeys to traverse the so-called Northeast and Northwest Passages thus resulted in the collection of numerous scientific 'specimens' (minerals, plants, birds, even occasional humans) and the naming of countless geographic features. Outside of Svalbard, Iceland and Antarctica, many of these places had long since been named, or were at least well known, by the indigenous peoples who inhabited them (Müller-Wille *et al.*, 1987). As with mountain climbers in alpine regions, there has always been special importance attached to 'being first'.

Then, much as today, arctic residents themselves tended to view the new arrivals as visitors or transients, with seemingly little incentive to stay for any length of time and high turnover among personnel, even at established stations. Perhaps this is also the nature of polar tourism. In Finnish Lapland, for example, domestic tourists are generally repeat visitors, whereas the majority of foreigners visit only once (J. Saarinen, personal communication 2003). For ship-borne tour operators in both polar regions, a significant percentage (25–30%) of tourists do return repeatedly, depending upon the itinerary/destination (A. Grenier, personal communication 2003). Outsiders tend to view the region with a sense of mystery and romance; something difficult to obtain but worth substantial cost and effort to visit at least once. It is no wonder that the marketing for tourism tends to revolve around the notion of the Arctic as one of 'the last wilderness frontiers' (Swaney, 1999), 'the final frontiers' (Cornwallis and Swaney, 1991) or 'the last great untouched wilderness areas on Earth' (Soublière, 1997). With its lack of an indigenous human population, the Antarctic is marketed as 'the loneliest of lands', as well as 'a spectacular wilderness' (Rubin, 1996).

The concept of 'wilderness' is itself a Western construct, with its roots in Judeo-Christian fundamentalism. Europeans brought this concept with them to North America as they set out to tame the ostensibly 'wild' lands of the continent's western frontier (Nash, 1982). In as much as it applies to polar environments, it is worth keeping in mind that arctic cultures have not recognized this concept, since they are traditionally at home in these so-called wild and barren arctic lands (Forbes, 2004). Interestingly, two decades after it was coined, 'ecotourism' remains a term with no mutually agreed meaning or value. Yet, without discussing semantics, it is apparent that ecotourism in polar lands has much to do with the desire of tourists to visit 'wilderness' or 'unspoiled nature' (Page and Dowling, 2002). Wilderness can be a formal designation sanctioned by the government, as it is in the USA (Klein, 2002), or more informal, as in marketing literature such as brochures and guide or handbooks (Bruemmer, 1993; Swaney, 1999). In either case, there is a necessary, if sometimes tacit, connection between ecotourism and the development of conservation strategies, e.g. protected areas (Bonner and Smith, 1985; Dingwall, 1995a; Ceballos-Lascuráin, 1996; Humphreys et al., 1998).

Management strategies are necessary if polar ecotourism is to be sustainable (Humphreys et al., 1998; Kaltenborn, 2000; Kaae, 2002). The reason is that tourism, in general, has expanded significantly in all sectors of the Arctic and Antarctic in recent decades. As a result there are widespread concerns about dilution of the tourists' 'wilderness' experience, at a minimum, in addition to degradation of the environment and indigenous cultures in the worst-case scenarios (De Poorter, 1996; Nuttall, 1998; Prokosch, 2001).

This chapter will provide an overview of the nature and breadth of tourism in polar environments. Special emphasis will be placed on ecological impacts associated with contemporary recreation activities in terrestrial arctic and subarctic ecosystems. The format will be geographical, organized by individual regions.

Geographic Regions

Alaska

Tourism has played an important role in the economic and cultural development of Alaska over the past 125 or more years. Although the resource-extractive industry has also been a major economic force during the same period, it is arguable that tourism and recreation has been a more consistent factor in the development and changes in the Alaskan landscape. In 2001, it is estimated that tourism generated over US$1.8 billion in visitor expenditures, with many of the visitors no doubt attracted to Alaska to experience the dramatic natural environment (Alaska Travel Industry Association, 2001). Tourism and total visitation continues to grow in the state despite the reputation of Alaska being more expensive than other areas (Nichols Gilstrap, 2000). For the purposes of this chapter, we will focus on ecotourism activities in arctic Alaska, with reference as appropriate to southern Alaska, where the majority of ecotourism operations currently take place (Colt et al., 2002).

The roots of tourism in Alaska can be traced back to at least the latter 1800s, where the coastal communities of south-east and south-central Alaska actively promoted and supported steam-ship tourists to explore the natural and cultural highlights of the area. Natural areas such as Glacier Bay and the Muir snowfield were primary attractions, as well as the cultural aspects of communities of Sitka and other areas. In the Arctic, the writings of Robert Marshall in the 1930s, regarding his expeditions to the Brooks Range, certainly increased the reputation of the area as the 'ultimate wilderness' (Marshall and Marshall, 1970). Today the state government and several industry organizations actively promote tourism and ecotourism as essential components of the economy. In particular, the Alaska Wilderness Recreation and Tourism Association, an organization of ecotourism professionals, has been active in organizing ecotourism activities and in promoting sustainable practices and policies (Alaska Wilderness Recreation and Tourism Association, 2002).

Northern Alaska remains a vast, wild landscape with opportunities for visitors to experience an arctic wilderness in as close to an untouched state as is possible in the 21st century. None the less, impacts from visitation do exist and continue to be a concern, particularly as visitors travel into new areas in potentially sensitive arctic environments. Despite the remoteness of the Alaskan Arctic, technological advances and increased access, combined with widespread marketing by the tourism industry, have driven substantial increases in visitation. In addition, activities with short histories, such as aircraft 'flightseeing', snowmobile use and mountaineering, are increasing, adding to the management challenges and impact concerns (Martin, 2003). While some ecotourism activities in north Alaska are limited to developed settings, such as lodges and other tourist facilities (Bettles Lodge, 2003), the many visitors to protected areas are primarily oriented towards backcountry travel in the wilderness parks and preserves (National Park Service, 2003). Outfitters and guides offer a range of activities including dog sledding, kayaking and river rafting, backcountry fishing, and hiking and climbing. As such, ecotourists are travelling and camping in wilderness environments, with the associated potential impacts from these activities being disturbance to vegetation, soils, wildlife and effects on water quality.

The Alaskan Arctic remained relatively free of human impact until petroleum exploration began in the 1940s (Walker *et al.*, 1987). Many studies have been conducted on the impacts of oil-field development (e.g. Oechel, 1989; Reynolds and Tenhunen, 1996; Truett and Johnson, 2000), some of which relate to possible tourism impacts, such as the consequences of vehicle disturbance on arctic tundra in summer (e.g. Bliss and Wein, 1972) and in winter (Felix *et al.*, 1992; Emers *et al.*, 1995; Emers and Jorgensen, 1997). Other disturbances related to tourism, such as the effects of sand and dust on tundra adjacent to gravel

roads, have also been examined (Auerbach *et al.*, 1997).

Actual applied research on impacts as a consequence of ecotourism and related activities in arctic Alaska is limited to a few published studies, and some ongoing monitoring efforts in several of the protected areas (e.g. Emers *et al.*, 1997). Impacts from backcountry use in the north were observed as early as 1976 in the Arrigetch Peaks Region of Gates of the Arctic National Park, an area of high visitor appeal and ecological importance (Cooper, 1986). Two studies have examined the ability of Alaskan tundra ecosystems to tolerate off-trail, dispersed recreation use, such as that from backcountry camping and hiking. An unpublished report by Reid and Schreiner (1985) investigated the consequences of low levels of trampling applied throughout the summer to three vegetation types in Denali National Park. The alpine community in this study, similar in composition to the *Dryas* tundra common in the arctic, was found to be relatively durable to human use. Monz (2002) investigated the tolerance of two common plant communities in arctic Alaska to hiking disturbance. Both the *Dryas* tundra and the tussock tundra were found to be moderately tolerant to hiking disturbance and, although specific responses varied between the two plant communities, pre-disturbance conditions had returned to all but the areas of highest disturbance after 4 years. This suggests that, with visitor use below impact threshold levels and with minimum-impact education programmes, it is possible to allow for primitive and unconfined recreation and to maintain these areas with a minimum of observable impact.

The issue of maintaining a high level of resource quality in protected areas of the Alaskan North will undoubtedly require future research and the careful management of visitors. The overall body of knowledge on visitor impacts to wildlands (Leung and Marion, 2000), and the current state of information on the Alaskan Arctic, suggest several areas where future efforts might be directed:

1. **Impacts associated with increased aircraft use**. In Alaska, aircraft (primarily small bush planes) have played an important role in allowing for visitor access to remote wilderness areas

largely devoid of roads. Recently, some concerns have been raised on the part of managers as to the appropriate levels of impact as a result of aircraft landing on tundra (Roger Kaye, personal communication 2000). Strategies for effective management of landing sites so that impacts are not long lasting, without compromising important visitor access, should be investigated.

2.   Impacts adjacent to the Dalton Highway. The opening of the Dalton Highway, connecting Fairbanks to Prudhoe Bay, to the public (c. 1994) has improved access to some areas of the region, and it is unclear if associated impacts have progressed (Monz, 2002). Assessment and monitoring of impacts and visitor trends will become more important as use increases in areas accessible from the highway.

3.   Dispersal versus containment strategies on arctic tundra for overnight camping. There is some evidence that dispersal camping strategies (where visitors are not required to camp in designated sites) are effective at minimizing impacts in arctic tundra ecosystems (Monz, 2002), but this should be investigated experimentally. Currently this is the primary backcountry camping management strategy in many areas in Alaska, and some additional specific minimum impact guidance would be beneficial.

Northern Canada/Greenland

As mentioned earlier, the first European visitors to northern Canada and southern Greenland were Norse, and later explorers and commercial whalers. The Hudson's Bay Company established the first arctic trading posts in Canada in the 1920s, as the fur trade expanded from the essentially boreal beaver (*Castor canadensis*) to include polar fox (*Alopex lagopus*). Actual settlements were not established until later, in the 1950s and 1960s (Wenzel, 1991).

Interest in national parks in subarctic and arctic Canada began already early in the twentieth century, with Wood Buffalo National Park established in 1922, straddling the 60th parallel in Alberta and the Northwest Territories, primarily to protect the bison (*Bison bison atha-*

bascae). The first truly arctic national park reserve was established on south-central Baffin Island in 1972 (Wilson, 1976), along with two subarctic park reserves at Kluane, Yukon Territory and Nahanni, Northwest Territories (Nelson, 1984). Despite this, tourism in the Northwest Territories, and what was to eventually become Nunavut, was generally considered insignificant until the 1980s (Hamley, 1991). By then, a second arctic park had been established on northern Ellesmere Island (McNamee, 1987), with several others under consideration, respectively, for northern Yukon, Banks Island, Bathurst Inlet, Wager Bay and northern Baffin and Bylot Islands (Hamre, 1993).

By the 1990s, tourism had become a major source of revenue in the summer months all across the Canadian North (Bone, 1992). Tourism continues to grow in importance to the northern economy because not only does it provide employment for local people in the service industries, it also improves sales of local crafts, such as soapstone carving, graphic prints, clothing made from traditional materials. In addition, each Inuit village is permitted to kill a specified number of polar bears annually, and these hunting rights may be sold to non-residents and thus provide cash for local guides and outfitters (Swaney, 1999). The main activities vary somewhat according to location, but tend to revolve around access to wildlife, spectacular landscapes and local culture. In a general study of the motivations of Canadian ecotourists, the importance of 'wilderness factors' and an undisturbed environment in which to undertake these activities emerged as dominant considerations (Page and Dowling, 2002). However, the fact that some of these tourists also engage in fishing and non-trophy hunting sets up potential conflicts with the subsistence activities of indigenous peoples (Bone, 1992), similar to the situation in Alaska (Nuttall, 1998). Certain Inuit communities of Nunavut see ecotourism as having the potential for replacing income lost through the European Community boycott on sealskin imports (Wenzel, 1995). In a post-modern twist, the ban was originally instigated by animal rights advocates ostensibly acting on 'ecological' principles (Wenzel, 1991).

Already during the planning phases, concerns were raised by scientists about the compatibility between the proposed northern national parks and other protected areas, the prospects for tourism, and the management and conservation of sensitive environments (Nelson, 1984). Given its unusual location in the High Arctic at the northernmost tip of North America, the park proposal for Ellesmere Island garnered serious criticism because of the stated intent of the territorial government and Parks Canada to establish a 'regional tourist vacation package' and to market the park as a tourist destination (England, 1982). The essential contradiction in this and other northern parks revolves around the fact that Canadian national parks are established for 'the dual purpose of enjoyment and the protection of a natural heritage' (England, 1983). These aims are in addition to the more political issues of national sovereignty and the land claims process (Fenge, 1986; McNamee, 1987). The challenge for ecotourism in the region was laid down by the lead scientist for the Natural Resource Inventory that necessarily preceded establishment of the park. He argued that future access should be tightly restricted to small numbers of tourists who would be subjected to a rigorous 2- to 3-day orientation programme to inform them about the importance of preserving archaeological sites and critical habitats for wildlife (England, 1982). Given its extreme remoteness and the high cost of transport, the park has proven, in reality, to be accessible 'for wealthy wilderness seekers only' (Swaney, 1999).

While the total number of tourists remains low relative to boreal and temperate regions, it has been observed that, even in the Low Arctic, noticeable trails can develop after 100–200 passes by hikers, depending on the type of terrain. According to Welch and Churchill (1986), 300–400 visitors per year had caused significant damage within 10 years to preferred hiking trails and camping locations in Auyuittuq National Park on Baffin Island. Overall, some 500–600 hikers use the main trail in Pangnirtung Pass each year and considerable erosion occurs on trails associated with sandy aeolian material (Tarnocai and Gould, 1998). In the High Arctic, Kevan *et al.* (1995) found that a single pass of a tracked vehicle when the ground was thawed was sufficient to cause significant damage to

wet sedge meadows and that foot trails from a handful of researchers were still visible after 13 years of disuse. More recent monitoring of foot traffic has found 'considerable human impact' in a 3–4 km radius around the Tanquary and Lake Hazen camps in Quttinirpaaq National Park on Ellesmere Island (Tarnocai *et al.*, 2001). Counter to expectations voiced during the park's planning phase, there was less visible impact on areas associated with trails than on areas with dispersed traffic. Thus, in the newly established park, dispersed traffic has already had a visible impact, the negative effects of which are expected to increase as the number of visitors increases in the next decade.

In Greenland, as in northern Canada, the early 1900s also marked the beginning of rapid population growth as settlements for fishing, hunting and sheep farming were established in the south and west (Born, 2001; R.O. Rasmussen, personal communication 2003). Organized tourism began in the late 1950s and increased steadily to about 7000 tourists annually during the 1960s. While statistics have been poorly kept in the past, this breaks down to approximately 3300–4000 land-based tourists, and the rest from cruise ships or 1-day flights from Iceland. Since then a concerted and highly ambitious effort has been made to increase the annual total of tourists to 35,000 by the year 2005 (Christensen, 1992). As of 1991, sustainable tourism has been one of three key issues in a commercial national development strategy established by the Greenlandic Home Rule government, and substantial public funds have been allocated to tourism development. It was stipulated that the developments must be environmentally and culturally responsible. To date, the expected income and job-generating effects have not been met (Kaae, 2002).

As in other northern regions, the industry is highly seasonal, with most tourists arriving in July and August. Greenland Tourism divides the country into four main geographical regions (north, south, east, west) (Kaae, 2002). As well, three different subzones within southern Greenland have been planned to accommodate a range of activities which all tend to focus strongly on nature-oriented qualities and activities. Some of these have been important in Greenland tourism for many years. Those which might be accommodated under the umbrella of ecotourism include mountaineering, hiking, rock-climbing, cross-country skiing, wildlife viewing (whales, muskox, wild reindeer), dog-sledging, sailing and iceberg-touring, visits to historical sites, and general sightseeing, including trips to view the inland ice cap (Christensen, 1992). Hunting permits for tourists are available, but are not valid for muskoxen, walrus, polar bears or whales (Helms, 1991). Kaae (2002) asserts that the tourists indeed come primarily to experience the unique 'arctic nature' and the Inuit culture, including local handicrafts. Interestingly, while some tourists may perceive of nature in Greenland as 'wilderness', the term 'wilderness' does not seem to appear in tourist brochures or within general Danish language (79% of the tourists come from Denmark), and no classifications such as 'wilderness' exist in current Danish nature classification systems.

Northeast Greenland National Park, the world's largest, was established in 1974 in the High Arctic. In addition, there are five smaller protected areas, based on legislation from 1980, and 11 so-called Ramsar areas for protecting wetlands and bird habitats, which are not legally recognized and allow for informally regulated hunting and fishing access. Given the requirement of special permission to visit, coupled with extreme remoteness, the National Park receives only 150 tourists a year. Instead, most tourists restrict their visits to the more accessible coastal subarctic and Low Arctic areas of southern, western and eastern Greenland. Tourism impacts have received little study to date, but an ongoing inter-Nordic study aims to map environmental impacts of the tourism industry in Greenland, Iceland and Svalbard. Initial results indicate that tourists respond negatively to visual pollution and that impacts result from local residents as much as from tourists (Kaae, 2002). Past research has addressed the impacts of patchy disturbances on tundra vegetation and soils, such as off-road vehicle traffic, transient housing (from the Norse period to more modern settlements) and experimental removal of the organic layer (Bay and Holt, 1983; Holt and Bay, 1983; Forbes *et al.*, 2001). Another area of concern is intentional or unwitting disturbance of wildlife, e.g. nesting peregrine falcons (Mordhorst, 1998).

Northern Fennoscandia and Svalbard

In northern Europe, adventure holidays began as early as the 19th century. Wealthy Europeans travelled to Norway to fish for salmon and hunt wild animals. There were people going on private cruises to Svalbard in the 1850s, while regular cruise traffic had begun by the 1870s – also stopping at North Cape – and a hotel catering to Svalbard's ship-borne tourists existed by 1896 (Fogg, 1998; Viken, 1998; Kaltenborn, 2000). Increasing tourist numbers soon led to the establishment of national parks, to preserve areas for the dual purposes of nature conservation and recreation. Nine national parks, for example Sarek, were founded in Sweden in 1909, being the first national parks in the whole of Europe. In Iceland, Thingvellir National Park was established in 1928, while in Finland the first parks, Pallas-Ounastunturi and Pyhätunturi, were founded 10 years later in 1938. Norway, perhaps with the longest history of nature tourism in Fennoscandian countries, established its first national park, Rondane, as late as 1962, whereas on Svalbard the parks were established in 1973.

At present, there are approximately 20 national parks in Fennoscandian Lapland. Parks in Norway, Svalbard and certain Swedish parks are especially popular destinations for adventure tours, while in Finnish national parks, with easier terrain and smoother mountains, hiking and cross-country skiing are the most popular forms of recreation. Svalbard is often characterized as 'the last European wilderness' (Kaltenborn and Emmelin, 1993). Some 20,000–25,000 tourists come to Svalbard yearly on overseas cruises, which is about one-quarter of all tourism in the circumpolar High Arctic (Hindrum, 1998; Kaltenborn, 2000). In Finnish Lapland, the largest national parks, UKK and Pallas-Ounastunturi, are visited annually by 150,000 and 100,000 visitors, respectively. In recent years, around 200,000–250,000 tourists have visited North Cape annually, and a total of 30,000–40,000 have visited Svalbard (Viken, 1998). Recreational activity is also extensive around large combined tourism–business areas, such as Finland's Saariselkä, Ylläs and Levi, which emphasize modern forms of winter recreation among their activities, such as downhill skiing and snowmobiling.

The first national parks were established in order to conserve landscapes of beautiful scenery and aesthetic value for recreational purposes. Nature conservation and recreation have long been regarded to benefit from each other. With the steady increase in tourist numbers over the years, however, conflicts have arisen between nature conservation, recreation and some traditional forms of land use, e.g. reindeer herding. The reasons include the amount of locally apparent degradation of vegetation and soils (erosion), disturbance to animals and increasing tourism-related infrastructure (roads, cabins, powerlines, etc.) (Bäck *et al.*, 1989; Helle and Särkelä, 1993; Vistnes *et al.*, 2001). According to Saarinen *et al.* (2000), during the 1970s and 1980s awareness of natural processes increased, and the emphasis of nature conservation was on threatened and rare species. Today, the protection of biodiversity and maintenance of ecosystem functions are the main rationales for conservation, instead of single species and habitats (Saarinen *et al.*, 2000). Attention is also paid to social and economical conditions of the local communities, which has brought back the role of recreation and tourism in the planning, administration and management of nature conservation areas.

The relative importance of tourism as a year-round source of income is constantly increasing in northern Fennoscandia, with the simultaneous relative decrease of traditional sources of livelihoods, such as forestry, farming, hunting and fishing. At present, the income from tourism exceeds the income from agriculture and forestry in many rural municipalities in Finland (Saastamoinen *et al.*, 2000). The beneficial impact of tourism on local economies has increased the positive attitudes of people towards visitors, although there may still be significant scepticism towards tourism in the more rural areas. Popular modern museums focusing on regional nature, culture and history now exist in northern Norway (e.g. Tromsø; Varangerbotn), Sweden (e.g. Jokkmokk) and Finland (e.g. Inari; Rovaniemi).

The right of public access has largely shaped the development of recreation and ecotourism throughout Fennoscandia. Known popularly as 'everyman's rights', this allows for free access to and use of both public and private land, provided no harm is caused to people,

animals or vegetation. Traditional outdoor activities, e.g. walking, skiing and biking, and gathering of berries and mushrooms, are allowed for everyone, whereas restrictions are made considering, for example, the use of motorized vehicles or camping for more than one night, use of firewood, etc. These rights show some variation among the Fennoscandian countries, with Svalbard, for example, posing less restrictions to the use of motorized vehicles compared with mainland Norway (Kaltenborn, 2000), Sweden and Finland. Despite the right of public access in unprotected areas, zoning has been used to limit access to the most sensitive sites in national parks and nature reserves. For example in Pallas-Ounastunturi National Park in Finnish Lapland, hiking in restricted zones is forbidden during summer, whereas in wilderness and basic-access zones, hiking and skiing are allowed. However, official trails are only located in the basic zones, which concentrates most recreational use within the least-sensitive habitats. On Svalbard, there is also concern about disturbance of wildlife in sensitive habitats; in particular, marine bird-cliffs (Umbreit, 1998) and beach-dwelling arctic terns (Stonehouse, 1998).

In Finnish national parks, local people are allowed to continue hunting and reindeer herding, but the increase in recreation may, in some parks, lead to restrictions on the possibilities to maintain these traditional activities. Ironically, as Beach (1994) points out, 'the tourist who sets out to experience the last great wilderness in Europe does not always appreciate that this "wilderness" is in fact the immemorial homeland of the indigenous Saami and the stamping grounds for a highly developed traditional reindeer herding'. The Saami have indeed been instrumental in creating their environment, which some conservationists wish to label as purely natural (Nuttall, 1998). The national parks are actually quite important for the reindeer, due to the availability of epiphytic lichens (*Alectoria* spp. and *Bryoria* spp.) during winter, during the calving period in spring, and for relief from insect harassment during summer, when the reindeer are willing to climb to the high fjells (Warenberg *et al.*, 1997). Reindeer herders have the right to use snowmobiles and all-terrain vehicles (ATVs) in conjunction with their work. Since recreation and reindeer herding occur in the same region, the vegetation in very sensitive fjell areas is subject to significant wear. Mobilized and more intensive reindeer herding has increased the numbers of reindeer, which has had a negative impact on the cover of certain lichens – via both consumption and trampling – as well as the regeneration of mountain birch (Lehtonen and Heikkinen, 1995), in addition to the negative effects on the terrain by the vehicles.

In Fennoscandia, scientific research on the ecological impacts of recreation started during the 1970s, which is considerably later than in North America and Great Britain, for example, where vegetation studies had already been published in the 1930s (Bates, 1935). Some monitoring of the impacts of recreation had been carried out earlier, but the information has not been published. In Finland, most published studies on ecological impacts of recreation have been carried out in southern or central parts of the country (Holmström, 1970; Kellomäki, 1973, 1977; Kellomäki and Saastamoinen, 1975; Nylund et al., 1979; Malmivaara et al., 2002), while the number of studies concentrating on Finnish Lapland is smaller. Hoogesteger investigated the vegetation changes around wilderness huts in Finnish and Swedish Lapland (Hoogesteger, 1976, 1984; Hoogesteger and Havas, 1976), while Tolvanen et al. (2001) have studied the impact of experimental trampling on regeneration of subarctic vegetation. In Swedish Lapland, regeneration of subarctic tundra heath vegetation was monitored for 3 years in an experimental study by Emanuelsson (1984). Norwegian studies have investigated, for example, the effects of arctic expeditions on heath vegetation and soil (Gellatly et al., 1986a,b), the influence of experimental or recreational trampling on the recovery of fen, grassland and heath vegetation (Arnesen, 1999a,b), or followed 22 years of natural regeneration following trampling within three vegetation types in arctic–alpine tundra (Wielgolaski, 1998).

Ecological changes are inevitable even after very low levels of visitor traffic. The direct impacts of recreation are invariably negative: the value of the environment decreases as a consequence of wear and decreased visual quality. A reduction in species cover and density occurs even at low trampling intensities,

after which the change is slower. On many trails, there are hundreds or thousands of users during a single summer. The main issue is to keep the spatial dimensions of the trails under control, i.e. prevent their further expansion. For example, at Finland's Saariselkä tourist resort, with over 150,000 day hikers per year, the width of trails varies between 1.4 and 3.6 m, the widest points being 8 m, which can also be seen from a distance of many kilometres. The deepest points can be over 30 cm, which may be partially a consequence of fluvial soil erosion, especially during the snowmelt period (Rautio et al., 2001). Camping has an even greater local impact on vegetation than hiking. In UKK National Park, the amount of altered vegetation area around wilderness huts had increased 2.5- to 19-fold in 1999 (Rautio et al., 2001) compared with measurements carried out at the same sites 25 years earlier (Hoogesteger, 1976). During this time period, summer visitor numbers had increased fivefold at some huts, from 1000 to 5000 people (Rautio et al., 2001).

The wear and tear on the environment reduces its value for recreation. Especially in areas of summer tourism, attempts have been made to protect the environment from further wear. Complete closure of the trail or addition of artificial structures, e.g. stairs, cover, duckboards, are probably the only methods to protect the environment. Zoning is used to limit access to the most sensitive sites within protected areas. For example, in Pallas-Ounastunturi National Park, hiking in restricted zones is forbidden during summer, whereas in wilderness and basic zones, hiking and skiing are allowed. However, official trails are only located in the basic zones, which concentrates most recreational use within these least-sensitive habitats.

Perhaps the most neglected areas today are those that concentrate on winter recreation, especially downhill skiing. Management of the slopes and the wear of the environment is not seen by visitors due to the snow cover in winter. In summer there is little interest among owners for costly restoration activities to improve the quality of the environment. According to a questionnaire made in Ylläs tourist resort in Finland, local residents were more concerned about the condition of their environment than were the visitors (Rautio, 1997). A restoration project was established in the area in 1994, due to public debate caused by the low visual quality of the downhill skiing centre. The project aimed at finding natural methods to improve the quality of the environment. The results showed that there are no rapid methods for the restoration of downhill skiing slopes with natural vegetation (Rautio, 1997). Perhaps these discouraging results have hampered the later restoration attempts of the skiing centre, while other centres, e.g. Levi, have used restoration activities as a method to improve their image.

Russia

The first protected areas in Russia were established as early as the reign of Peter the Great (1696–1725), although national parks have existed only since 1983. Until very recently the strict nature reserves, so-called Zapovedniks, were off-limits to the general public, with a complete ban on all economic and other activities, including ecotourism (Fogg, 1998). But new rules allow for the designation of special zones within Zapovedniks where tourist nature trails can be established. As in North America and Fennoscandia, national parks serve a variety of purposes, including protection of natural complexes and cultural heritage, as well as maintaining public access for hiking, camping, skiing and other recreational pursuits, in addition to environmental education.

So far, tourism linked to protected areas is on a minute scale. Yet nature tourism is considered to offer one of the few opportunities in modern Russia to raise money for conservation. Income generation through ecotourism is expected to be easier for national parks than for the four other types of protected areas, because recreation falls within their mandate. The Bering Straits region has already begun to attract visitors via Alaskan ecotourism companies, and large numbers of tourists go ashore from boats to visit archaeological sites, native villages, and seabird and walrus colonies (Wells and Williams, 1998). In addition, the Northeast Passage offers substantial opportunities for developing ship-borne tourism (Johnston and Hall, 1995). At least one observer has pointed out the irony of 'eco' tourists accessing some of the most sensitive terrestrial habitats of

the High Arctic via Russian nuclear-powered icebreakers through the very shipping ports and marine zones where Russia has utterly failed to safely dispose of its nuclear waste (Umbreit, 1998).

There is concern that the level of impact from tourism and recreation (including sport hunting and fishing) is rising, and in the near future might put significant pressure on northern ecosystems (Vlassova, 2002). Many unique areas of Siberia and the Russian Far East, including the Russian portion of the Arctic, were closed to foreigners until 1989–1991. Scientific or 'knowledge-oriented' tourism is seen as one possible form of sustainable tourism, overlapping with the other forms of 'environmentally friendly' tourism, such as ecotourism, adventure tourism and cultural tourism (Ilyina and Mieczkowski, 1992). Examples of scientific tourism include the unpaid participation of tourists in archaeological excavations, icebreaker expeditions, expert evaluations of large development projects, etc.

It is believed that non-consumptive (mainly visual) use and a high degree of ecological and cultural literacy of the participants can guarantee minimal negative environmental and socio-cultural impact (Ilyina and Mieczkowski, 1992). On the other hand, indigenous groups have voiced concern that accelerated development, in general, means increased access to remote areas by people unfamiliar with the local culture and the existence of sacred sites which merit strict protection (Haruchi *et al.*, 2002). While afforded some protection for subsistence livelihoods under the Czarist and Soviet systems, indigenous people have historically lacked legal rights over most aspects of land use in northern Russia. Considering the economic free-for-all that took place after 1991, Osherenko (2001) argues that some measure of control over industrial development within their traditional homelands – including tourism – is essential to indigenous cultural survival. However, there are good reasons to believe that simply establishing more Zapovedniks may not be the answer, as these can impinge upon the traditional subsistence activities of northern minorities (Bolshakov and Klokov, 2000).

Relative to neighbouring Fennoscandia, 'wilderness' tourism in the European portion of the Russian North remains on a much smaller scale, and is likely to be so for many years to come (Viken *et al.*, 1995). As a result, there are very few studies on the ecological impacts of tourism. While in some places the vegetation of arctic–alpine tundra has been transformed into secondary anthropogenic meadows, the mountainous area of the Polar Urals is, overall, in rather good condition. One study of recreational impact reports that, as expected, lichens are the most sensitive component of tundra plant communities (Andreyashkina and Peschkova, 1997). One year after pedestrian trampling, lichen cover was almost completely destroyed under a load of 800 steps/m². Mosses and vascular plants were more resistant to the same level of trampling. Moss cover was only lightly damaged in dwarf-shrub tundra, whereas in *Sphagnum* tundra moss biomass was reduced by 50% at a level of 800 steps/m² and *c.* 60–70% at 2000 steps/m². At the higher level of impact, the vascular species composition did not change despite a loss of 60–70% of biomass compared to control plots, mainly because of rapid re-sprouting from underground organs. However, when the load reached 4000 steps/m², both above-ground and below-ground organs were damaged (Andreyashkina and Peschkova, 1997).

In another recent survey of the subalpine and alpine zones in the Urals, recreation and tourist travel were found to have significant effects on the 'synanthropization' of the vegetation, both in the north and in the south. In the alpine zone in the Polar Urals, only one so-called 'anthropophyte' was found (*Poa annua*). At lower elevations, *P. annua* was joined by other typical cosmopolitan ruderal plants, such as *Taraxacum officinale, Plantago* spp., *Cirsium* spp., *Polygonum aviculare*. Otherwise, the observed homogenization of vegetation composition in polar and alpine tundra along tourist routes and in camps was entirely derived from the indigenous flora (Gorchakovskii and Korobeinikova, 1997).

Antarctica/sub-Antarctic islands

As in the circumpolar Arctic, while overall numbers remain small relative to other regions, tourism in Antarctica has increased dramati-

cally in recent years. The same is true of the widely scattered sub-Antarctic islands, which occur in ten recognized groups and belong to six nations (Hall and Johnston, 1995; Valencia, 1995). Tourists now far outnumber scientists, and the management of visitors and monitoring of varied human impacts on ecosystems remains inconsistent, presenting certain challenges to the multinational Antarctic Treaty System (Dingwall, 1995b; Hall and Johnston, 1995). Organized tourism began in the mid to late 1950s, via both aircraft and ship. As of the 1990s, 19 out of 20 tourists are ship-borne 'adventure travellers', with special interests in scenery and natural history and, although exact numbers are difficult to determine, in recent years tourists have averaged somewhere between 4800 and 8000 annually (Hall and Johnston, 1995). While it has no true national parks, the Antarctic region has many areas set aside for scientific research (Stonehouse and Crosbie, 1995), and as wildlife sanctuaries, e.g. subantarctic Macquarie Island (Selkirk *et al.*, 1990).

Tourism can be encouraged by national governments on the premise that it enhances protection, yet most visitors arrive during the on-shore breeding season for marine mammals and birds, creating opportunities to maximize disturbance of wildlife and wildlife habitat (Pitman, 1990). Under the Antarctic Treaty, Agreed Measures for the Conservation of Antarctic Flora and Fauna with relevance for tourism prohibit 'harmful interference with the normal living conditions of native mammals and birds'. These may include allowing dogs to run free near bird and seal colonies, or any disturbance of animal concentrations during the breeding season, such as driving vehicles unnecessarily close, or persistent attention by persons on foot. Other ongoing problems are the collection of native plants and the introduction of non-native plants and animals (Bonner and Smith, 1985). As such, research on visitor impacts has focused particularly on disturbance of wildlife (Stonehouse, 1992), vegetation (Kappen, 1984; Scott and Kirkpatrick, 1994) and, for several decades now, the status of exotic and occasionally invasive species, ranging from mites to grasses to reindeer (Holdgate and Wace, 1961; Walton, 1975; Block *et al.*, 1984; McKerchar and Devine,

1984; Smith and Smith, 1987; Leader-Williams *et al.*, 1989; Abbott and Benninghoff, 1990; Frenot *et al.*, 2001). Hall and Johnston (1995) have suggested that, given the relatively small numbers of tourists, the amount of research and management interest appears to be 'all out of proportion' to these numbers. Nevertheless, a recent workshop on conservation in the region, while recognizing tourism as a legitimate activity, recommended legal provisions for the regulation and management of tourism. Included was a recommendation for strict protection from any tourism activities on unmodified or near-pristine islands (Dingwall, 1995b).

Conclusion

It is difficult to generalize about the impacts of ecotourism within and among regions as environmentally, economically and culturally diverse as the Arctic and Antarctic. The main commonality seems to be the development of easier, if often costly, access to even the most remote areas, and a concomitant increase in numbers of annual visitors, regardless of the intended activities upon reaching the final destination. Another seemingly accepted wisdom is that tourism in both of these regions is considered to play an important role in strategies for both sustainable development and environmental conservation.

In the Arctic, perhaps nothing has done more to promote 'ecotourism' than the establishment of a large circumpolar network of national parks and other types of protected areas (Baldursson and Zöckler, 2001). While the purpose of national parks has been well debated in, for example, Canada (Fenge, 1986), the concept of protected areas as conservation tools seems to have developed without supporting documentation, and often in contrast to the available evidence. It is a commonplace remark that tourism contributes to social change and the eventual destruction of the very things that the industry both promotes and depends on, such as local cultures and the natural environment (Nuttall, 1998). Studies cited here (e.g. Welch and Churchill, 1986; Tarnocai *et al.*, 2001) have, in fact, shown immediate and significant local degradation of Low and High Arctic vegetation and soils from hiking

and camping by as few as 100 tourists annually, with somewhat higher thresholds evident in subarctic regions (Gnieser, 2000; Tolvanen *et al.*, 2001). Surprisingly, and in contrast to evidence from other research (Monz, 2002), strategies for dispersing traffic that expected to reduce impacts were proven to actually increase visible degradation.

In the Antarctic, the establishment of national parks has been seriously debated, but is problematic because of the international management regime in place. Nevertheless, as in the Arctic, tourists are attracted to a number of favoured areas, primarily for viewing wildlife and scenery. In contrast to the Arctic, virtually all of these tourists arrive by ship, spend only brief periods on land, and never encounter indigenous communities. Important concerns comprise the disturbance of wildlife, particularly during the breeding season, degradation of the extremely limited cover of vegetation, and the introduction of non-native flora and fauna.

With the possible exception of Greenland, the marketing of ecotourism in both polar regions tends to revolve around Western concepts of pristine 'wilderness'. Outside of Antarctica, Iceland, Svalbard and a few smaller remote islands, this promotion directly contradicts the immemorial function of these 'wilderness' areas as homelands for a diverse array of indigenous cultures (Forbes, 2004). Interestingly, increasing numbers of tourists to the Arctic now cite indigenous culture as the main attraction after scenery and wildlife (Nuttall, 1998). The reality is that indigenous groups are often left out of discussions leading to the creation of protected areas, and can find that their livelihoods or cultural heritage (e.g. archaeological and sacred sites) are negatively affected by otherwise well-meaning tourists, including those who hunt and fish during their stay (Bone, 1992; Nuttall, 1998; Bolshakov and Klokov, 2000; Haruchi *et al.*, 2002). In yet another postmodern twist, Nuttall (1998) recently reported that some 'Native-owned tour companies play on the idea of the Arctic as a wilderness and last frontier to attract tourists seeking to experience both landscape and traditional Native culture'.

Whoever operates future tours in either the Arctic or Antarctic, the onus will be on the governing bodies to mandate appropriate guidelines, and the tour leaders and guides to carefully educate and monitor their groups before allowing tourists to explore potentially sensitive areas. In some cases, prohibiting access altogether may be merited when the risks of damage (e.g. species introductions, wildlife or habitat disturbance) are simply too great. Certainly, the future of ecotourism in the polar regions holds many such challenges.

References

Abbott, S.B. and Benninghoff, W.S. (1990) Orientation of environmental change studies to the conservation of antarctic ecosystems. In: Kerry, K.R. and Hempel, G. (eds) *Antarctic Ecosystems: Ecological Change and Conservation.* Springer-Verlag, Berlin, Germany, pp. 394–403.

Alaska Travel Industry Association (2001) Fact sheet: Benefits of Alaska tourism. Available at website http://www.alaskatia.org (verified June 2003).

Alaska Wilderness Recreation and Tourism Association (AWRTA) (2002) Available at website http://www.awarta.org (verified June 2003).

Andreyashkina, N.I. and Peschkova, N.V. (1997) Comparative characterization of the stability of mountain-tundra communities of the Urals to recreational impact. *Russian Journal of Ecology* 28, 52–54.

Armstrong, T., Rogers, G. and Rowley, G. (1978) *The Circumpolar North.* Methuen, London, UK.

Arnesen, T. (1999a) Vegetation dynamics following trampling in grassland and heathland in Solendet Nature Reserve, a boreal upland area in Central Norway. *Nordic Journal of Botany* 19, 47–69.

Arnesen, T. (1999b) Vegetation dynamics following trampling in rich fen at Solendet, Central Norway; a 15 year study of recovery. *Nordic Journal of Botany* 19, 313–327.

Auerbach, N.A., Walker, M.D. and Walker, D.A. (1997) Effects of roadside disturbance on substrate and vegetation properties in arctic tundra. *Ecological Applications* 7, 218–235.

Bäck, L., Josefsson, M. and Strömquist, L. (1989) Land capability, recreational land-use and conservation strategies in a sensitive mountain environment. *Uppsala Naturgeografiska Institutionen* 73, 1–68.

Baldursson, S. and Zöckler, C. (2001) The circumpolar protected areas network (CPAN). In: Kankaanpää, P., Huntington, H., Baldursson, S., Sippola, A.L., Kaitala, S., Zöckler, C., Gunn, A., Mirutenko, M., Prokosch, P. and Tishkov, A.

(eds) *Arctic Flora and Fauna: Status and Conservation.* Edita, Helsinki, pp. 78–79.

Bates, G. (1935) The vegetation of footpaths, sidewalks, cart-tracks and gateways. *Journal of Ecology* 23, 470–487.

Bay, C. and Holt, S. (1983) *Effects of an All Terrain Vehicle on Plant Communities in Jameson Land, NE Greenland.* Grønlands Botaniske Undersøgelse, Copenhagen.

Beach, H. (1994) The Saami of Lapland. In: Minority Rights Group (ed.) *Polar Peoples: Self-Determination and Development.* Minority Rights Publications, London, UK.

Bettles Lodge (2003) Available at website http://www.alaska.net/~bttlodge (verified June 2003).

Bliss, L.C. and Wein, R.W. (1972) Plant community responses to disturbances in the western Canadian Arctic. *Canadian Journal of Botany* 50, 1097–1109.

Block, W., Burn, A.J. and Richard, K.J. (1984) An insect introduction to the maritime Antarctic. *Biological Journal of the Linnean Society* 23, 33–39.

Bolshakov, N.N. and Klokov, K.B. (2000) Protected areas in the north of Russia and problems of northern minorities. In: Ebbinge, B.S., Mazourov, Yu, L. and Tomkovich, P.S. (eds) *Heritage of the Russian Arctic: Research, Conservation and International Co-operation.* Ecopros Publishers, Moscow, pp. 572–576.

Bone, R.M. (1992) *The Geography of the Canadian North.* Oxford University Press, Oxford, UK.

Bonner, W.N. and Smith, R.I.L. (eds) (1985) *Conservation Areas in the Antarctic.* SCAR/ICSU Press, Cambridge, UK.

Born, E.W. (2001) Population growth and patterns of resource exploitation. In: Born, E.W. and Böcher, J. (eds) *The Ecology of Greenland.* Atuakkiorfik Education, Nuuk, pp. 331–333.

Bruemmer, F. (1993) Introduction. In: Hamilton, W.R. (ed.) *The Baffin Handbook: Travelling in Canada's Eastern Arctic.* Nortext, Iqaluit, pp. 1–3.

Ceballos-Lascuráin, H. (1996) *Tourism, Ecotourism and Protected Areas: the State of Nature-Based Tourism around the World and Guidelines for its Development.* IUCN, Gland and Cambridge.

Christensen, T. (1992) Greenland wants tourism. *Polar Record* 28, 62–63.

Colt, S., Martin, S., Mieren, J. and Tomeo, M. (2002) *Recreation and Tourism in South-Central Alaska: Patterns and Prospects.* GTR PNW-GTR-551. USDA Forest Service, Pacific Northwest Research Station.

Cooper, D.J. (1986) The Arrigetch Peaks region of the central Brooks Range, Alaska: ecosystems and human use. In: Lucas, R. (comp.) *National*

Wilderness Research Conference: Current Research. General Technical Report INT 212, USDA Forest Service, Intermountain Research Station, Ogden, Utah, pp. 129–165.

Cornwallis, G. and Swaney, D. (1991) *Iceland, Greenland and the Faroe Islands.* Lonely Planet Publications, Hawthorne, Australia.

De Poorter, M. (1996) Environmental Issues. In: Rubin, J. (ed.) *Antarctica.* Lonely Planet Publications, Hawthorne, Australia, pp. 145–156.

Dingwall, P.R. (ed.) (1995a) *Progress in Conservation of the Subantartcic Islands.* IUCN/SCAR, Gland and Cambridge.

Dingwall, P.R. (1995b) Subantarctic island tourism: discussion and recommendations. In: Dingwall, P.R. (ed.) *Progress in Conservation of the Subantarctic Islands.* IUCN/SCAR, Gland and Cambridge, pp. 205–207.

Emanuelsson, U. (1984) Ecological effects of grazing and trampling on mountain vegetation in northern Sweden. PhD thesis, Department of Plant Ecology, University of Lund, Sweden.

Emers, M. and Jorgensen, J.C. (1997) Effects of winter seismic exploration on tundra vegetation and the soil thermal regime in the Arctic National Wildlife Refuge, Alaska. In: Crawford, R.M.M. (ed.) *Disturbance and Recovery in Arctic Lands.* Kluwer Academic Publishers, The Netherlands, pp. 443–454.

Emers, M., Jorgensen, J.C. and Raynolds, M.K. (1995) Response of arctic tundra plant communities to winter vehicle disturbance. *Canadian Journal of Botany* 73, 905–917.

Emers, M., Jorgensen, J. and Reitz, B. (1997) Recreation impact monitoring in the Arctic National Wildlife Refuge. *Recreational Impacts in Alaskan Ecosystems Conference Abstracts.* The National Outdoor Leadership School Research Program, Lander, Wyoming.

England, J. (1982) Tourism on Ellesmere: what's inside the package? *Northern Perspectives* 10(4), 1–7.

England, J. (1983) Ellesmere Island needs special attention. *Canadian Geographic* 103(3), 8–17.

Felix, N.A., Raynolds, M.K., Jorgensen, J.C. and Du Bois, K.E. (1992) Resistance and resilience of tundra plant communities to disturbance by winter seismic vehicles. *Arctic and Alpine Research* 24(1), 69–77.

Fenge, T. (1986) National Parks to conserve the Northwest Territories? *Park News* 22(2), 4–9.

Fogg, G.E. (1998) *The Biology of Polar Habitats.* Oxford University Press, Oxford, UK.

Forbes, B.C. (2004) Wilderness. In: Nuttall, M. (ed.) *Encyclopedia of the Arctic.* Routledge, New York.

Forbes, B.C., Ebersole, J.J. and Strandberg, B. (2001) Anthropogenic disturbance and patch dynamics in circumpolar arctic ecosystems. *Conservation Biology* 15, 954–969.

Frenot, Y., Gloaguen, J.C., Masse, L. and Lebouvier, M. (2001) Human activities, ecosystem disturbance and plant invasions in subantarctic Crozet, Kerguelen and Amsterdam Islands. *Biological Conservation* 101, 33–50.

Gellatly, A.F., Whalley, W.B. and Gordon, J.E. (1986a) Footpath deterioration in the Lyngen Peninsula, north Norway. *Mountain Research and Development* 6, 167–176.

Gellatly, A.F., Whalley, W.B., Gordon, J.E. and Ferguson, R.I. (1986b) An observation on trampling effects in north Norway: thresholds for damage. *Norsk Geografiska Tidsskrift* 40, 163–168.

Gnieser, C.H. (2000) Ecological consequences of recreation on subarctic-alpine tundra: Experimental assessment and predictive modeling as planning tools for sustainable visitor management in protected areas. PhD thesis, University of Calgary, Alberta, Canada.

Gorchakovskii, P.L. and Korobeinikova, V.P. (1997) Synanthropization of vegetation in the upper belts of the Urals. *Russian Journal of Ecology* 28, 323–329.

Hall, C.M. and Johnston, M.E. (1995) Introduction: Pole to pole: Tourism issues, impacts and the search for a management regime in polar regions. In: Hall, C.M. and Johnston, M.E. (eds) *Polar Tourism: Tourism in the Arctic and Antarctic Regions.* John Wiley & Sons Ltd, Chichester, UK, pp. 1–26.

Hamley, W. (1991) Tourism in the Northwest Territories. *Geographical Review* 81, 89–99.

Hamre, G. (1993) Creation of Canadian national parks in concert with settlement of aboriginal land claims. In: Hendee, J.C. and Martin, V. (eds) *Proceedings of the Symposium on International Wilderness Allocation, Management and Research, 5th World Wilderness Congress.* Wild Foundation and University of Idaho Wilderness Research Center, Moscow, Idaho, USA, pp 1–6.

Haruchi, S., Sohlberg, S. and Sulyandziga, P. (2002) *The Conservation Value of Sacred Sites of Indigenous Peoples of the Arctic: a Case Study in Northern Russia.* RAIPON, Moscow.

Helle, T. and Särkelä, M. (1993) The effects of outdoor recreation on range use by semi-domesticated reindeer. *Scandinavian Journal of Forest Research* 8, 123–133.

Helms, H.J. (1991) Nature conservation in Greenland. In: Andreasen, C. *et al.* (eds) *Nature Conservation in Greenland.* Atuakkiorfik, Nuuk, pp. 11–19.

Hindrum, R. (1998) Opportunities and problems associated with the development of arctic tourism: a case study from Svalbard. In: Humphreys, B., Pedersen, Å.Ø., Prokosch, P., Smith, S. and Stonehouse, B. (eds) *Linking Tourism and Conservation in the Arctic.* Norsk Polarinstitutt, Tromsø, pp. 75–79.

Holdgate, M.W. and Wace, N.M. (1961) The influence of man on the floras and faunas of southern islands. *Polar Record* 10, 475–493.

Holmström, H. (1970) *Eräiden Etelä-Suomen Vapaa-aika-alueiden Kasvillisuuden Kulutuskestävyyden Tutkimus.* Uudenmaan Seutukaavaliitot.

Holt, S. and Bay, C. (1983) *Effects of an All Terrain Cycle on Fen Vegetation in Jameson Land, NE Greenland.* Report prepared for Greenland Fisheries Investigations and Greenland Botanical Survey, Copenhagen, 9 pp.

Hoogesteger, M. (1976) Changes in vegetation around the wilderness huts in Koilliskaira [in Finnish with English summary]. *Silva Fennica* 10, 40–53.

Hoogesteger, M. (1984) The effect of trampling on vegetation at four cottages in Torne Lapland, northern Sweden. *Reports from the Kevo Subarctic Research Station* 19, 25–34.

Hoogesteger, M. and Havas, P. (1976) Luonnon kulutuskestävyydestä ja virkistyskäytön kanavoinnista Pohjois-Suomen suunnitelluissa kansallispuistoissa. *Terra* 88, 31–34.

Humphreys, B., Pedersen, Å.Ø., Prokosch, P., Smith, S. and Stonehouse, B. (eds) (1998) *Linking Tourism and Conservation in the Arctic.* Norsk Polarinstitutt, Tromsø, Norway.

Ilyina, L. and Mieczkowski, Z. (1992) Developing scientific tourism in Russia. *Tourism Management* 12, 327–331.

Johnston, M.E. and Hall, C.M. (1995) Visitor management and the future of tourism in polar regions. In: Hall, C.M. and Johnston, M.E. (eds) *Polar Tourism: Tourism in the Arctic and Antarctic Regions.* John Wiley & Sons Ltd, Chichester, UK, pp. 297–313.

Kaae, B.C. (2002) Nature and tourism in Greenland. In: Watson, A.E., Alessa, L., and Sproull, J. (eds) *Wilderness in the Circumpolar North: Searching for Compatibility in Ecological, Traditional, and Ecotourism Values.* US Department of Agriculture, Forest Service, Rocky Mountain Research Station, pp. 43–53.

Kaltenborn, B.P. (2000) Arctic–alpine environments and tourism: can sustainability be planned? *Mountain Research and Development* 20, 28–31.

Kaltenborn, B.P. and Emmelin, L. (1993) Tourism in the high north: management challenges and recreation opportunity spectrum planning in Svalbard, Norway. *Environmental Management* 17, 41–50.

Kappen, L. (1984) Ecological aspects of exploitation of the non-living resources of the Antarctic continent. In: Wolfrum, R. (ed.) *Antarctic Challenge.* Duncker & Humbolt, Berlin, pp. 211–217.

Kellomäki, S. (1973) Ground-cover response to trampling in a spruce stand of *Myrtillus* type. *Silva Fennica* 7, 96–113.

Kellomäki, S. (1977) Deterioration of forest ground cover during trampling. *Silva Fennica* 11, 153–161.

Kellomäki, S. and Saastamoinen, J. (1975) Trampling tolerance of forest vegetation. *Acta Forestalia Fennica* 147, 1–22.

Kevan, P.G., Forbes, B.C., Behan-Pelletier, V. and Kevan, S. (1995) Vehicle tracks on high arctic tundra: their effects on the soil, vegetation and soil arthropods. *Journal of Applied Ecology* 32, 656–669.

Klein, D.R. (2002) Perspectives on wilderness in the Arctic. In: Watson, A.E., Alessa, L. and Sproul, J. (eds) *Wilderness in the Circumpolar North: Searching for Compatibility in Ecological, Traditional and Ecotourism Values.* RMRS-P-26, USDA, Forest Service, Ogden, Utah, pp. 1–6.

Leader-Williams, N., Walton, D.W.H. and Prince, P.A. (1989) Introduced reindeer on South Georgia – a management dilemma. *Rangifer* 9, 59–65.

Lehtonen, J. and Heikkinen, R.K. (1995) On the recovery of mountain birch after *Epirrita* damage in Finnish Lapland, with a particular emphasis on reindeer grazing. *Écoscience* 2, 349–356.

Leung, Y. and Marion, J.L. (2000) Recreation impacts and management in wilderness: a state-of-knowledge review. In: Cole, D.N., McCool, S.F., Borrie, W.T. and O'Loughlan, J. (comps) *Wilderness Science in a Time of Change Conference – Volume 5: Wilderness Ecosystems, Threats and Management.* Proceedings RMRS-P-15-Vol-5, USDA Forest Service, Rocky Mountain Research Station, pp. 23–48.

Malmivaara, M., Lofstrom, I. and Vanha-Majamaa, I. (2002) Anthropogenic effects on understorey vegetation in *Myrtillus* type urban forests in southern Finland. *Silva Fennica* 36, 367–381.

Marshall, R. and Marshall, G. (eds) (1970) *Alaska Wilderness: Exploring the Central Brooks Range.* University of California Press, Berkeley.

Martin, S.P. (2003) Coming out of the country: Alaska's National Parks in a New Century. *Abstracts of the George Wright and Cultural Heritage Society 2003 Conference.* George Wright Society, Hancock, Mitchigan, USA.

McKerchar, N.D.R. and Devine, W.T. (1984) The Campbell Island story: the management challenge of subantarctic islands. In: McNeely, J.A.

and Miller, K.R. (eds) *National Parks, Conservation and Development: the Role of Protected Areas in Sustaining Society.* Smithsonian Institution Press, Washington, DC, pp. 376–385.

McNamee, K. (1987) Ellesmere Island National Park Reserve established. *Park News* 22(4), 7–9.

Monz, C.A. (2002) The response of two arctic tundra plant communities to human trampling disturbance. *Journal of Environmental Management* 64, 201–217.

Mordhorst, J. (1998) Planning for ecotourism in Kangerlussuaq, Søndre Strømfjord, Greenland. In: Humphreys, B., Pedersen, Å.Ø., Prokosch, P., Smith, S. and Stonehouse, B. (eds) *Linking Tourism and Conservation in the Arctic.* Norsk Polarinstitutt, Tromsø, pp. 87–89.

Müller-Wille, L. in conjunction with the Inuit Elders of Nunavik and Avataq Cultural Institute (1987) *Gazetteer of Inuit Place Names in Nunavik (Quebec, Canada).* Avataq Cultural Institute, Inukjuak, Quebec, Canada.

Nash, R. (1982) *Wilderness and the American Mind.* Yale University Press, New Haven, Connecticut.

National Park Service, US Department of Interior (2003) NPS visitation database. Available at website http://www.nature.nps.gov/mpur/index.cfm (verified May 2003).

Nelson, J.G. (1984) Living with exploitation in the subarctic and arctic of Canada. In: McNeely, J.A. and Miller, K.R. (eds) *National Parks, Conservation and Development: the Role of Protected Areas in Sustaining Society.* Smithsonian Institution Press, Washington, DC, pp. 527–533.

Nichols Gilstrap, Inc. (2000) Strategic marketing and planning analysis for Alaska tourism. Available at website http://www.dced.state.ak.us/cbd/toubus/pub/marketinganalysis2000.pdf (verified June 2003).

Nuttall, M. (1998) *Protecting the Arctic: Indigenous Peoples and Cultural Survival.* Routledge, London.

Nylund, M., Nylund, L., Kellomäki, S. and Haapanen, A. (1979) Deterioration of forest ground vegetation and decrease of radial growth of trees on camping sites. *Silva Fennica* 13, 343–356.

Oechel, W.C. (1989) Nutrient and water flux in a small arctic watershed: an overview. *Holarctic Ecology* 12, 229–237.

Osherenko, G. (2001) Indigenous rights in Russia: is title to land essential for cultural survival? *The Georgetown International Environmental Law Review* 13, 695–733.

Page, S.J. and Dowling, R.K. (2002) *Ecotourism.* Pearson Education Ltd, Harlow, UK.

Pitman, T. (1990) Macquarie Island – Australia's southernmost wilderness. *Wilderness News* 11(4), 11–13.

Prokosch, P. (2001) Tourism: threat or benefit to conservation? In: Kankaanpää, P., Huntington, P., Baldursson, S., Sippola, A.L., Kaitala, S., Zöckler, C., Gunn, A., Mirutenko, M., Prokosch, P. and Tishkov, A. (eds) *Arctic Flora and Fauna: Status and Conservation.* Edita, Helsinki, pp. 102–103.

Rautio, J. (1997) Yllästunturin laskettelurinteiden maisemointi. MSc thesis, Department of Geography, University of Oulu, Finland.

Rautio, J., Helenius, M. and Saarinen, J. (2001) Urho Kekkosen kansallispuiston kuluneisuus: luontomatkailun ympäristövaikutusten seuranta ja mittaaminen. Summary: Measuring the impacts of nature based tourism in Urho Kekkonen National Park in Finnish Lapland – methods and problems. *Finnish Forest Research Institute, Research Papers* 796, 111–124.

Reid, R.S. and Schreiner, E.S. (1985) Long-term experimental trampling on plant communities in Denali National Park, Alaska, USA. Resource Management Office, Denali National Park, Alaska. Unpublished report.

Reynolds, J.F. and Tenhunen, J.D. (eds) (1996) *Landscape Function and Disturbance in Arctic Tundra.* Springer-Verlag, Berlin, Germany.

Rubin, J. (ed.) (1996) *Antarctica.* Lonely Planet Publications, Hawthorne, Australia.

Saarinen, J., Jortikka, S. and Virtanen, E. (2000) Luonnonsuojelualueet ja matkailu. *Finnish Forest Research Institute, Research papers* 760, 5–12.

Saastamoinen, O., Loven, L. and Sievänen, T. (2000) Nature-based tourism in forested North-Europe – case of Finland. *Finnish Forest Research Institute, Research Papers* 792, 7–17.

Scott, J.J. and Kirkpatrick, J.B. (1994) Effects of human trampling on the sub-Antarctic vegetation of Macquarie Island. *Polar Record* 30, 207–220.

Selkirk, P.M., Seppelt, R.D. and Selkirk, D.R. (1990) *Subantarctic Macquarie Island: Environment and Biology.* Cambridge University Press, Cambridge, UK.

Smith, V.R. and Smith, R.I.L. (1987) The biota and conservation status of subantarctic islands. *Environment International* 13, 95–104.

Soublière, M. (ed.) (1997) *The 1998 Nunavut Handbook: Travelling in Canada's Arctic.* Nortext Multimedia Inc., Iqaluit.

Stonehouse, B. (1992) Monitoring shipborne visitors in Antarctica: a preliminary study. *Polar Record* 28, 213–218.

Stonehouse, B. (1998) Polar ship-borne tourism: do guidelines and codes of conduct work? In:

Humphreys, B., Pedersen, Å.Ø., Prokosch, P., Smith, S. and Stonehouse, B. (eds) *Linking Tourism and Conservation in the Arctic*. Norsk Polarinstitutt, Tromsø, pp. 49–58.

Stonehouse, B. and Crosbie, K. (1995) Tourist impacts and management in the Antarctic Peninsula area. In: Hall, C.M. and Johnston, M.E. (eds) *Polar Tourism: Tourism in the Arctic and Antarctic Regions*. John Wiley & Sons Ltd, Chichester, UK, pp. 217–233.

Sugden, D. (1982) *Arctic and Antarctic: a Modern Geographic Synthesis*. Barnes & Noble Book, Totowa, New Jersey.

Swaney, D. (1999) *The Arctic*. Lonely Planet Publications, Hawthorne, Australia.

Tarnocai, C. and Gould, J. (1998) *Ecosystem and Trafficability Monitoring for Auyuittuq National Park Reserve*. Prepared for Auyuittuq National Park Reserve by the Research Branch (ECORC, BRC), Agriculture and Agri-Food Canada, Ottawa, Canada.

Tarnocai, C., Gould, J., Broll, G. and Achuff, P. (2001) *Ecosystem and Trafficability Monitoring for Quttinirpaaq National Park: 11-year Evaluation*. Prepared for Quttinirpaaq National Park by the Research Branch (ECORC), Agriculture and Agri-Food Canada, Ottawa, Canada.

Tolvanen, A., Forbes, B., Rytkönen, K. and Laine, K. (2001) Regeneration of dominant plants after short-term pedestrian trampling in sub-arctic plant communities. In: Wielgolaski, F.E. (ed.) *Nordic Mountain Birch Ecosystems. Man and the Biosphere Series*. UNESCO, Paris and The Parthenon Publishing Group, pp. 361–370.

Truett, J.C. and Johnson, S.R. (eds) (2000) *The Natural History of an Arctic Oil Field: Development and the Biota*. Academic Press, San Diego, California.

Umbreit, A. (1998) The frame conditions for ecologically acceptable tourism and its guidelines on Svalbard. In: Humphreys, B., Pedersen, Å.Ø., Prokosch, P., Smith, S. and Stonehouse, B. (eds) *Linking Tourism and Conservation in the Arctic*. Norsk Polarinstitutt, Tromsø, Norway, pp. 100–107.

Valencia, J. (1995) Issues in the management of tourism on subantarctic islands. In: Dingwall, P.R. (ed.) *Progress in Conservation of the Subantarctic Islands*. IUCN/SCAR, Gland and Cambridge, pp. 203–204.

Viken, A. (1998) Tourism regulation-cultural norms or legislation? Outdoor life and tourism regulation in Finnmark and on Svalbard. In: Humphreys, B., Pedersen, Å.Ø., Prokosch, P., Smith, S. and Stonehouse, B. (eds) *Linking Tourism and Conservation in the Arctic*. Norsk Polarinstitutt, Tromsø, Norway, pp. 63–74.

Viken, A., Vostryakov, L. and Davydov, A. (1995) Tourism in northwest Russia. In: Hall, C.M. and Johnston, M.E. (eds) *Polar Tourism: Tourism in the Arctic and Antarctic Regions*. John Wiley & Sons, Chichester, UK, pp. 101–114.

Vistnes, I., Nellemann, C., Jordhøy, P. and Strand, O. (2001) Wild reindeer: impacts of progressive infrastructure development on distribution and range use. *Polar Biology* 24, 531–537.

Vlassova, T.K. (2002) Human impacts on the tundra–taiga zone dynamics: the case of the Russian lesotundra. *Ambio Special Report* 12, 30–36.

Walker, D.A., Cate, D., Brown, J. and Racine, C. (1987) *Disturbance and recovery of Arctic Alaskan Tundra Terrain: a review of recent investigations*. US Army Cold Regions Research and Engineering Laboratory CRREL Report 82-27. Hanover, New Hampshire.

Walton, D.W.H. (1975) European weeds and other alien species in the Subantarctic. *Weed Research* 15, 271–282.

Warenberg, K., Danell, Ö., Gaare, E. and Nieminen, M. (1997) *Porolaidunten Kasvillisuus*. WSOY, Helsinki.

Welch, D.M. and Churchill, J. (1986). Hiking trail conditions in Pangnirtung Pass, 1984, Baffin Island, Canada. Unpublished report, Parks Canada, Ottawa, Canada.

Wells, M.P. and Williams, M.D. (1998) Russia's protected areas in transition: route of the impacts of perestroika, economic reform and the move towards democracy. *Ambio* 27, 198–206.

Wenzel, G.W. (1991) *Animal Rights Human Rights: Ecology, Economy and Ideology in the Canadian Arctic*. University of Toronto Press, Toronto, Canada.

Wenzel, G.W. (1995) Warming the Arctic: environmentalism and Canadian Inuit. In: Peterson, D.L. and Johnson, D.R. (eds) *Human Ecology and Climate Change: People and Resources in the Far North*. Taylor & Francis, London.

Wielgolaski, F.E. (1998) Twenty-two years of plant recovery after severe trampling by man through five years in three vegetation types at Hardangervidda. *Norges Teknisk-Naturvitenskapelige Universitet, Vitenskapsmuseet, Rapport Botanisk Serie* 1998(4), 26–29.

Wilson, R. (ed.) (1976) *The Land that Never Melts: Auyuittuq National Park*. Peter Martin Associates, Toronto.

10

Ecological Impacts and Management of Tourist Engagements with Cetaceans

James Higham[1] and David Lusseau[2]

[1]Department of Tourism and [2]Department of Zoology, University of Otago, Dunedin, New Zealand

Introduction

The whale-watching industry, which originated in California (USA), dates to 1950. As of 1998, there were 492 communities, spread over 87 countries, involved in whale-watching activities (Hoyt, 2001). While much commercial whale-watching takes place in the USA and Canada, whale-based ecotourism has proliferated rapidly throughout the world, most recently at venues in various parts of the Caribbean and in Japan. Whale-watching activities are a major player in coastal tourism, with revenue of more than US$1 billion in 1998 and 9 million participants (Hoyt, 2001). These figures do not include companies that are not dedicated whale-watching operations, yet many scenic cruises rely on cetaceans as a key natural resource (Lusseau, 2002a). Through this course of development emerges a raft of effects or consequences, both positive and/or negative (depending primarily on point of view in some cases), that are broadly classified as social, political, cultural, economic and environmental. This chapter is primarily concerned with the environmental impacts of tourist engagements with whales and dolphins, the significance of those impacts, and the development of techniques aimed at managing this domain of human activity. The chapter also seeks to demonstrate that understanding and managing the ecological impacts of whale-watch tourism operations can not take place in isolation from the social, cultural and political context of the destination. Thus the relevance of issues such as resource-use conflicts, contested cultural values associated with whales and the politics of managing natural resources in remote communities is an important element in the discussions that follow.

The Whale-watch Industry

The coastal environment has long been a venue for leisure, recreation and tourism. Tourism development in marine contexts is a more recent phenomenon (Orams, 1999). Exponential growth in tourist activities that take place on, in and under water has been a notable feature of tourism development in the late 20th and early 21st centuries. Marine mammal-based tourism operators have been among the most prominent forms of marine tourism development during this time. Tourist engagements with marine mammals most commonly include encounters with cetaceans, but may also include species such as polar bear, dugong, seals (various species), sealions, sea elephants, walrus and sea otters, among others (e.g. the whale shark). Within the marine mammal-based tourism industry, this chapter specifically addresses the ecological impacts and management of tourist engagements with cetaceans.

The status of cetaceans as 'charismatic megafauna' partly explains the popularity and increasing profile of whale-watching in the contemporary tourism industry.

Until recently many countries commercially hunted whales and dolphins for their blubber (fat), their baleen and their meat (Hoyt and Hvenegaard, 2002). Some populations of cetaceans were also considered pests, and bounties were placed on them (e.g. killer whales along the US and Canadian Pacific north-western coast). Commercial hunting still exists in a few countries, including Norway, where an annual minke whale hunt takes place during a restricted season, and the Faroe Islands (pilot whales). Japan contentiously conducts whale hunting in the name of science, and continues an inshore drive fishery for dolphins (mainly bottlenose dolphins) and porpoises. Iceland, Malaysia, the Philippines, Chile and some Caribbean countries also engage in occasional inshore fisheries. The Solomon Islands and Mexico may be included on this list, given the recent hunting and commercial exportation of live bottlenose dolphins to Cancun (Mexico) to display as tourist attractions.

Many other communities have moved towards the non-destructive use of natural marine resources (Duffus and Dearden, 1990; Hoyt, 2001; Hoyt and Hvenegaard, 2002). Evolving leisure, recreation and tourism preferences have played an important part in changing values associated with the marine environment. These values are manifest in the transition from destructive (e.g. fishing and oil exploitation) to non-consumptive uses of marine resources. The latter include leisure travel, marine sports and recreation, adventure pursuits and ecotourism (in its various forms), among others.

This transition has offered coastal communities the challenge of discontinuing traditional industries that have commonly been associated with resource overexploitation, and the opportunities associated with new avenues of economic development. Some have been spectacularly successful in maintaining or enhancing their socio-economic status through the pursuit of non-consumptive resource utilities. However, the challenge remains to ensure that management errors made with industries such as commercial fisheries are not replicated in non-consumptive commercial sectors. While

many would agree that marine mammal-based tourism is preferable to the consumptive use of marine resources, it can not be assumed that such activities are benign in the ecological impacts that they may cause.

The industry that originated in California in 1950 boasts an extended and uninterrupted sequence of exponential growth since 1980 (Fig. 10.1). Through this course of development, marine mammal tour operations have diversified to the greatest possible extent. All marine mammal species, ranging from blue whales (Hoyt, 2001) to polar bears (Polar Bears Alive, 2003) are targeted by commercial ecotourism businesses. Whale-watching activities, that is, ventures targeting one or more of the 83 species of whales and dolphins, are diverse. All 83 species are currently targeted by whale-watching activities in one form or another. These species can be viewed from helicopters, planes, small vessels, kayaks, inflatable boats, large ships, or from land. It is also possible to interact with numerous species of marine mammals in 'swim-with' activities. Some common species, such as humpback whales, killer whales or bottlenose dolphins, are the focus of more activities than others. The success of communities that have developed as whale-watching tourism destinations relies on the predictable presence of one or two key species of cetaceans. Both the scale and rationale of most of these activities classify them as ecotourism (Weaver, 2001), but mass tourism companies (such as cruise ships) utilize whales and dolphins as well. In most locations where whale-watching activities have been established for several decades, there is a tendency for the industry to move towards fewer, larger vessels that can take more passengers (Hoyt, 2001). Most activities take place in coastal waters and take advantage of the inshore distribution of coastal dolphins and the seasonal use of this habitat by most whales (breeding and feeding grounds) and pelagic dolphins (nursery areas). This affords companies the opportunity to operate short daily tours, often several tours per day, and reliably find the targeted species on each tour. In a few locations pelagic species can be observed inshore year-round. For example, sperm whales can be viewed every day in Kaikoura, New Zealand (Richter et al., 2002), or in Andenes, Norway (Hoyt, 2001). Offshore operations are under-

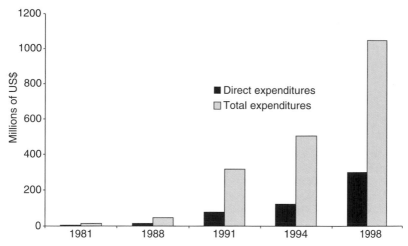

Fig. 10.1. The growth of the whale-watching industry worldwide (adapted from Hoyt, 2001).

taken in a few locations where the occurrence of spectacular species, such as blue whales, can be predicted. Multi-week cruises run in Antarctic waters dedicated to watching large whales. It is possible to view blue whales in Californian offshore waters during their summer migration. Again, these offshore trips rely on the predictability of these animals being present in these locations.

The Ecological Effects of Tourism Activities on Whales and Dolphins (Cetaceans)

It may be argued that the most critical element of sustainability in this type of tourism activity lies within the ecological dimension of marine tourism. It is difficult to assess the impact of human activities on marine mammals because they live in a different environment and use their senses differently to humans. Strict methodologies are necessary to interpret responses to anthropogenic impacts objectively. For the past 10 years there has been increasing interest in studying the effects of tourism activities on cetaceans. Unfortunately, most studies have examined only one aspect of the problem, without considering the potential interactions between several variables, for example acoustic communication and behavioural state. Few data have been gathered on the long-term

impacts associated with boat disturbance. Some studies have been able to relate changes in habitat use as well as avoidance of previously preferred areas to an increase in boat traffic (Baker *et al.*, 1988; Salden, 1988; Corkeron, 1995; Lusseau, 2002b).

Several short-term studies have shown a variety of responses. Most studies have focused on behavioural changes depending on the presence and the density of boats. In most cases schools of animals tend to tighten when boats are present (e.g. Blane and Jaakson, 1995; Barr, 1996; Nowacek *et al.*, 2001). Some species show signs of active avoidance. Responses range from changes in movement patterns (Edds and MacFarlane, 1987; Salvado *et al.*, 1992; Campagna *et al.*, 1995; Bejder *et al.*, 1999; Nowacek *et al.*, 2001), increases in dive intervals (Baker *et al.*, 1988; Baker and Herman, 1989; Blane, 1990; MacGibbon, 1991; Janik and Thompson, 1996) and increases in swimming speed (Blane and Jaakson, 1995; Williams *et al.*, 2002). These signs of avoidance can be a result of not only the presence of boats, but also the manoeuvring of boats, including sudden changes in vessel speed or rapid approaches (MacGibbon, 1991; Gordon *et al.*, 1992; Constantine, 2001).

The presence and density of boats (Briggs, 1985; Kruse, 1991; Barr, 1996) and the distance between boats and individuals (Corkeron, 1995) can also affect the frequency or

Fig. 10.2. One of the dolphins bearing scars from a propellor strike in Milford Sound.

occurrence of behaviours. Humpback whales in Alaska have been seen reacting to vessels up to 4 km away from the pod (Baker *et al.*, 1988). In addition, the behavioural state of cetacean groups interacting with tourist vessels can be affected and changed (Ritter, 1996; Constantine and Baker, 1997; Lusseau, 2003). For example interactions with boats led to a decrease in resting behaviour in spinner dolphins in Hawaii (Würsig, 1996). Resting behaviour seems to be the most sensitive state to boat interactions (Lusseau, 2003).

Hearing is the primary sense of cetaceans. They use vocalizations not only to communicate and maintain group cohesion (Janik and Slater, 1998), but also to locate prey and navigate using echolocation (Popper, 1980). Vocalization patterns are also altered by the presence of tour boats. In the case of humpback whales in Hawaii, the presence of boats has been found to affect the song phase and unit duration (Norris, 1994). The production of an 'alarm signal' as well as an increase in silence time has been related to the presence of boats in belugas and narwhals (Finley *et al.*, 1990). An increase in whistling rate has also been linked to the maintenance of group cohesion during interactions with boats in different species of dolphins (Scarpaci *et al.*, 2000; Van Parijs and Corkeron, 2001).

More obvious impacts, such as injuries from collisions, have also been observed. In Milford Sound, New Zealand, four bottlenose dolphins bore propeller scars and one 2-week

calf died after being run over by a tour boat in 2002 (Lusseau, 2002a). In 2000, a humpback whale was hit by a vessel in the popular Stellwagen Bank, New England, USA. The erratic navigation of vessels causing propeller strikes obviously affects the mortality and morbidity of individuals within a population (Fig. 10.2).

More and more studies show that the navigation of vessels interacting with animals is a key parameter in the intrusiveness of the interaction (Nowacek *et al.*, 2001; Lusseau, 2002b; Williams *et al.*, 2002). The more boats are manoeuvred unpredictably and erratically, the more animals try to elude them. The observed avoidance strategies are similar to typical anti-predator responses (Howland, 1974). Given the recent history of the whaling industry, it is not surprising that whales and dolphins employ anti-predator techniques when a vessel targets them, especially when the vessel attempts to out-manoeuvre or impair their movement.

Measuring and Understanding Biological Significance

It is generally recognized that one critical, but largely unresolved, issue centres on the consequences of observed marine mammal avoidance responses. These need to be scientifically researched and understood in terms of biological significance. The biological consequences of increased dive times, decreased blow intervals, changes in travel directions, disruption of important behaviours and increases in aggressive behaviours are not adequately understood. It is necessary to relate the effects of the responses observed to standardized parameters, such as the energetic budget of the species, to assess their biological significance. However, we lack the basal energetic information that can often only be collected in a controlled environment, to relate the changes observed to energetic expenses. Remote sensors that can be deployed in the field are short-lived (their life span is measured in hours). Therefore, they provide controversial results because it is impossible to know whether the animal had recovered from the stress of being tagged during the sampling process. However, new avenues of scientific research are opening due to the discovery of the emergent properties of metabolism and cellular functions (Darveau *et al.*, 2002). Due to this theoretical work, it may be possible to extrapolate values, such as metabolic rate, measured in some species to species that can only be observed in the field. Moreover, observing the impacts of tourism on the behavioural budget of different populations offers the opportunity to link observational data to energetic budget (Lusseau, 2003). The behavioural budget of a population is directly linked to its energetic budget (Lusseau, 2002b). It is therefore possible to assess the energetic cost of avoiding interactions with boats by observing the changes in the proportion of time engaged in different behavioural states (e.g. resting, socializing, feeding, milling and travelling). New analytical techniques are opening this avenue of research and will afford more rigorous insights into the true biological significance of responses observed (Lusseau, 2003). This also means that a precautionary approach should be applied to the management of cetacean-watching activities until the real extent of the problem is understood scientifically.

Relating the effects observed to their energetic cost would allow the comparison of the impacts of ecotourism on cetaceans as they vary between focal species. Such comparisons would allow the establishment of simple management schemes on a population-specific basis. This would also allow a more proactive approach to the management of cetacean-watching activities, by establishing operator guidelines and operational quotas before the development pressure of the industry reaches levels that cannot be sustained.

The Diversity of Impacts: Complex Issues of Sustainability

The whale-watching industry presents specific challenges relating to sustainability. It has been noted that the growth of whale-watching internationally has raised concerns for the impacts of this activity upon the focal species being viewed (Gordon *et al.*, 1992). Questions regarding the environmental sustainability of whale-watching vary between specific whale-watch contexts, and also vary with the scale of the industry, and the form that this activity takes (e.g. land- and marine-based viewing platforms). Concerns for the biological significance of tourist impacts upon whales have been discussed alongside the generally positive economic impacts achieved, most notably, by the communities where marine mammal-watching takes place (Hoyt, 2001; Orams, 2002). The socio-cultural impacts of whale-watching have also been debated by academics. It has been argued that whale-watching is a platform for public environmental education (Hoyt, 2001), which might foster values that conform with a new environmental paradigm (Duffus and Dearden, 1990; Orams, 1997). Whether or not whale-watching does bring with it positive implications for cetaceans, or nature conservation generally, remains an open question (Duffus and Dearden, 1990), although this point is lauded as an important justification for development of this form of tourism (Orams, 1997; Higham and Carr, 2002). Bearing this in mind, remarkably little research has been committed to answering this question (Orams, 1995a,b).

Whales and dolphins are also the subject of varied and conflicting cultural values. It may be argued that the varied cultural values associated with whales present a perplexing challenge to sustainable tourism development. The dominant Western environmental paradigm views whales as intelligent creatures with sophisticated communication systems. Symbolic representations, which carry similar meanings and associations for members of a society, are commonly associated with iconic species such as the large whales. Media representations of whales are also the products of a cultural context (Smestad, 1997). Significant divergence from the dominant Western paradigm exists in cultural values associated with whales. In Norway the hunting of minke whales during an annual 6-week season is viewed as an important part of the fisheries industry and represents a cornerstone of Norwegian coastal culture (Henriksen, 2002).

In this case, the whale is a symbol of a broad-ranging and diverse subsistence economy. It is also a symbol of the right to harvest from a range of natural resources in a sustainable way. The harvesting of fish stocks, the gathering of down, birds eggs and the hunting of game, including game birds, within different seasonal contexts, collectively form parts of this coastal culture. The diversity of these resources is seen as an effective safeguard against economic and ecological fluctuation. The centralization of control over these resources has become a critical issue to peripheral high-latitude coastal communities, and the minke whale hunt is seen to symbolize the complex issues associated with political centralization (Smedstad, 1997; Henriksen, 2002). Clearly, the dominant Western view of whales is not shared universally (Ris, 1993). The fact that the International Whaling Committee (IWC) 1982 moratorium banning all commercial whale hunting exempts aboriginal subsistence whaling (including Greenland Inuit, and native peoples in Alaska and Siberia, among others) based on cultural grounds confirms this point (Smestad, 1997).

Similarly, Orams (2002) notes that the indigenous Maori living in the vicinity of Kaikoura (New Zealand) have a long-standing and important spiritual relationship with whales, which are viewed as a *taonga* (treasure). The Treaty of Waitangi (1840), which set out the relationship between indigenous Maori and the European colonists, established the rights of Maori to have *rangatiratanga* (control or sovereignty) and *kaitiakitanga* (guardianship) over *taonga*. This right, including exclusive access to whales in the Kaikoura area for commercial tourism, was addressed by the High Court and Court of Appeal in 1994 and 1995 (Orams, 2002). The outcome of this case was one of support for 'rights pertaining to economic development for

indigenous peoples [which] were becoming recognised and accepted in international jurisprudence' (Orams, 2002, pp. 343–344).

Sustainable tourism development therefore requires recognition of and respect for traditional cultural values associated with whales. Orams (2002, p. 343) notes that 'one of the more challenging aspects of ecotourism has been the argument that this kind of tourism development should be inclusive of, sensitive to, and beneficial for indigenous peoples'. This raises the possibility that cultural dimensions of ecotourism may present situations that are reprehensible or offensive to tourists. Hinch (1998) observes that longstanding traditional cultural practices may offend the sensitivities of predominantly Western ecotourists. The hunting, slaughter and processing of traditional food sources, including otter, beaver, seals, walrus and whale, by indigenous Arctic communities, many of which may be harnessing ecotourism as an economic development option, demonstrates this point (Hinch, 2001).

Potential for Resource Use Conflicts

It is apparent that differing cultural values associated with marine mammals may be the basis of challenging and complex resources-use issues. For example, small dolphins, such as bottlenose dolphins, are used both by whale-watching activities and by drive fisheries in Japan. In this case there exists a direct conflict of interest because the drive fisheries (i.e. vessels driving dolphins in shallow bays to slaughter them) directly consume the resource that whale-watching activities rely upon. Indeed, in the whale-watch community of Andenes (Norway) there exist numerous licensed local restaurants and cafés offering menus that include whale meat (Henriksen, 2002). This community is not unique in offering visitors the seemingly contradictory experiences of whale-watch tours and whale cuisine (albeit different species being watched and hunted – sperm and minke whales, respectively).

Many commercial marine mammal tour operations take place in inshore waters, where great potential exists for conflict with other human activities. At one level these conflicts may exist between tourism and non-tourism resource utilities, the latter including aquaculture, marine transport and communications and commercial fisheries. However, conflicts may also arise between separate tourism and recreational interests, such as private/recreational boating and fishing interests, scenic cruises and fishing charters. Conflicting activities such as these may detrimentally affect the satisfaction level of visitors engaging in whale-watching. Similarly, incidental by-catch of small cetaceans (e.g. Hector's dolphins, harbour porpoises, Chilean dolphins and vaquitas) in coastal set nets indirectly consumes the natural resources that whale-watching operators utilize. In some extreme cases (e.g. Hector's dolphins in New Zealand) recreational fishing can be involved in the destruction of these key resources (Slooten *et al.*, 2000). In other words, the economic viability of the ecotourism sector is undermined by activities that have no economic contribution to the country. It is apparent that exclusive access to the marine resource by tourism operations is rarely the case. As such multiple resource demands may pose the potential for resource-use conflicts to exist, and these need to be managed carefully (see case study).

Management Responses

The management of whale-watching, most particularly in the case of inshore rather than pelagic operations, is determined to a large degree by the domestic legislative framework in place. The legislative framework differs from one national/regional context to the next (Davis *et al.*, 1997). Historically, the enactment of legislation governing whale-watching has been developed retrospectively, as the speed of growth in the whale-watch sector has raced ahead of the development of management frameworks. Once in place, the legislative context may also prove to be inadequate in practice (see case study). The adequacy of legislation may be determined by the status of the marine environments within which tourism and marine mammal encounters take place. Where tourism–wildlife encounters take place in marine protected areas, the capacity for conservation agencies to oversee a sustainable marine mammal-watching industry may be enhanced.

Licensing or permitting may also be operationalized under relevant conservation legislation. Such a framework may allow the implementation of guidelines to oversee the sustainable use of a resource (Edington and Edington, 1986). In these instances it is perhaps necessary (but rarely the case) that guidelines are developed on a species-specific basis. This situation is also complicated where multiple and conflicting resource uses coincide. It is generally recognized that licensing of vessels encountering marine mammals, rather than operations that specialize in marine mammal-watching, should take place (Davis *et al.*, 1997). The alternative is to risk the management of specialized marine mammal-watching operations, while others (e.g. scenic cruise operators) remain outside the regulatory framework. This situation is undesirable when both types of operations interact with marine mammal populations, providing visitor experiences that, at least in tourism of animal encounters and resource management, are identical.

The licensing or permit regime may dictate various aspects of the marine mammal-watching phenomenon, including numbers of vessels, duration of encounters and the manoeuvring of vessels. It is critical that aspects of marine mammal tourism, such as the navigation of vessels (e.g. speed, direction and engine speed/noise) and the management of visitor behaviours (e.g. where swimming with dolphin experiences are offered), are regulated through the licensing and/or permitting process. The economic context of the regulation process is an important aspect of the management of marine mammal-watching. Where regulatory agencies are under-resourced to police the conduct of commercial operators, or pursue avenues of legal enforcement, the management framework may be regarded with impunity.

Even in cases where the regulatory management framework is developed successfully and implemented effectively, the need for further management intervention may be necessary. Where marine sanctuaries are in place, it may also be desirable actively to manage the spatio-ecological dimensions of marine mammal-watching. It has been demonstrated that marine mammal species may be prone to significant impacts (as measured in terms of the energetic budget of individuals within a population) in some behavioural states more so than others (Lusseau, 2002b). Under these circumstances, it is necessary to achieve rigorous insights into where these behaviours are most likely to take place, and to zone these areas appropriately in order to afford members of the population adequate protection when engaged in the most vulnerable behavioural states. This point indicates that the financial context of this phenomenon should extend to the funding of scientific research and monitoring of focal marine mammal species. The collection of longitudinal data has been widely recognized as a critical element of sustainable wildlife tourism (Higham, 1998). In the absence of longitudinal data, a rigorous scientific appreciation of dynamics within the focal species, and the biological significance of changes in all aspects of wildlife behaviour, becomes an impossibility.

Managing Tourism Engagements with Marine Mammals in Remote Communities

Many remote communities situated in the economic periphery have been transformed economically by the development of whale-watching. Kaikoura (New Zealand), Húsavík (Iceland), Friday Harbour (Washington, USA) and Hervey Bay (Australia) are examples that demonstrate this point (Hoyt, 2001). Many such communities are either located far from the centralized (regional or national) managing agencies, or they are communities that have a history of strong interdependence, such as fishing communities (Levine and Levine, 1987; Smith and Hanna, 1993; Sawada and Minami, 1997). Members of remote communities are, typically, fiercely independent and resist external influences that may be perceived to compromise collective or individual values, attitudes and identities.

People derive part of their self-worth and esteem from the groups they belong to (Hogg and Abrams, 1988). Shared community values create a strong community identity that may be quite distinct from that of the rest of the country/region they belonged to (Brewer and Kramer, 1986). It is difficult to apply national management schemes to industries that are located within such communities where man-

agement plans may be viewed as an attempt to overrule the decisions of the closed group (van Vugt, 2002). There is a sense that because the community is special and unique, in the eyes of the people belonging to it, the rules that apply to the management of its activities have to be special and unique as well.

One way management agencies around the globe have tried to mitigate this social issue has been by decentralizing the management of natural resources (Agrawal and Gibson, 1999; Millich, 1999; Lal *et al.*, 2001). However, generally, the laws on which this management is based are still central. The local management bodies are therefore often perceived by peripheral communities as minions of the central government, and are therefore discredited. The alienation of management agencies and tourism operators has emerged as a significant barrier to effective management in many marine mammal tourism contexts.

Case Study: Doubtful Sound, New Zealand

Managing dolphin-watching in a diverse marine-based tourism sector

Doubtful Sound is the second largest of the 14 fjords that compose the Fiordland region in south-western South Island, New Zealand (Fig. 10.3). It is home to a small resident population of bottlenose dolphins (*Tursiops* spp.) that rarely leaves the fjord for more than a few hours (Williams *et al.*, 1993; Schneider, 1999; Lusseau *et al.*, 2002). Scenic cruises that operate on this fjord rely significantly on bottlenose dolphins as a key natural resource (Lusseau, 2002a). No Doubtful Sound visitation data currently exists. Researcher estimates indicate that visitor numbers in the high and low seasons range between 400 and 500 people/day, and 150 and 180 people/day, respectively. This estimate would indicate annual visitor numbers to Doubtful Sound in the vicinity of 75,000–95,000 people. Such figures reflect the presence of new, and expansion of existing, commercial tourism businesses in Doubtful Sound. The tourism pressure in Doubtful Sound has increased dramatically over the past 2 years (Lusseau, 2002a) and is planned to increase fur-

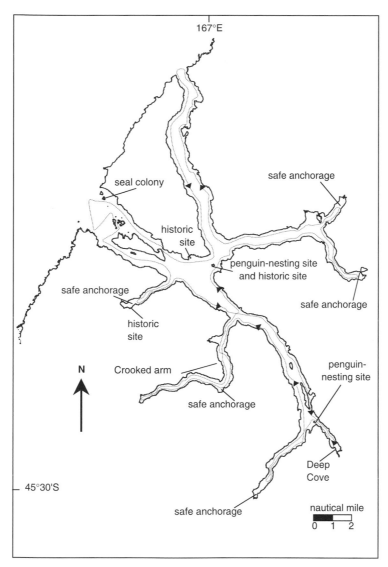

Fig. 10.3. Map of Doubtful Sound, Fiordland (south-western New Zealand), showing the locations of resources utilized by tour operators (penguin-nesting sites, seal colony and historic sites). The dolphin survey route is displayed with a dotted line (arrows showing the direction).

ther in the near future. This expansion and intensification of anthropogenic pressure on Doubtful Sound, and consequently on the bottlenose dolphin population, has heightened the need for management responses aimed at impact mitigation.

In this case, as in many others, marine mammal operations are only one aspect of the marine-based tourism industry at the location

(Lusseau, 2002a). In New Zealand all tourism companies fall under one piece of national legislation, the Resource Management Act (RMA), 1991 (New Zealand Government, 1991), which is administered by local regional councils. In addition, whale-watching activities are managed under the Marine Mammal Protection Act (MMPA), 1978 (New Zealand Government, 1978) and the Marine Mammal Protection

Regulations (MMPR), 1992 (New Zealand Government, 1992). These laws fall under the jurisdiction of the Department of Conservation, a national governmental department, and are managed by the regional conservancy offices of this governmental agency. Marine mammal tour operators aside, the sound is also plied by fishing charter, scenic cruise and adventure operators (plus, increasingly, private boat owners). None of these companies/private groups are dedicated dolphin watchers, yet dolphins are a key resource in this location and are encountered daily by the scenic cruises (Lusseau, 2002b). Under these circumstances, visitors may partake in a scenic cruise, because it is cheaper than marine mammal-watching tours, in anticipation of the equal probability of engaging in dolphin encounters. Despite the expanding and diversifying tourism and recreation interests in the region (many of which engage with the resident population of bottlenose dolphins on a regular, perhaps daily occurrence), only those operators that specialize in marine mammal-watching are subject to management under the RMA, MMPA and MMPR. The exceptions, which represent the majority of tour operations (permitted marine mammal tour operators being the exception), spend a significant amount of time with dolphins (Lusseau, 2002), yet are managed only under the RMA.

Because of the remoteness of the area, it is difficult and expensive to carry out policing activities. Moreover, the MMPR do not prevent non-permitted vessels from interacting with marine mammals if they happened to encounter them. Therefore the prosecution of non-permitted operators can only take place where intentional interactions with dolphin schools can be demonstrated. This legal impracticality effectively undermines marine mammal protection legislation, a situation that understandably fosters tension between permitted and non-permitted tour operators. The former naturally argue that there is no benefit in holding a permit because other operators can freely access the same target resource. Moreover, there are considerable commercial disadvantages associated with holding a permit, because it ties operators to national responsibilities and an extra level of management. Thus, the operations of non-permitted companies can be freely expanded (that is, increase the number of trips

per day and the number of boats the company operates) under the regional management plan, while permit owners cannot do so because of the national guidelines under the MMPR.

In Doubtful Sound misinterpretation or neglect of the guidelines provided in the MMPR on how to interact with dolphins has led to unparalleled levels of MMPR violations (Lusseau, 2002a). Conservative attitudes towards boat navigation, interactions with dolphins and legislated regulations have proved a major barrier to effective management. The imposition of guidelines by centralized management authorities without adequate consultation, dialogue or explanation of the rationale behind guidelines, regulations and restrictions would appear to explain a large part of the problem.

Management intervention: a multi-level marine sanctuary

Recent studies show that interactions with vessels in Doubtful Sound disrupt the behaviours, and therefore threaten to unbalance the energy budget, of the dolphin population (Lusseau, 2003). Lusseau (2002) demonstrates that the presence of vessels typically causes dolphins to discontinue resting and socializing behaviours and, in most cases, to begin travelling. Such behaviour changes have significant implications for the energetic budget of the population. This suggests that management interventions should seek to minimize or prevent boat interactions when dolphins are socializing and, most particularly, when dolphins are resting (Lusseau, 2003). It has also been demonstrated that the critical behaviours take place predominantly in specific locations within the range of the population (Lusseau, 2003). In this particular case, the creation of a multi-level marine mammal sanctuary in Doubtful Sound emerges as a logical management response (Lusseau et al., 2002). The MMPA overrides regional management in cases where a marine mammal species is at risk (New Zealand Government, 1978). This may result in the creation of marine mammal sanctuaries to protect the populations at risk. The establishment of sanctuaries is a flexible tool that affords the involvement of commu-

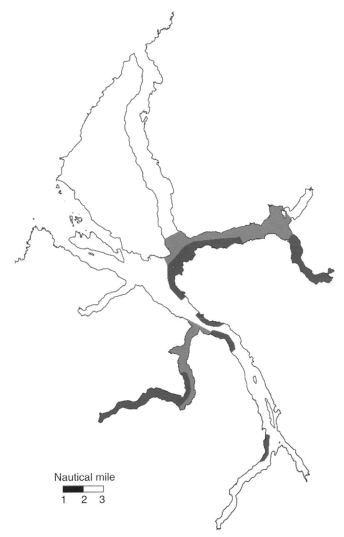

Fig. 10.4. Proposed multi-level marine mammal sanctuary in Doubtful Sound. Dark grey areas correspond to no-boat zones. Light grey areas correspond to location that only tour operators possessing a dolphin-watching permit and researchers may access.

nities and interested groups at various stages of the management process.

The designation of a multi-level sanctuary allows differentiated management zones to exist at a minimum of three levels:

1. Zones that are accessible to all commercial tour operators and private boat users.
2. Zones that are accessible only to permit holders and scientific researchers.
3. Zones that are excluded from any access.

In the Doubtful Sound context, such a sanctuary would close to boat access all zones that are predominantly used to rest, and most zones that are predominantly used to socialize (Fig. 10.4). In addition, it would establish secondary zones that only permitted marine mammal tour operators and permitted scientific researchers could utilize. These zones would be in locations where the highest probability of dolphin encounters exists. It would also include areas where some socializing behaviour is likely to

Table 10.1. Guidelines for the delineation and management of critical habitats.

Rule 1: all critical resting regions need to be allocated a no-boat zone status

Rule 2: most critical socializing regions need to be allocated a no-boat zone status

Rule 3: the boundaries of protected areas need to be at least 400 m away from most resting and socializing sightings in a region and, at best, 1 km away, because dolphins were observed reacting to the presence of vessels at these distances (Lusseau, 2003)

Rule 4: the restriction to access other natural resources (penguin-nesting sites, seal colony, significant scenery and historic sites) must be minimal

Rule 5: the restriction to access safe anchorage locations and safe navigation routes must be minimal

Rule 6: tour operators that possess watching permits, and researchers, must be able to access more locations where dolphins are likely to be seen than other operators

Rule 7: tour operators that possess watching permits, and researchers, must be able to access some locations where some socializing can be observed, to match the expectation of their tourists (and meet study requirements in the case of researchers)

be observed. It is necessary that any restrictions in access do not undermine the economic viability of other tour companies (e.g. scenic cruise operators). In the Doubtful Sound case the primary (no access) and secondary (permit holder access only) management zones would collectively represent less than 15% of the total area of the fjord (Fig. 10.3) (Lusseau, 2002a). Zoning takes into consideration the use of Doubtful Sound by tour operators. The zoning process requires that a set of rules, designed to provide guidance to the zoning system, is established in consultation with stakeholders, including tour operators (Table 10.1).

This management option restores the benefits of holding a dolphin-watching permit. It limits the number of vessels likely to interact with dolphins, and minimizes the likelihood of non-permitted vessels interacting with dolphins. It also minimizes the impact of interactions because locations where sensitive behaviours (resting and socializing) are most likely to take

place are closed to boats. The creation of a sanctuary also clarifies the process of policing regulations. 'Intent' would no longer have to be demonstrated. Moreover, it would diminish tensions between permitted and non-permitted operators. As the zoning process involves input from the local community into the management process, the community is more likely to value, understand and respect the resultant management guidelines. Finally, the creation of a sanctuary may, in the long-term, increase the intrinsic economic value of the area and its attractiveness, by increasing its wilderness value (Davis and Tisdell, 1996; Higham *et al.*, 2001; Sloan, 2002), providing a long-term benefit for the tour operators and the local community.

This approach is easy to implement and police because it minimizes the number of regulations and guidelines and manages the industry under one piece of legislation. It provides a sustainable solution for tourism engagement with marine mammals because it incorporates environmental, economic and social needs. Such a framework could be applied easily to other locations where dolphins and whales are utilized by different sectors of the tourism industry to different degrees.

Current research confirms that the guidelines of the MMPR, if respected, minimize the impact of boat interactions with dolphins in Doubtful Sound (Lusseau *et al.*, 2002). Clear explanation of the rationale behind the guidelines (such as maintaining slow speed within 300 m of a school of dolphins) resulted in significant improvements in the interactions of vessels and dolphins observed in Doubtful Sound (Lusseau *et al.*, 2002). In this case, open dialogue between the management agency (Department of Conservation regional office) and the tour operators, perhaps in the form of a road show, public lectures, seminar presentations and/or research updates during meetings, clearly increases respect for, and compliance with, regulations. Independent research is critical to the effectiveness of this approach. The host community often considers researchers as 'part-time', or honorary members of the community because they spend a significant amount of time in the location. Moreover, because of their independent status, they are not perceived to be imposing a national management agenda upon the community. Researchers can therefore act as an effective link between regional management bodies, the community, and the tourism industry, given their often advantageous position achieved through the 'give-and-take' paradigm of social identity (van Vugt, 2002). This scenario has been demonstrated in the case of dolphin-watch management in the Bay of Islands (New Zealand) (Constantine, 1999).

Conclusions

The proliferation and diversification of marine mammal tour operations presents significant challenges relating to sustainable development. The ecological impacts of anthropogenic change emerge as a critical issue in this field. These may include pod tightening, increases in dive intervals and increases in travelling speed. These signs of avoidance can be a result of the presence of boats or, more particularly, erratic and changeable boat speed, noise and manoeuvring. The presence and density of boats and the distance between boats and individuals can also affect the frequency or occurrence of behaviours. Additionally, the behavioural state of cetacean groups interacting with tourist vessels can be affected and changed. Typically this results in a decrease in resting, which seems to be the most sensitive behavioural state to boat interactions (Würsig, 1996; Lusseau, 2003). The presence of vessels also influences vocalizations, with implications for communication, group cohesion, the location of prey and navigation (Popper, 1980; Janik and Slater, 1998). Human engagements with marine mammals may also result in injury to the latter due to collisions.

The complexity of the marine mammal tourism context, like other forms of wildlife tourism management, requires carefully designed and site/species-specific management interventions, drawing on a suite of management techniques. Few management techniques appear to be adequate when implemented in isolation. The legislative framework, including the designation of marine protected areas and multi-level sanctuaries within protected areas, is a critical requirement (Davis *et al.*, 1997). A permitting framework that is comprehensive (rather than selective) in coverage, reasonable and enforceable is important. Such a framework must be

responsive to a dynamic tourism context in which management deficiencies may emerge over time. So, too, is a commitment on the part of commercial operators and management agencies to an ongoing monitoring research programme. Management agencies face the challenge of achieving effective management within socio-cultural, economic and political contexts that are, in many cases, complex. The geographically remote, economically peripheral and politically conservative nature of many whale-watch communities (e.g. Lofoten and Andamen, Norway) may present resistance to politically centralized management and regulatory structures that can paralyse the best intended management interventions. These agencies must also be responsive to research findings and efficient in their adoption of management recommendations, based on rigorous scientific research (Davis *et al.*, 1997; Higham, 1998). It is questionable whether at present any marine mammal tourism contexts meet all of these management criteria adequately.

References

Agrawal, A. and Gibson, C.C. (1999) Enchantment and disenchantment: the role of community in natural resource conservation. *World Development* 27(4), 629–649.

Baker, C.S. and Herman, L.M. (1989) *Behavioural Responses of Summering Humpback Whales to Vessel Traffic: Experimental and Opportunistic Observations*. Final Report to the National Park Service, Alaska Regional Office: Anchorage, Alaska.

Baker, C.S., Perry, A. and Vequist, G. (1988) Humpback whales of Glacier Bay, Alaska. *Whalewatcher* Fall, 13–17.

Barr, K. (1996) Impacts of tourist vessels on the behaviour of dusky dolphins (*Lagenorhynchus obscurus*) at Kaikoura. MSc thesis, Department of Marine Sciences, University of Otago, Dunedin, New Zealand.

Bejder, L., Dawson, S.M. and Harraway, J.A. (1999) Responses by Hector's Dolphins to boats and swimmers in Porpoise Bay, New Zealand. *Marine Mammal Science* 15(3), 738–750.

Blane, J.M. (1990) Avoidance and interactive behaviour of the Saint Lawrence beluga whale (*Delphinapterus leucas*) in response to recreational boating. MA thesis, University of Toronto, Canada.

Blane, J.M. and Jaakson, R. (1995) The impact of eco-tourism boats on the Saint Lawrence Beluga Whales. *Environmental Conservation* 21(3), 267–269.

Brewer, M.B. and Kramer, R.M. (1986) Choice behavior in social dilemmas: effects of social identity, group size and decision framing. *Journal of Personality and Social Psychology* 3, 543–549

Briggs, D.A. (1985) Report on the effects of boats on the orcas in the Johnstone Strait from July 11, 1984–September 1, 1984. Unpublished report, UCSC, Santa Cruz, California.

Campagna, C., Rivarola, M.M., Greene, D. and Tagliorette, A. (1995) Watching southern right whales in Patagonia. Unpublished report to UNEP, Nairobi.

Constantine, R. (1999) Effects of tourism on marine mammals in New Zealand. *Science for Conservation* 106. Department of Conservation, Wellington, New Zealand.

Constantine, R. (2001) Increased avoidance of swimmers by wild Bottlenose Dolphins (*Tursiops truncatus*) due to long-term exposure to swim-with-dolphin tourism. *Marine Mammal Science* 17(4), 689–702.

Constantine, R. and Baker, C.S. (1997) Monitoring the commercial swim-with-dolphin operations in the Bay of Islands. *Science and Research Series* 104. Department of Conservation: Wellington, New Zealand.

Corkeron, P.J. (1995) Humpback Whales (*Megaptera novaeangliae*) in Hervey Bay, Queensland: behaviour and responses to whale-watching vessels. *Canadian Journal of Zoology* 73, 1290–1299.

Darveau, C.A., Suarez, R.K., Andrews, R.D. and Hochachka, P.W. (2002) Allometric cascade as a unifying principle of body mass effects on metabolism. *Nature* 417(6885), 166–170.

Davis, D. and Tisdell, C. (1996) Economic management of recreational scuba diving and the environment. *Journal of Environmental Management* 48, 229–248.

Davis, D., Banks, S., Birtles, A., Valentine, P. and Cuthill, M. (1997) Whale sharks in Ningaloo Marine Park: managing tourism in an Australian marine protected area. *Tourism Management* 18(5), 259–271.

Duffus, D.A. and Dearden, P. (1990) Non-consumptive wildlife-oriented recreation: a conceptual framework. *Biological Conservation* 53, 213–231.

Edds, P.L. and MacFarlane, J.A.F. (1987) Occurrence and general behaviour of balaenopterid cetaceans summering in the Saint Lawrence Estuary, Canada. *Canadian Journal of Zoology* 65, 1363–1376.

Edington, J.M. and Edington, M.A. (1986) *Ecology, Recreation and Tourism.* Cambridge University Press, Cambridge, UK.

Finley, K.J., Miller, G.W. and Davis, R.A. (1990) Reactions of belugas, *Delphinapterus leucas*, and narwhals, *Monodon monoceros*, to ice-breaking ships in the Canadian high Arctic. *Canadian Bulletin of Fisheries and Aquatic Science* 224, 97–117.

Gordon, J., Leaper, R., Hartley, F.G. and Chappell, O. (1992) Effects of whale watching vessels on the surface and underwater acoustic behaviour of sperm whales off Kaikoura, New Zealand. *Science and Research Series* 52. Department of Conservation, Wellington, New Zealand.

Henriksen, I. (2002) Whales, tourism and coastal culture in Norway: Issues of sustainability. Unpublished Masters thesis. Norwegian School of Hotel Management, Stavanger, Norway.

Higham, J.E.S. (1998) Tourists and albatrosses: the dynamics of tourism at the Northern Royal Albatross Colony, Taiaroa Head, New Zealand *Tourism Management* 19(6), 521–533.

Higham, J.E.S. and Carr, A. (2002) Ecotourism visitor experiences in Aotearoa/New Zealand: challenging the environmental values of visitors in pursuit of pro-environmental behaviour. *Journal of Sustainable Tourism* 10(4), 277–294.

Higham, J., Carr, A. and Gale, S. (2001) *Ecotourism in New Zealand: Profiling Visitors to New Zealand Ecotourism Operations.* Research Paper No. 10, Dunedin, New Zealand. Department of Tourism, University of Otago, Dunedin, New Zealand.

Hinch, T.D. (1998) Ecotourists and indigenous hosts: diverging views on their relationship with nature. *Current Issues in Tourism* 1(1), 120–124.

Hinch, T.D. (2001) Indigenous territories. In: Weaver, D. (ed.) *The Encyclopedia of Ecotourism.* CAB International, Wallingford, UK.

Hogg, M.A. and Abrams, D. (1988) *Social Identifications.* Routledge, London.

Howland, H.C. (1974) Optimal strategies for predator avoidance: the relative importance of speed and manoeuvrability. *Journal of Theoretical Biology* 47, 333–350.

Hoyt, E. (2001) Whale watching 2001. Unpublished report to IFAW and UNEP, London.

Hoyt, E. and Hvenegaard, G.T. (2002) A review of whale-watching and whaling with applications for the Caribbean. *Coastal Management* 30(4), 381–399.

Janik, V.M. and Slater, P.J.B. (1998) Context-specific use suggests that Bottlenose Dolphin signature whistles are cohesion calls. *Animal Behaviour* 56, 829–838.

Janik, V.M. and Thompson, P.M. (1996) Changes in

surfacing patterns of Bottlenose Dolphins in response to boat traffic. *Marine Mammal Science* 12, 597–602.

Kruse, S. (1991) The interactions between Killer Whales and boats in Johnstone Strait, B.C. In: Norris, K.S. and Pryor, K. (eds) *Dolphin Societies: Discoveries and Puzzles.* University of California Press, California, pp. 149–159.

Lal, P., Lim-Applegate, H. and Scoccimarro, M. (2001) The adaptive decision-making process as a tool for integrated natural resource management: focus, attitudes, and approach. *Conservation Ecology* 5(2), 11. Available at website http://www.consecol.org/vol5/iss2/art11 (verified 30 December 2003).

Levine, H.B. and Levine, M.W. (1987) *Steward Island: Anthropological Perspectives on a New Zealand Fishing Community.* Victoria University Occasional Papers in Anthropology, 1. Victoria University of Wellington, Department of Anthropology, Wellington, New Zealand.

Lusseau, D. (2002a) The state of the scenic cruise industry in Doubtful Sound in relation to a key natural resource: Bottlenose Dolphins. *Proceedings of the Ecotourism, Wilderness and Mountain Tourism conference* August 27–29, 2002. University of Otago, Dunedin, New Zealand, pp. 106–117.

Lusseau, D. (2002b) The effects of tourism activities on Bottlenose Dolphins (*Tursiops* spp.) in Fiordland. PhD thesis, University of Otago, Dunedin, New Zealand.

Lusseau, D. (2003) The effects of tour boats on the behavior of Bottlenose Dolphins: using Markov chains to model anthropogenic impacts. *Conservation Biology* 17(6), 1785–1793.

Lusseau, D., Slooten, E., Higham, J.E.S. and Dawson, S.M. (2002) *The Effects of Tourism Activities on Bottlenose Dolphins in Fiordland: Towards a Sustainable Solution.* Final report to the Department of Conservation, Wellington, New Zealand.

MacGibbon, J. (1991) Responses of sperm whales (*Physeter macrocephalus*) to commercial whale watching boats off the coast of Kaikoura. Unpublished report to the Department of Conservation. University of Canterbury, Christchurch, New Zealand.

Millich, L. (1999) Resource mismanagement versus sustainable livelihoods: the collapse of the Newfoundland Cod Fishery. *Society and Natural Resources* 12(7), 625–642.

New Zealand Government (1978) *New Zealand Marine Mammal Protection Act 1978.* New Zealand Government Printer, Wellington, New Zealand.

New Zealand Government (1991) *New Zealand Resource Management Act 1991.* New Zealand Government Printer, Wellington, New Zealand.

New Zealand Government (1992) *Marine Mammal Protection Regulations 1992.* New Zealand Government Printer, Wellington, New Zealand.

Norris, T. (1994) Effects of boat noise on the acoustic behavior of Humpback Whales. *Journal of the Acoustic Society of America* 96(5-2), 3251.

Nowacek, S.M., Wells, R.S. and Solow, A.R. (2001) Short-term effects of boat traffic on Bottlenose Dolphins, *Tursiops truncatus,* in Sarasota Bay, Florida. *Marine Mammal Science* 17(4), 673–688.

Orams, M.B. (1995a) Using interpretation to manage nature-based tourism. *Journal of Sustainable Tourism* 4(2), 81–94.

Orams, M.B. (1995b) Towards a more desirable form of ecotourism. *Tourism Management* 16(1), 3–8.

Orams, M.B. (1997) The effectiveness of environmental education: can we turn tourists into 'Greenies'? *Progress in Tourism and Hospitality Research* 3, 295–306.

Orams, M.B. (1999) *Marine Tourism: Development, Impacts and Management.* Routledge, London.

Orams, M.B. (2002) Marine ecotourism as a potential agent for sustainable development in Kaikoura, New Zealand. *International Journal of Sustainable Development* 5(3), 338–354.

Polar Bears Alive (2003) *Polar Bears Alive.* Available at website http://www.polarbearsalive.org/tours.htm (verified 21 March 2003).

Popper, A.N. (1980) Sound emission and detection by Delphinids. In: Herman, L.M. (ed.) *Cetacean Behaviour: Mechanisms and Functions.* John Wiley & Sons, New York, pp. 1–52.

Richter, C., Dawson, S.M. and Slooten, E. (2002) The impacts of whale-watching activities in Kaikoura. Unpublished report to the Department of Conservation, Wellington, New Zealand.

Ris, M. (1993) Conflicting cultural values: whale tourism in Northern Norway. *Arctic* 46(2), 156–163.

Ritter, F. (1996) Abundance, distribution and behaviour of cetaceans off La Gomera (Canary Islands) and their interaction with whale-watching boats and swimmers. Unpublished Diploma thesis, University of Bremen, Germany.

Salden, D.R. (1988) Humpback whales encounter rates offshore of Maui, Hawaii. *Journal of Wildlife Management* 52(2), 301–304.

Salvado, C.A.M., Kleiber, P. and Dizon, A.E. (1992) Optimal course by dolphins for detection avoidance. *Fishery Bulletin* 90, 417–420.

Sawada, H. and Minami, H. (1997) Peer group play and co-childrearing in Japan: a historical ethnography of a fishing community. *Journal of*

Applied Developmental Psychology 18(4), 513–526.

Scarpaci, C., Bigger, S.W., Corkeron, P.J. and Nugegoda, D. (2000) Bottlenose Dolphins (*Tursiops truncatus*) increase whistling in the presence of 'swim-with-dolphin' tour operations. *Journal of Cetacean Research and Management* 2(3), 183–185.

Schneider, K. (1999) Behaviour and ecology of bottlenose dolphins in Doubtful Sound Fiordland, New Zealand. Unpublished PhD Thesis, University of Otago, Dunedin, New Zealand.

Sloan, N.A. (2002) History and application of the wilderness concept in marine conservation. *Conservation Biology* 16(2), 294–305.

Slooten, E., Fletcher, D. and Taylor, B. (2000) Accounting for uncertainty in risk assessment: case study of Hector's Dolphin mortality due to gillnet entanglement. *Conservation Biology* 14(5), 1264–1270.

Smestad, T.H. (1997) Images of whales, whaling and whalers: a rhetorical study of the controversies over Norwegian minke whaling. Unpublished Master of Arts thesis, University of Maastricht.

Smith, C.L. and Hanna, S.S. (1993) Occupation and community as determinants of fishing behaviors. *Human Organisation* 52 (3), 299–303.

Van Parijs, S.M. and Corkeron, P.J. (2001) Boat traffic affects the acoustic behaviour of Pacific humpback dolphins, *Sousa chinensis. Journal of the Marine Association UK* 81, 533–538.

Van Vugt, M. (2002) Central, individual, or collective control? Social dilemma strategies for natural resource management. *American Behavioral Scientist* 45(5), 783–800.

Weaver, D. (ed.) (2001) *The Encyclopedia of Ecotourism.* CAB International, Wallingford, UK.

Williams, J.A., Dawson, S.M. and Slooten, E. (1993) The abundance and distribution of bottlenosed dolphins (*Tursiops truncatus*) in Doubtful Sound, New Zealand. *Canadian Journal of Zoology* 71, 2080–2088.

Williams, R., Trites, A.W. and Bain, D. (2002) Behavioural responses of Killer Whales (*Orcinus Orca*) to whale-watching boats: opportunistic observations and experimental approaches. *Journal of Zoology* 256, 255–270.

Würsig, B. (1996) Swim-with-dolphin activities in nature: weighing the pros and cons. *Whalewatcher* 30(1), 11–15.

11

Impacts of Ecotourism on Birds

Ralf Buckley

International Centre for Ecotourism Research, Griffith University, Gold Coast,
Queensland, Australia

Introduction

Birds are a major feature of many ecotourism marketing materials. Bird logos, bird photographs, bird diversity, bird-viewing opportunities and bird checklists are commonplace in ecotour brochures, websites and trip or lodge documents. Birdwatching is a large and growing specialist sector of the ecotourism industry (Jones and Buckley, 2000), and provides much of the customer base for manufacturers of high-end binoculars.

All forms and aspects of ecotourism have some impacts on birds, both resident and migratory species, but these impacts differ enormously in size, scale and significance. In many cases the impacts of ecotourism on birds may not be apparent to the ecotourists, or tour operators themselves. There are also examples, however, where impacts on spectacular bird populations have reduced the attractiveness of entire tourist destinations. Perhaps best known of these are the flamingoes of the Camargue, France (Feltwell, 1996).

This chapter reviews published scientific literature on such impacts in an attempt to identify any general patterns and to illustrate the degree of variation. It draws on two previous reviews (Hockin *et al.*, 1992; Liddle, 1997) as well as more recent and additional literature. In particular, it relies on these authors for citations to studies published in European languages other than English.

Little of this literature refers specifically to ecotourism, but rather to various forms of outdoor recreation and related human activities. Some boundaries must therefore be drawn to define what is considered as ecotourism for the purposes of this review. Such definition is not always straightforward (Buckley, 1994, 2001, 2003a, pp. 223–235). This review includes impacts from vehicles, boats and small-scale infrastructure, since many ecotourism products make use of these. Larger-scale high-impact tourism developments and activities, however, are not included. Thus, for example, golf courses can have major impacts on birds through ingestion of pesticides, sometimes leading to large-scale mortality (Cox, 1991; Kendall *et al.*, 1992; Rainwater *et al.*, 1995). Similarly, ski resorts have impacts through habitat clearance, obstructed visibility, noise and lights, and elevated cables. In France, for example, there are many instances where black grouse have been killed through collisions with cables at ski resorts (Miquet, 1990).

Hunting and shooting is also excluded. In some instances, hunting reserves may potentially contribute to conservation if they prevent clearance of land for agriculture. Even in reserves set aside for gamebird shooting, however, only the relatively common target gamebird species are conserved. Other bird species, which may prey on or compete with the gamebirds, are commonly killed by managers or gamekeepers. Golden eagles on grouse moors in the UK, for example, are routinely shot by gamekeepers (Watson *et al.*, 1989). Shooting is a major cause of mortality for target species such as migratory duck. Besides birds bagged as game, other individuals may die by ingesting lead shot. In addition, both target and non-target species are repeatedly disturbed from feeding in areas where hunting occurs. This increases mortality and decreases reproductive success, especially for migratory species (Béchet *et al.*, 2003).

In developing nations particularly, tourism may be associated with illegal trade in endangered species and a consequent increase in poaching, as recorded for green peafowl in Asia (van Balen *et al.*, 1995). Even in developed nations, illegal collection of birds and eggs is widespread, largely for international trade in rare species. On Cat Island in Victoria, Australia, however, fisherman have been recorded taking little penguins as bait (Harris and Norman, 1981). Clearly, this is not ecotourism.

In other cases, however, the distinction is not so clear-cut. Tourists in off-highway vehicles may behave as ecotourists, or they may not (Buckley, Chapter 6, this volume). Sailboats, yachts and canoes may be used for ecotourism or purely for adventure-based outdoor recreation. Small-scale angling for food may be treated as part of an ecotourism experience in some parts of the world, such as sea kayak expeditions in the Arctic or river float trips in Russia. Elsewhere, angling is an afternoon or weekend pastime for urban residents with no particular interest in the environment except as a source of fish and bait. Similar considerations apply for horse-riding. Many people who would consider themselves ecotourists own dogs, but hikers with dogs commonly produce much higher impacts on birds and other wildlife than hikers without dogs. Most protected area agencies and ecotours oppose the deliberate feeding of birds for or by tourists, but many individual people and some well-known ecolodges do routinely feed birds. Possible consequences, both for the species fed and their predators, prey and competitors, remain largely unknown.

As far as possible, therefore, this review attempts to include all outdoor recreation activities and associated human disturbances which are incorporated into ecotourism products, at least in some parts of the world. The responses of birds to human disturbance have been known to bird hunters and egg collectors from time immemorial, whether the muttonbird collectors on the islands of the Bass Strait, Australia, or hunters in search of bird-of-paradise feathers in New Guinea. The first documented record of impacts associated specifically with recreation, however, appears to be that of Schick (1890), who noted that the number of osprey along a beach in New Jersey, USA, declined from 100 to 25 pairs as woodlands were cleared for beach cottages. Since that date there have been over 300 published records of recreation impacts on birds, albeit with a strong focus on certain species and geographic areas.

But are these disturbances ecologically significant for the species concerned? Recreational hunting was apparently a major factor in the extinction of the passenger pigeon (Schorger, 1973). While, clearly, this did not qualify as ecotourism, there are several more recent examples where particular bird species are threatened by forms of outdoor recreation that could indeed fall within the broader definition of ecotourism as propounded by tourism promotion agencies (Buckley, 1994; Weaver, 2000). Over 90% of the remaining population of Heerman's gull, for example, nests on a single island in the Gulf of California, and recreational disturbance has reduced the number of offspring per adult by 75%, from 0.18 per year to 0.045 (Palacios and Mellink, 1996). Over 75% of the North American population of canvasback duck use Lake Onalaska in the upper Mississippi River as a staging area during migration, and recreational boats frequently disturb large flocks which circle for up to an hour before alighting again to feed (Korschgen *et al.*, 1985). Given that the energetic balance of migratory waterfowl is commonly very tight (Tucker, 1971), this extra energy expenditure and loss of feeding time increases mortality during migration. On a more local scale, the impacts of recreational off-road driving have caused complete failure of individual breeding colonies of least terns in the Gulf of California (Palacios and Mellink, 1996). Visiting tourists have also caused complete failure of breeding colonies of least terns in South Carolina (Gaddy and Kohlsaat, 1987), king shag in Argentina

(Kury and Gochfeld, 1975) and brown pelicans in the Gulf of California (Anderson and Keith, 1980). Perhaps most significant of all, tourists to particularly isolated areas, such as Antarctica, may bring diseases that could decimate previously thriving colonies of resident birds, penguins in this instance (Anderson, 1998).

The impacts of ecotourism on birds may be classified by various criteria, including: the source of impact or type of activity; the mechanism or severity of impact; or the bird species or family involved (Liddle, 1997; Buckley, 2003b). Since this volume focuses on the impacts and management of ecotourism, rather than the life histories and ecology of birds, the primary division in this chapter is between fixed-site activities which modify bird habitat, and mobile activities which affect individual birds. Since impacts on breeding success are of particular significance for the survival of bird populations, these are distinguished from disturbance to non-breeding birds. These categories are not clear-cut. At what point, for example, does a mobile disturbance which is repeated frequently and routinely in the same place, effectively become a habitat modification? Likewise, disturbances to non-breeding birds may later affect their reproductive success. Commonly, however, birds respond differently when breeding, so the distinction is useful.

Table 11.1 lists the English and scientific names of birds mentioned in this chapter.

Modification to Bird Habitats

Ecotourism activities can modify avian habitats in many ways. Some of the more common include:

- clearance or more open vegetation at lodges, campgrounds, trails;
- reduced visibility from lodges, windbreaks, etc.;
- lights at night from lodges, vehicles, boats;
- continual noise from lodges, vehicles, boats, etc.;
- more or fewer nesting, roosting or perching points;
- removal of nest sites through firewood collection and tentsite clearance;

- more or less open water, e.g. from water-supply or recreational dams;
- changes to aquatic vegetation on lakes and riverbanks;
- changes to plant cover from changed fire regimes;
- changes to vegetation through inadvertent introduction of weeds or diseases;
- increased predator access along roads and tracks;
- increased food supplies from scraps at lodges and campgrounds;
- increased food supplies from planting of native fruit- or nectar-bearing trees;
- reduced food supplies from erosion of soil and plant litter;
- reduced food supplies from compaction of marshes or shores;
- reduced food supplies from loss of water-weeds and streambank vegetation;
- reduced food supplies through collection of bait, etc.;
- changed food supplies for insect-eating birds where insect fauna is modified by vegetation change or clearance.

Construction of cottages on lakeshores, for example, reduces the local populations of birds such as osprey (Schick, 1890) and loon (Lehtonen, 1970; Vermeer, 1973; Bundy, 1979; Andersson *et al.*, 1980; Heimberger *et al.*, 1983). Birds flying at night are disorientated by artificial lights and may collide with buildings or other structures (Imber, 1975; Verheijen, 1980, 1981; Elkins, 1983; Mead, 1983; Reed *et al.*, 1985; Telfer *et al.*, 1987). Pink-footed geese in Denmark avoid areas with obstructed visibility where they may be unable to see predators approaching (Madsen, 1985).

Forest-edge bird species, including predators and brood parasites such as blue jay and brown-headed cowbird, use recreational tracks and trails to enter forest-core areas in reserves in Illinois, USA (Hickman, 1990). Eggs in nests near recreational trails along lowland streams in the Colorado Front Range suffered 95% predation rate (Miller and Hobbs, 2000). Forest-edge species increase in relative density near campgrounds in lodgepole pine forest at 2600 m elevation in Yosemite National Park, and forest-core species decrease (Garton *et al.*, 1977). Scavenger species increase in density near

Table 11.1. Index of English and scientific names.

Table 11.1. *Continued*

sandpiper, common	*Actitis hypoleucos*	teal, cotton	*Nettapus*
sandpiper, semipalmated	*Calidris pusilla*		*coromandelianus*
shag, king	*Phalacrocorax*	tern, common	*Sterna hirundo*
	albiventer	tern, least	*Sterna antillarum*
shelduck, common	*Tadorna tadorna*	tern, roseate	*Sterna dougallii*
shelduck, ruddy	*Tadorna ferruginea*	tern, sooty	*Sterna fuscata*
skimmer, black	*Rynchops niger*	thrush, hermit	*Catharus guttatus*
snowgoose, greater	*Chen caerulescens*	titmouse, tufted	*Parus bicolor*
	atlantica	tree duck, lesser	*Dendrocygna javanica*
sparrowhawk	*Accipiter nisus*	tropicbird, redbilled	*Phaethon aethereus*
stork, openbill	*Anastomus oscitans*	warbler, Townsend's	*Dendroica townsendi*
stork, wood	*Mycteria americana*	warbler, willow	*Phylloscopus trochitus*
swallow, sand martin	*Riparia riparia*	wren, canyon	*Catherpes mexicanus*
swan, Bewick's	*Cygnus columbianus*		

campgrounds in Scotland (Watson, 1976). Seven tree-nesting scavenger species increase in abundance around campgrounds by two rivers in Utah, USA, whereas seven ground-nesting bird species decrease in abundance (Blakesley and Reese, 1988). Areas near campgrounds are abandoned completely by rarer bird species in Coconino National Forest, Arizona, USA (Aitchison, 1977). In The Netherlands, the density of 8 out of 13 woodland bird species decreases in areas with heavier recreational use (van der Zande *et al.*, 1980, 1984); and the number of birds nesting in hedges near lakes decreases where more people walk along the lakeshore (van der Zande and van der Vos, 1984).

Disturbance to Adult Birds

Activities

Disturbance to adult birds has been recorded for a wide variety of recreational activities and a wide variety of species. Some activities, responses and taxa have been studied much more intensively than others. Activities causing disturbance include:

- hikers, walkers and joggers, on- or off-trail;
- anglers on foot or wading, bait collectors;
- people with riding animals, packstock or pets;
- off-road vehicles of various types, from mountain bikes to all-terrain vehicles (ATVs);

- watercraft, including canoes, rafts, rowboats, sailboats, sailboards, motorized canoes, jet skis or personal water craft (PWCs), and powerboats;
- light aircraft and helicopters.

The effects of disturbances from any of these activities may depend on a wide variety of characteristics, such as speed, sudden movements, colour, noise, height (for aircraft), season, time of day, frequency, and combination with other activities. These factors together constitute a disturbance regime.

The impacts of people on foot, including anglers and bait collectors, have been recorded for a wide variety of birds, including: bitterns, boobies, cormorants, curlews, dotterels, ducks, gallinules, geese, grebes, gulls, eagles, egrets, flamingoes, frigatebirds, herons, ibis, oystercatchers, pelicans, penguins, plovers, rails, sandpipers, storks, terns, tropicbirds and various songbirds (Grier, 1969; Hume, 1972; Cooke, 1975; Werschkul *et al.*, 1976; Batten, 1977; Stalmaster and Newman, 1978; Jungius and Hirsch, 1979; Burger, 1981, 1986, 1988, 1994; de Roos 1981; Tuite *et al.*, 1983, 1984; van der Zande and van der Vos, 1984; Bell and Austin, 1985; Hubner and Putzner, 1985; Owens *et al.*, 1986; Paruk 1987; van den Heiligenberg, 1987; Cryer *et al.*, 1987; Hobson *et al.*, 1989; Yalden and Yalden, 1990; Buehler *et al.*, 1991; Yalden, 1992; Holmes *et al.*, 1993; Pierce *et al.*, 1993; Rodgers and Smith, 1995; Burger and Gochfeld, 1998; Fitzpatrick and Bouchez, 1998; Giese, 1998; Giese *et al.*,

1999; Shepherd and Boates, 1999; Mori et al., 2001; Verhulst et al., 2001). Most of these records are for people walking along shorelines and other open areas. There are rather few studies of hikers in montane, forest and woodland ecosystems.

Off-road vehicle (ORV) disturbance of feeding birds has been recorded especially on beaches and shorelines (Blodget, 1978; Pfister et al., 1992; Watson et al., 1996; Fisher et al., 1998), but also in deserts and marshes (Berry, 1980). Ecological thresholds for noise and visual disturbance can be quite low. Areas in Denmark visited only by a single car every few days, for example, are abandoned completely by pink-footed geese (Madsen, 1985). ATVs provide the main threat to least terns on beaches in the Gulf of California, for example (Palacios and Mellink, 1996), and have led to the complete failure of tern colonies. ORVs also kill oystercatchers, terns and plovers in the beaches of the Alexandria Dunefield at Algoa Bay in South Africa (Watson et al., 1996). Vehicle collisions are also a significant source of mortality for cassowaries in the tropical rainforest of north-east Queensland (Crome and Moore, 1990). Off-highway vehicles travelling at speed on unpaved roads may kill birds in a wide variety of ecosystems, as indicated by roadkill in arid and savanna landscapes in Australia, south-western USA and sub-Saharan Africa (Buckley, Chapter 6, this volume).

Disturbance to waterbirds, shorebirds and shore-nesting birds of prey has been recorded for a wide variety of boats, bird species and ecosystems. The impacts of recreational sailing on ducks, geese, coots and swans in Europe have been studied with particular intensity (Hume, 1972; Cooke, 1975; Batten, 1977; Tuite, et al., 1983, 1984; Bell and Austin, 1985; Pfluger and Ingold, 1988; Peltzer, 1989; Keller, 1991; Madsen, 1998). Ducks, geese and swans will move into shallow areas at lake edges, away from deep water used by sailboats. However, on lakes and reservoirs where the shorelines are also used by anglers, the birds leave the area entirely. Species such as loon, eider and greater crested grebe in the cool temperate lakes of Canada and Scandinavia are disturbed by recreational canoes and other boats, especially if the boaters land on the islands (Titus and van Druff, 1981; Keller, 1989, 1991).

Often they completely avoid lakes used by recreational boaters. Similar responses are reported for cormorants in The Netherlands (Lok and Bakker, 1988). Canoes also disturb bald eagles in the Nooksack River of Washington State, USA (Knight, 1984), and ruddy shelduck on rivers in Nepal (Hulbert, 1990). In the latter case, however, the birds suffered relatively little disturbance from canoes paddling downriver midstream, and considerably more from canoes being dragged back upstream along the riverbank. Pedestrians onshore also caused more disturbance than boats offshore to eiders in Scotland (Keller, 1991), and the same applied for 15 species of waterbirds in Florida (Rodgers and Smith, 1995), and for seabirds on islands in the Gulf of California (Tershy et al., 1997). On the coastal beaches of the northwestern USA, boats are one source of disturbance for a number of terns and other shoreline species (Burger et al., 1982, 1995; Burger, 1995, 1998, 2000).

Where comparisons have been made, motorized watercraft commonly produce more severe impacts than non-motorized craft. This applies even for motorized as compared to non-motorized canoes (Titus and van Druff, 1981), but particularly for faster power-boats (Hume, 1972) and especially for jet skis (Burger, 1998; Burger and Leonard, 2000). Impacts on birds have even been recorded for model power-boats used for recreation on a small lake (Bamford et al., 1990). Noise, speed and suddenness all seem to be factors. Airboats in Wisconsin, USA also cause severe disturbance to Canadian geese (Bartelt, 1987). In this case there is also a secondary impact: disturbance by recreational airboats breaks up family groups of the geese, which are then more susceptible to hunters.

Responses of birds to aircraft range from panic to complete habituation. At some airports and airstrips, birds using nearby marshes or other vegetation pose a hazard to aircraft. Least terns have been recorded nesting next to military jetpads (Altman and Grano, 1984). Red-tailed hawks have also been reported nesting under low-altitude helicopter routes in Colorado, USA (Anderson et al., 1989). Cliff-nesting seabirds may also remain on their nests when aircraft pass overhead (Dunnet, 1977). More commonly, however, aircraft provoke alarm responses

(Owens, 1977; Burger, 1981; Hockin *et al.*, 1992). Greater snowgeese, for example, are driven completely away from feeding areas with two or more aircraft overflights per day (Bélanger and Bedard, 1989). Smaller aircraft at low altitude generally cause more severe disturbance than, for example, commercial passenger aircraft at high altitude, as reported for brent geese by Owens (1977). Aircraft disturbance is recorded for a range of seabird species (Dunnet, 1977; Burger, 1981; Brown, 1990), ducks and geese (Harms *et al.*, 1997; Conomy *et al.*, 1998; Ward *et al.*, 1999), and eagles (Watson, 1993). As with other forms of disturbance, even similar or related bird species may respond differently. Conomy *et al.* (1998), for example, found that black duck can become habituated to military aircraft, but that wood duck do not. Severe disturbances by helicopter overflights have been recorded for various species, including Pacific black brant geese (Miller, 1994) and emperor penguins (Giese and Riddle, 1999).

Responses

Responses of adult birds to disturbance by human recreational activities can usefully be considered along a continuum, as follows:

- avoid disturbed areas completely;
- leave area when disturbed and do not return;
- leave area temporarily, return later on same or subsequent day;
- leave feeding, perching or roosting site within area;
- evade disturbance by local movement within area;
- alarm behaviour such as alarm calls or running to and fro;
- alert responses, including physiological changes.

Any of these may be ecologically significant for the population of the species concerned. Temporary interruption of feeding, for example, or increased metabolic rate associated with an alert response, may affect the energetic balance of migratory or overwintering birds, so that they may not complete their migration, survive till spring, or produce a new brood of offspring.

A considerable proportion of past research has focused on so-called flushing behaviour: i.e. birds escaping from human disturbance by taking flight, running, swimming or diving. There have been numerous studies of threshold distances at which human activities trigger flushing by various bird species, and the distances that birds travel when flushed.

Both the type of response, and the threshold and flush distances, may depend on: the bird species concerned; the history and lifecycle stage of the individual birds affected; flock size; visibility, substrate and topography; and disturbance factors such as the human activity, its speed and suddenness, presence of other animals, such as dogs (Burger and Galli, 1980; Yalden and Yalden, 1989, 1990), approach angle and even colour of clothing (Gutzwiller and Marcum, 1993).

Complete avoidance of areas used by tourists has been recorded for, for example, bald eagles in Maryland, USA (Buehler *et al.*, 1991) and Mississippi, USA (Paruk, 1987); common sandpiper in the UK (Yalden and Yalden, 1990) and piping plover in north-eastern coastal USA (Burger, 1994); and shelduck (Cooke, 1980; Hulbert, 1990) and various other ducks in Europe (Tuite *et al.*, 1983, 1984). In Joshua Tree National Park, USA, four bird species completely avoid cliff areas used for recreational climbing (Camp and Knight, 1998): the canyon wren, Townsend's warbler, Lazuli bunting and long-eared owl. Raptors also avoid cliffs used by climbers in Europe (Giuliano, 1994). Areas near roads are avoided by various bird species (Buckley, Chapter 6, this volume) including ducks and geese in Europe (Mooij, 1982; Madsen, 1985; Keller, 1990). In Denmark, for example, pink-footed geese avoid areas within 500 m of roads and tracks travelled by more than 20 vehicles daily (Madsen, 1985).

Displacement from a disturbed area for at least the remainder of the day has been recorded for a variety of species, including eagles (Stalmaster and Newman, 1978; Craig *et al.*, 1988; Anthony and Isaacs, 1989), ducks and waders (Bell and Austin, 1985; Korschgen *et al.*, 1985; Yalden, 1992). Some birds may leave even if others stay. When overwintering bald eagles on the Nooksack River in Washington State, USA, were disturbed, 92% left the area (Stalmaster and Newman, 1978).

Similarly, disturbance to greater snowgeese in Quebec, Canada, caused only part of the flock to leave (Bélanger and Bedard, 1989).

In each of these cases, other individual eagles or snowgeese also took flight, but returned later that day. Bald eagles studied by Stalmaster and Newman (1978) returned to their feeding sites after several hours' absence. Various ducks and geese move away from feeding or roosting areas if disturbed (Owens, 1977; Tuite *et al.*, 1983, 1984; Galhoff *et al.*, 1984; Owens *et al.*, 1986; Cryer *et al.*, 1987; Norris and Wilson, 1988; Morton *et al.*, 1989). The same applies for shorebirds such as curlew, plover, redshank and oystercatcher (de Roos, 1981; van der Zande *et al.*, 1984), and other species such as storks (Datta and Pal, 1993). Up to 75% of the entire North American population of canvasback duck use Lake Onalaska in the upper Mississippi as a staging area, and when the ducks are disturbed by sport fishermen in boats, they leave the lake in flocks of up to 25,000 birds, circling high above the lake for up to an hour before re-alighting (Korschgen *et al.*, 1985).

There do appear to be some broad general patterns for flushing thresholds and flight distances, but these are far from definitive or universal (Hulsman, 1984). Larger bird species such as raptors generally seem to flush at greater distances from human disturbance and to fly further (Cooke, 1980; Skagen *et al.*, 1991; Holmes *et al.*, 1993; Knight and Cole, 1995). For some species, larger flocks may flush at greater distances (Owens, 1977; Madsen, 1985), whereas for other species the opposite effect occurs (Gutzwiller *et al.*, 1998). In any given area, migratory species may flush at greater distances than resident species, as shown for 38 species in Florida (Klein *et al.*, 1995) and 138 species in India (Burger and Gochfeld, 1991). Rural populations for 13 out of 14 European species examined by Cooke (1980) flushed at greater distances than urban populations of the same species, though this difference was only statistically significant for six species. Bird species of open landscapes, such as ocean shores, commonly flush at greater distances than birds living in dense woodland, though whether this is due to visibility or to the size or behavioural patterns of the species is not known. Carolina chickadee,

tufted titmouse and American goldfinch, however, fled or hid sooner from hikers wearing orange vests than from those in more sombre-coloured clothing (Gutzwiller and Marcum, 1993). Many bird species flush at greater distances from people with dogs than from unaccompanied hikers, as noted for golden plover by Yalden and Yalden (1989, 1990) and five species of gulls by Burger and Galli (1980). For bald eagles on Gulkana River in Alaska, flush distance also depends on the age of the individual bird and the height of its perch (Steidl and Anthony, 1996).

Typical flushing distances vary considerably from one bird species or family to another. Shorebirds such as golden plover may flush at distances below 50 m (Yalden and Yalden, 1990), whereas eagles may flush at distances >250 m and fly over 1 km away (Fraser *et al.*, 1985; Grubb and King, 1991; Steidl and Anthony, 1996). Ducks and geese in the UK flush at 250–450 m from sailing dinghies (Batten, 1977). Brent geese flush at <500 m from quiet unpowered watercraft (Owens, 1977), but 1–2 km from motor boats.

Even where birds do not take flight or other evasive action, they may still stop feeding or otherwise exhibit alarm or alert responses. Brent geese and shelduck studied by Martin (1973), for example, ceased feeding when humans came within 200 m. Piping plover on the north-eastern coast of the USA spend 90% of their time feeding when undisturbed, but this was reduced to 50% by disturbance from beachgoers (Burger, 1994). Dotterel chicks in northern New Zealand also spend less time feeding if humans are present (Lord *et al.*, 1997), and New Zealand dabchicks spend more time alert and less feeding (Bright *et al.*, 2003). Rail, gallinules, ibis and heron in the Florida Everglades stopped feeding when tourists approached (Burger and Gochfeld, 1998), as do greater snowgeese in Canada (Bélanger and Bedard, 1989). Flamingoes in Yucatan, Mexico reduced feeding time from 40% to 24% when disturbed by tour boats (Galicia and Baldassarre, 1997). Some species may be able to compensate for such disturbance by feeding for a longer period, or feeding at night, but this compensation is rarely complete and also increases risks of predator attack while feeding.

An alert response to disturbance may be

indicated by a behavioural change, such as standing still, looking at an intruder, or species-specific behaviour such as beak-clattering; or it may produce physiological changes which are not detectable to a guide or tourist. An increase in heart rate in response to approaching humans, for example, has been recorded for blue-footed booby, frigatebirds and waved albatross (Jungius and Hirsch, 1979), black duck (Harms *et al.*, 1997) and Adelie penguins (Giese, 1998; Giese *et al.*, 1999). For albatross and penguins in particular, these authors specifically noted that increases in heart rate occurred before any detectable behavioural change. For the penguins, for example, heart rate increased when humans reached 15 m away, whereas behavioural changes did not commence until humans were only 5 m from the birds.

Other physiological indicators of stress have also been measured on a few occasions. Regel and Putz (1997), for example, showed that disturbance by humans caused a 1.5–2.6°C rise in stomach temperature for emperor penguins. Similarly, disturbance by humans to Magellanic penguins in Argentina caused an increase in the stress-related hormone, corticosterone (Fowler, 1999).

Finally, there are a few bird species which respond to human disturbance by attack rather than evasion. The main examples are larger raptors such as some owls and eagles, especially when nesting (Grubb, 1976; Sherrod *et al.*, 1976).

Responses to disturbance may depend strongly on the past history of the individual bird, as well as factors outlined above. Birds which have been subject to hunting become more easily alarmed, whereas those which have been fed become more easily attracted. Birds with a history of neutral interactions with human recreational activities may become habituated, i.e. they show less response to disturbance than would otherwise be the case. Birds learn to use sanctuary areas protected from shooting (Madsen, 1994); to avoid heavily used recreational areas. (Titus and van Druff, 1981; Keller, 1989, 1990); to move back to feeding areas once humans leave (Cooke, 1975); to visit areas where food may be available from humans (Watson, 1976; author, personal observation) and to ignore repeated harmless disturbances (Swenson, 1979; Cooke, 1980; Poole, 1981). Ducks (Schneider, 1986), Bewick's swans (Scott, 1980) and sandhill cranes (Lovvorn and Kirkpatrick, 1981) all aggregate in refuge areas protected from hunting. Of 150 recorded attacks on humans by cassowaries, 75% were by birds that had been fed previously (Kofron, 1999); and bald eagles that had previously been disturbed flew further with successive disturbances (Fraser *et al.*, 1985).

Energetic consequences

The energetic consequences of disturbance to birds by ecotourists or other human activities can be quite significant. Golden plover alarmed by walkers in the UK, for example, have to spend an extra hour a day foraging for food (Yalden and Yalden, 1990). Piping plover in north-eastern USA lose over half their normal feeding time when alarmed (Burger, 1994). When semipalmated sandpiper feeding in the Bay of Fundy, Canada, are disturbed by bait collectors, they lose 68.5% of their foraging time, and this decreases their fat reserves so much that they cannot survive over winter (Shepherd and Boates, 1999). Greater snowgeese staging near Quebec during their autumn migration typically incur a 5.3% increase in energy expenditure and a 1.6% reduction in energy intake if they take off when disturbed but then resume feeding later (Bélanger and Bedard, 1990). If they cease feeding, energy expenditure increases by 3.4%, but energy intake decreases by 3–20%. Geese disturbed during the day may feed at night to offset their energy losses, but night feeding does not fully compensate for the loss of daytime feeding. Similar, or more serious, impacts also occur for other migratory waterfowl (Tucker, 1971; Korschgen *et al.*, 1985; Havera and Boens, 1992).

The energetic balance of migratory birds often allows only a very small margin of safety (Tucker, 1971). For most migratory flocks, a proportion of the individual birds have insufficient energy reserves and die during the migration. If feeding opportunities at pre-migration or staging areas are reduced even by a relatively small proportion, this can lead to a large increase in the proportion of birds dying during migration. The same applies for birds with limited sources of food during overwintering. Each winter some die, and if human disturbance reduces their feeding opportunities or increases their energy expenditure, many more die in consequence. In addition, birds may be more susceptible to disturbance when feeding than when resting, as shown for overwintering bald eagles in Washington State, USA (Knight, 1984). Even resting birds with no apparent response may suffer increased energy expenditure from human disturbance. When emperor penguins are approached by tourists, for example, their physiological alert response leads to an increase in stomach temperature and metabolic activity which increases their daily energy expenditure by up to 10% (Regel and Putz, 1997).

Breeding birds can also be particularly susceptible to energetic impacts. Black ducks, for example, use 3.4 times as much energy when laying (Wooley and Owen, 1978). Female eider do not eat for 25 days when incubating their eggs, and lose 40% of their body weight during this period (Gabrielsen and Smith, 1995). Any disturbance increases energy consumption, so that they may be unable to complete incubation, or may have insufficient energy reserves to guard their chicks once hatched. In addition, birds suffering energy depletion during migration, overwintering or breeding may become differentially vulnerable to disease and predation.

Impacts on Breeding Bird Populations

The impacts of ecotourism and recreation are particularly significant when birds are breeding. Many birds have relatively short life spans and only a few opportunities to produce offspring. If tourism and recreation reduce the number of adult birds breeding, the number of eggs they lay and hatch successfully, or the number of chicks that survive to maturity, then the population will decline. For rare or endemic species where breeding is concentrated in a small number of populations, repeated disturbance can soon threaten the survival of the entire species. Colony-nesting birds are particularly susceptible, since a single disturbance may cause widespread egg and chick mortality for many nests at once. Even the adult

birds are more vulnerable during breeding, both because of increased energy requirements and because the need to guard their nests and checks makes them vulnerable to predators. There are many recorded instances, for example, where birdwatchers and photographers have inadvertently revealed nests to predators (including humans), which then take eggs or chicks (Liddle, 1997).

There are many different mechanisms for ecotourists to cause impacts on breeding birds. These include:

- reduction of nesting habitat by clearance, damage, building or continual disturbance;
- reduction in the number of adult birds which breed in a particular year;
- displacement of breeding pairs from more- to less-favourable nesting habitat, where breeding success is reduced;
- damage to nests;
- complete abandonment of nests and sometimes entire breeding colonies;
- adults spending less time on nest;
- adults providing less food for chicks;
- predators using tourists as cues to find nests and chicks;
- death of eggs or chicks through excessive heat or cold if adults are forced to flee nests;
- adults crushing and killing their own eggs and chicks during panic take-off if disturbed suddenly;
- adults failing to hide their nests if disturbed suddenly, increasing the risk of predation;
- predation of eggs and chicks by gulls, skuas, jaegers, fox, etc., when adults are forced from nests even briefly;
- predation of eggs and chicks by other adults of the same species, especially colony-breeding predator species such as gulls, when adults are forced off nests;
- increased energy expenditure by parent birds, forcing them to spend more time off the nest and increasing risks to chicks;
- chicks leaving nest site and suffering death through predation, injury, dehydration or starvation.

There are many instances where a reduction in breeding success has been noted for birds disturbed by tourism and recreation, but the precise mechanism has not been determined. Such observations have been made for a variety of different bird species and families. The overall reproductive success of bald eagles studied by Bangs *et al.* (1982) was reduced from 88% to 23% by canoe campers. Reduced reproductive success in bald eagles was also reported by Mathisen (1968) and Grubb and King (1991). For golden eagles in Maine, USA, 95% of nest losses were due to human disturbance (Bocker and Ray, 1971). Disturbance reduced nesting success for osprey in various parts of the world (Reese, 1972; Levenson and Koplin, 1984). In Idaho, USA, ospreys produced fewer young if human activities encroached within 1500 m (van Daele and van Daele, 1982). Red kites in Wales suffered reduced breeding success if subject to disturbance (Newton *et al.*, 1981).

Reductions in breeding success through disturbance by tourists has been recorded for a wide variety of seabirds and shorebirds, both individual and colony-nesting. These include, for example: herring, glaucous-winged and western gulls (Hunt, 1972; Gillett *et al.*, 1975; Robert and Ralph, 1975); least terns (Gaddy and Kohlsaat, 1987; Rodgers and Smith, 1995); brown pelicans (Anderson, 1988); black skimmer (Safina and Burger, 1983); various waders (Frederick and Collopy, 1989); pied oystercatcher and redcapped plover disturbed by vehicles and campers on Fraser Island, Australia (Fisher *et al.*, 1998); least and crested auklets in Alaska (Piatt *et al.*, 1990); black guillemot (Cairns, 1980); fulmar (Ollason and Dunnet, 1980); ringed, little ringed and piping plovers (Pienkowski, 1984; Flemming *et al.*, 1988; Putzer, 1989); and Adelie penguins (Giese, 1996). Similar effects are recorded for freshwater birds such as mallard (Balat, 1969), loon (Robertson and Flood, 1980; Titus and van Druff, 1981; Gotmark *et al.*, 1989; Hockin, *et al.*, 1992) and great crested grebe (Keller, 1989; Putzer, 1989); and also for stork, egret, heron, ibis, cormorant and black skimmer in the Florida Everglades (Rodgers and Smith, 1995).

An extensive set of records is tabulated by Hockin *et al.* (1992). Human disturbance during breeding, even on a single occasion, commonly reduced breeding success by 40% or more. For example, human disturbance reduced hatching success by: 47% for Adelie penguins in the Antarctic (Giese, 1996); 54% for herring gulls in Maine, USA (Hunt, 1972); 62% for bald eagles in North America (Bangs *et al.*, 1982); 80% for arctic loon in Sweden (Götmark *et al.*, 1989); and 75–100% for least terns in South Carolina, USA (Gaddy and Kohlsaat, 1987).

Clearance and damage to vegetation at campsites and lodges affects a relatively small area. Much larger areas can be affected through noise, fire or frequent human use. This may either drive adult birds away completely, as discussed above; or it may prevent them nesting, even if they use the area otherwise; or it may render the area less attractive as nesting habitat, so that older birds seek territories elsewhere, and only younger birds use the disturbed areas. Masked, red-footed and blue-footed boobies may perch at 2–6 m from walking trails in the Galapagos Islands, Ecuador, for example, but there are fewer nests within 10 m of trails than at greater distances (Burger and Gochfeld, 1993). The density of breeding birds decreases with increased recreational use for 8 of 13 European species examined by van der Zande *et al.* (1984). Only young male willow warblers, with lower reproductive success, nest within 200 m of roads in Europe (Reijnen and Foppen, 1994; Reijnen *et al.*, 1995). Loon, grebe and eider rarely nest on lakeshores or islands subject to significant recreational use (Titus and van Druff, 1981; Pfluger and Ingold, 1988; Keller, 1989, 1990; Laurila, 1989).

Ducks do not breed at all on lakes used for recreation in Wisconsin (Jahn and Hunt, 1964), and fewer ducks breed in areas used by anglers in Europe (Reichholf, 1970, 1975, 1976; Tuite, 1981). Common sandpipers do not nest in areas used by anglers in the UK (Yalden and Yalden, 1990). Piping plovers nest less in lakeshores used by ATVs in North Dakota (Prindiville-Gains and Ryan, 1988). Nesting shorebirds generally avoid areas used by ATVs in Massachusetts, USA (Blodget, 1978). Nesting golden plover and curlew avoid moorland areas used for recreation in the UK (Haworth and Thompson, 1990). Oystercatchers in The Netherlands nest preferentially in areas closed to recreation and tourism (de Roos and Schaafsma, 1981). Note that this reduction in effective nesting habitat areas would not generally be obvious to ecotourists, or even specialist birdwatchers, unless they are very familiar with the whole local area throughout several seasons.

A wide variety of raptors avoid nesting in areas used for tourism and recreation. Buzzards, sparrowhawk, hobby, kestrel, tawny owl and longeared owl in The Netherlands nest only in areas completely closed to the public (Saris, 1976). Kestrel (van der Zande and Verstrael, 1985) and Spanish Imperial eagle (Gonzalez et al., 1992) avoid disturbed areas completely for nesting. Osprey in Minnesota USA, which nest within 100 m of shorelines in undisturbed areas, move to 1.2–4.8 km inland in areas with tourist development (Fraser et al., 1985). This reduces their access to food for themselves and their nestlings, increases the time they must spend off the nest for foraging, and reduces their ability to watch their nests while searching for food.

Various gulls, terns and other shorebirds in eastern USA move their nest sites from barrier island beaches to abnormal sites, such as dredge spoil islands, when their preferred sites are used by tourists (Buckley and Buckley, 1975; Parnell and Soots, 1975; Burger and Shisler, 1979; Erwin, 1980, 1989; Jackson and Schardien-Jackson, 1985; Kotliar and Burger, 1986). Roseate and sooty terns in the Virgin Islands even move their nest sites from beaches to cliffs (Dewey and Nellis, 1980). Loons in Canada move their nests from islands to marshes when islands are used by canoeists (Alvo, 1981). A breeding colony of northern royal albatross on Taiaroa Heads, New Zealand, has been visited by birdwatchers for many years, but is now used as one stop on the itineraries of commercial coach tours whose clients are generally uninterested in albatross and unaware of their impacts on the nesting birds (Higham, 1998). As a result of this continual disturbance, the birds have been driven gradually from their preferred area to a less protected area, where adults, eggs and chicks are subject to increased heat stress and many more chicks die. On a more local scale, openbill storks in India (Datta and Pal, 1993), black-billed magpie in the USA (Knight and Fitzner, 1985; Dhindsa and Kamer, 1988), and various songbirds in the USA (Gutzwiller et al., 1998) move their nests to higher and/or less accessible trees if they are disturbed by humans.

Subtle impacts on breeding behaviour have also been recorded on occasion. Trumpeter swans, for example, modify their breeding behaviour in the presence of recreational disturbance (Henson and Grant, 1991). Human intrusion was also found to modify the seasonal timing of birdsong in some species (Gutzwiller et al., 1997), with consequent effects on courtship and pairing. Disruption of courtship displays and callings has also been noted for bowerbirds in the gorges of Purnululu World Heritage Area, Australia, which are subject to tourist overflights in helicopters and light aircraft (author, personal observation).

Even if birds continue to use disturbed areas for nesting, their nests may be destroyed by tourists. Species such as terns, plovers and oystercatchers nesting on shorelines used by ORVs are particularly vulnerable (Burger, 1981; Jeffery, 1987; Buick and Paton, 1989; Burger and Gochfield, 1990). ATVs and hikers can also crush or collapse nest burrows for species such as mutton birds and some penguins. Wash from boats on lakes and rivers can flood or damage waterbird nests. Even in woodland areas, campers can destroy nests by breaking branches for firewood or to clear tent sites. At campgrounds in Coconino National Forest, Arizona, USA, for example, 30% of Steller's jay nests and 20% of American robin nests were destroyed in this way (Aitchison, 1977).

Abandonment of nests following disturbance by tourists has been recorded for a wide variety of bird species, including osprey (Ames and Mesereau, 1964), bald eagle (Fraser et al., 1985), brown pelican (Anderson, 1988), wood stork (Gonzalez, 1999), loon (Titus and van Druff, 1981; Götmark et al., 1989), tufted puffin (Pierce and Simons, 1986), black-crowned night heron (Tremblay and Ellison, 1979) and jackass penguins (Hobson and Hallinan, 1981). Abandonment may not be immediate, especially for colony-nesting species. Wood stork colonies in Venezuela disturbed by humans, for example, suffered successively increasing predation from crested caracara (Gonzalez, 1999), which ultimately led them to abandon the entire colony. There seems to be a general tendency amongst most bird species that nests are more likely to be abandoned at earlier stages before eggs are laid or hatched, than at later stages when the adults have invested heavily in feeding their chicks.

Even where adult birds remain with their nests, there are many mechanisms by which human disturbance can interfere with reproductive success. Adults may hatch fewer chicks, as shown for lapwing by Iversen (1986) and white pelican by Boellstroff *et al.* (1988). They may feed their nestlings less, as shown for marsh harrier by Fernandez and Azkona (1993), and sand martin. They may stay away from nests for longer periods, as shown for herons by Vos *et al.* (1985), and eggs may take longer to incubate. Chicks may develop more slowly, and may leave the nest at a more immature stage (Nisbet and Drury, 1972; Hulsman, 1984).

When adult herring gulls on islands off Maine, USA, are driven from their nests by picnickers, their eggs overheat, addle and die (Hunt, 1972). For peregrine falcon and golden eagle in Scotland (Watson, 1976) and Adelie penguin in the Antarctic (Giese, 1998), eggs die of cold when adults are frightened away from their nests by tourists, even for a short period. When nesting adults are disturbed suddenly they may crush and kill their own eggs or chicks during a panic take-off, as recorded for both brown pelican (Anderson and Keith, 1980) and white pelican (Bunnell *et al.*, 1981) disturbed by aircraft. When greater crested grebes are scared away suddenly by recreational boaters, they do not have time to hide their eggs with vegetation according to their normal practice (Keller, 1989), increasing predation risks.

Increased predation on eggs and chicks when brooding adults are driven off the nest by tourists or other human disturbance, has immediate and major impacts on reproductive success for a wide range of bird species. In many cases, predators have learnt to use birdwatchers or other tourists as cues to find hidden nests (Liddle, 1997). This has been shown, for example, for Canada geese (MacInnes and Misra, 1972), eider (Götmark and Åhlund, 1984) and coot (Salathe, 1987). In Chubut, Argentina, predatory dolphin gulls have learnt to follow human intruders as they approach nesting king shag rookeries (Kury and Gochfeld, 1975), preying on eggs and chicks as adult birds are distracted. After only a few disturbance events, the gulls eliminate the shag colonies entirely.

Predators such as gulls, skuas, jaegers, ravens and foxes are extremely efficient at attacking bird nests. For solitary-nesting species, such as loon, grebe and eider, the only protection is in concealment. For colony-nesting species, such as many geese, terns, gulls, cormorants and other waterbirds, however, the main protection is through vigilance and physical defence. In many cases, these breeding colonies are continually surrounded by predators waiting for an opportunity. If tourists lead adult birds to desert their nests or relax their guard, even for seconds, those predators will take eggs or small chicks. Examples include: Canada geese in Hudson Bay (MacInnes and Misra, 1972); various seabirds (Hand, 1980; Randell and Randell, 1981; Gutzwiller, 1995); cormorants and shags (Kury and Gochfeld, 1975; Verbeek, 1982); Atlantic puffin (Finney *et al.*, 2003); eider in Sweden (Joensen, 1973; Åhlund and Götmark, 1989; Laurila, 1989) and velvet scoter in Finland (Mikola *et al.*, 1994). Gulls are the most commonly recorded predators. When velvet scoter ducks in Finland were disturbed a few times each day, over 50% of ducklings were taken by gulls in the first 3 weeks after hatching, with the frequency of gull attacks increasing 3.5 times during human disturbances (Mikola *et al.*, 1994). When loons in Sweden were disturbed by boats, gull predation increased by a factor of 200–300 times (Åhlund and Götmark, 1989). Experimentally reducing the density of gulls improves the reproductive success of Atlantic puffin (Finney *et al.*, 2003).

Many gull species also prey on nests of other individuals from the same species, if those individuals are disturbed by tourists. This has been recorded for glaucous-winged gulls in the San Juan Islands National Wildlife Refuge, USA (Gillett *et al.*, 1975), western gulls on Farallon Island, California (Robert and Ralph, 1975) and in the Gulf of California (Hand, 1980), Heermann's gull (Anderson and Keith, 1980) and ring-billed gull (Fetterolf, 1983). There is also a positive feedback effect, in that individual gulls that have lost their brood as a result of disturbance are no longer restricted by the need to defend their own nests, so they become more aggressive predators (Hand, 1980). Even if chicks are not killed by predators when brooding adults are disturbed, they may still die of injury, dehydration or starvation if they leave unattended nests.

Conclusions

By far the majority of recorded impacts on birds from ecotourism, recreation and associated human disturbance are negative, often strongly so (Hockin et al., 1992; Liddle, 1997; Carney and Sydeman, 1999). There are a few exceptions, including: birds that habituate to loud noises (Murton, 1971; Altman and Grano, 1984; Anderson et al., 1989); birds that nest close to tourist accommodation (Hill and Rosier, 1989); and birds that maintain reproductive success despite limited human disturbance (Hull and Wilson, 1996; Cobley and Shears, 1999). Recreation is not the only factor affecting bird populations, which may increase on occasion even despite recreational impacts (Gerrard et al., 1993). But these cases are very much the exception; and even if one species increases in numbers, others may decrease in consequence.

Much more commonly, a single small disturbance, or series of low-key disturbances, can cause far-reaching impacts which may not be discernible to the people involved. A single angler prevents ducks in Germany breeding on lakes smaller than 1 ha in area (Reichholf, 1976). A single aircraft flying over a colony of white pelican chicks in Canada led to the death of 88% of the entire colony's chicks (Bunnell et al., 1981). Areas visited by only one car every week are abandoned by pink-footed geese in Denmark (Madsen, 1985). Very low-level use of subalpine forests in Wyoming, at 1 person/ha/week, led to a 46–57% decline in the density of mountain chickadee, American robin and hermit thrush (Gutzwiller and Anderson, 1999). For waterbirds such as ducks (Putzer, 1989) or cormorants (Hubner and Putzer, 1985) a single boater drives away most of the flock. For the various species suffering increased egg and chick predation, as summarized above, one or two human disturbances cause large-scale mortality or even the complete failure of the colony. For migratory and overwintering birds, even a low-key disturbance reduces feeding time significantly, which can tip the birds over the threshold from survival to starvation and death. Major ecological consequences from minor tourism disturbance are commonplace, not unusual.

Different bird species respond very differently to similar impacts (Foin et al., 1977; Robertson and Flood, 1980; van der Zande et al., 1980; Burger et al., 1982; Clark et al., 1984; Hulsman, 1984; Tuite et al., 1984; Pfluger and Ingold, 1988; Hill and Player, 1992; Hockin et al., 1992; Burger and Gochfeld, 1993; Liddle, 1997; Carney and Sydeman, 1999). There are some broad patterns under which birds of the same family, size, diet or migratory habits may respond to disturbance in similar ways, but those patterns are not nearly strong enough to be able to generalize from one bird species to another. In addition, for some bird species at least, disturbance responses of individual birds depend strongly on preconditioning: fear, habituation or attraction. To determine the impacts of ecotourism or recreation on birds in any given area, with sufficient confidence for conservation and visitor management, requires extended expert observations or rigorously designed scientific study on the particular species, ecosystems and human activity concerned.

Such information available currently is heavily concentrated in particular geographic areas, notably Europe and North America. It is also concentrated on particular groups of bird species, such as: gulls and terns; waders and shorebirds; geese, ducks and divers; and raptors. In the southern hemisphere, penguins are beginning to receive attention, but tourism impacts on the vast majority of land birds in the southern hemisphere continents remain almost entirely unknown.

The identification and quantification of the ecological impacts of ecotourism and recreation on birds, at a population scale, are not necessarily straightforward. Some impacts may be immediately apparent, such as roadkill or nesting birds flushed by dogs. Few tourists, or perhaps even land managers, however, will have sufficient understanding and information to appreciate ecological consequences through, for example, effects on energy balances of adult birds, delayed predation on eggs and chicks, or avoidance of disturbed habitat areas. More subtle secondary impacts are unlikely to be detected except by experienced bird ecologists, yet they may be highly significant for overall impacts. Examples include: use of humans as visual cues by predators; increased vulnerability of younger birds from family groups disrupted by disturbance; increased predation on smaller birds where additional food supplies increase the densities of larger and more aggressive species; predation on forest-core birds by forest-edge species which move into campgrounds and trail-edge habitats; and many more.

Ecotourism and outdoor recreation have less impact than major land-use changes such as clearance for agriculture (Haworth and Fielding, 1988). They are, however, often targeted specifically at rarer species of higher value both for tourism and for conservation. They can be highly significant for the survival of local and sometimes global populations of particular species. And for most species worldwide, they are largely unknown. As land use in protected areas continues to change from protection and conservation towards recreation and tourism, knowledge of tourist impacts on birds needs to be increased greatly.

Acknowledgements

The database of literature on which this review is based has been constructed since 1991 by staff of the International Centre for Ecotourism Research at Griffith University (www.gu.edu.au/centre/icer/staff). It is currently maintained by Karen Sullivan, who also kindly checked references and citations. Coverage, opinions, errors and omissions in this chapter remain my own responsibility.

References

Åhlund, M. and Götmark, F. (1989) Gull predation on eider ducklings *Somateria mollissima*: effects of human disturbance. *Biological Conservation* 48,115–127.

Aitchison, S.W. (1977) Some effects of a campground on breeding birds in Arizona. In: Johnson, R.R. and Jones, D.A. (eds) *Importance, Preservation and Management of Riparian Habitat*. USDA Forest Service, Fort Collins, Colorado, pp. 175–182.

Altman, R.L. and Grano, R.D. (1984) Least terns nesting alongside Harrier jet pad. *Journal of Field Ornithology* 55, 108–109.

Alvo, R. (1981) Marsh nesting of common loons *Gavia immer*. *Canadian Field Naturalist* 95, 357.

Ames, P.L. and Mersereau, G.S. (1964) Some factors in the decline of osprey in Connecticut. *Auk* 81, 173–185.

Anderson, D.E., Rongstad, O.J. and Mytton, W.R. (1989) Response of nesting red-tailed hawks to helicopter overflights. *Condor* 91, 296–299.

Anderson, D.W. (1988) Dose–response relationship between human disturbance and brown pelican breeding success. *Wildlife Society Bulletin* 16, 339–345.

Anderson, D.W. and Keith, J.O. (1980) The human influence on seabird nesting success: conservation implications. *Biological Conservation* 18, 65–80.

Anderson, I. (1998) With people come plagues: tourists and scientists could be bringing deadly diseases to Antarctica's wildlife. *New Scientist* 159, 4.

Andersson, A.P., Lindberg, P., Nilsson, S.G. and Petersson, A. (1980) Breeding success of the black-throated diver *Gavia artica* in Swedish lakes. *Var Fagelvarld* 39, 85–94.

Anthony, G.R. and Isaacs, F.B. (1989) Characteristics of bald eagle nest sites in Oregon. *Journal of Wildlife Management* 53, 148–159.

Balat, F. (1969) Influence of repeated disturbance on the breeding success in the mallard *Anas platyrhynchos*. *Zoologicke* 18, 247–252.

Bamford, A.R., Davies, S.J.J.F. and van Delft, R. (1990) The effects of model power boats on waterbirds at Herdsman Lake, Perth, Western Australia. *Emu* 90, 260–265.

Bangs, E.E., Spraker, T.H., Berns, V.D. and Baily, T.N. (1982) Effects of increased human populations on wildlife resources of the Kenai Peninsula, Alaska, USA. In: Sabal, V. (ed.) *Transactions of the North American Wildlife and Natural Resources Conference 47*. Wildlife Management Institute, Washington, DC, pp. 605–616.

Bartelt, G.A. (1987) Effects of disturbance and hunting on the behavior of Canada goose family groups in east central Wisconsin. *Journal of Wildlife Management* 51, 517–522.

Batten, L.A. (1977) Sailing on reservoirs and its effects on water birds. *Biological Conservation* 11, 49–58.

Béchet, A., Girouz, J.E., Gauthier, G., Nichols, J.D. and Hines, J.E. (2003) Spring hunting changes the regional movements of migrating greater snow geese. *Journal of Applied Ecology* 40, 553–564.

Bélanger, L. and Bedard, J. (1989) Responses of staging greater snow geese to human disturbance. *Journal of Wildlife Management* 53, 713–719.

Bélanger, L. and Bedard, J. (1990) Energetic cost of man-induced disturbance to staging snow geese. *Journal of Wildlife Management* 54, 36–41.

Bell, D.V. and Austin, L.W. (1985) The game-fishing season and its effects on overwintering wild-fowl. *Biological Conservation* 33, 65–80.

Berry, K.H. (1980) *A Review of the Effects of Off-road Vehicles on Birds and Other Vertebrates.* Management of Western Forests and Grasslands for Nongame Birds, Salt Lake City.

Blakesley, J.A. and Reese, K.P. (1988) Avian use of campground and non-campground sites in riparian zones. *Journal of Wildlife Management* 52, 399–402.

Blodget, B.G. (1978) *The effect of off-road vehicles on least terns and other shore birds.* National Park Service Cooperative Research Unit Report No. 26, Institute for Man and the Environment, University of Massachusetts, Amherst.

Bocker, E.L. and Ray, T.D. (1971) Golden eagle population studies in the south west. *Condor* 73, 463–467.

Boellstroff, D.E., Anderson, D.W., Ohlendorf, H.M. and O'Neill, F.J. (1988) Reproductive effects of nest-marking studies in an American white pelican colony. *Colonial Waterbirds* 11, 215–219.

Bright, A., Reynolds, G.R., Innes, J. and Wass, J.R. (2003) Effects of motorised boat passes on the time budgets of New Zealand dabchick, *Poliocephalus rufopectus. Wildlife Research* 30, 237–244.

Brown, A.L. (1990) Measuring the effect of aircraft noise on sea birds. *Environment International* 16, 587–592.

Buckley, R.C. (1994) Ecotourism: a framework. *Annals of Tourism Research* 21, 661–669.

Buckley, R.C. (2001) Environmental impacts of ecotourism. In: Weaver, D. (ed.) *Encyclopaedia of Ecotourism.* CAB International, Wallingford, UK, pp. 374–394.

Buckley, R.C. (2003a) *Case Studies in Ecotourism.* CAB International, Wallingford, UK.

Buckley, R.C. (2003b) Ecological indicators of tourist impacts in parks. *Journal of Ecotourism* 2, 54–66.

Buckley, P.A. and Buckley, F.G. (1975) The significance of dredge spoil islands to colonially nesting waterbirds in certain national parks. In: Parnell, J. and Soots, R. (eds) *Proceedings of a Conference on Management of Dredge Islands in North Carolina Estuaries.* Sea Grant Publications, North Carolina State University, Raleigh, North Carolina, p. 35.

Buehler, D.A., Mersmann, T.J., Fraser, J.D. and Seegar, J.K.D. (1991) Effects of human activity on bald eagle distribution on the Northern Chesapeake Bay. *Journal of Wildlife Management* 55, 282–290.

Buick, A.M. and Paton, D.C. (1989) Impact of off-road vehicles on the nesting success of hooded plovers *Charadrius ruficollis* in the Coorong Region of South Australia. *Emu* 89, 159–172.

Bundy, C. (1979) Breeding and feeding observations on the black-throated diver. *Bird Study* 26, 33–36.

Bunnell, E.I., Dunbar, D., Koza, L. and Ryder, G. (1981) Effects of disturbance on the productivity and numbers of white pelicans in British Columbia – observations and models. *Colonial Waterbirds* 4, 2–11.

Burger, J. (1981) The effect of human activity on birds at a coastal bay. *Biological Conservation* 21, 231–241.

Burger, J. (1986) The effect of human activity on shorebirds in two coastal bays in Northeastern United States. *Environmental Conservation* 13, 123–130.

Burger, J. (1988) Effects of demolition and beach clean-up operations on birds on coastal mudflat in New Jersey, USA. *Estuarine, Coastal and Shelf Science* 27, 95–108.

Burger, J. (1994) The effect of human disturbance on foraging behaviour and habitat use in Piping Plover. *Estuaries* 17(3), 695–701.

Burger, J. (1995) Beach recreation and nesting birds. In: Knight, R.L. and Gutzwiller, K.J. (eds) *Wildlife and Recreationists: Coexistence Through Management and Research.* Island Press, Washington, DC, pp. 281–295.

Burger, J. (1998) Effects of motorboats and personal watercraft on flight behavior over a colony of common terns. *Condor* 100, 528–534.

Burger, J. (2000) Landscapes, tourism and conservation. *Science of the Total Environment* 249, 39–49.

Burger, J. and Galli, J. (1980) Factors affecting distribution of gulls (*Larus* spp.) on two New Jersey coastal bays. *Environmental Conservation* 7, 59–65.

Burger, J. and Gochfield, M. (1981) Discrimination of the threat of direct versus tangential approach to the nest by incubating herring and great black-backed gulls. *Journal of Comparative Physiology and Psychology* 95, 676–684.

Burger, J. and Gochfeld, M. (1990) Nest site selection in least terns (*Sterna antillarum*) in New Jersey and New York. *Colonial Waterbirds* 13, 31–40.

Burger, J. and Gochfeld, M. (1991) Human distance and birds: tolerance and response distances of resident and migrant species in India. *Environmental Conservation* 18, 158–165.

Burger, J. and Gochfeld, M. (1993) Tourism and short-term behavioral responses of nesting masked, red-footed and blue-footed boobies in the Galapagos. *Environmental Conservation* 20, 255–259.

Burger, J. and Gochfeld, M. (1998) Effects of ecotourists on bird behaviour at Loxahatchee National Wildlife Refuge, Florida. *Environmental Conservation* 25, 13–21.

Burger, J. and Leonard, J. (2000) Conflict resolution in coastal waters: the case of personal watercraft. *Marine Policy* 24, 61–67.

Burger, J. and Shisler, J.K. (1979) The immediate effects of ditching a saltmarsh on nesting herring gulls *Larus argentatus*. *Biological Conservation* 15, 85–103.

Burger, J., Gochfeld, M. and Niles, T.H.B. (1995) Ecotourism and birds in coastal New Jersey: contrasting responses of birds, tourists and managers. *Environmental Conservation* 22, 56–65.

Burger, J., Shisler, J. and Lesser, F.H. (1982) Avian utilisation of six marshes in New Jersey. *Biological Conservation* 23, 187–122.

Cairns, D. (1980) Nesting density, habitat structure and human disturbance as factors in black guillemot reproduction. *Wilson Bulletin* 92, 352–361.

Camp, R.J. and Knight, R.L. (1998) Rock climbing and cliff bird communities at Joshua Tree National Park, California. *Wildlife Society Bulletin* 26, 892–898.

Carney, K.M. and Sydeman, W.J. (1999) A review of human disturbance effects on nesting colonial waterbirds. *Waterbirds* 2, 68–79.

Clark, K.L., Euler, D. and Armstrong, E. (1984) Predicting avian community response to lakeshore cottage development. *Journal of Wildlife Management* 48, 1239–1247.

Cobley, N.D. and Shears, J.R. (1999) Breeding performance of gentoo penguins (*Pygoscelis papua*) at a colony exposed to high levels of human disturbance. *Polar Biology* 21, 355–360.

Conomy, J.T., Dubovsky, J.A., Collazo, J.A. and Fleming, W.J. (1998) Do black ducks and wood ducks habituate to aircraft disturbance? *Journal of Wildlife Management* 62, 1135–1142.

Cooke, A.S. (1975) The effects of fishing on waterfowl at Grafham Water. *Cambridge Bird Club Report* 48, 40–46.

Cooke, A.S. (1980) Observations on how close certain passerine species will tolerate an approaching human in rural and suburban areas. *Biological Conservation* 18, 85–88.

Cox, C. (1991) Pesticides on golf courses: mixing toxins with play. *Journal of Pesticide Reform* 11, 2–4.

Craig, R.J., Mitchell, E.S. and Mitchell, J.E. (1988) Time and energy budgets of bald eagles wintering along the Connecticut River. *Journal of Field Ornithology* 59, 22–32.

Crome, F.H.J. and Moore, L.A. (1990) Cassowaries in Northeastern Queensland: report on a survey and a review and assessment of their status and conservation and management needs. *Australian Wildlife Research* 17, 369–385.

Cryer, M., Linley, N.W., Ward, R.M., Stratford, J.O. and Anderson, P.F. (1987) Disturbance of overwintering wildfowl by anglers at two reservoir sites in south Wales. *Bird Study* 34, 191–199.

Datta, T. and Pal, B.C. (1993) The effect of human interference on the nesting of the openbill stork *Anastomus oscitans* at the Raiganj Wildlife Sanctuary, India. *Biological Conservation* 64, 149–154.

De Roos, G. (1981) *The Impact of Tourism upon some Breeding Wader Species on the Isle of Vlieland in The Netherlands Wadden Seas*. Mededelingen Landbouwhogesschool, Wadeningen, pp. 81–114.

De Roos, G.T. and Schaafsma, W. (1981) Is recreation affecting the number of breeding bird's nests? *Statistica Neerlandica* 85, 69–90.

Dewey, R.A. and Nellis, D.W. (1980) Seabird research in the US Virgin Islands. *The 45th North American Wildlife Conference*. Wildlife Management Institute, Washington, DC, pp. 445–452.

Dhinda, M.S. and Komer, P.E. (1989) Nest height of black-billed magpies: is it determined by human disturbance or habitat type? *Canadian Journal of Zoology* 67, 228–232.

Dunnet, G.M. (1977) Observations on the effects of low-flying aircraft at seabird colonies on the coast of Aberdeenshire, Scotland. *Biological Conservation* 12, 55–64.

Elkins, N. (1983) *Weather and Bird Behaviour*. T & A.D. Poyser, Calton, UK.

Erwin, R.M. (1980) Breeding habitat use by colonially nesting waterbirds in two mid-Atlantic US regions under different regimes of human disturbance. *Biological Conservation* 18, 39–51.

Erwin, R.M. (1989) Responses to human intruders by birds nesting in colonies: experimental results and management guidelines. *Colonial Waterbirds* 12, 104–108.

Feltwell, J. (1996) Tourisme mort Camargue. *Biologist* 43, 181–183.

Fernandez, C. and Azkona, P. (1993) Human disturbance affects parental care of marsh harriers and nutritional status of nestlings. *Wildlife Management* 57, 602–607.

Fetterrolf, P.M. (1983) Effects of investigator activity on ring-billed gull *Larus delawarensis* behaviour and reproductive performance. *Wilson Bulletin* 95, 23–41.

Finney, S.K., Harris, M.P., Keller, L.F., Elston, D.A., Monaghan, P. and Wanless, S. (2003) Reducing the density of breeding gulls influences the pattern of recruitment of immature Atlantic puffins

Fratercula arctica to a breeding colony. *Journal of Applied Ecology* 40, 545–552.

Fisher, F., Hockings, M. and Hobson, S. (1998) Recreational impacts on waders on Fraser Island. *The Sunbird* 28, 11.

Fitzpatrick, S. and Bouchez, B. (1998) Effects of recreational disturbance on the foraging behaviour of waders on a rocky beach. *Bird Study* 45, 157–171.

Flemming, S.P., Chisson, R.D., Smith, P.C., Austin-Smith, P. and Bancroft, R.P. (1988) Piping plover status in Novia Scotia related to its reproductive and behavioral responses to human disturbance. *Journal of Field Ornithology* 59, 321–330.

Foin, T.C., Garton, E.O., Bowen, C.W., Everingham, J.M., Schultz, R.O. and Holton, B. (1977) Quantitative studies of visitor impacts on environments of Yosemite National Park, California, and their implications for park management policy. *Journal of Environmental Management* 5, 1–22.

Fowler, G.S. (1999) Behavioral and hormonal responses of Magellanic penguins (*Spheniscus magellanicus*) to tourism and nest site visitation. *Biological Conservation* 90, 143–149.

Fraser, J.F., Frenzel, L.D. and Mathison, J.E. (1985) The impact of human activities on breeding bald eagles in north-central Minnesota. *Journal of Wildlife Management* 49, 585–592.

Frederick, P.C. and Collopy, M.W. (1989) Researcher disturbance in colonies of wading birds: effects of frequency of visit and egg-marking on reproductive parameters. *Colonial Waterbirds* 12, 152–157.

Gabrielsen, G.W. and Smith, E.N. (1995) Physiological responses of wildlife to disturbance. In: Knight, R.L. and Gutzwiller, K.J. (eds) *Wildlife and Recreationists: Coexistence Through Management and Research.* Island Press, Washington, DC, pp. 95–108.

Gaddy, L.L. and Kohlsaat, T.L. (1987) Recreational impacts on the natural vegetation, avifauna and herpetofauna of four south Carolina Barrier Islands, USA. *Natural Areas Journal* 7, 55–64.

Galhoff, H., Sell, M. and Abs, M. (1984) Akitivatätsrhythmus, Verteilungs-muster und Ausweichfluge von Tafelenten *Aythya ferina* L. in einem norwestdeutschen Ueberwinterungsquartier (Ruhrstausee Kemnade). *Anz. orn. Ges. Gayern* 23, 133–147 [cited in Hockin *et al.*, 1992].

Galicia, E. and Baldassarre, G.A. (1997) Effects of motorized tour boats on the behavior of non-breeding American flamingos in Yucatan, Mexico. *Conservation Biology* 11, 467–481.

Garton, E.O., Bowen, C.W. and Foin, T.C. (1977) The impact of visitors on small mammal commu-

nities of Yosemite National Park. In: Foin, T.C. Jr (ed.) *Visitor Impacts on National Parks: The Yosemite Ecological Impact Study.* Vol. 10, Institute of Ecology, University of California, Davis, pp. 44–50.

Gerrard, J.M., Dzus, G.R. and Gerrard, P.N. (1993) Water-bird population changes in 1976–1990 on Besnard Lake, Saskatchewan: increases in loons, gulls and pelicans. *Canadian Journal of Zoological* 71, 1682–1686.

Giese, M. (1996) Effects of human activity on Adelie penguin *Pygoscelis adeliae* breeding success. *Biological Conservation* 75, 157–164.

Giese, M. (1998) Guidelines for people approaching breeding groups of Adelie penguins. *Polar Record* 34, 287–292.

Giese, M. and Riddle, M. (1999) Disturbance of emperor penguin *Aptenodytes forsteri* chicks by helicopters. *Polar Biology* 22, 366–371.

Giese, M., Handsworth, R. and Stephenson, R. (1999) Measuring resting heart rates in penguins using artificial eggs. *Journal of Field Ornithology* 70, 49–53.

Gillett, W.H., Hayward, J.L. and Stout, J.F. (1975) Effects of human activity on egg and chick mortality in a glaucous-winged gull colony. *Condor* 77, 492–495.

Giuliano, W. (1994) The impact of hiking and rock-climbing in mountain areas. *Environmental Conservation* 21, 278–279.

Gonzalez, J.A. (1999) Nesting success in two wood stork colonies in Venezuela. *Journal of Field Ornithology* 70, 18–27.

Gonzalez, L.M., Bustamante, J. and Hiraldo, F. (1992) Nesting habitat selection by the Spanish imperial eagle *Aquila adalberti. Biological Conservation* 59, 45–50.

Götmark, F. and Åhlund, M. (1984) Do field observers attract nest predators and influence nesting success of common eiders? *Journal of Wildlife Management* 48, 381–387.

Götmark, F., Neergaard, A. and Åhlund, M. (1989) Nesting ecology and management of the arctic loon in Sweden. *Journal of Wildlife Management* 53, 1025–1031.

Grier, J.W. (1969) Bald eagle behaviour and productivity responses to climbing to nests. *Journal of Wildlife Management* 33, 961–966.

Grubb, T.G. (1976) Nesting bald eagle attacks researcher. *Auk* 93, 842–843.

Grubb, T.G. and King, R.M. (1991) Assessing human disturbance of breeding bald eagles with classification tree models. *Journal of Wildlife Management* 55, 500–511.

Gutzwiller, K. (1995) Recreational disturbance and wildlife communities. In: Knight, R.L. and Gutzwiller, K. (eds) *Wildlife and Recreationists*

Coexisting Through Management and Research. Island Press, Washington, DC, USA, pp. 169–182.

Gutzwiller, K.J. and Anderson, S.H. (1999) Spatial extent of human-intrusion effects on subalpine bird distributions. *Condor* 101, 378–389.

Gutzwiller, K.J. and Marcum, H.A. (1993) Avian responses to observer clothing color: caveats from winter point counts. *Wilson Bulletin* 105, 628–629.

Gutzwiller, K., Kroese, E., Anderson, S. and Wilkins, C. (1997) Does human intrusion alter the seasonal timing of avian song during breeding periods? *Auk* 114, 55–65.

Gutzwiller, K., Clements, K.L., Marcum, H.A., Wilkins, C.A. and Anderson, S.H. (1998) Vertical distributions of breeding-season birds: is human intrusion influential? *Wilson Bulletin* 110, 497–503.

Hand, J.L. (1980) Human disturbance in western gull *Larus occidentalis livens* colonies and possible amplification by intraspecific predation. *Biological Conservation* 18, 59–63.

Harms, C.A., Fleming, W.J. and Stoskopf, M.K. (1997) A technique for dorsal subcutaneous implantation of heart rate biotelemetry transmitters in black ducks – application in an aircraft noise response study. *Condor* 99, 231–237.

Harris, M.P. and Norman, F.I. (1981) The distribution and status of coastal colonies of seabirds in Victoria, Australia. *Natural History Museum of Victoria* 42(2), 89–106.

Havera, S.P. and Boens, L.R. (1992) Human disturbance of waterfowl on Keokuk Pol, Mississippi River. *Wildlife Society Bulletin* 20, 290–298.

Haworth, P.F. and Fielding, A. (1988) Conservation and management implications of habitat selection in the merlin *Falco columbarius* L. in the South Pennines, UK. *Biological Conservation* 46, 247–260.

Haworth, P.F. and Thompson, D.B.A. (1990) Factors associated with the breeding distribution of upland birds in the South Pennines, England. *Journal of Applied Ecology* 27, 562–577.

Heimberger, M., Euler, D. and Barr, J. (1983) The impact of cottage development on common loon *Gavia immer* reproductive success in central Ontario, Canada. *Wilson Bulletin* 95, 431–439.

Henson, P. and Grant, A. (1991) The effects of human disturbance on trumpeter swan breeding behaviour. *Wildlife Society Bulletin* 19, 248–257.

Hickman, S. (1990) Evidence of edge species attraction to nature trails within deciduous forest. *Natural Areas Journal* 10, 3–5.

Higham, J.E.S. (1998) Tourists and albatrosses: the dynamics of tourism at the Northern Royal Albatross colony, Taiaroa Head, New Zealand. *Tourism Management* 19, 521–531.

Hill, D.A. and Player, A. (1992) Behavioral responses of black-headed gulls and avocets to two methods of control of gull productivity. *Bird Study* 39, 34–42.

Hill, G. and Rosier, J. (1989) Wedgetailed shearwaters, white-capped noddies and tourist development on Heron Island, Great Barrier Reef Marine Park, Australia. *Journal of Environmental Management* 29, 107–114.

Hobson, K.A., Knapton, R.W. and Lysack, W. (1989) Population, diet and reproductive success of double-crested cormorants breeding on Lake Winnipeg, Manitoba, Canada, in 1987. *Colonial Waterbirds* 12, 191–197.

Hobson, P.A.R. and Hallinan, J. (1981) Effect of human disturbance on the breeding behaviour of jackass penguins *Spheniscus demersus. South African Journal of Wildlife Research* 11, 59–62.

Hockin, D., Ounsted, M., Gorman, M., Hill, D., Keller, V. and Barker, M.A. (1992) Examination of the effects of disturbance on birds with reference to its importance in ecological assessment. *Journal of Environmental Management* 36, 253–286.

Holmes, T.L., Knight, R.L. and Stegall, L. (1993) Responses of wintering grassland raptors to human disturbance. *Wildlife Society Bulletin* 21, 461–468.

Hubner, T. and Putzer, D. (1985) Störungsökologische Untersuchungen rastender Kormorane an niederrhei-nischen Kiesseen bei Störungen druch Kiestranport, Segel-Surf-und Angelsport. *Seevogel* 6, 122–126 [cited in Hockin *et al.*, 1992].

Hulbert, I.A.R. (1990) The response of ruddy shelduck *Tadorna ferruginea* to tourist activity in the Royal Chitwan National Park of Nepal. *Biological Conservation* 52, 113–123.

Hull, C.L. and Wilson, J. (1996) The effect of investigators on the breeding success of royal, *Eudyptes schegeli*, and rockhopper penguins, *E. chrysocome*, at Macquarie Island. *Polar Biology* 16, 335–337.

Hulsman, K. (1984) *Seabirds of the Capricornia Section, Great Barrier Reef Marine Park.* Royal Society of Queensland Symposium, pp. 53–60.

Hume, R.A. (1972) Reactions of goldeneyes to boating. *British Birds* 69, 178–179.

Hunt, G.L. Jr (1972) Influence of food distribution and human disturbance on the reproductive success of herring gulls. *Ecology* 53, 1051–1061.

Imber, M.J. (1975) Behaviour of petrels in relation to the moon and artificial light. *Notornis* 22, 302–306.

Iversen, F.M. (1986) The impact of disturbance on the lapwing's *Vanellus vanellus* incubation. *Danisk Ornithologisk Forenings Tidsskrist* 80, 97–102.

Jackson, J.A. and Schardien-Jackson, B.J. (1985) Status, dispersion and population changes of the least tern *Sterna antillarum* in coastal Mississippi, USA. *Colonial Waterbirds* 8, 54–62.

Jahn, L.R. and Hunt, R.A. (1964) *Duck and Coot Ecology and Management in Wisconsin.* Technical Bulletin No. 33, Wisconsin Conservation Department, Wisconsin, USA.

Jeffery, R.G. (1987) Influence of human disturbance on the nesting success of African black oystercatchers. *South African Journal of Wildlife Research* 17, 71–72.

Joensen, A.H. (1973) The breeding of the eider (*Somateria mollissima*) in Denmark. *Danske Viltundersogelser* 20, 5–36.

Jones, D.N. and Buckley, R.C. (2000) *Birdwatching Tourism in Australia.* Wildlife Tourism Research Report Series No. 10. CRC for Sustainable Tourism, Gold Coast, Australia.

Jungius, J. and Hirsch, U. (1979) Herzfrequenzänderungen bei Brutvoglen in Galapagos als Folge von Storungen durch Besucher. *Journal of Ornithology* 120, 299–310 [cited in Hockin *et al.*, 1992].

Keller, V. (1989) Variations in the response of great crested grebes *Podiceps cristatus* to human disturbance – a sign of adaption? *Biological Conservation* 49, 31–45.

Keller, V.E. (1990) The effect of disturbance from roads on the distribution of feeding sites of geese (*Anser brachyrhynchus, A. anser*) wintering in northeast Scotland. *Ardea* 79, 229–232.

Keller, V.E. (1991) Effects of human disturbance on eider ducklings *Somateria mollissima* in an estuarine habitat in Scotland. *Biological Conservation* 58, 213–228.

Kendall, R.J., Brewer, L.W., Hitchcock, R.R. and Mayer, J.R. (1992) American wigeon mortality associated with turf application of diazinon AG 500. *Journal of Wildlife Diseases* 28, 263–267.

Klein, M.L., Humphrey, S.R. and Percival, H.F. (1995) Effects of ecotourism on distribution of waterbirds in a wildlife refuge. *Conservation Biology* 9, 1454–1465.

Knight, R.L. (1984) Responses of wintering bald eagles to boating activity. *Journal of Wildlife Management* 48, 999–1004.

Knight, R.L. and Cole, D.N. (1995) Factors that influence wildlife reponses to recreationists. In: Knight, R.L. and Gutzwiller, K.H. (eds) *Wildlife and Recreationists: Coexistence through Management and Research.* Island Press, Washington, DC, pp. 71–80.

Knight, R.L. and Fitzner, R.E. (1985) Human disturbance and nest site placement in black-billed magpies *Pica pica. Journal of Field Ornithology* 56, 153–157.

Kofron, C.P. (1999) Attacks to humans and domestic animals by the southern cassowary (*Casuarius casuarius johnsonii*) in Queensland, Australia. *Journal of Zoology* (London) 249, 375–381.

Korschgen, C.E., George, L.S. and Green, W.L. (1985) Disturbance of diving ducks by boaters on a migration staging area. *Wildlife Society Bulletin* 13, 290–296.

Kotliar, N.B. and Burger, J. (1986) Colony site selection and abandonment by least terns *Sterna antillarum* in New Jersey, USA. *Biological Conservation* 37, 1–22.

Kury, C.R. and Gochfeld, M. (1975) Human interference and gull predation in cormorant colonies. *Biological Conservation* 8, 23–34.

Laurila, T. (1989) Nest site selection in the common eider *Somateria mollissima*: differences between the archipelago zones. *Ornis Fennica* 66, 100–111.

Lehtonen, L. (1970) Zur biologie des Prachttauchers, *Gavia. a. artica. Annales Zoologica Fennici* 7, 25–60.

Levenson, H. and Koplin, J. (1984) Effects of human activity on productivity of nesting ospreys. *Journal of Wildlife Management* 48, 1374–1377.

Liddle, M.J. (1997) *Recreation Ecology: the Ecological Impact of Outdoor Recreation.* Kluwer Academic Publishers, Dordrecht, The Netherlands.

Lok, C.M. and Bakker, L. (1988) Seasonal use of feeding grounds by cormorants *Phalacrocorax carbo* at Voorne, The Netherlands. *Limosa* 61, 7–12.

Lord, A., Waas, J.R. and Innes, J. (1997) Effects of human activity on the behaviour of northern New Zealand Dotterel *Charadrius obscurus aquilonius* chicks. *Biological Conservation* 82, 15–20.

Lovvorn, J.R. and Kirkpatrick, C.M. (1981) Roosting behaviour and habitat of migrant greater sandhill cranes *Grus canadensis tabida. Journal of Wildlife Management* 45, 842–857.

MacInnes, C.D. and Misra, R.K. (1972) Predation on Canada goose nests at McConnell River, northwest territories. *Journal of Wildlife Management* 36, 414–422.

Madsen, J. (1985) Impact of disturbance on field utilisation of pink-footed geese in west Jutland, Denmark. *Biological Conservation* 33, 53–63.

Madsen, J. (1994) Impacts of disturbance on migratory waterfowl. *Ibis* 137, 67–74.

Madsen, J. (1998) Experimental refuges for migratory waterfowl in Danish wetlands. II. Tests of hunting disturbance effects. *Journal of Applied Ecology* 35, 398–417.

Martin, P.S. (1973) The discovery of America. *Science* 179, 969–974.

Mathisen, J.E. (1968) Effects of human disturbance on nesting of bald eagles. *Journal of Wildlife Management* 32, 1–6.

Mead, C.M. (1983) *Bird Migration.* Country Life Books, Middlesex, UK.

Mikola, J., Miettinen, M., Lehikoinen, E. and Lehtilä, K. (1994) The effects of disturbance cause by boating on survival and behaviour of velvet scoter *Melanitta fusca* ducklings. *Biological Conservation* 67, 119–124.

Miller, J.R. and Hobbs, N.T. (2000) Recreational trails, human activity, and nest predation in lowland riparian areas. *Landscape and Urban Planning* 50, 227–236.

Miller, M.W. (1994) Route selection to minimize helicopter disturbance of molting pacific black brant – a simulation. *Arctic* 47, 341–349.

Miquet, A. (1990) Mortality in black grouse *Tetrao tetrix* due to elevated cables. *Biological Conservation* 54, 349–355.

Mooij, J.H. (1982) Die Auswirkungen von Strassen auf die Avifauna einer offenen Landschaft am unteren Niederrhein (Nordrhein-Westfalen), untersucht am Verhalten von Wildgänsen. *Charadrius* 18, 73–92 [cited in Hockin *et al.*, 1992].

Mori, Y., Sodhi, N.S., Kawanishi, S. and Yamagishi, S. (2001) The effect of human disturbance and flock composition on the flight distances of waterfowl species. *Journal of Ethology* 19, 115–119.

Morton, J.M., Fowler, A.C. and Kirkpatrick, R.L. (1989) Time and energy budgets of American black ducks in winter. *Journal of Wildlife Management* 53, 401–410.

Murton, R.K. (1971) *Man and Birds.* Collins, London.

Newton, I., Davis, P.E. and Moss, D. (1981) Distribution and breeding of red kites *Milvus milvus* in relation to land use in Wales, UK. *Journal of Applied Ecology* 18, 173–186.

Nisbet, I.C.T. and Drury, W.H. (1972) Measuring breeding success in common and roseate terns. *Bird Banding* 43, 97–106.

Norris, D.W. and Wilson, H.J. (1988) Disturbance and flock size changes in whitefronted geese wintering in Ireland. *Wildfowl* 39, 63–70.

Ollason, J.C. and Dunnet, G.M. (1980) Nest failures in the fulmar: the effect of observers. *Journal of Field Ornithology* 51, 39–54.

Owens, M., Atkinson-Willes, G.L. and Salmon, D. (1986) *Wildfowl in Great Britain.* Cambridge University Press, Cambridge, UK.

Owens, N.W. (1977) Responses of wintering brent geese to human disturbance. *Wildfowl* 28, 5–14.

Palacios, E. and Mellink, E. (1996) Status of the least tern in the Gulf of California. *Journal of Field Ornithology* 67, 48–58.

Parnell, J. and Soots, R. (eds) (1975) *Proceedings of a Conference on Management of Dredge Islands in North Carolina Estuaries.* Sea Grant Publications, North Carolina University, Raleigh.

Paruk, J.D. (1987) Habitat utilization by bald eagles wintering along the Mississippi River, USA. *Transactions of the Illinois State Academy of Science* 80, 333–343.

Peltzer, R.H.M. (1989) The impact of recreation on nature in the Netherlands. *Proceedings of the Leisure Studies Association Annual Conference.* Leisure Studies Association, Maastricht, pp. 125–149.

Pfister, C., Harrington, B.A. and Lavine, M. (1992) The impact of human disturbance on shorebirds at a migration staging area. *Biological Conservation* 60, 115–126.

Pfluger, D. and Ingold, P. (1988) Zur Empfindlichkeit von Blasshühnern und Haubentauchern gegenüber Störungen vom Wasser und vom Land. *Review of Swiss Zoology* 95, 1171–1178 [cited in Hockin *et al.*, 1992].

Piatt, J.F., Roberts, B.D., Lidster, W.W., Wells, J.L. and Hatch, S.A. (1990) Effects of human disturbance on breeding least and crested auklets at St Lawrence Island, Alaska. *Auk* 107, 342–350.

Pienkowski, M.W. (1984) Breeding biology and population dynamics of ringed plovers *Charadrius hiaticula* in Britain and Greenland: nest predation as a possible factor limiting distribution and timing of breeding. *Journal of Zoology* 202, 83–114.

Pierce, D.J. and Simons, T.R. (1986) The influence of human disturbance on tufted puffin *Fratercula cirrhata* breeding success. *Auk* 103, 214–216.

Pierce, G.C., Spray, C.J. and Stuart, E. (1993) The effect of fishing on the distribution and behaviour of waterbirds in the Kukut area of Lake Songkla, Southern Thailand. *Biological Conservation* 66, 23–24.

Poole, A. (1981) The effect of human disturbance on osprey reproductive success. *Colonial Waterbirds* 4, 20–27.

Prindiville-Gains, E. and Ryan, M.R. (1988) Piping plover habitat use and reproductive success in North Dakota, USA. *Journal of Wildlife Management* 52, 266–273.

Putzer, D. (1989) Wirkung and Wichtung menschlicher Anwesenheit und Storung am Beispiel bestansbedrohter, and Feuchtgebiete gebundener Vogelharten. *Schriftenreihe fur Landschaftspflege und Naturschurz* 29, 169–194 [cited in Hockin *et al.*, 1992].

Rainwater, T.R., Leopold, V.A., Hooper, M.J. and Kendall, R.J. (1995) Avian exposure to organophosphorus and carbamate presticides on a coastal

South Carolina golf course. *Environmental Toxicology and Chemistry* 14, 2155–2161.

Randell, R.M. and Randell, B.M. (1981) Roseate tern breeding biology and factors responsible for low chick production in Algoa Bay, South Africa. *Ostrich* 52, 17–24.

Reed, J.R., Hailman, J.P. and Sincock, J.L. (1985) Light attraction in procellariform birds: reduction by shielding upward radiation. *Auk* 102, 377–383.

Reese, J.G. (1972) Osprey nesting success along the Choptank River, Maryland. *Chesapeake Science* 13, 233–235.

Regel, J. and Putz, K. (1997) Effect of human disturbance on body temperature and energy expenditure in penguin. *Polar Biology* 18, 246–253.

Reichholf, J. (1970) Der Einfluss von Storungen durch Angler auf den Entenbrutbestand auf den Altwassern am Unteren Inn. *Vogelwelt* 91, 68–72.

Reichholf, J. (1975) Der Einfluss von Erholungsbetrieb, Angelsport und Jagd auf das Wasservogel-Schutzgebiet am Unteren Inn und die Möglichkeiten und Chancen zur Steuerung der Entwicklung. *Schriftenreihe für Landschaftspflege und Naturschutz* 12, 109–116 [cited in Hockin *et al.*, 1992].

Reichholf, J. (1976) The influence of recreational activities on waterfowl. In: Smart, M. (ed.) *Proceedings of the International Conference on the Conservation of Wetlands and Waterfowl.* International Waterfowl Research Bureau, Slimbridge, UK, pp. 364–369.

Reijnen, R. and Foppen, R. (1994) The effects of car traffic on breeding bird populations in woodland. I. Evidence of reduced habitat quality for willow warblers (*Phylloscopus trochilus*) breeding close to a highway. *Journal of Applied Ecology* 31, 85–94.

Reijnen, R., Foppen, R., Braak, C.T. and Thissen, J. (1995) The effects of car traffic on breeding bird populations in woodlands. III. Reduction of density in relation to the proximity of main roads. *Journal of Applied Ecology* 32, 187–202.

Robert, H.C. and Ralph, C.J. (1975) Effects of human disturbance on the breeding success of gulls. *Condor* 77, 495–499.

Robertson, R.J. and Flood, N.J. (1980) Effects of recreational use of shorelines on breeding bird populations. *Canadian Field Naturalist* 94, 131–138.

Rodgers, J.A. and Smith, H.T. (1995) Set-back distances to protect nesting bird colonies from human disturbance in Florida. *Conservation Biology* 9, 89–99.

Safina, C. and Burger, J. (1983) Effect of human disturbance on reproductive success in the black skimmer. *Condor* 85, 164–171.

Salathe, T. (1987) Crow predation on coot eggs: effects of investigator disturbance, nest cover and predator learning. *Ardea* 75, 221–230.

Saris, F.J.A. (1976) *Breeding Populations of Birds and Recreation in the Duivelsberg.* Free University Working Paper No. 66, Institute for Environmental Studies, Brussels.

Schick, C.S. (1890) Birds found breeding on Seven Mile Beach, New Jersey. *Auk* 7, 326–329.

Schneider, M. (1986) Auswirkungen eines Jagdschöngebietes auf die Wasservögel im Ermatinger Becken (Bodensee). *Ornithologische Jahreschafte für Baden-Württenberg* 2, 1–46.

Schorger, A.W. (1973) *The Passenger Pigeon: its Natural History and Extinction.* University of Oklahoma, USA.

Scott, D.K. (1980) The behaviour of Bewick's swans at the Welney Wildfowl Refuge, Norfolk, and on the surrounding fens: a comparison. *Wildfowl* 31, 5–18.

Shepherd, P.C.F. and Boates, J.S. (1999) Effects of a commercial baitworm harvest on semipalmated sandpipers and their prey in the Bay of Fundy Hemispheric Shorebird Reserve. *Conservation Biology* 13, 347–356.

Sherrod, S.K., White, C.M. and Williamson, F.S.L. (1976) The biology of the bald eagle on Amchitka Island, Alaska, USA. *Living Bird* 15, 143–182.

Skagen, S.K., Knight, R.L. and Orians, G.H. (1991) Human disturbance of an avian scavenging guild. *Ecological Applications* 1, 215–225.

Stalmaster, M.V. and Newman, J.R. (1978) Behavioral responses of wintering bald eagles to human activity. *Journal of Wildlife Management* 42, 506–513.

Steidl, R.J. and Anthony, R.G. (1996) Responses of bald eagles to human activity during the summer in interior Alaska. *Ecological Applications* 6, 482–491.

Swenson, J.E. (1979) Factors affecting status and reproduction of ospreys in Yellowstone National Park. *Wildlife Management* 43, 495–601.

Telfer, T.C., Sincock, J.L., Vernon Byrd, G. and Reed, J.R. (1987) Attraction of Hawaiian seabirds to lights: conservation efforts and effects of moon phase. *Wildlife Society Bulletin* 15, 406–413.

Tershy, B.R., Breese, D. and Croll, D.A. (1997) Human perturbations and conservation strategies for San Pedro Martir Island, Islas del Golfo de California Reserve, Mexico. *Environmental Conservation* 24, 261–270.

Titus, J.R. and van Druff, L.W. (1981) Response of the common loon to recreational pressure in the Boundary Waters Canoe Area, north eastern Minnesota. *Wildlife Monographs* 79, 4–59.

Tremblay, J. and Ellison, L. (1979) Effects of human disturbance on breeding of black-crowned night herons. *Auk* 96, 364–369.

Tucker, V.A. (1971) Flight energetics in birds. *American Zoologist* 11, 115–124.

Tuite, C.H. (1981) *The Impact of Water-based Recreation on the Waterfowl of Enclosed Inland Waters in Britain. A Report to the Sports Council and the Natural Conservancy Council.* The Wildfowl Trust, Nature Conservancy Council and Sport Council. Slimbridge, UK.

Tuite, C.H., Owen, M. and Paynter, D. (1983) Interaction between wildfowl and recreation at Llangorse Lake and Talybont Reservoir, South Wales. *Wildfowl* 34, 48–63.

Tuite, C.H., Hanson, P.R. and Owen, M. (1984) Some ecological factors affecting winter wildfowl distribution on inland waters in England and Wales, and the influence of water-based recreation. *Journal of Applied Ecology* 21, 41–62.

Van Balen, S., Prawiradilaga, D.M. and Indrawan, M. (1995) The distribution and status of green peafowl *Pavo muticus* in Java. *Biological Conservation* 71, 289–297.

Van Daele, L.J. and van Daele, H.A. (1982) Factors affecting the productivity of ospreys nesting in West-Central Idaho. *Condor* 84, 292–299.

Van den Heiligenberg, T. (1987) Effects of mechanical and manual harvesting of lugworms *Arenicola marina* L. on the benthic fauna of tidal flats in the Dutch Wadden sea. *Biological Conservation* 39, 165–178.

Van der Zande, A.N. and van der Vos, P. (1984) Impact of semi-experimental increase in recreation intensity on the densities of birds in groves and hedges on a lake shore in the Netherlands. *Biological Conservation* 30, 237–259.

Van der Zande, A.N. and Verstrael, T.J. (1985) Impacts of outdoor recreation upon nest-site choice and breeding success of the kestrel *Falco tinnunculus*. *Ardea* 73, 90–98.

Van der Zande, A.N., TerKeurs, W.J. and van der Weijden, W.J. (1980) The impact of roads on the densities of four bird species in an open field habitat – evidence of a long-distance effect. *Biological Conservation* 18, 299–321.

Van der Zande, A.N., Berkhuizen, J.C., van Latesteijn, H.C., Ter Keurs, W.J. and Poppelaars, A.J. (1984) Impact of outdoor recreation on the density of a number of breeding bird species in woods adjacent to urban residential areas. *Biological Conservation* 30, 1–39.

Verbeek, N.A.M. (1982) Egg predation by north western crows: its association with human and bald eagle activity. *Auk* 99, 347–352.

Verheijen, F.J. (1980) The moon: a neglected factor in studies on collisions of nocturnal migrant birds with tall lighted structures and with aircraft. *Die Vogelwarte* 30, 305–320.

Verheijen, F.J. (1981) Bird kills at tall lighted structures in the USA in the period 1935–1973 and kills at a Dutch lighthouse in the period 1924–1928, show similar lunar periodicity. *Ardea* 69, 199–203.

Verhulst, S.R., Oosterbeek, K. and Ens, B.J. (2001) Experimental evidence for effects of human disturbance on foraging and parental care in oystercatchers. *Biological Conservation* 101, 373–380.

Vermeer, K. (1973) Some aspects of the nesting requirements of the common loons in Alberta. *Wilson Bulletin* 85, 429–435.

Vos, D.K., Ryder, R.A. and Graul, W.D. (1985) Response of breeding great blue herons *Ardea herodias* to human disturbance in north central Colorado, USA. *Colonial Waterbirds* 8, 13–22.

Ward, D.H., Stehn, R.A., Erickson, W.P. and Derkesen, D.V. (1999) Response of fall-staging brent and Canada geese to aircraft overflights in southwestern Alaska. *Journal of Wildlife Management* 63, 373–381.

Watson, A. (1976) Human impact on animal populations in the Cairngorms. *Landscape Research News* 1, 1–14.

Watson, A., Payne, S. and Rae, R. (1989) Golden eagles *Aquila chrysetos*: land use and food in northeast Scotland. *Ibis* 131, 336–348.

Watson, J.J., Kerley, G.I.H. and McLachlan, A. (1996) Human activity and potential impacts on dune breeding birds in the Alexandria coastal dunefield. *Landscape and Urban Planning* 34, 315–322.

Watson, J.M. (1993) Responses of nesting bald eagles to helicopter surveys. *Wildlife Bulletin Society* 21, 171–178.

Weaver, D. (2000) *Encyclopedia of Ecotourism.* CAB International, Wallingford, UK.

Werschkul, D.F., McMahon, E. and Leitschuk, M. (1976) Some effects of human activities on the great blue heron in Oregon. *Wilson Bulletin* 88, 660–662.

Wooley, J.B. and Owen, R.B. (1978) Energy costs of activity and daily energy expenditure in the Black Duck. *Journal of Wildlife Management* 42, 739–745.

Yalden, D.W. (1992) The influence of recreational disturbance on common sandpipers *Actitis hypoleucos* breeding by an upland reservoir, in England. *Biological Conservation* 61, 41–49.

Yalden, D.W. and Yalden, P.E. (1989) The sensitivity of breeding golden plovers *Pluvialis apricaria* to human intruders. *Bird Study* 36, 49–55.

Yalden, P.E. and Yalden, D.W. (1990) Recreational disturbance of breeding golden plovers *Pluvialis apricarius*. *Biological Conservation* 51, 243–262.

12

Impacts of Ecotourism on Terrestrial Wildlife

Ralf Buckley

International Centre for Ecotourism Research, Griffith University, Gold Coast, Queensland, Australia

Introduction

The focus of this review is on disturbance to terrestrial vertebrates by people engaged in recreational activities where enjoyment of nature is a significant attraction. It also examines the consequences of such disturbance at individual and population scale, to the extent that these have been studied. This review does not include impacts on wildlife caused by hunting (Caro *et al.*, 1998; Bauer and Giles, 2002) and fishing, except in so far as: (i) hunting makes wildlife wary of humans (Wathery, 1969; Weinberg *et al.*, 1997); (ii) habituation to tourists makes wildlife vulnerable to poachers (Buckley, 2003, pp. 221–212); or (iii) hunting of a prey species affects the ability of tourists to watch its predators (Gasaway *et al.*, 1983; Kilgo *et al.*, 1998; Novaro *et al.*, 2000).

Impacts of large-scale tourist infrastructure are not considered here, nor are those from outdoor recreation activities which rely principally on physical features of the nature environment, and where the primary attraction is excitement rather than contemplation. The effects of aircraft noise (e.g. Dewey, 1994; Larkin *et al.*, 1996) are considered briefly. The impacts of off-road vehicles are reviewed by Buckley (Chapter 6, this volume) and are therefore not considered here. The same applies for impacts of ecotourism on birds (Buckley, Chapter 11, this volume) and marine mammals (Higham and Lusseau, Chapter 10, this volume). Disturbance to terrestrial

reptiles and amphibians is included here, but has been subject to relatively little research. Invertebrates are not considered here except briefly: the impacts of trampling are included in the chapter by Cole (Chapter 4, this volume). Other impacts on invertebrates are reviewed by Liddle (1997) and Buckley (2001). There has also been limited research on recreational impacts on shoreline invertebrates (Beauchamp and Gowing, 1982; Ghazanshahi *et al.*, 1983; Bally and Griffiths, 1989; Povery and Keough, 1991; Wynberg and Branch, 1997; Kelaher *et al.*, 1998a,b).

Previous reviews of this topic include: classic texts by Edington and Edington (1986, 1977); bibliographies by Boyle and Samson (1983, 1985) and Hall and Dearden (1984); a specialist book by Knight and Gutzwiller (1995); a report by Roe *et al.* (1997); several chapters in the comprehensive work by Liddle (1997); and a summary by Green and Higginbottom (2000, 2001). Impacts on wildlife are also discussed in more general reviews and texts, such as Wang and Miko (1997), Hammitt and Cole (1987), Buckley (2001), Newsome *et al.* (2001, pp. 95–124) and Hendee and Dawson (2002, pp. 321–349, 423–424).

Various schemes have been proposed to classify the impacts of tourism on wildlife (e.g. Pomerantz *et al.*, 1988; Duffus and Dearden, 1990; Anderson, 1995; Gutzwiller, 1995; Whittaker and Knight, 1998; Gill *et al.*, 1996; Liddle, 1997; Hendee and Mattson, 2002).

Knight and Cole (1995), for example, divided impacts into harvesting, habitat modification, disturbance and pollution. This review focuses on impacts through habitat modification and direct disturbance. Most of the data available refer to effects at the scale of individual animals rather than entire populations, but a distinction may be drawn between breeding and non-breeding individuals.

The impacts of ecotourism and outdoor recreation on wildlife may, in many cases, be much less significant than major habitat changes associated with agriculture, forestry or extractive industries (Mattson, 1997; Green and Catterall, 1998); large dams (Sheppe, 1985); or direct impacts from hunting and poaching (Ottichilo, 1987). In other cases, however, disturbance by tourists may have a major effect on wildlife survival and reproduction, particularly for species and populations in conservation reserves which are largely protected from other human activities. As one example, tourism in middle-altitude rainforest in Madagascar produces more impacts on wildlife than small-scale subsistence logging by local residents (Stephenson, 1993a). Where wildlife species survive only in protected areas, increased disturbance from ecotourists and other wildlife watchers, especially during critical periods such as breeding, migration and overwintering, may have significant consequences for conservation of the species concerned. Such population-scale impacts have not often been quantified, but examples of population decline associated with increased recreation cross a wide spectrum of species: wood turtles in Connecticut, USA (Garber and Berger, 1995), grasshoppers in Austria (Ilich and Haslett, 1994), monkeys in Costa Rica (Lippold, 1990), rodents and tenrecs in Madagascar (Stephenson, 1993a,b), and bats in Mexico.

Table 12.1 lists the English and scientific names of animals mentioned in this chapter.

Habitat Modification

Wildlife habitat may be modified by: tracks and trails; barriers; campsites and lodges; new sounds and smells; fire and weeds; provision or removal of food and water sources; and provision, removal or damage to refuges and breeding sites. Such effects may be complex and

indirect, especially for species dependent on different food and habitat at different seasons or ages (Buckley and McDonald, 1991).

Roads and tracks can act as barriers to the movement of wildlife, both large and small (Buckley, Chapter 6, this volume). Some wildlife tourism ventures, especially private reserves, use fences deliberately to keep watchable species close to tourist areas. Elsewhere, roads can block or modify movement patterns. Examples include: small cryptic species (Adams and Geis, 1983; Andrews, 1990; Burnett, 1992; Goosem, 2000); larger herbivores (Ward et al., 1973; Reed et al., 1975; Singer and Doherty, 1985) and large predators (Boitani et al., 1984; Thiel, 1985; Mech et al., 1988; Brody and Pelton, 1989; van Sickle and Lindzey, 1992; Foster and Humphrey, 1995; Yanes et al., 1995; Lovallo and Anderson, 1996; Gibeau and Heuer, 1996; Gunther et al., 1998; Ruediger, 1998; Tewes and Blanton, 1998; Tewes and Hughes, 2001).

In addition, many animals avoid roads, tracks and trails. Even a narrow hiking trail, therefore, may effectively modify habitat over a broad area. White-tailed deer, for example, move away from trails used by oversnow vehicles even at low-intensity use, two vehicles per day (Dorrance et al., 1975). Grizzly bears in the Rocky Mountains generally stay at least 250m from roads, reducing effective habitat area by 8.7% (McLellan and Shackleton, 1988). Grizzly bears in north-western Montana, USA, avoid trails even if they cross the best foraging areas (Kasworm and Manley, 1990). Similar behaviour has been reported by Mattson et al. (1987), Gunther (1990), Olson and Gilbert (1994) and Mattson (1997). Hanuman langurs in Shimla, India, avoid areas of human habitation, though rhesus macaques do not (Ross et al., 1993). Large mammals in the rainforests of Sumatra behave differently near trails (Griffiths and van Schaik, 1993), even when behaviour is recorded by camera traps and is hence not affected by human presence. These losses of available habitat area are particularly significant where the areas affected are important for feeding or breeding; for example, where roads run along narrow valley floors in mountainous areas. Tracks, trails and boardwalks also modify small-scale habitat features such as woody debris, affecting food and refuge sites for smaller vertebrates such as lizards (Martín and

Table 12.1. Alphabetical list of common and scientific names.

baboon, hamadryas	*Papio hamadryas*	lemming, northern bog	*Synaptomys b*
badger, European	*Meles meles*	lizard, flat-tailed horned	*Phrynosoma m.___*
bat, Indiana	*Myotis sodalis*	lizard, Iberian rock	*Lacerta monticola*
bear, black	*Ursus americanus*	macaque, Barbary	*Macaca sylvanus*
bear, brown or grizzly	*Ursus arctos*	macaque, rhesus	*Macaca mulatta*
bear, polar	*Ursus maritimus*	markhor, Heptner's	*Capra falconeri*
bison	*Bison bison*		*heptneri*
blackbuck	*Antilopa cervicapra*	marmot, alpine	*Marmota marmota*
bobcat	*Lynx rufus*	marmot, Vancouver	*Marmota*
caiman, Paraguayan	*Caiman yacare*	Island	*vancouverensis*
caribou	*Rangifer tarandus*	monkey, howling	*Alouatta palliata*
chimpanzee	*Pan troglodytes*	monkey, whitefaced	*Cebus capucinus*
chipmunk, Colorado	*Eutamias quadrivittatus*	moose, North American	*Alces alces*
chital	*Axis axis*	muskox	*Ovivos moschatus*
cougar, mountain lion,	*Felis concolor*	possum, brushtail	*Trichosurus vulpecula*
panther		possum, ringtail	*Pseudocheirus*
coyote	*Canis latrans*		*peregrinus*
deer, mule	*Odocoileus virginiatus*	quoll, eastern	*Dasyurus viverrinus*
deer, red	*Cervus elaphus*	rat, broad-toothed	*Mastacomys fuscus*
deer, roe	*Capreolus capreolus*	rattlesnake, eastern or	*Sistrutus catenatus*
deer, white-tailed	*Odocoileus hemionus*	massasauga	*catenatus*
devil, Tasmanian	*Sarcophilus laniarius*	reindeer, Svalbard	*Rangifer tarandus*
elephant, African	*Loxodonta africana*		*platyrhynchus*
elephant-shrew, eastern	*Elephantulus myurus*	rhinoceros, Asian	*Rhinoceros unicornis*
rock		sheep, (Rocky Mtn)	*Ovis canadensis*
elk, American	*Cervus canadensis*	bighorn	
fox, red or silver	*Vulpes vulpes*	sheep, dall	*Ovis dalli*
gazelle, Thomson's	*Gazella thomsoni*	skink, five-lined	*Eumeces fasciatus*
goat, (Rocky) mountain	*Oreamnos americanus*	squirrel, Columbian	*Spermophilus*
gorilla, mountain	*Gorilla gorilla berengei*	ground	*columbianus*
hyrax, rock	*Procavia capensis*	squirrel, grizzled giant	*Ratufa macroura*
kangaroo, grey	*Macropus fuliginosus*	tortoise, desert	*Gopherus agasizii*
langur, Hanuman	*Presbytis entellus*	vole, California	*Microtus californicus*

Salvador, 1995; Hecnar and M'Closkey, 1998). Compaction under trails may crush burrows in soil or snow, or reduce their insulation (Schmid, 1970; Layser and Burke, 1973; Mainini *et al.*, 1993). Modifications to cave entrances, even gates or grids intended to reduce disturbance from tourists, can cause tenfold reductions in the populations of cave-dwelling bats (Churchill, 1987; White and Seginak, 1987). Torch batteries discarded by cavers can affect the fauna of cave streams (Edington and Edington, 1977, 1986).

Avoidance Behaviour

While some animals avoid areas with habitat modifications, such as tracks and trails, others respond more directly to people using such areas. Elk and moose, for example, move away from cross-country skiers on ski trails (Ferguson and Keith, 1982). The elk return once the skiers leave, but the moose do not. Elk in Yellowstone National Park move away from tourists, often into poorer foraging areas (Cassirer *et al.*, 1992). Elk in Wyoming avoid campers, picnickers and anglers; 80% of a herd of 400 stayed at least 800 m away (Ward, 1973). Chamois in the Swiss Alps avoid trails being used by hikers, joggers and mountain bikes (Gander and Ingold, 1997). Chamois in Austria move to cliffs when there are skiers on the slopes (Hamr, 1988). Brown bear in Europe have become very secretive, avoiding areas with any human habitation or activity (Elgmork, 1983, 1987; Liddle, 1997). The same applies for cougar in south-western USA (van Dyke *et al.*, 1986; Beier, 1995). Rainforest wildlife in Sumatra leave trail areas when tourists arrive (Griffiths and van Schaik, 1993). Howling monkey in Costa Rica moved out of a reserve area once ecotourists started to visit it (Lippold, 1990). Flat-tailed horned lizards in Arizona move away from areas used by off-road vehicles (Beauchamp *et al.*, 1998).

Where animals cannot leave disturbed areas completely, they may change the timing of activities to avoid tourists in time rather than space. Captive elephant shrew, for example, become more nocturnal if disturbed during the day (Woodall *et al.*, 1989). Similar effects, incidentally, have been recorded for birds (Buckley, Chapter 11, this volume). Red-necked wallabies in south-eastern Queensland, Australia, forage diurnally in protected areas but nocturnally on private rural landholdings where they are disturbed by people and dogs (author, personal observation).

Physiological Disturbance

Disturbance to wildlife from the sight, sound or smell of humans and their artefacts and activities has been recorded for a wide range of species. Most of the responses recorded, however, are behavioural. Physiological indicators of stress, such as temperature and heart rate, are more difficult to measure and have not often been recorded (Gabrielsen and Smith, 1995). Perhaps the classic study is that of MacArthur *et al.* (1982), who used remote telemetry to detect increases in heart rate for mountain bighorn sheep approached by hikers. Increases of up to 20 beats/min were recorded when unaccompanied hikers approached within 30 m from a nearby road. Where hikers approached from the opposite direction, or were accompanied by dogs, this threshold distance rose to 200 m. Remote heart-rate telemetry on desert bighorn sheep was later reported by Giest *et al.* (1985). Several studies have showed increases in heart rate during aircraft overflights (Larkin *et al.*, 1996; Weisenberger *et al.*, 1996; Krausman *et al.*, 1998). Interestingly, for captive desert mule deer and mountain sheep subjected to simulated jet aircraft noise, behavioural responses persisted for 4–5 min, whereas heart rate re-

turned to normal after 3 min (Weisenberger *et al.*, 1996). Hormonal levels were not measured.

Instead of heart rate, Humphrey (1978) and Bakken *et al.* (1999) used body temperature as an indicator of stress. Captive silver foxes suffered stress-induced hyperthermia when disturbed either by approaching humans or by aircraft overflights, but the former produced greater effects (Bakke *et al.*, 1999). Hibernating Indiana bats showed an increase in body temperature in response to lights, photographic flashes, human speech and other sounds, and especially physical contact (Humphrey, 1978).

Alert and Alarm Behaviour

Where physiological evidence is not available, the first signs that wildlife are disturbed by ecotourists or other people are behavioural changes, which indicate that the animal has detected the person and is alert. These changes may be obvious, such as standing erect and gazing fixedly at the intruder; or much more subtle, such as an animal keeping an eye on people while continuing to feed. For species which routinely live in social groups, alert behaviour may be indicated by changes in the relative position of different individuals, e.g. juveniles moving closer to their mothers or a lead individual moving to the side of the group nearest the tourists or adopting a guard or lookout position (Pedevillano and Wright, 1987). Alternatively, alertness may be indicated by changes in vocalizations, whether specialized sounds (e.g. between parents and offspring); decreased calling, as for pygmy marmosets in north-eastern Ecuador (de la Torre *et al.*, 2000); increased calling, as for chimpanzees approached by larger tourist groups in Uganda (Grieser-Johns, 1996); or alarm calls, as for alpine marmot in Europe (Mainini *et al.*, 1993).

Alert behavioural responses may occur at considerable distance, e.g. 640 m for reindeer that hear oversnow vehicles. Median alert distance for chamois disturbed by hikers and bikers in the Swiss Alps is 180 m (Gander and Ingold, 1997). Asian rhino, however, allow tourists to approach within 30 m before reacting (Lott and McCoy, 1995). Some species respond more to people on foot, others to vehicles, others to aircraft (Ward *et al.*, 1973; Singer, 1978; Krausman and Hervert, 1983; Lewis, 1986).

Alert and alarm behaviour is commonly more intense, and triggered at larger distances, where tourists are accompanied by dogs. The effects of dogs have been recorded for a wide range of species including, red, roe and mule deer; pronghorn antelope; chamois; bighorn sheep; marmots and badgers (MacArthur *et al.*, 1982; Berger *et al.*, 1983; Cederna and Lovari, 1986; Freddy *et al.*, 1986; Aaris-Sorensen, 1987; Jeppesen 1987a,b; Smith and Krausman, 1988; Humphries *et al.*, 1989; Bullock *et al.*, 1993; Mainini *et al.*, 1993).

Evasive Behaviour

Perhaps the most commonly reported response to human disturbance, especially by larger mammals in open terrain, is simply to move away, either gradually or abruptly: they run and/or hide. This response is readily observed and hence often reported. It may be triggered by tourists on foot, in vehicles (Buckley, Chapter 6, this volume) or by low-flying aircraft, including helicopters.

Both the approach distance which causes animals to move away, and the distance they then move, can differ greatly between species, populations and individual animals. These distances also depend on the terrain, the type and magnitude of the disturbance, and the history or habituation of the animals concerned. Various authors, for example, have reported elk, mule deer and white-tailed deer moving away from hikers and cross-country skiers in North America, but with considerable differences in detail (Behrend and Lubeck, 1968; Dorrance *et al.*, 1975; Eckstein *et al.*, 1979; Ferguson and Keith, 1982; Freddy *et al.*, 1986; Cassirer *et al.*, 1992). In Yellowstone National Park, for example, elk at two sites moved away from cross-country skiers at a median approach distance of 400 m, and travelled up to 1700 m away, commonly into an adjacent drainage. Most did not return for 2 days or more. At another site, however, elk did not begin to move away until skiers approached within 15 m (Cassirer *et al.*, 1992).

Behrend and Lubeck (1968) reported that white-tailed deer move away from hikers at 17–54 m, and Freddy *et al.* (1986) that mule deer move away at 133 m, travelling up to 330 m. In these cases, disturbance was due to small numbers of slow-moving people. European orienteering events with several hundred runners, in contrast, led moose, roe and red deer to run up to 6 km away, often out of the protective forest cover into open ground (Sennstam and Stalfelt, 1976; Jeppesen, 1984, 1987a,b). Some of the animals died in consequence (Sennstam and Stalfelt, 1976). Some individual animals, however, hid instead of running (Jeppesen, 1984, 1987a).

Chamois in Switzerland also run from hikers, with a median escape distance of 103 m (Gander and Ingold, 1997). In the Sierra Nevada, 7 of 10 groups of desert bighorn sheep ran from hikers (Hicks and Elder, 1979), and six of these left their pasture areas. Grizzly bear generally run from hikers (Schneider, 1977; Jacobs and Schloeder, 1992; Titus *et al.*, 1994), with 70% of bears running over 1 km (McLellan and Shackleton, 1989). Marmots in the Swiss Alps run to their burrows (Ingold *et al.*, 1993). Asian rhinoceros in Nepal run if tourists approach within 10 m (Lott and McCoy, 1995). Grizzled giant squirrel in southern India run and then freeze (Joshua and Johnsingh, 1994). A variety of native fauna in the UK, the Alps and Zimbabwe are all disturbed by hikers (Holroyd, 1967; von Petrak, 1988; Yalden, 1990; Harris *et al.*, 1995; Potts *et al.*, 1996).

Disturbance by helicopters and other low-flying aircraft has been described for caribou, muskox, deer, goats, sheep, bears and other species (Price and Lent, 1972; Miller and Gunn, 1979; Krausman and Hervert, 1983; Sindiyo and Pertet, 1984; Bleich *et al.*, 1990, 1994; Stockwell *et al.*, 1991; Dewey, 1994; Cote, 1996; Larkin *et al.*, 1996; Krausman *et al.*, 1998). Dall sheep in Alaska run up to 800 m uphill if disturbed by helicopters 1 km away (Price and Lent, 1972). When mountain bighorn sheep are disturbed by low-flying aircraft, 1 in 5 individuals moves into a different habitat type (Krausman and Hervert, 1983). Desert bighorn sheep in the Grand Canyon also run uphill when disturbed by helicopter or light aircraft (Stockwell *et al.*, 1991). Lion and buffalo run and hide when balloons pass overhead, but elephants are apparently not disturbed (Sindiyo and Pertet, 1984).

Aggressive Responses

Interactions between humans and wildlife are not often reported in the popular press and other mass media. When they are, however, the focus is on attacks by dangerous beasts: bears and cougar in North America, dingo and crocodiles in Australia, Big Five in Africa. And certainly, such attacks do occur (Singer and Bratton, 1980; Herrero and Fleck, 1990; Beier, 1991; Qui, 1996). To judge from the published scientific literature, however, they are relatively rare.

Aggression also appears to be strongly correlated with feeding. Increased aggressive behaviour from animals subject to feeding has been recorded for, for example, coyote in the USA (Bounds and Shaw, 1994); dingo in Australia; black bear in Yosemite National Park (Herrero, 1976; Edington and Edington, 1977; Hammitt and Cole, 1987); grizzly bear in Yellowstone National Park (Gunther, 1992) and Denali National Park (Albert and Bowyer, 1991); baboons in Tanzania (Wrangham, 1974); hamadryas baboon in Saudi Arabia (Kamal *et al.*, 1997); macaque in Thailand (Aggimarangsee, 1993) and rock hyrax in Tsitsikamma National Park, South Africa (Crawford and Fairall, 1984). From personal experience, I can corroborate aggressive behaviour by black bears, baboons, various monkeys, dingo, hyrax (on Mt Kenya) and even small and generally inoffensive species such as possums and gliders in Australia.

Some of the larger predatory species may indeed attack humans as prey. This includes, for example, the large cats such as cougar, tiger, lion and leopard; polar bear and leopard seal; and alligators and crocodiles. People are also occasionally attacked and eaten by species that eat both live prey and carrion, such as bears and hyena.

However, many injuries to tourists by wildlife are from entirely herbivorous species acting defensively when approached. In several North American towns, for example, tourists are warned to avoid overwintering elk, which may become aggressive. I myself have been attacked (many years ago) by monkeys in Thailand and by a gemsbok in Namibia, though since the latter was a solitary individual which had lost a horn, perhaps it was unusually aggressive.

Buffalo, rhino and elephant are amongst Africa's Big Five (along with lion and leopard), because of the danger they pose to hunters and other humans, even though they are entirely herbivorous.

Food and Water

There are many instances where the behaviour of wildlife has been modified quite considerably by provision of food or water, either deliberate or unintentional (Doenier *et al.*, 1997). In some cases the opportunity to feed animals is sold as part of the experience, though this would not generally be viewed as ecotourism. Other tour operators feed animals out of view of their clients so as to increase the reliability of sightings. Examples include wallabies in Tasmania, and fox and polar bear in Hudson Bay, Canada (Buckley, 2003, p. 178).

There are many more examples where animals have learnt that tourists can provide food, either directly or through scraps, leftovers and garbage. Examples include mice, raccoons, coatis, elephants, macaques, baboons and vervet monkeys (Edington and Edington, 1986; Green and Higginbottom, 2000), and both black and grizzly bears (Cole, 1974; Beeman, 1975; Merrill, 1978; Gilbert and Krebs, 1981; Boyle and Samson, 1985).

In Yosemite National Park, for example, black bears historically used to obtain up to 50% of their total food supplies from tourists (Graber and White, 1978). Currently, education programmes and bear-resistant garbage containers are used in protected areas throughout bear habitat areas in Canada and the USA. In some, such as Denali National Park in Alaska, hikers must pass a bear safety test, which includes food and cooking, before they receive a backcountry permit (Buckley, 2003, p. 184). They must also carry their food in bear-resistant food containers issued by the parks agency.

While these programmes may be motivated more by concerns over tourist safety than wildlife or ecosystem health, there are also instances where feeding has been shown to affect wildlife populations. In campgrounds in Colorado, USA, for example, the availability of extra food leads to increased populations of Colorado chipmunk and deer mice, though not of four other species studied (Clevenger and Workman, 1977; Foin *et al.*, 1977). In Yosemite National Park, generalist-feeding deer mice increase in numbers at campground sites, whereas specialist-feeding mountain mice decrease (Garton *et al.*, 1977). Indirect effects have also been recorded on occasion. Black-buck populations in India decrease where food is available, for example, because of competition from other species (Raman *et al.*, 1996). And in the Australian Alps, increases in the introduced European fox have led to increased predation on the native broad-toothed rat (Green, 2003).

A range of physiological and behavioural responses has been described. Grizzly bears denied access to garbage, for example, have expanded their range, suggesting that the provision of food had previously caused range contraction (Blanchard and Knight, 1991). In the Galapagos Islands, feeding of land iguanas caused complete collapse of their territorial system, leading to a failure in breeding (Harris, 1973; Edington and Edington, 1986). A review by Boutin (1990) indicated that in 33 of 39 cases, supplementary food led to extension of the breeding season for the species concerned. And for California vole (Ford and Pitelka, 1984) and Columbian ground squirrel (Dobson and Kjelgaard, 1985), animals with extra food supplies began breeding at an earlier age.

Supplementary water supplies may have similar effects to supplementary food, especially in arid areas (Leslie and Douglas, 1980; Edington and Edington, 1986). Artificial watering can also affect herbivores by producing particularly lush vegetation, as shown for red deer in Scotland (Watson, 1979). Supplementary water in arid regions does generally improve survival of herbivores (Parker and Witkowski, 1999).

Lights, Noise, Disease, Roadkill

Wildlife-watching tours in several continents, but notably Africa and Australia, often include spotlighting at night, both to search for nocturnal animals and to observe nocturnal behaviour by animals also active during the day. Potential impacts include behavioural disturbance and disruption, especially where the

more susceptible nocturnal species are temporarily dazzled. In Australia, for example, Lindenmayer and Press (1989) have demonstrated that spotlights do indeed affect night vision for nocturnal marsupials. Wilson (1999) found that reducing the intensity of spotlights from 30 W to 22.5 W yielded twice as many sightings of the ringtail possum. Wildlife may also be affected by fixed lights, such as those on lodges and aircraft landing fields. Potential consequences, such as increased vulnerability to predation, or disruption to breeding behaviour or parental care, remain almost entirely unstudied worldwide.

Similarly, although the reaction of various species to noise sources such as vehicles (Buckley, Chapter 6, this volume) and aircraft (see above) have been documented to some degree, the effects of noise as such (Radle, 1999), are not well known. In particular, many animals rely on sound to communicate with each other and to warn against predator attacks. If these sounds are masked by human interference, the consequences could well be significant. In addition, many animals can hear sounds which humans cannot (Bowles, 1995). Some animal species use natural sounds as development cues, and these, too, can be disrupted. Spadefoot toads studied by Brattstrom and Bondello (1983), for example, survive dry seasons buried underground, emerging when the sound of thunder heralds rain. Deceived by the sound of off-road vehicles, the toads emerged, but without water in which to survive or breed.

Tourist traffic may be a significant contributor to roadkill in many areas (Gunther *et al.*, 1998; Finder *et al.*, 1999). In Cradle Mountain National Park, Tasmania, for example, sealing a tourist access road allowed vehicles to travel considerably faster, leading to complete extinction of the local population of eastern quolls, and a 50% reduction in the local population of Tasmanian devils (Jones, 2000). When a new road was opened in the Warrambungle Ranges, Australia, the entire local population of rock wallabies became extinct (Fox, 1982). Roadkill of grey kangaroos is also reported by Coulson (1982) in Victoria, Australia. On a 32 km stretch of road in southern Texas, 25 bobcats were killed by vehicles over 2 years (Cain *et al.*, 2003).

In 1967, three brown bears from a total population of 70 were killed in vehicle collisions in Abruzzi National Park, Italy (Zunino and Herrero, 1972). From 1984 to 1986, eight black bears from a total population of 56 in North Carolina, USA, were also killed by vehicles (Hellgren and Vaughan, 1989). Roadkill has also been recorded as a significant cause of mortality for white-tailed deer (Finder et al., 1999) and grizzly bears (Cole, 1974).

Individual animals may also be killed deliberately, whether the 'problem bears' of North America which became aggressive after finding that tourists could provide food, or the black rhino shot by a trail guide in Africa who was concerned for the safety of his clients (Curzon, 1996). Perhaps more significant ecologically, tourists may transmit disease to wildlife (Hall and Dearden, 1984; Hall, 1992; Goltsman et al., 1996). Human-transmitted disease killed a number of habituated lowland gorillas in The Congo (Butynski and Kalina, 1998). There are similar concerns for chimpanzees and mountain gorillas (Shackley, 1996; Buckley, 2003, p. 39). Disease also seems to be more prevalent amongst Australian marsupials subject to supplementary feeding (Green and Higginbottom, 2000, 2001), although this is believed to be due principally to stress and crowding. Of course, wildlife can also transmit diseases to tourists, whether rabies or hantavirus.

Predisposition

Many of the impacts and responses outlined above may depend considerably on the history of the individual animals concerned: whether they have previously been hunted or harassed, fed or merely photographed. The effects of predisposition, positive or negative, have been demonstrated for a wide range of animal species (Tracy, 1977; Schultz and Bailey, 1978; Boyle and Samson, 1985; Liddle, 1997). These include, for example, various deer (Douglas, 1971; Dorrance et al., 1975; Eckstein et al., 1979; Krausman et al., 1986); caribou (Calef, 1976); chamois (Patterson, 1989); mountain bighorn sheep (MacArthur et al., 1982) bears (McCullough, 1982; Jope, 1985; McLellan and Shackleton, 1988, 1989; Fagen and Fagen, 1994; Olson et al., 1997); chimpanzees

(Griffiths and van Schaik, 1993); barbary macaques (Oleary and Fa, 1993); the rainforest fauna of Sumatra (Grieser-Johns, 1996); and pygmy marmosets in Ecuador (de la Torre et al., 2000).

Not surprisingly, animals that have been hunted or pursued become more wary, even of non-hunters; those that have been fed become more tame or even aggressive; and those that have encountered many humans with no effect, generally learn to ignore them. This, in turn, may have severe impacts if it makes them more vulnerable to poachers, as for elephant in Tanzania (Buckley, 2003, pp. 211–212) or bears in Kamchatka, Russia (Russell and Enns, 2002; author, personal observation, 2003).

This conflict between hunting and wildlife viewing presents difficulties in the development of wildlife-based ecotourism in many areas. Tour operators and guides work hard to habituate local populations for their clients, but this is difficult where the animals are also hunted, and dangerous if they are subject to poaching. Examples from various regions indicate that many mammals, like birds (Buckley, Chapter 6, this volume) quickly learn where they are safe from hunters. This, however, makes them all the more vulnerable to poachers.

Different individual animals in the same populations may have different human interaction histories and hence respond differently to a new disturbance. When a seasonally used lodge in Alaska was occupied for longer than usual one year, for example, individual habituated bears fished for salmon as in other years, but non-habituated adults waited an additional 17 days before they moved to the salmon stream near the lodge (Olson et al., 1997). During this period, the number of juvenile bears fishing was higher than usual, perhaps because they are normally driven away by adults. In Glacier National Park, USA, individual mountain goats continue to use a mineral lick even when tourists are nearby (Pedevillano and Wright, 1987; author, personal observation).

Energetic Consequences

Disturbance from tourism and recreation can affect the energy balance of affected animals, either by increasing energy expenditure or reducing energy intake (Moen, 1976; Parker *et al.*, 1984; White *et al.*, 1999). Where the animals do not have the opportunity to compensate, this may lead to death through starvation, or to reduced breeding success. Many species of cool temperate, arctic and alpine areas, for example, store up food or fat reserves during summer and deplete them gradually over winter. If they are driven from feeding areas, or spend more time watchful and less time feeding in summer, or have to expend energy avoiding tourists in winter, they may die. Even if they survive, they will be less competitive against better-fed animals in breeding populations and less able to feed and protect offspring.

Grizzly bears in Montana, USA, for example, lose preferred foraging areas since they avoid trails used by hikers (Kasworm and Manley, 1990). Roe deer in northern Europe have barely enough energy reserves to overwinter (Drozdz and Osiecki, 1973), and moose and deer which flee from orienteering events may die (Sennstam and Stalfelt, 1976; Jeppesen, 1987a,b). Elk in Yellowstone National Park must spend 5.5% of their total daily winter energy expenditure in moving away from cross-country skiers (Cassirer *et al.*, 1992). As a result they need to eat an additional 0–3 kg of dry forage each day, but in moving away from skiers they are forced into areas where forage is harder to obtain. Disturbance by skiers also reduces the energy reserves of overwintering marmots on Vancouver Island, Canada (Dearden and Hall, 1983).

Hibernating species, such as bats, are also particularly vulnerable to energetic losses (Harvey, 1975, 1980; Edington and Edington, 1977; Humphrey, 1978; Tuttle, 1979; Churchill, 1987; Speakman *et al.*, 1991). When six species of bat were disturbed experimentally by human speech, lights and photography, for example, their body temperatures increased and their energy expenditure increased by 49 joules, reducing total hibernating time by 4.5 h (Speakman *et al.*, 1991). If tourists actually touched the bats, however, the additional energy expenditure rose to 2038 J, corresponding to 104 h of hibernation time.

Breeding Populations

Tourist disturbance to breeding has been recorded for a range of terrestrial vertebrate species. Disruption can occur at any stage of the reproductive cycle. Thomson's gazelles, for example, leave breeding areas if disturbed, reducing their reproductive success. Tourists disturb the social behaviour of pygmy marmosets in Ecuador (de la Torre *et al.*, 2000), and break down the breeding territories of land iguanas in the Galapagos Islands (Harris, 1973; Edington and Edington, 1986). Kangaroos fleeing from tourists may eject their joeys from the pouch and/or abandon them (Stuart-Dick, 1987). Female black bears disturbed by skiers may abandon their dens and cubs (Goodrich and Berger, 1994), and the same applies for polar bears disturbed by oversnow vehicles or aircraft (Amstrup, 1993). Wolves and coyotes disturbed by tourists move their pups to different dens (Harrison and Gilbert, 1985; Ballard *et al.*, 1987). For smaller species, such as marmots, breeding burrows may be completely destroyed by tourists (Mainini *et al.*, 1993). Offspring of various species may be separated from their mothers, sometimes with fatal consequences, when herds move in response to tourist disturbance (van Lawick-Goodall and van Lawick-Goodall, 1970; Singer, 1978; Maier *et al.*, 1998; Bakken *et al.*, 1999). Egg-laying reptiles, such as caiman, crocodiles and alligators, lose their eggs to predators such as coatis, raccoons, baboons, hyaenas and monitor lizards when nesting females are disturbed by tourists (Cott, 1969; Crawshaw and Schaller, 1980; Dietz and Hines, 1980; Jacobs and Kushlan, 1986). Gravid female rattlesnakes also show behavioural changes if disturbed (Parent and Weatherhead, 2000), though apparently without any effect on litter size.

Conclusions

Perhaps the most remarkable feature of the information summarized above is that there is so little of it. There are hundreds or thousands of wildlife species worldwide, which are watched and approached by tourists, and most of these species will run or hide if approached too close. A large part of the skills of wildlife tourism guides is in understanding the behaviour of particular species, and indeed individual animals, well enough to approach them without triggering either flight or attack. In addition to published quantitative studies as above, therefore, there is no doubt a considerable body of expert knowledge amongst naturalists and wildlife guides, but this remains largely unrecorded.

Many colonial burrow-dwelling mammals, for example, behave in a similar way to the marmots studied by Ingold *et al.* (1993) and Dearden and Hall (1983). They use sentinels to watch for danger and alarm signals to alert other individuals. When alerted they look around, move close to their burrows, and/or take refuge underground. This applies for a wide variety of rabbits, squirrels, gophers, pikas, mongooses, and also more solitary species, such as weasels, badgers and even aardwolf, as well as many skinks and other lizards. Yet none of these seem to have been studied.

Likewise, there are native deer, goats, bears, and many other species throughout Asia; llama and vicuna in South America; marsupials in Australia and a wide variety of game animals throughout Africa. Many of these are significant tourist attractions and many are also endangered. Individual guides, scientists and local residents no doubt know a great deal about approach distances and evasive behaviour, but nowhere does this seem to be documented. Even journals such as the *Ecological Journal* produced by Conservation Corporation Africa, which records wildlife observations by CCA staff, focus on the undisturbed behaviours of the animals concerned, rather than the effects of disturbance. This is not surprising, since CCA prides itself on low-impact wildlife watching. But in order to achieve that goal, its staff have learned a lot about the response of wildlife to approaching tourists, and this, too, deserves documentation.

The case studies summarized above show that disturbance need not be dramatic to produce significant ecological consequences. If hibernating bats lose 4.5 h of hibernation with every tourist visit, then just one visit a day would soon cause local extinction, even though the bats show no apparent response to each visit. Few studies, however, have quantified these effects, or attempted to estimate their consequences at population level. Decreased feeding time, or avoidance of prime feeding areas that are used by tourists, can tip an animal's annual energy balance from positive to negative. Brief disturbance by skiers or hikers can lead denning females to abandon an entire year's investment in offspring.

However, quantitative estimates such as these seem to be the exception. In addition, most of them are in North America. Even there, very few species have been studied and even for those species, there are only a few independent studies. In the rest of the world, and for other species, there is simply no information.

Historically, this may be since conservation biologists and animal ecologists saw the impacts of ecotourism and outdoor recreation as negligible compared to factors such as habitat destruction, feral predators, hunting and poaching, and disease. And, indeed, none of those factors has decreased in importance. But meanwhile, tourism in protected areas has increased to the point where the impacts of ecotourism on wildlife can no longer be ignored.

Acknowledgements

The database of literature on which this review is based has been constructed since 1991 by staff of the International Centre for Ecotourism Research at Griffith University (www.gu.edu.au/centre/icer/staff). It is currently maintained by Karen Sullivan, who also kindly checked references and citations. Coverage, opinions, errors and omissions in this chapter remain my own responsibility.

References

Aaris-Sorensen, J. (1987) Past and present distribution of badgers (*Meles meles*) in the Copenhagen area. *Biological Conservation* 41, 159–165.

Adams, L.W. and Geis, A. (1983) Effects of roads on small mammals. *Journal of Applied Ecology* 20, 403–415.

Aggimarangsee, N. (1993) Survey for semi-tame colonies of macaques in Thailand. *Natural History Bulletin of the Siam Society* 40, 103–166.

Albert, D.M. and Bowyer, R.T. (1991) Factors related to grizzly bear–human interactions in Denali

National park. *Wildlife Society Bulletin* 19, 339–349.

Amstrup, S.C. (1993) Human disturbances of denning polar bears in Alaska. *Arctic* 48, 246–250.

Anderson, S.H. (1995) Recreational disturbance and wildlife populations. In: Knight, R.L. and Gutzwiller, K.J. (eds) *Wildlife and Recreationists: Coexistence Through Management and Research.* Island Press, Washington, DC, pp. 157–168.

Andrews, A. (1990) Fragmentation of habitat by roads and utility corridors: a review. *Australian Zoologist* 26, 130–141.

Bakken, M., Oppermann Moe, R., Smith, A.J. and Eriksroed Selle, G.M. (1999) Effects of environmental stressors on deep body temperature and activity levels in silver fox vixens (*Vulpes vulpes*). *Applied Animal Behavioral Science* 64, 141–151.

Ballard, W.B., Whitman, J.S. and Gardiner, C.L. (1987) Ecology of an exploited wolf population in south central Alaska. *Wildlife Monograph* 98, 1–54.

Bally, R. and Griffiths, C.L. (1989) Effects of human trampling on an exposed rocky shore. *International Journal of Environmental Studies* 34, 115–125.

Bauer, J. and Giles, J. (2002) *Recreational Hunting: an International Perspective.* Wildlife Tourism Research Report No. 13, Status Assessment of Wildlife Tourism in Australia Series. CRC for Sustainable Tourism, Gold Coast, Queensland, Australia.

Beauchamp, B., Wone, B., Bros, S. and Kutilek, M. (1998) Habitat use of the flat-tailed horned lizard (*Phrynosoma mcallii*) in a disturbed environment. *Journal of Herpetology* 32, 210–216.

Beauchamp, K.A. and Gowing, M.M. (1982) A quantitative assessment of human trampling effects on a rocky intertidal community. *Marine Environmental Research* 7, 279–293.

Beeman, L.E. (1975) Population characteristics, movements, and activities of the black bear (*Ursus americanus*) in the Great Smoky Mountains National Park. PhD Dissertation, University of Tennessee, Knoxville.

Behrend, D.F. and Lubeck, R.A. (1968) Summer flight behaviour of whitetailed deer in two Adirondack forests. *Journal of Wildlife Management* 32, 615–618.

Beier, P. (1991) Cougar attacks on humans in the United States and Canada. *Wildlife Society Bulletin* 19, 403–412.

Beier, P. (1995) Dispersal of juvenile cougars in fragmented habitat. *Wildlife Management* 59, 228–237.

Berger, J., Daneke, D., Johnson, J. and Berwick, S.H.

(1983) Pronghorn foraging economy and predator avoidance in a desert ecosystem: implication for the conservation of large mammalian herbivores. *Biological Conservation* 25, 193–208.

Blanchard, B.M. and Knight, R.R. (1991) Movements of Yellowstone grizzly bears. *Biological Conservation* 58, 41–67.

Bleich, V.C., Bowyer, R.T., Pauli, A.M., Vernoy, R.L. and Anthes, R.W. (1990) Responses of mountain sheep to helicopter surveys. *California Fish and Game* 76, 197–204.

Bleich, V.C., Bowyer, R.T., Pauli, A.M., Nicholson, M.C. and Anthes, R.W. (1994) Mountain sheep *Ovis canadensis* and helicopter surveys – ramifications for the conservation of large mammals. *Biological Conservation* 70, 1–7.

Boitani, L., Barrasso, P. and Grimod, I. (1984) Ranging behaviour of the red fox in Gran Paradiso National Park (Italy). *Bollettino di Zoologia* 51, 275–284.

Bounds, D.L. and Shaw, W.W. (1994) Managing coyotes in U.S. National Parks: human–coyote interactions. *Natural Areas Journal* 14, 280–284.

Boutin, S. (1990) Food supplementation experiments with terrestrial vertebrates: patterns, problems and the future. *Canadian Journal of Zoology* 68, 203–220.

Bowles, A.E. (1995) Responses of wildlife to noise. In: Knight, R.L. and Gutzwiller, K.J. (eds) *Wildlife and Recreationists: Coexistence through Management and Research.* Island Press, Washington, DC, pp. 109–156.

Boyle, S.A. and Samson, F.B. (1983) *Nonconsumptive Outdoor Recreation: an Annotated Bibliography of Human–Wildlife Interactions.* Special Science Report on Wildlife No. 252. US Department of the Interior Fish and Wildlife Service, Washington, DC.

Boyle, S.A. and Samson, F.B. (1985) Effects of nonconsumptive recreation wildlife: a review. *Wildlife Society Bulletin* 13, 110–116.

Brattstrom, B.H. and Bondello, M.C. (1983) Effects of off-road vehicle noise on desert vertebrates. In: Webb, R.H. and Wilshire, H.G. (eds) *Environmental Effects of Off-road Vehicles: Impact and Management in Arid Regions.* Springer Verlag, New York, USA, pp. 167–206.

Brody, A.J. and Pelton, M.R. (1989) Effects of roads on black bear movements in western North Carolina. *Wildlife Society Bulletin* 17, 5–10.

Buckley, R.C. (2001) Environmental impacts. In: Weaver, D. (ed.) *Encyclopaedia of Ecotourism.* CAB International, Wallingford, UK, pp. 374–394.

Buckley, R.C. (2003) *Case Studies in Ecotourism.* CAB International, Wallingford, UK.

Buckley, R.C. and McDonald, J. (1991) Science

and law: the nature of evidence. *Search* 22, 94–95.

Bullock, D.J., Kerridge, F.J., Hanlon, A. and Arnold, R.W. (1993) Short-term responses of deer to recreational disturbances in two deer parks. *Communications from the Mammal Society* 66, 327–332.

Burnett, S.E. (1992) Effects of a rainforest road on movements of small mammals: mechanisms and implications. *Wildlife Research* 19, 95–104.

Butynski, T.M. and Kalina, J. (1998) Gorilla tourism: a critical look. In: Milner-Gulland, E.J. and Mace, R. (eds) *Conservation of Biological Resources*. Blackwell Science Ltd, London.

Cain, A.T., Tuovila, V.R., Hewitt, D.G. and Tewes, M.E. (2003) Effects of a highway and mitigation projects on bobcats in Southern Texas. *Biological Conservation* 114, 189–197.

Calef, G.W. (1976) Numbers beyond counting, miles beyond measure. *Audubon* 78, 42–61.

Caro, T.M., Pelkey, N., Borner, M., Severre, E.L.M., Campbell, K.L.I., Huish, S.A., Kuwai, J.O., Farm, B.P. and Woodworth, B.L. (1998) The impact of tourist hunting on large mammals in Tanzania: an initial assessment. *African Journal of Ecology* 36, 321–346.

Cassirer, E.F., Freddy, D.J. and Ables, E.D. (1992) Elk responses to disturbance by cross-country skiers in Yellowstone National Park. *Wildlife Society Bulletin* 20, 375–381.

Cederna, A. and Lovari, S. (1986) The impact of tourism on chamois feeding activities in an areas of the Abruzzo National Park, Italy. In: Lovari, S. (ed.) *Biology of Mountain Ungulates*. Croom Helm, UK.

Churchill, S. (1987) The conservation of cave fauna in the top end. *Australian Ranger Bulletin* 4, 10–11.

Clevenger, G.A. and Workman, G.W. (1977) The effects of campgrounds on small mammals in Canyonlands and Arches National Parks, Utah. *Transactions of North American and Natural Resources Conference* 42, 473–484.

Cole, G.F. (1974) Management involving grizzly bears and humans in Yellowstone National Park, 1970–1973. *Bioscience* 24, 1–11.

Cote, S.D. (1996) Mountain goat responses to helicopter disturbance. *Wildlife Society Bulletin* 24, 681–685.

Cott, M.B. (1969) Tourists and crocodiles in Uganda. *Oryx* 10, 153–160.

Coulson, G.M. (1982) Road-kills of macropods on a section of highway in Central Victoria. *Australian Wildlife Research* 9, 21–26.

Crawford, R.J.M. and Fairall, N. (1984) Male rock hyraxes (*Procavia capensis*) return to former

home ranges after translocation. *Koedoe* 27, 151–153.

Crawshaw, P.G.J. and Schaller, G.B. (1980) Nesting of Paraguayan caiman *Caiman yacare* in Brazil. *Auulsos Zoologica* (Sao Paulo) 33, 283–292.

Curzon, C. (1996) Black rhino versus trailists. *African Wildlife* 50, 19–23.

de la Torre, S., Snowdon, C. and Bejarano, M. (2000) Effects of human activities on wild pygmy marmosets in Ecuadorian Amazonia. *Biological Conservation* 94, 153–163.

Dearden, P. and Hall, C. (1983) Non-consumptive recreation pressures and the case of the Vancouver Island marmot (*Marmota vancouverensis*). *Environmental Conservation* 10, 63–66.

Deitz, D.C. and Hines, T.C. (1980) Alligator nesting in North-Central Florida. *Copeia* 2, 249–258.

Dewey, R. (1994) *Unfriendly Skies, the Threat of Military Overflights to National Wildlife Refuges*. Defenders of Wildlife, Washington, DC.

Dobson, F.S. and Kjelgaard, J.D. (1985) The influence of food resources on life history of in Columbian ground squirrels. *Canadian Journal of Zoology* 63, 2105–2109.

Doenier, P.B., Delgiudice, G.D. and Riggs, M.R. (1997) Effects of winter supplemental feeding on browse consumption by white-tailed deer. *Wildlife Society Bulletin* 25, 235–243.

Dorrance, M.J., Savage, P.J. and Huff, D.E. (1975) Effects of snowmobiles on white-tailed deer. *Journal of Wildlife Management* 39, 563–569.

Douglas, M.J.W. (1971) Behaviour responses of red deer and chamois to cessation of hunting. *New Zealand Journal of Science* 14, 506–518.

Drozdz, A. and Osiecki, A. (1973) Intake and digestibility of natural feeds by roe deer. *Bialowieza* 18, 81–91.

Duffus, D.A. and Dearden, P. (1990) Non-consumptive wildlife oriented recreation: a conceptual framework. *Biological Conservation* 53, 213–232.

Eckstein, R.G., O'Brien, T.F., Rongstad, O.J. and Bollinger, J.G. (1979) Snowmobile effects on movements of white-tailed deer: a case study. *Environmental Conservation* 6, 45–51.

Edington, J.M. and Edington, M.A. (1977) *Ecology and Environmental Planning*. Chapman & Hall, London.

Edington, J.M. and Edington, M.A. (1986) *Ecology, Recreation and Tourism*. Cambridge University Press, Cambridge, UK.

Elgmork, K. (1983) Influence of holiday cabin concentrations on the occurrence of brown bears (*Ursus arctos* L.) in south-central Norway. *Acta Zoology Fennica* 174, 161–162.

Elgmork, K. (1987) The cyptic brown bear populations of Norway. *Proceedings of the International*

Conference on Bear Research Management 7, 13–16.

Fagen, J.M. and Fagen, R. (1994) Interactions between wildlife viewers and habituated brown bears, 1987–1992. *Natural Areas Journal* 14, 159–164.

Ferguson, M.A.D. and Keith, L.B. (1982) Influence of nordic skiing on distribution of moose and elk in Elk Island National Park, Alberta. *Canadian Field Naturalist* 96, 69–78.

Finder, R.A., Roseberry, J.L. and Woolf, A. (1999) Site and landscape conditions at white-tailed deer/ vehicle collision locations in Illinois. *Landscape and Urban Planning* 44, 77–85.

Foin, T.C., Garton, E.O., Bowen, C.W., Everingham, J.M., Schulta, R.O. and Holton, B. Jr (1977) Quantitative studies of visitor impacts on environments of Yosemite National park, California, and their implications for park management policy. *Journal of Environmental Management* 5, 1–22.

Ford, R.G. and Pitelka, F.A. (1984) Resource limitation in populations of the California vole. *Ecology* 65, 122–136.

Foster, M.L. and Humphrey, S.R. (1995) Use of highway underpasses by Florida panthers and other wildlife. *Wildlife Society Bulletin* 23, 95–100.

Fox, A. (1982) Conservation vs. recreation: national parks at the crossroads. *Australian Science Magazine* (Apr/May/June), 16–19.

Freddy, D.J., Bronaugh, W.M. and Fowler, M.C. (1986) Responses of mule deer to disturbance by persons afoot and snowmobiles. *Wildlife Society Bulletin* 14, 63–68.

Gabrielsen, G.W. and Smith, E.N. (1995) Physiological responses of wildlife to disturbance. In: Knight, R.L. and Gutzwiller, K.J. (eds) *Wildlife and Recreationists: Coexistence Through Management and Research*. Island Press, Washington, DC.

Gander, H. and Ingold, P. (1997) Reactions of male alpine chamois *Rupicapra r. rupicapra* to hikers, joggers and mountainbikers. *Biological Conservation* 79, 107–111.

Garber, S.D. and Burger, J. (1995) A 20-yr study documenting the relationship between turtle decline and human recreation. *Ecological Applications* 5, 1151–1162.

Garton, E.O., Bowen, C.W. and Foin, T.C. (1977) The impact of visitors on small mammal communities of Yosemite national park. In: Foin, T.C. (ed.) *Visitor Impacts on National Parks: the Yosemite Ecological Impact Study*, Vol. 10. Institute of Ecology, University of California, pp. 44–50.

Gasaway, W.C., Stephenson, R.O., Davis, J.L., Sheperd, P.E.K. and Burris, O.E. (1983) Interrelationships of wolves, prey, and man in interior Alaska. *Wildlife Monographs* 84, 1–50.

Ghazanshahi, J., Huchel, T.D. and Devinny, J.S. (1983) Alteration of southern California rocky shore ecosystems by public recreational use. *Journal of Environmental Management* 16, 379–394.

Geist, V., Stemp, R.E. and Johnston, R.H. (1985) Heart rate telemetry in bighorn sheep as a means to investigate disturbances. In: Bayfield, N.G. and Barrow, G.C. (eds) *The Ecological Impact of Outdoor Recreation on Mountain Areas in Europe and North America*. Recreational Ecology Research Groups Report No. 9, Wye College, Wye, UK.

Gibeau, M.L. and Heuer, K. (1996) Effects of transportation corridors on large carnivores in the Bow River Valley, Alberta. In: Evink, G.L., Garrett, P., Zeigler, D. and Berry, J. (eds) *Trends in Addressing Transporation Related Wildlife Mortality*. State of Florida Department of Transport, Tallahassee, Florida.

Gilbert, B.S. and Krebs, C.J. (1981) Effects of extra food on *Peromyscus* and *Clethrionomys* populations in the southern Yukon Canada. *Oecologia* 51, 326–331.

Gill, J.A., Sutherland, W.J. and Watkinson, A.R. (1996) A method to quantify the effects of human disturbance on animal populations. *Journal of Applied Ecology* 33, 786–792.

Goltsman, M., Kruchenkova, E.P. and Macdonald, D.W. (1996) The Mednyi Arctic foxes: treating a population imperilled by disease. *Oryx* 30, 251–258.

Goodrich, J.M. and Berger, J. (1994) Winter recreation and hibernating black bears *Ursus americanus. Biological Conservation* 67, 105–110.

Goosem, M. (2000) Effects of tropical rainforest roads on small mammals: edge of effects in community composition. *Wildlife Research* 27, 151–163.

Graber, D. and White, M. (1978) Management of black bears and humans in Yosemite National Park. *California and Nevada Wildlife* 1978, 42–51.

Green, K. (2003) Altitudinal and temporal differences in the food of foxes (*Vulpes vulpes*) at alpine and subalpine altitudes in the Snowy Mountains. *Wildlife Research* 30, 245–253.

Green, R.J. and Catterall, C.P. (1998) The effects of forest clearing and regeneration on the fauna of Wivenhoe Park, southeast Queensland. *Wildlife Research* 25, 677–690.

Green, R.J. and Higginbottom, K. (2000) The effects of non-consumptive wildlife tourism on free-ranging wildlife: a review. *Pacific Conservation Biology* 6, 183–197.

Green, R.J. and Higginbottom, K. (2001) *The*

Negative Effects of Wildlife Tourism on Wildlife. Wildlife Tourism Research Report No. 5, Status Assessment of Wildlife Tourism in Australia Series. CRC for Sustainable Tourism, Gold Coast, Queensland, Australia.

Grieser-Johns, B. (1996) Responses of chimpanzees to habituation and tourism in the Kibale Forest, Uganda. *Biological Conservation* 18, 257–262.

Griffiths, M. and van Schaik, C.P. (1993) The impact of human traffic on the abundance and activity periods of Sumatran rainforest wildlife. *Conservation Biology* 7, 623–626.

Gunther, K.A. (1990) Visitor impact on grizzly bear activity in the Pelican Valley, Yellowstone National Park. *International Conference on Bear Research and Management* 8, 73–78.

Gunther, K. (1992) Changing problems in bear management: Yellowstone National Park twenty years after the dumps. In: *Proceedings of the Ninth Annual International Bear Conference, Missoula, Montana, February.*

Gunther, K.A., Beil, M.J. and Robison, H.L. (1998) Factors influencing the frequency of road killed wildlife in Yellowstone National Park. In: Evink, G.L., Garrett, P., Zeigler, D. and Berry, J. (eds) *Proceedings of the International Conference on Wildlife Ecology and Transportation.* State of Florida Department of Transportation, Tallahassee, Florida.

Gutzwiller, K.J. (1995) Recreational disturbance and wildlife communities. In: Knight, R.L. and Gutzwiller, K.J. (eds) *Wildlife and Recreationists: Coexistence through Management and Research.* Island Press, Washington, DC, pp. 169–182.

Hall, C.M. (1992) Tourism in Antarctica: activities, impacts and management. *Journal of Travel Research* 30, 2–10.

Hall, C. and Dearden, P. (1984) *The Impact of 'Non-consumptive' Recreation on Wildlife: an Annotated Bibliography.* Public Administration Series: Bibliography. Vance Bibliographies, Monticello, Illinois, p. 1485.

Hammitt, W.E. and Cole, D. (1987) *Wildlife Recreation: Ecology and Management.* John Wiley & Sons, New York, USA.

Hamr, J. (1988) Disturbance of behaviour of chamois in alpine tourist area of Austria. *Mountain Research and Development* 8, 65–73.

Harris, L.K., Krausman, P.R. and Shaw, W.W. (1995) Human attitudes and mountain sheep in a wilderness setting. *Wildlife Society Bulletin* 23, 66–72.

Harris, M.P. (1973) Evaluation of tourist impact and management in the Galapagos. *World Wildlife Fund, Yearbook 1973.* WWF, Morges, Switzerland, pp. 178–179.

Harrison, D.J. and Gilbert, J.R. (1985) Denning ecology and movements of coyotes in Maine during pup rearing. *Journal of Mammalogy* 66, 712–719.

Harvey, M.J. (1975) Endangered Chiroptera of the southeastern United States. In: *Proceedings of the Annual Conference of Southeastern Association of Game and Fishery Commission* 29, 429–433.

Harvey, M.J. (1980) Status of the endangered bats *Myotis sodalis, M. grisescens,* and *Plecotus townsendii tingens* in the southern Ozarks. In: Wilson, D.E. and Gardner, A.L. (eds) *Proceedings of the Fifth International Bat Research Conference.* Texas Tech Press, Lubbock, pp. 221–223.

Hecnar, S.J. and M'Closkey, R.T. (1998) Effects of human disturbance on five-lined skink, *Eumeces fasciatus,* abundance and distribution. *Biological Conservation* 85, 213–222.

Hellgren, E.C. and Vaughan, M.R. (1989) Demographic analysis of a black bear population in the Great Dismal Swamp. *Journal of Wildlife Management* 53, 969–977.

Hendee, J.C. and Dawson, C.P. (eds) (2002) *Wilderness Management,* 3rd edn. WILD Foundation and Fulcrum Publishing, Colorado.

Hendee, J.E. and Mattson, D.J. (2002) Wildlife in wilderness: a North American and international perspective. In: Hendee, J.C. and Dawson, C.P. (eds) *Wilderness Management,* 3rd edn. WILD Foundation and Fulcrum Publishing, Colorado, pp. 321–349.

Herrero, S. (1976) Conflicts between man and grizzly bears in the national parks of North America. *International Conference on Bear Research and Management* 3, 121–145.

Herrero, S. and Fleck, S. (1990) Injury to people inflicted by black, grizzly, or polar bears: recent trends and new insights. *International Conference on Bear Research and Management* 8, 25–32.

Hicks, L.L. and Elder, J.M. (1979) Human disturbance of Sierra Nevada bighorn sheep. *Journal of Wildlife Management* 43, 909–915.

Holroyd, J.C. (1967) Observations of Rocky Mountain goats on Mount Wardle, Kootenay National Park. *Canadian Field Naturalist* 81, 1–78.

Humphrey, S.R. (1978) Status, winter habitat, and management of the endangered Indiana bat, *Myotis sodalis. Florida Science* 41, 65–76,

Humphries, R.E., Smith, R.H. and Sibly, R.M. (1989) Effects of human disturbance on the welfare of park fallow deer. *Deer* 7, 458–463.

Ilich, I.P. and Haslett, J.R. (1994) Responses of assemblages of Orthoptera to management and use of ski slopes on upper sub-alpine meadows in the Austrian Alps. *Oecologia* 97, 470–474.

Ingold, P., Huber, B., Neuhaus, P., Mainini, B., Marbacher, H., Schnigrig-petrig, R. and Zeller, R. (1993) Tourism and sport in the alps – a serious problem for wildlife? *Revue Suisse de Zoologie* 100, 529–545.

Jacobs, M.J. and Schloeder, K.A. (1992) Managing brown bears and wilderness recreation on the Kenai Peninsula, Alaska, USA. *Environmental Management* 16, 249–254.

Jacobsen, T. and Kushlan, J.A. (1986) Alligators in natural areas: choosing conservation policies consistent with local objectives. *Biological Conservation* 36, 667–679.

Jeppesen, J.L. (1984) Human disturbance of roe deer and red deer: preliminary results. In: Sastamoiren, O., Hultman, S.G., Elerstioch, N. and Mattisson, L. (eds) *Multiple-use Forestry in the Scandinavian Countries*. Communication Institute Forests, pp. 113–118. (Cited in Liddle, 1997.)

Jeppesen, J.L. (1987a) Impact of human disturbance on home range, movements and activity of red deer (*Cervus elaphus*) in a Danish environment. *Danish Review of Game Biology* 13(2), 1–8.

Jeppesen, J.L. (1987b) The disturbing effects of orienteering and hunting on roe deer (*Capreolus capreolus*). *Danish Review of Game Biology*. 13(3), 1–24.

Jones, M.E. (2000) Road upgrade, road mortality and remedial measures: impacts on a population of eastern quolls and Tasmanian devils. *Wildlife Research* 27, 289–296.

Jope, K.L. (1985) Implications of grizzly bear habituation to hikers. *Wildlife Society Bulletin* 13, 32–37.

Joshua, J. and Johnsingh, J.T. (1994) Impact of biotic disturbances on the habitat and population of the endangered grizzled giant squirrel *Ratufa macroura* in South India. *Biological Conservation* 68, 29–34.

Kamal, K.B., Boug, A. and Brain, P.F. (1997) Effects of food provisioning on the behaviour of commensal hamadryas baboons, *Papio hamadryas*, at Al Hada Mountain in western Saudi Arabia. *Zoology in the Middle East* 14, 11–22.

Kasworm, W.F. and Manley, T.L. (1990) Road and trail influences on grizzly bears and black bears in northwest Montana. *Conference on International Bear Research and Management*. Vancouver, British Columbia, Canada, pp. 79–80.

Kelaher, B.P., Chapman, M.G. and Underwood, A.J. (1998a) Changes in benthic assemblages near boardwalks in temperate urban mangrove forests. *Journal of Experimental Marine Biology and Ecology* 228, 291–307.

Kelaher, B.P., Underwood, A.J. and Chapman, M.G. (1998b) Effect of boardwalks on the semaphore crab *Heloecius cordiformis* in temperate urban mangrove forests. *Journal of Experimental Marine Biology and Ecology* 227, 281–300.

Kilgo, J.C., Labisky, R.F. and Fritzen, D.E. (1998) Influences of hunting on the behavior of white-tailed deer: implications for conservation of the Florida panther. *Conservation Biology* 12, 1359–1364.

Knight, R.L. and Cole, D.N. (1995) Factors that influence wildlife responses to recreationists. In: Knight, R.L. and Gutzwiller, K.J. (eds) *Wildlife and Recreationists: Coexistence through Management and Research*. Island Press, Washington, DC, pp. 71–80.

Knight, R.L. and Gutzwiller, K.H. (1995) *Wildlife and Recreationists: Coexistence through Management and Research*. Island Press, Washington, DC.

Krausman, P.R. and Hervert, J.J. (1983) Mountain sheep responses to aerial surveys. *Wildlife Society Bulletin* 11, 372–375.

Krausman, P.R., Leopold, B.D. and Scarborough, D.L. (1986) Desert mule deer response to aircraft. *Wildlife Society Bulletin* 14, 68–70.

Krausman, P.R., Wallace, M.C., Hayes, C.L. and DeYoung, D.W. (1998) Effects of jet aircraft on mountain sheep. *Journal of Wildlife Management* 62, 1246–1254.

Larkin, R.P., Pater, L.L. and Tazik, D. (1996) *Effects of Military Noise on Wildlife: a Literature Review*. US Department of Commerce Washington, DC.

Layser, E.F. and Burke, T.E. (1973) Northern bog lemming and its unique habitat in north eastern Washington. *Murrelet* 54, 7–8.

Leslie, D.M.J. and Douglas, C.L. (1980) Human disturbance at water sources of bighorn sheep. *Wildlife Society Bulletin* 8, 284–290.

Lewis, D.M. (1986) Disturbance effects on elephants feeding: evidence for compression in Luangwa Valley, Zambia. *African Journal of Ecology* 24, 227–241.

Liddle, M.J. (1997) *Recreation Ecology: the Ecological Impact of Outdoor Recreation*. Kluwer Academic Publishers, Dordrecht, The Netherlands.

Lindenmayer, D. and Press, K. (1989) *Spotlighting Manual*. Australian Capital Territory Parks and Conservation Service, Canberra, Australia.

Lippold, L.K. (1990) Primate population decline at Cabo Blanco Absolute Nature Reserve, Costa Rica. *Brenesia*. 34, 145–152.

Lott, D.F. and McCoy, M. (1995) Asian rhinos *Rhinoceros unicornis* on the run? Impact of tourist visits on one population. *Biological Conservation* 73, 23–26.

Lovallo, M.J. and Anderson, E.M. (1996) Bobcat movements and home ranges relative to roads in Wisconsin. *Wildlife Society Bulletin* 24, 71–76.

MacArthur, R.A., Giest, V. and Johnston, R.H. (1982) Cardiac and behavioural responses of mountain sheep to human disturbance. *Journal of Wildlife Management* 46, 351–358.

Maier, J.A.K., Murphy, S.M., White, R.G. and Smith, M.D. (1998) Responses of caribou to overflights by low-altitude jet aircraft. *Journal of Wildlife Management* 62, 752–766.

Mainini, B., Neuhaus, P. and Ingold, P. (1993) Behaviour of marmots (*Marmota marmota*) under the influence of different hiking activities. *Biological Conservation* 64, 161–164.

Martín, J. and Salvador, A. (1995) Microhabitat selection by the Iberian rock lizard *Lacerta monticola*: effect on density and spatial distribution of individuals. *Biological Conservation* 79, 303–307.

Mattson, D.J. (1997) Wilderness-dependent wildlife: the large and the carnivorous. *International Journal of Wilderness* 3, 34–38.

Mattson, D.J., Knight, R.R. and Blanchard, B.M. (1987) Human impacts on bear habitat use. *International Conference on Bear Research and Management* 8, 33–56.

McCool, S.M. (1996) Wildlife viewing, natural area protection and community sustainability and resilience. *Natural Areas Journal* 16, 147–151.

McCullough, D.R. (1982) Behavior, bears and humans. *Wildlife Society Bulletin* 10, 27–33.

McLellan, B.N. (1989) Dynamics of a grizzly bear population during a period of industrial resource extraction. II. Mortality rates and causes of death. *Canadian Journal of Zoology* 67, 1861–1864.

McLellan, B.N. and Shackleton, D.M. (1988) Grizzly bears and resource extraction industries: effects of roads on behaviour, habitat use and climography. *Journal of Applied Ecology* 25, 451–460.

McLellan, B.N. and Shackleton, D.M. (1989) Immediate reactions of grizzly bears to human activities. *Wildlife Society Bulletin* 17, 269–274.

Mech, L.D., Fritts, S.H., Radde, G.L. and Paul, W.J. (1988) Wolf distribution and road density in Minnesota. *Wildlife Society Bulletin* 16, 85–87.

Merrill, E.H. (1978) Bear depredations at backcountry campgrounds in Glacier National Park. *Wildlife Society Bulletin* 6, 123–126.

Miller, F.L. and Gunn, A. (1979) *Responses of Peary Caribou and Muskoxen to Helicopter Harassment*. Canadian Wildlife Service Ontario Canada, Occasional Paper 40.

Moen, A.N. (1976) Energy conservation by white-tailed deer in the winter. *Ecology* 57, 192–198.

Newsome, D., Moore, S.A. and Dowling, R.K. (2001) *Natural Area Tourism: Ecology Impacts and Management*. Channel View, Clevedon, UK.

Novaro, A.J., Funes, M.C. and Walker, R.S. (2000) Ecological extinction of native prey of a carnivore assemblage in Argentine Patagonia. *Biological Conservation* 92, 25–33.

Oleary, H. and Fa, J.E. (1993) Effects of tourists on Barbary macaques at Gibraltar [review]. *Folia Primatologica* 61, 77–91.

Olson, T.L. and Gilbert, B.K. (1994) Variable impacts of people on habitat use, movements and activity of brown bears on an Alaskan river. *International Conference on Bear Research and Management* 9, 97–106.

Olson, T.L., Gilbert, B.K. and Squibb, R.C. (1997) The effects of increasing human activity on brown bear use of an Alaskan river. *Biological Conservation* 82, 95–99.

Ottichilo, W.K. (1987) The causes of the recent heavy elephant mortality in the Tsavo ecosystem, Kenya, 1975–80. *Biological Conservation* 41, 279–289.

Parent, C. and Weatherhead, P.J. (2000) Behavioral and life history responses of eastern massasauga rattlesnakes (*Sistrutus catenatus catenatus*) to human disturbance. *Oecologia* 125, 170–178.

Parker, A.H. and Witkowski, E.T.F. (1999) Long-term impacts of abundant perennial water provision for game on herbaceous vegetation in a semi-arid African savanna woodland. *Journal of Arid Environments* 41, 309–321.

Parker, K.L., Robbins, C.T. and Hanley, T.A. (1984) Energy expenditures for locomotion in mule deer and elk. *Journal of Wildlife Management* 48, 474–488.

Patterson, I.J. (1989) Responses of Apennine chamois to human disturbance. *Zeitschrift fur Saugetierk* 53, 245–252.

Pedevillano, C. and Wright, R.G. (1987) The influence of visitors on mountain goat activities in Glacier National Park, Montana. *Biological Conservation* 39, 1–11.

Pomerantz, G.A., Decker, D.J., Goff, G.R. and Ourdy, K.G. (1988) Assessing impact of recreation on wildlife: a classification scheme. *Wildlife Society Bulletin* 16, 58–62.

Potts, F.C., Goodwin, H. and Walpole, M.J. (1996) People, wildlife and tourism around Hwange National Park, Zimbabwe. In: Price, M.F. (ed.) *People and Tourism in Fragile Environments*. John Wiley & Sons, Chichester, UK, pp. 199–219.

Povey, A. and Keough, M.J. (1991) Effects of trampling on plant and animal populations on rocky shores. *Oikos* 61, 355–368.

Price, R. and Lent, P.C. (1972) Effects of human disturbance on Dall sheep. *Alaska Co-operative Wildlife Research Unit Quarterly Report* 23, 23–28.

Qui, M.J. (1996) Tiger–human conflict in southeastern Tibet. *Oryx* 30, 5–6.

Radle, A.L. (1999) The effect of noise on wildlife: a literature review. *World Forum for Acoustic Ecology*, University of Oregon, Eugene, Oregon.

Raman, T.R.S., Menon, R.K.G. and Sukumar, R. (1996) Ecology and management of chital and blackbuck in Guindy National Park, Madras. *Journal of the Bombay Natural History Society* 93, 178–192.

Reed, D.F., Woodard, T.M. and Pojar, T.M. (1975) Behavioral response to mule deer to a highway underpass. *Journal of Wildlife Management* 39, 361–367.

Roe, D., Leader-Williams, N. and Dalal-Clayton, B. (1997) *Take Only Photographs, Leave Only Footprints: the Environment Impacts of Wildlife Tourism*. IIED Wildlife and Development Series No. 10. International Institute for Environment and Development, London.

Ross, C., Srivastava, A. and Pirta, R.S. (1993) Human influences on the population density of Hanuman langurs *Presbytis entellus* and rhesus macaques *Macaca mulatta* in Shimla, India. *Biological Conservation* 65, 159–163.

Ruediger, B. (1998) Rare carnivores and highways – moving into the 21st century. In: Evink, G.L., Garrett, P., Zeigler, D. and Berry, J. (eds) *Proceedings of the International Conference on Wildlife Ecology and Transportation* (FL-ER-69-98). Florida Department of Transportation, Tallahassee, Florida, pp. 10–16.

Russell, C. and Enns, M. (2002) *Grizzly Heart*. Island Press, Washington, DC.

Schmid, W.D. (1970) Modification of the Sunivian microclimate by snow mobiles. In: Haugen, A.O. (ed.) *Proceedings, Symposium on Snow and Ice in Relation to Wildlife*. Iowa Co-operative Wildlife Research Unit, Iowa State University, USA, pp. 251–257.

Schneider, W. (1977) *Where the Grizzly Walks*. Mountain Press, Missoula, Montana.

Schultz, R.D. and Bailey, J.A. (1978) Responses of national park elk to human activity. *Journal of Wildlife Management* 42, 91–100.

Sennstam, B. and Stalfelt, F. (1976) Rapport angaende 1975 ars femdanger-sorienterings inverkan pa klouviltet. *Rapport* 12, 35.

Shackley, M. (1996) *Wildlife Tourism*. International Thomson Business Press, London.

Sheppe, W.A. (1985) Effects of human activities on Zambia's Kafue Flats ecosystems. *Environmental Conservation* 12(1), 49–57.

Sindiyo, D.M. and Pertet, F.N. (1984) Tourism and its impact on wildlife conservation in Kenya. *UNEP Industry and the Environment* January–March (a), 14–19.

Singer, F.J. (1978) Behaviour of mountain goats in relation to US Highway 2, Glacier National Park, Montana. *Journal of Wildlife Management* 42, 591–597.

Singer, F.J. and Bratton, S.P. (1980) Black bear/human conflicts in the Great Smoky Mountains National Park. In: Martinka, C.J. and McArthur, K.L. (eds) *Bears – Their Biology and Management*. IUCN Publication. New Series 40. IUCN, Giland Switzerland, pp. 137–139.

Singer, F.J. and Doherty, J.L. (1985) Managing mountain goats in a highway crossing. *Wildlife Society Bulletin* 13, 469–477.

Smith, N.S. and Krausman, P.R. (1988) Desert bighorn sheep: a guide to selected management practices. A literature review and synthesis including appendices on assessing condition, collecting blood, determining age, constructing water catchments and evaluating bighorn range. *US Fish Wildlife Service Biology Report* 88, 1–27.

Speakman, J.R., Webb, P.I. and Racey, P.A. (1991) Effects of disturbance on the energy expenditure of hibernating bats. *Journal of Applied Ecology* 1087–1104.

Stephenson, P.J. (1993a) The impacts of tourism on nature reserves in Madagascar – Perinet, a case-study. *Environmental Conservation* 20, 262–265.

Stephenson, P.J. (1993b) The small mammal fauna of Reserve Speciale Danalamazaotra, Madagascar – the effects of human disturbance on endemic species diversity. *Biodiversity and Conservation* 2, 603–615.

Stockwell, C.A., Bateman, G.C. and Berger, J. (1991) Conflicts in national parks: a case study of helicopters and bighorn sheep time budgets at the Grand Canyon. *Biological Conservation* 56, 317–328.

Stuart-Dick, R.I. (1987) Parental investment in the eastern grey kangaroo. PhD thesis, University of New England, Armidale, New South Wales.

Sukumar, R. (1991) The management of large mammals in relation to male strategies and conflict with people. *Biological Conservation* 55, 93–102.

Tewes, M.E. and Blanton, D.R. (1998) Potential impacts of international bridges on ocelots and jaguarundis along the Rio Grande wildlife corridor. In: Evink, G.L., Garrett, P., Zeigler, D. and Berry, J. (eds) *Proceedings of the International Conference on Wildlife Ecology and Transportation* (FL-ER-69-98). Florida Department of Transportation, Tallahassee, Florida, pp. 135–139.

Tewes, M.E. and Hughes, R.W. (2001) Ocelot management and conservation along transportation corridors in southern Texas. *Proceeding of the International Conference on Ecology and Transportation, 24–28 September, Keystone, Colorado,* pp. 559–564.

Thiel, R.P. (1985) Relationship between road densities and wolf habitat suitability of Wisconsin. *American Midland Naturalist* 113, 404–407.

Titus, K., Trent, J.N., Aumiller, L.D., Westlund, J.H. and Sigman, M. (1994) Managing brown bears as both game and nongame: past experience and future prospects. *Wildlife Management Institution of North American Wildlife and Natural Resource 59th Conference, Anchorage.*

Tracy, D.M. (1977) Reactions of wildlife to human activity along Mount McKinley National Park road. MS thesis, University of Alaska, Fairbanks.

Tuttle, M.D. (1979) Status, causes of decline, and management of endangered gray bats. *Journal Wildlife Management* 43, 1–17.

Van Dyke, F.G., Brocke, R.H. and Shaw, H.G. (1986) Use of road track counts as indices of mountain lion presence. *Journal of Wildlife Management* 50, 102–109.

Van Lavick-Goodall, H. and Van Lavick-Goodall, J. (1970) *Innocent Killers.* Collins, London.

Van Sickle, W.D. and Lindzey, F.G. (1992) Evaluation of road track survey for cougars (*Felis concolor*). *Great Basin Naturalist* 52, 232–236.

Von Petrak, M. (1988) Cross country skiing and red deer (*Cervus elephus* Linne 1758) in the Eifel. *Zeitschift fur Jagdwissenschaft.* 34, 105–114.

Wang, C. and Miko, P.S. (1997) Environmental impacts of tourism on US National Parks. *Journal of Travel Research* 35, 31–36.

Ward, A.L. (1973) Elk behaviour in relation to multiple use on the Medicine Bow National Forest. *Proceedings of the Annual Conference of the Western Association of the State Game and Fish Commissioners* [as cited in Liddle, 1997].

Ward, A.L. and Cupal, J.J. (1979) Telemetered heart rate of three elk as affected by activity and human disturbance. In: Dowling, K. (ed.) *Symposium on Dispersed Recreation and Natural Resource Management.* Utah State University, Logan, pp. 47–56.

Ward, A.L., Cupal, J.J., Lea, A.L., and Oakley, C.A. and Weeks, R.W. (1973) Elk behavior in relation to cattle grazing, forest recreation, and traffic. *Transactions of North American Wildlife and Natural Resources Conference* 39, 327–337.

Wathery, F.P. (1969) Flight behaviour and avoidance of predators in Thomson's gazelle (*Gazella thomsoni* Guenther 1884). *Behaviour* 34, 184–221.

Watson, A. (1979) Bird and mammal numbers in relation to human impacts at ski lifts on Scottish Hills. *Journal of Applied Ecology* 16, 753–764.

Weinberg, P.I., Valdez, R. and Fedosenko, A.K. (1997) Status of the Heptner's markhor (*Capra falconeri heptneri*) in Turkmenistan. *Journal of Mammalogy* 78, 826–829.

Weisenberger, M.E., Krausman, P.R., Wallace, M.C., Deyoung, D.W. and Maughan, O.E. (1996) Effects of simulated jet aircraft noise on heart rate and behavior of desert ungulates. *Journal of Wildlife Management* 60, 52–61.

White, D.H. and Seginak, J.T. (1987) Cave gate designs for use in protecting endangered bats. *Wildlife Society Bulletin* 15, 445–449.

White, D., Kendall, K.C. and Picton, H.D. (1999) Potential energetic effects of mountain climbers on foraging grizzly bears. *Wildlife Society Bulletin* 27, 146–151.

Whittaker, D. and Knight, R.L. (1998) Understanding wildlife responses to humans. *Wildlife Society Bulletin* 26, 312–317.

Wilson, R. (1999) Possums in the spotlight. *Nature Australia* Autumn, 35–41.

Woodall, P.F., Woodall, L.B. and Bodero, D.A.V. (1989) Daily activity patterns in captive elephant shrews (Macroscelididae). *African Journal of Ecology* 27, 63–76.

Wrangham, R.W. (1974) Artificial feeding of chimpanzees and baboons in their natural habitat. *Animal Behaviour* 22, 83–93.

Wynberg, R.P. and Branch, G.M. (1997) Trampling associated with bait-collection for sand prawns *Callianassa kraussi* Stebbing: effects on the biota of an intertidal sandflat. *Environmental Conservation* 24, 139–148.

Yalden, D.W. (1990) Recreational disturbance of large mammals in the Peak District. *Journal of Zoology, London* 221, 293–298.

Yanes, M., Velasco, J.M. and Suarez, F. (1995) Permeability of roads and railways to vertebrates: the importance of culverts. *Biological Conservation* 71, 217–222.

Zunino, F. and Herrero, S. (1972) The status of the brown bear (*Ursus arctos*) in Abruzzo National Park, Italy, 1971. *Biological Conservation* 4, 263–273.

13

Environmentally Sustainable Trail Management

Jeffrey L. Marion[1] and Yu-Fai Leung[2]

[1]Patuxent Wildlife Research Center, US Geological Survey, Virginia Tech/Forestry (0324), Blacksburg, Virginia, USA; [2]Parks, Recreation and Tourism Management, North Carolina State University, Raleigh, North Carolina, USA

Introduction

A trail system that facilitates access to remote ecotourism destinations, provides safe, high quality recreational experiences, and concentrates traffic on durable treads maintained to minimize resource degradation can only result from professional planning and management. This chapter outlines and reviews the essential ingredients of trail management programmes from a resource protection perspective. This begins with planning considerations for selecting and developing a sustainable system of trails, decision frameworks for balancing resource protection and recreation provision objectives, trail construction and maintenance, and visitor management. All aspects are considered important to avoid common trail impact problems, including unacceptable impacts from poorly located trails, deficient construction or trail maintenance, and lack of trail condition standards and monitoring.

In the absence of effective trail management, resource degradation along trails often occurs, ranging in both type and severity. Vegetation loss along the primary tread is generally expected but, in response to other trail impacts (e.g. muddiness or erosion), can extend to adjacent areas through trail widening and braiding. Compositional changes in trailside vegetation may also occur, including the introduction and spread of invasive exotic species.

Similarly, loss of organic litter and soil, and compaction of mineral soil, is generally expected on designated trails, but can extend to trailside areas or to alternative visitor-created paths when the main tread becomes degraded. Common problems include soil erosion that may expose rocks and roots or create deep rutting, and muddiness, including muddy treads and mud-holes with standing water. Trail widening and braiding generally follow – avoidable resource impacts that can substantially expand the cumulative spatial extent of disturbance. Other impacts include sedimentation of water resources (Fig. 13.1) and disturbance of wildlife. More extensive reviews of these impacts and the trail degradation literature are provided by Cole (1987), Leung and Marion (1996, 2000), Liddle (1997), Hammitt and Cole (1998) and Newsome et al. (2002).

Trail Planning

The management of environmentally sustainable trails begins with preparation of a trail system plan that provides direction and guidance to all trail management decision-making. An exceptional trail plan should address four general topics: (i) management guidance, including goals, objectives and desired resource and social condition statements; (ii) identification of a decision-making framework, including

Fig. 13.1. Erosion of soil into a stream, Big South Fork National River and Recreation Area, USA.

indicators, standards, monitoring methods and alternative management actions; (iii) evaluation of existing trail resources in light of administrative and recreational needs intended for the trail system; and (iv) description of the actions and resources necessary to develop and manage the trail system (see Table 13.1). Developed for a World Heritage area, Tasmania Parks and Wildlife Service (1998) provides a good example of what a comprehensive trail management plan might include.

General planning guidance can be found by contacting major land management agencies, guidance specific to trails is provided by Flink and Olka (2000) for urban/suburban multiple-use trails, by Birchard and Proudman (2000) and Demrow and Salisbury (1998) for backcountry trails, and by Vogel (1982) for equestrian trails. An important step omitted in many trail plans is the specification of prescriptive management objectives and desired resource and social conditions for the trail system, generally by management zone (NPS, 1998). Application of zoning allows different classifications of guidance for social, physical and managerial settings and spatial segregation of conflicting uses (Forest Service, 1982). For example, zone 'x' will provide for low-intensity human-powered activities

on primitive trails with few facilities and pristine resource conditions, while zone 'y' will provide for high use, including equestrians, on designated routes with crushed stone (aggregate) surfacing, bridges for stream crossings, and allowance for greater levels of resource degradation. Comprehensive and specific desired condition statements provide improved management guidance, particularly for identifying the type and extent of trail development, justifying requests for additional resources, or need for controversial management actions.

Desired resource and social conditions can be sustained by employing planning and decision frameworks such as the Limits of Acceptable Change (LAC) (Stankey et al., 1985; NPS, 1997a,b; Farrell and Marion, 2002). These permit inclusion of indicators and standards of quality, and monitoring to gauge management success in achieving prescriptive objectives. Conditions that exceed management standards prompt an evaluation of the impact problem and selection and implementation of corrective actions (Anderson et al., 1998). Omitting this step and these frameworks greatly increases the subjectivity of management decisions and can permit a spiralling decline in social and resource conditions beyond acceptable levels.

Table 13.1. Elements of a potential trail plan.

Goals, prescriptive objectives, and specific desired resource and social condition statements for the trail system and zones related to recreational opportunities and resource conditions

Evaluation and specification of appropriate recreational opportunities

Incorporation/description of a decision-making framework to guide and justify management actions

Identification of indicators, standards and monitoring protocols needed to sustain high-quality resource conditions and recreational experiences. Description of alternative management actions that may be applied to achieve desired conditions

Inventory of existing trails and roads for their suitability to sustain intended types and amounts of uses. Consider management zoning; environmental sensitivity; recreational and administrative needs; distribution, design and condition of existing trails; and facility/maintenance features

Evaluation of proposed uses in relation to the existing network, to identify deficiencies. Description of the actions and resources necessary to address deficiencies (e.g. new trail construction, reconstruction, relocations) and to manage the proposed trail system (e.g. support trail maintenance and visitor management)

Trail standards specifying the general level of trail development, including tread widths, substrates, grades, difficulty, maintenance features, and corridor width and height

An exceptional trail is almost always the result of good planning, one designed to meet the specific requirements of its intended types and amounts of recreational uses, level of difficulty, and physical characteristics of the land (Hesselbarth and Vachowski, 2000). Unfortunately, most protected area managers inherit a trail system opportunistically patched together from a network of old roads and trails with varied origins and purposes. Many trails were visitor-created, others were constructed for logging, fire fighting, or to provide vehicular access to remote locations. Few were designed as recreational trails, and most were probably not carefully planned and constructed to sustain high use, limit resource degradation, or

fulfil recreation objectives (Leung and Marion, 1996). Furthermore, managers often find they have more trails than are truly needed or that can be maintained in acceptable condition.

These issues are best addressed through a trail system assessment process, conducted to evaluate existing trails for suitability and retention in a formal trail system. We suggest a three-tiered approach, beginning with a fatal flaw analysis to omit trail segments that are inherently harmful to natural or cultural resource protection. This evaluation is designed to identify trails that could threaten sensitive flora, fauna, cultural/historic sites, contain significant degradation requiring expensive re-routes or reconstruction work, or include significant public safety hazards. Next, trail suitability can be evaluated from an array of perspectives, including needs for administrative and public access to backcountry features and locations, and recreational objectives for different zones and visitor activities. Finally, ground-based technical assessments of trail suitability based on existing trail locations, construction methods, maintenance and resource conditions can identify those trails most able to sustain heavy recreational traffic with limited maintenance.

Trails found to be unsuitable from such reviews may be unnecessary, while others will require re-routeing, reconstruction, or maintenance to be included in a formal trail system. In spite of the controversial nature of such decisions, we emphasize that closing trails that threaten resource protection objectives, are unnecessary, highly degraded, unsafe, or unsuitable is more professionally responsible than leaving them open to continued use and degradation. Trails intended for inclusion within the system should not be reopened until needed re-routeing or reconstruction work is completed. A negative public response may even be useful in garnering additional funding to construct and maintain an improved trail system.

Trail Location and Design

Many trail impact problems are the result of poor planning and location rather than higher impacting types or amounts of use (Cole, 1987; Leung and Marion, 1996, 2000). Many trails have sections ranging from good to poor condition, yet each trail likely receives the same types and amounts of use. Thus, problems like muddy soils or eroded treads are primarily a function of trail routeings through wet soils or up steep slopes. Applying tread reconstruction and maintenance solutions to such problems can be expensive, effective for only a short time, and give the trail a more 'developed' appearance that can alter the nature of recreational experiences. Short trail re-routes or larger relocations are a more effective long-term solution for sustaining traffic while minimizing resource impacts and maintenance. The following topics highlight some important trail location and design considerations to promote sustainable trail development.

Trail grade

An important goal of trail layout and design is to minimize the number of tread structures (e.g. drainage features, steps, tread armouring) and tread maintenance (Birchard and Proudman, 2000). The most important design specification for limiting soil erosion is keeping trail grades below 10% (Hooper, 1988) or 12% (Agate, 1996; Hesselbarth and Vachowski, 2000). A design grade of less than 9% is recommended for equestrian trails (Vogel, 1982). Crushed stone (aggregate) will migrate downslope at unacceptable rates when applied to trail grades over 8% (The Footpath Trust, 1999). Trail segments with steeper grades should be re-routed wherever possible, particularly those receiving moderate to heavy use. When topographic features prohibit relocation, more extensive tread work, involving steps, drainage and armouring with rock (stone pitching), will be essential to prevent excessive erosion.

Slope alignment angle

The orientation of the trail to the prevailing slope, termed slope alignment angle, determines the ease with which water can be removed from a trail (Leung and Marion, 1996). Trails that directly ascend a slope have a low slope alignment angle (irrespective of trail grade) and will be difficult or impossible to

Fig. 13.2. It is impossible to drain water out of this entrenched trail in Zion National Park, USA, due to its low slope alignment angle. Re-routeing is recommended to avoid the need for extensive tread work involving erosion control measures and steps on the existing alignment.

drain water from if they become incised (Fig. 13.2). Re-routeing these sections is generally the most effective long-term solution. Sidehill trails on the contour or at oblique orientations (45–90°) are easily drained to minimize muddiness and erosion, and their steeper sideslopes confine use to a narrow tread.

Stream crossings

A good trail design will minimize the number of stream crossings and carefully plan the locations where crossings are necessary. Trails approaching stream crossings often directly descend steep slopes and are prone to erosion, the sediments from which can drain into streams (Fig. 13.1). The employment of a sidehill design across slopes permits control of trail grades and drainage. Adequate tread drainage in the vicinity of streams prevents the buildup of larger, more erosive volumes of water. Tread outsloping is a recommended tread drainage method near streams, because runoff is slowed and evenly distributed, allowing adjacent organic litter and vegetation to filter out soil particles before reaching streams. Bridges are also critical resource protection facilities on horse and motorized trails, uses that are more apt to loosen tread soils, making them more susceptible to erosion.

Soil type/limitations

Soil properties, including soil wetness, texture, structure and depth, influence the ability of soil to withstand a given type and amount of traffic (Demrow and Salisbury, 1998; Scottish Natural Heritage, 2000). Avoid soils that are seasonally wet and poorly drained, or be prepared to employ trail construction techniques such as boardwalks, turnpikes, causeways, puncheon or geosynthetics to sustain traffic and avoid muddiness (Hesselbarth and Vachowski, 2000). Loam and sandy-loam soils, because of their even mixture of silt, clay and sand, provide the fewest limitations for trails (Demrow and Salisbury, 1998; Hammitt and Cole, 1998). Removal of organic litter and soils during trail construction to expose underlying mineral soil creates a more durable tread, less prone to muddiness. Rock and gravel in the mineral soil further strengthens them to support heavy traffic while resisting erosion and muddiness. Where possible, avoid soils high in silt and clay, which become muddy when wet, or cracked and dusty when dry.

Soil depth to bedrock of greater than 1 m is preferred – shallower soils may become saturated and subject to muddiness. Extremely thin soils in alpine terrain are easily eroded, so contain traffic on clearly marked treads (Demrow and Salisbury, 1998). Repeated traffic will alter soil structure, compressing the arrangement of soil aggregates and decreasing air and water infiltration (Pritchett, 1979). However, compacted treads provide a more stable and resistant surface, which sheds water to resist muddiness and minimizes the potential for soil erosion.

Sensitive resource considerations

The critical habitats of rare, threatened and endangered plants and animals, or sensitive resources, such as fragile vegetation, important wildlife habitat or irreplaceable archaeological or cultural sites, are best protected through their avoidance. Routeing trails away from such areas is preferable, unless they are an appropriate destination for visitors. In such cases, employing boardwalks and railings can protect resources while permitting visitor access.

Design for special uses

Special uses, particularly more impacting motorized or horse traffic, require special design considerations. These include, for example, tread surfacing with crushed stone (Fig. 13.3), wider trails and cleared trail corridors, a wider radius at turns, hitching posts, and staging areas for loading/unloading animals or equipment and parking trailers. Parking capacity can be limited to the capacity of the trail to sustain the planned types of uses. Refer to the following, more specialized references for further guidance (Vogel, 1982; Keller, 1991; McCoy and Stoner, 1991; Wernex, 1993).

Trail Construction

Sidehill trails

Trails with a high slope alignment angle (sidehill trails) are always the most preferred design (Birchard and Proudman, 2000) (Fig. 13.3b). A properly constructed sidehill trail design allows the greatest control over trail grades and effectively minimizes the most common and significant trail degradation problems: tread erosion, muddiness, widening, and secondary treads (Agate, 1996; Demrow and Salisbury, 1998; Birchard and Proudman, 2000; Hesselbarth and Vachowski, 2000). However, sidehill construction is more difficult, particularly on steep slopes. The amount of excavation on slopes greater than 50% is considerable and treads will slump or erode unless shored up with retaining walls (Birchard and Proudman, 2000). Regardless, the benefits of avoiding or minimizing future

(a)   (b)

Fig. 13.3. (a) Extensive rockwork and application of gravel are employed to sustain traffic in reconstructing this highly used trail at Acadia National Park, USA. (b) While gravel can be visually obtrusive when initially applied, over time it sinks in and combines with soil to produce the highly resistant tread shown on this trail in Shenandoah National Park, USA.

resource degradation and the cumulative costs of repetitive short-term maintenance clearly make sidehill trails the preferred design for resource protection and sustainable use.

Sidehill trail construction requires excavating the trailbed into the slope to create a gently outsloped bench. A trail crossing slopes up to 10% may require only the removal of organic litter and soils to expose mineral soil, which will remain drier and is more resistant to traffic than organic materials. Sideslopes of 10–30% can employ a half-bench design, where half the tread rests on original mineral soil exposed by excavation and half is on compacted mineral soil dug from upslope (Hesselbarth and Vachowski, 2000). A three-quarter or full-bench construction will be more sustainable and is preferred, particularly on slopes above 30%.

Outsloping treads 5% (2.5 cm drop for every 46 cm of width) during construction allows water to drain across and off the tread, rather than accumulate and run down the trail to erode soil (Hooper, 1988; Birchard and Proudman, 2000). However, natural processes and trail use eventually compromise tread outsloping, so additional measures are needed to remove water from treads. The most effective and sustainable method for removing water from trails is the Coweeta or grade dip, also known as terrain dips or rolling grade dips (Birchard and Proudman, 2000; Hesselbarth and Vachowski, 2000). These are constructed by reversing the trail's grade periodically to force all water off the tread. These must be planned during initial construction so that a descending trail's grade levels off and ascends for 3–5 m before resuming its descent. A sufficient frequency of grade dips, particularly on steeper trail grades and in mid-slope positions, is necessary to prevent the accumulation of sufficient water to erode tread surfaces. Additional methods for removing water on previously constructed trails are described under Trail Maintenance.

Techniques for wet soils

Areas with wet soils require more expensive initial construction and continuing maintenance and should be avoided whenever possible. When wet soils do need to be traversed, large stepping stones are a preferred method for short stretches, including small stream crossings. Constructing parallel drainage ditches can also be effective by draining water away from tread soils. More expensive options include turnpike and puncheon construction, which elevate the trail above wet ground. A turnpike is constructed by placing mineral soil excavated from two parallel trailside ditches between rows of rot-resistant logs or rocks (Steinholtz and Vachowski, 2001). Geosynthetics (described in a following section) can be used under the fill material or to encapsulate gravel or rock to improve drainage and trafficability (Monlux and Vachowski, 2000). Puncheons are elevated wooden walkways ranging from primitive bog bridging (Demrow and Salisbury, 1998) to more elaborate structures with wooden stringers and decking (Steinholtz and Vachowski, 2001). Puncheon has much higher initial and recurring costs, so it is generally used only in locations where suitable mineral soil or gravel is unavailable for turnpike construction (Birchard and Proudman, 2000). Puncheon must also be well-anchored in areas prone to flooding and may burn during dry season forest fires. More elaborate elevated boardwalks and bridges are required when deeper water or ravines must be traversed (Steinholtz and Vachowski, 2001).

Tread hardening

A number of tread-hardening techniques may also be employed during original trail construction or during subsequent reconstruction and maintenance. Wet soils can be capped with crushed stone or excavated and replaced with crushed stone or other suitable fill material (Meyer, 2002). Large stones are often used to form a stable base in wet soils, often capped with crushed stone and 'crusher fines'

or 'whin dust' (screened material less than 6 mm) to provide a smoother tread surface that can be periodically hand or machine graded (Scottish Natural Heritage, 2000). In Scotland, aggregate placed on top of geosynthetics has been used to effectively 'float' trails over deep peat substrates (Bayfield and Aitken, 1992; The Footpath Trust, 1999). Even soils that are not seasonally wet may require capping with crushed stone to create a tread surface capable of sustaining heavy horse or motorized traffic.

Special measures are required when trails must be constructed with grades over 10%. Wood or rock staircases (Fig. 13.4) and features for removing water from trail treads are critical. Regardless of construction materials, steps must be stout, well-anchored and immobile to sustain heavy traffic. Broken rock makes the most suitable fill material above steps, as angular edges interlock yet allow drainage, providing a stable base for soil or crushed stone tread substrates. Water must be removed from treads quickly to prevent its buildup and erosive force. Outsloped treads, or alternating steps with water bars, are two common methods. Trails with low slope alignment angles must have extensive rockwork armouring with little exposed soil, or severe erosion is inevitable.

Other options for steep slopes include aggregate with rock anchors positioned flush with the path surface to prevent the downward migration of gravel (The Footpath Trust, 1999). Rounded (natural) gravel has little cohesion, requiring closely spaced anchors and limiting its application on steeper grades. Angular crushed stone with crusher fines included contains a mix of particle sizes that pack tightly to form a hard, durable surface when dry (Fig. 13.3a). With a sufficient number of stone anchors and adequate drainage, crushed stone can be applied to slopes up to 16% (Bayfield and Aitken, 1992; The Footpath Trust, 1999). Stone-pitched paths, consisting of well-anchored rockwork across the entire tread surface, are another alternative for steep slopes (The Footpath Trust, 1999). Additional options for exceptionally steep pitches include crib ladders, pinned rock or wooden steps, log ladders, and even wooden staircases constructed from dimensional lumber (Demrow and Salisbury, 1998).

(a)

(b)

Fig. 13.4. (a) A rock staircase was constructed to replace several damaging and eroded visitor-created trails on these Mayan ruins at Altun Ha, Belize. (b) A wooden staircase prevents erosion while permitting access to a waterfall at the Monteverde Cloud Forest Reserve, Costa Rica.

Geosynthetics

Monlux and Vachowski (2000) and Bayfield and Aitken (1992) describe a diverse array of geosynthetics that are available to enhance the effectiveness of construction methods and reduce the amount of fill material needed:

- Geotextiles – construction fabrics made from long-lasting synthetic fibres, primarily used for separation and reinforcement. They

support loads through tensile strength and allow water, but not soil, to pass through.

- Geonets – composite materials with a thin polyethylene drainage core sandwiched between geotextile layers. These can provide separation, reinforcement and drainage.

- Sheet drains – similar to geonets but more rigid and with a wider egg-crate shape to enhance drainage. Less fill is needed due to their greater rigidity.

Fig. 13.5. Geosynthetics are applied on this trail in the Daniel Boone National Forest, USA, to improve trafficability for all-terrain vehicles and horses.

- Geogrids – polyethylene sheeting configured into an open grid with high tensile strength. They are used for reinforcement and often placed on top of a layer of geotextile to provide separation.
- Geocells – polyethylene strips bonded together to make a three-dimensional honeycomb structure. Fill material placed within the cells stabilizes and reinforces soil by confining substrates in cells to prevent lateral movement.
- Turf reinforcement – semi-rigid three-dimensional products designed for installation at or near the soil surface to reinforce vegetation mats and increase resistance to shear stress. These 'wear-and-carry' surfaces can be used in porous pavement systems.

Geosynthetics are particularly effective in increasing the trafficability of treads in wet soils (Fig. 13.5) (Meyer, 2002). Due to their tensile strength and/or rigidity, these materials increase the substrate's load bearing capacity by distributing loads over a larger area (Meyer, 2002). Geosynthetics are also available for limiting erosion on steep slopes, though none were found

that are specifically designed or recommended for supporting trail traffic. Two-dimensional natural fibre and synthetic mats can be applied over soil to retard erosion and enhance vegetative growth. Three-dimensional geosynthetics can be filled with soil to stabilize and reinforce steep slopes and protect vegetative growth. Experimentation and research is needed to evaluate the efficacy of alternative geosynthetics employed to stabilize recreational trail surfaces with grades in excess of 8%. Regardless, the high cost of geosynthetics will generally restrict their use to problem areas where other practices have been ineffective.

Reinforcing/augmenting soil structure

Materials can also be added to existing tread substrates to improve their engineering characteristics (Bayfield and Aitken, 1992; Meyer, 2002). Chemical binders are commercial liquid concentrates formulated to increase the density, cementation, moisture resistance, bearing and shear strength, and stability of compacted earth materials. These include organic products (e.g. Road Oyl, Stabilizer), and latex polymer products (e.g. PolyPavement, Soil Sement) (Bergmann, 1995; Meyer, 2002). Physical binders are fine-textured native soils that can be mixed with coarsely textured aggregate to fill voids and help 'bed' the larger material. Examples include Bentonite, a natural clay material, and class C Flyash, a powdery by-product from coal combustion, containing quicklime, that reacts chemically to cement soil or crushed stone particles.

Trail Maintenance

Trail maintenance work addresses post-construction trail management needs – from routine maintenance to the resolution of severely degraded treads. First, analyse and understand the root cause of existing problems, such as perennially wet soils, low slope alignment angles, steep grades, lack of tread drainage features, or heavy traffic (Bayfield and Aitken, 1992). Take a long-term perspective and consider whether the trail should be relocated to avoid future degradation and repetitive high maintenance, or if tread reconstruction, drainage work or hardening will suffice. Options such as seasonal or type-of-use restrictions and controlled (restricted) use should also be considered (Meyer, 2002). Also recognize that resolving problems with wet soils, deeply incised treads, or uneven tread surfaces will likely also reduce associated problems with trail widening and braiding.

Tread shaping

Over time, trails will often lose their constructed cross-sectional 'shape' or 'profile'. Most trail treads are constructed with outsloped treads, but soil, rock and organic material generally accumulate along both sides of trails, causing water to run down the trail and erode tread substrates. Slough material on the up-slope side of the trail should be removed and the original outsloped tread surface should be re-established (Birchard and Proudman, 2000). Berm material on the downslope side should also be cleared when present, allowing water to more quickly move across and off the tread. Non-organic slough and berm material may be used to fill in eroded ruts, or over exposed roots and rocks. Some trails are insloped to a ditch and others, particularly in flat terrain, are crowned – re-establishing and maintaining these profiles are critical to removing the erosive effects of water from trails.

Treads may also creep downhill from their original alignments. Trail creep is caused by a natural tendency for trail users to travel the downslope edges of side-hill trails (Hesselbarth and Vachowski, 2000). Trails should be returned to their original alignments through side-hill tread reconstruction work and by the strategic placement of embedded anchor rocks on the downhill edges of trails. Trail users will seek to avoid the rocks, centring their use along the tread. Crib walls to support treads may be necessary for sections that traverse particularly steep slopes.

Tread shaping can also address problems with trail widening and development of multiple treads. Both problems generally occur in flatter terrain in places where woody trailside vegetation provides insufficient deterrence. Reshape treads to improve their trafficability while piling rocks and woody debris along braided treads to discourage further use and prevent erosion. Strategic, yet naturally appearing, guide rocks can also be embedded along trail edges, particularly adjacent to drainage features, to confine traffic to the designed tread width. Lining the tread with rock scree in alpine areas may appear artificial but will be more effective in containing traffic to a single narrow tread than a trail marked with cairns (Demrow and Salisbury, 1998). If such measures are ineffective, consider relocating the segment out of flat terrain where possible.

Surface water control

Two of the very worst trail problems, soil erosion and muddiness, are caused by water accumulating on trail treads. Water removal should be a top trail maintenance priority, one that cannot be deferred without the potential for suffering significant long-term and, possibly irreversible, trail degradation. Grade dips and tread outsloping are the best and most sustainable methods for water removal – both should be original design features and may be difficult to add during routine trail maintenance work (Hesselbarth and Vachowski, 2000). Subsequent trail maintenance seeks to enhance the ability of natural features, or to construct and maintain artificial features that divert water from tread surfaces. Natural features may be roots, rocks, or low points where water can be drained from the trail. Minor ditching at these sites can increase their ability to remove water. Some authors refer to these as 'bleeders' (Birchard and Proudman, 2000). Artificial tread drainage features include water bars and drainage dips, which are designed to intercept and drain water to the lower sides of trails.

Numerous authors provide guidance on the installation and maintenance of water bars and drainage dips (Agate, 1996; Demrow and Salisbury, 1998; Birchard and Proudman, 2000; Hesselbarth and Vachowski, 2000). The US Forest Service (1984, 1991) provides specifications for these installations and other trail construction techniques. Key considerations include their frequency, trail angle, size and stability. Water bars may be constructed of rock or wood, including a wheel-friendly design with a protruding flexible rubber strip bolted between buried treated lumber (Birkby, 1996). Drainage dips are shallow angled channels dug into the tread to drain water with an adjacent downslope berm of soil to increase their effectiveness and longevity. US Forest Service guidance specifies tread drainage frequencies based on trail grade and soil type; for example, every 30 m for loam soil at 6% grade, every 15 m for loam soil at 10% grade, and every 45 m for clay soil at 10% grade (Forest Service, 1991).

The angle at which water bars and drainage dips are installed relative to the trail alignment is also critical. An angle of 45–60° ensures that water will run off the trail with sufficient speed to carry its sediment load (Hesselbarth and Vachowski, 2000). Larger angles will cause water to pool first, dropping sediment loads and filling in drainage channels. Cleaning and reconstruction of tread drainage features must be done one to three times/year to maintain their effectiveness. Effective water bars must be of sufficient length to extend across the trail and be anchored beyond tread boundaries. This will discourage trail users and surface water from seeking to circumvent the drainage feature. For log water bars, a diameter of >6 inches (15.2 cm) allows 2–3 inches (5.1–7.6 cm) to be embedded, with sufficient above-ground material left to divert water from larger storm events. Stability is also critical, rock and wood water bars must be sufficiently anchored to sustain heavy traffic from hikers or horses.

Publications from England and Scotland (Agate, 1996; The Footpath Trust, 1999) place an emphasis on designing an integrated trail drainage system that includes off-path drainage with ditching, culverts and stone cross-drains or culverts, and on-path drainage with stone cross-drains, stone water bars, and Letts drains (bleeders). Though used less frequently, drainage ditches, check dams and culverts can be important elements of a water drainage and erosion control system. Their use is described best by Birkby (1996) Hesselbarth and Vachowski (2000), and Birchard and Proudman (2000).

Vegetation management

Sustained vegetation management efforts are essential to the utility, safety and natural condition of trail corridors. Annual vegetation clearing maintains an open and passable trail corridor. Hazard trees and tree falls can be hazardous to the safety of trail users and when not cleared, also promote trail widening and braiding. Proper vegetation clearing to design dimensions can centre and constrain traffic to a specified tread width. Management of exotic plant populations along trail corridors is also an increasing activity and concern in the USA.

Visitor Management

While natural processes can degrade trails that receive no use, visitor traffic breaks down protective vegetative and organic cover, exacerbates muddiness and increases tread susceptibility to soil erosion. Trail management therefore necessarily includes managing the type, amount, behaviour and timing of visitor use, to ensure resource protection. We provide a limited summary of this topic here and direct readers to more comprehensive treatments in

Table 13.2. Description and purpose for four trail survey methods.

Survey type	Description and purpose	Citations
Trail inventory	Document general physical attributes (e.g. location, lengths, trail features) and/or trail conditions	Cole (1983), Williams and Marion (1992)
Prescriptive work log	Identify tread deficiencies and prescribe engineering solutions to direct work crews and provide cost and staffing estimates	Williams and Marion (1992), Demrow and Salisbury (1998)
Trail condition monitoring	Systematic procedures for assessing trail conditions to monitor trends, understand trail degradation and assess efficacy of management actions	Cole (1983), Leung and Marion (1999), Marion and Leung (2001)
Use assessment	Assesses types and amounts of trail uses	Hollenhorst et al. (1992), Watson et al. (2000)

the literature: Manning (Chapter 16, this book), Cole *et al.* (1987), Anderson *et al.* (1998), Leung and Marion (2000), and Hendee and Dawson (2002).

Trampling research has shown that the majority of resource impact on trails, excepting construction, occurs with relatively low use levels (Cole, 1987; Leung and Marion, 2000). Above moderate-use levels, the per capita impact associated with increasing visitation diminishes substantially, so dispersing or restricting use to control trail impacts may be an ineffective management strategy. Some exceptions include higher impact types of use (e.g. horses or motorized uses) and trail use during wet seasons. For example, the substantially greater susceptibility of trails to muddiness and erosion during wet seasons has led some managers to issue wet-weather restrictions on all or certain types of trail uses.

Trail impact research has revealed the importance of numerous other factors that are as, or more, important than use level in determining trail conditions (Cole *et al.*, 1987; Leung and Marion, 1996). These include trail grade, slope alignment angle and construction and maintenance work, that are reviewed in this chapter, and rainfall, infiltration rates and vegetation type, that are not (see Leung and Marion, 1996).

Special management of visitor uses that have a greater potential to degrade trails is generally necessary to minimize resource impacts. For example, horse users may be restricted to a subset of trails specially selected, constructed and maintained to sustain that type of use (for further discussion see Chapter 5, this volume).

Higher-impacting visitor behaviours may also be modified to minimize impacts, through visitor education or regulation. Examples include Leave No Trace skills and ethics (http://www.LNT.org), educational messages that promote staying on and travelling down the centre of designated trails, or regulations prohibiting livestock grazing or requiring use of weed-free feed (Hendee and Dawson, 2002).

Educational or regulatory actions may also be implemented to avoid or lessen recreational conflicts or crowding (Anderson *et al.*, 1998). Conflicting uses may be separated by travel zone or trail, incompatible uses may be restricted or prohibited (Cole *et al.*, 1987). Similarly, amount of use on trails or within zones may be influenced or regulated to achieve different use levels, providing solitude in some areas and higher density use in others (Manning, 1999).

Trail Surveys: Maintenance Needs, Conditions and Use

Several types of trail surveys can yield information of value to trail managers, including basic trail inventories, prescriptive work logs, trail condition monitoring and use assessments (Table 13.2). The most basic of these is the trail system inventory, generally accomplished with a measuring wheel or global positioning system (GPS) unit to gather basic data about trail location, physical or maintenance attributes, and condition (Fig. 13.6a). A prescriptive work log survey can document the work and materials needed to address trail impacts or facility

Fig. 13.6. Trail surveyors employ a GPS unit to inventory trails (a), and trail condition assessment methods to document resource conditions (b) in Zion National Park, USA.

needs, but requires the expertise of an experienced trail maintainer. Monitoring surveys periodically apply standardized trail condition assessment procedures to document and track trail degradation (Fig. 13.6b). Carrying capacity decision frameworks require such data to evaluate indicator standards of quality. Use assessment surveys can provide information about visitor use on trails: types, amounts and spatial/ temporal distribution. All of these types of information can assist managers in professionalizing their trail planning, management and decision-making.

Conclusion

This chapter has reviewed trail impacts and management practices with an emphasis on professional trail planning and management. Trails able to sustain heavy tourism use will require planning, careful location and construction, visitor management, and an ongoing programme of maintenance. Successful trail management programmes require all of these elements. Trails that are poorly located will either require prohibitive development and maintenance to protect natural resources, or will quickly degrade to a state that is both difficult and unsafe for intended uses. Similar consequences will occur on trails that are properly located and constructed but that lack a sustained programme of maintenance and/or visitor management. And management of trail systems in the absence of decision frameworks with indicator standards and monitoring programmes run the risk of permitting long-term or irreversible degradation, unsafe use and a declining quality of visitor experiences.

Fortunately there is a substantial and growing literature on trail planning and management that can aid ecotourism and protected area managers in professionalizing their trail-management programmes. We sought to highlight the core attributes of an exceptional trail management programme and to introduce readers to available literature in this chapter. With the continued growth of tourism visitation worldwide, improved trail management is becoming critical at most high-use tourism destinations.

References

Agate, E. (1996) *Footpaths: a Practical Handbook*. British Trust for Conservation Volunteers. The Eastern Press Ltd, London.

Anderson, D.H., Lime, D.W. and Wang, T.L. (1998) *Maintaining the Quality of Park Resources and Visitor Experiences: a Handbook for Managers*. Publication TC-777. University of Minnesota, Department of Forest Resources, Cooperative Park Studies Unit, St Paul, Minnesota.

Bayfield, N.G. and Aitken, R. (1992) *Managing the Impacts of Recreation on Vegetation and Soils:*

a Review of Techniques. ITE Project T0 2050V1, Institute of Terrestrial Ecology, Brathens, Banchory, UK.

Bergmann, R. (1995) *Soil Stabilizer for Use on Universally Accessible Trails*. Publication 9523-1804-MTDC-P, USDA Forest Service, Technology and Development Program, Missoula, Montana.

Birchard, W. and Proudman, R.D. (2000) *Appalachian Trail Design, Construction, and Maintenance*, 2nd edn. Appalachian Trail Conference, Harpers Ferry, West Virginia.

Birkby, R.C. (1996) *Lightly on the Land: the SCA Trail-Building and Maintenance Manual*. Student Conservation Association, Inc. The Mountaineers, Seattle, Washington, DC.

Cole, D.N. (1983) *Assessing and Monitoring Backcountry Trail Conditions*. Research Paper INT-303, USDA Forest Service, Intermountain Forest and Range Experiment Station, Ogden, Utah.

Cole, D.N. (1987) Research on soil and vegetation in wilderness: a state-of-knowledge review. In: Lucas, R.C. (comp.) *Proceedings – National Wilderness Research Conference: Issues, State-of-Knowledge, Future Directions; Fort Collins, Colorado*. General Technical Report INT-220, USDA Forest Service, Intermountain Research Station, Ogden, Utah, pp. 135–177.

Cole, D.N., Petersen, M.E. and Lucas, R.C. (1987) *Managing Wilderness Recreation Use: Common Problems and Potential Solutions*. General Technical Report INT-230, USDA Forest Service, Intermountain Research Station, Ogden, Utah.

Demrow, C. and Salisbury, D. (1998) *The Complete Guide to Trail Building and Maintenance*, 3rd edn. Appalachian Mountain Club Books, Boston, Massachusetts.

Farrell, T.A. and Marion, J.L. (2002) The Protected Area Visitor Impact Management (PAVIM) Framework: a simplified process for making management decisions. *Journal of Sustainable Tourism* 10(1), 31–51.

Flink, C.A. and Olka, K. (2000) *Trails for the Twenty-first Century: Planning Design and Management Manual for Multi-Use Trails*, 2nd edn. Island Press, Washington, DC.

Footpath Trust (1999) *Upland Pathwork: Construction Standards for Scotland*. The Footpath Trust for the Path Industry Skills Group. Scottish Natural Heritage, Battleby, Redgorton, Perth, UK.

Forest Service (1982) *ROS Users Guide*. USDA Forest Service, Washington, DC.

Forest Service (1984) *Standard Specifications for Construction of Trails*. USDA Forest Service, Engineering Staff, Washington, DC.

Forest Service (1991) *Trails Management Handbook*. USDA Forest Service, Washington, DC.

Hammitt, W.E. and Cole, D.N. (1998) *Wildland Recreation: Ecology and Management*, 2nd edn. John Wiley & Sons, New York, USA.

Hendee, J. and Dawson, C.D. (2002) *Wilderness Management: Stewardship and Protection of Resources and Values*, 3rd edn. Fulcrum Publishing, Golden, Colorado.

Hesselbarth, W. and Vachowski, B. (2000) *Trail Construction and Maintenance Notebook*. Publication 0023-2839-MTDC-P, USDA Forest Service, Technology and Development Program, Missoula, Minnesota.

Hollenhorst, S.J., Whisman, S.A. and Ewert, A.W. (1992) *Monitoring Visitor Use in Backcountry and Wilderness: a Review of Methods*. General Technical Report PSW-GTR-134, USDA Forest Service, Pacific Southwest Research Station. Berkeley, California.

Hooper, L. (1988) *National Park Service Trails Management Handbook*. USDI National Park Service, Denver Service Center, Denver, Colorado.

Keller, K. (1991) *Mountain Bikes on Public Lands: a Managers Guide to the State of the Practice*. Bicycle Federation of America, Washington, DC, USA.

Leung, Y.-F. and Marion, J.L. (1996) Trail degradation as influenced by environmental factors: a state-of-the-knowledge review. *Journal of Soil and Water Conservation* 51(2), 130–136.

Leung, Y.-F. and Marion, J.L. (1999) Assessing trail conditions in protected areas: application of a problem assessment method in Great Smoky Mountains National Park, U.S.A. *Environmental Conservation* 26(4), 270–279.

Leung, Y.-F. and Marion, J.L. (2000) Recreation impacts and management in wilderness: a state-of-knowledge review. In: Cole, D.N. and others (eds) *Proceedings: Wilderness Science in a Time of Change*. Vol 5. *Wilderness Ecosystems, Threats, and Management, May 23-27, 1999, Missoula, Minnesota*. Proceedings RMRS-P-15-Vol-5, USDA Forest Service, Rocky Mountain Research Station, Ogden, Utah, pp. 23–48.

Liddle, M. (1997) *Recreation Ecology: the Ecological Impact of Outdoor Recreation and Ecotourism*. Chapman & Hall, London.

Manning, R. (1999) *Studies in Outdoor Recreation: Search and Research for Satisfaction*, 2nd edn. Oregon State University Press, Corvallis, Oregon.

Marion, J. and Leung, Y.-F. (2001) Trail resource impacts and an examination of alternative assessment techniques. *Journal of Park and Recreation Administration* 19(3), 17–37.

McCoy, M. and Stoner, M. (1991) *Mountain Bike*

Trails: Techniques for Design, Construction and Maintenance. Bikecentennial, Missoula, Minnesota.

Meyer, K.G. (2002) *Managing Degraded Off-highway Vehicle Trails in Wet, Unstable, and Sensitive Environments*. Publication 0223-2821-MTDC, USDA Forest Service, Technology and Development Program, Missoula, Minnesota.

Monlux, S. and Vachowski, B. (2000) *Geosynthetics for Trails in Wet Areas: 2000 Edition*. Publication 0023-2838-MTDC, USDA Forest Service, Technology and Development Program, Missoula, Minnesota.

National Park Service (1997a) *A Summary of the Visitor Experience and Resource Protection (VERP) Framework*. Publication NPS D-1214, USDI National Park Service, Denver Service Center, Denver, Colorado.

National Park Service (1997b) *The Visitor Experience and Resource Protection (VERP) Framework: a Handbook for Planners and Managers*. Publication No. NPS D-1215, USDI National Park Service, Denver Service Center, Denver, Colorado.

National Park Service (1998) *Director's Order 2 for Park Planning Sourcebook*. USDI, National Park Service, Washington, DC. Available at website http://planning.nps.gov/document/do2.pdf (verified 22 December 2003).

Newsome, D., Moore, S.A. and Dowling, R.K. (2002) *Natural Area Tourism: Ecology, Impacts and Management*. Channel View Publications, Clevedon, UK.

Pritchett, W.L. (1979) *Properties and Management of Forest Soils*. John Wiley & Sons, New York.

Scottish Natural Heritage (2000) *A Technical Guide to the Design and Construction of Lowland Recreation Routes*. Scottish Natural Heritage, Battleby, Redgorton, Perth, UK.

Stankey, G.H., Cole, D.N., Lucas, R.C., Petersen, M.E. and Frissell, S.S. (1985) *The Limits of Acceptable Change (LAC) System for Wilderness Planning*. General Technical Report INT-176, USDA Forest Service, Intermountain Forest and Range Experiment Station, Ogden, Utah.

Steinholtz, R.T. and Vachowski, B. (2001) *Wetland Trail Design and Construction*. Publication 0123-2833-MTDC, USDA Forest Service, Technology and Development Program, Missoula, Minnesota.

Tasmania Parks and Wildlife Service (1998) *Walking Track Management Strategy for the Tasmanian Wilderness World Heritage Area* (3 Vols). Tasmania Department of Environmental and Land Management, Parks and Wildlife Service, Hobart, Tasmania.

Vogel, C. (1982) *Trails Manual*, 2nd edn. Equestrian Trails, Sylmar, California.

Watson, A.E., Cole, D.N., Turner, D.L. and Reynolds, P.S. (2000) *Wilderness Recreation Use Estimation: a Handbook of Methods and Systems*. General Technical Report RMRS-GTR-56, USDA Forest Service, Rocky Mountain Research Station, Ogden, Utah.

Wernex, J. (1993) *Off-highway Motorcycle and ATV Trails: Guidelines for Design, Construction, Maintenance and User Satisfaction*, 2nd edn. American Motorcyclist Association, Westerville, Ohio.

Williams, P.B. and Marion, J.L. (1992) Trail inventory and assessment approaches applied to trail system planning at Delaware Water Gap National Recreation Area. In: Vander Stoep, G.A. (ed.) *Proceedings of the 1992 Northeastern Recreation Research Symposium, Saratoga Springs, NY*. General Technical Report NE-176, USDA Forest Service, Northeastern Forest Experiment Station, Broomall, Pennsylvania, pp. 80–83.

14

Managing Impacts of Camping

Yu-Fai Leung[1] and Jeffrey L. Marion[2]

[1]Parks, Recreation and Tourism Management, North Carolina State University, Raleigh, North Carolina, USA; [2]Patuxent Wildlife Research Center, US Geological Survey, Virginia Tech/Forestry (0324), Blacksburg, Virginia, USA

Introduction

Overnight accommodation is an essential element of ecotourism experiences in natural and protected areas. A wide variety of forms of ecotourism accommodation exist, ranging from primitive campsites to vernacular eco-lodges (Gardner, 2000). For developed or permanent accommodation structures such as eco-lodges and buildings, environmental impacts are primarily a result of facility construction and operations. In particular, site selection and construction, solid waste disposal and sewage treatment are often major environmental management issues (Tribe *et al.*, 2000; Mehta *et al.*, 2002). Impacts induced by visitor activities at these hardened sites are generally minimal. An area's management objectives and funding/staffing resources largely determine the appropriateness and feasibility of providing developed structures and facilities.

In contrast, environmental impacts at primitive campsites, car campgrounds or at primitive camping structures often result from visitor activities and behaviour associated with site creation and use, including the proliferation and expansion of disturbance at these sites, vegetative and soil impacts, pollution of water resources, and disturbance of wildlife. This chapter addresses management of resource impacts on overnight sites for ecotourists with no or minimal construction of permanent structures (hereafter referred to as 'campsites').

The Significance of Camping Impacts

Campsites play an important role in protecting natural resources while providing comfortable places for overnight visitation. Visitors often prefer that campsites be attractive, relatively accessible, close to water sources, have adequate space and flat surfaces for tents, a place to cook or have a campfire, and privacy from other visitors (Brunson and Shelby, 1990). In contrast, managers prefer that campsites be located on resistant surfaces away from water resources and other campsites (Marion *et al.*, 1993).

Camping-related impact problems frequently occur in areas that receive intensive camping activities. Common forms of impact include campsite proliferation (increasing number of sites), expansion of campsite size, tree damage, disturbance or loss of vegetation cover, degradation of soils and soil fauna, and improperly disposed human waste. These problems have been reported in both North American protected areas and ecotourism destinations (Obua, 1997; Zabinski and Gannon, 1997; Gajda *et al.*, 2000; Leung and Marion, 2000). In the USA, camping-related impacts are a major concern among national park managers (National Park Service, 2001). Compared to other types of human impact, the aggregate extent of campsite-related impacts are usually less than 1% of the total park area (Leung and Marion, 2000; Cole, 2002). Nevertheless, camping has the potential for generating

Table 14.1. Spatial and temporal approaches to managing campsite impacts (adapted from Leung and Marion, 1999).

Impact management strategy	Spatial approach	Temporal approach
I. Segregation/zoning	Match types and levels of camping use with resource capabilities in different locations	Match types and levels of camping use with resource capabilities in different seasons
II. Dispersal	Spread campsites and related activities across a large area to maintain low frequency of use per unit area	Spread camping use throughout the year to maintain low frequency of use per unit area
III. Containment	Concentrate campsites and related activities on a limited number of established or resistant locations	Concentrate camping use within a limited period of time throughout the year
IV. Configuration	Reduce unnecessary visitor impacts through judicious spatial arrangement of camping sites and facilities	Not applicable

substantial impacts to the environment due to the nature and high intensity of activities, such as trampling, campfires and firewood collection (Hammitt and Cole, 1998; Newsome et al., 2001). Campsite impacts also have social significance as ecotourists spend a substantial amount of time on and around campsites. A number of recent studies have also identified that degraded campsite conditions can diminish the quality of visitor experiences (Roggenbuck et al., 1993; Chin et al., 2000; Hillery et al., 2001).

Management Objectives and Decision Making

In order to manage campsite impacts effectively, management objectives must be clearly defined. Common protected area management objectives call for minimizing the aggregate spatial extent of inevitable ground disturbance associated with camping, particularly the loss of vegetation cover and organic materials which results in exposure of mineral soil. Common management problems associated with these objectives are campsite proliferation and campsite expansion. Other important management objectives include the avoidance of unnecessary or avoidable impacts, such as damage to trees and pollution of water resources. Common management problems

associated with these objectives include campfire-related impacts and improperly disposed human waste. Finally, management objectives frequently call for the provision of high-quality recreation experiences and social conditions. Thus, in addition to resource management concerns, managers seek to minimize camping-related problems with visitor crowding and conflicts (Parks Canada, 1992).

Camping management can be proactive or reactive. Proactive management seeks to minimize camping impact problems before they occur, by implementing a suite of actions, including judicious selection of campsites to proper site maintenance. In contrast, reactive management responds to problems after they occur, often when resource and social conditions at campsites have become unacceptable and difficult or expensive to rectify. Examples for such rectification include closure of heavily degraded campsites or relocation of poorly located sites.

Planning and decision-making frameworks, such as Limits of Acceptable Change (LAC) and Visitor Experience and Resource Protection (VERP), are useful mechanisms through which effective campsite impact management practices can be developed and implemented (McCool and Cole, 1997). More decision-making frameworks tailored for rural tourism settings and for protected areas in developing countries have been proposed

Fig. 14.1. A camping dispersal strategy can be implemented by encouraging visitors to select a previously unused site on durable surfaces, such as this dry, grassy site in the Jefferson National Forest, USA. A single night of use should not produce any visible disturbance 1 year later.

recently (Hall and McArthur, 1998; Tribe *et al.*, 2000; Farrell and Marion, 2002). These models share a great deal of similarities, particularly relating to iterative decision processes, definition of clear management objectives, identification of indicators, establishment of standards, and implementation of monitoring or audit programmes.

Campsite Impact Management Strategies

The diversity of campsite impact management strategies and actions has been reviewed (Newsome *et al.*, 2001). Strategies are referred to as broad approaches to management, while actions are specific measures taken to achieve a certain management strategy. Some common classifications of impact management strategies include site versus visitor management (Hammitt and Cole, 1998), dispersal versus containment (Cole, 1981), and macro- versus micro-techniques (Ryan, 2003). Leung and Marion (1999) organized various campsite management strategies into four primary types: segregation/zoning, dispersal, containment

and configuration. Table 14.1 provides a concise description of each strategy. Three of these strategies could be extended to the temporal dimension. Each strategy may be implemented using different actions for the entirety or portions of a protected area or destination (Anderson *et al.*, 1998). We focus our discussion on two primary strategies: campsite dispersal or campsite containment (Leung and Marion, 1999), since the debate of these two strategies has dominated the recreation ecology literature (Hammitt and Cole, 1998). Specifically we examine some effective management actions for addressing common camping impacts, such as site proliferation, site expansion, tree damage and human waste, under each of these two strategies.

Campsite Dispersal

One common approach to campsite impact management is to disperse ecotourists to a large number of campsites over the landscape, so that frequency of use on each site is so low that substantial impacts are avoided (Fig. 14.1). Conceptually, this approach can be applied to a

Fig. 14.2. The US Leave No Trace programme's educational practices direct visitors to 'Travel and Camp on Durable Surfaces'. Rocks and non-vegetated leaf litter provide a resistant location for cooking activities, to avoid intensive trampling disturbance.

temporal scale, with camping use being spread out throughout a year. There are a variety of ways by which a campsite dispersal strategy can be implemented (Hammitt and Cole, 1998; Leung and Marion, 1999). For example, campers can be educated to select a camping spot that shows no sign of previous camping use, or they can be required to camp beyond a certain distance from water bodies or trail corridors.

Successful implementation of the campsite dispersal strategy hinges on its assumptions, of which many, if not most, protected areas have difficulty meeting. These conditions include extremely low use, a sufficient area for large numbers of potential campsites, a highly tolerant and/or resilient environment, and the practice of minimum-impact outdoor ethics such as Leave No Trace (LNT) by visitors (http://www.LNT.org) (Fig. 14.2). Recreation ecology studies have shown that impacts could be modest if frequency of use is kept at an extremely low level within a resilient environment, in which site recovery can occur very quickly. Above low use levels, however, most resource impacts exhibit a curvilinear relationship with amount of use. In other words, substantial levels of resource impacts occur at low to moderate levels of use, while additional use

generates fewer cumulative impacts (Leung and Marion, 2000; Cole, 2002). This non-linear relationship acts against management success when a campsite dispersal strategy is applied.

The campsite dispersal strategy in its various forms was common among protected areas in North America, but it has proved to be ineffective in reducing camping impacts in most situations, due to the failure of meeting one or more of the above assumptions. Table 14.2 compares areal measures of campsite impact in a number of US protected areas with different management strategies. Unregulated and dispersed camping strategies tend to be ineffective at moderate to high use levels. Many protected areas have re-examined their campsite management practices and adopted containment and/or configuration strategies (Marion, 1995; Marion and Farrell, 2002).

Two additional factors of a successful dispersal strategy are effective management of campfires and human waste disposal. Due to the spatial extensiveness of visitor use under the dispersal strategy, campfires must be strictly controlled, either through a campfire ban or adoption of low-impact campfire practices. Such policies can minimize potential fire hazards and potential damage caused by firewood

Table 14.2. Campsite size and use statistics for selected park and wilderness areas (source: Marion and Farrell, 2002).

Area name and state	Campsite size (m^2) (mean/sum)[a]	Disturbed area (m^2)/ overnight stay[b]	Overnight visitors/ year	Camping policy	Citation
Isle Royale National Park, MI	68 16,539	0.35	46,625	Designated sites	Farrell and Marion (1997)
Apostle Islands National Lakeshore, WI	275 17,309	1.13	15,321	Designated	Smith (1998)
Boundary Waters Canoe Area Wilderness, MN	220 NA	NA	NA	Designated	Marion and Merriam (1985)
Great Smoky Mountains National Park, TN/NC	157 51,192	0.53	96,459	Designated areas	Marion and Leung (1997)
Delaware Water Gap National Recreation Area, PA/NJ – 1986	243 28,140	0.86	32,399	Designated areas	Marion (1994)
Delaware Water Gap National Recreation Area, PA/NJ – 1991[c]	165 14,020	0.43	33,184	Designated sites	Marion (1994)
Shenandoah National Park, VA	37 26,410	0.66	40,000	Dispersal	Williams and Marion (1995)
New River Gorge National River, WV	706 84,083	2.14	39,410	Unregulated	Marion (1990)
Jefferson National Forest Wildernesses, VA[d]	56 6,137	NA	NA	Unregulated	Leung and Marion (1995)
Eagle Cap Wilderness, OR	206 NA	NA	NA	Unregulated	Cole and Hall (1992)
Bob Marshall Wilderness, MT	315 NA	NA	NA	Unregulated	Cole and Hall (1992)

NA = Not available.
[a] Mean size and sum of all site sizes (survey was a census or near-census).
[b] Calculated by dividing the sum of site sizes for an area by its overnight stays for the year sites were monitored.
[c] Monitoring in 1991 followed several measures taken in 1987 to reduce campsite impacts.
[d] Including 11 wilderness areas, all of which receive low levels of use.

collection, fire site construction and the actual fire (Fig. 14.3).

Human waste disposal is another challenge, as the dispersal strategy encourages camping use on a large number of sites in remote areas. The cat-hole method for human waste disposal is usually suggested in suitable environment types, such as forested areas and mountains with sufficient soil depth (Meyer, 1994; Cilimburg *et al.*, 2000). Specific guidelines for the cat-hole method vary among ecosystem types, but it is generally recommended that human waste be buried in a 15–20 cm hole created at least 60 m from the closest water source. However, the cat-hole method is not suitable for environments with thin or no soils

or covered with snow (Hampton and Cole, 2003). In such environments human waste should be carried out. Such practices can be implemented by tour operators who provide portable toilets for their customers, or by visitors using commercially available personal waste disposal kits.

Campsite Containment

In contrast with the dispersal approach, a campsite containment strategy seeks to reduce the total extent of impacts by concentrating camping use to a small number of campsites, which receive a higher frequency of use.

Fig. 14.3. Campsite impacts such as tree damage are entirely avoidable if visitors use camping stoves or leave axes and saws at home and collect only dead and downed firewood.

Conceptually this approach can be applied to a temporal scale, with camping use being concentrated during specified seasons or times. This strategy, increasingly common in protected areas, is sometimes referred to as a 'honey-pot' or 'sacrifice area' approach (Ryan, 2003). This management strategy is targeted to resolve the problems associated with proliferating numbers of campsites and their expansion.

The effectiveness of the campsite containment strategy has been demonstrated in a substantial number of recreation ecology studies. In the Selway-Bitterroot Wilderness of Idaho, Spildie and others (2000) evaluated a confinement strategy for overnight camping involving packstock animals. They found that this strategy substantially reduced the areal disturbance of camping/packstock impacts, including tree scarring and mineral soil exposure (Spildie *et al.*, 2000). Similar success was reported by Marion (1995), who identified a 50% reduction

in areal disturbance by designating campsites and installation of fire grates.

The containment strategy can be implemented through different actions, such as education and information, regulations and provision of structures or facilities that serve as attractants for activity concentration (Fig. 14.4). A key element of the containment strategy is to minimize site proliferation. This problem can be resolved by adopting a designated or established site camping policy in which visitors are instructed or required to camp only on designated (posted) campsites or on pre-existing campsites. Education materials such as brochures and maps are useful in guiding visitors to appropriate sites. The amount of use, particularly during peak use periods, should be regulated, so that designated or established campsites can accommodate overnight visitation demand while avoiding creation or use of overflow sites.

Another key element of a successful containment strategy is to select campsite locations that are resistant to resource damage and site expansion (Fig. 14.5). As impacts to high-use campsites are inevitable, environmental resistance is more critical in site selection than resilience. Flat and dry ground near water and trails have been favourite locations for campsites, but these sites are also particularly vulnerable to resource and social impacts. Large, flat stream benches, gaps and ridge tops are common camping locations, but they do little to discourage site proliferation and expansion, and often encourage the development of dense clusters of sites that contribute to visitor crowding and conflicts. Table 14.3 provides an example of campsite selection criteria designed to minimize both resource and social impacts.

Distance regulations and/or site definition are often used to ensure activity concentration, addressing campsite expansion problems. For example, campers could be required to restrict camping activities within 7 m of a campsite post or sign. In addition to distance regulations, campsites can be developed with boundaries physically defined by wood logs or scree walls. Such visual cues often help to concentrate use within the physical boundaries (Johnson and Clark, 2000). Campsite expansion within car campgrounds can be restricted through site design and facilities, such as barriers and gravel

Fig. 14.4. A camping containment strategy can be implemented by carefully selecting designated campsites that will resist site expansion, such as this site in Glacier National Park, USA.

placed to identify a parking spot, and permanently anchored picnic tables and fire grates to enhance the spatial concentration of camping activities (Fig. 14.5b).

Natural topography may also be utilized to restrict campsite expansion. For instance, selection of sidehill positions for campsite development has proved to be effective in limiting the potential of site expansion. Marion and Farrell (2002) described how this method was applied in Isle Royale National Park in Michigan, USA. Small campsites were constructed in modestly sloping (10–15%) terrain, using standard cut-and-fill practices to create small benches for tenting and cooking areas. The cut-and-fill techniques are similar to those used for trail construction. Rock or rot-resistant logs can support fill material. Tent sites should be gently crowned to facilitate water drainage.

The containment strategy can be integrated with the spatial configuration strategy to enhance the spatial concentration of camping activities, particularly when new campsites are designed and constructed. By arranging campsites and access trails in an appropriate spatial layout, the problem of site proliferation, site expansion and social trail creation may be minimized since campers' activity patterns are

matched by the site layout (Fig. 14.6). The effectiveness of this integrated strategy hinges on the understanding of campers' needs and their activity patterns.

Campsites can be maintained to enhance and sustain their durability and their desirability to visitors. Marion and Sober (1987) illustrate several types of maintenance performed on campsites in Boundary Waters Canoe Areas Wilderness, Minnesota. Some of these measures include improving tent sites in core areas and closure/revegetation of unnecessary use areas. Such measures sustain the serviceability and attractiveness of the campsite to visitors, who are less likely to expand campsites or create additional sites (Marion and Sober, 1987). In Hollands Wood of New Forest, England, camping impacts on soil are ameliorated by rotavation and adding of topsoil (Johnson and Clark, 2000).

Under the containment strategy, managers should close campsites that are deemed unsuitable for ecological or social reasons, to avoid further use. While natural recovery of closed campsites would be ideal, assisted site restoration may be needed in less resilient environments such as alpine or desert zones. Recent research has evaluated rehabilitation

(a)

(b)

Fig. 14.5. Providing facilities, such as tenting platforms, in this primitive camping area (a) or designated parking spots and anchored picnic tables and fire rings in this car-accessible campsite (b), can help to attract and spatially concentrate visitor activities to reduce the areal extent of impact.

techniques, including compost amendments, seeding and soil scarification, for impacted campsites, with considerable success (Zabinski and Cole, 2000; Zabinski *et al.*, 2002).

There are some specific impact concerns associated with the containment strategy. For example, campfire-related impacts are of concern, since higher amounts of use on campsites are promoted. Firewood collection for campfires is more extensive in the proximity of campsites, and soil and vegetation damage due to fire effects can be more intensive (Bratton *et*

Table 14.3. Examples of campsite selection criteria recommended for designated and established site camping policies (source: Williams and Marion, 1995).

Points	Campsite selection criteria
	A. *Campsite location*
2	Campsite is located more than 800 m from a road or permanent building (other than trail shelters); 50 m from the formal trail or a shelter/hut, 30 m from another campsite
1	Campsite is located out of sight (during summer months) from the formal trail
1	Campsite is located out of sight (during summer months) from shelters/huts or other campsites
1	Campsite is located 30 m from any water source
	B. *Expansion potential*
2	Poor expansion potential: off-site areas are completely unsuitable for any expansion due to natural elements, such as topography, rockiness, dense vegetation, and/or poor drainage
1	Moderate expansion potential: off-site areas are moderately unsuitable for any expansion due to the factors listed above
−1	Good expansion potential: off-site areas are suitable for campsite expansion. Natural elements listed above provide no effective resistance to campsite expansion
	C. *Campsite slope*
2	Most campsite areas have gentle slopes (2–4%), or they can be easily created
	D. *Ground vegetation*
2	Ground vegetation around the campsite is predominantly grasses or sedges, as opposed to broad-leafed herbs, or off-site vegetation cover is very sparse (less than 20%)

al., 1982; Newmark and Nguye, 1991; Byers and Banskota, 1992; Hall and Farrell, 2001). The high frequency of use on concentrated campsites also necessitates the provision of toilet facilities to handle human waste. Additional information about campsite selection and development can be found in Fay *et al.* (1977), Leonard *et al.* (1981) and Gardner (2000).

Similar to the dispersal strategy, specific campfire management actions can be implemented to deal with this problem, ranging from campfire bans, to education and provision of fire grates. If campfires are allowed in a containment strategy, fire grills or rings can be anchored permanently at a resistant location to ensure activity concentration and avoid development of user-created fire sites. Table 14.4 illustrates common options for addressing this and other camping-related impacts, such as littering and human waste.

Impact Monitoring as a Management Tool

One useful approach to campsite impact management, regardless of the strategy chosen, is the establishment of straightforward, but consistent, monitoring or site review procedures (Leung and Marion, 2000; Tribe *et al.*, 2000). Monitoring programmes are particularly essential for sensitive, natural/pristine or protected zones with high conservation value (Fig. 14.7). When applied consistently over time, campsite impact monitoring programmes can detect impact trends and evaluate the effectiveness of management strategies and actions (Marion, 1995).

Monitoring techniques can range from simple ordinal-scale condition class systems (Frissell, 1978) to multiple-indicator systems with either ordinal ratings (Cole, 1983) or quantitative measurements (Marion, 1995; Smith and Newsome, 2002). Impact conditions can be portrayed by maps with the help of GIS to facilitate evaluation of patterns (Gajda *et al.*, 2000; Johnson and Clark 2000). Key elements of such programmes include identification of good indicator measures and development of useful and efficient field techniques. Indicator selection will inevitably vary, depending on the nature of the natural resources and uses in the area. Some common indicator measures applied in various settings include: campsite size, groundcover vegetation loss, exposure of bare soil, visitor-induced tree damage, and number of social trails connected to campsites (Newsome *et al.*, 2001). Monitoring data can be employed within a decision-making process (discussed previously) for an ecotourism destination, to evaluate

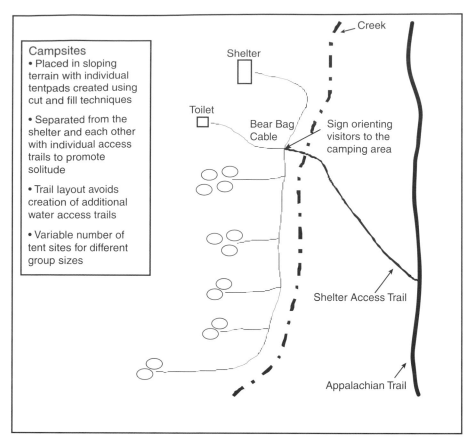

Fig. 14.6. Example of a preferred spatial arrangement of campsites and related facilities.

whether campsite conditions remain within acceptable limits.

Concluding Remarks

This chapter has reviewed campsite impacts, the need for defining management objectives and a decision-making process, some common campsite impact management strategies and actions, and monitoring as a management tool. A containment strategy is generally most effective and recommended, although dispersal can be effective in very low-use and highly resistant and resilient environments. Containment and dispersal strategies can also be integrated when applied to different management zones. Alternately, campsites can be located in a dispersed manner for social reasons, while visitor activ-

ities are spatially contained within each site to enhance resource protection. Similar to managing trails, effective campsite management also requires careful site selection and planning, and establishment of a systematic decision-making process that includes indicators, standards and monitoring/evaluation programmes.

With the growth of interest and participation in ecotourism, camping impacts and their management will inevitably become a more significant area of concern among ecotourism researchers and professionals. Recreation ecology research can provide immediate input to campsite management in ecotourism settings (Leung *et al.*, 2001). Unlike trail-impact research, campsite impacts have, until recently, received research attention almost exclusively from North America (Morin *et al.*, 1997; Smith

Table 14.4. Examples of management actions for specific camping-related impacts.

Camping-related impact	Visitor management measures	Site management measures
Campfires/firewood collection	• Campfire ban • Spatial restrictions on fire location • Permit only stove or portable grill fires • Prohibit firewood collection • Education: low-impact fire practices	• Provision of fire grates or grills
Litter	• Pack-it-in, pack-it-out regulations or education	• Provision of trash receptacles
Human waste	• Education: cat-hole techniques • Pack-it-in, pack-it-out regulations (e.g. portable toilets)	• Provision of toilets
Tree damage	• Prohibit axes, hatchets and saws • Prohibit campfires • Education: low-impact firewood-gathering practices	• Site location and design

Fig. 14.7. Field staff assess the condition of this campsite in Patagonia's Torres del Paine National Park, Chile, as part of a monitoring programme. Data are used to track long-term changes in site conditions and to establish and monitor standards of quality for resource conditions.

and Newsome, 2002). There is an urgent need for research on other ecosystems that are attracting ecotourists. Research is also needed for improving our understanding of social reasons of illegal site creation and other non-compliance to camping regulations or guidelines. Until an improved understanding of potential camping-related impacts is developed, it is preferable to adopt a precautionary principle and act conservatively in locating and developing campsites.

The need for efficient management sometimes tempts managers to adopt a 'quick' fix, often involving facility development or rest rotation. Rest rotation is rarely an effective management solution, because impacts occur quickly yet recover very slowly. Developing campsites with facilities and site-hardening practices can be a quick and effective solution, but this often entails irreversible changes to the environment and to the nature of ecotourist experiences. While highly developed camp-sites and car campgrounds may support more visitation, visitor experiences may be compro-mised. Therefore, consideration of an area's zoning and management objectives, and care-ful evaluation of camping impact problems, will ultimately lead to the most judicious solu-tions. Developed facilities are sometimes nec-essary when undeveloped or less-developed accommodation options are inappropriate due to environmental sensitivity. In such instances, managers should select and employ the most sustainable options in terms of design, con-struction, operations and maintenance.

References

Anderson, D.H., Lime, D.W. and Wang, T.L. (1998) *Maintaining the Quality of Park Resources and Visitor Experiences: a Handbook for Managers.* University of Minnesota, Department of Forest Resources, Cooperative Park Studie Unit, St Paul, Minnesota.

Bratton, S.P., Stromberg, L.L. and Harmon, M.E. (1982) Firewood-gathering impacts in back-country campsites in Great Smoky Mountains National Park. *Environmental Management* 6(1), 63–71.

Brunson, M. and Shelby, B. (1990) A hierarchy of campsite attributes in dispersed recreation set-tings. *Leisure Sciences* 12(2), 197–209.

Byers, A.C. and Banskota, K. (1992) Environmental impacts of backcountry tourism on three sides of Everest. In: Thorsell, J. (comp.) *World Heritage: Twenty Years Later.* IUCN, Gland, Switzerland, pp. 105–122.

Chin, C.L.M., Moore, S.A., Wallington, T.J. and Dowling, R.K. (2000) Ecotourism in Bako National Park, Borneo: Visitors' perspectives on environmental impacts and their management. *Journal of Sustainable Tourism* 8(1), 20–35.

Cilimburg, A., Monz, C.A. and Kehoe, S.K. (2000) Human waste disposal in wilderness: A review of problems, practices, and concerns. *Environmental Management* 25(6), 587–598.

Cole, D.N. (1981) Managing ecological impacts at wilderness campsites: an evaluation of tech-niques. *Journal of Forestry* 79(2), 86–89.

Cole, D.N. (1983) *Monitoring the Condition of Wilderness Campsites.* Research Paper INT-302,

USDA Forest Service, Intermountain Research Station, Ogden, Utah.

Cole, D.N. (2002) Ecological impacts of wilderness recreation and their management. In: Hendee, J.C. and Dawson, C.P. (eds) *Wilderness Management*, 3rd edn. Fulcrum Publishing, Golden, Colorado, USA, pp. 413–459.

Cole, D.N. and Hall, T.E. (1992) *Trends in Campsite Condition: Eagle Cap Wilderness, Bob Marshall Wilderness, and Grand Canyon National Park.* Research Paper INT-453, USDA Forest Service, Intermountain Research Station, Ogden, Utah.

Farrell, T.A. and Marion, J.L. (1997) *An Evaluation of Camping Impacts and Their Management at Isle Royale National Park.* Final Management Report, US Geological Survey, Virginia Tech Cooperative Park Studies Unit, Blacksburg, Virginia.

Farrell, T.A. and Marion, J.L. (2002) The Protected Area Visitor Impact Management (PAVIM) Framework: a simplified process for making management decisions. *Journal of Sustainable Tourism* 10(1), 31–51.

Fay, S.C., Rice, S.K. and Berg, S.P. (1977) *Guidelines for Design and Location of Overnight Backcountry Facilities.* USDA Forest Service, Northeastern Forest Experiment Station, Durham, New Hampshire, UK.

Frissell, S.S. (1978) Judging recreation impacts on wilderness campsites. *Journal of Forestry* 76(8), 481–483.

Gajda, A.M.T., Brown, J., Peregoodoff, G. and Bartier, P. (2000) Managing coastal recreation impacts and visitor experience using GIS. In: Cole, D.N., McCool, S.F., Borrie, W.T. and O'Loughlin, J. (comps) *Wilderness Science in a Time of Change Conference. Vol. 5. Wilderness Ecosystems, Threats, and Management.* USDA Forest Service, Rocky Mountain Research Station, Ogden, Utah, pp. 115–123.

Gardner, J. (2000) Accommodations. In: Weaver, D.B. (ed.) *The Encyclopedia of Ecotourism.* CAB International, Wallingford, UK, pp. 525–534.

Hall, C.M. and McArthur, S. (1998) *Integrated Heritage Management: Principles and Practices.* The Stationery Office, London.

Hall, T.E. and Farrell, T.A. (2001) Fuelwood depletion at wilderness campsites: extent and potential ecological significance. *Environmental Conser-vation* 28(3), 241–247.

Hammitt, W.E. and Cole, D.N. (1998) *Wildland Recreation: Ecology and Management*, 2nd edn. John Wiley & Sons, New York.

Hampton, B. and Cole, D. (2003) *Soft Paths: How to Enjoy the Wilderness without Harming It*, 3rd edn. Stackpole Books, Harrisburg, Pennsylvania.

Hillery, M., Nancarrow, B., Griffin, G. and Syme, G.

(2001) Tourist perception of environmental impact. *Annals of Tourism Research* 28(4), 853–867.

Johnson, D. and Clark, A. (2000) A review of ecology and camping requirements in the ancient woodlands of the New Forest, England. In: Font, X. and Tribe, J. (eds) *Forest Tourism and Recreation: Case Studies in Environmental Management.* CAB International, Wallingford, UK, pp. 93–102.

Leonard, R.E., Spencer, E.L. and Plumley, H.J. (1981) *Guidelines for Backcountry Facilities: Design and Maintenance.* Appalachian Mountain Club, Boston, Massachusetts.

Leung, Y.-F. and Marion, J.L. (1995) *A Survey of Campsite Conditions in Eleven Wilderness Areas of the Jefferson National Forest.* USDI National Biological Service, Virginia Tech Cooperative Park Studies Unit, Blacksburg, Virginia.

Leung, Y.-F. and Marion, J.L. (1999) Spatial strategies for managing visitor impacts in national parks. *Journal of Park and Recreation Administration* 17(4), 20–38.

Leung, Y.-F. and Marion, J.L. (2000) Recreation impacts and management in wilderness: a state-of-knowledge review. In: Cole, D.N., McCool, S.F., Borrie, W.T. and O'Loughlin, J. (comps) *Wilderness Science in a Time of Change Conference.* Vol. 5. *Wilderness Ecosystems, Threats, and Management.* USDA Forest Service, Rocky Mountain Research Station, Ogden, Utah, pp. 23–48.

Leung, Y.-F., Marion, J.L. and Farrell, T.A. (2001) The role of recreation ecology in sustainable tourism and ecotourism. In: McCool, S.F. and Moisey, R.N. (eds) *Tourism, Recreation and Sustainability: Linking Culture and Environment.* CAB International, Wallingford, UK, pp. 21–39.

Marion, J.L. (1990) *Inventory and Impact Monitoring of River Recreation Sites Within the New River Gorge.* Technical Report NPS/MAR/NRTR-90/047, USDI National Park Service, Mid-Atlantic Regional Office, Philadelphia, Pennsylvania.

Marion, J.L. (1994) *Changes in Campsite Condition: Results From Campsite Monitoring at Delaware Water Gap National Recreation Area.* Technical Report NPS/MARDEWA/NRTR-94/063, USDI National Park Service, Mid-Atlantic Region, Philadelphia, Pennsylvania.

Marion, J.L. (1995) Capabilities and management utility of recreation impact monitoring programs. *Environmental Management* 19(5), 763–771.

Marion, J.L. and Farrell, T.A. (2002) Management practices that concentrate visitor activities:

Camping impact management at Isle Royale National Park, USA. *Journal of Environmental Management* 66, 201-212.

Marion, J.L. and Leung, Y.-F. (1997) *An Assessment of Campsite Conditions in Great Smoky Mountains National Park.* Research/Resources Management Report, USDI National Park Service, Southeast Regional Office, Atlanta, Georgia.

Marion, J.L. and Merriam, L.C. (1985) *Recreational Impacts on Well-Established Campsites in the Boundary Waters Canoe Area Wilderness.* Station Bulletin AD-SB-2502, University of Minnesota, Agricultural Experiment Station, St Paul, Minnesota.

Marion, J.L. and Sober, T. (1987) Environmental impact management in the Boundary Waters Canoe Area Wilderness. *Northern Journal of Applied Forestry* 4(1), 7–10.

Marion, J.L., Roggenbuck, J.W. and Manning, R.E. (1993) *Problems and Practices in Backcountry Recreation Management: a Survey of National Park Service Managers.* Natural Resources Report NPS/NRVT/NRR-93/12, USDI National Park Service, Natural Resources Publication Office, Denver, Colorado.

McCool, S.F. and Cole, D.N. (comps) (1997) *Proceedings – Limits of Acceptable Change and Related Planning Processes: Progress and Future Directions.* USDA Forest Service, Intermountain Research Station, Ogden, Utah.

Mehta, H., Baez, A.L. and O'Loughlin, P. (2002) *International Ecolodge Guidelines.* The International Ecotourism Society, Burlington, Vermont.

Meyer, K. (1994). *How to Shit in the Woods: an Environmentally Sound Approach to a Lost Art,* revised edn. Ten Speed Press, Berkeley, California.

Morin, S.L., Moore, S.A. and Schmidt, W. (1997) Defining indicators and standards for recreation impacts in Nuyts Wilderness, Walpole-Nornalup National Park, Western Australia. *CALM Science* 2(3), 247–266.

National Park Service (2001) *Backcountry Recreation Management.* National Park Service Reference Manual #77 – Natural Resources Management, USDI National Park Service, Washington, DC. Available at website http://www.nature.nps.gov/rm77/backcountry.htm (verified 22 December 2003).

Newmark, W.D. and Nguye, P.A. (1991) Recreational impacts of tourism along the Marangu route in Kilimanjaro National Park. In: Newmark, W.D. (ed.) *The Conservation of Mount Kilimanjaro.* IUCN, Gland, Switzerland and Cambridge, UK, pp. 47–51.

Newsome, D., Moore, S.A. and Dowling, R.K. (2001) *Natural Area Tourism: Ecology, Impacts, and Management.* Channel View Books, Clevedon, UK.

Obua, J. (1997) The potential, development and ecological impact of ecotourism in Kibale National Park, Uganda. *Journal of Environmental Management* 50(1), 27–38.

Parks Canada (1992) *Camping Manual.* Parks Canada, Hull, Canada.

Roggenbuck, J.W., Williams, D.R. and Watson, A.E. (1993) Defining acceptable conditions in wilderness. *Environmental Management* 17(2), 187–197.

Ryan, C. (2003) *Recreational Tourism: Demand and Impacts,* 2nd edn. Channel View Publications, Clevedon, UK.

Smith, A.J. and Newsome, D. (2002) An integrated approach to assessing, managing and monitoring campsite impacts in Warren National Park, Western Australia. *Journal of Sustainable Tourism* 10(4), 343–359.

Smith, G.M. (1998) *Campsite Monitoring (1989–1997), Apostle Islands National Lakeshore.* USDI National Park Service, Apostle Islands National Lakeshore, Bayfield, Wisconsin.

Spildie, D.R., Cole, D.N. and Walker, S.C. (2000) Effectiveness of a confinement strategy in reducing packstock impacts at campsites in the Selway-Bitterroot Wilderness, Idaho. In: Cole, D.N., McCool, S.F., Borrie, W.T. and O'Loughlin, J. (comps.) *Wilderness Science in a Time of* *Change Conference. Vol. 5. Wilderness Ecosystems, Threats, and Management.* USDA Forest Service, Rocky Mountain Research Station, Ogden, Utah, pp. 199–208.

Tribe, J., Font, X., Griffiths, N., Vickery, R. and Yale, K. (2000) *Environmental Management for Rural Tourism and Recreation.* Cassell, London, UK.

Williams, P.B. and Marion, J.L. (1995) *Assessing Campsite Conditions for Limits of Acceptable Change Management in Shenandoah National Park.* Technical Report NPS/MARSHEN/NRTR-95/071, USDI National Biological Service, Virginia Tech Cooperative Park Studies Unit, Blacksburg, Virginia.

Zabinski, C.A. and Cole, D.N. (2000) Understanding the factors that limit restoration success on a recreation-impacted subalpine site. In: Cole, D.N., McCool, S.F., Borrie, W.T. and O'Loughlin, J. (comps) *Wilderness Science in a Time of Change Conference.* Vol. 5. *Wilderness Ecosystems, Threats, and Management.* USDA Forest Service, Rocky Mountain Research Station, Ogden, Utah, pp. 216–221.

Zabinski, C.A. and Gannon, J.E. (1997) Effects of recreational impacts on soil microbial communities. *Environmental Management* 21(2), 233–238.

Zabinski, C.A., DeLuca, T.H., Cole, D.N. and Moynahan, O. (2002) Restoration of highly impacted subalpine campsites in the Eagle Cap Wilderness, Oregon. *Restoration Ecology* 10, 275–281.

15

Visitor Perceptions of Recreation-related Resource Impacts

Robert E. Manning, Steven Lawson, Peter Newman, Megha Budruk, William Valliere, Daniel Laven and James Bacon

Park Studies Laboratory, School of Natural Resources, University of Vermont, Burlington, Vermont, USA

Introduction

As preceding chapters in this volume have clearly described, visitors to parks and protected areas – ecotourists – can cause significant impacts to important natural resources that are vital to ecotourism. For example, visitor use can compact and erode soils, trample fragile vegetation, pollute surface water and disturb sensitive wildlife (Hammitt and Cole, 1998). Such impacts may ultimately threaten the ecological integrity of ecotourism sites. These impacts can also have important aesthetic consequences, ultimately degrading the quality of the visitor experience. To what extent do visitors perceive environmental impacts of ecotourism? How important are these impacts in defining the quality of the visitor experience? Do visitors have standards regarding the acceptable level of environmental impacts in parks and protected areas? This chapter examines these and related questions.

Perceived Environmental Impact

A small group of early studies in outdoor recreation began to explore visitor perceptions of environmental impacts, particularly those caused by recreation use. A review of this literature suggested that visitor perceptions of recreational impacts tend to be limited, particularly when compared to those of managers or other 'expert' opinion (Lucas, 1979). With the exception of litter, visitors rarely reported complaints about site conditions and usually rated the environmental conditions of recreation sites as 'good' or better. This appears true for impacts on campsites and trails, as well as other resource impacts, such as water pollution and wildlife disturbance. A study in the Boundary Waters Canoe Area, Minnesota, for example, found that campers seldom commented on campsite impacts other than litter, and that there was no correlation between visitor ratings of campsite physical conditions and expert ratings of the severity of environmental impacts (Merriam and Smith, 1974). Hikers in the Selway-Bitterroot Wilderness Area, Idaho and Montana, reported that they were satisfied with trail conditions, despite the fact that some trails were clearly eroded (Helgath, 1975). Only 1% of floaters on the Pine River in the Manistee National Forest, Michigan, were concerned with streambank erosion (which was judged by researchers as prominent in places); litter was far and away the most objectionable environmental condition reported by users (Solomon and Hansen, 1972). The only impact reported by more that 50% of visitors to roaded forest lands in the US Pacific Northwest was litter (Downing and Clark, 1979). Finally, only one in four campers reported vegetation impacts as a problem at four heavily used developed campgrounds in Pennsylvania (Moeller *et al.*, 1974).

Standards of Environmental Quality

While this early research suggests that many visitors may not be especially sensitive to recreation-related impacts, at least compared to managers' or experts' judgement, this may be changing. Increasing recreation use may be causing greater levels of environmental impacts, and visitors may be becoming more sensitive to the ecological conditions in parks and protected areas, particularly visitors who may be motivated by ecotourism-related objectives. Do contemporary park and protected-area visitors have standards for the maximum acceptable level of recreation-related impacts?

Recent research has begun to apply normative theory and related empirical techniques to help develop standards of quality for the maximum acceptable level of visitor-caused environmental impacts in parks and protected areas. This research has been designed to help apply park and protected-area management frameworks, such as Limits of Acceptable Change (LAC) (Stankey *et al.*, 1985) and Visitor Experience and Resource Protection (VERP) (National Park Service, 1997; Manning, 2001). These frameworks rely on formulation of indicators and standards of quality (Manning, 1999, 2001). Indicators of quality are measurable, manageable variables that help define the quality of park resources and the visitor experience. Standards of quality define the minimum acceptable condition of indicator variables. Once indicators and standards of quality are formulated, LAC, VERP and related management frameworks require long-term monitoring of indicator variables and management action to ensure that standards of quality are maintained.

One of the most problematic issues in this contemporary approach to park and outdoor recreation management has been setting standards of quality. Such standards may be based on a variety of sources, including legal and administrative mandates, agency policy, historic precedent, expert judgement, interest-group politics, and public opinion, especially that derived from outdoor recreation visitors.

This latter source has special appeal because it involves those most directly interested in, and affected by, management actions.

Research on visitor-based standards of quality has focused increasingly on personal and social norms. Developed in the discipline of sociology, norms have attracted considerable attention as a theoretical construct and empirical framework in outdoor recreation research and management. In particular, normative theory has special application to setting standards of quality for the recreation experience. As applied in outdoor recreation, norms are generally defined as standards that individuals and groups use for evaluating behaviour and social and environmental conditions (Vaske *et al.*, 1986; Shelby and Vaske, 1991; Donnelly *et al.*, 1992). If visitors have normative standards concerning relevant aspects of recreation experiences, then such norms can be measured and used as a basis for formulating standards of quality.

Application of visitor-based standards of quality in outdoor recreation is most fully described in Shelby and Heberlein (1986), Vaske *et al.* (1986), Shelby *et al.* (1996) and Manning (1999). These applications have relied on the work of Jackson (1965), who developed a methodology – return-potential curves – to measure norms. Normative research in outdoor recreation has focused largely on the issue of crowding (e.g. Shelby, 1981; Heberlein *et al.*, 1986; Vaske *et al.*, 1986; Whittaker and Shelby, 1988; Patterson and Hammitt, 1990; Williams *et al.*, 1991; Manning *et al.*, 1996, 1999, 2000, 2002a,b), but has also been expanded to include other potential indicators of quality, including ecological impacts at wilderness campsites (Shelby *et al.*, 1988), wildlife-management practices (Vaske and Donnelly, 1988) and minimum stream flows (Shelby and Whittaker, 1990). A recent series of studies in the US national park system has begun to apply this research approach to a range of recreation-related impacts, including trail erosion, social trails, campsite condition and litter.

Trail erosion/social trails

Visitor surveys at the Schoodic Peninsula and Isle au Haut sections of Acadia National Park,

Fig. 15.1. Trail erosion photographs, Acadia National Park.

Maine, found that many visitors felt recreation use was causing damage to soils and vegetation, and that trail conditions were important in affecting the quality of the recreation experience (Manning *et al.*, 2002c, 2003a). Thus, trail erosion and social trails were identified as potential indicators of quality. Subsequent visitor surveys were designed to measure normative standards of quality for those indicator variables. A visual approach was employed by preparing two series of computer-edited photographs of a range of trail impacts on generic sections of trail (Manning *et al.*, 1996). Trail erosion and social trails photographs are shown in Figs 15.1 and 15.2, respectively. Representative

samples of visitors were asked to rate the acceptability of each photograph on a scale that ranged from +4 ('very acceptable') to –4 ('very unacceptable') with a neutral point of 0.

Study findings for trail erosion are shown in Fig. 15.3, which graphs mean acceptability ratings – a norm curve – for each of five study photographs. It is clear that visitors find increasing levels of trail erosion increasingly unacceptable. The point at which the norm curve crosses the neutral point of the acceptability scale – represented by a trail erosion level approaching that shown in photograph 3 – is the point at which aggregate visitor ratings fall out of the acceptable range and into the unacceptable

Fig. 15.2. Social trails photographs, Acadia National Park.

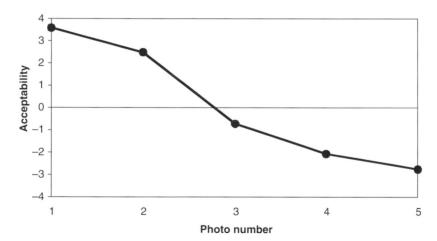

Fig. 15.3. Social norm curve for trail erosion.

range. This might be interpreted as a minimum acceptable trail condition.

Respondents were also asked to select the photograph that best represented: (i) the trail condition they would prefer to experience ('preference'); (ii) the trail condition that was so eroded that they would no longer hike on the trail ('displacement'); and (iii) the maximum level of trail erosion that the National Park Service should allow before limiting visitor use ('management action'). Findings are shown in Table 15.1 and represent a range of potential standards of quality for trail conditions, depending upon the management objectives for the area.

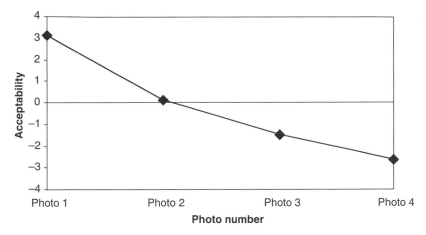

Fig. 15.4. Social norm curve for social trails.

Table 15.1. Alternative standards of quality for trail erosion.

Standard of quality	Mean photo number
Preference	1.3
Management action	2.7
Displacement	3.7

Table 15.2. Alternative standards of quality for social trails.

Standard of quality	Mean photo number
Preference	1.2
Management action	2.0
Displacement	3.4

Comparable study findings for social trails are shown in Fig. 15.4 and Table 15.2. These data provide an empirical basis for formulating standards of quality for this indicator variable. The norm curve for social trails falls out of the acceptable range and into the unacceptable range at photograph 2. Alternative standards of quality based on the evaluative dimensions of 'preference', 'management action' and 'displacement' are shown in Table 15.2.

Table 15.3. Alternative standards of quality for campsite condition.

Standard of quality	Mean photo number
Preference	2.1
Management action	3.8
Displacement	4.3

Campsite condition

Research in the wilderness portion of Yosemite National Park, California, was designed to explore visitor norms for several resource and social indicators of quality, including campsite condition (Newman *et al.*, 2001, 2002; Newman 2002). A series of five photographs was prepared that illustrated a range of campsite impacts that corresponded to the park's 'condition class' monitoring programme (Frissell, 1978; Hammitt and Cole, 1998; Boyers *et al.*,

1999). These photographs are shown in Fig. 15.5. A representative sample of overnight wilderness visitors was administered a diary survey, asking them to report their normative standards for campsite conditions (using the study photographs) for each night of their trip. Normative standards varied by wilderness zone, and study findings for the 'threshold' zone are shown in Table 15.3. Visitors would prefer the campsite condition to be in the range of that illustrated in photograph 2, would choose not to return to this area once campsite condition deteriorated substantially beyond that represented in photograph 4, and would support restrictions on

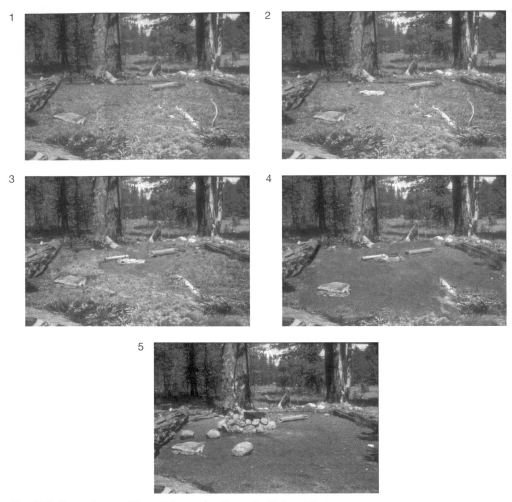

Fig. 15.5. Campsite condition photographs, Yosemite National Park.

visitor use as campsite condition approaches the level of impact illustrated in photograph 4.

Litter

An initial survey of visitors to Boston Harbor Islands National Recreation Area, Massachusetts, found several potential indicators of quality, including the amount of litter on park lands (Manning *et al.*, 2003b). As noted earlier in this chapter, other studies have found that park visitors are sensitive to litter, but no standards for the acceptable amount of litter have been explored. A second visitor survey at Boston Harbor Islands

incorporated a series of questions addressing normative standards of quality for litter. Adapting procedures developed by Keep America Beautiful, a national non-profit organization, a photometric index (PI) approach to measuring litter was incorporated in the study (Keep America Beautiful, 2001). In this approach, a standardized [16 × 6 ft (4.9 × 1.8 m)] horizontal grid of 96 cells is overlaid on a park scene. Litter accumulation is measured according to the number of cells occupied by litter. Each of the 96 cells count equally towards a PI rating of 0 to 96. If the same piece of litter covers multiple cells, each cell counts towards the scale value. In this study, the grid created was overlaid on a series of four park

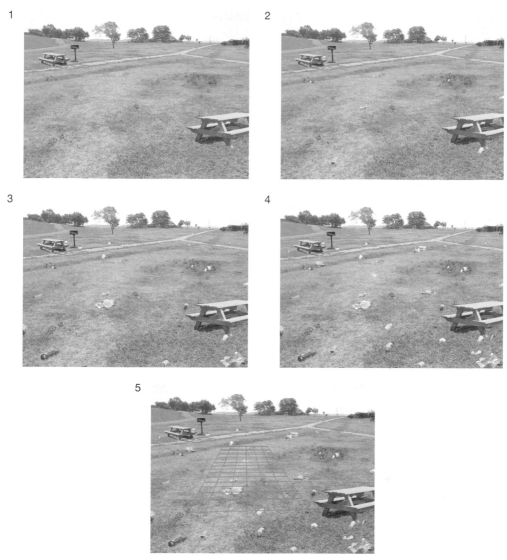

Fig. 15.6. Litter photographs, Boston Harbor Islands National Recreation Area.

scenes, depicting increasing amounts of litter accumulation. The four photographs used are shown in Fig. 15.6 and represented litter PI ratings of 0, 4, 8 and 12. Litter PI ratings were selected to represent a range of realistic levels of litter in the park.

Respondents were asked to rate litter PI photographs on a scale of −4 ('very unacceptable') to +4 ('very acceptable'), with a neutral point of 0. Respondents were also asked to indicate the photographs that represented the amount of litter they: (i) preferred; (ii) found so unacceptable they would not visit the park again; and (iii) felt the National Park Service should allow before limiting visitor use. The norm curve for litter is shown in Fig. 15.7 and indicates that aggregate visitor evaluations of litter fall out of the acceptable range and into the unacceptable range at a PI level of approximately 4. The data in Table 15.4 indicate that visitors would prefer to see a PI level of 0.2, would not visit the park again at a PI of 9.3, and

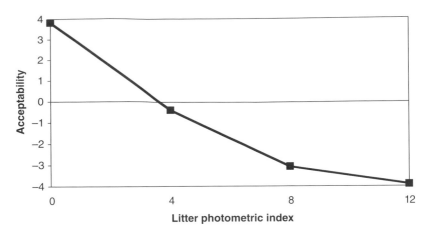

Fig. 15.7. Social norm curve for litter.

Table 15.4. Alternative standards of quality for litter.

Standard of quality	Photometric index
Preference	0.2
Management action	3.9
Displacement	9.3

think the National Park Service should not allow litter to accumulate beyond a PI level of 3.9.

Relative Importance of Environmental Impacts

How important are selected environmental impacts of recreation (e.g. trail erosion, social trails, campsite condition, litter) compared to other recreation-related environmental and social impacts? Which impacts are the most important in defining the quality of the visitor experience in parks and protected areas? Recent research has begun to explore this issue through stated-choice analysis.

Stated-choice analysis has been developed in the fields of psychometrics, econometrics and consumer marketing, to evaluate public preferences or attitudes (Green and Srivivasan, 1978). There is a growing body of literature describing the application of stated-

choice analysis to outdoor recreation management issues in parks and related areas (Louviere and Woodworth, 1985; Louviere and Timmermans, 1990b; Schroeder *et al.*, 1990). In stated-choice analysis, respondents are asked to make choices among alternative configurations of a multi-attribute good (Louviere and Timmermans, 1990a). Each alternative configuration is called a profile and is defined by varying levels of selected attributes of the good (Mackenzie, 1993). For example, respondents may be asked to choose between alternative recreation settings that vary in the number of other groups encountered, the quality of the natural environment, and the intensity of management regulations imposed on visitors. Respondents' choices among the alternatives are evaluated to estimate the relative importance of each attribute to the overall utility or satisfaction derived from the recreational setting. Further, stated choice models are used to estimate public preferences or support for alternative combinations of the attribute levels (Dennis, 1998).

A recent application of stated-choice analysis was used to develop a decision-making model to inform judgements about the management of social, resource and managerial attributes of the Denali National Park (Alaska) wilderness (Lawson and Manning, 2001, 2002). Specifically, stated-choice analysis was used to evaluate the choices Denali overnight wilderness visitors make when faced with trade-offs among the conditions of selected

Table 15.5. Example of Denali wilderness setting comparison.

Backcountry Setting A	Backcountry Setting B
• Encounter up to two other groups per day while hiking	• Encounter up to four other groups per day while hiking
• Able to camp out of sight and sound of other groups *all* nights	• Able to camp out of sight and sound of other groups *most* nights
• Hiking is along continuous, *single track* trails developed from prior human use	• Hiking is along intermittent, animal-like trails
• Camping sites have *some* signs of human use – light vegetation damage, a few moved rocks	• Camping sites have *some* signs of human use – light vegetation damage, a few moved rocks
• Required to camp at *designated sites*	• Required to camp at *designated sites*
• Only a minority of visitors are able to get a backcountry permit	• Most visitors are able to get a backcountry permit for their *preferred* trip

social, resource and managerial attributes of the wilderness portion of the park.

In the stated-choice analysis study, a set of six Denali wilderness setting attributes were selected to define a series of hypothetical Denali wilderness settings. Attributes selected to reflect the social conditions of the Denali wilderness included the number of other groups encountered per day while hiking and the likelihood of being able to camp out of sight and sound of other groups. Two attributes related to the resource conditions of the Denali wilderness were selected: the presence and extent of trails and the amount of human impact at campsites. The intensity of restrictions regarding where wilderness visitors are allowed to camp and the level of difficulty of obtaining a permit for an overnight wilderness trip were selected as attributes to reflect the management conditions of the Denali wilderness. An experimental design was used to combine the six attributes at varying levels into a set of paired comparison questions, each consisting of two hypothetical Denali wilderness settings. An example of a representative Denali wilderness setting comparison is presented in Table 15.5.

The stated choice analysis survey was administered to visitors returning from an overnight wilderness trip. Respondents to the survey were presented with a series of nine paired comparison questions, each containing two hypothetical Denali wilderness settings. In each question, respondents were asked to read through each setting description and indicate which they preferred.

Responses to the survey were analysed

using logistic regression. The coefficients of the logistic regression analysis are presented in Table 15.6 and Fig. 15.8. Results of the data analysis provide information about the relative importance wilderness visitors place on the selected social, resource and managerial attributes of the Denali wilderness. The magnitude of the regression coefficients presented in Table 15.6 reflects the relative importance of the corresponding level of the attribute to Denali overnight wilderness visitors. Specifically, visitors are more sensitive to levels of attributes with relatively large positive or negative coefficient values (e.g. 'Little or no sign of human us at campsites', 'Extensive signs of human use at campsites') than levels of attributes with relatively small positive or negative coefficient values (e.g. 'Most get a permit for their preferred trip', 'Required to camp in designated sites'). Further, the study results suggest that visitors may be particularly sensitive to changes in Denali wilderness setting attributes when they deteriorate beyond certain thresholds. For example, visitor utility or satisfaction drops sharply as campsites deteriorate from having 'some signs of human use' to 'extensive signs of human use', and this may represent a threshold or potential standard of quality (Fig. 15.8).

Conclusions

Initial research in outdoor recreation suggested that many visitors may not be highly perceptive of recreation-related environmental impacts. However, subsequent research suggests that

Table 15.6. Coefficient estimates for Denali wilderness setting attributes.

Variable	Coefficient
Encounters with other groups per day while hiking:	
0 other groups	0.439
Up to 2 other groups	0.065
Up to 4 other groups	−0.504*
Able to camp out of sight and sound of other groups:	
All nights	0.295
Most nights	0.145*
A minority of nights	−0.440*
Hiking is along:	
Intermittent, animal like trails	0.319
Single track trails developed from human use	−0.028
Multiple track trails developed from human use	−0.291*
Camping sites have:	
Little or no signs of human use	0.582
Some signs of human use	0.207*
Extensive signs of human use	−0.790*
Regulation of camping:	
Allowed to camp in any zone on any night	0.072
Required to camp in specified zones	0.140*
Required to camp in designated sites	−0.212*
Chance visitors have of receiving a permit:	
Most get a permit for their preferred trip	0.073
Most get a permit for at least their second choice	0.143*
Only a minority get a permit	−0.216*

* Statistically significant at 0.05 level or better. To avoid overidentification, the first level of each attribute was excluded from the statistical model. The coefficient of the excluded level for each attribute equals the negative sum of the coefficients on the other two levels of the attribute.

visitors may have normative standards for environmental conditions experienced in parks and protected areas, and that findings from such studies may provide an empirical basis for helping to formulate standards of quality for selected indicator variables. Moreover, research also suggests that recreation-related impacts to park and wilderness resources can be important to visitors in defining the quality of the recreation experience. This research can help support application of park and protected area management frameworks, such as LAC and VERP, designed to protect the quality of park resources and the visitor experience. Application of these management frameworks and related programmes of research are important in helping to assure long-term vitality, sustainability and ecological and social integrity of ecotourism.

Findings from the studies described above are suggestive of several other conclusions and implications regarding visitor perceptions of recreation-related resource impacts. First, it

may be wise to involve visitors in decisions about acceptable levels of recreation-related resource impacts. Early research in outdoor recreation suggests that managers and other 'experts' may be substantially more perceptive and less tolerant of such impacts than visitors. Visitor-based perceptions should be explicitly considered when planning and managing parks, protected areas and other ecotourism attractions.

Secondly, visitors may be willing to accept restrictions on visitor use designed to limit resource impacts. In fact, visitors may prefer such restrictions, when and where they are needed, to maintain acceptable levels of resource impacts.

Thirdly, it is not feasible to eliminate all resource impacts associated with recreation and ecotourism. Ecological research suggests that many types of resource impacts may occur quickly, even under relatively light levels of recreation use (Hammitt and Cole, 1998).

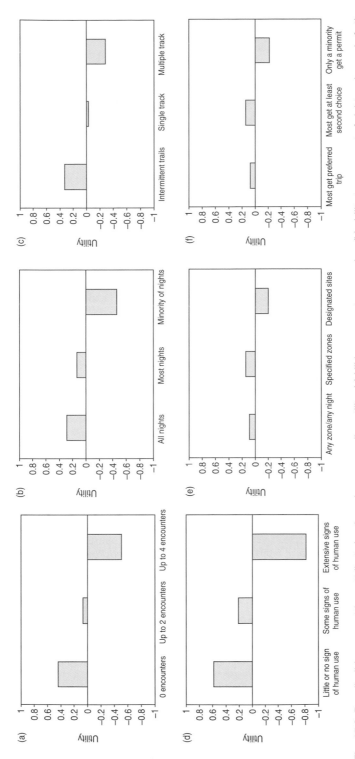

Fig. 15.8. Denali wilderness setting, attribute levels and corresponding utility. (a) Hiking encounters per day; (b) ability to camp out of sight and sound of others; (c) extent and character of trials; (d) extent of campsite impacts; (e) camping regulations; and (f) availability of permits.

Moreover, visitors may *prefer* some resource impact at developed facilities, such as trails and campsites. By definition, these facilities are designed to accommodate visitor use and its associated impacts.

Finally, the data on normative standards for recreation-related resource impacts presented in this chapter should be considered 'place-based'. That is, they reflect the judgements of visitors to specific sites within the US national park system. Not enough of these types of studies have been conducted over a diverse enough set of parks and protected areas to apply these findings to ecotourism more generally.

References

Boyers, L., Fincher, M. and van Wagtendonk, J. (1999) Twenty-eight years of wilderness campsite monitoring in Yosemite National Park. *Proceedings: Wilderness Science in a Time of Change*. USDA Forest Service RMRS-P-000.

Dennis, D. (1998) Analyzing public inputs to multiple objective decisions on national forests using conjoint analysis. *Forest Science* 44, 421–429.

Donnelly, M.P., Vaske, J. and Shelby, B. (1992) Establishing management standards: selected examples of the normative approach. In: Shelby, B., Stankey, G. and Shindler, B. (eds) *Defining Wilderness Quality: the Role Of Standards in Wilderness Management*. General Technical Report PNW-305, USDA Forest Service.

Downing, K. and Clark, R. (1979) Users' and managers' perceptions of dispersed recreation impacts: a focus on roaded forest lands. *Proceedings of the Wildland Recreation Impacts Conference*. USDA Forest Service, Pacific Northwest Region, R-6-001-1979, pp. 18–23.

Frissell, S. (1978) Judging recreation impacts on wilderness campsites. *Journal of Forestry* 76, 481–483.

Green, P. and Srivivasan, V. (1978) Conjoint analysis in consumer research: issues and outlook. *Journal of Consumer Research* 5, 103–123.

Hammitt, W. and Cole, D. (1998) *Wildland Recreation: Ecology and Management*. John Wiley & Sons, New York.

Heberlein, T.A., Alfano, G.E. and Ervin, L.H. (1986) Using a social carrying capacity model to estimate the effects of marina development at the Apostle Islands National Lakeshore. *Leisure Sciences* 8, 257–274.

Helgath, S. (1975) *Trail Deterioration in the Selway-Bitterroot Wilderness*. Research Note INT-193, USDA Forest Service.

Jackson, J. (1965) Structural characteristics of norms. In: Steiner, I.D. and Fishbein, M.F. (eds) *Current Studies in Social Psychology*. Holt, Rinehart, Winston, New York.

Keep America Beautiful (2001) *Pre-certification Manual*, pp. 143–192.

Lawson, S. and Manning, R. (2001) Crossing experiential boundaries: visitor preferences regarding tradeoffs among social, resource, and managerial attributes of the Denali wilderness experience. *The George Wright Forum* 18(3), 10–27.

Lawson, S. and Manning, R. (2002) Tradeoffs among social, resource, and management attributes of the Denali wilderness experience: a contextual approach to normative research. *Leisure Sciences* 24, 297–312.

Louviere, J. and Timmermans, H. (1990a) Stated preference and choice models applied to recreation research: a review. *Leisure Sciences* 12, 9–32.

Louviere, J. and Timmermans, H. (1990b) Using hierarchical information integration to model consumer responses to possible planning actions: recreation destination choice illustration. *Environment and Planning* 22, 291–308.

Louviere, J. and Woodworth, G. (1985) *Models of Park Choice Derived from Experimental and Observational Data: a Case Study in Johnston County, Iowa*. Technical Report, University of Iowa, Iowa City, Iowa.

Lucas, R. (1979) Perception of non-motorized recreational impacts: a review of research findings. *Recreational Impact on Wildlands*. USDA Forest Service, Pacific Northwest Region, R-6-001-1979, pp. 24–31.

Mackenzie, J. (1993) A comparison of contingent preference models. *American Journal of Agricultural Economics* 75, 593–603.

Manning, R. (1999) *Studies in Outdoor Recreation: Search and Research for Satisfaction*. Oregon State University Press, Corvallis.

Manning, R. (2001) Visitor experience and resource protection: a framework for managing the carrying capacity of national parks. *Journal of Park and Recreation Administration* 19, 93–108.

Manning, R., Lime, D., Freimund, W. and Pitt, D. (1996) Crowding norms at frontcountry sites: a visual approach to setting standards of quality. *Leisure Sciences* 18, 39–59.

Manning R., Valliere, W., Wang, B. and Jacobi, C. (1999) Crowding norms: alternative measurement approaches. *Leisure Sciences* 21, 97–115.

Manning R., Valliere, W., Minteer, B., Wang, B. and Jacobi, C. (2000) Crowding in parks and outdoor recreation: a theoretical, empirical and managerial analysis. *Journal of Park and Recreation Administration* 18, 57–72.

Manning, R., Wang, B., Valliere, W., Lawson, S. and Newman, P. (2002a) Research to estimate and manage carrying capacity of a tourist attraction: a study of Alcatraz Island. *Journal of Sustainable Tourism* 10, 388–464.

Manning, R., Lawson, S., Newman, P., Laven, D. and Valliere, W. (2002b) Methodological issues in measuring crowding-related norms. *Leisure Sciences* 24, 339–348.

Manning, R., Lawson, S., Valliere, W., Bacon, J. and Laven, D. (2002c) *Schoodic Peninsula, Acadia National Park Visitor Study 2000–2002.* University of Vermont, Burlington, Vermont.

Manning, R., Lawson, S., Valliere, W., Budruk, M., Bacon, J., Laven, D. and Wang, B. (2003a) *Research to Support Carrying Capacity Analysis and Management at Isle au Haut, Acadia National Park.* University of Vermont, Burlington, Vermont.

Manning, R., Leung, Y. and Budruk, M. (2003b) *Research to Support Carrying Capacity Analysis and Management at Boston Harbor National Park Area.* University of Vermont, Burlington, Vermont.

Merriam, L. Jr and Smith, C. (1974) Visitor impact on newly developed campsites in the Boundary Waters Canoe Area. *Journal of Forestry* 72, 627–630.

Moeller, G., Larson, R. and Morrison, D. (1974) *Opinions of Campers and Boaters at the Allegheny Reservoir.* Research Paper NE-307, USDA Forest Service.

National Park Service (1997) *VERP: the Visitor Experience and Resource Protection (VERP) Framework – a Handbook for Planners and Managers.* National Park Service Technical Report, Denver, Colorado.

Newman, P. (2002) Integrating social, ecological and managerial indicators of quality into carrying capacity decision making in Yosemite National Park wilderness. Unpublished Doctoral Dissertation, University of Vermont, Burlington, Vermont.

Newman, P., Marron, J. and Cahill, K. (2001) Integrating resource, social and managerial indicators of quality into carrying capacity decision making. *The George Wright Forum* 18(3), 28–40.

Newman, P., Manning, R. and Valliere, W. (2002) Integrating resource, social and managerial indicators of quality into carrying capacity decision making. *Proceedings of the 2001 Northeastern Recreation Research Symposium.* General Technical Report NE-289, USDA Forest Service, pp. 233–238.

Patterson, M.E. and Hammitt, W.E. (1990) Backcountry encounter norms, actual reported encounters, and their relationship to wilderness solitude. *Journal of Leisure Research* 22, 259–275.

Schroeder, H., Dwyer, J., Louviere, J. and Anderson, D. (1990) *Monetary and Nonmonetary Trade-offs of Urban Forest Site Attributes in a Logit Model of Recreation Choice.* General Technical Report RM-197, USDA Forest Service.

Shelby, B. (1981) Crowding models for backcountry recreation. *Land Economics* 56, 43–55.

Shelby, B. and Heberlein, T.A. (1986) *Carrying Capacity in Recreation Settings.* Oregon State University Press, Corvallis.

Shelby, B. and Vaske, J.J. (1991) Using normative data to develop evaluative standards for resource management: a comment on three recent papers. *Journal of Leisure Research* 23, 173–187.

Shelby, B. and Whittaker, D. (1990) Recreation values and instream flow needs on the Delores River. Paper presented at the Third Conference on Society and Resource Management, College Station, Texas.

Shelby, B., Vaske, J.J. and Harris, R. (1988) User standards for ecological impacts at wilderness campsites. *Journal of Leisure Research* 20, 245–256.

Shelby, B., Vaske, J.J. and Donnelly, M. (1996) Norms, standards, and natural resources. *Leisure Sciences* 18, 103–123.

Solomon, M. and Hansen, E. (1972) *Canoeists' Suggestions for Stream Management in the Manistee National Forest in Michigan.* Research Paper NC-77, USDA Forest Service.

Stankey, G., Cole, D., Lucas, R., Peterson, M., Frissell, S. and Washburne, R. (1985) *The Limits of Acceptable Change (LAC) System for Wilderness Planning.* General Technical Report INT-176, USDA Forest Service.

Vaske, J.J. and Donnelly, M.P. (1988) Normative evaluations of wildlife management. Paper presented at the Annual Congress of the National Recreation and Park Association, Indianapolis, Indiana.

Vaske, J., Graefe, A., Shelby, B. and Heberlein, T. (1986) Backcountry encounter norms: Theory, method, and empirical evidence. *Journal of Leisure Research* 18, 137–153.

Whittaker, D. and Shelby, B. (1988) Types of norms for recreation impacts: Extending the social norm concept. *Journal of Leisure Research,* 20, 261–273.

Williams, D., Roggenbuck, J. and Bange, S. (1991) The effect of norm-encounter compatibility on crowding perceptions, experience and behavior in river recreation settings. *Journal of Leisure* 23, 154–172.

16

Managing Impacts of Ecotourism Through Use Rationing and Allocation

Robert E. Manning

Recreation Management Program, School of Natural Resources, University of Vermont, Burlington, Vermont, USA

Introduction

Preceding chapters of this book clearly demonstrate a range of environmental (and related social) impacts that can arise from ecotourism. These impacts require management to ensure that significant natural and cultural resources of destination areas are protected, a fundamental principle of ecotourism (Lindberg *et al.*, 1998). Moreover, degradation of natural and cultural resources may undermine the quality of visitor experiences, and this, too, may ultimately threaten the concept and practice of ecotourism.

Recreation Management Practices

Theoretically, there are many practices that might be applied to managing environmental impacts of ecotourism. It is useful to organize these management practices into classification systems to illustrate the broad spectrum of alternatives available. One classification system defines alternatives on the basis of management strategies (Manning, 1979). Management strategies are basic conceptual approaches to management that relate to achievement of desirable objectives. Four basic strategies can be identified for managing outdoor recreation, as illustrated in Fig. 16.1. Two strategies deal with supply and demand: the supply of recrea-

tion opportunities may be increased to accommodate more use, or the demand for recreation may be limited through restrictions or other approaches. The other two basic strategies treat supply and demand as fixed, and focus on modifying either the character of recreation to reduce its adverse impacts, or the resource base to increase its durability.

There are a number of sub-strategies within each of these basic management strategies. The supply of outdoor recreation areas, for example, can be increased in terms of both space and time. With respect to space, new areas may be added or existing areas might be used more effectively through additional access or facilities, such as trails and campsites. With respect to time, some recreation use might be shifted to off-peak periods. Within the strategy of limiting demand, restrictions might be placed on the total number of visitors that are allowed or their length of stay. Alternatively, certain types of use that can be demonstrated to have high environmental and/or social impacts might be restricted. The third basic management strategy suggests reducing the environmental or social impacts of existing use. This might be accomplished by modifying the type of character of use or by dispersing or concentrating use according to resource capability or user compatibility. A final basic management strategy involves increasing the durability of the resource. This might be accomplished by hardening the

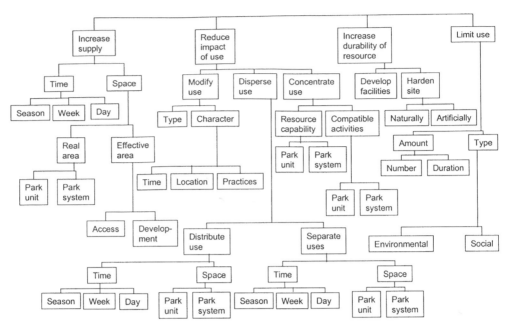

Fig. 16.1. Strategies for managing impacts of ecotourism (from Manning, 1979, 1999).

resource itself (through intensive maintenance, for example) or developing facilities (such as boardwalks or tent pads) to accommodate use more directly.

A second system of classifying management alternatives focuses on tactics or actual management practices. Management practices are actions or tools applied by managers to accomplish the management strategies described above. Restrictions on length of stay, differential fees, and use permits, for example, are management practices designed to accomplish the strategy of limiting recreation demand or rationing. Management practices are often classified according to the directness with which they act on visitor behaviour (Gilbert *et al.*, 1972; Lime, 1977; Peterson and Lime, 1979; Chavez, 1996). As the term suggests, direct management practices act directly on visitor behaviour, leaving little or no freedom of choice. Indirect management practices attempt to influence the decision factors upon which visitors base their behaviour. A conceptual diagram illustrating direct and indirect recreation management practices is shown in Fig. 16.2. As an example, a direct management practice aimed at reducing campfires in a wilderness

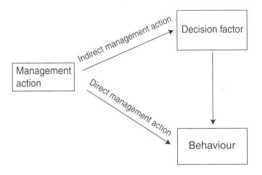

Fig. 16.2. Direct and indirect management practices (adapted from Peterson and Lime, 1979).

environment would be a regulation barring campfires, and enforcement of this regulation. An indirect management practice would be an education programme designed to inform visitors of the undesirable ecological and aesthetic impacts of campfires and to encourage them to carry and use portable stoves instead. A series of direct and indirect management practices is shown in Table 16.1.

A growing body of research has focused on

Table 16.1. Direct and indirect management practices (adapted from Lime, 1977, 1979).

Type	Example
Direct (emphasis on regulation of behaviour; individual choice restricted; high degree of control)	Impose fines
	Increase surveillance of area
	Zone incompatible uses spatially (hiker-only zones, prohibit motor use, etc.)
	Zone uses over time
	Limit camping in some campsites to one night, or some other limit
	Rotate use (open or close roads, access points, trails, campsites, etc.)
	Require reservations
	Assign campsites and/or travel routes to each camper group in backcountry
	Limit usage via access point
	Limit size of groups, number of horses, vehicles, etc.
	Limit camping to designated campsites only
	Limit length of stay in area (maximum/minimum)
	Restrict building of campfires
	Restrict fishing or hunting
Indirect (emphasis on influencing or modifying behaviour; individual retains freedom to choose; control less complete, more variation in use possible)	Improve (or not) access roads, trails
	Improve (or not) campsites and other concentrated use areas
	Improve (or not) fish and wildlife populations (stock, allow to die out, etc.)
	Advertise specific attributes of the area
	Identify the range of recreation opportunities in surrounding area
	Educate users to basic concepts of ecology
	Advertise underused areas and general patterns of use
	Charge consistent entrance fee
	Charge differential fees by trail, zone, season, etc.
	Require proof of ecological knowledge and recreational activity skills

selected recreation management practices and their potential effectiveness. Much of this research has examined two of the most common management practices: (i) use of rationing and allocation; and (ii) information and education. This chapter addresses the former.

to the basic objective of providing public access to parks and related areas (Hendee and Lucas, 1973, 1974; Behan, 1974, 1976; Dustin and McAvoy, 1980). However, limits on use may be needed to protect the integrity of critical park and ecotourism resources and to maintain the quality of the recreation experience.

Use Rationing and Allocation

Substantial attention has been focused on the management strategy of limiting the amount of use that parks and related ecotourism areas receive. Use rationing is controversial and is often considered to be a management approach of 'last resort' because it runs counter

Rationing and Allocation Practices

Five basic management practices have been identified in the literature to ration and allocate recreation use (Stankey and Baden, 1977; Fractor, 1982; Shelby et al., 1989; McLean and Johnson, 1997). These include: (i) reservation systems; (ii) lotteries; (iii) first-come, first-served or queuing; (iv) pricing; and (v) merit. A reservation system requires potential visitors to reserve a space or permit in advance of their visit. A lottery also requires potential visitors to request a permit in advance, but allocates permits on a purely random basis. A first-come, first-served or queuing system requires potential visitors to 'wait in line' for available permits. A pricing system requires visitors to pay a fee for a permit which may 'filter out' those who are unable or unwilling to pay. A merit system requires potential visitors to 'earn' the right to a permit by virtue of demonstrated knowledge or skill.

Each of these management practices has potential advantages and disadvantages, which are summarized in Table 16.2. For example, reservation systems may tend to favour visitors who are willing and able to plan ahead, but these systems may be difficult and costly to administer. Lotteries are often viewed as eminently 'fair', but can also be cumbersome and costly to administer. Although relatively easy to administer, first-come, first-served systems may favour visitors who have more leisure time or who live relatively close to a park or related areas. Pricing is a commonly used practice to allocate scarce resources in free-market economies, but may discriminate against potential visitors with low incomes. Merit systems are rarely used, but may lessen the environmental and social impacts of use.

Several principles or guidelines have been suggested for considering and applying use rationing and allocation practices (Stankey and Baden, 1977). First, emphasis should be placed on the environmental and social impacts of recreation use, rather than the amount of use *per se*. Some types of recreation use may cause more impacts than others. To the extent that such impacts can be reduced, rationing use of recreation areas can be avoided, or at least postponed. Secondly, as noted above, rationing use should probably be considered a management practice of last resort. Less direct or 'heavy-handed' management practices would seem more desirable where they can be demonstrated to be effective. Thirdly, good information is needed to implement use rationing and allocation. Managers must be certain that environmental and/or social problems dictate use rationing, and that visitors are understood well enough to predict the effects of alternative allocation systems. Fourthly, combinations of use-rationing systems should be considered. Given the advantages and disadvantages of each use-allocation practice, hybrid systems may have special application. For example, half of all permits might be allocated on the basis of a reservation system and half on a first-come, first-served basis. This would serve the needs of potential visitors who can and do plan vacations in advance as well as those whose jobs or lifestyles do not allow for this. Fifthly, use rationing should establish a linkage between the probability of obtaining a permit and the value of the recreation opportunity to potential visitors. In other words, visitors who value the opportunity highly should have a chance to 'earn' a permit through pricing, advance planning, waiting time or merit. Finally, use-rationing practices should be monitored and evaluated to assess their effectiveness and fairness. Use rationing for recreation is relatively new and is likely to be controversial. Special efforts should be made to ensure that use-rationing practices accomplish their objectives.

Fairness

A critical element of use-rationing and allocation practices is 'fairness' (Dustin and Knopf, 1989). Parks, outdoor recreation areas and other ecotourism sites administered by federal, state and local agencies are public resources. Use-rationing and allocation practices must be seen as both efficient and equitable. But how are equity, fairness and related concepts defined? Several studies have begun to develop important insights into this issue. These studies have outlined several alternative dimensions of equity and measured their support among the public.

One study identified four dimensions of an overall theory of 'distributive justice' (Shelby *et al.*, 1989). Distributive justice is defined as an ideal whereby individuals obtain what they 'ought' to have, based on criteria of fairness. A first dimension is 'equality', and suggests that all individuals have an equal right to a benefit, such as access to parks and outdoor recreation. A second dimension is 'equity', and suggests that benefits be distributed to those who 'earn'

Table 16.2. Evaluation of five recreation use rationing practices (adapted from Stankey and Baden, 1977).

	Reservation	Lottery	First come, first served	Pricing	Merit
Clientele group benefited by system	Those able and/or willing to plan ahead; i.e. persons with structured lifestyles	No one identifiable group benefited; those who examine probabilities of success at different areas have better chance	Those with low opportunity cost for their time (e.g. retired, unemployed); also favours users who live nearby	Those able or willing to pay entry costs	Those able or willing to invest time and effort to meet requirements
Clientele group adversely affected by system	Those unable or unwilling to plan ahead; e.g. persons with occupations that do not permit long-range planning, such as many professionals	No one identifiable group discriminated against; can discriminate against the unsuccessful applicant to whom the outcome is important	Those persons with high opportunity cost of time; also those persons who live some distance from areas; the cost of time is not recovered by anyone	Those unwilling or unable to pay entry costs	Those unable or unwilling to invest time and effort to meet requirements
Experience to date with use of system	Main type of rationing system used in both US National Forests and National Parks	Limited; however, it is a common method for allocating big-game hunting permits	Used in US National Parks for many services; often used with reservation systems	Little; entrance fees sometimes charged, but not to limit use	Little; merit is used to allocate use for some specialized activities such as mountain climbing and river running
Acceptability of system to users[a]	Generally high; good acceptance in areas where used; seen as best way to ration by users in areas not currently rationed	Low	Low to moderate	Low to moderate	Not clearly known; could vary considerably, depending on level of training required to attain necessary proficiency and knowledge level
Difficulty for administrators	Moderately difficult; requires extra staffing, expanded hours; record-keeping can be substantial	Difficult to moderately difficult; allocating permits over an entire use season could be very cumbersome	Low difficulty to moderately difficult; could require development of facilities to support visitors waiting in line	Moderate difficulty; possibly some legal questions about imposing a fee for wilderness entry	Difficult to moderately difficult; initial investments to establish licensing programme could be substantial

Continued

Table 16.2. *Continued*

	Reservation	Lottery	First come, first served	Pricing	Merit
Efficiency – extent to which system can minimize problems of suboptimization	Low to moderate; underutilization can occur because of 'no shows', denying entry to others; allocation of permits has little relationship to value of the experience as judged by the applicant	Low; because permits are assigned randomly, persons who place little value on an opportunity stand as good a chance of gaining entry as those who place high value on it	Moderate; because system rations primarily through a cost of time, it requires some measure of worth by participants	Moderate to high; imposing a fee requires user to judge worth of experience against costs; uncertain as to how well use could be 'fine-tuned' with price	Moderate to high; requires user to make expenditures of time and effort (and maybe dollars) to gain entry
Principal way in which use impact is controlled	Reducing visitor numbers; controlling distribution of use in space and time by varying number of permits available at different trailheads or at different times	Reducing visitor numbers; controlling distribution of use in space and time by number of permits available at different places or times, thus varying probability of success	Reducing visitor numbers; controlling distribution of use in space and time by number of persons permitted to enter at different places or times	Reducing visitor numbers; controlling distribution of use in space and time by using differential prices	Some reduction in numbers as well as shifts in time and space; major reduction in per capita impact
How system affects user behaviour[b]	Affects both spatial and temporal behaviour	Affects both spatial and temporal behaviour	Affects both spatial and temporal behaviour; user must consider cost of time of waiting in line	Affects both spatial and temporal behaviour; user must consider cost in dollars	Affects style of user's behaviour

[a] Based upon actual field experience as well as upon evidence reported in visitor studies (Stankey, 1973).
[b] This criterion is designed to measure how the different rationing systems would directly impact the behaviour of users (e.g. where they go, when they go, how they behave, etc.).

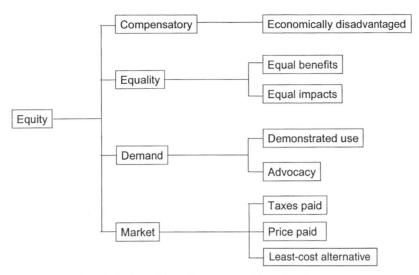

Fig. 16.3. Dimensions of equity (adapted from Crompton and Lue, 1992).

them through some investment of time, money or effort. A third dimension is 'need', and suggests that benefits be distributed on the basis of unmet needs or competitive disadvantage. A final dimension is 'efficiency', and suggests that benefits be distributed to those who place the highest value upon them.

Insights into these dimensions of distributive justice were developed through a survey of river runners on the Snake River in Hell's Canyon, Idaho, USA (Shelby *et al.*, 1989). Visitors were asked to rate the five use-allocation practices described above – reservation; lottery; first-come, first-served; pricing; and merit – on the basis of four criteria: perceived chance of obtaining a permit, perceived fairness of the practice, acceptability of the practice and willingness to try the practice. Results suggest that visitors use concepts of both fairness and pragmatism in evaluating use-rationing practices. However, pragmatism – the perceived ability on the part of the respondent to obtain a permit – had the strongest effect on willingness to try each of the allocation practices. These findings suggest that managers have to convince potential visitors that proposed use allocation practices are not only 'fair', but that they will provide them with a reasonable chance to obtain a permit.

A second series of studies has examined a more extended taxonomy of equity dimensions that might be applied to provision of a broad

spectrum of park, recreation and ecotourism opportunities (Wicks and Crompton, 1986, 1987, 1989, 1990; Wicks, 1987; Crompton and Wicks, 1988; Crompton and Lue, 1992). Eight potential dimensions of equity are identified, as shown in Fig. 16.3. A first dimension is compensatory and allocates benefits on the basis of economic disadvantage. The second two dimensions are variations of equality and allocate benefits to all individuals equally, or ensure that all individuals ultimately receive equal total benefits. The fourth and fifth dimensions are based on demand and allocate benefits to those who make greatest use of them or those who advocate most effectively for them. The final three dimensions of equity are market-driven and distribute benefits based on amount of taxes paid, the price charged for services, or the least-cost alternative for providing recreation services.

These dimensions of equity were described to a sample of residents in the US State of California, and respondents were asked to indicate the extent to which they agreed or disagreed with each dimension of equity as a principle for allocating public park and recreation services (Crompton and Lue, 1992). A majority of the sample agreed with only three of the dimensions. These dimensions were, in decreasing order, demonstrated use, price paid and equal benefits.

Visitor attitudes and preferences

Despite the complex and controversial nature of use rationing and allocation, there appears to be considerable support for a variety of such management practices among visitors (Stankey, 1973, 1979; Fazio and Gilbert, 1974; Lucas, 1980, 1985; McCool and Utter, 1981, 1982; Utter *et al.*, 1981; Shelby *et al.*, 1982, 1989; Schomaker and Leatherberry, 1983; Glass and More, 1992; Watson, 1993; Watson and Niccolucci, 1995). Research suggests that even most individuals who have been unsuccessful at obtaining a permit continue to support the need for use rationing (Fazio and Gilbert, 1974; Stankey, 1979; McCool and Utter, 1982). A study of visitors to three wilderness areas in the US State of Oregon found that support for use restrictions was based on concerns for protecting both resource quality and the quality of the visitor experience (Watson and Niccolucci, 1995). Support by day hikers was influenced most strongly by concerns with crowding, while support by overnight visitors was influenced by concern for both crowding and environmental impacts.

Preferences among alternative use-rationing practices have been found to be highly variable, based on both location and type of user (Magill, 1976; McCool and Utter, 1981; Shelby *et al.*, 1982, 1989; Glass and More, 1992). Support for a particular use-allocation practice appears to be related primarily to which practices respondents are familiar with, and the extent to which they believe they can obtain a permit. A study of river managers found that first-come, first-served and reservation systems were judged the two most administratively feasible allocation practices, and were also the most commonly used practices (Wilke, 1991).

In keeping with the generally favourable attitude towards use limitation described above, most studies have found visitor compliance rates for mandatory permits to be high, ranging from 68% to 97%, with most areas in the 90% range (Lime and Lorence, 1974; Godin and Leonard, 1977; van Wagtendonk and Benedict, 1980; Plager and Womble, 1981; Parsons *et al.*, 1982). Moreover, permit systems that have incorporated trailhead quotas have been found to be effective in redistribut-ing use both spatially and temporally (Hulbert and Higgins, 1977; van Wagtendonk, 1981; van Wagtendonk and Coho, 1986).

Pricing

Among the use-rationing and allocation practices described above, pricing has received special attention in the literature. Pricing is the primary means of allocating scarce resources in a free-market economy. Economic theory generally suggests that higher prices will result in less consumption of a given good or service. Thus, pricing may be an effective approach to limiting use of parks and related ecotourism areas. However, park and recreation services in the public sector have traditionally been priced at a nominal level, or have been provided free of charge. The basic philosophy underlying this policy is that access to park and recreation services is important to all people and no one should be 'priced out of the market'. Interest in instituting or increasing fees at parks and outdoor recreation areas has generated a considerable body of literature that ranges from philosophical to theoretical to empirical (Anderson and Bonsor, 1974; Gibbs, 1977; Manning and Baker, 1981; Driver, 1984; Manning *et al.*, 1984, 1996; Rosenthal *et al.*, 1984; Cockrell and Wellman, 1985a,b; Dustin, 1986; Manning and Koenemann, 1986; Martin, 1986; McCarville *et al.*, 1986; Walsh, 1986; Daniels, 1987; Dustin *et al.*, 1987; Harris and Driver, 1987; Leuschner *et al.*, 1987; McCarville and Crompton, 1987; McDonald *et al.*, 1987; Wilman 1988; Bamford *et al.*, 1988; Reiling *et al.*, 1988, 1992, 1996; Schultz *et al.*, 1988; Fedler and Miles, 1989; Stevenson, 1989; Manning and Zwick, 1990; Kerr and Manfredo, 1991; Peterson 1992; Christensen *et al.*, 1993; Reiling and Cheng, 1994; Scott and Munson, 1994; Emmett *et al.*, 1996; Lundgren, 1996; McCarville, 1996; Reiling and Kotchen, 1996; Bowker and Leeworthy, 1998). Legislation authorizing extended application of fees and higher fees at US national parks and other federal public lands (popularly known as the 'Fee Demonstration Program') has generated especially intense interest, and has given rise to an expanded body of scholarly and professional literature, including special issues of the *Journal of Leisure Research* [31(3)] and the *Journal of Park and Recreation Administration* [17(3)].

Studies of pricing have tended to focus on several issues related to its potential as a recreation management practice. First, to what extent does pricing influence use of parks and related areas? Several studies have found an inverse relationship between price and use (Lindberg and Aylward, 1999; Richer and Christensen, 1999; Schroeder and Louviere, 1999). For example, a study of day users at six US recreation areas administered by the Army Corps of Engineers found that 40% of respondents reported they would no longer use these areas if a fee was instituted (Reiling *et al.*, 1996). However, other studies have shown little or no effects of pricing on recreation use levels (Manning and Baker, 1981; Becker *et al.*, 1985; Leuschner *et al.*, 1987; Rechisky and Williamson, 1992). The literature suggests that the influence of fees on recreation use is dependent upon several factors, including:

1. The 'elasticity of demand' for a park or recreation area. Elasticity refers to the slope of the demand curve that defines the relationship between price and quantity consumed (or visitation). This issue is illustrated in Fig. 16.4. The demand for some recreation areas is relatively elastic, meaning that a change in price has a comparatively large effect on the quantity consumed (or visitation). The demand for other recreation areas is relatively elastic, meaning that a change in price has a comparatively small effect on the quantity consumed (or visitation).
2. The significance of the recreation area. Parks of national significance, such as Yellowstone National Park in the USA, are likely to have a relatively inelastic demand, suggesting that pricing is not likely to be effective in limiting use unless price increases are quite dramatic. Parks that are less significant are likely to be characterized by more elastic demand, and pricing may be an effective use-allocation practice.
3. The percentage of total cost represented by the fee. In cases where the fee charged represents a relatively high percentage of the total cost of visiting a recreation area, pricing is likely to be a more effective use-limiting

approach. However, where the fee charged represents only a small percentage of the total cost, pricing is not likely to be an effective use-limiting approach.
4. The type of fee instituted. Pricing structure can be a potentially important element in determining the effectiveness of fees as a management practice. For example, a daily-use fee might be more effective in limiting total use than an annual pass that allows unlimited use opportunities for a flat fee.

A second issue addressed in the literature is the acceptability of fees to potential visitors. Again, study findings are mixed, though they often suggest that there is a substantial willingness to pay for park and recreation services (Bowker *et al.*, 1999; Krannich *et al.*, 1999; Vogt and Williams, 1999; Williams *et al.*, 1999; Winter *et al.*, 1999). However, research suggests that the acceptability of fees is at least partially dependent on several factors, including:

1. Dispensation of resulting revenues. If revenues derived from fee programmes are retained by the collecting agency and reinvested in recreation facilities and services, then fees are often judged to be more acceptable to park visitors.
2. Initiation of fee or increase in existing fee. Public acceptance of new fees where none were charged before tends to be relatively low compared to increases in existing fees.
3. Local or non-local visitors. Local visitors tend to be more resistant to new fees or increased fees than non-local visitors. As described above, this is probably because fees represent a larger percentage of the total cost of visiting a recreation area for local visitors. Moreover, local residents are likely to visit a given recreation area more often than non-local residents.
4. Provision of comparative information. Visitor acceptance of a fee is likely to be greater when information is provided on the costs of competing or substitute recreation opportunities, and when visitors are made aware of the costs of providing recreation opportunities.

A third issue concerns the potential for pricing to discriminate against certain groups in soci-

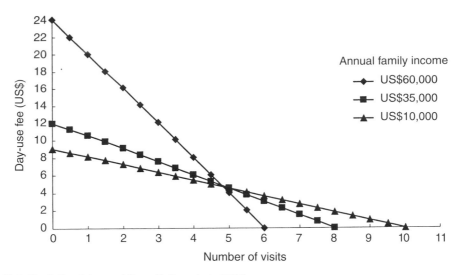

Fig. 16.4. Elasticity of demand (from Reiling *et al.*, 1996).

ety, particularly those with low incomes and minority racial and ethnic groups. Once again, research on this issue is mixed. For example, one study examined the socio-economic characteristics of visitors to two similar outdoor recreation areas in the US state of Virginia, one of which charged an entrance fee, and the other did not (Leuschner *et al.*, 1987). No differences were found in income levels, suggesting the fee had no discriminatory effect. However, several studies have found evidence of discriminatory effects (Mak and Moncur, 1998; Bowker and Leeworthy, 1998; Bowker *et al.*, 1999; Schneider and Budruk, 1999). For example, two studies of willingness to pay recreation fees at state parks and Army Corps of Engineers day-use areas in the US found that lower-income visitors had a more elastic demand curve than did high-income users, as illustrated in Fig. 16.4 (Reiling *et al.*, 1992, 1994). This suggests that pricing may discriminate against lower-income visitors.

A final issue concerns the use of differential pricing to influence recreation use patterns. Differential pricing consists of charging higher or lower fees at selected times and locations. Research demonstrates that outdoor recreation tends to be characterized by relatively extreme 'peaking'. That is, certain areas or times are used very heavily, while other times or areas are relatively lightly used. Can pricing be used to even out such recreation use patterns? Research is suggestive of this potential use of pricing (LaPage *et al.*, 1975; Willis *et al.*, 1975; Manning *et al.*, 1982). For example, studies of experimental differential campsite pricing at state parks in Vermont, USA, documented significant shifts in campsite occupancy patterns (Manning *et al.*, 1984; Bamford *et al.*, 1988).

Conclusion

Environmental impacts of ecotourism demand management action to protect significant natural and cultural resources, as well as the quality of the visitor experience. Managers have at their disposal an array of management actions that range from indirect, light-handed approaches, such as information/education, to direct, more heavy-handed approaches, such as rationing and allocation. While the former may be preferred, the latter may ultimately be required, at least in some places at some times. A growing body of research offers guidance concerning the range of management actions that might be used to ration and allocate use of parks and related ecotourism sites, their potential advantages and disadvantages, and differential effects they may have on selected groups in society.

References

Anderson, F. and Bonsor, N. (1974) Allocation, congestion, and the valuation of recreational resources. *Land Economics* 50, 51–57.

Bamford, T., Manning, R., Forcier, L. and Koenemann, E. (1988) Differential campsite pricing: an experiment. *Journal of Leisure Research* 20, 324–342.

Becker, R., Berrier, D. and Barker, G. (1985) Entrance fees and visitation levels. *Journal of Park and Recreation Administration* 3, 28–32.

Behan, R. (1974) Police state wilderness: a comment on mandatory wilderness permits. *Journal of Forestry* 72, 98–99.

Behan, R. (1976) Rationing wilderness use: an example from Grand Canyon. *Western Wildlands* 3, 23–26.

Bowker, J. and Leeworthy, V. (1998) Accounting for ethnicity in recreation demand: a flexible count data approach. *Journal of Leisure Research* 30(1), 64–79.

Bowker, J., Cordell, H. and Johnson, C. (1999) User fees for recreation services on public lands: a national assessment. *Journal of Park and Recreation Administration* 17(3), 1–14.

Chavez, D. (1996) Mountain biking: direct, indirect, and bridge building management styles. *Journal of Park and Recreation Administration* 14, 21–35.

Christensen, N., Stewart, W. and King, D. (1993) National forest campgrounds: users willing to pay more. *Journal of Forestry* 91, 43–47.

Cockrell, D. and Wellman, J. (1985a) Democracy and leisure: reflections on pay-as-you-go outdoor recreation. *Journal of Park and Recreation Administration* 3, 1–10.

Cockrell, D. and Wellman, J. (1985b) Against the running tide: democracy and outdoor recreation user fees. In: *Proceedings of the 1985 National Outdoor Recreation Trends Symposium, Volume II*. US National Park Service, Atlanta, Georgia, pp. 193–205.

Crompton, J. and Lue, C. (1992) Patterns of equity preferences among Californians for allocating park and recreation resources. *Leisure Sciences* 14, 227–246.

Crompton, J. and Wicks, B. (1988) Implementing a preferred equity model for the delivery of leisure services in the U.S. context. *Leisure Studies* 7, 287–304.

Daniels, S. (1987) Marginal cost pricing and the efficient provision of public recreation. *Journal of Leisure Research* 19, 22–34.

Driver, B. (1984) Public responses to user fees at public recreation areas. In: *Proceedings: Fees for Outdoor Recreation on Lands Open to the Public*. Appalachian Mountain Club, Gorham, New Hampshire, pp. 47–51.

Dustin, D. (1986) Outdoor recreation: a question of equity. *Forum for Applied Research and Public Policy* 1, 62–67.

Dustin, D. and Knopf, R. (1989) Equity issues in outdoor recreation. *Outdoor Recreation Benchmark 1988: Proceedings of the National Outdoor Recreation Forum*. General Technical Report SE-52, USDA Forest Service, pp. 467–471.

Dustin, D. and McAvoy, L. (1980) 'Hardening' national parks. *Environmental Ethics* 2, 29–44.

Dustin, D., McAvoy, L. and Schultz, J. (1987) Beware of the merchant mentality. *Trends* 24, 44–46.

Emmett, J., Havitz, M. and McCarvill, R. (1996) A price subsidy policy for socioeconomically disadvantaged recreation participants. *Journal of Park and Recreation Administration* 14, 63–80.

Fazio, J. and Gilbert, D. (1974) Mandatory wilderness permits: some indications of success. *Journal of Forestry* 72, 753–756.

Fedler, A. and Miles, A. (1989) Paying for backcountry recreation: understanding the acceptability of use fees. *Journal of Park and Recreation Administration* 7, 35–46.

Fractor, D. (1982) Evaluating alternative methods for rationing wilderness use. *Journal of Leisure Research* 14, 341–349.

Gibbs, K. (1977) Economics and administrative regulations of outdoor recreation use. *Outdoor Recreation: Advances in Application of Economics*. General Technical Report WO-2, USDA Forest Service, pp. 98–104.

Gilbert, G., Peterson, G. and Lime, D. (1972) Towards a model of travel behavior in the Boundary Waters Canoe Area. *Environment and Behavior* 4, 131–157.

Glass, R. and More, T. (1992) *Satisfaction, Valuation, and Views Toward Allocation of Vermont Goose Hunting Opportunities*. Research Paper NE-668, USDA Forest Service .

Godin, V. and Leonard, R. (1977) *Permit Compliance in Eastern Wilderness: Preliminary Results*. USDA Forest Service Research Note NE-238.

Harris, C. and Driver, B. (1987) Recreation user fees: pros and cons. *Journal of Forestry* 85, 25–29.

Hendee, J. and Lucas, R. (1973) Mandatory wilderness permits: a necessary management tool. *Journal of Forestry* 71, 206–209.

Hendee, J. and Lucas, R. (1974) Police state wilderness: a comment on a comment. *Journal of Forestry* 72, 100–101.

Hulbert, J. and Higgins, J. (1977) BWCA visitor distribution system. *Journal of Forestry* 75, 338–340.

Kerr, G. and Manfredo, M. (1991) An attitudinal-based model of pricing for recreation services. *Journal of Leisure Research* 23, 37–50.

Krannich, R., Eisenhauer, B., Field, D., Pratt, C. and
    Luloff, A. (1999) Implications of the National
    Park Service Recreation Fee Demonstration
    Program for Park operations and management:
    Perceptions of NPS Managers. *Journal of Park
    and Recreation Administration* 17(3), 35–52.
LaPage, W., Cormier, P., Hamilton, G. and Cormier,
    A. (1975) *Differential Campsite Pricing and
    Campground Attendance*. Research Paper NE-
    330, USDA Forest Service.
Leuschner, W., Cook, P., Roggenbuck, J. and
    Oderwald, R. (1987) A comparative analysis for
    wilderness user fee policy. *Journal of Leisure
    Research* 19, 101–114.
Lime, D. (1977) When the wilderness gets crowded
    . . . ? *Naturalist*, 28, 1–7.
Lime, D. (1979) Carrying capacity. *Trends* 16, 37–40.
Lime, D. and Lorence, G. (1974) *Improving Estimates
    of Wilderness Use from Mandatory Travel
    Permits*. Research Paper NC-101, USDA Forest
    Service.
Lindberg, K. and Aylward, B. (1999) Price responsive-
    ness in the developing country nature tourism
    context: review and Costa Rican case study.
    Journal of Leisure Research 31(3), 281–299.
Lindberg, K., Wood, M. and Engeldrum, D. (1998)
    *Ecotourism: a Guide for Planners and
    Managers*. The Ecotourism Society, North
    Bennington, Vermont.
Lucas, R. (1980) *Use Patterns and Visitor
    Characteristics, Attitudes, and Preferences in
    Nine Wilderness and Other Roadless Areas*.
    Research Paper INT-253, USDA Forest Service.
Lucas, R. (1985) Recreation trends and management
    of the Bob Marshall Wilderness Complex.
    *Proceedings of the 1985 National Outdoor
    Recreation Trends Symposium*, Volume II. US
    National Park Service, Atlanta, Georgia, pp.
    309–316.
Lundgren, A. (ed.) (1996) *Recreation Fees in the
    National Park Service-Issues, Policies and
    Guidelines for Future Action*. University of
    Minnesota Cooperative Park Studies Unit, St
    Paul, Minnesota.
Magill, A. (1976) *Campsite Reservation Systems: The
    Campers' Viewpoint*. Research Paper PSW-121,
    USDA Forest Service.
Mak, J. and Moncur, J. (1998) Political economy of
    protecting unique recreational resources:
    Hanauma Bay, Hawaii. *Ambio* 27(3), 217–223.
Manning, R. (1979) Strategies for managing recrea-
    tional use of national parks. *Parks* 4, 13–15.
Manning, R. (1999) *Studies in Outdoor Recreation*.
    Oregon State University Press, Corvallis, Oregon.
Manning, R. and Baker, S. (1981) Discrimination
    through user fees: fact or fiction? *Parks and
    Recreation* 16, 70–74.

Manning, R. and Koenemann, E. (1986) Differential
    campsite pricing: an experiment. *Camp-
    grounds: New Perspectives on Management*.
    Southern Illinois University, Carbondale, Ilinois,
    pp. 39–48.
Manning, R. and Zwick, R. (1990) The relationship
    between quality of outdoor recreation opportu-
    nities and support for recreation funding. *Pro-
    ceedings of the 1989 Northeastern Recreation
    Research Symposium*. General Technical Report
    NE-145, USDA Forest Service, pp. 13–18.
Manning, R., Powers, L. and Mock, C. (1982)
    Temporal distribution of forest recreation: prob-
    lems and potential. *Forest and River Recreation:
    Research Update*. Miscellaneous Publication
    18, University of Minnesota Agricultural
    Experiment Station, St Paul, Minnesota, pp.
    26–32.
Manning, R., Callinan, E., Echelberger, H.,
    Koenemann, E. and McEwen, D. (1984)
    Differential fees: raising revenue, distributing
    demand. *Journal of Park and Recreation
    Administration* 2, 20–38.
Manning, R., LaPage, W., Griffall, K. and Simon, B.
    (1996) Suggested principles for designing and
    implementing user fees and charges in the
    National Park System. *Recreation Fees in the
    National Park System*. University of Minnesota
    Cooperative Park Studies Unit, St Paul,
    Minnesota, pp. 134–136.
Martin, B. (1986) Hiker's opinions about fees for
    backcountry recreation. *Proceedings – National
    Wilderness Research Conference: Current
    Research*. General Technical Report INT-212,
    USDA Forest Service, pp. 483–488.
McCarville, R. (1996) The importance of price last
    paid in developing price expectations for a
    public leisure service. *Journal of Park and
    Recreation Administration* 14, 52–64.
McCarville, R. and Crompton, J. (1987) Propositions
    addressing perception of reference price for
    public recreation services. *Leisure Sciences* 9,
    281–291.
McCarville, R., Reiling, S. and White, C. (1986) The
    role of fairness in users' assessments of first-time
    fees for a public recreation service. *Leisure
    Sciences* 18, 61–76.
McCool, S. and Utter, J. (1981) Preferences for allo-
    cating river recreation use. *Water Resources
    Bulletin* 17, 431–437.
McCool, S. and Utter, J. (1982) Recreation use lotter-
    ies: outcomes and preferences. *Journal of
    Forestry* 80, 10–11, 29.
McDonald, C., Noe, F. and Hammitt, W. (1987)
    Expectations and recreation fees: a dilemma for
    recreation resource administrators. *Journal of
    Park and Recreation Administration* 5, 1–9.

McLean, D. and Johnson, R. (1997) Techniques for rationing public recreation services. *Journal of Park and Recreation Administration* 15, 76–92.

Parsons, D., Stohlgren, T. and Kraushaar, J. (1982) Wilderness permit accuracy: differences between reported and actual use. *Environmental Management* 6, 329–335.

Peterson, G. (1992) Using fees to manage congestion at recreation areas. *Park Visitor Research for Better Management: Park Visitor Research Workshop.* Phillip Institute of Technology, Canberra, Australia, pp. 57–67.

Peterson, G. and Lime, D. (1979) People and their behavior: a challenge for recreation management. *Journal of Forestry* 77, 343–346.

Plager, A. and Womble, P. (1981) Compliance with backcountry permits in Mount McKinley National Park. *Journal of Forestry* 79, 155–156.

Rechisky, A. and Williamson, B. (1992) Impact of user fees on day use attendance at New Hampshire State parks. *Proceedings of the 1991 Northeastern Recreation Research Symposium.* General Technical Report NE-160, USDA Forest Service, pp. 106–108.

Reiling, S. and Cheng, H. (1994) Potential revenues from a new day-use fee. *Proceedings of the 1994 Northeastern Recreation Research Symposium.* General Technical Report NE-198, USDA Forest Service, pp. 57–60.

Reiling, S. and Kotchen, M. (1996) Lessons learned from past research on recreation fees. *Recreation Fees in the National Park Service: Issues, Policies and Guidelines for Future Action.* University of Minnesota Cooperative Park Studies Unit, St Paul, Minnesota, pp. 49–69.

Reiling, S., Criner, G. and Oltmanns, S. (1988) The influence of information on users' attitudes toward campground user fees. *Journal of Leisure Research* 20, 208–217.

Reiling, S., Cheng, H. and Trott, C. (1992) Measuring the discriminatory impact associated with higher recreational fees. *Leisure Sciences* 14, 121–137.

Reiling, S., McCarville, R. and White, C. (1994) *Demand and Marketing Study at Corps of Engineers Day-Use Areas.* Army Corps of Engineers Waterways Experiment Station, Vicksburg, Mississippi.

Reiling, S., Cheng, H., Robinson, C., McCarville, R. and White, C. (1996) Potential equity effects of a new day-use fee. *Proceedings of the 1995 Northeastern Recreation Research Symposium.* General Technical Report NE-218, USDA Forest Service, pp. 27–31.

Richer, J. and Christensen, N. (1999) Appropriate fees for wilderness day use: pricing decisions for recreation on public land. *Journal of Leisure Research* 31(3), 269–280.

Rosenthal, D., Loomis, J. and Peterson, G. (1984) Pricing for efficiency and revenue in public recreation areas. *Journal of Leisure Research* 16, 195–208.

Schneider, I. and Budruk, M. (1999) Displacement as a response to the Federal Recreation Fee Program. *Journal of Park and Recreation Administration* 17(3), 76–84.

Schomaker, J. and Leatherberry, E. (1983) A test for inequity in river recreation reservation systems. *Journal of Soil and Water Conservation* 38, 52–56.

Schroeder, H. and Louviere, J. (1999) Stated choice models for predicting the impact of user fees at public recreation sites. *Journal of Leisure Research* 31(3), 300–324.

Schultz, J., McAvoy, L. and Dustin, D. (1988) What are we in business for? *Parks and Recreation* 23, 52–53.

Scott, D. and Munson, W. (1994) Perceived constraints to park usage among individuals with low incomes. *Journal of Park and Recreation Administration* 12, 79–96.

Shelby, B., Danley, B., Gibbs, M. and Peterson, M. (1982) Preferences of backpackers and river runners for allocation techniques. *Journal of Forestry* 80, 416–419.

Shelby, B., Whittaker, D. and Danley, M. (1989) Allocation currencies and perceived ability to obtain permits. *Leisure Sciences* 11, 137–144.

Stankey, G. (1973) *Visitor Perception of Wilderness Recreation Carrying Capacity.* Research Paper INT-142, USDA Forest Service.

Stankey, G. (1979) Use rationing in two southern California wildernesses. *Journal of Forestry* 77, 347–349.

Stankey, G. and Baden, J. (1977) *Rationing Wilderness use: Methods, Problems, and Guidelines.* Research Paper INT-192, USDA Forest Service.

Stevenson, S. (1989) A test of peak load pricing on senior citizen recreationists: a case study of Steamboat Lake State Park. *Journal of Park and Recreation Administration* 7, 58–68.

Utter, J., Gleason, W. and McCool, S. (1981) User perceptions of river recreation allocation techniques. *Some Recent Products of River Recreation Research.* General Technical Report NC-63, USDA Forest Service, pp. 27–32.

Van Wagtendonk, J. (1981) The effect of use limits on backcountry visitation trends in Yosemite National Park. *Leisure Sciences* 4, 311–323.

Van Wagtendonk, J. and Benedict, J. (1980) Wilderness permit compliance and validity. *Journal of Forestry* 78, 399–401.

Van Wagtendonk, J. and Coho, P. (1986) Trailhead quotas: rationing use to keep wilderness wild. *Journal of Forestry* 84, 22–24.

Vogt, C. and Williams, D. (1999) Support for wilderness recreation fees: the influence of fee purpose and day versus overnight use. *Journal of Park and Recreation Administration* 17(3), 85–99.

Walsh, R. (1986) *Recreation Economic Decisions.* Venture Publishing, State College, Pennsylvania.

Watson, A. (1993) *Characteristics of Visitors Without Permits Compared to Those With Permits at the Desolation Wilderness, California.* Research Note INT-414, USDA Forest Service.

Watson, A. and Niccolucci, M. (1995) Conflicting goals of wilderness management: natural conditions vs. natural experiences. *Proceedings of the Second Symposium on Social Aspects and Recreation Research.* General Technical Report PSW-156, USDA Forest Service, pp. 11–15.

Wicks, B. (1987) The allocation of recreation and park resources: the courts' intervention. *Journal of Park and Recreation Administration* 5, 1–9.

Wicks, B. and Crompton, J. (1986) Citizen and administrator perspectives of equity in the delivery of park services. *Leisure Sciences* 8, 341–365.

Wicks, B. and Crompton, J. (1987) An analysis of the relationships between equity choice preferences, service type and decision making groups in a U.S. city. *Journal of Leisure Research* 19, 189–204.

Wicks, B. and Crompton, J. (1989) Allocation services for parks and recreation: a model for implementing equity concepts in Austin, Texas. *Journal of Urban Affairs* 11, 169–188.

Wicks, B. and Crompton, J. (1990) Predicting the equity preferences of park and recreation department employees and residents of Austin, Texas. *Journal of Leisure Research* 22, 18–35.

Wilke, T. (1991) Comparing rationing policies used on rivers. *Journal of Park and Recreation Administration* 9, 73–80.

Williams, D., Vogt, C. and Vitterso, J. (1999) Structural equation modeling of users' response to wilderness recreation fees. *Journal of Leisure Research* 31(3), 245–268.

Willis, C., Canavan, J. and Bond, R. (1975) Optimal short-run pricing policies for a public campground. *Journal of Leisure Research* 7, 108–113.

Wilman, E. (1988) Pricing policies for outdoor recreation. *Land Economics* 64(3), 234–241.

Winter, P., Palucki, L. and Burkhardt, R. (1999) Anticipated responses to a fee program: the key is trust. *Journal of Leisure Research* 31(3), 207–226.

17

Using Ecological Impact Measurements to Design Visitor Management

Ralf Buckley

International Centre for Ecotourism Research, Griffith University, Southport, Queensland, Australia

Introduction

Protected areas worldwide are becoming more and more crowded, with more and more people visiting them for more and more different activities. This applies to all types of protected areas, but particularly to IUCN Category II areas, referred to here as national parks, or simply parks. Visitors include private individuals, non-profit groups and commercial tour clients. Global demand for nature and adventure tourism and recreation continues to grow, and parks provide one of the main opportunities. Parks agencies now have to devote a considerable proportion of their time and resources to visitor management; often, much more than they can now devote to conservation management. Their research and information needs have changed accordingly. The same applies for other public and private owners and managers of land with high recreational use.

In parks with low visitation, the major monitoring requirements relate to external environmental threats, such as: weeds and feral animals entering the park from neighbouring properties and becoming established; unscheduled fires; outbreaks of plant or animal diseases; illegal human activities, such as poaching, logging or seed collecting; and air or water pollution in the park from external sources upwind or upstream. In parks and other land with high levels of visitation, land manag-

ers also need information on visitor characteristics, visitor impacts and the effectiveness of visitor management tools. Visitor characteristics may include numbers, origins, activities, expectations and satisfaction, and are determined principally from on-site visitor surveys, sometimes coupled with automatic counters and similar approaches. The effectiveness of visitor management tools can be assessed both in terms of increased visitor satisfaction, and reduced visitor impacts.

Monitoring visitor impacts requires somewhat different approaches from monitoring impacts of external threats, though many of the impact mechanisms, environmental parameters affected, and sampling or measurement techniques are the same. The significance of ecological impacts from tourism and recreation has been recognized widely by protected area management agencies (Parks Canada, 2001; USNPS, 2001), environmental non-government organizations (GYC, 2001) and researchers (Leung and Marion, 2000; Buckley, 2001, 2002, 2003; Sirakaya *et al.*, 2001; Newsome *et al.*, 2002). However, the practical issues involved in monitoring these impacts still seem to be problematical for many agencies. For tourism in parks, there are many lists of potential ecological indicators that have not been implemented in practice, many systems of management indicators with little ecological basis, and many ecological studies of recreational impacts which do not provide management indicators. Indicators that are both scientifically defensible and feasible and valuable in management, however, are very rare.

Context for Indicators

Uses of indicators

Broadly, parks agencies use environmental indicators in order to: determine what impacts tourists and other visitors are having on the park's natural environments; compare them with impacts from other sources; and undertake and evaluate management responses. In particular, environmental degradation caused by local visitor impacts can be addressed most effectively by managing the visitors, whereas those caused by other external impacts can only be addressed by management of natural resources directly. Commonly, individual protected area management agencies have specific administrative frameworks within which they collect and use such indicators. For example, some parks agencies have policies or requirements to produce regular reports on the state of the parks, whereas others may use impact indicators to allocate funds for infrastructure and rehabilitation work.

Green cf. brown indicators, local and global scales

The effects of the human economy on the natural environment may conveniently be classified into two major categories, known respectively as green and brown (or grey) impacts. Broadly, green impacts are those that involve consumption of biological resources, e.g. by the forestry sector, with consequent loss of biodiversity and ecosystem area. Brown impacts damage the natural environment though discharge of wastes. Burning fossil fuels to generate electricity or drive cars, for example, releases greenhouse gases and various other atmospheric pollutants. Energy consumption can thus be used as an aggregate measure of global atmospheric impacts. Brown indicators such as these are therefore used widely in environmental performance measurement and accreditation schemes, including those in the tourism industry (Font and Buckley, 2001).

For tourism in protected areas, however, local-scale but proportionally large impacts on in-park biodiversity are more significant ecologically than broad-scale but proportionally smaller impacts on global air quality. Certainly, tourists can have considerable impacts on air and water quality in some parks, but these are ecologically significant more because of local-scale effects on vegetation and aquatic ecosystems, than because of their contribution to global pollution. Generic indicators of brown impacts are therefore not particularly relevant for managing tourism in parks, unless they are carefully selected and customized for a particular waste management issue of immediate ecological significance to conservation of the natural environment in the park concerned.

For example, at a global scale, burning wood for small-scale heating generally produces less total environmental impacts than burning highly refined petroleum products. In a number of heavily used parks in the Himalayas, however, collecting firewood for trekkers has caused widespread deforestation, whereas the quantity of fuel needed to replace fires with fuel stoves is very small on a global scale. In this instance, therefore, fuel stoves are environmentally preferable.

Local-scale indicators of green impacts, in contrast, while of little relevance for airlines or urban hotels, are critical for tourism and recreation in protected areas and similar fragile environments. The many generic guidelines, checklists, indicators and accreditation schemes for sustainability in tourism overall, therefore, are of little use for tourism and recreation in parks. A very different set of indicators is needed, focusing on local-scale green rather than global-scale brown impacts, and devised by biologists and ecologists rather than engineers and social scientists. Many potential indicators have been identified (Leung and Marion, 2000; Sirakaya *et al.*, 2001; Newsome *et al.*, 2002), but rarely have they been implemented in practice.

Baselines and benchmarks

Impacts can only be detected as a change relative to a prior baseline. Even indicators that measure environmental quality rather than environmental impacts can only be used for management if there is a benchmark to compare them against. Benchmarks are also needed if environmental degradation or management at one park is to be assessed in a national, regional or global context. And if indicators of different types are to be aggregated to yield an overall comparative measure of environmental quality, impact or management performance, they must first be expressed as numerical measures with similar means, range and variance; and normalization against a benchmark is generally the first step. Standardization can be useful in comparing different indicators against each other, e.g. to determine which changed the most or the fastest. Aggregate indices compiled from a suite of standardized indicators are useful for comparisons between parks in the same geographic region or legal jurisdiction; for comparisons between regions and countries; and for tracking trends over time, whether locally or globally. The availability of baselines or benchmarks, or the feasibility of establishing them, is hence a significant consideration in selecting specific indicators of tourism impacts in parks.

Fluctuation, cycles and trends

Most environmental parameters that are responsive enough to serve as indicators of tourist impacts are also likely to experience considerable natural variation. A baseline for such parameters is hence not a single fixed numerical value, but a pattern of variation in space and time, with defined confidence limits. Depending on its purpose, a benchmark may need to be defined in a similar way. Relevant patterns of variation will typically include: seasonal cycles, and perhaps also diurnal and multi-year cycles; fluctuations related to events such as floods, frosts or fires; spatial patterns related to terrain and geology; and spatial patterns associated with internal processes such as the formation and regeneration of gaps in forest cover caused by the death of individual trees, or periodic fires regulated by the gradual accumulation of plant biomass. In addition to natural sources of variation, many environmental indicator parameters may also be affected by a range of anthropogenic factors not associated with tourism or recreation; and these must also be quantified and taken into account in establishing and using indicators of tourism impacts specifically. For example, air and water quality in a protected area may be subject to off-park impacts from nearby roads or factories, or towns or farmland upstream. In most countries, for example, the proportion of watercourses which effectively retain wilderness water quality is extremely small. Indicators of environmental quality to be used in, for example, state-of-the-park or state-of-the-environment reporting, need to include impacts from all sources, including those off-park. Indicators to be used in managing tourists and other visitors, however, need to differentiate clearly between impacts associated with tourism and recreation, and those associated with other human activity.

Users, ecosystems and impact types

Different types of user engaged in different types of activity have different types of impact in different types of ecosystem. To be useful in management, indicators in any particular protected area need to focus on impacts which are ecologically significant for its particular ecosystem, and which reflect the particular characteristics and activities of its users. For example, if a park is free of a particular weed or pathogen species, but at risk that visitors may import it on their clothing, livestock or vehicles, then the distribution of the weed or pathogen in areas around the park, and the effectiveness of visitor quarantine measures, become particularly important indicators. In a park where wildlife suffer significant disturbance in winter from off-track recreational snowmobiling, with potential effects on individual energetic balance and overwinter survival, then indicators of snowmobile noise and activity patterns, and animal stress and response, will be more critical.

Short- cf. long-term impacts

Some of the effects of tourism and recreation on the natural environment are lasting, others evanescent. This applies both to immediate and

direct impacts, and to their indirect consequences. For example, the sound of an engine
backfire or a pneumatic tool is sharp but short.
If repeated sufficiently, however, it may drive
wildlife away from the area for an entire season
or longer, particularly if the species concerned
are also subject to hunting; and this may have
long-term effects on the species populations.
Similarly, if a toxin is discharged into a river or
a coral reef, its effects on aquatic ecosystems
may last long after the toxin itself has been
flushed away. Indicators for short-term impacts,
therefore, need to be able to detect individual
events and, if possible, quantify both their
magnitude and frequency. For longer-lasting
impacts, the time when indicators are measured is less critical. Detecting a change relative
to a baseline or benchmark, however, may
often require a more subtle sampling scheme
than for short-term effects.

Types of Indicator

Priority conservation values

Most protected areas are protected in order to
conserve particular species or ecosystems. In
some cases, notably World Heritage Areas,
these specific conservation values are defined
both in the nomination process and as an
adjunct to establishing legislation. In this case,
managers of the areas concerned need indicators for those specific priority conservation
values, irrespective of the particular factors that
may be affecting them. Such indicators might
include, for example, areas of remaining undisturbed vegetation or animal habitat or of particular ecosystems, such as mangroves or vine
thickets; physicochemical indicators of stream
water quality; or the number of individuals in a
local population of an endangered species.

Even where priority conservation values
are not defined in established legislation or
management plans, protected area agencies
may require broadscale environmental quality
indicators such as those listed above. In parks
where external threats are a major management
consideration, indicators that show the intensity or effects of these threats may be particularly important. These might include, for
example, populations of feral animal species,

or indicators of water quality immediately
upstream of a park boundary.

Management process indicators

A second major category of indicator includes
those relating to management processes, effort
and outcome. Indicators of management processes, for example, may include: the existence
of a management plan, and the level of detail it
contains; existence and detail of implementation plans for specific management issues such
as weed control or visitor education; emergency
response procedures and equipment; and visitor infrastructure and interpretation programmes. Budget processes and allocations,
staffing processes and numbers, management
targets and monitoring programmes can all be
used as indicators of environmental management processes. The extent, quality and maintenance of tracks, fences, signs, parking and other
visitor facilities may also be useful indicators,
particularly if related to targets in implementation plans. Other indicators of frontcountry
management effort include, for example, management expenditure per unit area or per visitor; weight or volume of litter removed or taken
to landfill; and staff time devoted to particular
activities. All of these are easy to measure and
easily modified by changed management practices; but they are only indirectly related to
either primary conservation values, or to the
specific impacts of tourism and recreation.

Indicators of backcountry ecological impacts

In managing recreation to minimize conservation impacts, the most valuable types of environmental indicator are those that measure
visitor impacts on backcountry areas directly.
Such indicators need to reflect ecological processes rather than management processes.
Common examples include: track erosion;
weed distribution; human noise; microlitter at
backcountry campsites; measures of stress,
individual mortality, behavioural changes or
population impacts for particular wildlife species; and analogous measures for particular
plant species.

Design of Impact-indicator Systems

Criteria for indicators

Selecting broad indicators of environmental quality, management efforts or tourism sustainability is relatively straightforward. Possible indicator parameters are tabulated by Manning (1999, pp. 123, 128–140), Sirakaya *et al.* (2001), and Newsome *et al.* (2002, pp. 270–272, 277, 281). Likewise, there are numerous research-level scientific studies of specific ecological impacts, reviewed by Liddle (1997), Leung and Marion (2000) and Buckley (2001); and manuals of ecological monitoring techniques, such as Elzinga *et al.* (2001).

Effective indicators of significant recreational impacts on protected area ecosystems, however, which are scientifically meaningful and defensible as well as useful in practical management, are more difficult to select. In general, the most useful ecological indicators for management will fit the following criteria:

- discriminating, so that they can differentiate the impacts of tourism from other natural or anthropogenic sources of variations;
- quantifiable, at least approximately or at a categorical level, so that management responses can be matched to the level of impact;
- actionable, so that if an impact is detected, something can be done about it;
- sensitive, so that a change in the degree of impact produces a clearly distinguishable change in the indicator;
- ecologically significant, so that any change indicates an effect that is important for the park's conservation values;
- integrated, so that the indicators used in a particular park, or set of parks, provide a balanced overall picture of the impacts of tourism and recreation;
- feasible, in the sense that resources and expertise can be made available to monitor them in practice.

Distinguishing tourism impacts

To detect an impact over a given time period in a given area from a specific source such as tour-

ists, generally requires: (i) a sampling pattern with unimpacted control sites as well as sites with impacts; and (ii) measurements before, during and after the time period concerned. To ecologists this is known as a BACI design: Before/After, Control/Impact. For statistical confidence, measurements need to be replicated for all four of these categories. In addition, to comply fully with the mathematical requirements of statistical tests, the sites should be allocated randomly between impacted 'treatment' sites and non-impacted 'control' sites. In practice, as with environmental impact monitoring in many sectors and circumstances, these requirements often cannot all be met. Sampling designs must be adapted to circumstances. The price is usually either higher sampling effort, or reduced reliability of results.

To distinguish visitor impacts from other sources of variations, several approaches are possible, separately or in combination. The first is to use an indicator which is specific to tourism and recreation, or at least where other sources are negligibly small in comparison, i.e. control values remain zero throughout the monitoring period. This approach is generally most practicable for physicochemical indicators. Examples include: concentrations of petroleum residues in water samples from otherwise undisturbed lakes used for recreational power boating; or atmospheric concentrations of nitrogen oxides, or other components of car exhausts, in a valley subject to heavy use by recreational vehicles; or the proportion of time during which engine noise from recreational vehicles such as snowmobiles, helicopters or jetskis is audible in an otherwise peaceful wilderness area. Biological and microbiological indicators where this approach can be used are less common. An example might include the frequency of horse droppings along a track in an area with no wild or feral horses. For most biological indicators, however, controls are required; and there are some, such as the first record of a new weed or pathogen in a given park, where even with controls it is difficult to determine whether the introduction was caused by visitors or other sources.

The second main approach is to use a very localized control, where it can be assumed that any natural variation between impacted and control site, over either space or time, is negligible compared to the impact of tourism and recreation. For example, soil compaction on a walking track or campsite might be compared with undisturbed off-track areas nearby. However, this approach can only be used if it can reasonably be assumed that without the impact, there would be no distinction between control and impacted sites. For a track crossing flat ground, with the same vegetation on both sides, such an assumption would be reasonable; for a track running along the boundary between subalpine forest and alpine meadow, it would not.

Similarly, for a vehicle ford across a uniform stretch of river, the impacts of the crossing on in-stream turbidity can be examined by comparing water quality immediately upstream and downstream of the ford. However, to test for the impacts of recreational swimming on a forest stream, it is not enough to compare water quality upstream and downstream of a swimming hole, because there might be systematic differences upstream and downstream of all pools in the stream, irrespective of swimmers. In such circumstances, the difference between water quality parameters upstream and downstream of the swimming hole must be compared with the corresponding difference for a similar and nearby pool in the same stream, but without swimmers (Warnken, 1996; Buckley *et al.*, 2001).

Even with a control of this type, strictly speaking, a single comparison can only test for an impact at the particular site concerned. To test whether the relevant impact occurs more generally, or to determine its magnitude and significance, would require a replicated set of relevant comparisons. This could be done, for example, for a set of swimming holes in the same creek, a set of creeks in the same catchment, or a set of tracks in the same forest or meadow. A broader-scale control, such as a comparison between different creeks with high and low levels of tourist use, will generally be more robust, in the sense that the results are likely to be reliable and broadly applicable. Smaller-scale controls, such as neighbouring pools in a single creek, will generally be more sensitive in the sense that they can detect a smaller degree of impact.

The third main approach is to measure the selected indicator parameter, or parameters, at a number of sites with known and different degrees of tourist activity, and to examine the effect of tourism activity on the environmental indicator through correlation or regression. If the indicator parameter is also subject to influences from other factors, and those factors can be quantified at each site, then the relative significance of tourism can be distinguished through multiple regression. This approach is generally most useful where a large number of potential monitoring sites are available; where the impacts of tourism are diffuse rather than localized; or where broadscale impacts over a relatively large geographical area are of greater interest. Examples include: the amount of microlitter at backcountry campsites, in relation to number of visitor nights; or the number of different weed species in different areas of similar terrain and vegetation, relative to the number, density and use of walking tracks.

Self-limiting cf. self-propagating impacts

Some types of impacts are self-limiting, in the sense that if the source of impacts is removed, its effects will gradually reduce. The time scale of recovery may be minutes, e.g. for noise disturbance to bird calls along a rainforest track; months, as for the introduction of a weed seed which germinates but does not survive over winter; decades, as for the recovery of vegetation on an abandoned walking track; or centuries, as for damage by off-road vehicles to cryptogamic crusts on desert soils. Other types of impacts are self-propagating, in the sense that once triggered by tourism, they continue to spread even if the source is subsequently removed. A fire started by a tourist's cigarette butt, campfire or car muffler can expand very rapidly in a period of minutes, hours or days. A weed or pathogen inadvertently introduced in a tourist's car or clothing, horse feed or human waste, may subsequently spread over following years and decades. Even an impact such as litter can sometimes effectively be self-propagating through a social or psychological mechanism, if tourists are more likely to discard litter in areas where it is already present than in areas where there is none.

Self-propagating impacts are commonly more critical in the design of indicator systems, because the chance of controlling them through management action is far greater if they are identified as soon as they first occur. For control of an established weed, for example, it will probably be useful to track its areal extent and rate of spread in relation to tourist corridors and other disturbances, using quantitative on-ground measurements and perhaps also aerial photography or remote sensing. For a new weed species, however, the critical issue is to find and identify it when it first arrives and there is still a possibility of eradicating it. If it is not yet present in the park, there is no opportunity to measure its in-park distribution; and even if it is present, remote sensing will not detect it until there is a sizeable patch with a recognizable signature. If the critical indicator is simply presence or absence, then no sampling technique can substitute for experienced field staff who can search areas of suitable habitat at intervals and identify the species reliably if they find it.

Note that particular types of impact may behave differently in different environments, being self-limiting in some but self-propagating in others. For example, fire only spreads in dry vegetation with a sufficient fuel load. Trampling vegetation on a steep downslope alpine track may cause expanding erosion gullies; whereas trampling a thicket of lawyer vine in subtropical rainforest is likely to injure the person more than the plant.

Indirect impact mechanisms

Where tourist infrastructure and activities affect plants and animal populations through indirect mechanisms, the first step in establishing an indicator system is to identify what those mechanisms are. This may be far from straightforward, particularly if similar mechanisms have not been identified previously elsewhere. It may not be immediately apparent to a land manager or tour operator that grooming snow on ski slopes can affect small montane mammals by crushing their undersnow burrows; that the noise of helicopter overflights in a scenic mountain range may affect the population of rare bird species by drowning out their territorial and courtship calls; that introduced weeds may affect native plant species by competing for insect pollinators; that an orienteering event

can cause major disturbance to deer populations; or that duck subject to recreational hunting may be killed not only by a direct hit, but by accidentally ingesting spent lead shot when feeding from bottom sediments. All or most of these impacts do occur, however, and many more besides.

Many more indirect ecological impacts associated with infrastructure development have been identified in various parts of the world, and some of these could apply equally well to tourism. For example, in one case on the west coast of the USA, a proposed real estate development would have cleared plants that serve as the only food source for the caterpillars of an endangered butterfly species during part of the year. Even if the butterflies were elsewhere when the vegetation was cleared, therefore, the real estate development would have caused the extinction of the butterfly population concerned (McDonald and Buckley, 1993). Another example is reported from the Brazilian Amazon, in an area where a network of tracks is dividing an area of forest into smaller patches. One of the characteristic bird species of the forest is an antbird, which gets its food by following the foraging columns of a particular species of army ant. The ants live in large colonies which require a minimum area of forest to survive. If the tracks divide the forest around a colony into a patch smaller than this minimum size threshold, the ant colony will move *en masse* to a larger forest fragment, crossing the tracks in order to do so. The antbirds, however, live only in undisturbed forests, and do not venture to the forest edge or out of the forest canopy. Therefore, if their ant colony crosses a track, the antbirds are unable to follow – once a patch of forest is too small to support an ant colony, the ants can move elsewhere but the antbirds die. Without a detailed knowledge of ant and antbird ecology, however, it would not be obvious that the disappearance of antbirds was due to tracks.

The point about these cases is not the particular mechanism involved, since this may be highly specific to the ecosystem or individual species concerned. It is simply to show that impacts that are not immediately obvious may in fact be quite commonplace, and may also be highly significant for the survival of particular species. A system of environmental indicators that is designed to quantify particular known tourist impacts is unlikely to detect previously unanticipated indirect impacts such as these, even though these impacts may be both ecologically significant, and caused by tourism. If a particular protected area, or other area of high conservation value which is used for tourism and recreation, is known to contain species or ecosystems of high conservation value, an effective environmental indicator programme also needs to monitor those components directly. And if land managers do not know what species occur in the areas for which they are responsible, as is indeed the case for many protected areas, then a system for environmental indicators of tourist impacts should start with relevant baseline studies before any tourism is permitted in the protected area concerned. Without such baseline information, land managers cannot tell whether tourism and recreation will damage the park's primary conservation function.

Ecological skills and knowledge

Approaches and information, such as those outlined above, are a fundamental part of the knowledge and skill base of any professional ecologist. Diagnostics on the function of any complex system generally require specialist information, training and experience if we want to know what is causing abnormal symptoms. In a human body, for example, we use a doctor to prescribe and interpret relevant physiological and pathological tests. Even for a far simpler structure, such as a gas pipeline, we insist on qualified specialist engineers to commission and assess non-destructive tests to determine whether the structure is still in good repair. Natural ecosystems are far more complex than either human bodies or any human mechanical device or social institution. We should therefore expect that diagnosing impacts of tourism in protected areas would require an ecologist with at least as much skill as a doctor, engineer or lawyer. And for any of these complex systems, we expect to seek specific professional advice for every separate symptom or checkup, incident or inspection. There are innumerable books in each of these fields, both popular and reference, but we do not expect these to

substitute for individual professional consultations. Why should it be any different for ecological expertise?

Of course, in any of these fields, expertise may be gained by experience as well as training. Some bush mechanics, paramedics and paralegals may be as competent as their more highly qualified colleagues, but this is the exception rather than the rule. Professional qualifications are intended as a guarantee of competence. Similarly, there are many naturalists and park rangers with a detailed knowledge and understanding of particular areas and environments, which can only be gained by long experience in the field; and for some types of tourist impact, their observations may be as least as valuable as more formal monitoring programmes. Such local expertise is becoming rarer, however, as financial pressures force protected area agencies to move rangers between regions more frequently, hire casual field staff during peak seasons, and use their most experienced rangers in administration. So if parks agencies are to monitor tourist impacts, they will need to hire ecologists, whether on staff or on contract. Note, incidentally, that hiring staff trained in tourism is not an adequate substitute: designing environmental indicators needs skills in science, not business. It is also far easier for an ecologist to learn how the tourism industry works than for a tourism graduate to become an ecologist.

Many tour operators in national parks do appreciate the significance of environmental indicators and are keen to assist in environmental monitoring. Some operators, indeed, trained as biologists before turning to the tourism business. Tour operator observations can be particularly useful where, for example, tours visit particular sites or areas repeatedly, perhaps more often than rangers; or where tour clients are keen to take part in environmental programmes as an educational experience. Similarly, parks agencies may be able to make use of environmental data compiled by other government agencies. Examples include aerial photographs and satellite imagery from, for example, national mapping authorities; or water-quality sampling conducted by health authorities. Whether or not these are sufficiently specific to distinguish the impacts of tourism and recreation is generally fortuitous, but sources such as these are often relevant for broadscale indicators of environmental quality.

Indicators in practice

As with management indicators of any type, environmental indicators of tourism impacts in parks are most valuable if there is an operational framework in which they are used. For example, many land-management agencies use management frameworks based on conceptual approaches, such as limited of acceptable change, recreational capacity, etc. (Stankey *et al.*, 1985; McCool and Cole, 1997; Buckley, 1998, 2000; Fennell, 1999, p. 124; Manning, 1999; Hockings *et al.*, 2000; Weaver 2001, pp. 82–84; Newsome *et al.*, 2002).

In establishing an indicator programme, therefore, the way in which results are used may be as important as they way in which they are collected. For example, if there are many different indicator programmes within a single parks agency, as is often the case, is there any routine coordination mechanism so that managers in different regions can easily find out what projects are under way elsewhere and with what outcomes? Is the same information available and accessible to volunteers, environmental groups or members of the public? Is the methodology fully specified so that the reliability of results can be assessed or audited? Is information on indicators shared across agencies, land tenures and legal jurisdictions, so that comparisons can be made or aggregate indices compiled? Are indicators used for testing the effectiveness of management tools, for routine reporting on the state of the protected area estate, or for budget allocation; and, if so, how are the results checked or audited before they are used? If these issues can be addressed at the design stage, they may influence the selection of indicator parameters and the way in which data are collected, analysed, stored and reported.

Conclusions

Several straightforward, but none the less significant, conclusions may be drawn from these considerations. The most basic is that you can't monitor impacts without a baseline, either measured or assumed. If you don't know what plant or animal species may live in the backcountry areas of your park, you won't be able to tell if visitors are affecting their populations. So basic biological surveys should be a high priority for any protected area monitoring system. And until this information is available no access should be granted unless it can easily be cancelled later; and no infrastructure should be built unless it can be fully removed and rehabilitated.

Another basic conclusion is that protected area agencies need field staff with training in ecology, and the ability to identify plant and animal species accurately and recognize changes in plant and animal communities. Detailed monitoring programmes do not substitute for the breadth of knowledge and observational skills of an experienced ranger. So, keep plenty of rangers in the backcountry, and keep them at the same park long enough to learn how it changes year-to-year.

The third major conclusion is that for effective ecological monitoring, hire ecologists. Ecology is a profession that requires learned skills and knowledge like any other. Indeed, it is considerably more complex than many other professions where we rely routinely on qualified specialists. Staff trained in tourism, management or education, for example, should not be expected to design or carry out quantitative ecological monitoring programmes; particularly those that test for more complex indirect impacts, or involve indicators that need to be measured using various instruments.

This does not mean that other parks staff, visitors and tour operators cannot take part, or assist in, ecological monitoring. There are many useful monitoring exercises that rely on volunteer labour and individual reporting systems. To be effective, however, these systems must usually be established and operated by ecologists, and, in addition, they will rarely be able to distinguish tourism impacts specifically.

There are many park rangers, and some tour operators, who do indeed have the interest and knowledge to recognize which of their observations can demonstrate a tourist-related impact and which do not. Science, it has been said, is only applied common sense; and distinguishing tourist impacts often needs only

common-sense science. But not all parks staff
have sufficient interest or practice for this
approach to be sufficient on its own. Systematic
volunteer observations are useful, common-
sense science by rangers is better, but the only
reliable way to monitor the ecological impacts
of tourism in parks is to hire ecologists.

Acknowledgements

A previous version of this chapter was published as Buckley (2003). Relevant sections are
reproduced with permission.

References

Buckley, R.C. (1998) Tools and indicators for manag-
    ing tourism in parks. *Annals of Tourism
    Research* 26, 207–210.
Buckley, R.C. (2000) Recreational capacity, carrying
    capacity and quotas: where angels fear to tread.
    In: Haas, G. and Manfredo, M. (eds)
    Recreational Carrying Capacity. Colorado State
    University, Fort Collins, Colorado.
Buckley, R.C. (2001) Environmental impacts. In:
    Weaver, D. (ed.) *The Encyclopaedia of
    Ecotourism.* CAB International, Wallingford,
    UK, pp. 379–394.
Buckley, R.C. (2002) Pay to play in parks: global
    issues and Australian Alps case study. In: Taylor,
    L. (ed.) *Human Use Management in Mountain
    Areas.* The Banff Centre, Banff, Canada pp.
    99–105.
Buckley, R.C. (2003) Ecological indicators of tourist
    impacts in parks. *Journal of Ecotourism* 2,
    54–66
Buckley, R.C., Ward, J. and Warnken, W. (2001)
    Tourism and World Heritage in the Central
    Eastern Rainforests of Australia. *Tourism
    Recreation Research* 26, 106–108.
Elzinga, C.L., Salzer, D.W., Willoughby, J.W. and
    Gibbs, J.P. (2001) *Monitoring Plant and Animal
    Populations.* Blackwell Science, Malden,
    Massachusetts.
Fennell, D.A. (1999) *Ecotourism: an Introduction.*
    Routledge, London.
Font, X. and Buckley, R.C. (eds) (2001) *Tourism
    Ecolabelling.* CAB International, Wallingford,
    UK.
Greater Yellowstone Coalition (2001) Available at

website   http://www.greateryellowstone.org
    (verified 29 August 2001).
Hockings, M., Stolten, S. and Dudley, N. (2000)
    *Evaluating Effectiveness: a Framework for
    Assessing the Management of Protected Areas.*
    IUCN, Cambridge, UK.
Leung, Y.F. and Marion, J.L. (2000) Recreation
    impacts and management in wilderness: a state-
    of-knowledge review. In: Cole, D.N., McCool,
    S.F., Borrie, W.T. and O'Loughlin, J. (eds)
    Wilderness Science in a Time of Change, Vol. 5.
    USDAFS, Rocky Mountain Research Station,
    Ogden, Utah, pp. 23–48.
Liddle, M. (1997) *Recreation Ecology.* Chapman and
    Hall, London.
Manning, R.E. (1999) *Studies in Outdoor Recreation,*
    2nd edn. Oregon State University Press,
    Corvallis.
McCool, S.E. and Cole, D.N. (comps.) (1997)
    *Proceedings – Limits of Acceptable Change and
    Related Planning Processes: Progress and
    Future Directions.* General Technical Report
    INT-GTR-371, USDAFS Rocky Mountain
    Research Station, Ogden, Utah.
McDonald, J. and Buckley, R.C. (1993) The taking
    offence and lawful activity defence under the
    Nature Conservation Act 1992 (Qld): when is
    habitat disturbance a taking? *Environmental
    Planning Law Journal* 10, 198–204.
Newsome, D., Moore, S.A. and Dowling, R.K. (2002)
    Natural Area Tourism. Channel View, Clevedon,
    UK.
Parks Canada (2001) Available at website http://
    parkscanada.pch.gu.ca/parks/main_e (verified
    29 August 2001).
Sirakaya, E., Jamal, T.B. and Choi, H.S. (2001)
    Development indicators for destination sustain-
    ability. In: Weaver, D. (ed.) *The Encyclopaedia
    of Ecotourism.* CAB International, Wallingford,
    UK, pp. 411–432.
Stankey, G.H., Cole, D.N., Lucas, R.C., Petersen,
    M.E. and Fussell, S.S. (1985) *The Limited of
    Acceptable Change (LAC) System for
    Wilderness Planning.* USDAFS, Ogden, Utah.
US National Parks Service (2001) The National Park
    Service Park Net. Available at website http://
    www.nps.gov (verified 29 August 2001).
Warnken, W. (1996) Threshold detection of ecotour-
    ism impact: microbiological and chemical
    indictors of recreational effects on water quality
    in a subtropical rainforest conservation reserve.
    PhD Thesis, Griffith University.
Weaver, D. (2001) *Ecotourism.* John Wiley & Sons,
    Milton, Queensland, Australia.

18

Reducing Impacts Through Interpretation, Lamington National Park

Carolyn J. Littlefair

International Centre for Ecotourism Research, Griffith University, Gold Coast, Queensland, Australia

Introduction

Increased visitation to natural areas has led protected-area managers to seek tools to minimize the environmental impacts of visitors. Interpretation is one such management tool.

Interpretation has many and varied definitions. One of the first, and most enduring, was given by Freeman Tilden, who defined interpretation as 'an educational activity which aims to reveal meanings and relationships through the use of original objects, by firsthand experience, and by illustrative media, rather than simply to communicate factual information' (Tilden, 1977, p. 8).

The management of impacts is not, however, the sole function of interpretation. Interpretation can have numerous objectives, commonly categorized into: promotion, recreation, education and management benefits (Beckmann, 1991). Management or conservation benefits may include: stimulating a behavioural change to minimize personal impacts on the environment; stimulating an environmental ethic or consciousness in visitors; or increasing the desire of visitors to contribute to conservation (Beckmann, 1991; Wearing and Neil, 1999). The assumption underlying the use of interpretation for management is that, if visitors understand the environment they are visiting, they will be concerned about and hence act responsibly towards the environment (Bramwell and Lane, 1993).

Interpretation is often a preferred management tool for park managers. According to Roggenbuck (1992), interpretation programmes are almost universally the first choice of managers as a management tool in natural areas. It is perceived to be a cost-effective method; it is a light-handed approach and allows visitors the freedom of choice; and it enhances visitor experiences and satisfaction (Roggenbuck, 1987; Bright, 1994; Beckmann, 1999).

Most evaluations of interpretation have focused on measuring knowledge and attitude (Orams, 1997; Knapp and Barrie, 1998; Woods and Moscardo, 1998; Beaumont, 2000). However, a change in knowledge or attitude does not necessarily result in a change in behaviour or a reduction in the impact (Roggenbuck, 1992). A few studies have attempted to assess the influence of interpretation on visitor behaviour (O'Loughlin, 1988; Manfredo and Bright, 1991; Brown et al., 1992; Dresner and Gill, 1994; Beaumont, 2000), but these have commonly used self-reported behaviour or intention to behave as the only measure of behavioural change. Previous evaluations of interpretation which have quantified actual visitor impacts have been conducted in non-terrestrial environments (Wagstaff and Wilson, 1988; Medio et al., 1997), used non-personal interpretive media (Cole, 1998), or have been conducted with non-guided activities (Orams and Hill, 1998; Widner and Roggenbuck, 2000).

Table 18.1. Components included in each interpretive programme.

Component	Interpretive programme				
	Control	Generic	Role Model	Appeal	Complete
Environmental interpretation		*	*	*	*
Role modelling by guide			*		*
Verbal appeals from guide				*	*

Methods

The aim of this research, therefore, was to assess the effectiveness of interpretation by measuring how much it reduced the actual environmental impacts of visitors on guided walks in a national park. This study seems to be the first such evaluation in a terrestrial environment, using a well-established commercial tour with a high standard of interpretation.

The research was conducted with the assistance of Binna Burra Mountain Lodge in Lamington National Park, which is part of the Central Eastern Rainforest Reserves (Australia) World Heritage area. A little over 200 km² in area, Lamington National Park lies about 100 km south of Brisbane. It is internationally renowned for its scenic beauty, with forested valleys and ranges, rivers and waterfalls, and contains significant stands of subtropical, temperate and dry rainforest communities (QPWS, 1999).

Binna Burra Mountain Lodge offers its guests a variety of guided walks in the national park. In particular, each week, their guides lead a walk along the Caves Circuit, a 5 km track through subtropical rainforest and open eucalypt forest, named after two large caves in an eroded cliff.

In this study a variety of potential impacts were examined. For practical experimental purposes, three proved both measurable and ecologically significant: shortcutting of corners at trail switchbacks; picking up litter on the track; and the noise level of groups.

Minimum impact messages in guided walks can be delivered in various ways, and can include direct appeals from the guide to modify a specific behaviour, or role modelling of the appropriate behaviour by the guide. The impacts of visitors on these guided walks were quantified experimentally under five different interpretive

programmes that were developed to utilize these components. For convenience these programmes will be referred to henceforth as the Control, Generic, Role Model, Appeal and Complete interpretive programmes (Table 18.1).

The Control programme had no environmental interpretation or minimum impact interventions. The visitor groups with this interpretive programme were accompanied by a guide, but solely to ensure the safety of the visitors and to maintain consistency across all interpretive programmes. The Generic programme was the foundation of all other interpretive programmes. It consisted of environmental interpretation on the influence of past volcanic activity in the region and how this relates to present landforms and vegetation. The programme incorporated the principles of good interpretation, such as engaging the senses of visitors, encouraging participation and interaction, and exploring bigger-picture issues. It did not, however, include any minimum impact messages.

The Role Model programme incorporated the same environmental interpretation as the Generic programme, with the addition of positive role modelling by the guide. The guide would display the appropriate behaviour relating to each of the impacts being measured. The Appeal programme had the same environmental interpretation as the Generic programme, with the addition of verbal appeals from the guide. The verbal appeals asked visitors to modify specific behaviours in order to minimize their impact. The Complete programme consisted of the same environmental interpretation as the Generic programme, with the addition of both the role modelling used in the Role Model programme and the verbal appeals from the Appeal programme.

Between 1999 and 2002, 41 walks, run by Binna Burra Mountain Lodge along the Caves Circuit, were examined. A total of 449 visitors

Table 18.2. Components included in each section for each interpretive programme.

Component	Section	Control	Generic	Role Model	Appeal	Complete
Environmental interpretation	1		*	*	*	*
	2		*	*	*	*
Role modelling by guide	1					
	2			*		*
Verbal appeals from guide	1					
	2				*	*

were included in the study, ranging in age from children to seniors. The size of each group varied from 2 to 32, with a mean group size of 11. The researcher went along on each tour as one of the visitors, which made it possible to observe group members and measure their impacts without influencing their behaviour.

Shortcutting was measured by discreet observation of the participants on each walk. At each of the 11 corners on the track, the number of participants that took a shortcut or stayed on the track, was recorded. Role modelling of the appropriate behaviour involved the guide always staying on the track, walking to the end of the switchback and staying at the front of the group. The verbal appeal asked visitors to always walk to the end of the track at switchbacks and explained the consequences and impacts of shortcutting. The results of the study were analysed using a chi-square test and odds ratios.

In measuring the amount of litter picked up, an internal control on each walk was necessary. The track was divided into two sections, with any interventions (role modelling and/or verbal appeal) occurring at the mid-point. During the first section of the track, interpretive programmes included only the basic descriptive information corresponding to the Generic programme, as above. Additional interpretation for the Generic, Role Model, Appeal and Complete programmes were provided during the second section of each walk (Table 18.2). The Control programme did not include any interpretation in either section.

To test the effectiveness of interpretive programmes in persuading visitors to pick up litter, it was necessary to ensure that there was always litter on the track. An assistant would therefore walk ahead of the group, out of sight, and place a standard set of litter in specific places in both sections before the group came along. After the tour group passed, the assistant would walk back along the track, note which litter had been picked up, and collect any that was remaining. The litter varied in size and colour and was typical of litter found along popular family walking tracks.

Role modelling involved the guide picking up litter, which took place at a location where the majority of the group could see the guide. Verbal appeals from the guide asked visitors to pick up any litter they saw on the track and explained the impacts that litter has in a national park, especially the effect on wildlife. During the appeal the guide also informed visitors that there were gloves that could be used to pick up anything they did not want to touch and a bag to put litter in so that they did not have to carry it out. The results were analysed using a logistic analysis and odds ratios.

To measure the noise level of each walk, a similar two-stage design was used as for measuring litter (Table 18.2). To measure noise, a micro-cassette recorder was taken on each walk, concealed in a pocket.

Role modelling involved the guide pausing the group so that everyone was quiet to look for wildlife. The guide would then talk quietly while walking along. The verbal appeals from the guide asked visitors not to shout or talk loudly, explaining the impact that noisy behaviour has on wildlife and that visitors would probably see more wildlife if they were quiet.

A continuous recording of the entire tour was taken for each walk. Following each walk, the tape was replayed and each 5-second interval was classified into one of 11 specific noise levels, defined by how many people were making noise and how loud this was. For the analysis these 11 levels were aggregated into three categories, namely: loud talking or shouting, quiet talking and no talking. Data were analysed using split-plot analyses.

Results

Shortcutting

Along the Caves Circuit there are 11 corners; however, the shape of the terrain meant that visitors only regularly shortcut three of these: corners A, B and C. The detailed analysis focused on these corners only.

Corner A

At corner A, 100% of visitors in the Control and Generic interpretive programmes took a shortcut, compared to 80% of visitors in the Role Model programme, 43% in the Appeal programme and 7% in the Complete interpretive programme (Fig. 18.1). These differences were highly significant ($P<0.001$, $\chi^2=241.14$, df=4).

The odds ratios showed that:

- there was no statistically significant difference between the odds of a visitor shortcutting in the Control programme compared to the odds of a visitor shortcutting in the Generic programme;
- the odds of a visitor shortcutting in the Generic programme were 45 times more likely than the odds of a visitor shortcutting in the Role Model programme;
- the odds of a visitor shortcutting in the Role Model programme were 5 times more likely than the odds of a visitor shortcutting in the Appeal programme; and
- the odds of a visitor shortcutting in the Appeal programme were over 9 times more likely than the odds of a visitor shortcutting in the Complete programme.

Corner B

At corner B, 100% of visitors in the Control interpretive programme took a shortcut, compared to 86% in the Generic programme, 37% in the Role Model programme, 27% in the

Appeal programme and 6% in the Complete interpretive programme (Fig. 18.2). These differences were highly significant ($P<0.001$, $\chi^2=178.08$, df=4).

The odds ratios showed that:

- there was no statistically significant difference between the odds of a visitor shortcutting in the Control programme compared to the odds of a visitor shortcutting in the Generic programme;
- the odds of a visitor shortcutting in the Generic programme were 10 times more than the odds of a visitor shortcutting in the Role Model programme;
- there was no statistically significant difference between the odds of a visitor shortcutting in the Role Model programme compared to the odds of a visitor shortcutting in the Appeal programme; and
- the odds of a visitor shortcutting in the Appeal programme were 6 times more than the odds of a visitor shortcutting in the Complete programme.

Corner C

At corner C, 100% of visitors in the Control interpretive programme took a shortcut, compared to 91% of visitors in the Generic programme, 64% in the Appeal programme, 29% in the Role Model programme and 10% in the Complete interpretive programme (Fig. 8.3). These differences were significant ($P<0.01$, $\chi^2=237.55$, df=4).

The odds ratios showed that:

- there was no statistically significant difference between the odds of a visitor shortcutting in the Control programme compared to the odds of a visitor shortcutting in the Generic programme;
- the odds of a visitor shortcutting in the Generic programme were 5 times more than the odds of a visitor shortcutting in the Appeal programme;
- the odds of a visitor shortcutting in the Appeal programme were 4 times more than the odds of a visitor shortcutting in the Role Model programme; and
- the odds of a visitor shortcutting in the Role Model programme were over 3 times

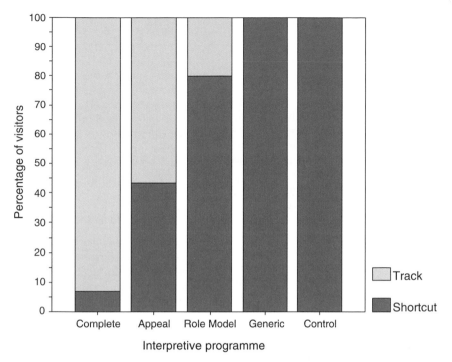

Fig. 18.1. Shortcutting at corner A for each interpretive programme.

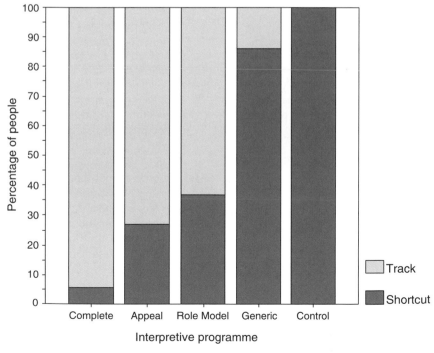

Fig. 18.2. Shortcutting at corner B for each interpretive programme.

more than the odds of a visitor shortcutting in the Complete programme.

Summary

For all three corners, the Complete programme consistently resulted in the least shortcutting, and visitors were always, statistically, less likely to shortcut than on all the other interpretive programmes. So the combination of environmental interpretation, role modelling by the guide and verbal appeals from the guide was always the most effective in reducing shortcutting.

The Generic and Control interpretive programmes yielded statistically indistinguishable results. Visitors receiving either a general environmental interpretation programme, or none at all, were equally likely to shortcut corners.

For all three corners, the Role Model and Appeal interpretation programmes were more effective than Generic or Control programmes, but less effective than the Complete programme. Verbal appeals were more effective than role modelling at corner A; at corner B, they were equally effective; and at corner C, role modelling was more effective than verbal appeals to reduce shortcutting. This result shows that adding either role modelling or verbal appeals does decrease the amount of shortcutting by visitors.

Litter

Analysis of the amount of litter picked up for each section (Fig. 18.4) showed that there was an influence from the interpretive programme, on how much litter was picked up ($P=0.023$, $\chi^2=11.3641$, df$=4$).

Odds ratios were calculated to compare:

- the amount of litter picked up in section 1 for each interpretive programme;
- the amount of litter picked up in section 1 of the track versus the amount of litter picked up in section 2, for each interpretive programme; and
- the amount of litter picked up in section 2 for each interpretive programme.

Section 1

Results of the analysis of litter picked up in section 1 by each interpretive programme showed that there was no significant difference in the odds of litter being picked up, between any of the interpretive programmes.

For section 1, the Generic, Role Model, Appeal and Complete interpretive programmes all had the same components (Table 18.2) and, not surprisingly, showed no difference in the amount of litter picked up between these programmes. But, there was also no difference in the odds that visitors in the Control programme would pick up litter when compared to visitors in the Generic programme.

Section 1 versus Section 2

When the amount of litter picked up in section 1 of the track was compared with the amounts of litter picked up in section 2, for each interpretive programme individually, odds ratios showed that:

- there was no significant difference between the odds of litter being picked up in section 2, compared to the odds of litter being picked up by the Control programme in section 1, for the Control, Generic and Role Model programmes;
- the odds of litter being picked up by the Appeal programme in section 2 was over 11 times more than the odds of litter being picked up by the Appeal programme in section 1; and
- the odds of litter being picked up by the Complete programme in section 2 was 14 times more than the odds of litter being picked up by the Complete programme in section 1.

The only programmes that increased the odds of litter being picked up were the Appeal programme (environmental interpretation, plus verbal appeals from the guide for visitors to pick up litter) and the Complete programme (environmental interpretation, verbal appeals, plus role modelling by the guide).

Section 2

When the amount of litter picked up by each interpretive programme in section 2 of the track was compared, odds ratios showed that:

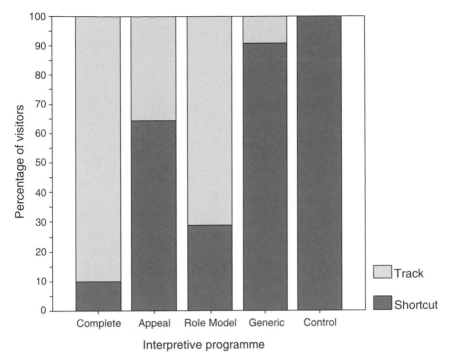

Fig. 18.3. Shortcutting at corner C for each interpretive programme.

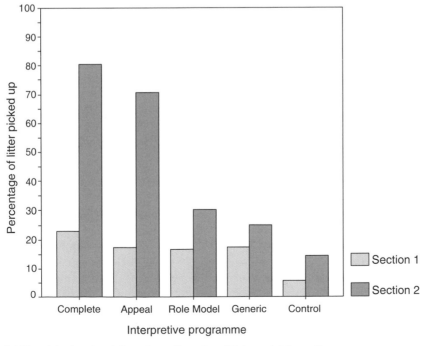

Fig. 18.4. Litter picked up by visitors, in sections 1 and 2, in each interpretive programme.

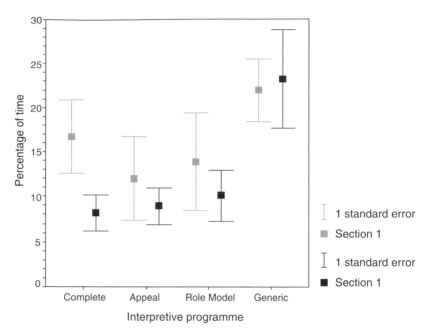

Fig. 18.5. Mean (±1 sᴇ) percentages that visitors in each interpretive programme were shouting or talking loudly, in sections 1 and 2.

- there was no significant difference between the odds that litter would be picked up by the Generic programme in section 2, compared to the odds of litter being picked up by the Control programme in section 2;
- there was no significant difference between the odds that litter would be picked up by the Role Model programme in section 2, compared to the odds of litter being picked up by the Generic programme in section 2;
- the odds of litter being picked up by the Appeal programme in section 2 was over 5 times more than the odds of litter being picked up by the Role Model programme in section 2; and
- there was no significant difference between the odds that litter would be picked up by the Complete programme in section 2, compared to the odds of litter being picked up by the Appeal programme in section 2.

The addition of role modelling in the Complete programme did not significantly increase the odds that litter would be picked up. This is based on the finding that visitors in the Complete programme (environmental interpretation, role modelling and verbal appeals) were equally likely to pick up litter in section 2 as visitors in the Appeal programme (environmental interpretation and verbal appeals). Additionally, there was no significant difference in the odds that visitors in the Role Model programme (environmental interpretation and role modelling) would pick up litter to a greater extent when compared to visitors in the Generic programme (environmental interpretation).

Summary

Verbal appeals from the guide were the only factor that influenced whether litter was picked up. The Complete programme and Appeal programme were the only interpretive programmes where visitors picked up more litter in section 2, after role modelling, than in section 1. Visitors in both of these programmes were found to be equally likely to pick up litter as each other, showing that the inclusion of role modelling in the Complete programme did not increase the odds that litter would be picked up.

The Role Model, Generic and Control programmes were all equally likely to pick up litter in section 2 as in section 1. This result confirms that role modelling did not increase the amount of litter picked up, as those in the Role Model programme were not more likely to pick up litter in section 2, after role modelling, compared to section 1. Visitors in the Control and Generic programmes were equally likely to pick up litter as each other, showing that the addition of environmental interpretation, compared to no environmental interpretation, did not increase the odds that litter would be picked up.

Noise

Both verbal appeals and role modelling by the guide focused principally on reducing shouting and loud talking, as this behaviour is considered to be inappropriate for a national park. For each walk, the amount and percentage of time that the group was shouting or talking loudly, in each section, was determined, and the mean value for each interpretive programme calculated (Fig. 18.5). The analysis showed that there was no significant difference between sections for each interpretive programme ($P=0.259$, $F=1.429$, $df=3$). The Control programme was removed from this analysis because the experimental conditions resulted in the dispersion of visitors away from the recorder, so the noise recorded was not considered to be an accurate representation of the influence of the interpretive programme.

Although not statistically significant, there does appear to be a trend that visitors in the Complete, Appeal and Role Model programmes, spent proportionately less time being noisy in section 2, after role modelling and/or verbal appeals, than in section 1. The Generic programme, which had no difference in the interpretive components between section 1 and 2 (Table 18.2) showed similar values in section 2 and section 1.

The analysis of the talking and quiet categories also showed no significant difference between section 1 and section 2 for each inter-

pretive programme ($P=0.179$ and $P=0.085$, respectively).

Summary

Three categories of noise behaviour were analysed: shouting and loud talking, talking and quiet. For all three noise categories, there was no significant difference between the interpretive programmes. Although not significant, there was a pattern of reduced shouting and loud talking following verbal appeals and/or role modelling in the Complete, Appeal and Role Model programmes. This result implies that interventions of role modelling and/or verbal appeals may reduce noisy behaviour.

It is likely that any pattern was not significant because of the high variation in time spent being noisy between the walks, despite the enormous volume of data collected (over 60,000 individual 5-second intervals). Future research, with a greater number of walks, may reduce variation and be able to detect any difference statistically.

Conclusion

There are two key implications from this study. The first implication is that environmental interpretation will not reduce visitor impacts unless it specifically addresses those impacts in the interpretive programme. Both the litter and shortcutting results show that the groups that had general environmental interpretation fared no differently (that is, no better or worse) to groups without any environmental interpretation. It was only when the impacts were specifically addressed by verbal appeals and/or role modelling that any reduction in the impact was found.

Secondly, where visitors may be unclear as to the specific actions needed to reduce impacts, role modelling by the guide is imperative in assisting the group to understand and engage in the correct behaviour. This outcome was seen in the shortcutting results, where role modelling played an important part. Prior to role modelling, many visitors were unsure of where the correct track was and, without being shown, even the visitor with the best intentions made mistakes.

This research demonstrated that environmental interpretation does have the potential to be used as an effective management tool to reduce visitor impacts. Interpretation is most effective in reducing impacts when those impacts are specifically addressed by the interpretation, and visitors have a positive role modelling of the appropriate behaviours. However, caution should be taken by natural resource managers, as interpretation is not necessarily the solution to reducing all impacts. The best approach may be the use of a number of management options that can reduce a particular impact.

Acknowledgements

I would like to acknowledge the advice and support from my supervisors, Professor Ralf Buckley, Associate Professor Stephen Wearing, and Dr Michael Arthur. I also wish to thank the staff at Binna Burra Mountain Lodge for their assistance and the CRC for Sustainable Tourism for supplementary funding, which allowed me to conduct this research.

References

Beaumont, N. (2000) The contribution of ecotourism education to environmental knowledge. In: McArthur, S. and Dowling, R. (eds) *Australia: the World's Natural Theme Park. The Ecotourism Association of Australia 1999 National Conference Proceedings.* Ecotourism Association of Australia, Brisbane, Australia.

Beckmann, E.A. (1991) Environmental interpretation for education and management in Australian national parks and other protected areas. PhD thesis, University of New England, Armidale, Australia.

Beckmann, E.A. (1999) Minimising the human factor: changing visitor impacts through interpretation. In: Interpretation Australia Association (ed.) *The Human Factor in Interpretation. Interpretation Australia Association National Conference Proceedings.* Interpretation Australia Association, Collingwood, Victoria, Australia, pp. 22–29.

Bramwell, B. and Lane, B. (1993) Interpretation and sustainable tourism. *Journal of Sustainable Tourism* 1(2), 71–80.

Bright, A.D. (1994) Information campaigns that enlighten and influence the public. *Parks and Recreation* 29(8), 49–54.

Brown, C.M., Halstead, J.M. and Luloff, A.E. (1992) Information as a management tool: an evalua-

tion of the Pemigewasset Wilderness Management Plan. *Environmental Management* 16(2), 143–148.

Cole, D.N. (1998) Written appeals for attention to low-impact messages on trailside bulletin boards: experimental evaluations of effectiveness. *Journal of Park and Recreation Administration* 16(1), 65–79.

Dresner, M. and Gill, M. (1994) Environmental education at a summer camp. *Journal of Environmental Education* 2(3), 35–41.

Knapp, D. and Barrie, E. (1998) Ecology versus issue interpretation: the analysis of two difference messages. *Journal of Interpretation Research* 3(1), 21–38.

Manfredo, M.J. and Bright, A.D. (1991) A model for assessing the effects of communication on recreationists. *Journal of Leisure Research* 23(1), 1–20.

Medio, D., Ormond, R.F.G. and Pearson, M. (1997) Effect of briefings on rates of damage to corals by SCUBA divers. *Biological Conservation* 79(1), 91–95.

O'Loughlin, T. (1988) *Wilderness Education Project Report.* Department of Lands, Parks and Wildlife (Tasmania) and Australian National Parks and Wildlife Service, Hobart, Australia.

Orams, M.B. (1997) The effectiveness of environmental education: can we turn tourists into 'greenies'? *Progress in Tourism and Hospitality Research* 3(4), 295–306.

Orams, M.B. and Hill, G.J.E. (1998) Controlling the ecotourist in a wild dolphin feeding program: is education the answer? *Journal of Environmental Education* 29(3), 33–38.

Queensland Parks and Wildlife Service (1999) *Lamington National Park Draft Management Plan.* Queensland Parks and Wildlife Service, Brisbane, Australia.

Roggenbuck, J.W. (1987) Park interpretation as a visitor management strategy. In: Royal Australian Institute of Parks and Recreation (ed.) *Metropolitan Perspectives in Parks and Recreation. Proceedings of the 60th National Conference of the Royal Australian Institute of Parks and Recreation.* Royal Australian Institute of Parks and Recreation, Canberra, Australia.

Roggenbuck, J.W. (1992) Use of persuasion to reduce resource impacts and visitor conflicts. In: Manfredo, M.J. (ed.) *Influencing Human Behavior: Theory and Applications in Recreation, Tourism, and Natural Resources Management.* Sagamore Publishing, Champaign, Illinois, pp. 149–208.

Tilden, F. (1977) *Interpreting our Heritage,* 3rd edn. The University of North Carolina Press, Chapel Hill, North Carolina.

Wagstaff, M.C. and Wilson, B.E. (1988) The evaluation of litter behavior modification in a river environment. *Journal of Environmental Education* 20(1), 39–44.

Wearing, S. and Neil, J. (1999) *Ecotourism: Impacts, Potentials and Possibilities.* Butterworth-Heinemann, Oxford, UK.

Widner, C.J. and Roggenbuck, R.W. (2000) Reducing theft of petrified wood at Petrified Forest National Park. *Journal of Interpretation Research* 5(1), 1–18.

Woods, B. and Moscardo, G. (1998) Researching interpretive techniques in tourism: an evaluation of pictorial symbols in reef tourist education. In: Faulkner, B., Tidswell, C. and Weaver, D. (eds) *Progress in Tourism and Hospitality Research 1998. Proceedings of the Eighth Australian Tourism and Hospitality Research Conference.* Bureau of Tourism Research, Canberra, Australia, pp. 320–333.

19

Campsite Impacts in Prince William Sound, Alaska, USA

Christopher A. Monz[1] and Paul Twardock[2]

[1]St Lawrence University, Canton, New York, USA; [2]Alaska Pacific University, Anchorage, Alaska, USA

Introduction

Wildland recreation and tourism use continues to increase in many protected areas in North America (Cole, 1996). In many coastal areas, activities such as sea-kayaking, sport-fishing and power-boating have become increasingly popular, leading to challenges for resource managers charged with maintaining natural conditions and quality visitor experiences. Although overall data are lacking, it has been widely reported that sea-kayak camping, in particular, has grown in popularity in the US in recent years (K. Cordell, Georgia, USA, personal communication, 2002), and coastal areas in Alaska offer the opportunity for extended sea-kayak expeditions with a high degree of solitude. In one of the areas known for quality kayaking and nature tourism experiences, Prince William Sound (PWS), total kayak visitor use days have nearly doubled between 1987 and 1998 (Twardock and Monz, 2000). Managing recreational resources in the PWS area is particularly difficult because visitor use is dispersed and unregulated, campsites are widely distributed geographically, and with travel being exclusively by boat, there are no identifiable trails leading to the sites. The popularity of PWS extends well beyond Alaska, as visitors are attracted from across the US, Canada and Europe. Sustainable ecotourism use requires that these wildland environments

be protected not only from large-scale threats such as development, but also from visitor activities with the potential to create long-lasting impacts to soil, vegetation, water and wildlife resources (Marion and Leung, 1998).

Assessment and monitoring of campsite conditions has been employed in many areas in the USA as an important component of an overall wildland management strategy (e.g. Frissell, 1978; Cole, 1983a,b; Marion, 1991; Monz, 1998). The loss of vegetation, soil erosion and associated aesthetic degradation of sites is a significant management concern, particularly when visitation is increasing. Moreover, impacted sites not only tend to increase in size with increasing use, but impacted areas can also proliferate, as campers move from degraded sites to unused areas. Since an overwhelming proportion of soil and plant impact tends to occur with the first few nights of visitation, this trend can cause a rapid increase in the total amount of impacted area (Hammitt and Cole, 1998). An initial assessment and subsequent, continued site monitoring can provide vital information to determine the extent and type of management actions needed to preserve the wilderness or pristine character of an area.

This project was initiated to assess the location and extent of visitor-created impacts in the PWS as a consequence of wildland tourism and recreation activities. Given the nature of visitor activities in the area, we focused our assessments on beaches readily accessible by sea kayak and motorboat, where camping was possible. Our goal was to establish a network of campsites for long-term impact monitoring and to identify areas of current and potential use.

Approach

Study area

Prince William Sound, Alaska is located roughly at 61°N 148°W, and spans a large geographic area of over 10,000 km². PWS is remote and accessible by road only from the towns of Valdez and Whittier, and boat from Cordova, Tatitlek and Chenega. The region is well known for the principal economic activities of commercial fishing and crude oil transportation, but, more recently, ecotourism and recreation activities have increased, with commercial sight-seeing tours, cruise lines and sea-kayak outfitters now operating extensively in the area. Many of the visitors are drawn by the wild nature and wilderness character of the sound – huge mountains and glaciers, abundant wildlife and opportunities for solitude.

Although PWS is an outstanding wilderness, the area has a long history of human use, starting with Natives using open boats and kayaks for travel. Today, human activities continue in such forms as hunting, fishing, mining, subsistence (living based on hunting, gathering and fishing), logging and water-based recreation. The US Forest Service (Chugach National Forest) manages most of the uplands of Prince William Sound, including the 800,000 ha Nellie Juan Wilderness Study Area. In addition to the National Forest, there are State Marine parks, Alaska native village and regional corporation lands, municipal lands, private lands and state university lands adjacent to the Sound.

Management of visitor use is complicated by the large and geographically complex nature of the region. While there are few access points, there are over 4000 km of shoreline, consisting of rocky cliffs interspersed with beaches of a grey sandstone ('graywacke') and slate (Lethcoe, 1990). Upland visitation in the temperate spruce/hemlock rainforest is limited due to the boggy nature of most soils above the beaches. The majority of use in western PWS occurs in the summer months, due to the wet, windy and cold conditions between September and April, although hunting may be a substantial off-season use. In May of 2000 a new road opened to Whittier, which was previously served only by railroad. This increased access was widely expected to result in an immediate and dramatic increase in overnight use on the sound from nearby Anchorage; however, to date, the expected use has not materialized. According to the Alaska State Department of Transportation, 119,000 people used the Whittier road between April 2001 and March 2002, well below the 600,000 projected visitors and slightly above the recent historical use via rail of approximately 100,000 (Dobyn, 2003). Anecdotal accounts report increases in kayak use, although no actual use estimates have been made since the road opened.

PWS is surrounded by a northern temperate spruce/hemlock rain forest with 60–300 inches of precipitation per year and moderate temperatures. Thin, wet, acidic soils overlay bedrock and gravel substrates. Beaches consist of graywacke and sand, with plant communities of dune grass (*Elymus mollis*), a perennial found in cobble and sand, and succulents such as seabeach sandwort (*Honkenya peploides*), beach pea (*Lathyrus maritimus*) and oysterleaf (*Mertensia maritima*). Uplands have open peat bogs and mixed stands of western hemlock (*Tsuga heterophylla*) and sitka spruce (*Picea sitchensis*). The beach/forest transition is a thick wall of sitka alder (*Alnus crispa*) and a variety of willow (*Salix* sp.). The forest understorey includes high bush blueberry (*Vaccinium ovalifolium*), ferns (*Athyrium filix* and *Dryopteris expansa*), horsetail (*Equisetium* spp.), dwarf dogwood (*Carnus canadensis*), devils club (*Oplopanax horridus*), wintergreen (*Pyrola asarifolia*), skunk cabbage (*Lysichiten americanum*) and peat mosses (*Sphagnum* spp.).

In 1989, the tanker *Exxon Valdez* ran aground on Bligh Reef, and the resulting spill oiled approximately 800 km of shoreline (Neff *et al.*, 1995). As a consequence of natural processes and clean-up efforts, little observable surface oil remained 2 years after the spill (Wiens *et al.*, 1996), although significant ecosystem components and processes remain impaired over 12 years later (*Exxon Valdez* Oil

Spill Trustees, 2002). The clean-up efforts introduced many thousands of workers and boats in areas that had previously received little human activity, and impacts such as the trampling of beach vegetation were observed.

Campsite assessment

This research utilized standard campsite assessment protocols (Monz, 2000), similar to those developed by the National Park Service (Marion, 1991) and the USDA Forest Service (Cole, 1983a,b) in many protected areas throughout the USA. Inventory parameters for each camping area (Table 19.1) allow for future relocation of campsites and provide basic descriptive information, while the impact parameters (Table 19.2) are an estimate of the departure from natural conditions. Additional methodological details are provided in Monz (1998) and Kehoe (2002).

For measurement of the campsite areas, we employed the radial transect method (Marion, 1991; Monz, 2000). Condition class measurements followed a standard categorical approach (e.g. 0 through 5 numerical ratings, from very low to very high impact) as suggested by Marion (1991) and detailed in Kehoe (2002).

A Garmin hand-held global positioning system (GPS) unit (model GPS 45, Garmin International, Lenexa, Kansas, USA) was utilized to obtain approximate latitude/longitude coordinates on all beaches. Photos were taken at each site to document impacts and to help with site relocation.

Data analysis

Campsite areas were determined geometrically from the radial transect data by utilizing a custom computer program (J. Marion, Virginia, USA, 2002). Relative vegetation cover loss was calculated by the following formula:

$$RC_L = 1 - \frac{\% \text{ cover in campsite}}{\% \text{ cover in control plots}} \times 100$$

All data were summarized and synthetic variables were calculated using Microsoft Excel (Microsoft Corporation, Bellvue, Washington,

Table 19.1. Inventory parameters.

Site number (designated) and name	Site location (GPS coordinates)
Substrate of landing area	Substrate of campsites
Number of campsites at beach	Compass orientation of beach

GPS, global positioning system.

Table 19.2. Impact assessment parameters.

Size of impacted area	Condition class
Vegetative ground cover on site	Vegetative cover off site
Mineral soil exposure	Tree damage
Root exposure	Number of tree stumps
Number of trails	Number of fire sites
Litter and trash present	Observable human waste

USA) and SPSS statistical software (SPSS Inc., Chicago, Illinois, USA).

Results

Over the duration of the project (1995–2000), campsite conditions at 138 campsites at some 94 beaches were assessed. Many additional areas, where camping was possible and no observable impact was found, were examined and mapped for future reference. Assessments were generally made in mid to late June of each year, a time when long-lasting impacts are more apparent, as it is relatively early in the visitor season. As has been reported previously (Monz, 1998), a large range of campsite conditions was found, with campsite condition classes ranging from 0–5 and the median condition class being 4 (Table 19.3). This indicates that sites tend to be moderately to highly impacted. There are also several important beaches where multiple impacted areas are forming, due to multiple parties camping simultaneously. Impacted area of campsites ranged from 8 to 257 m², with the median campsite size being 35 m². Sites exhibited substantial

Table 19.3. Summary of campsite conditions in Prince William Sound. Values are medians followed by minimum and maximum values.

Impact parameter	Prince William Sound study area
Number of sites inventoried	138
Condition class[a]	4 (0–5)
Relative vegetation cover loss (RC_L)[b]	58% (0–97)
Mineral soil exposure	19% (2.5–98)
Tree damage rating[c]	0 (0–2)
Root exposure rating[c]	0 (0–2)
Number of tree stumps/ damaged shrubs	0 (0–14)
Number of trails	2.0 (0–9)
Number of fire rings	0 (0–5)
Litter/trash rating[c]	1 (0–3)
Area of observable impact	35 m^2 (8–257)

[a] Follows Marion (1991), except as noted in Methods.
[b] Calculated as described in Methods.
[c] Rating systems were the following scale:
1 = 'little/none'; 2 = 'moderate' and 3 = 'severe'.

Table 19.4. Frequency of observation of impact problems at the PWS. Values are the percentage of sites that demonstrate the indicated impact parameter.

Impact parameter	Frequency
≥ Moderate tree/shrub damage	37
≥ Moderate root exposure	27
Cut tree stumps/cut shrubs	41
Multiple trailing	72
Fire impacts observable	34
Significant presence of camping trash	43
Observable human waste	9
Campsites larger than 50 m^2	34

relative vegetation cover loss (median = 58%) compared to adjacent control plots (Table 19.3). Mineral soil exposure was not as extensive, at 19%.

Multiple trailing, cut trees and shrubs, and the presence of camping trash were the most frequent impacts observed, being found on 72, 41 and 43% of the sites inventoried, respectively (Table 19.4). Other impacts were somewhat less prevalent, with substantial root exposure found at 27% and fire scars and rings at 34% of the sites inventoried. Evidence of improperly disposed of human waste was found at only 9% of the sites surveyed. Excessively large campsites, with impacted areas greater than 50 m^2, were found at 34% of the sites inventoried.

Campsites were found on four primary substrate types: (i) a coarse beach gravel substrate ('graywacke') dominated by beach grasses and succulents; (ii) a highly organic soil in the forest understorey dominated by mosses and forbs; (iii) areas of beach cobble (stones of 2–4 cm in diameter) with low densities of beach grasses; and (iv) sand with diverse plant cover. Sites on sand were the least frequent in the study area, but vegetation loss on these sites

was the least of the four types investigated (Table 19.5).

The greatest vegetation loss, highest mineral soil exposure, and highest condition class ratings were observed on gravel substrates, suggesting that the beach grass community was the most susceptible to impact (Table 19.5). No significant differences were observed in the overall size of the impacted area among the four substrate types, but the size varied widely, from a mean of 37 m^2 on the gravel sites to 73 m^2 on the sand. A subset of sites were re-measured during the study and a comparison of the primary and secondary assessments for 12 sites revealed no significant change in five impact parameters over a 3–4-year period (Table 19.6).

Discussion

Assessment and monitoring of campsite conditions is an important information-gathering step in the overall management of resource conditions. Monitoring programmes have been applied and effectively utilized in many natural areas (e.g. Frissell, 1978; Cole, 1983b; Marion and Leung, 1997), and are a fundamental component in the application of long-term planning frameworks, such as Limits of Acceptable Change (Stankey *et al.*, 1985) or Visitor Experience and Resource Protection (National Park Service, 1997). Assessment work often highlights the need for management actions, and monitoring can help ascertain their effectiveness. None the less, difficult decisions must be made from a management standpoint, and

Table 19.5. A comparison of selected impact parameters on campsites of differing substrate types.

Impact parameter	Substrate type*			
	Organic soil	Gravel	Cobble	Sand
Relative vegetation cover loss (%) (RC_L)	42a	84c	58b	16a
Condition class	2.2a	3.5b	2.5a	1.6a
Mineral soil exposure (%)	10a	80c	55bc	37ab
Area of observable impact (m^2)	42.8[NS]	37.1[NS]	57.3[NS]	72.7[NS]
N	49	23	45	7

* Values are means. Means followed by the same letter are not significantly different with Scheffei's multiple comparison test at P≤0.05. NS, no significant difference found.

Table 19.6. An examination of change in conditions on 12 campsites during a 3–4-year period for selected impact parameters.

Impact parameter	Assessment[a]		t value[b]	P value[b]
	Primary	Secondary		
RC_L (%)	75.5	79.6	−0.500	0.627
Condition class	3.8	3.1	2.0	0.071
Soil exposure (%)	64.7	69.3	−0.455	0.658
Trash rating	1.5	1.6	−0.616	0.551
Area of observable impact (m^2)	54.8	58.0	−0.633	0.561

[a] Values are means. Primary assessment is the initial assessment, secondary assessments are measurements conducted 3 or 4 years afterward.
[b] t and P values reported are from the paired t-test, N=12.

monitoring can inform, but not accomplish, the decision process.

Campsites in Prince William Sound tend to fall in the moderately impacted range, showing a high level of cover loss, damage to adjacent trees and a significant number of additional trails (Tables 19.3 and 19.4). These results support the previous, preliminary work in PWS, which reported similar findings (Monz, 1998). It should be noted that we also collected descriptive and photographic information, which has now been catalogued and archived for future reference. This information will prove valuable in future efforts of re-assessment and for very general qualitative comparison.

Hammitt and Cole (1998) describe a general relationship between the amount of use and the loss of vegetation cover. In general, the initial use tends to result in the majority of disturbance to plant/soil communities and these observations have led to the recommendation of camping in sites that are already highly disturbed. Once the impact has occurred, little

additional impact accrues on these disturbed areas. Leung and Marion (2000) expand on this principle by comparing the total impact of dispersal verses containment strategies, that is, comparing repeated camping on impacted sites verses selecting new, pristine areas. In general, use must be very low or substrates highly resistant for dispersal to be effective, otherwise impacts can proliferate extensively. These principles are illustrated in this study with the beach grass community existing on the gravel and cobble substrates. Although the vegetation is highly susceptible to initial use (probably due to the ease of stem breakage of the tall grasses), areas devoid of vegetation are then highly resistant to any further impact, because of the gravel substrate with little or no organic soil that remains. This is contrasted with the soil that in the forested areas adjacent to beaches, which showed a trend of less relative cover loss initially, but may continue to be susceptible to disturbance because of the thick, soft organic horizon and the potentially slow plant re-growth. We observed that the soils in the forest understorey were easily displaced and disturbed by hiking boots, and therefore visitors still possibly affect even sites normally considered beyond susceptibility to additional impact. At most beaches, camping is possible on both beach gravel and forest understorey surfaces, and often very functional campsites can be found on beach gravel within a few metres of the forest interface. An important management implication of these findings is to make every effort to: (i) have visitors camp on the gravel surfaces whenever possible; (ii) avoid any additional disturbance to the intact beach grass community; and (iii) avoid substantial travel and camping in the forest understorey, even in areas previously disturbed.

Comparison of primary and secondary measurements at a subset of sites suggests that overall impacts are not changing significantly (Table 19.6). This should be interpreted with caution, as relatively few sites were re-measured extensively over the duration of the project. Our observations at many additional areas revisited but not re-measured would also support this finding. This trend should be monitored carefully if reported trends of increased visitation continue (Twardock and Monz, 2000). Impacts can proceed rapidly if visitors do not camp on bare gravel substrates and instead select vegetated areas for new camps, regardless of the vegetation type.

Recent studies have contrasted dispersal versus containment strategies in forested ecosystems of the eastern US (Williams and Marion, 1995; Marion and Leung, 1997). These and other results indicate that, in general, in areas where use levels tend to be low and resistant soil/plant communities exist, dispersal can be an effective strategy. In areas with higher use and with sensitive soil/plant communities, such as those found in both the beach grass and forest understorey areas in PWS, containment strategies can be a more effective method of avoiding overall increases in disturbance. Traditional containment practices involve developing a system whereby overnight visitors are required to camp in designated sites or in a certain zone, and a certain level of site development (e.g. site numbers, hardened surfaces, fire grates) often accompanies this strategy. This approach is advantageous in limiting resource impacts, but changes the visitor experience

somewhat, with a more developed camping feel.

Our results and observations over the duration of this project suggest that in PWS, it may be possible to limit future impacts by directing visitors away from vegetated areas susceptible to impact, to the abundant, highly resistant exposed beach gravel for overnight camping. Given the ease with which the beach grass vegetation is disturbed, visitors need to diligently avoid plants when landing, camping and hiking along the beaches, and should also avoid storing their kayaks on vegetated areas. Recently, the US Forest Service has initiated an extensive visitor education programme with interpretive information at the put-in sites in Whittier and Valdez and at the National Forest visitor centre. If effective, this approach could maintain the 'pristine' site camping experience, minimize resource impacts, and, although costs of the education programme have been incurred, reduce the need for, and cost of, site maintenance in the field. Future re-measurement of the sites established in this study will enable the evaluation of the effectiveness of this education programme and overall management strategy.

As suggested in the previous work on campsite impact in PWS (Monz, 1998), additional questions beyond the scope of this study remain. One important question from a managerial context is the resiliency of both the beach grass vegetation and the forest understorey with site closure following significant impact. Observations in the field suggest that regeneration may be significant for some plant species; an experimental study with applied levels of disturbance would clarify this issue.

Conclusions

Primitive camping beaches in the PWS area have experienced some resource degradation due to visitor activities and, should visitation continue to increase, it is likely that additional impacts will occur. The results and observations presented here suggest that visitor impacts, although substantial and widespread, are not increasing significantly, although future assessments should be made, given the possibility of increased use. Perhaps most importantly, this work has documented the extent, location and characteristics of the current resource impacts in an effort to support ongoing, appropriate management and visitor education strategies.

Vegetation loss was high in both the beach grass and forest understorey communities. However, once established, sites on the exposed beach gravel are highly resistant to additional use and, whenever possible, visitors should camp on these sites exclusively. Multiple trailing, damage to trees and the presence of camping trash were noted at a substantial number of sites, and these impacts are being addressed by managers through a visitor education programme. Periodic re-measurement of the network of sites is recommended to evaluate the effectiveness of current management strategies.

Acknowledgements

The authors thank Bill Ewing for his dedication to the many weeks of fieldwork. Don Ford and the National Outdoor Leadership School (NOLS) Alaska staff provided considerable help with the study design and logistical support. Sharon Kehoe and Michelle Escodera also helped with the field assessments. This study was supported by funding from the NOLS Research Program and by NOLS Alaska.

References

Cole, D.N. (1983a) *Monitoring the Condition of Wilderness Campsites.* Research Paper INT-302, US Department of Agriculture Forest Service, Intermountain Forest and Range Experiment Station, Ogden, Utah.

Cole, D.N. (1983b) *Campsite Conditions in the Bob Marshall Wilderness, Montana.* Research Paper INT-312, US Department of Agriculture Forest Service, Intermountain Forest and Range Experiment Station. Ogden, Utah.

Cole, D.N. (1996) Wilderness Recreation Use Trends, 1965 Through 1994. Research Paper INT-RP-488, US Department of Agriculture Forest Service, Intermountain Forest and Range Experiment Station. Ogden, Utah.

Dobyn, P. (2003) Whittier nuisance hulk may become plush resort. *Anchorage Daily News,* 26 February.

Exxon Valdez Oil Spill Trustee Council (2002*)* Exxon Valdez *Oil Spill Restoration Plan: Update on*

Injured Resources and Services. Exxon Valdez Oil Spill Trustee Council, Anchorage, Alaska.

Frissell, S.S. (1978) Judging recreational impacts on wilderness campsites. *Journal of Forestry* 76, 481–483.

Hammitt, W. and Cole, D.N. (1998) *Wildland Recreation,* 2nd edn. John Wiley & Sons, New York.

Kehoe, S. (2002) *A Procedural Manual for Monitoring Campsite Conditions in Prince William Sound, Alaska.* NOLS Research Program, Lander, Wyoming.

Lethcoe, J. (1990) *Geology of Prince William Sound, Alaska.* Prince William Sound Books, Valdez, Alaska.

Leung, Y. and Marion, J.L. (2000) Recreation impacts and management in wilderness: a state-of-knowledge review. In: Cole, D.N., McCool, S.F., Borrie, W.T. and O'Loughlan, J. (eds) *Wilderness Science in a Time of Change Conference. Vol. 5. Wilderness Ecosystems, Threats and Management.* Proceedings RMRS-P-15-Vol-5, USDA Forest Service, Rocky Mountain Research Station, Ogden, Utah, pp. 23–48.

Marion, J.L. (1991) *Developing a Natural Resource Inventory and Monitoring Program for Visitor Impacts on Recreational Sites: a Procedural Manual.* Natural Resources Report PS/NRVT/NRR-91/06.S, USDI National Park Service, Natural Resources Publication Office, Denver, Colorado.

Marion, J.L. and Leung, Y. (1997) An Assessment of Campsite Conditions in Great Smoky Mountains National Park. USDI National Park Service, Southeast Regional Office, Atlanta, Georgia.

Marion, J.L. and Leung, Y. (1998) International impact research and management. In: Hammitt, W.E. and Cole, D.N. (eds) *Wildland Recreation.* John Wiley & Sons, New York.

Monz, C.A. (1998) Monitoring recreation resource impacts in two coastal areas of western North America: an initial assessment. In: Watson, A.E., Alphet, G. and Hendee, J.C. (eds) *Personal, Societal and Ecological Values of Wilderness: Sixth World Wilderness Congress Proceedings on Research, Management, and Allocation. Vol. I.* Proc. RMRS-P-4. US Department of Agriculture, Forest Service, Rocky Mountain Research Station, Ogden, Utah.

Monz, C.A. (2000) Recreation resource and monitoring techniques: examples from the Rocky Mountains, USA. In: Godde, P., Price, M. and Zimmermann, F. (eds) *Tourism and Development in Mountain Regions.* CAB International, Wallingford, UK.

National Park Service (1997) *VERP: The Visitor*

Experience and Resource Protection Framework – a Handbook for Planners and Managers. Publication NPS D- 121, NPS Denver Service Center, Denver, Colorado.

Neff, J.M., Owens, E.H., Stoker, S.S. and McCormick, D.M. (1995) Shoreline oiling conditions in Prince William Sound following the Exxon Valdez oil spill. In: Wells, G., Butler, J.N. and Hughes, J.S. (eds) *Exxon Valdez Oil Spill: Fate and Effects in Alaskan Waters.* ASTM Special Technical Publication 1219. American Society for Testing and Materials, Philadelphia, Pennsylvania.

Stankey, G.H., Cole, D.N., Lucas, R.C., Peterson, M.E. and Frissel, S.S. (1985) *The Limits of Acceptable Change (LAC) System for Wilderness Planning.* General Technical Report INT-176, USDA Forest Service, Intermountain Forest Experiment Station. Ogden, Utah.

Twardock, P. and Monz, C.A. (2000) Recreational kayak visitor use, distribution, and economic value in Prince William Sound, Alaska USA. In: Cole, D.N., McCool, S.F., Borrie, W.T. and O'Loughlan, J. (comps) *Wilderness Science in a Time of Change Conference. Vol. 4. Wilderness Visitors, Experiences, and Visitor Management.* Proceedings RMRS-P-15-Vol-4, USDA Forest Service Rocky Mountain Research Station, Ogden, Utah, pp. 175–180.

Wiens, J.A., Crist, T.O., Day, R.H., Murphy, S.M. and Hayward, G.D. (1996) Effects of the *Exxon Valdez* oil spill on the marine bird communities in Prince William Sound. *Alaska Ecological Applications* 6(3), 826–841.

Williams, P.B. and Marion, J.L. (1995) *Assessing Campsite Conditions for Limits of Acceptable Change Management in Shenandoah National Park.* Technical report NPS/MARSHEN/NRTR-95/071, USDI National Biological Service, Virginia Tech Cooperative Park Studies Unit, Blacksburg, Virginia.

20

The Role of Tourism in Spreading Dieback Disease in Australian Vegetation

Ralf Buckley, Narelle King and Tatia Zubrinich
International Centre for Ecotourism Research, Griffith University, Gold Coast, Queensland, Australia

Introduction

Commercial tourism and private recreation in national parks and other areas of high conservation value are continuing to grow in both economic and environmental significance (Buckley, 2000a). Some impacts are local, others diffuse; some immediately obvious, others not; some ecologically significant, others less so; some recover if tourists are removed, whereas others continue to increase; some are easily controlled and managed, others not (Buckley, 2000b). The most serious are those that are important but insidious: diffuse, not immediately obvious, self-propagating, irreversible and damaging to conservation. Prime examples include feral animals, weeds and pathogens; and one such pathogen is the oomycete *Phytophthora cinnamomi*, commonly known as jarrah dieback or cinnamon fungus. A number of other *Phytophthora* and *Pythium* species also cause plant dieback diseases (Erwin and Ribeiro, 1996; Podger and Keane, 2000; Shearer and Smith, 2000) but *P. cinnamomi* is particularly virulent and easily spread.

Historically, construction of logging and mining roads into production forests has been of particular concern in spreading *P. cinnamomi* (Newhook and Podger, 1972; Podger *et al.*, 1996). More recently, however, the role of tourism and recreation in dispersing dieback disease into protected areas has received increased attention (Shearer, 1990; Podger *et al.*, 1996). It is this role that we review here. To provide an appreciation for its significance, however, the life history, distribution and ecological effects of *P. cinnamomi* are first summarized below.

Life History, Distribution and Impacts

P. cinnamomi has been isolated from over 900 plant species in 67 countries (Zentmeyer, 1980; Irwin *et al.*, 1995). It is one of the most damaging plant pathogens in recorded history: in some Australian plant communities, it can eliminate 50–75% of plant species (Weste and Marks, 1987). It occurs in all Australian States and Territories, but its impacts are particularly severe in woody vegetation in the south-west and south-east, where it is a longstanding management concern in many parks and forests (Newhook and Podger, 1972; Shearer, 1990, 1994; Hill *et al.* 1994, 1995; Barker and Wardlaw, 1995; Castello *et al.*, 1995; Irwin *et al.*, 1995; Podger *et al.*, 1996; Shearer and Dillon, 1996; Cahill, 1999; Podger and Keane, 2000). It spreads by direct mycelial growth between plant roots and by zoospores in surface and subsurface soil water, and survives adverse conditions within its plant hosts and by producing resistant chlamydospores (Weste and

Vithanage, 1979; Shea *et al.*, 1980; Kennedy and Weste, 1986; Kinal *et al.*, 1993; Hill *et al.*, 1994; Cahill, 1999). Symptoms include chlorosis, cankers and collar rot on the stem, root rot and death, shoot wilting and dieback, stem shrinkage, crown dieback and plant death, commonly within 3 years of infection (Weste and Marks, 1987; Davison and Shearer, 1989; Newell and Wilson, 1993; Davison and Tay, 1995a,b; Shearer and Dillon, 1995; Shanahan *et al.*, 1996; Shearer and Smith, 2000). Plants may also be infected asymptomatically (Pratt and Heather, 1973). Susceptibility differs greatly between species and genotypes, with trees and shrubs in the *Proteaceae*, *Myrtaceae* and *Epacridaceae* particularly affected, and forbs, grasses and sedges least (Cho, 1983; Marks and Smith, 1991; Wills, 1992; Cahill *et al.*, 1993; Stukey and Crane, 1994; Wills and Keighery, 1994; Irwin *et al.*, 1995; Tynan *et al.*, 1998). The most heavily affected plant communities are temperate heaths, woodlands and forests on infertile sandy and gravelly soils with low organic content and microbial activity, especially where subject to flooding because of topography or impermeable subsurface horizons. Resistance is also reduced by other stresses such as drought, salinization, hypoxia, waterlogging, fire, insects or other pathogens (Shea *et al.*, 1980; Weste and Marks, 1987; Marks and Smith, 1991; Davison, 1994; Davison *et al.*, 1994; Barker and Wardlaw, 1995; Bunny *et al.*, 1995; Castello *et al.*, 1995; Shearer and Dillon, 1995, 1996; Brasier, 1996; Podger *et al.*, 1996; Burgess *et al.*, 1999a,b; Podger and Keane, 2000; Aberton *et al.*, 2001; Wilson *et al.*, 2003). Sporulation and mycelial growth generally require warm, moist soils, so the pathogen is uncommon in arid and cold montane regions. In some areas the pathogen is active year-round, but with seasonal variations; in others it is only active during part of the year (Shea *et al.*, 1980; Hill *et al.*, 1994; Duncan and Keane, 1996). The areas affected by *P. cinnamomi* are likely to increase as global climate change increases temperatures, ultraviolet radiation and carbon dioxide concentrations in southern Australia (Brasier, 1996; Chakrabarty *et al.*, 2000).

Historically and currently, *P. cinnamomi* has caused greatest damage to parks and forests in temperate southern Australia: south-western Western Australia, Mount Lofty and Kangaroo Island in South Australia; and non-alpine Victoria and Tasmania (Newhook and Podger, 1972; Anon, 1975; Havel, 1979; Underwood and Murch, 1984; Kennedy and Weste, 1986; Davison and Shearer, 1989; Podger *et al.*, 1990; Weste and Ashton, 1994; Barker and Wardlaw, 1995; Hill *et al.*, 1995; Shearer and Dillon, 1995; Duncan and Keane, 1996; Newell, 1998; Wilson *et al.*, 2000). It is generally absent or insignificant in the arid inland areas of central Western Australia, southern Northern Territory, northern South Australia, and western New South Wales. It occurs widely in the tropical north, but to date appears to have caused only localized damage, e.g. to *Eucalyptus tetrodonta* in the Northern Territory (Weste, 1983) and a small number of rainforest sites in Queensland (Davison and Shearer, 1989; Daly, 1998; Brown, 1999; Pryce *et al.*, 2002).

It is not clear whether it is native to Australia; and if so, to what regions (Pratt and Heather, 1973; Brown, 1976, 1999; Palzer, 1985; Goosem and Tucker, 1999; Podger and Keane, 2000). There seem to be four main possibilities: (i) it has long been widespread, but has become damaging over recent decades in south-western Western Australia, Victoria and Tasmania because of logging and road construction; or (ii) it has long been present in areas where it occurs but currently causes little damage, such as Queensland and New South Wales, and has been spread in recent decades into the high-damage areas of south-western Western Australia, Victoria and Tasmania; or (iii) it has long been present in the high-damage area of south-western Western Australia, has spread more recently into new high-damage areas in Victoria and Tasmania, and is now spreading into new areas in New South Wales and Queensland, which will suffer high damage in future; or (iv) it is spreading into the tropics and subtropics, but has little impact because soil microflora and plant mycorrhizae are more diverse and abundant.

There appears to be evidence both for and against each of these propositions. For example, many Australian plant communities are subject to periodic fires, floods and droughts, irrespective of human influences. Again, mycorrhizae are also particularly prevalent in infertile sandy soils. According to Podger and

Keane (2000), 'colonisation of Australian landscapes by *P. cinnamomi* is almost certainly in its third century and the pathogen is now established in a mosaic over millions of hectares of native vegetation'. Shearer and Smith (2000) argue that there is 'strong evidence it was introduced to vulnerable forests in the south from tropical vegetation further north'.

Similarly, it is not clear to what degree the pre-European distribution of plant species and communities in Australia reflect the long-term influence of *P. cinnamomi*. These issues are important for management, since different strategies are likely to be effective or ineffective in areas where *P. cinnamomi* is a new and robust invader, attacking plant communities with no resistance or immunity, cf. areas where plant communities are in a long-term balanced equilibrium between *P. cinnamomi* attack and plant resistance, with the balance recently tipped towards *P. cinnamomi* through human activities. In the temperate south, the former seems to apply, with highly visible dieback fronts and patches in newly infected areas, particularly along roads. In the wet tropics and subtropics the pathogen currently appears less aggressive, but there are a number of infestations and no grounds for complacency.

In heavily affected areas, the effect of *P. cinnamomi* is to reduce cover and abundance of woody plants and increase those of forbs, grasses and sedges; often completely changing the character of the vegetation (Kennedy and Weste, 1986; Wills, 1992; Wills and Keighery, 1994; Peters and Weste, 1997). Rare plant species may be threatened (Gadek, 1999). Initial changes can produce positive feedback effects as a thinning tree canopy increases soil temperature, reduces humus and microbial activity, lowers transpiration and increases runoff – all favourable to *P. cinnamomi* (Anon, 1975; Davison *et al.*, 1994; Duncan and Keane, 1996)

These changes in vegetation also affect animal communities: the smaller mammals of closed-canopy forests and dense shrubland are replaced by larger open-country grazers, and nectar-feeding birds and arboreal mammals decrease in abundance and diversity (Kennedy and Weste, 1986; Wills, 1992; Castello *et al.*, 1995; Er, 1997; Newell, 1998). Soil invertebrate faunas and microbiota may also be modified (Newell, 1997). As one example of faunal impacts, *Antechinus stuartii* decreased in abundance in areas affected by *P. cinnamomi* in the Brisbane Ranges, Victoria (Newell and Wilson, 1993; Newell, 1998): *A. stuartii* nest sites in *Eucalyptus* were not affected, but the pathogen caused a decline in *Xanthorrhoea australis*, where *A. stuartii* forages for insects.

Tourism Impacts and Management

Tourism contributes to the spread of *P. cinnamomi* dieback both by spreading spores, mycelium and infected plant material, and by changing conditions in ways which increase plant stress and susceptibility (Shea *et al.*, 1980; Weste, 1983; WACALM, 1992; Kinal *et al.*, 1993; Gillen and Napier, 1994; Castello *et al.*, 1995; Podger *et al.*, 1996; Shearer and Dillon, 1996; Podger and Keane, 2000; Shearer and Smith, 2000). Direct dispersal of spores is much more significant in most areas. Spores may be spread in fill, construction, gravel, sand and other materials used for infrastructure construction, track building and landscaping. Spores are also carried in mud, soil and water on earth-moving and construction machinery, and on vehicles belonging to land-management agencies, maintenance crews, commercial tour operators and private individuals. Spores can be dispersed along roads and tracks by trucks, buses and cars; and off-road by public, private and commercially owned four- and six-wheel drive (4WD and 6WD) vehicles, trail bikes, mountain bikes, horses and human footwear. Spores can be carried across lakes and along rivers by boats; and into backcountry and wilderness areas on hikers' boots and camping equipment such as trowels and tent pegs. Once introduced, *P. cinnamomi* can continue to spread through plant-to-plant transmission, transport of spores in surface and subsurface water flows, and on both native and feral animals (Kinal *et al.*, 1993; Brown, 1999). This may become apparent immediately, or it may remain hidden until the area concerned is affected by fire, heavy rain, drought, insect pests or other pathogens.

Ideally, mapping should be the first step in any management strategy, but this is not always straightforward, since the effects of the pathogen may take some time to become apparent in newly infected areas. Mapping techniques include aerial survey and photography, ground survey, floristic community analysis and direct sampling of individual plants or soil (Western Australia Forests Department, 1982; Kennedy and Weste, 1986; Cahill and Hardham, 1994; Fouche, 1995; Newell, 1998; Goosem and Tucker, 1999; Podger and Keane, 2000; Shearer and Smith, 2000; Pryce *et al.*, 2002). Because of technical difficulties and costs in accurate mapping, the boundaries between infected and uninfected areas are rarely demarcated with any precision. In addition, the distribution of the pathogen can be very patchy at a small scale (Pryce *et al.*, 2002). Hence a negative assay may not necessarily indicate conclusively that an area is uninfected.

A number of chemical treatments have been trialled, but they are only partially effective, may have phytotoxic and other side-effects and are generally too expensive for broadscale use (Shea *et al.*, 1980; Weste and Marks, 1987; Hardy *et al.*, 1994; Aberton *et al.*, 1999; Pegg, 1999; Jackson *et al.*, 2000). Chemical agents tested to date include phosphonates and phosphites (Aberton *et al.*, 1999; Jackson *et al.*, 2000) and metalaxyl (Irwin *et al.*, 1995). Attempts at biological control using bacteria and fungi antagonistic to *P. cinnamomi* have not proved effective in the field (Newhook and Podger, 1972; Hardy *et al.*, 1994; Irwin *et al.*, 1995; El-Tarabily *et al.*, 1996; You *et al.*, 1996; Li *et al.*, 1997; Cahill, 1999).

In relatively dry, level areas where *P. cinnamomi* spreads plant-to-plant, it can be blocked by clearing vegetation from a barrier zone and keeping this bare for several years (Hill *et al.*, 1994). Small, heavily affected areas may be revegetated with resistant species or cultivars (Cahill *et al.*, 1993; Weste and Ashton, 1994; Stukely and Crane, 1994; Irwin *et al.*, 1995; Weste *et al.*, 1999; Wilson *et al.*, 2000). Management actions that accelerate the spread of the pathogen, such as burning off, thinning, track and infrastructure construction and maintenance, and other disturbances, can be restricted to seasons of low *Phytophthora* activity (Shea *et al.*, 1980; Hardy *et al.*, 1994). Secondary spread of *P. cinnamomi* spores can be restricted by improving drainage in areas prone to waterlogging, by locating roads and tracks in valleys rather than on ridges, and by

sealing roads and hardening paths (Weste and Marks, 1987; Gillen and Napier, 1994; Hill *et al.*, 1994). Such approaches are only likely to be effective if applied on a catchment scale, including public or private land outside protected area boundaries (Barker *et al.*, 1996; Peters and Weste, 1997).

Realistically, in most areas there is no effective way to control *P. cinnamomi* once it has been introduced into a new catchment or susceptible area of vegetation. The only effective management strategy is to quarantine areas that are unaffected from those that are already infected (Wilson *et al.*, 2000). The only reliable quarantine approach is to ban access completely to uninfected catchments. Even this may not be effective if animals can spread spores across watersheds. Where access restriction is not feasible for legal, political or practical reasons, the most effective approach is a programme of strict hygiene to mimimize the spread of spores. This approach is also valuable in catchments where only small areas have, as yet, been affected. Hygiene approaches require complete sterilization of all materials used in road and track construction and similar infrastructure; thorough washdown and disinfection of all wheeled vehicles, both motorized and unmotorized, every time they enter an unaffected area; and systems for cleaning horses' hooves, hikers' footwear and camping equipment (Chester, 1999; Wilson *et al.*, 2000). These approaches are used in national parks in south-western and south-eastern Australia, but their effectiveness has not been tested experimentally. In particular, it seems unlikely that vehicle washdown and hiker boot-scrubbing stations are used by 100% of drivers and hikers, whether private or commercial; or that they remove 100% of spores from vehicle undercarriages, tyres, hooves and boots.

A parallel approach, which has been used in Tasmania for a number of years, is to encourage tourists to visit uninfected sites before they visit areas known to carry *P. cinnamomi* infestations. Maps of areas known to be affected by dieback are shown at national park entrance stations and trailheads. However, by the time visitors are made aware of this information, it may be too late in practice for them to redesign their itineraries. Therefore, although this educational approach is valuable, it needs to reach domestic and international tourists and visitors sooner if it is to prove effective in the long term.

Current management approaches, especially in Western Australia, focus on complete quarantine of so-called protectable areas where *P. cinnamomi* is not yet present and which are likely to remain uninfected if strictly isolated (Podger and Keane, 2000). Hygiene-based attempts to slow or limit the spread of the disease into areas that will probably become infected eventually, seem to have been dismissed as ineffective.

Conclusion

Phytophthora dieback is very significant for the Australian tourism industry because affected areas lose their scenic attraction, and because quarantine requirements may restrict access for commercial operators and individual visitors. Not surprisingly, tour operators and industry associations have lobbied against any restrictions on access (Chester, 1999), arguing instead for approaches based on hygiene. However, whether they would be prepared to invest the capital and incur the operating expenses to make such approaches work in practice, is far from clear. For example, one obvious approach would be to halt all external vehicles at the boundary of a national park or an uninfected area, and transfer passengers to other vehicles which remain permanently within the uninfected zone. However, this would require major investment in vehicles, garaging, refuelling, security and so on. It also relies on identifying the boundaries between infected and uninfected areas, which is commonly problematic. Similarly, hikers and bushwalkers might be required to scrub down their boots, tent pegs, etc. at the park entrance, dip them in disinfectant and or phosphonate, and have them inspected by a ranger before continuing. Before such systems are instituted, however, it will be necessary to test how effective they are in removing *P. cinnamomi* spores: both to assure land managers that they are useful management techniques, and to convince private and commercial users that the effort is worth making. Currently, the only effective management approach seems to be a complete access ban and strict quarantine for protectable areas,

rendering such areas entirely off limits for both individual recreation and commercial tourism, as well as any other users.

References

Aberton, M.J., Wilson, B.A. and Cahill, D.M. (1999) The use of potassium phosphonate to control *Phytophthora cinnamomi* in native vegetation at Anglesea, Victoria. *Australasian Plant Pathology* 28, 225–234.

Aberton, M.J., Wilson, B.A., Hill, J. and Cahill, D.M. (2001) Development of disease caused by *Phytophthora cinnamomi* in mature *Xanthorrhoea australis*. *Australian Journal of Botany* 49, 1–11.

Anon. (1975) Salt problems in Perth's hills. *Ecos* 5, 3–12.

Barker, P.C.J. and Wardlaw, T.J. (1995) Susceptibility of selected Tasmanian rare plants to *Phytophthora cinnamomi*. *Australian Journal of Botany* 43, 379–386.

Barker, P.C.J., Wardlaw, T.J. and Brown, M.J. (1996) Selection and design of *Phytophthora* management areas for the conservation of threatened flora in Tasmania. *Biological Conservation* 76, 187.

Brasier, C.M. (1996) *Phytophthora cinnamomi* and oak decline in southern Europe. Environmental constraints including climate change. *Annales Des Sciences Forestieres* 53, 347–358.

Brown, B. (1976) *Phytophthora cinnamomi* associated with patch death in tropical rain forests in Queensland. *Australian Plant Pathology Society Newsletter* 5, 1–4.

Brown, B. (1999) Occurrence and impact of *Phytophthora cinnamomi* and other *Phytophthora* species in rainforests of the Wet Tropics World Heritage Area, and of the Mackay region, Queensland. In: Gadek, P.A. (ed.) *Patch Deaths in Tropical Queensland Rainforests: Association and Impact of* Phytophthora cinnamomi *and other Soil Borne Organisms*. CRC Rainforest, Cairns, Australia, pp. 41–76.

Buckley, R.C. (2000a) NEAT trends: current issues in nature, eco and adventure tourism. *International Journal of Tourism Research* 2, 437–444.

Buckley, R.C. (2000b) Tourism and biodiversity: land-use, planning and impact assessment. *Journal of Tourism Studies* 10, 47–56.

Bunny, F.J., Crombie, D.S. and Williams, M.R. (1995) Growth of lesions of *Phytophthora cinnamomi* in stems and roots of jarrah (*Eucalyptus marginata*) in relation to rainfall and stand density in mediterranean forest of Western Australia. *Canadian Journal of Forest Research* 25, 961–969.

Burgess, T., McComb, J.A., Colquhoun, I. and Hardy, St J. G.E. (1999a) Hypoxia and its effects on root morphology and lesion development in *Eucalyptus marginata* infected with *Phytophthora cinnamomi*. *Plant Pathology* 48, 786–796.

Burgess, T., McCombe, J.A., Colquhoun, I. and Hardy, St J. G.E. (1999b) Increased susceptibility of *Eycalyptus marginata* to stem infection *Phytophthora cinnamomi* resulting from hoot hypoxia. *Plant Pathology* 48, 797–806.

Cahill, D. (1999) General biology and ecology of *Phytophthora* with special reference to *Phytophthora cinnamomi*. In: Gadek, P.A. (ed.) *Patch Deaths in Tropical Queensland Rainforests: Association and Impact of Phytophthora cinnamomi and other Soil Borne Organisms.* CRC Rainforest, Cairns, Australia, pp. 21–26.

Cahill, D.M. and Hardham, A.R. (1994) A dipstick immunoassay for the specific detection of *Phytophthora cinnamomi* in soils. *Phytopathology* 84, 1284–1292.

Cahill, D.M., Bennett, I.J. and McComb, J.A. (1993) Mechanisms of resistance to *Phytophthora cinnamomi* in clonal, micropropagated *Eucalyptus marginata*. *Plant Pathology* 42, 865–872.

Castello, J.D., Leopold, D.J. and Smallidge, P.J. (1995) Pathogens, patterns, and processes in forest ecosystems: Pathogens influence and are influenced by forest development and landscape characteristics. *BioScience* 45, 16–24.

Chakrabarty, S., Tiedemann, A.V. and Teng, P.S. (2000) Climate change: potential impact on plant diseases. *Environmental Pollution* 108, 317–326.

Chester, G. (1999) *Phytophthora cinnamomi:* tourism industry considerations. In: Gadek, P.A. (ed.) *Patch Deaths in Tropical Queensland Rainforests: Association and Impact of* Phytophthora cinnamomi *and other Soil Borne Organisms.* CRC Rainforest, Cairns, Australia, pp. 17–20.

Cho, J.J. (1983) Variability in susceptibility of some *Banksia* species to *Phytophthora cinnamomi* and their distribution in Australia. *Plant Disease* 67, 869–871.

Daly, D. (1998) *Using Rainforest Research: Rainforest Masks a Deadly Disease.* CRC Rainforest, Cairns, Australia.

Davison, E.M. and Tay, F.C.S. (1995a) Predictions of where minimal damage to jarrah roots could result in tree death. *New Phytopathology* 131, 393–401.

Davison, E.M. and Tay, F.C.S. (1995b) Damage to surface roots of *Eucalyptus marginata* trees at sites infested with *Phytophthora cinnamomi*. *Australian Journal of Botany* 43, 527–536.

Davison, E.M. (1994) Role of environment in dieback of jarrah: effects of waterlogging on jarrah and *Phytophthora cinnamomi* and infection of jarrah by *P. cinnamomi*. *Journal of the Royal Society of Western Australia* 77, 123–126.

Davison, E.M. and Shearer B.L. (1989) *Phytophthora* spp. in indigenous forests in Australia. *New Zealand Journal of Forestry Science* 19, 277–289.

Davison, E.M., Stukely, M.J., Crane, C.E. and Tay, F.C.S. (1994) Invasion of phloem and xylem of woody stems and roots of *Eucalyptus marginata* and *Pinus radiata* by *Phytophthora cinnamomi*. *Phytopathology* 84, 335–340.

Duncan, M.J. and Keane, P.J. (1996) Vegetation changes associated with *Phytophthora cinnamomi* and its decline under *Xanthorrhoea australis* in Kinglake National Park, Victoria. *Australian Journal of Botany* 44, 355–369.

El-Tarabily, K.A., Sykes, M.L., Kurtböke, I.D., Hardy, St. J.G.E., Barbosa, A.M. and Dekker, R.F.H. (1996) Synergistic effects of a cellulase-producing *Micromonospora carbonacea* and an antibiotic-producing *Streptomyces violascens* on the suppression of *Phytophthora cinnamomi* root rot of *Banksia grandis*. *Canadian Journal of Botany* 74, 618–624.

Er, K.B.H. (1997) Effects of eucalypt dieback on bird species diversity in remnants of native woodland. *Corella* 21, 101–111.

Erwin, D.C. and Ribeiro, O.K. (1996) *Phytophthora Diseases Worldwide*. The American Phytopathology Society, St Paul, Minnesota.

Fouche, P.S. (1995) The use of low-altitude infrared remote sensing for estimating stress conditions in tree crops. *South African Journal of Science* 91, 500–502.

Gadek, P.A. (ed.) (1999) *Patch Deaths in Tropical Queensland Rainforests: Association and Impact of* Phytophthora cinnamomi *and Other Soil Borne Organisams.* Cooperative Research Centre for Tropical Rainforest Ecology and Management, Cairns, Australia.

Gillen, K. and Napier A. (1994) Management of access. *Journal of the Royal Society of Western Australia* 77, 163–168.

Goosem, S. and Tucker, N. (1999) Current concerns and management issues of *Phytophthora cinnamomi* in the rainforests of the Wet Tropics. In: Gadek, P.A. (ed.) *Patch Deaths in Tropical Queensland Rainforests: Association and Impact of* Phytophthora cinnamomi *and other Soil Borne Organisms.* CRC Rainforest, Cairns, Australia, pp. 9–15.

Hardy, St. J.G.E.; O'Brien, P.A. and Shearer, B.L. (1994) Control options of plant pathogens in native plant communities in south-western Australia. *Journal of the Royal Society of Western Australia* 77, 169–177.

Havel, J. (1979) Identification of vulnerable communities and prediction of disease spread. In: Old, K.M. (ed.) *Phytophthora and Forest Management in Australia*. CSIRO, Melbourne, Australia, pp. 64–72.

Hill, T.C.J., Tippett, J.T. and Shearer, B.L. (1994) Invasion of bassendean dune *Banksia* woodland by *Phytophthora cinnamomi*. *Australian Journal of Botany* 42, 725–738.

Hill, T.C., Tippett, J.T. and Shearer, B.L. (1995) Evaluation of three treatments for eradication of *Phytophthora cinnamomi* from deep, leached sands in southwest Australia. *Plant Disease* 79, 122–127.

Irwin, J.A.G., Cahill, D.M. and Drenth, A. (1995) *Phytophthora* in Australia. *Australian Journal of Agricultural Research* 46, 1311–1337.

Jackson, T.J., Burgess, T., Colquhoun, I. and Hardy, G.E.S. (2000) Action of the fungicide phosphite on *Eucalyptus marginata* inoculated with *Phytophthora cinnamomi*. *Plant Pathology* 49, 147–154.

Kennedy, J. and Weste, G. (1986) Vegetation changes associated with invasion by *Phytophthora cinnamomi* on monitored sites in the Grampians, western Victoria. *Australian Journal of Botany* 34, 251–279.

Kinal, J., Shearer, B.L. and Fairman, R.G. (1993) Dispersal of *Phytophthora cinnamomi* through lateritic soil by laterally flowing subsurface water. *Plant Disease* 77, 1085–1090.

Li, H., White, D., Lamza, K.A., Berger, F. and Leifert, C. (1997) Biological control of *Botrytis*, *Phytophthora* and *Pythium* by *Bacillus subtilis* Cot1 and CL27 on micropropagated plants in high-humidity fogging glasshouses. In: Cassells, A.C. (ed.) *Pathogen and Microbial Contamination Management in Micropropagation*. Kluwer Academic Publishers, Dordrecht, The Netherlands.

Marks, G.C. and Smith, I.W. (1991) The cinnamon fungus in Victorian forests: history, distribution, management and control. *Lands and Forests Bulletin* 31, 33.

Newell, G.R. (1997) The abundance of ground-dwelling invertebrates in a Victorian forest affected by 'dieback' (*Phytophthora cinnamomi*) disease. *Australian Journal of Ecology* 22, 206–217.

Newell, G.R. (1998) Characterization of vegetation in an Australian open forest community affected by cinnamon fungus (*Phytophthora cinnamomi*): implications for faunal habitat quality. *Plant Ecology* 137, 55–70.

Newell, G.R. and Wilson, B.A. (1993) The relationship between cinnamon fungus (*Phytophthora cinnamomi*) and the abundance of *Antechinus stuartii* (Dasyuridae, Marsupialia) in the Brisbane Ranges, Victoria. *Wildlife Research* 20, 251–259.

Newhook, F.J. and Podger, F.D. (1972) The role of *Phytophthora cinnamomi* in Australian and New Zealand forests. *Annual Review of Phytopathology* 10, 299–325.

Palzer, C. (1985) *Environmental Impact Statement on Tasmanian Woodchip Exports Beyond 1988*. Forestry Commission of Tasmania, Hobart.

Pegg, K. (1999) *Phytophthora cinnamomi* in tropical rainforest – management of outbreaks. In: Gadek, P.A. (ed.) *Patch Deaths in Tropical Queensland Rainforests: Association and Impact of* Phytophthora cinnamomi *and other Soil Borne Organisms*. CRC Rainforest, Cairns, Australia, pp. 85–89.

Peters, D. and Weste, G. (1997) The impact of *Phytophthora cinnamomi* on six rare native tree and shrub species in the Brisbane Ranges, Victoria. *Australian Journal of Botany* 45, 975–995.

Podger, F.D. and Keane, P.J. (2000) Management of disease in native eucalypt forests and woodlands. In: Keane, P.J., Kile, G.A., Podger, F.D. and Brown, B.N. (eds) *Diseases of Pathogens and Eucalypts*. CSIRO Publishing, Victoria, Australia, pp. 445–475.

Podger, F., Palzer, C. and Wardlaw, T. (1990) A guide to the Tasmanian distribution of *Phytophthora cinnamomi* and its effects on native vegetation. *Tasforests* 2, 13–20.

Podger, F.D., James, S.H. and Mulcahy, M.J. (1996) *Review of Dieback in Western Australia*. Report to the Minister of Environment, Government of Western Australia, Perth, Australia.

Pratt, B.H. and Heather, W.A. (1973) The origin and distribution of *Phytophthora cinnamomi* Rands in Australian native plant communities and the significance of its association with particular plant species. *Australian Journal of Biological Science* 26, 559–573.

Pryce, J., Edwards, W. and Gadek, P.A. (2002) Distribution of *Phytophthora cinnamomi* at different spatial scales: when can a negative result be considered positively? *Austral Ecology* 27, 459–462.

Shanahan, K., Weste, G. and Guest, D. (1996) *Phytophthora cinnamomi* in the common heath, *Epacris impressa*. *Australasian Plant Pathology* 25, 141.

Shea, S.R., Gillen, K.J. and Leppard, W.I. (1980) Seasonal variation in population levels of *Phytophthora cinnamomi* Rands in soil in diseased, feely-drained *Eucalyptus marginata* Sm sites in the northern Jarrah forest of south-western Australia. *Protection Ecology* 2, 135–156.

Shearer, B.L. (1990) Dieback of native plant communities caused by *Phytophthora* species – a major factor affecting land use in southwestern Australia. *Land and Water Research News* 5, 15–26.

Shearer, B.L. (1994) The major plant pathogens occurring in native ecosystems of south-western Australia. *Journal of the Royal Society of Western Australia* 77, 113–122.

Shearer, B.L. and Dillon, M. (1995) Susceptibility of plant species in *Eucalyptus marginata* forest to infection by *Phytophthora cinnamomi*. *Australian Journal of Botany* 43, 113–134.

Shearer, B.L. and Dillon, M. (1996) Impact and disease centre characteristics of *Phytophthora cinnamomi* infestations of banksia woodlands on the Swan Coastal Plain, Western Australia. *Australian Journal of Botany* 44, 79–90.

Shearer, B.L. and Smith, I.W. (2000) Diseases of eucalypts caused by soilborne species of *Phytophthora* and *Pythium*. In: Keane, P.J., Kile, G.A., Podger, F.D. and Brown, B.N. (eds) *Diseases of Pathogens and Eucalypts*. CSIRO Publishing, Victoria, Australia, pp. 259–291.

Stukely, M.J.C. and Crane, C.E. (1994) Genetically based resistance of *Eucalyptus marginata* to *Phytophthora cinnamomi*. *Phytopathology* 84, 650–656.

Tynan, K.M., Scott, E.S. and Sedgley, M. (1998) Evaluation of *Banksia* species for response to *Phytophthora* infection. *Plant Pathology* 47, 446–455.

Underwood, R.J. and Murch, J.L. (1984) Hygienic logging in the northern jarrah forests. *Australian Forestry* 47, 39–44.

Weste, G. (1983) Dieback and death of *Eucalyptus tetradonta* due to *Phytophthora cinnamomi* in native forest at Nhulunbuy, N.T. *Australasian Plant Pathology* 12, 42–44.

Weste, G. and Ashton, D.H. (1994) Regeneration and survival of indigenous dry sclerophyll species in the Brisbane Ranges, Victoria, after a *Phytophthora cinnamomi* epidemic. *Australian Journal of Botany* 42, 239–253.

Weste, G. and Marks, G.C. (1987) The biology of *Phytophthora cinnamomi* in Australasian forests. *Annual Review of Phytopathology* 25, 207–229.

Weste, G. and Vithanage, K. (1979) Survival of chlamydospores of *Phytophthora cinnamomi* in several non-sterile, host-free forest soils and gravels at different soil water potentials. *Australian Journal of Botany* 27, 1–9.

Weste, G., Walchhuetter, T. and Walshe, T. (1999) Regeneration of *Xanthorrhoea australis* following epidemic disease due to *Phytophthora cinnamomi* in the Brisbane Ranges, Victoria. *Australasian Plant Pathology* 28, 162–169.

Western Australia, Conservation and Land Management. (1992) *Dieback Disease: Hygiene Manual*. WACALM, Perth, Australia.

Western Australia, Forests Department (1982) *Dieback Policy 1982: Adopted as a Consequence of the 1982 Dieback Review*. Western Australia Forests Department, Perth, Australia.

Wills, R.T. (1992) The ecological impact of *Phytophthora cinnamomi* in the Stirling Range National Park, Western Australia. *Australian Journal of Ecology* 17, 145–159.

Wills, R.T. and Keighery, G.J. (1994) Ecological impact of plant disease on plant communities. *Journal of the Royal Society of Western Australia* 77, 127–131.

Wilson, B.A., Aberton, J.A. and Cahill, D.M. (2000) Relationships between site factors and distribution of *Phytophthora cinnamomi* in the Eastern Otway Ranges, Victoria. *Australian Journal of Botany* 48, 247–260.

Wilson, B.A., Lewis, A. and Aberton, J. (2003) Spatial model for predicting the presence of cinnamomi fungus (*Phytophthora cinnamomi*) in sclerophyll vegetation communities in south-eastern Australia. *Australian Ecology* 28, 108–115.

You, M.P., Sivasithamparam, K. and Kurtboke, D.I. (1996) Actinomycetes in organic mulch used in avocado plantations and their ability to suppress *Phytophthora cinnamomi*. *Biological Fertility of Soils* 22, 237–242.

Zentmeyer, G.A. (1980) Phytophthora cinnamomi *and The Diseases it Causes*. Monograph 10, The American Phytopathological Society, St Paul, Minnesota.

21

Instream Bacteria as a Low-threshold Management Indicator of Tourist Impacts in Conservation Reserves

Wiebke Warnken and Ralf Buckley

International Centre for Ecotourism Research, Griffith University, Gold Coast, Queensland, Australia

Introduction

National parks, World Heritage areas and other conservation reserves protect biological diversity and provide clean water. Most jurisdictions also permit recreation in reserve areas. In some countries, tourism may contribute to the establishment and maintenance of reserves. The use of reserves for individual and commercial tourism and recreation is increasing very rapidly worldwide. The ecological impacts of this use, and the resources required to manage those impacts, are increasing correspondingly. Quantitative monitoring data on the types, extent and degree of such impacts, in relation to the types, timing and intensity of tourist activities, are hence vital, in order to manage reserves for their primary conservation purpose. Most importantly, reserve managers need early-warning indicators of tourist impacts, before those impacts reach the threshold of irreversible damage.

Different types of impact have different relative significance in different ecosystems. Trampling by hikers does less lasting damage to vegetation in mesic than extreme environments, but weed seeds and fungal spores are more likely to establish. Human voices are a major disturbance to fauna in subtropical rainforest, but not on snowcapped mountaintops. Human wastes can cause a far greater increase in nutrient concentrations in small alpine ponds or desert waterholes than in higher-

volume rivers. Hence different ecological parameters are more critical indicators of tourist impacts in different conservation reserves. Here, therefore, we describe an iterative approach to identifying a low threshold early-warning indicator of human recreational impacts for one such reserve.

Specifically, the aim of this project was to test the effectiveness of microbiological water quality parameters as an early-warning indicator of the environmental impacts of tourism and recreation in a subtropical rainforest national park.

Study Site

Lamington National Park is a World Heritage subtropical rainforest conservation reserve about 70 km inland, in south-east Queensland, Australia. It lies at approximately 153° 04′W and 28°17′S, and has a total area of 22,000 ha. It has not been logged, has no human impact other than tourism and recreation, and is of very considerable conservation significance. It is well known internationally and receives around about 300,000 visitors annually.

The park is a part of an eroded volcanic massif, a plateau sloping gently north, bounded to the south by a steep erosion rim, and dissected by the deep gorges of two northward-flowing river systems, the catchments of which lie entirely within the park. Annual rainfall has ranged from 1000 to over 2500 mm over the past decade. Monthly rainfall ranges from 50 mm in August and September to 250 mm in April. The main wet season runs from December to May. Summer storms can deposit over 100 mm in 24 h.

The volcanic soils support three principal vegetation types. Along the southern escarpment there is a narrow band of southern beech forest dominated by *Nothofagus cunninghamii* and also characterized by *Telopea* spp. The drier east-facing spurs support tall brush-box forest dominated by *Lophostemon conferta*, with a relatively open rainforest understorey. The remainder of the park supports a very dense and diverse multistorey rainforest, with numerous vines, epiphytes and buttresses. Along the rivers and their tributaries, treeferns and large epiphytic ferns are particularly prevalent.

The park is an important habitat area for a number of rare, endangered, threatened, endemic and restricted animal species, including the Lamington blue spiny crayfish (*Euastacus sulcatus*); various endangered frogs such as the Fleay's barred frog (*Mixophyes fleayi*) and the cascade tree frog (*Litonia pearsoniana*); the Hastings river mouse (*Pseudomys oralis*), Albert's lyrebird (*Menura alberti*) and the magnificent riflebird (*Ptiloris magnificus*), as well as less conspicuous species.

The two access roadheads into Lamington National Park have accommodation and associated facilities. Elsewhere in the park, hiking (unrestricted) and overnight bush camping (with a permit) are the only activities allowed. Pets, firearms and open fires are banned, and rock climbing and abseiling are restricted. The park is crossed by a series of tracks, and most hikers stay on these, since off-track progress can be slow and painful, through hook-spined lawyer vines (*Calamus* spp.) and stinging trees (*Dendrocnide excelsa*). Comfortable campsites are very limited, and overnight camping along the tracks is restricted to designated sites.

The main impacts of tourists in Lamington National Park are hence: the introduction of weeds and possibly pathogens, principally along tracks; noise disturbance to native fauna, including marsupials and birds; and contamination of watercourses. Here we focus on the last of these, for the following reasons: (i) water quality in streams is a good integrative measure of impacts in their entire catchments; (ii) the streams and rivers are one of the main tourist attractions and some sections are heavily visited; (iii) some of the park's more significant species, such as the rare spiny crayfish and frogs, live in the streams; and (iv) stream water is used by visitors and needs to be of potable quality.

Canungra Creek, the main river in the western part of the park, has two branches of very similar length, streamflow, sinuosity, geology, soils and vegetation, known as West Fork and East Fork. The West Fork is heavily visited, with many tracks along the river and elsewhere in its catchment. The East Fork is relatively inaccessible and rarely visited, with no tracks. The park's most popular recreational swimming area is Blue Pool on the West Fork, easily accessible by a half-day hike from the western roadhead.

Tourism activity in the Canungra Creek catchment is relatively low-key: day hikes along formed trails, and swimming and picnicking, principally at Blue Pool. Camping at Blue Pool itself is not permitted. There is a rarely used flat area, large enough for a single tent, at the junction of the East and West Forks, and another (flooded at high water) halfway from Blue Pool to the junction. There are multi-tent camping areas, designated by the park management agency, above the boundary of the Canungra Creek catchment, on the rim of the Lamington plateau, but these drain southwards, away from Canungra Creek. There is a heavily visited tourist lodge and car camping area at the roadhead west of Canungra Creek West Fork, but again this drains outside the Canungra Creek catchment. There are public toilets at the carpark, but they flush to fully sealed tanks with no external drainage. Recreational impacts on water quality are hence derived almost entirely from day visitors.

These tourists could therefore affect water quality by: eroding soil on tracks; leaving food scraps and other litter in or near watercourses, and rinsing out food containers in the creek; direct contact with the water by swimmers of all ages, including babies still in nappies; disturbance of streambed sediment; and urination and defecation in the catchment. We have observed all these behaviours. Their most likely immediate impacts on water quality are to increase concentrations of suspended sediment, organic matter, nitrogen and phosphorus, and microorganisms from the human gut. The increase in nitrogen and phosphorus may also increase biomass of benthic algae and sessile aquatic invertebrates, as occurs in the oligotrophic freshwater lakes of Fraser Island (Hadwen *et al.*, 2003). However, both in Canungra Creek and other freshwater bodies in the region (Arthington *et al.*, 1989; Bunn *et al.*, 1995, 1997; Pusey *et al.*, 1995), these biomass parameters are subject to such high natural variability that they cannot detect human impacts at the low level occurring in Lamington National Park.

We therefore focused on the principal nutrients, nitrogen and phosphorus; and on the major gut bacteria from humans and other mammals, coliforms and enterococci. These parameters are sufficiently specific for human impacts to be detectable, but sufficiently broad to affect instream ecology. A number of other microbiological indicators were also considered, notably: pathogenic bacterial species; protozoa and viruses; and new detection methods based on molecular techniques (Tsai *et al.*, 1993; McDaniels *et al.*, 1996; Venkateswaran *et al.*, 1996, 1997; Jinru *et al.*, 1998). Such approaches were not adopted because of site access considerations, sample size and laboratory requirements, the prohibitive costs of achieving adequate replication, and the experimental nature of the techniques concerned. One of the aims of this study was to develop and test an approach that can be used by managers of conservation reserves worldwide. Simplicity, reliability, low costs and robustness are therefore critical.

Many other possible measures of water quality were rejected because they are either too coarse to reflect human impact, or too fine to reflect ecosystem function. Basic physicochemical factors, such as temperature and turbidity, are simple to record and replicate, but the information they provide about ecosystem functions is very coarse. Population parameters for individual animal species in aquatic ecosystems should, in theory, provide a much finer indication of ecosystem function, but are often subject to considerable natural variation, so that the time scale required to detect a human

impact reliably may be longer than the time scale over which the impact occurs. In addition, quantitative measurements of aquatic animal populations, as an indicator of recreational impacts, may well disrupt these populations more than the recreational activities themselves. Concentrations of particular chemical species, such as the active constituents from insect repellents or from detergents, can distinguish human impacts unambiguously, but only very specific ones. Identification of DNA from human viruses may provide a very specific indication of past human presence in the water catchment, but little or no information on how this may have modified the ecosystem concerned.

Methods

We tested for human impacts on water quality by comparing sites with different levels of visitor use, at two scales. At a broad catchment scale we compared the heavily visited West Fork of Canungra Creek, with the rarely visited East Fork. We sampled both branches immediately above their junction. At a much finer scale we sampled at the inflow and outflow of Blue Pool. To distinguish tourist impacts from natural streamflow variations we also sampled at the inflow and outflow of a very similar control pool immediately upstream, which is much less accessible and very rarely visited.

All sites are accessible only on foot. The catchment-scale comparison involves a 9-hour round-trip hike from the roadhead. We sampled all sites throughout 3 years, 1992–1995 inclusive; 1993 was an atypically dry year, with peak monthly rainfall (in March) <300 mm, as compared to 470 mm in 1992 and 600 mm in 1994. At Blue Pool and its control pool we sampled every 1 or 2 months, to establish broad seasonal patterns, and intensively every day, or every second day, during the period of highest visitor use, over Christmas. The precise dates depend on the onset of the wet-season rains, which change the recreational character of the park very rapidly. These sites were sampled on 68 days in all. Sites on East Fork and West Fork we sampled less frequently, on 15 days in all. All samples at Blue Pool and control pool were taken between 12.00 and 14.00 hours, when visitors numbers peak at Blue Pool. During each sampling event, three replicate 250 ml samples were taken at each site sampled, and three replicate subsamples were taken from each bottle.

In addition to nutrients and bacteria, we measured air and water temperatures, streamflow, pH, dissolved oxygen and turbidity. For each 2-hour sampling period at Blue Pool we counted the total number of visitors, the total number of swimmers, and the maximum number of swimmers at any one time. Rainfall and other weather data were obtained from the Bureau of Meteorology records for Green Mountain (the western roadhead), and for the nearby Springbrook Plateau. We also measured bacterial concentrations in streambed sediments and streambank soils.

All water samples were collected and analysed according to the standard protocols of the American Public Health Association (APHA, 1992) and US Environment Protection Agency (USEPA, 1986). Samples for nutrient and turbidity analysis were collected in new acid-washed high-density polyethylene (HDPE) bottles manufactured by Nalgene®. Those for bacterial analysis were collected in sterilized glass bottles. Sample bottles were immersed with their apertures open upstream. Sediment and soil samples were collected by pushing sterilized 250 ml Schott® glass containers into the top 2 cm of sediment or soil until completely full. New sterile disposable vinyl gloves were worn while collecting all water, sediment and soil samples. All sample bottles were packed in ice, carried to a field vehicle equipped with a refrigerator, and driven immediately to the laboratory.

Samples for nutrient analysis were frozen at $-80°C$ and analysed by the Queensland Government Chemical Laboratories (QGCL), accredited by the National Association of Testing Authorities (NATA). Samples for bacterial analysis were treated immediately in our own laboratories, within 6 h of collection. They were filtered through Millipore® membranes with pore size 0.45 μm and diameter 47 mm, using APHA procedures. Filtered membranes were transferred on to selective culture media: the Sartorius® Teepol® medium for total coliforms (TCF) and faecal coliforms (FCF), Oxoid® Membrane Lauryl Sulphate® medium for

Escherichia coli, and Sartorius® Azide® medium for enterococci. Plates for TCF and FCF were incubated for 4 h at 35°C, followed by 18 h at 37°C; those for *E. coli* for 4 h at 35°C and 18 h at 44.5°C; and those for enterococci for 4 h at 30°C followed by 48 h at 35°C. Confirmation tests for TCF, FCF and *E. coli* were carried out with the Vitek® Microbact 12E® test kit, and those for enterococci with the Oxoid® Streptococcal Grouping Kit®. A clinical pathology laboratory provided final confirmation on colony identification.

We tested the sensitivity of results to variations in: (i) the precise location of sampling sites; (ii) the use of ice for initial transport of samples from the sampling sites to the field vehicle; and (iii) the time delay between sampling and analysis. We also tested the survival time of individual bacterial species (Tassoula, 1997) in the aquatic environment at the study site, and the precise ability of culture media to distinguish between *E. coli* and other faecal coliforms.

Small changes in precise sampling location had no significant effect on bacterial counts. Failure to chill samples immediately on collection increased bacterial counts by approximately 7.5% ($P<0.001$). All samples were therefore carried on ice from the time of collection until the time of analysis. Storage of samples at 4°C for 12 h (overnight) increased bacterial counts by 6% on average ($P<0.001$). All samples were therefore treated immediately on returning to the laboratory.

For water samples held at ambient temperature, concentrations of each of the four principal bacterial indicators increased by 10–30% during the first 24 h after sampling, and then decayed exponentially, with concentrations falling below 10% of the maximum within 7 days in each case. The survival time for *E. coli* and faecal coliforms was slightly shorter than for total coliforms.

The Sartorius® Teepol® culture medium does not distinguish accurately between total and faecal coliforms. In particular, only about half (53.6%) of the colonies identified as presumptive faecal coliforms by the Teepol test were confirmed as faecal coliforms by biochemical tests. The Sartorius® Azide® agar was similarly inaccurate, with 52% false positives. Confirmation tests on the Oxoid® Membrane

Lauryl Sulphate (MLS) test for *E. coli* showed that, on average, this technique was over 80% accurate. Confirmation tests were carried out on 70 faecal coliform colonies, 90 total coliform, 60 enterococci and 108 *E. coli*.

All bacteria concentrations were log-transformed to normalize distributions for further statistical analysis.

Results

Visitor numbers

Large numbers of people visit Lamington National Park all year round. Not surprisingly, however, the Blue Pool swimming hole is a popular walking destination only during the warmer summer months, and only prior to the onset of the wet season. During the peak visitor season, up to 100 people were counted over the sampling period at Blue Pool. The peak visitation period is from 12.00 to 14.00 hours. Not all visitors swim: up to 30 swimmers were recorded each day during this peak visitation period. Rarely, however, were more than five or six people in the water at any one time. On 56% of sampling days, there were fewer than five swimmers.

Physical and chemical parameters

Mean monthly air temperature ranged from 4°C in June, July and August to 15°C in January and February. The monthly maximum air temperatures ranged from 15°C to 29°C, respectively. There are very occasional frosts in winter, and summer temperatures can exceed 37°C. Water temperature ranged from approximately 7°C in mid-winter to 25°C in mid-summer. The mean water temperature over the summer sampling period was 18.5°C. Instream pH ranged from 5.5 to 8.0, with a mean value of 7.3, and no consistent seasonal variations.

Most rain falls in heavy, short bursts: 145 mm of rain fell on 11 January 1994, and 86 mm on 21 January 1994. Water quality samples were taken on both these days. Rainfall on other sampling days was less than 25 mm in all cases. Stream flow velocity ranged from 0.63 to 2.01 m/s. Mean stream flow was lower in summer 1993/94 than 1994/95. Average stream flow velocity was 1.25 m/s, corresponding to approximately 185 l/s. Mean nephelometric turbidity over the entire sampling period was 1.93 NTU. The maximum value measured was 10 NTU after 1 day of heavy rainfall. Compared to other rivers, this is a very low turbidity level (Queensland, Department of the Environment and Heritage, 1993).

The mean concentration of nitrates and nitrites in the Canungra Creek system was 0.12 mg/l, as nitrogen ($n = 336$). Except during floods, the range was 0.1–0.2 mg/l with no significant differences between years or seasons. During the flood event of 11 January 1994, however, nitrate and nitrite concentrations increased to 0.76 mg/l. Ammonium concentrations ranged from 0.002 to 0.014 mg/l, with a mean of 0.005 mg/l as N. Concentrations were significantly higher during the summer months ($P < 0.05$). Phosphorus concentrations ranged from 0.002 to 0.048 mg/l, with a mean of 0.034 mg/l, expressed as P. Concentrations were higher in summer. A total of 336 nitrate and nitrite, ammonium and phosphorus determinations were made.

Phosphate and ammonium concentrations increased significantly with water temperature and air temperature, whereas nitrate and nitrite concentrations decreased significantly. There were no significant patterns in nutrient concentrations associated with the number of recreational swimmers.

Bacterial parameters

A total of 3510 bacterial determinations were made in all. Results are summarized in Tables 21.1 and 21.2. For the Canungra Creek system, ranges were 20–2200 CFU/100 ml (mean 1700) for total coliforms; 5–1300 CFU/100 ml (mean 275) for faecal coliforms; 40–4000 CFU/100 ml (mean 730) for enterococci; and 1–2000 CFU/100 ml (mean 64) for *E. coli*. Compared with water-quality guidelines for recreational waters, these levels are relatively high, albeit safe. Since they are equally high in the undisturbed East Fork catchment, however, they do not indicate a human impact of concern for management.

Concentrations were corrected for false-positive identifications where appropriate, and

Table 21.1. Visitor numbers, streamflow and water quality at Blue Pool, 1992–1995.

Date	No. of visitors	No. of swimmers	Rainfall (mm/day)	Stream-flow (m/s)	Mean log$_{10}$ total coliforms CFU/100 ml (n=9) inflow	outflow	Mean log$_{10}$ faecal coliforms CFU/100 ml (n=9) inflow	outflow	Mean log$_{10}$ E. coli CFU/100 ml (n=9) inflow	outflow	Mean log$_{10}$ enterococci CFU/100 ml (n=9) inflow	outflow	NH$_3$ (mg/l)	P (mg/l)	NO$_x$ (mg/l)
2/10/92			0.0		2.46	2.49	2.05	2.24					0.005	0.031	0.130
1/11/92			0.3		2.39	2.38	2.38	2.28					0.004	0.037	0.108
15/11/92			1.8		2.63	2.61	2.50	2.40					0.002	0.036	0.120
29/11/92	42	7	0.1		3.17	3.28	2.16	2.18					0.005	0.042	0.150
13/12/92	33	1	0.0		2.86	2.84	2.68	2.60					0.004	0.041	0.120
28/12/92	31	6	0.0		3.03	3.20	2.62	2.78					0.006	0.041	0.093
30/12/92	29	9	2.7		3.07	3.21	2.69	2.64					0.008	0.043	0.098
1/01/93	73	9	0.0		3.14	3.27	2.51	2.57					0.007	0.044	0.110
4/01/93	63	7	0.0		3.01	3.16	2.36	2.63					0.005	0.041	0.127
14/01/93	56	16	0.0		3.11	3.20	2.29	2.44					0.009	0.036	0.107
26/01/93	15	3	9.0		3.81	3.95	2.84	2.86					0.004	0.036	0.160
31/01/93	22	6	17.4		3.62	3.72	2.85	2.92							
13/02/93	20	0	0.0		2.84	2.84	2.66	2.58					0.004	0.027	0.130
21/02/93	17	0	1.9		3.43	3.46	2.96	2.99					0.002	0.025	0.140
8/04/93	10	0	0.0		3.16	3.04	2.69	2.68					0.003	0.026	0.130
12/04/93	80	4	0.3		3.21	3.22	2.87	2.79							
18/09/93	35	2	0.0		2.38	2.27	1.71	1.67							
24/10/93	48	0	2.4		2.06	2.25	1.88	1.85							
7/11/93	40	0	0.0		2.18	2.25	1.70	1.83							
14/11/93	20	5	16.3	1.36	1.54	2.50	1.35	1.62	1.20	1.22			0.004	0.031	0.094
21/11/93	18	0	18.8	1.37	2.68	2.63	1.98	1.96	1.71	1.79			0.004	0.029	0.098
28/11/93	43	5	0.0	1.20	2.17	2.36	1.03	1.43	1.03	0.81			0.004	0.030	0.094
5/12/93	18	4	0.0	1.17	2.89	2.88	1.78	1.55	1.19	1.00			0.005	0.027	0.100
7/12/93	10	1	7.8	1.39	2.81	2.83	2.03	2.02	1.13	0.95			0.005	0.030	0.092
12/12/93	36	0	5.0	1.38	2.07	2.17	1.68	1.86	1.54	1.59	2.00	2.00	0.012	0.036	0.110
19/12/93	64	3	0.0	1.39	2.44	2.45	1.64	1.68	1.17	1.22	1.77	1.81	0.012	0.023	0.100
21/12/93	25	5	0.0	1.28	2.48	2.55	1.52	1.58	1.37	1.27	2.27	2.49	0.005	0.024	0.090
23/12/93	0	0	0.0	1.21					1.42	1.35	2.19	1.66	0.006	0.025	0.085
26/12/93	84	12	0.0	1.18	2.50	2.78	1.72	1.97	1.26	1.63	2.13	2.50	0.007	0.027	0.100

Date															
28/12/93	94	29	0.0	1.20					1.10	1.71	2.15	2.09	0.008	0.033	0.097
30/12/93	55	14	0.0	1.19					0.54	1.40	2.19	2.23	0.008	0.028	0.110
1/01/94	49	26	0.0	1.09	2.61	3.15	2.09	2.43	1.04	1.45	2.24	2.56	0.007	0.028	0.110
4/01/94	52	16	0.0	1.12							3.13	3.23	0.012	0.030	0.116
6/01/94	47	18	0.0	1.09					0.84	1.18	2.79	2.89	0.008	0.033	0.110
9/01/94	63	22	0.0	1.08	2.87	3.23	2.14	2.46	1.40	1.69	2.80	2.91	0.008	0.035	0.039
11/01/94	3	0	145.4	1.51					3.24	3.30	3.60	3.48	0.005	0.037	0.756
13/01/94	19	4	0.2	1.33					1.91	2.04	3.40	3.34	0.014	0.021	0.156
16/01/94	29	5	9.2	1.31					1.76	1.82	3.34	3.21	0.006	0.031	0.083
18/01/94	21	9	1.2	1.31					1.37	1.33	2.97	2.98	0.002	0.029	0.077
20/01/94	0	0	85.8	1.33					2.18	2.24	2.02	2.16	0.003	0.044	0.170
26/01/94	21	1	16.5	1.57					1.75	1.83	3.17	3.12	0.003	0.029	0.100
2/02/94	0	0	3.0	1.83					1.70	1.59			0.004	0.028	0.120
9/02/94	2	0	0.3	1.65					1.45	1.40			0.004	0.023	0.116
6/03/94	3	0	22.8	1.99					1.76	1.67			0.011	0.018	0.180
31/03/94	0	0	9.8	1.89					1.11	1.22			0.004	0.016	0.160
2/04/94	30	2	0.3	2.01					1.34	1.10			0.004	0.015	0.173
3/06/94	3	0	1.7	2.00					0.60	0.66			0.003	0.023	0.180
16/07/94	20	0	0.0	1.12					0.65	0.68			0.003	0.025	0.183
28/07/94	4	0	0.0	0.94					0.20	0.15			0.004	0.024	0.170
24/08/94	0	0	0.0	0.79					0.10	0.03			0.007	0.027	0.160
28/10/94	9	0	0.2	0.63					1.17	1.01	1.69	2.55	0.004	0.030	0.057
17/11/94	0	0		1.04	3.03	3.15	1.81	1.89	1.60	1.61	2.53		0.004	0.040	0.170
11/12/94	0	0	20.0	1.21					1.47	1.53			0.002	0.030	0.090
21/12/94	0	0	0.0	1.05					1.18	1.11	2.05	2.14	0.004	0.030	0.071
24/12/94	20	20	0.0	0.98	2.95	3.12	2.46	2.71	0.65	1.29			0.006	0.032	0.100
25/12/94	2	1	19.0	1.08	3.55	3.61	2.51	2.28	1.60	1.74	2.83	2.72	0.005	0.035	0.130
26/12/94	19	3	0.0	0.93	3.38	3.30	2.53	2.38	1.66	1.51			0.003	0.037	0.150
27/12/94	28	8	0.0	1.03	3.22	3.40	2.31	2.69	1.03	1.50	2.66	2.79	0.007	0.035	0.120
28/12/94	34	12	0.0	1.02	3.33	3.24	2.51	2.39	1.15	1.68			0.003	0.033	0.120
29/12/94	34	29	0.0	0.88	3.07	3.46	2.58	2.70	0.87	1.48	2.87	2.94	0.008	0.037	0.133
30/12/94	30	11	0.0	0.92	3.85	3.72	2.48	2.53	1.06	1.59			0.008	0.038	0.140
31/01/94	16	13	15.8	1.13	3.41	3.59	2.82	2.86	1.29	1.60	2.74	2.75	0.005	0.036	0.130
1/01/95	25	8	0.4	0.81	2.99	3.27	2.53	2.73	0.81	1.38	3.41	3.40	0.005	0.033	0.120
7/01/95	27	5	16.7	1.20	3.95	4.34	2.65	3.12	2.08	2.13			0.003	0.043	0.147
16/01/95	7	4	0.0	1.20					0.79	1.03			0.005	0.035	0.140

Table 21.2. Visitor numbers, streamflow and water quality at control pool, 1992–1995.

Date	No. of visitors	No. of swimmers	Rainfall (mm/day)	Stream-flow (m/s)	Mean $\log_{10}$ total coliforms CFU/100 ml ($n=9$) inflow	outflow	Mean $\log_{10}$ faecal coliforms CFU/100 ml ($n=9$) inflow	outflow	Mean $\log_{10}$ E. coli CFU/100 ml ($n=9$) inflow	outflow	Mean $\log_{10}$ enterococci CFU/100 ml ($n=9$) inflow	outflow	NH_3 (mg/l)	P (mg/l)	NO_x (mg/l)
14/11/93	20	5	16.3	1.36	1.30	1.60	1.13	1.28	1.05	1.04			0.004	0.029	0.098
21/11/93	18	0	18.8	1.37	2.86	2.61	1.87	1.90	1.68	1.68			0.004	0.030	0.094
28/11/93	43	5	0.0	1.20	2.29	2.25	1.14	1.28	0.95	0.79			0.005	0.027	0.100
5/12/93	18	4	0.0	1.17	2.94	2.90	1.69	1.59	0.95	0.95			0.005	0.030	0.092
7/12/93	10	1	7.8	1.39	2.93	2.84	1.99	2.10	0.95	0.95					
12/12/93	36	0	5.0	1.38	1.88	1.74	0.73	1.36	1.72	1.61	1.74	1.68	0.012	0.036	0.110
19/12/93	64	3	0.0	1.39	2.31	2.49	1.72	1.75	1.20	0.95	1.93	1.65	0.012	0.023	0.100
21/12/93	25	5	0.0	1.28	2.55	2.49	1.48	1.54	1.04	1.30	2.30	2.01	0.005	0.024	0.090
23/12/93	0	0	0.0	1.21					1.22	1.34	2.15	1.65	0.006	0.025	0.085
26/12/93	84	12	0.0	1.18	2.71	2.46	1.75	1.71	1.28	1.46	2.45	1.93	0.007	0.027	0.100
28/12/93	94	29	0.0	1.2					1.15	1.28	2.28	2.41	0.008	0.033	0.097
30/12/93	55	14	0.0	1.19					1.10	1.10	2.26	2.31	0.008	0.028	0.110
1/01/94	49	26	0.0	1.09	2.59	2.57	2.01	1.96	1.26	1.04	2.43	2.43	0.007	0.028	0.110
4/01/94	52	16	0.0	1.12							3.24	3.21	0.012	0.030	0.116
6/01/94	47	18	0.0	1.09					1.03	0.90	2.96	2.79	0.008	0.033	0.110
9/01/94	63	22	0.0	1.08	2.77	2.84	2.15	2.19	1.18	1.26	2.83	2.80	0.008	0.035	0.039
11/01/94	3	0	145.4	1.51					3.28	3.14	3.49	3.57	0.005	0.037	0.756
13/01/94	19	4	0.2	1.33					1.92	1.96	3.15	3.22	0.014	0.021	0.156
16/01/94	29	5	9.2	1.31					1.89	1.86	3.18	3.26	0.006	0.031	0.083
18/01/94	21	9	1.2	1.31					1.32	1.40	2.89	2.93	0.002	0.029	0.077
20/01/94	0	0	85.8	1.33					2.24	2.20	2.14	2.02	0.003	0.044	0.170
26/01/94	21	1	16.5	1.57					1.99	1.86	3.31	3.26	0.003	0.029	0.100
2/02/94	0	0	3.0	1.83					1.48	1.45			0.004	0.028	0.120
9/02/94	2	0	0.3	1.65					1.42	1.48			0.004	0.023	0.116
6/03/94	3	0	22.8	1.99					1.78	1.75			0.011	0.018	0.180
31/03/94	0	0	9.8	1.89					1.29	1.24			0.004	0.016	0.160
2/04/94	30	2	0.3	2.01					1.43	1.40			0.004	0.015	0.173
3/06/94	3	0	1.7	2.00					0.65	0.75			0.003	0.023	0.180
16/07/94	20	0	0.0	1.12					0.51	0.57			0.003	0.025	0.183

Date															
28/07/94	4	0	0.94	0.0	3.05	3.09	1.97	1.88	0.00	0.10			0.004	0.024	0.170
24/08/94	0	0	0.79	0.0					0.26	0.15	1.79	1.78	0.007	0.027	0.160
28/10/94	9	0	0.63	0.2					1.36	1.23	2.48	2.51	0.004	0.030	0.057
17/11/94	0	0	1.04	20.0					1.69	1.64			0.004	0.040	0.170
11/12/94	0	0	1.21	0.0					1.58	1.54	2.29	2.30	0.002	0.030	0.090
21/12/94	0		1.05	0.0					1.12	1.07			0.004	0.030	0.071
24/12/94	20	20	0.98	19.0	3.28	3.42	2.77	2.69	0.65	0.55			0.006	0.032	0.100
25/12/94	2	1	1.08	0.0	3.57	3.59	2.51	2.30	1.65	1.69			0.005	0.035	0.130
26/12/94	19	3	0.93	0.0	3.64	3.50	2.56	2.51	1.64	1.67	2.61	2.66	0.003	0.037	0.150
27/12/94	28	8	1.03	0.0	3.23	3.18	2.41	2.31	1.25	1.14			0.007	0.035	0.120
28/12/94	34	12	1.02	0.0	3.22	3.65	2.44	2.72	1.16	1.12	2.51	2.55	0.003	0.033	0.120
29/12/94	34	29	0.88	0.0	3.30	3.21	2.55	2.61	0.94	0.83			0.008	0.037	0.133
30/12/94	30	11	0.92	0.0	3.59	3.63	2.58	2.75	1.04	0.89	3.15	3.02	0.008	0.038	0.140
31/12/94	16	13	1.13	15.8		3.50	2.94	2.98	1.38	1.42			0.005	0.036	0.130
1/01/95	25	8	0.81	0.4	3.05	3.03	2.50	2.53	0.87	0.81	2.73	2.78	0.005	0.033	0.120

log-transformed to normalize distributions. Concentrations of all bacterial indicators were weakly correlated with water temperature, streamflow and nitrates. Large-scale analysis of variance for aggregated data did not reveal any statistically significant differences in total coliform concentrations between sampling sites.

For individual days, however, comparisons using the nine replicate determinations from each sampling site and occasion show a statistically significant increase in total coliform concentrations from pool inflow to pool outflow on 19 of 41 sampling days at Blue Pool, but 0 of 41 for the control pool. At a catchment scale, total coliform concentrations were significantly higher in the heavily frequented West Fork of Canungra Creek on 50% of days sampled. Similarly, concentrations of faecal coliforms were significantly higher at the outflow than the inflow of Blue Pool on 12 out of 41 sampling days, with no significant differences at the control pool. Corresponding patterns occurred for enterococci on 6 of 25 sampling days.

For *E. coli*, concentrations at the outflow of Blue Pool were significantly higher ($P<0.001$) than those at the inflow on 21 of 45 sampling days, and significantly lower on 3 sampling days. Again, there were no significant differences at the control pool. On these 21 days, *E. coli* concentrations increased by approximately a factor of three between inflow and outflow, or between 5 and 25 CFU/100 ml. This represents only 1% of natural seasonal variation.

The top 1 cm of streambed sediment at the experimental sites contained from 100 to 1000 *E. coli* per gram of sediment (dry weight). This sediment is easily resuspended in the water column by physical disturbance of the streambed, temporarily increasing bacterial concentrations in the overlying water column. Experimental disturbance of this sediment increased concentrations of *E. coli* from a baseline of approximately 50 CFU/100 ml, to a maximum of approximately 150 CFU/100 ml; but when the disturbance ceased, *E. coli* concentrations fell to 75 CFU/100 ml within 1 or 2 min, and back to baseline within an hour. Surface soils near the margin of Canungra Creek contain from 7×10^3 to 10×10^3 *E. coli* per gram. Total coliforms in the streambed sediments

ranged from 0.075×10^6 to 2.0×10^6 CFU/100 ml ($n=20$), approximately $1000 \times$ the concentration in the water column.

Storm events, seasonal cycles and swimmer impacts

The largest changes in water quality are those associated with storm flood events. During the storm of 11 January 1994, turbidity was five times higher than at any time during non-flood flow; nitrate and nitrite, four times higher; and total coliforms and *E. coli* concentrations, 20 times higher. Storm events overwhelm seasonal cycles and swimmer impacts. They are short-lived, and occur principally at the onset of the wet season.

There are also large seasonal cycles in microbiological water quality. Total coliform concentrations change by up to $1000 \times$ between dry and wet seasons, and *E. coli* and enteroccoci by up to $100 \times$. Impacts of swimmers must be considered against this natural stream flow variation.

Independent of human activity in their respective catchments, both the heavily visited West Fork and the undisturbed East Fork of Canungra Creek contain significant numbers of coliform bacteria, including faecal coliforms and *E. coli*. If there are any catchment-scale differences in water quality associated with the different intensity of recreational use in the catchments of West Fork and East Fork of Canungra Creek, they are not reliably detectable against natural background variation.

At the scale of individual pools, in contrast, recreational swimmers have a definite and unequivocal effect on the concentrations of enteric bacteria in the water column. On 21 separate and independent occasions, there was a significant increase in *E. coli* concentrations from inflow to outflow of the experimental pool, but not the control pool. The days on which such significant differences occurred were all in summer before the onset of the wet season. Once the rains begin, any human effects were masked by flood runoff.

Differences between days on which there was a significant increase in *E. coli* concentrations in the experimental pool, but not the control pool, and days on which there was no significant difference between inflow and out-flow of the experimental pool, were not asso-ciated with any consistent differences in physicochemical parameters, except for a weak positive correlation with air temperature and ammonia concentrations, and a weak negative correlation with rainfall. Such correlations are expected because ammonia concentrations increase with water temperature, and swimmer numbers increase with temperature and decrease with rainfall. Hence it is clear that these increases in bacterial concentrations are due solely or principally to the effect of swim-mers. This was confirmed by multiple regres-sion of log-transformed *E. coli* concentrations on the days concerned against swimmer num-bers and streamflow.

For days with fewer than five swimmers, there were either: no significant differences in bacterial concentrations between inflow and outflow; a significant but small decrease; or a significant but small increase. For days with more than five swimmers, there was a consis-tently significant and larger increase (Fig. 21.1).

For this particular ecosystem and test site, there is a clear threshold effect at approxi-mately five swimmers. Similar, though less well-defined threshold effects are apparent for total and faecal coliforms. For enterococci, there is a weaker threshold at approximately 15 swimmers per day. All these thresholds are sta-tistically significant at $P < 0.001$ for coliforms and $P < 0.005$ for enterococci (Fisher's Exact Test).

For *E. coli*, above this threshold, increasing the numbers of swimmers does not increase the ratio between *E. coli* concentrations at the out-flow and those at the inflow of the experimen-tal pool, though it does increase the absolute difference. This may be because, even on days with 30 swimmers per day, there were rarely more than five or six swimmers in the water at once. In any event, the precise threshold is pre-sumably associated with specific characteris-tics of the site and activity, and has little general significance.

The issue of general significance is that recreational swimmers do produce a detect-able impact on microbiological indicators of water quality, at a relatively low threshold of use. In addition, since the size of the impact is small relative to natural seasonal variations, this approach provides an indicator of human impact at a level below that where manage-ment action is required.

Discussion

This study, carried out from 1991 to 1994, was apparently the first time that human recrea-tional impacts on water quality have been detected in a flowing stream, with no infra-structure and individual day-use only, against much larger background variations, and at such a low threshold of use, providing an indicator of impact well below the threshold where man-agement action is required. Similar results were reported in 1996 for streams in Tropical Queensland, Australia (Butler *et al.*, 1996).

The actual increases in *E.coli* concentra-tions at the Blue Pool swimming hole ranged from 10 to 30 CFU/100 ml. The precise mecha-nism causing this effect was beyond the scope of this investigation. The concentration of coli-form bacteria in the streambed sediment is approximately $1000\times$ greater than that in the overlying water column, and swimmers stir up sediment. Even at high swimmer numbers, however, turbidity in the experimental pool is low, and below the threshold of detection by filtration and weighing. On the basis of nephel-ometric turbidity measurements and the gravi-metric detection threshold, the resuspension of streambed sediment by swimmers could in-crease *E. coli* concentrations in the water column by up to 100 CFU/100 ml.

Hence it is impossible to determine at pre-sent whether the increases were due to a direct physical input of bacteria from swimmers' bodies, or solely to resuspension of bacteria in streambed sediments. The precise mechanism, however, is of secondary significance.

Although the precise threshold, and, indeed, the most sensitive indicator parameter, are likely to be specific to the ecosystem and tourist activity concerned, the approach adopted is applicable to the management of ecotourism and outdoor recreation in conser-vation reserves and wilderness areas world-wide.

This is of considerable significance for the conservation of biodiversity and water quality worldwide. Tourism and travel is the world's

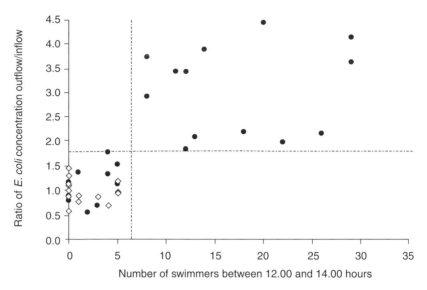

Fig. 21.1. Effect of swimmer numbers on *E. coli* concentrations in Blue Pool. ●, Days with a significant difference in bacterial concentration; ◇, days with no significant difference in bacterial concentration.

largest industry sector; nature-based tourism is its fastest-growing subsector, and nature-based tourism is concentrated in areas of high conservation value, principally conservation reserves and other relatively pristine natural environments. Recreational use of such areas has increased greatly, and in many cases exponentially, in recent years. This growth has increased tourism infrastructure, such as roads and accommodation; commercial tours and ecotours, both mechanized and non-mechanized; and individual recreational use of national parks and similar areas.

The impacts of localized high-intensity tourism developments such as hotels and resorts are relatively well known (Warnken and Buckley, 1998); the impacts of dispersed non-mechanized activities much less so. In addition, most research to date on broad-scale effects has focused on impacts and parameters which are highly visible and easy to quantify, such as trampling of tracks, rather than those with the greatest potential significance for ecosystem function, such as the introduction of non-native species, effects on the population dynamics of rare plants and animals, or contamination of water bodies. Many impacts of this type are undetectable to the untrained observer, but have potentially far-reaching and

irreversible consequences (Papadakis *et al.*, 1997).

Land-management agencies have a suite of tools to control the impacts of tourism and recreation in conservation reserves and other fragile environments. The principal tools are: restrictions on numbers, equipment or activities, either in time or space; minimal-impact education programmes; and hardening of the environment in high-use areas. For efficient use, all of these require accurate information on the quantitative impacts of different types and levels of use in different ecosystems. In addition, for effective planning, land managers must either be able to predict impacts accurately for a very wide range of specific circumstances; or be able to detect impacts at subcritical levels, before they reach a threshold where they are either irreversible or self-perpetuating.

There are many different potential indicators for these purposes, and different parameters will be more effective in different ecosystems and for different types of tourist activity. Most research to date has been in open environments with low vegetation, especially northern-hemisphere arctic-alpine and estuary shoreline areas; whereas the research described here was in sub-tropical rainforest, a much less-studied ecosystem. The most salient feature, however, is that we searched specifically for an indicator parameter that could detect tourist effects at the lowest threshold. It is this general approach, rather than the specific ecosystem, tourist activity, indicator parameter or impact threshold, which is likely to hold particular promise for the application of ecological data in the management of tourism.

References

American Public Health Association (APHA) (1992) *Standard Methods for the Examination of Water and Waste Water*, 18th edn. American Public Health Association, Washington, DC.

Arthington, A.H., Miller, G.J. and Outridge, P.M. (1989) Water quality, phosphorus budgets and management of dune lakes used for recreation in Queensland (Australia). *Water Science Technology* 21, 111–118.

Bunn, S.E., Kerby, B.M. and Hughes, J.M. (1995) Factors influencing drift in small forest streams, south-eastern Queensland. *Marine and Freshwater Research* 46, 1101–1108.

Bunn, S.E., Hughes, J.M., Hurwood, D.A., Choy, S. and Pearson, R.G. (1997) Genetic differentiation among populations of *Caridina zebra* (Decapoda: Atyidae) in tropical rainforest streams, northern Australia. *Freshwater Biology* 36, 289–296.

Butler, G., Birtles, A., Pearson, R. and Jones, K. (1996) *Ecotourism, Water Quality and Wet Tropics Streams*. Australian Centre for Tropical Freshwater Research, James Cook University, Townsville, p. 79.

Hadwen, W.L., Arthington, A.H. and Mosich, T.D. (2003) The impact of tourism on dune lakes on Fraser Island, Australia. *Lakes and Reservoirs: Research and Management* 8, 15–26.

Jinru, C., Johnson, R. and Griffiths, M. (1998) Detection of verotoxigenic *Escherichia coli* by magnetic capture-hybridization PCR. *Applied Environmental Microbiology* 64, 147–152.

McDaniels, A.W., Rice, E.W., Reyes, A.L., Johnson, C.H., Haugland, R.A. and Stelma, G.N. Jr (1996) Confirmational identification of *Escherichia coli*, a comparison of genotypic and phenotypic assays for glutamate decarboxylase and beta-D-glucuronidase. *Applied Environmental Microbiology* 62, 3350–3354.

Papadakis, J.A., Marridon, A., Richarson, S.C., Lampiri, M. and Marcelon, U. (1997) Bather-related microbial and yeast populations in sand and seawater. *Water Resources* 31, 799–804.

Pusey, B.J., Arthington, A.H. and Read, M.G. (1995) Species richness and spatial variation in fish assemblage structure in two rivers of the Wet Tropics of Northern Queensland, Australia. *Journal of Environmental Biology of Fishes* 42, 181–199.

Queensland, Department of the Environment and Heritage (1993) *Water Quality Summary Report – Albert River, Canungra Creek and the Logan River Estuary*. Environmental Technical Report No. 4. QDEH, Brisbane, Australia.

Tassoula, E.A. (1997) Growth possibilities of *E.coli* in natural waters. *International Journal of Environmental Studies* 52, 67–73.

Tsai, Y.L., Palmer, C.J. and Sangermano, L.R. (1993) Detection of *Escherichia coli* in sewage and sludge by polymerase chain reaction. *Applied Environmental Microbiology* 59, 353–357.

US Environmental Protection Agency (USEPA) (1986) *Bacteriological Ambient Water Quality Criteria for Marine and Fresh Recreational Waters*. Cincinnati, Ohio.

Venkateswaran, K., Murakoshi, A. and Satake, M. (1996) Comparison of commercially available kits with standard methods for the detection of coliforms and *Escherichia coli* in foods. *Applied Environmental Microbiology* 62, 2236–2243.

Venkateswaran, K., Kamijoh, Y., Ohashi, E. and Nakanishi, H. (1997) A simple filtration technique to detect enterohemorrhagic *Escherichia coli* O157:H7 and its toxins in beef by multiplex PCR. *Applied Environmental Microbiology* 63, 4127–4131.

Warnken, J. and Buckley, R.C. (1998) Scientific quality of tourism environmental impact assessment. *Journal of Applied Ecology* 35, 1–8.

22

Four-wheel Drive Vehicle Impacts in the Central Coast Region of Western Australia

Julianna Priskin

School of Earth and Geographical Sciences, The University of Western Australia, Crawley, Western Australia, Australia

Introduction

Four-wheel drive (4WD) vehicles provide the main means of access to the dry and sparsely settled sandy coastlines of Western Australia for ecotourists and other visitors alike. This has created an extensive network of tracks through dune and foreshore vegetation. Most previous studies of 4WD vehicle impacts have focused on local-scale impacts (Anders and Leatherman, 1987; Lonsdale and Lane, 1994; Kutiel *et al.*, 2000). In areas such as these dry sandy coastlines, however, the local impacts are straightforward: destruction of vegetation cover and destabilization of the sand surface. The critical issue is the aggregate impact at a regional scale, the proportion of the landscape where vegetation has been removed. For the narrow band of foreshore vegetation immediately above the high-tide mark, the best indicator of impact is the density of access points: the number of tracks that cut through foreshore vegetation, per kilometre of beach. For the broader band of dune vegetation behind the beach, the simplest indicator is the total length of track per kilometre of coastline, since all the tracks are of similar width. And the most effective way to quantify both beach access points and length of track is from aerial photographs. This paper, therefore, compares access-point and track-length statistics derived from airphoto coverage in 1965 and 1999, a period of 33 years.

The area studied is known as the Central Coast Region, which extends approximately 300 km north of Perth, the State capital of Western Australia (Fig. 22.1). The Central Coast includes extensive protected areas and other open space and crosses the jurisdictions of five local government authorities (LGAs). Its landward margin is delimited informally by a major highway, the Brand Highway. The area is accessed by 4WD vehicles for private recreation, off-road clubs, commercial ecotours, and local farmers and fishers (Priskin, 2003a,b).

Sandy dune soils and their vegetation are generally susceptible to recreational disturbances (Liddle and Moore, 1974; Liddle and Greig-Smith, 1975; Hosier and Eaton, 1980; Hylgaard and Liddle, 1981). Impacts differ in detail across the dune profile between the shoreline and landward dunes (Hylgaard, 1980; Bowels and Maun, 1982; Gallet and Roze, 2001). Areas closest to the shore are more vulnerable to damage but regenerate more quickly. Many of the plant species in these areas are herbaceous succulents, and tolerate salt spray, sand blast, sand burial, and high wind speeds (Anders and Leatherman, 1987; Rickard *et al.*, 1994; Andersen, 1995). Further landward, there is more woody vegetation, which takes longer to recover from damage by 4WD vehicles.

Destruction of plant cover leaves a bare sand surface which is susceptible to wind

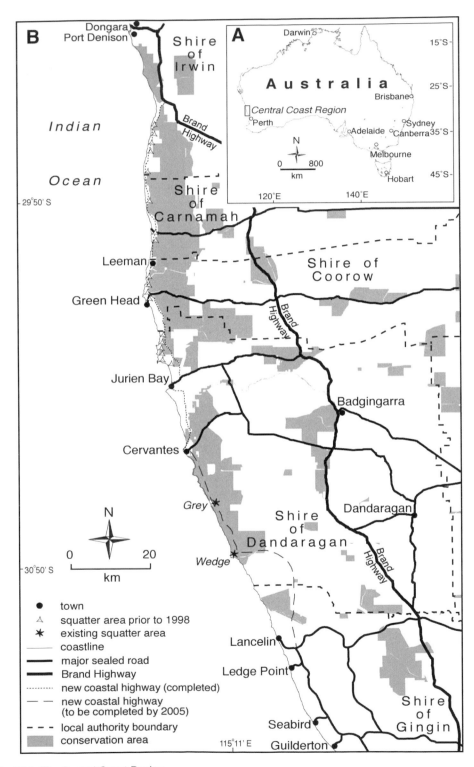

Fig. 22.1. The Central Coast Region.

erosion and dune destabilization (Godfrey and Godfrey, 1980; Hosier and Eaton, 1980; Carlson and Godfrey, 1989; Chapman *et al.*, 1989; Kutiel *et al.*, 1999). Where this leads to a steeper foreshore profile it may also be exacerbated by wave erosion (Anders and Leatherman, 1987). These impacts are prevalent throughout much of the Central Coast Region (Priskin, 2001), although in some areas they have been addressed by costly coastal management measures. The degradation of Western Australia's sandy coastlines by recreational 4WD use has been reported repeatedly (House of Representatives Standing Committee on Environment and Conservation, 1977; Majer, 1980; Clarke, 1983; O'Brien and MacRae, 1992), especially in the Central Coast Region (Eliot, 1999; Landvision *et al.*, 1999).

The Central Coast Region

The Central Coast Region of Western Australia has a Mediterranean climate (Gentilli, 1971), which encourages coastal recreation throughout the year. The region extends over a broad coastal plain, which consists of Holocene shoreline deposits backed by hills of Late Pleistocene dune limestone (Searle and Semeniuk, 1985). Limestone landforms include cliffs, headlands and offshore reefs. The latter run parallel to the entire Central Coast shoreline and exert a strong influence on nearshore morphodynamics (Sanderson and Eliot, 1996). Dune landforms include foredune plains, shore-parallel ridges, parabolic dunes, deflation plains, beach-ridge plains, and extensive mobile sand sheets that migrate up to 10 m a year (Department of Planning and Urban Development, 1994).

Between Lancelin and Flat Rock (Fig. 22.1) the coast is exposed and the beaches are high-energy, wave-dominated with an annual modal wave height greater than 1 m. During the summer these beaches are over 50 m wide and are suitable for beach driving for both commercial tour operators and private recreationists. In winter, these beaches erode and become impassable. The dune field at Lancelin (Fig. 22.1) is one of the few official public areas allocated to off-road driving activities in Western Australia (Clarke, 1983). Elsewhere,

the coast is sheltered and annual modal wave height is less than 0.5 m (Hegge *et al.*, 1996). These low-energy beaches are generally less than 25 m wide and have a steep profile. The coast between Flat Rock and Grey and north of Green Head (Fig. 22.1) is rocky, albeit intermittently, with limestone cliffs, bluffs and headlands that separate pockets of sandy beaches. The beaches offer secluded swimming and snorkelling areas as well as camping sites. The elevated bluffs and headlands are less than 10 m high and offer scenic vistas to offshore waters, reefs and islands. This area represents a part of the coast that has been traditionally popular for establishing squatter shacks (Fig. 22.1).

The vegetation of the region consists of low, dense scrub and heaths (Hopkins *et al.*, 1983). Foredune areas support grasses and herbaceous vegetation <1 m high, whereas swale areas between older dunes support dense shrubs up to 5 m tall. Annual rainfall decreases from 749 mm/year in the south to 460 mm/year in the north (Fig. 22.1), with a corresponding gradient in floristic composition. Both marine and terrestrial ecosystems of the Central Coast Region form part of one of the 25 global biodiversity hotspots (Myers *et al.*, 2000; Roberts *et al.*, 2002).

European settlement of the area occurred approximately 150 years ago, but it was not until the 1950s that the first townships were declared (Department of Planning and Urban Development, 1994). The towns serviced a growing fishing industry and broad-acre farming in the hinterland. Population density of the region has always been low, distributed in ten coastal settlements and hinterland locations along the Brand Highway (Fig. 22.1). In 1981, the regional population was 5100, rising to 7700 by 1991 and around 10,000 by 2000 (Western Australian Planning Commission, 2000).

Until the late 1990s there were no transport routes connecting the settlements directly along the coast (Department of Planning and Urban Development, 1994). Instead, each town was linked only to the Brand Highway, located 30–40 km to the east. However, by 1998 a sealed coastal highway had been partially constructed between Dongara and Jurien Bay (Fig. 22.1). Significant portions lie within

Table 22.1. Length of four-wheel drive (4WD) track.

	Length of coast (km)	Coast as % of Central Coast Region	Total track length 1965 (km)	Total track length 1998 (km)	Change in track length (km)	Change in track length (%)
Coastal setting						
Straight coast	57	21	88	140	52	60
Sandy bays between small salients	73	27	156	250	94	60
Sandy bays between forelands	40	15	70	84	14	20
Cuspate forelands	32	12	41	111	70	171
Rocky promontories and small bays	25	9	74	70	−4	−5
Alternating rocky coast and sandy bays	44	16	88	146	58	66
Beach type						
High-energy, exposed	94	35	145	307	162	112
Low-energy, sheltered	177	65	372	494	122	33
Dune type						
Foredune plain	59	22	168	190	23	13
Low-moderate foredune ridge	110	41	217	312	95	44
High foredune ridge	50	18	59	129	70	118
Deflation plain or mobile sand	53	20	72	168	96	134

conservation reserves (Western Australian Planning Commission, 1996). The main economic activity is fishing. Tourism is still a small industry in the region, although it is growing steadily, and currently contributes approximately 5% to the local economy of the area (Pracsys Management Consultants, 2002). Visitor numbers to the region are estimated at 250,000 per annum, including commercial nature-based and ecotour companies as well as private recreationists. Approximately 50% of all visitors to the region arrive in a 4WD vehicle (Priskin, 2003b).

The region also has a long history of 4WD use by individuals who occupy illegal squatter shacks (Fig. 22.1). Squatter shacks were constructed primarily of corrugated iron sheeting on a concrete pad. Originally established in the 1960s, shacks served farmers from the hinterland during their holidays (Department of Planning and Urban Development, 1994). Many of the current townships, including Guilderton, Seabird, Ledge Point, Lancelin, Cervantes and Green Head (Fig. 22.1) were originally squatter shack settlements. In 1984 there were an estimated 676 squatter shacks occupying prime coastal sites along the Central

Coast (Department of Planning and Urban Development, 1994), increasing to over 1000 by the late 1980s and approximately 1200 by 1990. The increased density of squatter shacks led to widespread destruction of dunes, erosion, the spread of weeds and the dumping of waste. In 1988 the State Government of Western Australia endorsed a Squatter Policy (Government of Western Australia, 1989), which required the removal of squatter shacks by 2001, as well as rehabilitation of damaged coastal areas. To date, all holiday squatters have been removed except at the largest settlements at Grey and Wedge (Fig. 22.1), where 130 and 370 shacks, respectively, have been allowed to remain until the completion of the new coastal highway, the Indian Ocean Drive, by 2005 (Department of Conservation and Land Management, 2000).

Methods

The spatial extent of 4WD tracks was obtained from analysis of aerial photographs for 1965 and 1998 (Priskin, 2003a), covering a 1 km band inland from the shoreline. 4WD tracks

Table 22.2. Number of four-wheel drive (4WD) access points.

	Length of coast (km)	Coast as % of Central Coast Region	Total track length 1965 (km)	Total track length 1998 (km)	Change in track length (km)	Change in track length (%)
Coastal setting						
Straight coast	57	21	55	103	48	87
Sandy bays between small salients	73	27	110	296	186	169
Sandy bays between forelands	40	15	67	94	27	40
Cuspate forelands	32	12	34	91	57	168
Rocky promontories and small bays	25	9	94	105	11	12
Alternating rocky coast and sandy bays	44	16	61	218	157	257
Beach type						
High-energy, exposed	94	35	105	260	155	148
Low-energy, sheltered	177	65	316	647	331	105
Dune type						
Foredune plain	59	22	145	266	121	83
Low-moderate foredune ridge	110	41	160	368	208	130
High foredune ridge	50	18	65	134	69	106
Deflation plain or mobile sand	53	19	51	139	88	173

and coastal access points were mapped along a 271 km stretch of the coast, excluding the townships of Guilderton to the south and Dongara and Port Denison to the north (Fig. 22.1). The photographs were analysed digitally using ARC/INFO and Arc/View Geographic Information Systems (Priskin, 2003a). The Central Coast Region was divided into 25 spatial units and each unit was categorized for the type of coastal setting, beach and dune type (Tables 22.1 and 22.2). Results were expressed as densities per kilometre of coastline (Fig. 22.2).

Results

The total length of 4WD tracks in 1998 was 813 km, as compared to 517 km in 1965 (Priskin, 2003a). This corresponds to an average of 3.0 km of 4WD vehicle tracks per km of coast in 1998, over 50% increase from the 1.9 km/km in 1965. The number of coastal access points also increased, from 421 in 1965 to 908 in 1998 (Priskin, 2003a). The majority of these impacts may be attributed to tourism and recreation, particularly for the 1998 data.

The pattern of tracks also changed between 1965 and 1998. Single tracks in 1965 had expanded to dense fan-shaped networks in 1998, especially at squatter shack communities (Fig. 22.3). Track densities in these areas are highest at the seaward side of the dunes. Many tracks are also braided, as new tracks are created alongside older ones. This occurs because strong winds erode old tracks, so drivers drive on vegetation to avoid bogging. Both aerial photography and field inspections showed that there are also many blind tracks, which become established by even a small number of vehicle passes. There are no maps or signs to help drivers distinguish blind tracks, so the tracks are constantly re-used and do not have the opportunity to regenerate.

The densities of tracks and access points differ between different landscape types in the region. There are six main landscape classes (Priskin, 2003a) (Tables 22.1 and 22.2). Stretches of coast characterized by sandy bays between small salients had the highest densities of 4WD tracks and access points in both 1965 and 1998 (Tables 22.1 and 22.2, Fig. 22.2). The greatest proportional increase over this period was 171%, for coastal sections

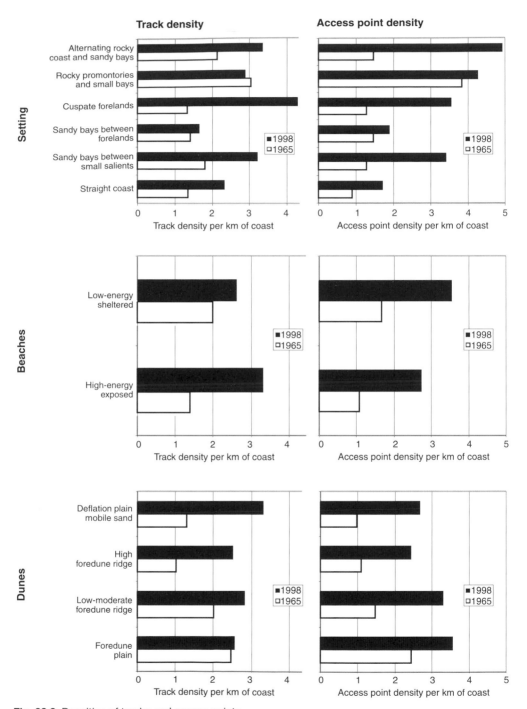

Fig. 22.2. Densities of tracks and access points.

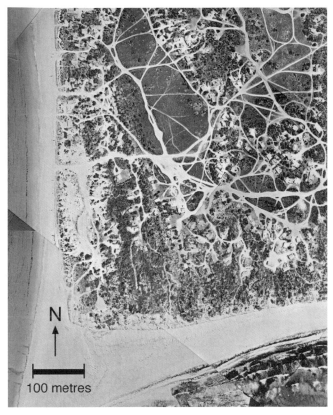

Fig. 22.3. Tracks at Wedge. Image from Western Australian Department of Land Administration (1997).

characterized by cuspate forelands, used preferentially for squatter settlements.

The greatest increase in the number of access points was 257%, for coastlines characterized as rocky coast and sandy bays. Low-energy coastlines had greater densities of tracks and access points than high-energy coastlines, but the latter experienced greater increases over the period studied. Sheltered sections of coast are less susceptible to wind erosion. Comparing the various dune types, greatest increases occurred in mobile sands, reflecting the increase in drivers seeking challenges to their vehicles and driving skills.

The Central Coast Region includes five local government areas, known as Shires, and the densities of 4WD tracks and access points differ between Shires (Priskin, 2003a). In 1965 the Shire of Coorow had the highest densities of tracks (2.74 km/km) and access points (2.61 per km). In 1998 the highest densities were in the Shire of Carnamah (3.92 km/km and 5.06 per km). The latter is the only one of the five shires without an established settlement (Fig. 22.1), so it has proved popular for bush camping and squatter shacks. Over the Central Coast Region as a whole, track densities are generally higher in more remote areas than close to settlements (Priskin, 2003a).

Management of 4WD Impacts

Most of the impacts from 4WD vehicles on beach and dune vegetation occur with only a few passes (Liddle, 1997; Buckley, Chapter 6 this volume), though successive passes do increase the time required for regeneration (Godfrey and Godfrey, 1980). The best management strategy to minimize impacts is hence to concentrate use on a small number of established routes and minimize the total length of track, the number of beach access points, and the extent of off-track use.

Rehabilitation of Western Australian coastline areas damaged by 4WD vehicles is expensive, labour intensive and time consuming (Kay and Alder, 1999). If degradation extends on either side of the track itself (Hosier and Eaton, 1980; Cole, 1993) then the total land area degraded by 4WD tracks in the Central Coast Region was 1550 km^2 in 1965 and 2500 km^2 in 1998. This is a conservative estimate, since impacts may often extend several metres from the track (Kutiel *et al.*, 1999).

Nominally, off-road driving in Western Australia is restricted by the Control of Vehicles (Off-Road Areas) Act 1978 (WA), but in practice there are no patrols in areas such as the Central Coast. Land managers may designate sacrificial areas for intensive use by off-road vehicles in order to protect the remainder, but many recreational drivers disregard such restrictions. Since much of the 4WD activity is associated with camping, provision of clearly marked campsites might reduce exploratory off-road vehicle use, and fences or barriers alongside tracks could reduce braiding.

Both restrictions on 4WD access, and rehabilitation of damaged areas, require management resources which need funding. One option to raise such funds would be to impose a tax or levy on registered 4WD vehicles. This would be unpopular both with owners of 4WD vehicles who do not use them off-road, and with farmers and fishermen who use theirs for commercial activity. Such a levy might, however, raise awareness of impacts amongst 4WD owners. Awareness can also be raised through voluntary codes of ethics, such as those promulgated by the Australian National Four-Wheel Drive Council, Tread Lightly Australia and others (Buckley, 2001). Off-road clubs have provided volunteer assistance with coastal clean-up campaigns. However, programmes that target existing clubs, associations and commercial tour operators may not reach individual drivers who cause the highest impacts.

Hardening of tracks across soft sandy areas, e.g. with rubber mats or chained planks, helps to keep vehicles on the tracks. However, these ground-cover techniques are expensive and visually intrusive, and may sometimes increase erosion. Perhaps the simplest approach would be to erect signs advising drivers to reduce tyre pressures, and to install compressed air stations at exit points so that drivers could easily re-inflate their tyres. This, however, would only be feasible at a limited number of sites, e.g. by ranger stations in national parks.

Conclusions

Use of 4WD vehicles for recreation and commercial ecotourism in the Central Coast Region of Western Australia is causing extensive and significant impacts on soils and vegetation, particularly of dunes and foreshores. The total length of 4WD track in a 271 km stretch of coastline has increased by 57% over the 33-year period, 1965–1998, from 517 to 813 km. The number of beach access points has increased by 116% during the same period, from 421 to 908. Tracks and access points are differentially abundant in particular landforms and local government areas, and those patterns have also changed. A range of management tools will be needed to address these impacts effectively.

Acknowledgements

This research was financed by the School of Earth and Geographical Sciences at The University of Western Australia and by the Central Coast Planning Co-ordinating Committee. The Department for Planning and Infrastructure and the Department of Conservation and Land Management provided sections of the aerial photographs for 1997/1998. I thank Ian Eliot, Julie Delaney, Lyal Harris and Gary Snook for assistance, and I also wish to express gratitude to the editor for having substantially edited this chapter.

References

Anders, F.J. and Leatherman, S.P. (1987) Effects of off-road vehicles on coastal foredunes at Fire Island, New York, USA. *Environmental Management* 11, 45–52.

Andersen, U.V. (1995) Resistance of Danish coastal vegetation types to human trampling. *Biological Conservation* 71, 223–230.

Bowels, J.M. and Maun, M.A. (1982) A study of the effects of trampling on the vegetation of Lake Huron sand dunes at Pinery Provincial Park. *Biological Conservation* 24, 273–283.

Buckley, R. (2001) *Green Guide for 4WD Tours.* CRC for Sustainable Tourism, Gold Coast, Australia.

Carlson, L.H. and Godfrey, P.J. (1989) Human impact management in a coastal recreation and natural area. *Biological Conservation* 49, 141–156.

Chapman, D.M., Whickam, H.G., Strike, T.M. and Clarke, P.J. (1989) *Coastal Dunes of New South Wales: Status and Management.* Coastal Studies Unit, The University of Sydney, Sydney, Australia.

Clarke, K. (1983) *Renewable Resource and Environmental Management in Western Australia: Off-road Vehicles.* Department of Civil Engineering, Department of Politics, Law School, The University of Western Australia, Nedlands, Australia.

Cole, D.N. (1993) Minimizing conflict between recreation and nature conservation. In: Smith, D.S. and Hallmund, P.C. (eds) *Ecology of Greenways: Design and Function of Linear Conservation Areas.* University of Minnesota Press, Minneapolis, pp. 105–122.

Department of Conservation and Land Management (2000) *Wedge and Grey Master Plan 2000.* Prepared by the Department of Conservation and Land Management for the National Parks and Nature Conservation Authority Western Australia, Perth, Australia.

Department of Planning and Urban Development (1994) *Central Coast Regional Profile.* Department of Planning and Urban Development, Perth, Australia.

Eliot, I.G. (1999) *Carnamah Coastal Strategy: a Plan for Landuse and Coastal Management in the Shire of Carnamah.* Report prepared for the Shire of Carnamah, Nedlands, Australia.

Gallet, S. and Roze, F. (2001) Resistance of Atlantic heathlands to trampling in Brittany (France): influence of vegetation type, season and weather conditions. *Biological Conservation* 97, 189–198.

Gentilli, J. (1971) *Climates of Australia and New Zealand.* Elsevier, Amsterdam.

Godfrey, P.J. and Godfrey, M. (1980) Ecological effects of off-road vehicles on Cape Cod. *Oceanus* 23, 56–67.

Government of Western Australia (1989) *Cabinet Endorsed State Government Squatter Policy.* Government of Western Australia, Perth, Australia.

Hegge, B., Eliot, I. and Hsu, J. (1996) Sheltered sandy beaches of southwestern Australia. *Journal of Coastal Research* 12, 748–760.

Hopkins, A.J.M., Keighery, G.J. and Marchant, N.G. (1983) Species-rich uplands of south-western Australia. *Proceedings of the Ecological Society of Australia* 12, 15–26.

Hosier, P.E. and Eaton, T.E. (1980) The impact of vehicles on dune and grassland vegetation on a south-eastern North Carolina barrier beach. *Journal of Applied Ecology* 17, 173–182.

House of Representatives Standing Committee on Environment and Conservation (1977) *Off-road Vehicles: Impact on the Australian Environment.* Australian Government Publishing Service, Canberra, Australia.

Hylgaard, T. (1980) Recovery of plant communities on coastal sand dunes disturbed by human trampling. *Biological Conservation* 19, 15–25.

Hylgaard, T. and Liddle, M.J. (1981) The effect of human trampling on a sand dune ecosystem dominated by *Epetrum nigrum. Journal of Applied Ecology* 18, 559–569.

Kay, R. and Alder, J. (1999) *Coastal Planning and Management.* Spon Press, London.

Kutiel, P., Zhevelev, H. and Harrison, R. (1999) The effect of recreational impacts on soil and vegetation of stabilised coastal dunes in the Sharon Park, Israel. *Ocean and Coastal Management* 42, 1041–1060.

Kutiel, P., Eden, S. and Zhevelev, Y. (2000) Effect of experimental trampling and off-road motorcycle traffic on soil and vegetation of stabilised coastal dunes, Israel. *Environmental Conservation* 27, 14–23.

Landvision, Eliot, I.G., Priskin, J., Environs Consulting and Evangelisti & Associates (1999) *Coastal Plan Incorporating Structure Plan and Design Guidelines for Coastal Development and Management for The Shire Of Dandaragan.* Landvision, Leederville.

Liddle, M.J. (1997) *Recreation Ecology.* Chapman and Hall, London.

Liddle, M.J. and Greig-Smith, P. (1975) A survey of tracks and paths in a sand dune ecosystem. I. Soils. *Journal of Applied Ecology* 12, 893–908.

Liddle, M.J. and Moore, K.G. (1974) The microclimate of sand dune tracks: the relative contribution of vegetation removal and soil compression. *Journal of Applied Ecology* 11, 1057–1068.

Lonsdale, W.M. and Lane, A.M. (1994) Tourist vehicles as vectors of weed in Kakadu National Park, Northern Australia. *Biological Conservation*, 69, 277–283.

Majer, J. (1980) Off-road vehicles hurt the bush, but drivers can learn to care. *Habitat* 8, 19–22.

McAtee, J.W. (1981) Human impacts on beach and foredune microclimate on North Padre Island, Texas. *Environmental Management* 5, 121–134.

Myers, N., Mittenmeier, R.A., Mittenmeier, C.G., da Fonseca, G.A.B. and Kent, J. (2000) Biodiversity hotspots for conservation priorities. *Nature* 403, 853–858.

Nelson, J.G. (1991) Sustainable development, conservation strategies and heritage. In: Mitchell, B. (ed.) *Resource Management and Development.* Oxford University Press, Toronto, pp. 246–267.

O'Brien, R. and MacRae, I. (1992) Planning for Western Australia's 12,000 km coastline. *Australian Planner* 30, 86–93.

Pracsys Management Consultants (2002) *The Indian Ocean Drive Economic and Social Impact Study.* Report prepared for the Wheatbelt Development Commission and the Department of Planning and Infrastructure. Pracsys Management Consultants, West Perth, Australia.

Priskin, J. (2001) Assessment of natural resources for nature-based tourism: the case of the Central Coast Region of Western Australia. *Tourism Management* 22, 637–648.

Priskin, J. (2003a) Physical impacts of four-wheel drive related tourism and recreation in a semi-arid, natural coastal environment. *Ocean and Coastal Management* 46, 127–155.

Priskin, J. (2003b) Characteristics and perceptions of coastal and wildflower nature-based tourists in the Central Coast Region of Western Australia. *Journal of Sustainable Tourism* 11(6), 535–564.

Rickard, C.A., McLachlan, A. and Kerley, G.I.H. (1994) The effects of vehicular and pedestrian traffic on dune vegetation in South Africa. *Ocean and Coastal Management* 23, 225–247.

Roberts, C.M., McClean, C.J., Veron, J.E.N., Hawkins, J.P., Allen, G.R., McAllister, D.E., Mittermeier, C.G., Schueler, F.W., S.F., Spalding, M., Wells, F., Vynne, C. and Werner, T.B. (2002) Marine biodiversity hotspots and conservation priorities for tropical reefs. *Science* 295, 1280–1284.

Sanderson, P.G. and Eliot, I. (1996) Shoreline salients, cuspate forelands and tombolos on the coast of Western Australia. *Journal of Coastal Research* 12, 761–773.

Searle, D.J. and Semeniuk, V. (1985) The natural sectors of the inner Rottnest Shelf coast adjoining the Swan Coastal Plain. *Journal of the Royal Society of Western Australia* 67, 116–136.

Western Australian Planning Commission (1996) *Central Coast Regional Strategy.* Western Australian Planning Commission, Perth, Australia.

Western Australian Planning Commission (2000) *Western Australia Tomorrow. Local Government Area Population Trends and Projections by Planning Regions.* Report 4. Western Australian Planning Commission, Perth, Australia.

23

Ecological Impacts of Ecotourist Visitation on Macroalgal Beds in Pacific Rim National Park Reserve

Lilian Alessa, Andrew Kliskey and Martin Robards

Department of Biological Sciences, University of Alaska Anchorage, Anchorage, Alaska, USA

Introduction

The coastal environment is the relatively narrow interface between land and sea. Functionally the coast can be defined as any area in which processes depending on the interaction between land and sea are most intense (Sorenson and McCreary, 1990). Coasts are robust and capable of absorbing natural and human disturbance, yet paradoxically are also fragile and susceptible to such disturbances. This is especially true along northern coastlines, which are allowed only a narrow window where biophysical variables are conducive to recovery after disturbance (Weslawski *et al.*, 1999). Uniquely, the coastal environment is a transitional zone between terrestrial and marine ecosystems, it acts as a buffer by absorbing high wind and wave energy, and is in a constant state of flux – it is not fixed in an absolute location unless it consists of rocky headlands which have evolved highly specialized assemblages of flora and fauna, such as macroalgal canopies and their associated invertebrate and vertebrate populations (EPAP, 1999). Different topographies, microclimates and oceanographic variables, such as currents, result in the establishment of specific, highly productive assemblages. Such areas may be considered 'functional zones' (FZs) upon which other biota, many distal to the FZ, such as those in the deep benthos and open ocean, rely. The precedent for growing concern for these FZs comes from historically recent transformation of many coastal areas, due not only to migrating populations but also to increased scales of resource extraction, global changes in climate and the ever-increasing desire of humans for recreation in these zones (Alessa and Bennett, 2001).

The ecological communities, and their dynamics, in the rocky intertidal zone are complex, due to natural, cyclic fluctuations, both temporally and spatially (Schiel and Taylor, 1999). Disturbance may play an important role in the distribution of the fauna and flora (Alessa and Bennett, 2001). Biotic and abiotic disturbances in the rocky intertidal zone leave bare space available for colonization, and thus increase diversity in a habitat otherwise dominated by a few species (Alessa and Bennett, 2001). Human activities, notably ecotourism, are considered a disturbance to natural environments (Laist *et al.*, 2001). This is particularly important since synergistic effects may occur with other disturbance pressures (Wipond and Dearden, 1988). In the nearshore, anthropogenic disturbance events vary in nature. Industrial discharges and ocean warming or cooling are more or less considered continual stresses (press disturbances). Other human activities are considered to be more variable in time and space (pulse disturbances).

Human activities in the intertidal zone may have a considerable negative impact on the biota there, particularly macroalgae. The altera-tion of critical algal communities often impacts, either directly or indirectly, the abundance of other organisms, mainly invertebrates, which are dependent on them for habitat and prey items (Addessi, 1994). The changes effected by human visitation may interact with serendipi-tous variables, such as weather and anthropo-genic inputs, to push habitats toward impairment, where resilience is decreased to the point that interseasonal recovery may no longer occur. These emerging trends highlight a gap that exists in research, which seeks to understand, mitigate and manage the effects of human disturbances on natural environments. Empirical approaches, which have fallen out of vogue for most disciplines, are crucial in this case, where the patterns created by humans are not well characterized and their complex feed-backs poorly understood. Such characterization is the first step in developing understanding through experimental design and manipulation that has meaning and context to real world sit-uations. Thus, one of the most prevalent bio-physical impacts in temperate coastal parks, where rocky headlands provide the substrata for intertidal and subtidal biota, is the removal of the base macroalgal canopy by trampling. This removal occurs through mechanical shear, which modifies both the canopy structure (i.e. through clearing) as well as the reproductive status of individuals that make it up (i.e. lower-ing the canopy's reproductive strength), by preferentially removing reproductive tissue (receptacles) from vegetative tissue (thallus). Since *Fucus* individuals only recruit within a few metres from the parent organism (Alessa and Bennett, 2001), the removal of reproductive tissue is significant.

The documentation of the removal of macroalgae by trampling is evident in the liter-ature (e.g. Schiel and Taylor, 1999); however, the details of recovery from the loss of algal tissue are diverse. Few report recovery as a con-sequence of vegetative growth from the remaining holdfast left behind (e.g. Schiel and Taylor, 1999). Few studies have examined the selective removal of reproductive tissue from the organism and the effects of use intensity on multi-year recovery cycles under conditions of complex patterns, such as those found in national parks and protected areas. In higher

latitude coastal parks with rocky headlands *Fucus* spp. (especially *gardneri*) macroalgae are important because these organisms engineer the intertidal zone in an otherwise marginal and hostile environment. They provide a com-plex canopied habitat which protects benthic fauna, including vertebrates, from stressors such as desiccation at low tide, predation, irra-diance, wave action, diurnal and seasonal tem-perature fluctuations and freshwater inputs. Moreover, the macroalgal canopy provides diverse niches which establish a complex and rich ecosystem that sustains both terrestrial and pelagic biota. Thus, by gaining an understand-ing of the variables that reduce the numbers and layering of these engineer organisms, we may be able to establish and monitor early indi-cators of approaching impairment thresholds; for example, a 'pre-threshold loss' for macroal-gal cover, close to which natural recovery is compromised. In this chapter we examine the effects of trampling by visitors on fucoid algae in the coastal environment of the Pacific Rim National Park Reserve (PRNPR), Canada.

Methods

Study site

PRNPR lies on the west coast of Vancouver Island in British Columbia, Canada. Together the three discontinuous units of the National Park, Long Beach, the West Coast Trail and Broken Group Islands (Fig. 23.1) protect a 125 km narrow strip of coastland (57% of Park) and ocean (43% of Park) covering approximately 51,986 ha. Of the three park units, the Long Beach Unit is the best known and most access-ible, particularly by road, and famous for its long, sandy beaches. The 500,000 to 1 million visitors per year represent the fifth highest number of visitors to a park in Canada. The Long-Beach unit is visited by approximately 800,000 people per year (60% from British Columbia, 25% from the rest of Canada, 10% from the United States, and 5% from other countries; Wilkinson, 2000). Approximately 90% of visitors travel to PRNPR between May and September. In a 1996 survey, Pacific Rim's 'overall ecological stress ranking' was ranked as 'most stressed' – one of only four parks in

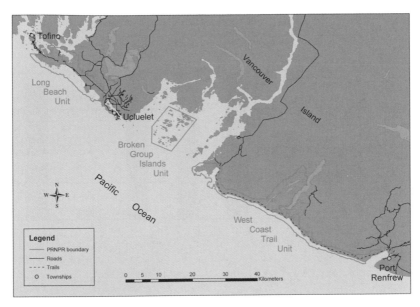

Fig. 23.1. Map of the Pacific Rim National Park Reserve.

Canada to receive such an assessment (Rollins, 1998).

Techniques

The impacts of visitor trampling on *Fucus* spp. macroalgae assemblages at PRNPR were measured before, during, and after four consecutive visitor seasons between 1999 and 2002. Use intensity in PRNPR is highly varied, and four rocky headland sites were chosen, representing different levels of human visitation. One high-impact site, one moderate-impact site, and two low-impact sites were chosen. Two low-level sites were chosen to ensure that measurement at this level of impact was distinguishable from background noise levels. All four sites were chosen following discussion with PRNPR staff, and the distinction between levels of impact were based on staff knowledge of visitation at the sites. Visitation levels at each site were ground-truthed before the measurement work commenced, to verify the differences in visitation and impact as conveyed by park staff. Throughout the measurement period, visitation levels were determined quantitatively by counting the number of visitors in each of four quadrants representing the total emersed (dry at the

lowest low tide) accessible area of each headland. Visitation levels were measured each day (sunrise to sunset) throughout season 1 (1999) and then at least every 3 days, including each day of a weekend, thereafter (2000–2002).

In addition to the visited sites, measurements were taken at four control sites which received no visitation during the entire study period. A control site was selected close to each of the four visited sites to ensure comparability in physical features (including wave exposure, aspect and topography). These were headlands that were not accessible by visitors, providing sites free of impacts resulting from visitation. Data collection activities by the field workers were conducted by swimming to each control site.

The percentage cover of *Fucus* spp. was measured at each site (visited and control) using 25 × 25 cm quadrats placed every 2 m along five 50 m transects. Measurements were made daily through the summer season and weekly outside of the summer. In addition, measurements were taken of the percentage cover of other dominant canopy organisms – barnacles (*Balanus* spp.) and anemones (*Anthropluera* spp.). The length of each frond of every *Fucus* spp individual in each quadrat was measured using a caliper ruler. The reproductive capacity of *Fucus* spp.

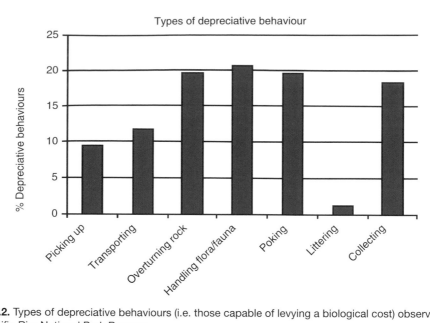

Fig. 23.2. Types of depreciative behaviours (i.e. those capable of levying a biological cost) observed in the Pacific Rim National Park Reserve.

was measured by counting terminal receptacles on each frond of every individual in each quadrat. Desiccation rates of *Fucus* canopy at each site were measured at three different tide heights (midzone, MZ; highzone, HZ; high highzone, HHZ) by placing 5-g pieces of *Fucus* on the substrate and measuring each piece at the outset and then every minute for up to 360 min. Each piece of *Fucus* consisted of thallus and receptacle.

Results

Use intensity

The four visited sites received visitation/impact levels of 0.28 ($\pm$0.13) persons/m^2/day for the high-impact site, 0.18 ($\pm$0.08) persons/m^2/day for the moderate impact site and 0.06 ($\pm$0.01) persons/m^2/day for the two low-impact sites, averaged over the four seasons. The types of activities in which visitors engaged at each of the sites were consistent (Fig. 23.2). These involved walking, collecting, disturbing and moving living organisms. The pattern of visitation to sites in PRNPR is typical of many national parks: heavy weekend visitation and

lighter weekday visitation, with intense overall visitation occurring almost exclusively during the summer months (May to September). It was observed that visitors did not walk purposefully across the headland, rather the patterns they created were complex and chaotic, with potentially multiple, non-linear feedbacks within and upon a given headland that result in unpredictable changes. Furthermore, visitors tended to stand in only a few spots and to move randomly within them as they explored other intertidal biota. The biological and management implications of this are beyond the scope of this chapter. Visitation is also coincidental with ambient conditions, such as weather, that can mitigate or exacerbate trampling effects. For example, a heavy rainfall during a weekend may limit the number of visitors to the rocky headland, whereas a sunny day will bring more out.

Effects of visitation on biotic cover

The percentage cover of *Fucus* in sites of low levels of impact remained high, in excess of 90%, and only marginally lower, approximately 5% less, than the averaged percentage cover for all four control sites (Fig. 23.3). These

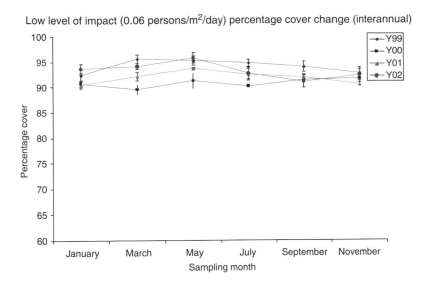

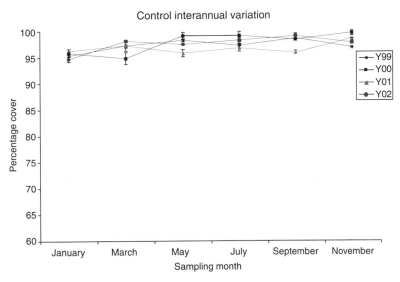

Fig. 23.3. Changes in percentage cover for *Fucus* spp. at Pacific Rim National Park Reserve over 4 years (1999–2002), at two sites of low levels of impact (visitation), compared to averaged percentage cover for all four control sites.

data suggest that low visitation does not result in progressive impairment. The percentage cover of *Fucus* at the site of moderate levels of impact ranged from 80 to 85% prior to a visitation season, decreasing over each season to 75–80% compared to the averaged control sites cover of 95% or higher (Fig. 23.4). These data indicate that moderate visitation pressure does result in progressive impairment, suggesting that a threshold exists between low visitation and moderate visitation. The percentage cover of *Fucus* at the site of high levels of impact ranged from 45–55% prior to a visitation season, decreasing over each season to 30–40% compared to the averaged control sites' cover of 95% or higher (Fig. 23.5). At sites

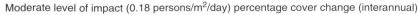

Moderate level of impact (0.18 persons/m²/day) percentage cover change (interannual)

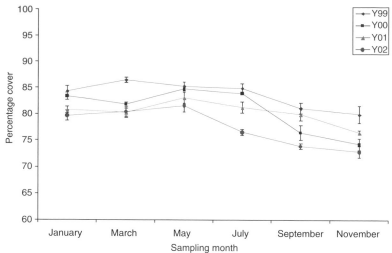

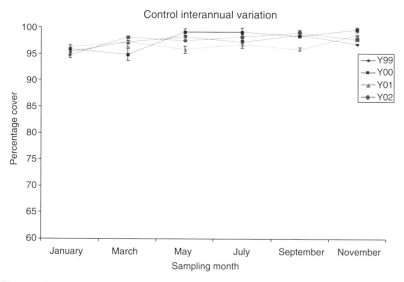

Fig. 23.4. Changes in percentage cover for *Fucus* spp. at Pacific Rim National Park Reserve over 4 years (1999–2002), at the site of moderate levels of impact (visitation), compared to averaged percentage cover for all four control sites.

of low levels of impact the percentage cover of biota was high and remained at a consistently high level annually and interannually. At sites of moderate levels of impact the biotic cover was reduced (approximately 5% of cover) through the visitor season and displayed an inability to recovery interannually (a 5% reduction over 4 years in the biotic cover available prior to the visitor season). At sites of high levels of impact the biotic cover was reduced significantly (approximately 15% of cover) during the visitor season and displayed an inability to recover interannually, similar to moderate levels of impact (a 5% reduction over 4 years in the biotic cover available prior to the visitor season).

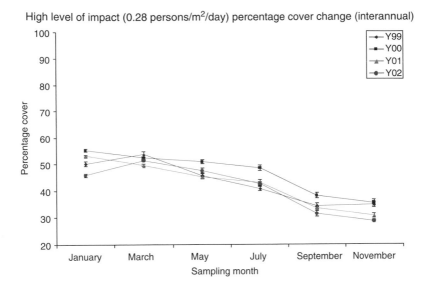

High level of impact (0.28 persons/m²/day) percentage cover change (interannual)

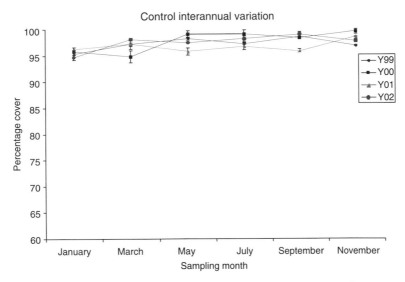

Control interannual variation

Fig. 23.5. Changes in percentage cover of *Fucus* spp. at Pacific Rim National Park Reserve over 4 years (1999–2002), at the site of high levels of impact (visitation), compared to averaged percentage cover for all four control sites.

In PRNPR, the percentage cover of the three dominant canopy species, *Fucus gardneri*, barnacle and anemone, in control sites versus visited sites reflects the overt removal of biota by foot traffic. In controls, *Fucus* forms a complex canopy, which overlaps barnacles and provides habitat for invertebrates, and the biotic cover comprising *Fucus* is close to 100% (Fig. 23.6).

However, in high-use sites, the percentage cover of *Fucus* and barnacles was significantly reduced, to below 50% (Fig. 23.7). This reduced pattern of biotic cover is not seen in any of the control sites but is observed in areas of high wave action, where large amounts of sediment are regularly redistributed (data not shown). This is not surprising when one considers that

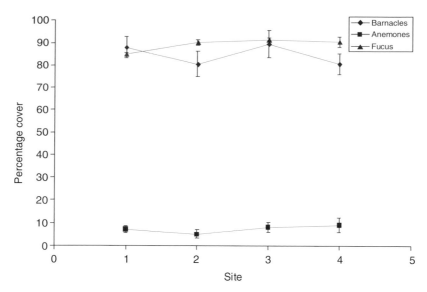

Fig. 23.6. Percentage cover of dominant canopy organisms for individual control sites (site 1, high visitation control; site 2, moderate visitation control; sites 3 and 4, low visitation controls).

the mechanical shear inherent in foot traffic may not be dissimilar to that caused by sediment transport in waves, despite the complexity of impact patterns. There is a trend towards biotic cover which more closely resembles that found in controls as use intensity decreases, and a strong correlation between decreasing density of people (per m²) and increased *Fucus* abundance ($r = 0.87$, $P < 0.0001$).

Effects of visitation on receptacle length

The lengths of the receptacles (reproductive fronds which contribute zygotes for recruitment) is correlated to the number of receptacles (gamete producing tissue) that an alga holds (Alessa and Bennett, 2001). The longer the frond, the more receptacles are present and the more gametes are produced. Thus, a reduction in the frond length will directly impact the number of gametes produced and the reproductive strength of the individual (Alessa and Bennett, 2001). Frond lengths were significantly shorter at the end of the season in the high use intensity site (Fig. 23.8). The decrease in frond lengths was a direct consequence of mechanical shear and, each season, numerous detached fronds were observed throughout the season in

the high use intensity site. The significant reduction in frond length reflects a decrease in total reproductive biomass and, hence, overall reproductive strength of the canopy.

Effects of use intensity on percentage reproductive fronds

The change in reproductive fronds demonstrates clearly that increasing use intensity has pronounced effects on the total biomass of functional reproductive tissue (Fig. 23.9). At the highest level of impact the percentage of reproductive fronds is well below 40 at all tide heights versus the controls, which range from approximately 65% at the HHZ to almost 90% in the HZ and MZ. There is a discrete and significant increase in the percentage of reproductive fronds across tide heights as use intensity drops to the moderate and low levels, where, for the latter, they most closely resemble those of the control.

Desiccation stresses as a consequence of trampling

The desiccation rates of *Fucus* were significantly higher at the high impact/visitation site

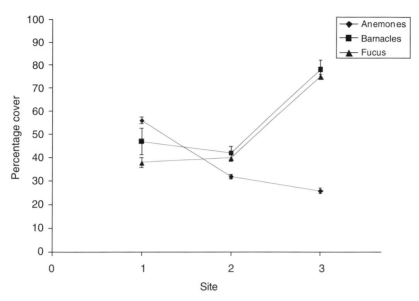

Fig. 23.7. Changes in percentage cover for dominant canopy organisms at visited sites (1, high impact/visitation site; 2, moderate impact/visitation site; 3, low impact/visitation sites).

than other visited sites, and higher at the moderate impact visitation site than the low impact/visitation sites (Fig. 23.10). These patterns in desiccation rates were consistent across all three tide heights (Fig. 23.10). Furthermore, during drier periods, the receptable-thallus attachment of *Fucus* became more brittle due to water loss and therefore easier to remove via mechanical shear resulting from foot traffic.

Discussion

The most biologically significant impact of visitation on rocky headlands of PRNPR is the removal and modification of the macroalgal canopy in the intertidal zone. An understanding of the mechanisms that affect and limit the reproductive success of *Fucus* spp. on the North Pacific coastline is essential to the management of these areas. Without these basic data, we will be unable to develop models that: (i) predict the sensitivity of specific nearshore locales to human impacts; (ii) identify variables that are indicative of stress for use by managers and scientists; and (iii) develop methods for, at least partial, restoration of highly impacted

areas. One of the goals for management in rocky coastal parks is the need to determine effects of use intensity on the removal of *Fucus* cover to help identify a use threshold (persons/m²/day) after which natural recovery can no longer occur, or is impaired, thus resulting in a macroalgal canopy which is highly vulnerable to change. The removal of receptacles will affect the total reproductive capacity of an individual alga and, hence, the ability of the canopy to recruit interseasonally, which is reflected in the observed progressive decrease in cover over 4 years of observation of differentially (i.e. low to high) impacted sites in PRNPR (see Figs 23.4, 23.5 and 23.6). The indication that frond lengths were shorter in visited sites than in control sites (Fig. 23.8) even prior to the height of visitation to a specific area may be an 'impact echo', which we propose represents a precondition of impairment resulting in a progressively deteriorating baseline. Frond lengths within the control sites did not change significantly over the 4 years of observation, which is expected in lieu of major disturbance such as severe storms or other events acutely capable of shearing algal tissue. Changes in frond lengths are observed across tide heights. These

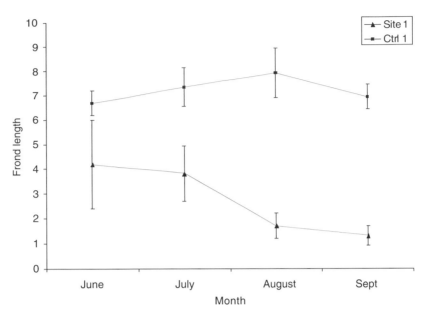

Fig. 23.8. Change in average frond length in Pacific Rim National Park Reserve, averaged for four summer seasons, at the high visitation site only, compared to the nearest control site only.

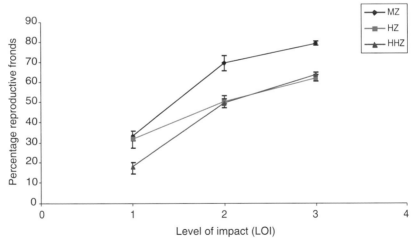

Fig. 23.9. Changes in the percentage of reproductive fronds by level of impact (1, high impact/visitation site; 2, moderate impact/visitation site; 3, low impact/visitation sites) across tide heights (MZ, midzone; HZ, highzone; HHZ, high highzone).

data need to be developed to provide indicators for use patterns that could preferentially affect specific tide zones, due to topographical impediments or the proximity to other organisms of visitor interest, such as starfish. The results of the effects of use intensity on repro-

ductive fronds (Fig. 23.9) indicate that increasing levels of human trampling reduce biotic cover at an increasing rate, while recovery from that trampling following a visitor season is inhibited once moderate or high levels of trampling are incurred.

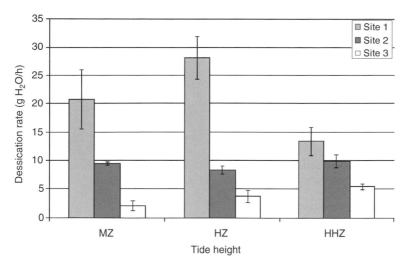

Fig. 23.10. Effects of clearing of *Fucus* canopy on desiccation rates across different tide heights (MZ, midzone; HZ, highzone; HHZ, high highzone) at different levels of impact (1, high visitation site; 2, moderate visitation site; 3, low visitation sites).

The complex canopied structure of the *Fucus* canopy in PRNPR results in microclimates that protect flora and fauna from desiccation during low tide. This is primarily due to the mitigation of evaporation. The removal of the macroalgal canopy, across tide heights, exposes mineral substrata where evaporation rates increase to levels where other biota cannot survive and where *Fucus* propagules cannot germinate and, hence, the canopy cannot self-recruit (Fig. 23.10). This process is exacerbated and the condition maintained through continuous visitation. The combination of the loss of reproductive strength (via the removal of reproductive fronds) and the creation of increasingly larger areas of high evaporation rates violates the tolerance limit of germination for *Fucus* propagules and results in a progressively impaired state.

Trampling impacts in parks such as PRNPR are likely the most significant cause of impairment of intertidal ecosystems – the primary attraction for ecotourism. Increasing levels of human trampling on intertidal biota result in susceptibility to damage and an inability of ecosystems to recover from that damage (Figs 23.3, 23.4 and 23.5). One of the main components that must be ascribed to an impact situation is that the recovery interval is greater than interseasonal. For example, if the biotic assemblages on a rocky headland are decimated

during the summer months but are restored (through self-recruitment) by the next summer, then the impact level is not significant in a long-term consideration. Ecotourism has the potential to push coastal assemblages beyond their ability to recover interseasonally. In this case study, we identified the direct relationship between tourist visitation (our proxies for ecotourism magnitude) and biophysical disturbance in a critical habitat, that is, in macroalgal canopies. Coupled with our understanding of the effects of visitors' knowledge and perception of ecosystem health on depreciative behaviour in the intertidal zone (Alessa *et al.*, 2003), these data provide park managers with information that allows them to manage the impacts of ecotourism and the behaviour leading to these impacts.

Acknowledgements

We gratefully acknowledge the staff and managers of Pacific Rim National Park Reserve, as well as the University of Canterbury (New Zealand), the University of Alaska Anchorage (USA), and the Earthwatch Institute (USA). We thank the Alaska Resource Library (ARLIS) staff, who were, as always, quick to help with reference materials.

References

Addessi, L. (1994) Human disturbance and long term changes on a rocky intertidal community. *Ecological Applications* 4(4), 786–797.

Alessa, L. and Bennett, S. (2001) A comparison of the impacts of human activity on *Fucus* gardneri in sites associated with recreation versus aquaculture. In: Ralonde, R. (ed.) *Proceedings of the On-Bottom Aquaculture Association, 'Assessing the Impacts of On-bottom Shellfish Aquaculture'*. National Oceanographic and Atmospheric Administration, University of Alaska Sea Grant, pp. 141–154.

Alessa, L., Bennett, S.M. and Kliskey, A.D. (2003) Effects of knowledge, personal attribution and perception of ecosystem health on depreciative behaviors in the intertidal zone of Pacific Rim National Park and Reserve. *Journal of Environmental Management* 68, 207–218

EPAP (1999) Ecosystem-based fishery management: A report to Congress by the Ecosystems Principles Advisory Panel, as mandated by the Sustainable Fisheries Act amendments to the Magnuson Stevens Fishery Conservation and Management Act 1996. US Department of Commerce, NOAA, National Marine Fisheries Service, Silver Spring, Maryland.

Laist, D.W., Knowlton, A.R., Mean, J.G., Collet, A.S. and Podesta, M. (2001) Collisions between ships and whales. *Marine Mammal Science* 17(1), 35–75.

Rollins, R. (1998) Managing for wilderness conditions on the West Coast Trail area of Pacific Rim National Park. In: Munro, N.W.P. and Willison, J.H.M. (eds) *Linking Protected Areas with Working Landscapes Conserving Biodiversity*. Proceedings of the Third International Conference on Science and Management of Protected Areas, 12–16 May 1997, Wolfville, Canada, pp. 643–654.

Schiel, D.R. and Taylor, D.I. (1999) Effects of trampling on a rocky intertidal algal assemblage in southern New Zealand. *Journal of Experimental Marine Biology and Ecology* 235, 213–235.

Sorenson, J.C. and McCreary, S.T. (1990) *Institutional Arrangements for Managing Coastal Resources and Environments*. Coastal Management Publication No. 1, NPS/US AID Series, National Park Service, Office of International Affairs, Washington, DC.

Weslawski, J.M., Szymelfenig, M., Zajaczkowski, M. and Keck, A. (1999) Influence of salinity and suspended matter on benthos of an Arctic tidal flat. *ICES Journal of Marine Science* 56(suppl.), 194–202.

Wilkinson, P.F. (2000) Protecting for ecological integrity in a coastal national park: visitor use in Pacific Rim National Park, Vancouver Island, Canada. *Biodiversity and Tourism Symposium – Placing Tourism in the Landscape of Diversities: a Dialogue between Nature and Culture, September 20–23*. Scientific Committee on Problems of the Environment (SCOPE), Paris, France.

Wipond, K. and Dearden, P. (1988) Obstacles to maintaining ecological integrity in Pacific Rim National Park Reserve. In: Munro, N.W.P. and Willison, J.H.M. (eds) *Linking Protected Areas with Working Landscapes Conserving Biodiversity*. Science and Management of Protected Areas Association, Wolfville, Nova Scotia, pp. 901–910.

24

Understanding Use and Users at Itatiaia National Park, Brazil

Teresa Cristina Magro[1] and Maria Isabel Amando de Barros[2]

[1]Departamento de Ciências Florestais, ESALQ/USP, Piracicaba, Brazil; [2]Outward Bound Brasil, São Paulo, Brazil

Introduction

Context

Although outdoor recreation activities in Brazil have not received widespread attention internationally, incentives for ecotourism and public visitation to conservation areas have increased significantly over recent years. Many conservation areas have experienced the pressure of an increasing number of visitors, often associated with a demand for diversified opportunities for recreation. Considered a specialized minority 30 years ago, nowadays there is an increasing group in search of activities such as hiking, camping, climbing and rafting. This is due to information becoming more easily accessible about what, how and where to practise, as well as the availability of good-quality equipment.

The increasing number of visitors seeking contact with the natural environment, and the need for diversity, increases the necessity for accommodating uses in protected areas. Planning and management actions need to be implemented in these areas, particularly strategies that control impacts to the environment and visitor experiences caused by recreation.

Although some countries have an extensive research history on recreation management in natural protected areas, Brazil has produced little on this topic. Increased impacts caused by recreation use are largely dealt with through restrictions in use, closure of areas, and greater regulation of activities, causing a reduction in alternative activities available and less visitor freedom.

The goal of this research is to help understand the relationship between visitor characteristics, behaviour and ecological impacts based on a case study in Itatiaia National Park (INP). The objectives of this study were: (i) to describe the actual conditions of ecological and social conditions in camping areas and trails; (ii) to obtain data about visitation and visitors – who they are, their previous experience and their knowledge of minimum impact techniques; and (iii) based on this knowledge, to propose guidelines for a visitor education programme that would minimize impacts.

The belief underlying this study is that better-informed and more responsible visitors will contribute to reducing impacts in these areas, enabling protected area policies to be less restrictive.

Recreation management in Brazil

Managers working in protected natural areas of Brazil constantly face problems related to impacts caused by recreation. Such impacts threaten the ability of these units to conserve their natural resources while providing recreational opportunities for visitors.

Professionals responsible for management in such areas, particularly parks, have been dealing with problems related to impacts caused by recreation for many years. They are in search of better solutions, but little progress has been made in many places. As a matter of fact, in most cases, use is simply prohibited, since better solutions require financial and human resource investments which are frequently not available.

According to Magro (2003), in the past, when public use of natural areas was not as intense, trail, campsites or area closures within some National Parks did not generate public reaction or were not even noticed. Significant increases in public use of parks and recreation areas, however, have created such pressure that public access to some closed areas has been re-established, creating new administrative problems. Public pressure, often from people involved in outdoor sports, to open new areas to new activities has also increased. In addition, historically there was a certain lethargy regarding public use of national parks, but now the situation is far more dynamic, with greater public participation. Public dissatisfaction has been observed when certain restrictive restoration measures were established, especially if they were of a permanent nature.

Visitors vary greatly in their demands and expectations. However, these demands and expectations need to become compatible with conservation goals. According to Barros and Dines (2000), the current attitude of simply ignoring these different demands has increased the impacts in these areas, because it foments illegal and uncontrolled use. These authors emphasize that wilderness outdoor activities have been increasing in the country at a time when the demand for protecting nature has also reached an unprecedented level.

According to Kinker (1999), public use is seen as an excellent opportunity for development and a source of income for many conservation units. Since tourism generates more visitation opportunities, it may bring economic benefits not only for the conservation unit itself but also for the surrounding communities. There has been a shift in the management of natural protected areas, fomented by interna-

tional cooperation agencies and banks and also by national pressure. This shift has been to move away from the ostracism which these areas have been subject to for years (for the sake of natural resources protection) and towards the establishment of centres of regional development. Therefore, public agencies in charge of these areas have been trying to open parks to recreation by providing physical infrastructure, and have also been setting up studies to analyse further ecotourism potential in parks and surrounding areas.

This strategy is time consuming and represents a long-term challenge. As a result, these areas continue to offer recreation opportunities for a large number of people without, however, fulfilling the expectations of visitors with respect to the quality of their experiences.

According to Jesus (2002), the appropriate strategy for conservation areas in Brazil may be the design of recreational plans that incorporate less conservative and more contemporary approaches to recreation activities. A contemporary approach acknowledges the new demand for activities in natural areas and their necessity for incorporation into the management of these conservation areas. It does not necessarily mean the immediate approval of all the activities, but the evaluation of whether each activity is appropriate for the area.

From policeman to educator

Many natural area managers and researchers consider environmental education a fundamental component for the long-term survival of these areas. Environmental education can provide information about natural areas; make people aware of nature's cultural, environmental and experimental value; and help to build a better human relationship with the natural environment (Gunderson et al., 2000).

According to Gunderson et al. (2000), environmental education includes methods and practices such as: creation of videos, publications and Internet information; minimal-impact materials and training, such as the Leave-No-Trace programme (Hampton and Cole, 1995); brochures and signs posted at the entrance of national parks; environmental interpretive programmes; local talks and presentations carried out by park staff and personnel; and environmental education curriculum for school students.

Visitor education has been considered the most desirable approach for public use management in natural areas, in Brazil and internationally (Indrusiak, 2000; Vasconcellos, 2002). According to Gunderson *et al.* (2000), wilderness managers in the USA prefer educational programmes that influence visitor behaviour in the direction of management goals, since education supports individuality and freedom of choice, characteristics not common to many other alternatives. Sixty per cent of managers working in wilderness areas in the USA were using educational strategies to deal with several management-related problems as early as the late 1970s (Washburne and Cole, 1983).

An educational emphasis has several advantages. One advantage is to move away from the policeman role, usually associated with managers when they prioritize regulations. Taking into account the high educational level observed in most visitors to Brazilian parks (Takahashi, 1998; Kinker, 1999), the educational approach presents a higher probability of being successful. Visitors should be able to use the information, deal with concepts and their relationships, and understand the reasons behind specific management strategies.

The main premises supporting an educational strategy towards management are: (i) many impacts and problems are due to careless behaviour and lack of information; (ii) visitors, once educated and informed, are willing to adopt appropriate behaviours; and (iii) many problems will be minimized by educating visitors about appropriate procedures, hence eliminating the need for more expensive regulatory strategies (Hammitt and Cole, 1998).

Visitor education is an important tool to consider amongst available management alternatives when dealing with certain problems. More studies are needed, however, to identify the essential information that should be provided to visitors and the best way to assemble and make it available; to determine whether education is effectively shifting behaviour in the expected direction; and, finally, to evaluate the performance of different educational strategies associated with other management strategies.

Methods

Study site

As described by Magro (2003), the Brazilian Federal Government acquired the lands of Itatiaia National Park (INP) in 1908, for the creation of two colonial towns. These towns were composed mainly of European immigrants, most commonly from Finland. Due to steep hillsides, these towns were not successful, and the land was returned to the Ministry of Agriculture. In 1929, a Biological Research Station was created and administered by the Botanical Garden of Rio de Janeiro (IBDF, 1982). In 1937, this land became the first Brazilian National Park, the Itatiaia National Park (INP). It is located in the south-west of Rio de Janeiro state, directly south of Minas Gerais (Figs 24.1 and 24.2). The park is 30,000 ha in area. One of the main attractions is Agulhas Negras Peak, 2787 m high and the fourth highest peak in Brazil. The average annual visitation to the whole park is approximately 100,000 visits. This is low relative to other Brazilian parks, such as Iguaçu or Tijuca National Parks, which each receive about 1 million visitors annually. However, visitation in Itatiaia is largely limited to one or two sites only, and occurs mostly on weekends, holidays and school vacations (Magro, 2003). The Itatiaia plateau, where this study was conducted, receives around 11,000 visitors every year, most of them from São Paulo and Rio de Janeiro.

Use of campsites and trails at INP plateau

There is only one official campsite in INP, located on the plateau near Rebouças Hut. Camping was suspended there in 1991, due to contamination of Campo Belo River springs. Even though closed for the public, the area has been used for military training. Other organizations, such as outdoor and climbing groups, also continued to use the area during this period. In the beginning of 1999, Rebouças Camping was reopened for use by other associations and groups (Magro *et al.*, 2001). The fact that the park campsite could only be used by some groups damaged the park's image, since

Fig. 24.1. Geographical location of Itatiaia National Park in Brazil.

the main technical justification of environmental contamination was discredited. Nowadays, the area is only open for the military.

Since the park administration did not offer alternatives for the demand for camping, visitors simply began to camp in other environmentally fragile areas elsewhere in the park. These areas soon became heavily used by visitors, since no authorization was required beforehand and no fees were payable. However, after a fire, caused by two visitors in 2001, INP administration prohibited all camping in and adjacent to the park, leaving camping visitors with only one alternative: the camping area at Hotel Alsene (Fig. 24.3).

As a result of these regulations, visitors' options have been reduced from those initially predicted for the park. Since first established, several activities have been prohibited or have become inactive, such as the use of huts, backpacking and camping. No alternatives for these activities have been implemented.

The most popular hiking trails in the plateau include: Pico das Prateleiras, receiving 27% of all visitors; Pico das Agulhas, with 24%

visitation; and the road leading to Rebouças Hut, with 21% of public visitation. Therefore, most visitation is concentrated at the two main plateau peaks, since the hiking trail leading to Rebouças Hut is a dirt road also used by vehicles. Since public use in the plateau is concentrated in only a few sites, the impacts are accentuated. This is reflected by the very major ecological and social trail impacts of the high visitor presence at these three sites.

Characteristics of visitors and visits

A profile of the visitors was needed for the highest visitation season. Accordingly, visitor and visit data collection began in February 2002 and was completed in October 2002.

Visitor and visit related data were obtained using a questionnaire, based on Kinker (1999), Takahashi (1998) and Cole et al. (1997a). The questionnaire obtained information about: (i) visit attributes, including group size, activities carried out by visitors and duration of visit; (ii) visitors' perceptions about conditions found

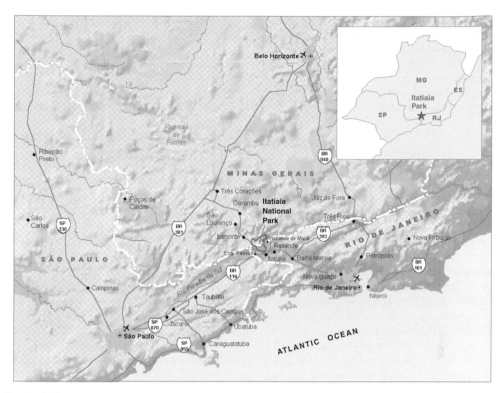

Fig. 24.2. The strategic location of Itatiaia National Park (INP), between two very important capitals (São Paulo and Rio de Janeiro), enhances visitation on weekends and holidays.

Fig. 24.3. Camping at the park's nearest hotel, within the Itatiaia National Park (INP) plateau.

during visitation; and (iii) visitor attributes, including previous experience, preferences and demographic information and knowledge about low-impact methods. Visitor knowledge of minimum impact techniques was assessed using tests developed by Confer *et al.* (2000) and Ramthun *et al.* (2000).

Trails assessment

The first survey of ecological impacts in the most heavily used INP trails was conducted by Magro (1999). Relevant data were collected in 1995 and 1996. After studying 12 possible impact indicators, the author selected three (slope, soil texture and trail profile) that best portrayed the degradation and restoration conditions in the studied area. Subsequently, Magro *et al.* (1999) carried out new studies, to assess the biophysical impact indicators in the trails and in the camping areas.

In the study reported here, more detailed data on ecological impacts were collected in 2002 along four trails on the INP plateau: Agulhas Negras (1300m); Prateleiras (2200m); Pico do Couto (1400m) and Cachoeira da Aiuruoca (6000m). Following methodology described by Hammitt and Cole (1998), information about trail conditions was collected at 100 sampling points distributed systematically along the trails.

The following indicators of impact were assessed, based on studies by Cole (1991), Takahashi (1998) and Magro (1999): soil compaction, trail width, total width of trail influence area, exposed soil, depth of tread, secondary trails and paths, and detractive factors. The detractive factors, assessed only as present or absent, were trail conditions such as steps, soil erosion, exposed rocks, soil disruption, exposed roots, drainage, muddiness or trash, that caused any harm to trail use.

From the data on trail width and depth, we were able to calculate the cross-sectional area, which is an important indicator of erosion. As noted by Hammitt and Cole (1998), width and depth are easily collected in the field, and are as efficient an indicator of erosion as full measurement of transverse area.

Campsite assessment

Impacts caused by recreational camping on the INP plateau were first examined by Magro *et al.* (1999), as part of a monitoring and planning programme for public use management. Between 1998 and 1999, a total of 35 camping areas were evaluated. These included all areas with evidence of use, both areas that were still in use and those that had been abandoned.

The present research used the same assessment methodology as in 1988 and 1999, with the following indicators of campsite impact: (i) vegetation, including bare soil areas, degraded vegetation, shrubs with broken branches and evidence of campfires; and (ii) sanitation, human excrement and trash. In addition to these basic indicators, the current research included a more detailed survey using multiple parameters, as recommended by Hammitt and Cole (1998) and Monz (1999). Following the methods of Cole (1982), Marion (1991); Cole and Hall (1992) and Takahashi (1998), the parameters used were as follows:

1. Area of the campsite. The area of each site was measured using the variable radial transect method developed by Marion (1991). A computer program (Autocad) was used to calculated campsite area, based on the transect measurements recorded. The total recreation site area was obtained by adding the area of any satellite sites and subtracting the area of any undisturbed islands within the overall campsite area.
2. Area of exposed mineral soil. An estimate of soil exposure, defined as ground with very little or no organic litter or vegetation cover, within the campsite boundaries and satellite areas was made using the geometric figure method, described by Marion (1991).
3. Tree damage. This measure was obtained by counting the number of trees and/or shrubs located inside each camping area, and in its immediate area of influence, which showed marks, initials, nails, broken branches and other scars caused by visitors.
4. Fire rings. We recorded each fire site within campsite boundaries, including satellite areas. This includes all old inactive fire sites, as exhibited by blackened rocks, charcoal or ashes.

5. Litter. Trash at each campsite was classified into three categories: low, none or less than a handful; medium, more than a handful but not enough to fill a 10-litre bucket; or large, more than a 10-litre bucket.

6. Social trails. These are informal trails that lead from the site to water, the main trail, other campsites, or satellite sites. This measure was obtained by counting the total number of social trails at each site.

7. Human waste. We followed all trails connected to each site to conduct a quick search of likely 'toilet' areas, typically areas just out of sight of the recreation site, and counted the number of individual human waste sites, defined as separate locations exhibiting toilet paper and/or human faeces.

8. Number of other visible sites. The number of other camping sites visible from the specific site under assessment.

9. Soil compaction. Five sampling points were established in each camping area, using a Lang penetrometer, with centre-to-edge distance randomly determined. Five readings were taken for each sampling point. The same procedure was used for a non-impacted control site adjacent to the camping area.

10. Photographs. A point with a good overview of the camping area was selected, emphasizing the boundaries used in delimiting the total area. The objective was to obtain a photograph including the largest possible area so as to permit the evaluation of local site conditions. Tripod height, azimuth, aperture and speed, were also recorded.

Results and Discussion

Group size and seasonality

Most visitors to INP plateau travel in groups, probably because of the area's rough terrain and difficult access. From a total of 605 individuals interviewed, 2% were travelling alone, 53% in a group of 2–4 persons, 29% in a 5–10-person group and 16% in a group of over 10 people. Although large groups constitute a small proportion of the total number of visitors, they may cause a significant impact on the quality of the experiences enjoyed by other visitors they encounter, besides making a major

Table 24.1. Visitor distribution at Itatiaia National Park from September 2001 to November 2002.

Attraction	Number of Visitors	Percentage of Total
Prateleiras Peak	2614	26.8
Base of Prateleiras Peak	527	5.4
Agulhas Negras Peak	2320	23.8
Base of Agulhas Negras Peak	267	2.7
Rebouças Hut	1994	20.4
End of Rebouças Hut access road	494	5.1
Couto Peak	787	8.0
Altar Peak	416	4.3
Others	346	3.5

contribution to ecological impacts such as trampling. According to Hampton and Cole (1995) any 'optimum' number is arbitrary, but most researchers and land managers consider that groups with more than 10 or 12 persons are large groups. Using this criterion, it appears that 84% of the individuals interviewed visit the park in small groups of 10 people or fewer, although the plateau does sometimes receive groups of up to 100 people at once.

The seasonal distribution of visitors is shown in Table 24.1, derived from park records for the period of September 2001 to November 2002. Most visitors go to the two main peaks, the Rebouças Hut and the road that accesses it. To reach Rebouças Hut itself requires a 3 km walk on a dirt road. Thus 25.5% of visitors to the park remain restricted to the Rebouças Hut access road and do not visit park attractions.

Visitor activities

When interviewed about their main activity during a visit: 41% of visitors responded that they were just hiking; 44% hiking and climbing to the peaks; 8% hiking and technical rock climbing; 4% hiking and camping; and 2% did not answer. These data also show that most visitors (84%) either come in search of the two most famous peaks in the plateau (Agulhas Negras and Prateleiras) or hike the trails leading to their base or the road leading to Rebouças Hut. There are several other options for day trips, such as Pico do Couto, Morro do

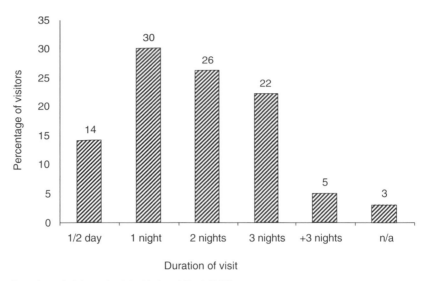

Fig. 24.4. Duration of visits at Itatiaia National Park (INP).

Altar and Cachoeira do Aiuruoca, but few visitors make use of these options. Instead, visitor activities are concentrated at the three sites mentioned above, increasing impacts in these areas. This pattern of use is caused mainly by the lack of information about other recreation options, since there are no visitor centres, trained personnel or information boards.

Hence, even though the INP plateau area is very attractive for backpacking, climbing and camping, its potential is not being fully realized, largely because of the lack of planning and access.

Length of stay

Figure 24.4 describes the duration of visitation at the INP plateau. We observed that 83% of visitors planned to stay overnight on the plateau, probably because of its difficult road access. It is a time-consuming drive and visitors are also interested in exploring all the attractions in the area, especially Pico das Agulhas Negras and Prateleiras. This contrasts with data reported by Takahashi (1998), which indicate that visits to parks in Parana State are generally short. At Itatiaia National Park, visitors made extended overnight visits, even though the number of opportunities for activities has

decreased over the years due to camping prohibition and some trail closures.

Visitor characteristics

Most of the visitors interviewed had a high level of education: 34% were college students, 19% had completed a college education, and 20% were taking, or had taken, postgraduate courses. These proportions far exceed the national averages, and also exceed the averages for the State where INP is located. This may contribute considerably to visitor acceptance of an educational programme, since individuals visiting the plateau will be in a position to understand and appreciate the significance of people's actions in protected areas.

Of the visitors interviewed, 51% were visiting the plateau for the first time, 40% visit the area at least three times a year and 72% stated they commonly visit other natural areas. This corresponds to a 'high level of previous experience' in the review by Roggenbuck and Lucas (1987), who examined the characteristics of visitors to wilderness in the USA. INP also has users with lengthy experience, given that 12% of all visitors have been visiting the park for 4–10 years and 18% have been visiting the park for more than 10 years.

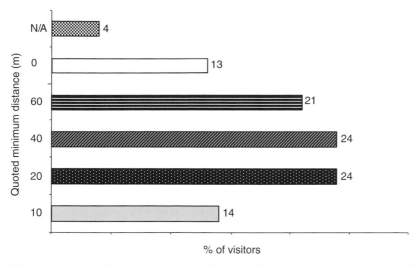

Fig. 24.5. Minimum distance of campsites from creeks and trails quoted by visitors interviewed in Itatiaia National Park (INP).

For 23% of visitors interviewed, camping is not the preferred option for overnight accommodation, even though they enjoy outdoor activities. Even though 70% of visitors interviewed reported previous camping experience, only 21% could identify the recommended minimum distance to set up tents from trails and creeks (Fig. 24.5). Correct procedures for trash disposal, on the other hand, were identified correctly by 92% of those interviewed.

Even though 88% agreed that it is more efficient to use camping stoves instead of campfires, the number of fires per camping site is high (5). Campfires have a strong social role amongst campers, and are commonplace despite the high fire risk. On average, campers cause one fire every year at INP. This will probably be one of the most difficult behaviours to modify through education.

Although, at 11,000 visitors per year, use of the plateau is not considered high, 35% of interviewees declared that the number of people they met during their visit was higher than they had previously expected. This may be due to the fact that surveys were conducted during the busiest visitation periods (Fig. 24.6). None the less, 50% of visitors noticed fewer impacts than they had expected.

Even though the questions about minimum impact techniques were relatively easy,

the average correct score was only 7%, indicating that users were quite unfamiliar with Leave-No-Trace (LNT) practices. This is a very low score compared with the results obtained by Confer *et al.* (2000), who reported an average score of 48%; and Cole *et al.* (1997b), with an average score of 33%. For the visitors interviewed at Itatiaia National Park, knowledge of minimal-impact practices was no higher, in general, for those who had made several previous visits. This reflects the lack of visitor education generally, not only at Itatiaia National Park.

Impacts along trails

Context for the present study was provided by the milestone work of Marion (1994), who measured impacts along 480 km of trails used by various types of visitor at several intensity levels. At Itatiaia National Park, the average trail width and depth do not indicate significant resource degradation. The majority of the trails consist of only one path, and its width accommodates single-row use. According to Marion (1994), measurements conducted on trails in protected areas show that the average width is ≥1 m and depth is ≥30 cm. The width of the trails at INP is close to this value but the depth is less, as shown in Table 24.2. Analysis of

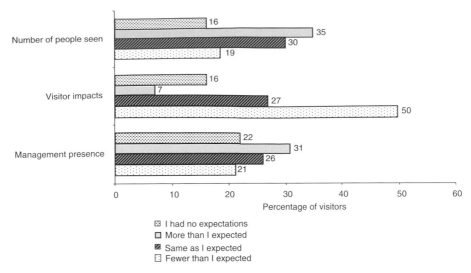

Fig. 24.6. Visitors' perception regarding encounters with other visitors, visitor impacts and management actions implemented at Itatiaia National Park (INP).

variance showed that trail width and the area of exposed soil were not significantly different among trails, except that there is less exposed soil on the Couto trail.

The impacts summarized in Table 24.2 may be compared with the visitor distribution data shown in Table 24.1, which indicate that 58.7% of visitors hike the trails to Agulhas Negras Peak and Prateleiras Peak, while 8% of visitors hike the Couto Peak trail. Trail width, depth and cross-sectional area are greater for the heavily used trails, though not proportionately so.

The most common detractive factors (Table 24.3) are erosion (except on the do Couto trail), steps, exposed rocks and drainage (especially on the Agulhas Negras trail). The other factors investigated, namely soil disruption, trash, vandalism and exposed roots, do not appear to present significant problems. It is notable that problems of this type are related principally to local terrain features, such as slope and soil type, and hence reflect trail location and planning more than visitor behaviour.

Vandalism is present only on Agulhas Negras trail, and is confined to knife-carved inscriptions on posted signs (Fig. 24.7): only one observation from a total of 100 points in the trail.

Impacts at campsites

The number of new campsites increased between the first survey in 1998 and the second in 1999, while camping was considered a legal activity (Table 24.4). However, the total campsite disturbance in 2002 is 42% lower than in 1999, showing the effects of camping prohibition after a fire in the Prateleiras area. Exposed mineral soil was the only campsite indicator showing an increase from 1999 to 2002. All other indicators exhibited a decrease in value, presumably due to closure of areas in August 2001.

Results from the detailed surveys of all campsite areas (Table 24.5) show considerable variation between maximum and minimum values for all parameters. Overall, the median area of campsites in INP, 61 m², is within the range of 40–188 m² reported for two areas in Oregon, USA (Cole *et al.*, 1997a). Differences between mean and median for total campsite areas and area of exposed soil reflect the skewed distribution of campsite size, with four large areas and numerous small campsites opened during the past few years. Indeed, over half of the camping areas in the plateau are <100 m² in area, and only two areas are >900 m². Since the area investigated was not initially planned for structured camping with

Table 24.2. Summary of trail characteristics.

	Agulhas Negras	Prateleiras	Aiuruoca	Couto
Total width of trail area (cm)	306.88 ± 21.62 ab	381.13 ± 25.58 a	286.14 ± 23.83 b	159.08 ± 11.44 c
Trail width (cm)	117.68 ± 6.25 a	113.67 ± 9.40 a	101.62 ± 17.75 a	81.02 ± 7.10 a
Width of exposed soil (cm)	60.00 ± 3.96 a	66.02 ± 4.82 a	76.84 ± 25.42 a	44.07 ± 2.75 a
Tread depth (cm)	15.22 ± 1.41 b	21.68 ± 1.88 a	9.41 ± 0.61 c	9.94 ± 0.83 c
Trail transverse area (cm²)[a]	1511.8 ± 176.46 ab	1867.1 ± 196.02 a	764.6 ± 100.28 c	974.1 ± 249.56 bc
Number of additional trail braids	0.87 ± 0.08 a	0.62 ± 0.07 b	0.48 ± 0.07 b	0.07 ± 0.02 c
Soil compaction inside trail (kgf/cm²)	11.19 ± 0.53 b	14.59 ± 0.36 a	13.55 ± 0.45 a	11.79 ± 0.35 b
Soil compaction outside trail (kgf/cm²)	4.52 ± 0.27 c	8.11 ± 0.28 a	6.91 ± 0.29 b	6.98 ± 0.30 b

The values are mean ± standard error. Means followed by the same letter are not statistically different using Tukey's HSD at $\alpha = 0.01$.
[a] Trail width times trail depth
kgf, kilogram force.

Table 24.3. Frequencies of detractive factors on major trails.

Detractive factor	Agulhas Negras		Prateleiras		Aiuruoca		Couto		P
	No.	%	No.	%	No.	%	No.	%	
Soil erosion	10	9.3	12	11.4	15	15	2	1.9	**0.012**
Steps	32	29.9	21	20	12	12	22	21.6	**0.018**
Soil disruption	0	0	0	0	2	2	1	1.0	0.272
Exposed rocks	39	36.4	7	6.7	10	10	24	23.5	**<0.0001**
Trash	0	0	3	2.9	1	1	0	0	0.113
Vandalism	1	1	0	0	0	0	0	0	0.411
Drainage	2	39.35	1	1	1	1	2	2.0	**<0.0001**
Exposed roots	3	2.8	2	1.9	0	0	2	2.0	0.459

The final column shows the probability that frequencies of the factor concerned are homogeneous across all trails, i.e. the trails differ in relative frequencies of erosion and steps at $P = 0.012$ and $P = 0.018$ respectively, and in relative frequencies of exposed rocks and drainage problems at $P < 0.0001$ in each case.

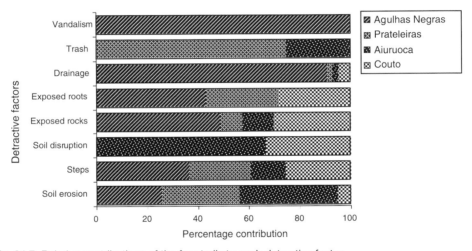

Fig. 24.7. Relative contributions of the four trails to each detractive factor.

defined tent sites, camping areas were created informally by visitors (Fig. 24.8). Most visitors prefer isolated sites that offer privacy for couples and small groups: 53% of the people interviewed were in a group of 2–4 people. Only the large groups deliberately select areas with a greater concentration of users.

As noted by Cole (1989), total area is one of the most straightforward indicators of impact at campsites: larger areas generally represent greater aggregate impacts. The four large camping areas at INP should therefore be managed to avoid further expansion and to minimize the impacts that have already occurred.

According to Leung and Marion (1999), the level of off-site disturbance and the potential for campsite expansion and proliferation may be inferred from the number of social trails radiating from a campsite. At INP campsites, the mean number of social trails is 5.4, indicating a very high potential for expansion. Indeed, such expansion was occurring until campsite areas were closed, since there was no management framework in place.

Whether the impacts described in the present study can be considered acceptable, will depend on the management objectives set for the area. In Itatiaia National Park, indicators such as damaged trees, social trails and human

Table 24.4. Basic impact indicators at plateau camping areas, 1998–2002.

Date		1998	1999	2002		
Number of campsites studied		16	19	19	2002–1999	% Change
Bare area	proportion of sites (%)	53	53	22	−31	−58
	largest area (m²)	288	474	1710	1236	260
	total area (m²)	1147	1094	3170	2076	190
Disturbance area	proportion of sites (%)	88	95	78	−17	−17
	largest area (m²)	6975	7515	5496	−2019	−27
	total area (m²)	13434	19517	11310	−8207	−42
Damaged trees	proportion of sites (%)	29	42	37	−5	−11
	highest numbers	100	30	3	−27	−90
Campfires	% of areas	53	74	63	−11	−14
	Maximum value	12	8	6	−2	−25
Human waste	proportion of sites (%)	6	58	26	−32	−55
	scarce (% sites)	6	37	16	−21	−57
	abundant (% sites)	–	21	11	−10	−47
Trash	% of areas	19	53	22	−31	−58

Table 24.5. Detailed impact indicators at 28 campsites, 2002.

Indicators	Median	Maximum	Minimum	Mean
Number of other sites visible	0	3	0	0.68
Number of trees damaged	9	28	1	11.07
Number of social trails	5	12	1	5.43
Number of fire rings	2	5	0	1.93
Trash	Low	–	–	Low
Occurrence of human waste	1	8	0	1.68
Number of satellite areas	0	2	0	0.5
Total camp area (m²)	61	1180	12	257
Bare area (m²)	20	413	0	42.4

waste should always have a tolerance limit close to zero, except at campsites.

Conclusions

Results from surveys carried out in trails and camping areas have two major implications for public use management at INP: one related to resource administration by park staff and the other related to visitor education. Results from the measurement of impact indicators on trails corroborate the visitor distribution data, which show that 59% of visitors hike the Agulhas Negras and Prateleiras Trails, while only 8% of visitors hike the Couto Peak Trail. However, many of these trail impacts are induced by poor trail design and maintenance rather than inappropriate visitor behaviour. Inappropriate beha-

viours, such as vandalism and littering, occur only at very low frequency. Therefore, management actions intended to influence visitor behaviour will have low effectiveness in improving the conditions along the trails studied. Erosion and drainage problems need to be addressed through improvements in trail design and regular trail maintenance.

The number of visitors to Itatiaia National Park Plateau has been increasing, reflecting an increasing demand for activities such as long hikes, camping and rock climbing. However, most visitation is concentrated at three locations: Agulhas Negras Peak, Prateleiras Peak and Rebouças Hut. The park's potential to offer a greater variety of recreational opportunities is not being developed, since visitors do not explore other feasible hikes and sites. One reason for this is the lack of information available

(a)

(b)

Fig. 24.8. When there is no definition of official camping sites, visitors open new camping areas in search of privacy. (a) Satellite area of a campsite that has been used for about 10 years. (b) Newly created non-official area.

to visitors, since the park does not have a visitor centre, trained personnel or information boards.

Impacts at overnight campsites are indeed due largely to visitor behaviour. The greatest problems are related to area expansions, number of social trails, tree disturbance, number of fire pits and inadequate disposal of human waste. The expansion of informal camp-sites has arisen from a legitimate demand which is poorly addressed. If the park's administration does not provide structured camping areas to meet the demand, then irregular unstructured use will continue. However, the results also show that visitors to INP have very poor knowl-edge of minimum-impact techniques. This sug-gests that visitor education programmes are also needed. A minimal-impact education programme will only be successful, however, if carried out as part of an overall integrated visitor management framework. Most of the people interviewed for this study recognized the importance of educational programmes for visitors, and believed that observed impacts are due principally to ignorance rather than vandalism. Park administration should be prepared to meet the demands of new users. Otherwise, illegal activities that increase local environmental damage will continue to occur.

Acknowledgements

This research was funded by the Fundação O Boticário de Proteção à Natureza (FBPN) and the MacArthur Foundation. We would like to thank Dr Alan Watson from the Aldo Leopold Wilderness Research Institute for reviewing the manuscript and assisting with revision.

Editor's Note

This chapter has been subject to further editorial rewriting. I trust that the content and opinions expressed by the authors remain unchanged.

References

Barros, M.I.A. and Dines, M. (2000) Mínimo impacto em áreas naturais: uma mudança de atitude. In: Serrano, C. (ed.) *A Educação pelas Pedras*. Editora Chronos, São Paulo, pp. 47–84 (in Portuguese).

Cole, D.N. (1982) *Wilderness Campsites Impacts: Effect of Amount of Use*. Research Paper-284, USDA, Forest Service Intermountain Research Station, Ogden, Utah.

Cole, D.N. (1989) *Low-impact Recreational Practices for Wilderness and Backcountry*. USDA, Forest Service Intermountain Research Station, Ogden, Utah.

Cole, D.N. (1991) *Changes on Trails in the Selway-Bitterroot Wilderness, Montana, 1978–89*. Research Paper INT – 550, USDA, Forest Service Intermountain Research Station, Ogden, Utah.

Cole, D.N. and Hall, T.E. (1992) *Trends in campsite condition: Eagle Cap Wilderness, Bob Marshal Wilderness and Grand Canyon National Park*. Research Paper INT-453, USDA, Forest Service Intermountain Research Station, Ogden, Utah.

Cole, D.N., Watson, A.E., Hall, T.E. and Spildie, D.R. (1997a) *High Use Destination in Wilderness: Social and Biophysical Impacts, Visitor Responses, and Management Options*. Research Paper INT- 496, USDA, Forest Service Intermountain Research Station, Ogden, Utah.

Cole, D.N., Hammond, T.P. and McCool, S.F. (1997b) Information quality and communication effectiveness: low impact messages on wilderness trailside bulletin boards. *Leisure Sciences* 19, 59–72.

Confer, J.J., Mowen, A.J., Graefe, A.R. and Absher, J.D. (2000) Magazines as wilderness information sources: assessing user's general wilderness knowledge and specific Leave No Trace knowledge. In: *Proceedings of Wilderness Science in a Time of Change Conference: Wilderness Visitors, Experiences, and Visitor Management*, 4. USDA, Forest Service, Fort Collins, Colorado, pp. 193–197.

Gunderson, K., Barns, C.V., Hendricks, W.W. and McAvoy L.H. (2000) Wilderness education: an updated review of the literature and new directions for research and practice. In: *Proceedings of Wilderness Science in a Time of Change Conference: Wilderness Visitors, Experiences, and Visitor Management*, 4. USDA, Forest Service, Fort Collins, pp. 253–259.

Hammitt, W.E. and Cole, D.N. (1998) *Wildland Recreation: Ecology and Management*. John Wiley & Sons, New York.

Hampton, B. and Cole, D.N. (1995) *Soft Paths – How to Enjoy the Wilderness Without Harming It*. Stackpole Books, Mechanicsburg.

IBDF (1982) *Plano de Manejo do Parque Nacional do Itatiaia*. M.A. – Instituto Brasileiro de Desenvolvimento Florestal, IBDF/FBCN, Brasília.

Indrusiak, C.B. (2000) Metodologia para avaliação do perfil do público em programas de educação ambiental para áreas protegidas. In: *Anais II Congresso Brasileiro de Unidades de Conservação*. FBPN, Campo Grande, pp. 243–247.

Jesus, F. de (2002) Plano de Uso Público: necessidade de atualização no planejamento. In: *Anais III Congresso Brasileiro de Unidades de Conservação*. Rede Nacional Pró-Unidades de Conservação: Fundação O Boticário de Proteção à Natereza: Associação Caatinga, Fortaleza, pp. 844–845.

Kinker, S.M.S. (1999) Ecoturismo e a Conservação da Natureza em Parques Nacionais Brasileiros: estudo de caso dos Parques Nacionais de Aparados da Serra e Caparaó. São Paulo, MSc Thesis, Universidade de São Paulo, São Paulo, Brazil.

Leung, Y-F. and Marion, J.L. (1999) Characterizing

backcountry camping impacts in Great Smoky National Park, USA. *Journal of Environmental Management* 57, 193–203.

Magro, T.C. (1999) Impactos do uso público em uma trilha no planalto do Parque Nacional do Itatiaia. PhD Thesis, Universidade de São Paulo, São Carlos.

Magro, T.C. (2003) Closure of trails: a restoration strategy or lack of management? In: Watson, A. and Sproull, J. (eds) *Proceedings of Seventh World Wilderness Congress Symposium: Science and Stewardship to Protect and Sustain Wilderness Values.* USDA Forest Service, Rocky Mountain Research Station, Ogden, Utah, pp. 257–261.

Magro, T.C., Freixêdas-Vieira, V.M. and Koury, C.G. (1999) *Manejo do Uso Público no Parque Nacional do Itatiaia: Projeto Planejamento Participativo no Manejo do INP.* FBDS & ESALQ/USP, Piracicaba.

Magro, T.C., Freixêdas-Vieira, V.M., Essoe, B. and Barros, M.I.A. (2001) *Plano de Uso Público – Parque Nacional do Itatiaia.* MMA/IBAMA, Brasília.

Marion, J.L. (1991) *Developing a Natural Resource Inventory and Monitoring Program for Visitor Impacts on Recreational Sites: A Procedural Manual.* Natural Resource Report NPS/NRVT/NRR-91/06, USDI, National Park Service, Cooperative Park Studies Unit, Denver, Colorado.

Marion, J.L. (1994) *An Assessment of Trail Conditions in Great Smoky Mountains National Park.* Research/Resources Management Report, USDI, National Park Service, Cooperative Park Studies Unit, Denver, Colorado.

Monz, C. (1999) *Recreation Resource Assessment and Monitoring Techniques: Examples from the Rocky Mountains, USA.* NOLS Research Program Annual Report, Lander.

Ramthun, R., Kersey, L. and Rogers, J. (2000) Information collection styles of wilderness users: a market segmentation approach. In: *Proceedings of Wilderness Science in a Time of Change Conference: Wilderness Visitors, Experiences, and Visitor Management, 4.* USDA, Forest Service, Fort Collins, pp. 217–220.

Roggenbuck, J.W. and Lucas, R.C. (1987) *Wilderness Use and User Characteristics: a State of Knowledge Review.* General Technical Report INT – 220, USDA, Forest Service Rock Mountain Research Station, Fort Collins, pp. 204–246.

Takahashi, L.Y. (1998) Caracterização dos visitantes, suas preferências e percepções e avaliação dos impactos da visitação pública em duas unidades de conservação do Estado do Paraná. PhD Thesis, Universidade Federal do Paraná, Curitiba.

Vasconcellos, J.M. de O. (2002) Educação Ambiental e Interpretação: o fortalecimento dos pilares das UCs. *Proceedings, Rede Nacional Pró-Unidades de Conservação: Fundação O Boticário de Proteção à Natereza.* Associação Caatinga, Fortaleza, pp. 846–847.

Washburne, R.F. and Cole, D.N. (1983) *Problems and Practices in Wilderness Management: a Survey of Managers.* Research Paper, INT – 304, USDA, Forest Service Intermountain Forest and Range Experiment Station, Ogden, Utah.

25

Impacts and Management of Hikers in Kavkazsky State Biosphere Reserve, Russia

Vera P. Chizhova

Faculty of Geography, Moscow State University, Moscow, Russia

Introduction

There are about 175 natural protected areas (NPAs) in Russia: 100 strictly protected reserves known as *zapovedniks*, 35 national parks and 40 nature parks. Until 1983, *zapovedniks* were devoted only to conservation and scientific research, but during the past two decades they have also been forced to open to limited ecotourism because of severe funding shortfalls (Chizhova, 2000).

Half of Russia's overall land area is mountainous and most of these NPAs are in the mountains, including all seven of Russia's natural World Heritage sites. Most are in the Caucasus, Altai, Kuznetsky Alatau and Sayan Ranges in southern Russia, and in the Kamchatka, Jugjur and Sikhote-Alin regions in the Far East. These mountain ecosystems have harsh climates with a long period of snow cover; steep, unstable and highly erodible landscapes with high frequency of avalanche, debris flow and rockfall; thin skeletal rocky soils; and complex mosaics of plant and animal habitats.

To maintain the conservation value of mountain *zapovedniks*, therefore, the number and activities of ecotourists must be regulated carefully in the light of natural processes and ecotourist impacts. Here I describe hiker impacts, recreational capacity calculations and management measures for one such area,

Kavkazsky State Biosphere Reserve, part of the Western Caucasus World Heritage Area.

In these mountainous landscapes, most human activities are concentrated along trails and associated campsites, rather than being diffused evenly over the entire area. Much of the earlier impact research in Russia, reviewed by Kazanskaya (1972), Taran and Spiridonov (1977) and Ivonin *et al.* (2000) has focused principally on broad-scale impacts, and may therefore not be immediately applicable. We have therefore examined impacts along hiking trails and sites in the Urals (Chizhova *et al.*, 1989); Kamchatka (Ivanov *et al.*, 1995); western Russia (Chizhova and Obolenskaya, 2000) and the Kuznetsky Alatau (Chizhova, 2002a).

As in similar mountain ecosystems in other continents (Cole, Chapter 4 this volume; Marion and Leung, Chapter 13 this volume), continued trampling along trails in these regions produces a broad and completely denuded track where soils are either compacted on level areas, or eroded by slopewash on steeper sections. Initial compaction and removal of vegetation cover leads to increased runoff, with further impacts on vegetation. At the margin of the bare area is a zone with reduced diversity of native plant species, often colonized by introduced weeds. The degree of modification to the original vegetation decreases with distance perpendicular to the track centre line. Disturbance to wildlife by human

sound and scents extends far beyond disturbance to vegetation.

Measuring Hiker Impacts on Trails and Campsites

Site and methods

In 2001 the Kavakzsky *zapovednik*, a UNESCO
Biosphere Reserve, was also designated as part
of the Western Caucasus World Heritage site.
There is a clear-cut altitudinal zonation from
the humid subtropical shorelines of the Black
Sea on the south-western side, to the glacial
landscapes of the watershed. The hiking route
studied runs 56 km from an area known as
Krasnaya Polyana, up the steep southern
slopes of the Great Caucasian Ridge, across
Pseashkho Mountain Pass and down the northern slopes to Camp Kholodny. The lower southern section of the trail lies within the reserve's
buffer zone, and the upper sections within the
reserve's core area. Currently, the trail is visited
by only 100–200 visitors per year, but with the
planned construction of a mountain sports
centre at Krasnaya Polyana, the number of visitors will increase greatly.

Pseashkho Pass lies on the boundary
between two geobotanical regions. The southern region is dominated by beech and fir forests
at lower altitudes, and sub-alpine long-grass
meadows at higher elevations, above the pass
itself. The northern region is dominated by a
type of alpine meadow known as *tipchak*, with
smaller areas of long-grass meadows, and
avalanche-affected birch forests. The aim of this
research was to assess the impacts of hikers
along the trail and at commonly used campsites
and halting areas, as a basis for calculating an
appropriate recreational capacity for the trails.
The campsites studied were on the long-grass
meadows at around 1700 m elevation, immediately above the treeline.

At each campsite, impacts on vegetation
are detectable over an approximately circular
area around 30 m in diameter. At the outer
edges of these areas, plant associations are
barely affected by recreational impacts: disturbance stage 2 in the 5-point scale proposed by
Kazanskaya (1972). We examined soil compaction, plant height and plant cover along radial

transects, and plant species assemblages in four
concentric zones within each site. Soil compaction was measured with a steel-cone micro-
penetrometer. Plant species were classified
either as locally native or locally introduced,
i.e. synanthropic, using floristic data from
Semagina (1999).

Results

Soil penetration resistance is five times higher
in the centre of the trampled campsites than at
the undisturbed periphery: $750 g/cm^2$ as compared to $150 g/cm^2$. At the outer periphery, the
grass cover is 1.5–2.0 m or more in height, with
100% projected foliage cover. At the centre the
grass is trampled down to 5 cm or less in height,
and 1–2% projected foliage cover. Impacts
decrease radially from the centre. Synanthropic
species such as *Poa annua*, *Trifolium repens*
and *Plantago major*, all relatively resistant to
trampling, are common in the central zones.
The peripheral zones support typical long-grass
meadow species together with species from the
beech and fir forests, such as *Rubus buschii*,
Matteuccia struthiopteris, *Solidago virgaurea*,
Hesperis vatonis, *Sorbus caucasica*, *Vaccinium
arctostaphylos*, and occasionally *Urtica dioica*
in wetter areas.

The trail itself is rather narrow in this mountainous area, with the zone of soil and vegetation impact extending only 0.5–1.0 m on each
side. This compares with an impact zone
extending 10–12 m on either side of tourist trails
in the flatlands of Middle Russia, for example.
In addition, this modified marginal zone,
beyond the heavily trampled track itself, is discernible along only 2–3% of the overall length
of trail between Krasnaya Polyana and Camp
Kholodny. Of course, that could soon change if
the number of hikers increases significantly.

Managing Impacts

Establishing permissible recreational loads

Permissible recreation load may be defined as
the number of tourists that can use the route, over
a given time period, without causing degrada-

Table 25.1. Major factors influencing permissible recreation loads in different types of natural protected area (Chizhova, 2002a).

Factors determining the loads	Recreation area	Nature park	National park	*Zapovednik*
Resistance of natural complexes to trampling (mechanical composition of soil, soil moisture, composition of plant community, etc.)	+++	++	+	–
Resistance of animals to disturbance	+	++	+++	+++
Route parameters (length, curving, forest density in the area, etc.)	–	+	+++	+++
Functional zoning of the territory	+	++	+++	(+)
Level of comfort of the territory	+++	++	+	–
Equipment of routes and tourist sites	–	++	+++	+++
Psychophysical comfort (frequency of contacts	+	++	++	+++
Dominating type of recreation	Mass recreation	Mass recreation and private trips	Managed and private ecotourism and trips	Managed ecotourism and guided trips
Average recreation loads	From 10 to 50 people/ha simultaneously	5–25 people/ha in the recreation zone and up to 10 guided groups for 1 route per day	1–3 tourist groups for 1 route per day	1–3 tourist groups for 1 route per week

Significance: +++ high; ++ medium; + low; (+) significant only in special cases.

tion of vegetation adjacent to the trail. This load depends on tourist impacts, management practices and ecosystem characteristics (Chizhova, 2002b). In many cases, ecological tolerances are exceeded in practice (Ganzer, cited in Luksh-chanderl, 1987, p. 114).

Noise disturbance to wildlife and damage to birch forests through firewood consumption and pollution of high-altitude lakes are also potentially significant impacts, but can be reduced considerably through appropriate minimal-impact practices. For example, hikers can carry stoves, or campsites can be supplied with firewood, so as to reduce damage to the birch forests. Trampling impacts, in contrast, depend strongly on the number of visitors and cannot easily be reduced.

In addition to these impacts on the natural environment, recreational capacity calculations need to consider social impacts of hikers on each other (Chizhova, 2001). Groups of hikers prefer not to see or hear other groups,

either on the trail or at campsites. To achieve this, groups need to be spaced along the trail. Spacing distances depend on trail factors such as curvature, complexity and safety, density of surrounding forest cover, number of observation sites, etc.; and on tourist factors such as group size, composition, fitness, time taken at observation sites, etc. Table 25.1 summarizes the relative importance of each of these factors in establishing permissible recreational loads for each of the four major categories of NPA in Russia (Chizhova, 2002b). Critical issues include the following:

- the ecological and physical factors that affect permissible recreation load need to be established separately for each individual tourist route;
- social and psychological factors need to be considered, as well as ecological and physical factors;
- the maximum permissible recreation load

should be determined by the most limiting ecological or social factor;

- routes should be monitored at least three times per year, i.e. before, during and after the main tourist season;
- permissible recreational loads should be adjusted each year in the light of monitoring results.

Different factors are more or less significant for different types of NPA. Impacts on wildlife, for example, are less critical for recreation areas because this type of NPA rarely supports native fauna. Trampling is generally less important for *zapovedniks* because there are strict management rules requiring visitors to stay on trails.

At current levels of use, hikers between Krasnaya Polyana and Camp Kholodny in Kavakzsky Biosphere Reserve, cause little disturbance to fauna because the species concerned are apparently habituated to such intermittent use. Introduction of weeds on hiking boots could be of concern, but does not seem to be significant to date. In particular, synanthropic species on trailsites and campsites do not seem to have spread into untrampled surrounding vegetation. Currently, there are no facilities along the trail, except at the beginning and end of the route, but this is in keeping with visitor expectations.

In view of all these factors, the recommended maximum permissible recreation load for the route as a whole is two groups per week of 8–10 people each. Currently, the route is used by hikers from June to September. It should be closed in early June, however, because the mountain passes and steeper slopes are still snowbound and hazardous. It should also be closed throughout September, because at that time bears descend from the mountain meadows to the lower forested slopes, in search of fruit. Since the bears use the same trails as the tourists, hikers can cause major disturbance to foraging bears. The overall hiking season should therefore extend over about 11 weeks, corresponding to a total load of around 200 visitors each season.

In addition to limiting the number of hikers on the trail, restrictions on activities, equipment and infrastructure are needed, so as to maintain the conservation status of the Kavakzsky *zapovednik* as a Biosphere Reserve and World Heritage site. This will be particularly critical if a mountain sports centre is constructed as proposed. For example, all shops, souvenir booths, kiosks, restaurants, etc. should be prohibited completely. Radios, music players, musical instruments, loudspeakers and loud singing or shouting should also be prohibited. Such restrictions should be straightforward, but seem to have been ignored in other parts of the Caucasus, such as Teberdinsky Biosphere Reserve and Prielbrussky and Sochinsky National Parks.

Monitoring and Further Research

A monitoring programme should be established that tracks:

- trail erosion: runoff intensity, slopewash losses, trailbed expansion;
- vegetation change: species diversity, weeds, physical damage;
- wildlife impacts: local population changes in disturbed areas;
- physical impacts: litter, fire rings, graffiti, etc.

Monitoring should be carried out at least three times each season: before, during and after the period of high tourist load. Management responses may include: modifications to the permissible recreational loads; trail repairs and maintenance; changes to trail route, lookouts, etc.; and/or environmental education programmes for visitors to the reserve.

Further research is also needed on tourist impacts other than trampling: for example, water pollution from campsites on the shores of mountain lakes. However, some of these lakes are avalanche pools which are completely emptied by avalanches almost every year, so tourist impacts may be insignificant in comparison.

Conclusions

The principal conclusions may be summarized as follows:

1. Mountain landscapes have particular characteristics, such as harsh climates and steep

slopes, which affect the impacts of ecotourism and outdoor recreation.

2. The impacts of recreational hikers in mountain landscapes are concentrated along linear routes, rather than spread out as in flatlands.

3. Visitor management needs to consider key sites such as look-outs, rest stops and campsites, as well as the location and maintenance of trails.

4. In the Kavkazsky area, where many of the prime sites for mountain hikers are close to the dwarf birch forests, hikers should be required to carry stoves or firewood and be forbidden to damage the birch forests.

5. Since most mountain lakes and pools are oligotrophic, washing in pools should be forbidden.

6. Minimal-impact education programmes are needed for all visitors.

Acknowledgements

The research described here was conducted under a scientific and technical cooperative agreement between the Kavkazsky State Biosphere Reserve and the Faculty of Geography, Moscow State University. It was also supported by Soros grant 941/1999 from the Open Society Institute Support Foundation.

Editor's Note

The chapter was rewritten by the editor from an English-language draft provided by the author. I trust that the sense, content and author's opinions are presented accurately.

References

Chizhova, V.P. (2000) The development of ecotourism in Nature Protected Areas (ecological and geographical aspects). *Problems of Regional Ecology. Social and Scientific Magazine* 4, 28–35 (in Russian).

Chizhova, V.P. (2001) Tourists in Zapovedniks: how and how many? *Environmental Protection. Quarterly Journal of the Moscow Wild Nature Protection Centre* 3(22), 35–38 (in Russian).

Chizhova, V.P. (2002a) Principles of organizing the flow of tourists in various types of Nature Protected Areas. In: *Ecological Problems of Preserving Historical and Cultural Heritage.* Records of the VII All-Russian Conference. Collection of articles. The Russian Heritage Institute, Moscow, pp. 390–405 (in Russian).

Chizhova, V.P. (2002b) Case studies of setting up ecotourist routes and ecotrails in the Altai-Sayans region. In: *Ecological Tourism on its Way to Russia. Basic Principles, Recommendations, Russian and Foreign Experience.* Griff & Co, Tula, pp. 157–170 (in Russian).

Chizhova, V.P. and Obolenskaya, M.A. (2000) The particulars of recreational impact on nature in Protected Areas. In: *The Problems and Perspectives of Tourism Development in Countries with Transition Economies: Conference Records.* Smolensk, pp. 282–286 (in Russian).

Chizhova, V.P., Dobrov, A.V. and Zahlebny, A.H. (1989) *The Learning Trails of Nature.* Agropromizdat, Moscow (in Russian).

Ivanov, A.N., Valebnaya, V.A. and Chizhova, V.P. (1995) The problems of recreation in nature protected areas (the case of the Geyser Valley). *Moscow State University Journal, Geography Series,* 6, 68–74.

Ivonin, V.M., Avdonin, V.E. and Penjkovsky, N.D. (2000) *Recreational Ecology of Mountain Forests in Russian Prichernomorje (Black Sea coast).* Published by SKNTz VSh, Rostov-na-Donu, 272 pp.

Kazanskaya, N.S. (1972) Research on recreational digression of natural plant formations. *Izv. Academy of Sciences of the USSR, Geographical Series,* 1, 52–59.

Lukshchanderl, L. (1987) *Save the Alps.* Translated from German. Progress, Moscow.

Semagina, R.N. (1999) In Tuniev, B.S. (ed). *The Flora of Kavkazsky State Biosphere Reserve.* Monograph. 'KZ' Publishing House, Sochi.

Taran, I.V. and Spiridonov, V.N. (1977) *Sustainability of Recreational Forests.* Nauka, Novosibirsk.

Conclusions

Ralf Buckley

International Centre for Ecotourism Research, Griffith University, Gold Coast, Australia

Data Are Sparse

There are now over 1000 individual published studies on the ecological impacts of human recreational activities, including commercial ecotourism. But there are hundreds of thousands of plant and animal species affected, and for each of these there are dozens of different effects which disturbance could produce. The multitudinous social science disciplines have not yet described the behaviour of our own species; and why should other vertebrates, at least, be any less complex? In addition, the ecological impacts of ecotourism include effects on the physical as well as the biological environment, and effects on ecosystems and species assemblages and interactions as well as direct disturbance to individual species. So even though 1000 studies might sound a lot in tourism research, from an ecological perspective the entire body of impact research to date is but a bare beginning in the discipline of recreation ecology.

For effective management of visitor impacts in areas of high conservation value, as has often been said (Buckley and Pannell, 1990; Buckley, 2001), we need quantitative information on the impacts of different numbers of visitors in groups of various sizes, engaged in a range of activities with corresponding equipment, over different periods at various seasons in a range of ecosystems, and subject to a variety of management regimes, on a number of ecosystem parameters and components, including individual species. To date we do have individual research studies which have addressed aspects such as visitor numbers and group size, activity and equipment, season and duration, ecosystem and management; but only in a small number of instances and for a small number of species and parameters.

Our need for knowledge may be likened to a vast multidimensional matrix linking all the various factors which may influence impacts on all the various ecosystem components. In each cell of the matrix we need replicated studies, quantitative data, measures of uncertainty and predictive models. Our total current knowledge, in contrast, lies entirely within a tiny proportion of these matrix cells, and not a single cell is entirely filled.

Data Are Clumped

The reviews and case studies in this volume aim to take stock of the current state-of-the-art in relevant research; and for the topics included, coverage is relatively comprehensive. This set of topics, however, reflects information available, which is neither complete nor even. Information currently available on the impacts of ecotourism is heavily biased to a few geographic areas, notably North America; and in consequence, to particular ecosystems, species and ecotourism activities. For some combinations of impact categories, such as the impacts of pedestrian trampling on temperate grassland and similar vegetation, there is an established body of English-language ecological research by internationally recognized experts. For other types of impacts, and other parts of the world, there are valuable case studies but as yet no coherent and cross-referenced body of research.

There may be corresponding bodies of impact research in other languages from other continents, but if so, there is very little cross-citation into the English-language literature. Chapters in this volume from Russia and Brazil do cite previous work published in Russian and Portuguese, respectively, but not in such quantity as other chapters cite work published in English. It would indeed be valuable for bilingual ecologists to compile English-language reviews of recreation-impact research published, for example, in Mandarin or Cantonese, or even in Spanish and French.

Intercontinental differences in the apparent depth and breadth of recreation ecology research, however, cannot be ascribed solely to incompatibilities in language. For example, the literature cited in many of the chapters of this book show that there has been far less impact research in Australia than in North America, even though Australian scientists are well represented in the ecological literature as a whole. This pattern has been noted previously by Newsome et al. (2001). Certainly, there are fewer people and proportionately fewer ecologists in Australia; and certainly, many ecologists in both continents perceive other ecological issues as more fundamental or urgent than measuring the impacts of ecotourism and outdoor recreation. At least equally critical, however, is access to research funding for applied recreation ecology. Much of the work in the USA and Canada has been carried out by a relatively small number of individuals supported by specialist institutions. In Australia, recreation ecologists were initially optimistic in the mid-1990s when the federal government invested well over US$10 million in a national Cooperative Research Centre for Sustainable Tourism (CRCST), over a 7-year period. In practice, however, CRCST allocated almost all its efforts to social sciences, with minuscule fund-

ing for research on ecological impacts. It remains to be seen whether this situation will improve now that CRCST has received additional funding for a further 7 years.

Because of the strong representation by North American researchers, some particular ecosystems and activities have been studied much more intensively than others. Perhaps the greatest concentration of quantitative experimental research has been on pedestrian trampling of ground-layer vegetation, especially in open landscapes such as alpine meadows. This research is indeed applicable in similar ecosystems on other continents (Whinam et al., 2003; Magro and de Barros, Chapter 24, this volume). In other ecosystems, however, pedestrian trampling may be far less significant ecologically than other impacts of hikers, such as noise disturbance to birds and wildlife, or introduction of weeds and pathogens (Buckley, 2001).

There is thus a strong need to expand research effort on the ecological impacts of ecotourism and outdoor recreation across a broader range of ecosystems and species. In particular, as many developing countries are currently promoting ecotourism as a means to fund protected area systems, it is important to extend recreation ecology research into relevant tropical and sub-tropical ecosystems so as to assist these countries in managing visitor access and activities.

In the developed nations, there is an additional trend, namely the expansion of outdoor sports and adventure recreation in public lands. Recreation ecology research therefore needs to devote additional attention to a broader range of activities by a broader range of people. For example, the increasing popularity of mountain-biking and rock-climbing has generated a pressing need for better data on their ecological impacts.

However, even for the most heavily studied impacts, such as pedestrian trampling on ground-layer vegetation or flushing distances for shorebirds, available data are still insufficient to yield quantitative predictive models except at the broadest scale. The only variable that Cole (1995a,b) could identify to compare the results of vegetation trampling studies, for example, was the number of passes needed to reduce plant cover to 50% of its original value. Even with such a broad parameter, available data are not sufficient to predict the value of that parameter for a plant community not previously studied. Similarly, even though the effects of trampling on plant cover have now been studied experimentally for a range of ecosystems (Cole, Chapter 4, this volume), there are very few where the effects of, for example, the distribution of hiker passes over time have been quantified. Again, even though there are some instances where soil as well as plant parameters have been measured for trampled areas, and even though there are cases where the influence of, for example, slope and moisture content on soil erosion have been considered, there are still not sufficient data to predict how many hikers can cross a specific hill before tracks start to erode out. There are guidelines for choosing low-impact hiking routes and guidelines for building erosion-resistant hiking trails, but these are based on experience, not on predictions from impact research. Suppose that hikers routinely cross a particular hillslope, and a land manager wants to know whether to divert them around it so as to avoid an erosion scar and expensive rehabilitation or track hardening works. To make that decision the land manager needs to know how many pedestrian passes will reduce plant cover to zero and initiate soil erosion, for a specific slope, soil type, plant cover and climate. Rarely, however, can we provide such an estimate with any degree of confidence. So the land manager must choose between caution and associated controversy from users, or waiting until damage has occurred and trying to repair it. For trampling of trails, perhaps waiting for damage is an acceptable management strategy: impacts can be detected easily and immediately, are generally only of local significance, and can be rehabilitated if required. For many other impacts, however, detection is difficult and delayed and ecological effects are diffuse and irreversible. If research data are so limited even for trampling, how much more serious is the deficiency for other types of ecological impact? Even for the relatively better-studied impacts, therefore, many more data are required before the mechanisms can be considered well understood.

Of course, even with considerable additional research effort, the ecological impact of ecotourism, as with any other human activity, will never be precisely predictable. Individual animals, for example, behave differently from others of the same species. Indeed, they may react differently to two successive and similar disturbances, even if their usual behaviour is broadly predictable. Both wildlife ecologists and wildlife tour guides learn to identify individual animals and distinguish their likely reactions under different circumstances.

Overall, however, it is a clear conclusion from this volume that a great deal of recreation ecology research is required in all continents, for a wide range of ecosystems, species and ecotourism activities.

Data are Crude

From an ecological perspective, most past studies of ecotourism impacts are rather crude. Relatively few researchers have used physiological indicators; calculated consequences at population scale; or examined impacts which are indirect, second-order, diffuse, evanescent, invisible to the naked eye, or delayed in onset. However, such effects may be very significant ecologically.

Day visitors to heavily used sites in national parks, for example, could inadvertently increase the food available to common predatory bird species; and these more aggressive birds might also attack the eggs and nestlings of smaller bird species, some of them rare. The significance of such effects for populations and survival of these smaller species remains largely untested (Buckley, Chapter 11 this volume). Tracks created by backcountry hikers would perhaps increase the success of predators, native or introduced, in stalking small native mammals and ground-foraging birds, even where the tracks are faint and little-travelled. Oversnow vehicles can crush the undersnow burrows of small mountain mammals; and helicopter overflights can drown out territorial, courtship and alarm calls by native birds.

In the Australian Alps, it has been suggested that habitat modification on ski slopes and hiking trails within Mt Kosciusko National Park has hastened the spread of particular introduced plant species, whose more showy flowers attract native insect pollinators away from endemic native species in the same plant family (Kelly *et al.*, 2003). Since the continued survival of the native species depends on their ability to produce more seed than are attacked by seed-parasitic insects, even a small reduction in pollination success could tip the balance towards extinction of the species concerned. To assess the ecological significance of this mechanism would require detailed long-term analyses by a plant reproductive ecologist, and this has not yet been done.

Indirect impacts such as these are difficult to identify without extensive field observations and almost impossible to quantify without carefully designed ecological studies. Such studies require ecological expertise, funding, equipment and time scales (Buckley, 2002). All of these are rare in tourism research. In compiling the reviews and case studies presented here, therefore, we hope to provide not just a ready reference and synthesis of existing information for use in management, but also a platform for future ecological research on diffuse, indirect but ecologically significant impacts such as those outlined above.

References

Buckley, R.C. (2001) Environmental impacts. In: Weaver, D. (ed.) *Encyclopaedia of Ecotourism.* CAB International, Wallingford, UK, pp. 374–394.

Buckley, R.C. (2002) Ecological indicators of tourist impacts in parks. *Journal of Ecotourism* 2, 54–66.

Buckley, R.C. and Pannell, J. (1990) Environmental impacts of tourism and recreation in national parks and conservation reserves. *Journal of Tourism Studies* 1, 24–32.

Cole, D.N. (1995a) Experimental trampling of vegetation. Relationship between trampling intensity and vegetation response. *Journal of Applied Ecology* 32, 203–214.

Cole, D.N. (1995b) Experimental trampling of vegetation. Predictors of resistance and resilience. *Journal of Applied Ecology* 32, 215–224.

Kelly, C., Pickering, C.M. and Buckley, R.C. (2003) Impacts of tourism on threatened plant taxa and communities in Australia. *Ecological Management and Restoration* 4, 37–44.

Newsome, D., Moore, S.A. and Dowling, R.K. (2001) *Natural Area Tourism: Ecology Impacts and Management.* Channel View, Clevedon, UK.

Whinam, J., Chilcott, N., Ling, R. and Wyatt, P. (2003) A method to calculate environmental sensitivity to walker trampling in the Tasmanian Wilderness World Heritage Area. In: Buckley, R.C., Pickering, C. and Weaver, D. (eds) *Nature-based Tourism, Environment and Land Management.* CAB International, Wallingford, UK, pp. 151–165.

Index